...PER'S COLLEGE

5

2

)05

To b

THE CITY READER

The City Reader brings together the very best on the city. Classic writings by such authors as Robert Park, Lewis Mumford, Raymond Unwin, Jane Jacobs, Le Corbusier, and Kevin Lynch meet the best contemporary writings of, among others, Peter Hall, Mike Davis, Saskia Sassen, Dolores Hayden, and Manuel Castells.

Fifty generous selections are included. Each piece is separately introduced with a brief intellectual biography, a review of the author's writings and related literature, and an explanation of how the piece fits into the broader context of urban theory and practice, competing ideological perspectives on the city, and the major current debates concerning race and gender, global restructuring, the impact of technology, and post-modernism.

Richard T. LeGates is Professor of Urban Studies at San Francisco State University. **Frederic Stout** is Lecturer in Urban Studies at Stanford University.

"This is the definitively complete reader on urban problems and policies, spanning urban development from the ancient Greeks to the Internet, ranging across the relevant contributory disciplines and comparing experiences in different continents and countries. It will immediately become a basic text for any course in urban studies and urban planning. Both teachers and students will celebrate its publication."

Peter Hall, Professor of Planning, University College London

"This book is long overdue. Cities and their fortunes have stimulated some of the finest thinking about the integration of society, economy and culture. But much of the best in urban studies is out of print and inaccessible. This book brings a collection of the best together in an engaging, readable way. It is bound to renew interest in the classic works of urban studies, and by placing some outstanding recent work alongside them, it shows that the field is as bounteous as ever."

David Wilmoth, Deputy Vice-Chancellor, Melbourne Institute of Technology

"With this anthology, urban studies has certainly come of age. Now, for the first time, the most significant works on urbanism are collected in one place. The authors' careful and wise selection of ageless scholarship documenting the growth and structure of cities, writings spanning over one hundred years, not only demonstrates the course of metropolitan development as explored by a variety of observers but also highlights the most current interpretations regarding urban life. This is a 'must-read' book – it is comprehensive, authoritative and just plain fun."

Eugenie Birch, Associate Provost, Hunter College of the City University of New York

THE CITY READER

edited by

Richard T. LeGates
and
Frederic Stout

London and New York

First published 1996
by Routledge
11 New Fetter Lane, London EC4P 4EE

Simultaneously published in the USA and Canada
by Routledge
29 West 35th Street, New York, NY 10001

Typeset in Sabon by Solidus (Bristol) Limited
Printed and bound in Great Britain by
Clays Ltd, St Ives PLC

British Library Cataloguing in Publication Data
A catalogue record for this book is available from the British Library

Library of Congress Cataloguing in Publication Data
The city reader / edited by Richard T. LeGates & Frederic Stout.
p.   cm.
1. Urban policy. 2. Cities and towns. 3. City planning.
I. LeGates, Richard T.   II. Stout, Frederic.
HT151.C586   1996
307.76—dc20   95-37262

ISBN 0–415–11900–6
0–415–11901–4 (pbk)

To Courtney Elizabeth LeGates
and Amy Catherine Stout

They are the future

CONTENTS

4 URBAN POLITICS, GOVERNANCE, AND ECONOMICS

5 URBAN PLANNING: VISIONS, THEORY, AND PRACTICE

6 THE FUTURE OF THE CITY

ACKNOWLEDGEMENTS

Many people contributed to this anthology. We owe a particular debt of gratitude to our editor at Routledge, Tristan Palmer, for his enthusiasm for this project, patience, encouragement, and insightful comments on the manuscript at every stage in its development. Matthew Smith at Routledge ably assisted Tristan and solved innumerable problems along the way. Our Routledge desk editor Caroline Cautley resolved many editorial problems quickly and insightfully as we prepared the manuscript for publication. Peter Harrison, the copy editor, proved extremely helpful in catching errors in the manuscript and developing a clear and consistent format.

When we set out to write an urban anthology appropriate for today's world we sought out advisers who are in touch with the best scholarship worldwide. Peter Hall, Bartlett Professor of City Planning at University College, London in the United Kingdom, Vice-chancellor David Wilmoth of the Royal Melbourne Institute of Technology in Australia, and Eugenie L. Birch, Professor of Urban Affairs and Planning and Acting Associate Provost of Hunter College in New York, subjected our initial proposal to their formidable critical review and made many suggestions to tighten up the final manuscript.

We received constant encouragements and many valuable suggestions, both for selections to include and approaches to critical commentary, from our colleagues. We wish particularly to thank Rufus Browning, Yong Cho, Roger Crawford, Rich DeLeon, Bill Issel, Debbie LeVeen, Raquel Pinderhughes, Norman Schneider, Genie Stowers, and David Tabb at San Francisco State University; Paul Turner, Leonard Ortolano, and James L. Gibbs, Jr. at Stanford University; Cheyney Ryan at the University of Oregon, and Chester Hartman at the Poverty and Race Research and Action Council; John Mollenkopf of the Graduate Center of the City University of New York; and Karen Christensen, Fred Collignon, Allan Jacobs, and Rolf Pendall at the University of California, Berkeley. Many additional colleagues made helpful suggestions.

A number of people helped us with scanning anthology selections and with technical aspects of producing the manuscript. Particularly helpful were John Palme, Thoreau Lovell, John Tait, and Kurt Annweiler at San Francisco State University, Kate Blood at the University of California, Berkeley, Institute of Urban and Regional Development, and John Dick, at the Stanford University Center for Teaching and Learning.

For unfailing courtesy and helpfulness we thank the staffs of the Cecil H. Green Library and the Henry Myer Memorial Library at Stanford, the J. Paul Leonard Library at San Francisco State University, the San Francisco Public Library, and the University of California, Berkeley, College of Environmental Design Library, Institute of Governmental Studies Library, Bancroft and Doe Libraries.

Joanne Fraser, Courtney LeGates, and Lisa Ryan provided patience and moral support, often in difficult circumstances.

This project grew out of years of classroom teaching and we would be severely remiss if we did not thank the countless students of the Stanford Program on Urban Studies, The San Francisco State University Urban Studies Program, and the University of California, Berkeley Department of City and Regional Planning who read and commented on the selections included and many which did not meet their high standards. They were the ultimate judges of what readings made the cut as "essential."

INTRODUCTION

During the past twenty-five years our students in Urban Studies and City Planning courses at Stanford University, San Francisco State University, and the University of California, Berkeley have often asked us what is the best writing on a given topic or what single new writing will let them know what is happening in a given area right now. Since there was no one source to which we could refer them each of us accumulated photocopies of what we considered to be *essential* writings and bibliographic references to many more. As time passed our colleagues began to come to us for suggested course readings and we in turn learned from them. We realized that a systematic organization of the best writings we use to meet both requests would make for a good anthology to introduce students of urban studies and city planning to the field and to supplement course texts used in these and other courses concerned with cities. Accordingly, the selections in this anthology represent both kinds of essential readings – enduring writings we use consistently and the most exciting new writings to which we point our students.

The book focuses on *essential* writings. We picked enduring issues in urban studies and planning across different cultures and times. In our courses we have found that H. D. F. Kitto's "The Polis" raises fundamental questions about individuals' relations with their community which are as relevant today as they were 2,400 years ago; that Robert Park's seventy-year-old essay "Urbanism as a Way of Life" speaks to our students trying to understand contemporary urban violence, economic dislocation, homelessness, and anomie; and that our students are excited by William Julius Wilson's theories on the Black underclass and Manuel Castells and Peter Hall's reflections on technopoles of the world. Most writings are from twentieth-century writers and about a third were written very recently.

This is an *international* anthology. In an increasingly global world students must learn from writers beyond the borders of their country of origin. In addition to work by North American writers, the anthology contains writings by scholars from England, Scotland, Australia, Spain, France, South America, Belgium, Greece, and internationalists whose countries of birth, academic training, and current residence are all different. Space limitations precluded including material whose primary focus is on African, Asian, or South American cities, but many of the urban realities and urban processes are applicable everywhere precisely because they have become so internationalized.

This is an *interdisciplinary* anthology. The disciplines in which writers in the anthology were trained or where they are located within universities include anthropology, architecture, archaeology, city planning, classics, demography, economics, English literature, geography, history, landscape architecture, political science, and sociology. But many of the writers blend insights from more than one discipline. And some of the best writing about cities such as Hall and Castells's writings about technopoles or Dolores Hayden's writings about gender and urban space do not fit in conventional disciplinary boxes.

The writings in this anthology seek to combine theory and practice. "Urban studies" is the most commonly used term to refer to the academic study of cities. Knowledge about cities generated by social scientists and others is sometimes taught in a single program, sometimes dispersed among academic departments. The goal of these courses is primarily to teach students to *understand* cities; only secondarily to empower them professionally to change them. On the other hand, professional city planning, town planning, and regional planning courses explicitly seek to train students to work as city planners. Often planning is taught as part of graduate or undergraduate professional degree programs; sometimes it forms part of courses given by Geography, Architecture or other departments in the social sciences or design. As indicated above, our approach in this anthology is to blend the goal of understanding cities with the goal of planning them. We feel planning should be informed by understanding and that understanding can be enhanced by studying planning.

This anthology includes material on race and gender issues in cities, both in the selection of writings and introductions. Diversity characterizes many cities throughout the world and writings need to include the situation, contributions, and perspective of women and people of color as an integral part of the writing. To produce more balanced coverage of issues of urban race and gender we have included a number of essential writings by and about women and people of color by women and people of color themselves. We also include consideration of diverse groups in our introductions to all the writings.

An anthology of essential writings on cities should have a flexible organization. There is no one best way to organize material on changing cities. Urban studies and city planning courses content vary widely and courses are organized in almost as many different ways as there are courses. This dictates a flexible structure for the book. Readings are grouped into six broad categories on the evolution of cities; urban form and design; urban society and culture; urban politics, governance, and economics; urban planning: visions, theory, and practice; and the future of the city. Using Christopher Alexander's concepts (p. 119), this anthology is a semi-lattice; not a tree!

The section on the evolution of cities is chronological and it works as a unit in the sequence in which the selections are presented, though some professors might pick and choose selections or use some selections as part of courses which do not have a chronological evolution section. The other groupings work well if selections are read in the order in which they are presented, but different sequencing may work equally well or better in the context of a given course. Professors experiment; students enjoy!

We made Kingsley Davis's article on the urbanization of the human population a prologue for all that follows. The evolution of cities section is first and the future of cities section last. The other four sections could be addressed in any order.

One goal in picking the selections was to expose students to great scholarship. Almost everything written on the emergence of cities acknowledges a debt to the meticulous empirical research and creative theory building of Australian/British archaeologist V. Gordon Childe, on the Greek cities to H. D. F. Kitto's delightfully written interpretation of the polis, or on medieval cities to Belgian historian Henri Pirenne's provocative theories on the relationship between the revival of trade and the emergence of medieval cities. Students can learn a great deal from the way Childe, Kitto, and Pirenne think and write beyond the substantive content of the work.

The anthology begins with the evolution of cities. We have found that even our brightest and most experienced students bring time- and place-specific cultural concepts to their study of cities. We warn them – and readers of this anthology – against too quickly assuming what a "suburb," or a "core city," or an "ancient city" or any other urban settlement is. Some of our San Francisco Bay Area students who grew up in the affluent, predominantly white, residential suburb of Palo Alto think of Palo Alto when they think of a suburb. Material on the evolution of cities enriches their understanding that there were suburbs in medieval European cities composed of traders free from the medieval guilds, a proliferation of horsecar and streetcar suburbs as nineteenth-century technology, entrepreneurship, and public tastes made them possible, and a great range of suburbs today – including working-class suburbs, Black suburbs, and technoburbs. Study of the evolution of cities sharpens awareness of these differences. And understanding is the key to successful city planning.

The second section deals with urban form and design. The physical form of cities is fundamental to planners, whose lifework will involve continuing to shape city space. Understanding form and design is also important for geographers, architects, landscape architects, urban designers, and anyone interested in cities. The great scholar of vernacular landscape, J. B. Jackson, has spent a lifetime decoding the meaning of ordinary landscapes. We begin Part 2, Perspectives on Urban Form and Design, with his description of the logic underlying the physical organization of a hypothetical ordinary town in the Western United States both for its intrinsic interest and to illustrate the kind of intellectual inquiry Jackson pioneered. We have included in this section other writings by sociologists, architects, and planners, from Lynch's fecund writings on the image of the city to Allan Jacobs and Donald Appleyard's notable "Urban Design Manifesto" and Mike Davis's rant against the oppressive design of fortress Los Angeles.

If there was a single most important insight that the great American intellectual Lewis Mumford emphasized in sixty years of tireless polemics against determinists of every stripe it was that a city is an expression of the human spirit: much more than a physical entity or a locus of economic activity. Accordingly we begin Part 3, Urban Society and Culture, with Lewis Mumford's essay "What Is a City?" Other writings in this section review some of the important contributions sociologists and anthropologists have made to our understanding of urban culture, explore the culture of poverty and underclass debates, and juxtapose liberal and conservative views on how to respond to urban poverty. We close Part 3 with a review of images of the city in literature.

The fourth part of the book is titled Urban Politics, Governance, and Economics. Several selections explore the way in which political scientists, sociologists, and others now think about urban politics and governance. We particularly emphasize the debate between pluralists and structuralists, Marxist and non-Marxist theories, and regime theory. Other selections in Part 4 emphasize the impact of global restructuring on cities and interconnections between urban economics, politics, and society. There follow articles by John Kasarda, Saskia Sassen, and Mike Savage and Alan Warde which attempt to explain the jobs–skills mismatch in cities in the developed world, cities in a global economy, and uneven urban development.

The fifth part is titled Urban Planning: Visions, Theory, and Practice. It begins with visions. We tell our beginning students that the best city planning is utopian and encourage them to envision urban futures that they would like to see. Part 5 begins with powerful visions of urban futures by Frederick Law Olmsted, Ebenezer Howard, Frank Lloyd Wright, and Le Corbusier which should challenge students to think through their own values about the importance of aesthetics, community, the relation of man to nature, efficiency, and other issues. We hope our students will not lose the power to dream as they tackle research methodology, computers, finance, computer-assisted design, and other necessary professional coursework. Rather, we hope that they will see this as necessary knowledge to translate their own visions into reality. We move from planning visions to planning theory and conclude Part 5 with material on planning practice.

The final section of the anthology picks up evolutionary themes from Part 1 and extends the visionary section of Part 5. What will, and what should, cities be like in the future? Here we include some writings by astute observers like Peter Calthorpe writing about "pedestrian pockets" and Manuel Castells and Peter Hall writing about technopoles of the world. We include writing describing what alternative urban futures might be like and normative selections like Constantin Doxiadis's dreams for Ecumenopolis: a global community of all mankind.

The text of selections is reproduced essentially as it appeared in the original. We did not change original wording of older selections that might strike some modern readers as antiquated or try to improve on writing in the original which we ourselves found awkward. Where we have included bibliographic references which were in the original selections they are reprinted as they appeared, even where we noted apparent errors or omissions in the original bibliographies as prepared by the selection authors themselves. Where we have edited selections, material omitted within a paragraph is indicated by ellipses (...). The omission of one or more paragraphs is indicated by ellipses within square brackets in the middle of the page [...]. Our own summaries of omitted material are enclosed by square brackets [ ]. We have included the bibliographic references for Peter Hall's "The City of Theory" and Leonie Sandercock and Ann Forsyth's "A Gender Agenda for Planning," which are particularly valuable guides for further reading for students of urban studies and planning interested in planning theory. Elsewhere we include bibliographic references only where the selections referred to them. We retained the footnotes for Dolores Hayden's "What Would a Non-sexist City be Like?" as requested by the author, but elsewhere footnotes are not included. We have not included photographs which accompanied some of the selections. Charts and graphs from Kingsley Davis's "The Urbanization of the Human Population" have also been omitted because they are somewhat dated. Dolores Hayden supplied revised, clearer graphics which have been substituted for the graphics that appeared in the previously published version of "What Would a Non-sexist City Be Like?"

We have said a good deal about the role of visions in urban studies and planning. We close with our own vision of how this anthology will be used. It is aimed primarily at students who will be encountering many of the writers and writings for the first time. We hope the writings touch responsive chords and inspire students to think more deeply and read more widely. To that end for each selection we point the way to other related writings by the same authors and other writers on the same subject. We hope *The City Reader* will prove a book that professionally oriented students, professors, and practitioners will keep and periodically reread. One test to which we put each of the essential writing included is that it should still be relevant to reread and enjoy in twenty years.

Richard LeGates
Frederic Stout
San Francisco, January 1996

Prologue

KINGSLEY DAVIS

"The Urbanization of the Human Population"

Scientific American (1965)

Editors' introduction   Demography – from the Greek demos "people" – is the study of human populations. Kingsley Davis (born 1908) pioneered the study of historical urban demography. He is particularly fascinated by the history of world urbanization: the increase in the proportion of a population that is urban as opposed to rural.

The following selection synthesizes Davis's conclusions about the big picture: how urbanization has occurred throughout the world during all of human history. Davis raises fundamental issues and lays out a clear framework for understanding population dynamics and urban growth.

Davis's extraordinary data on how tiny European urban settlements were, and how slowly they grew throughout the Middle Ages and early modern period, provides the demographic backdrop for historian Henri Pirenne's account of the nature of medieval cities (p. 38). During the long period of medieval urbanization the proportion of the population which was urban as opposed to rural changed very slowly. In sharp contrast, Davis concludes that as the Industrial Revolution occurred in England, rapid population growth combined with rural–urban shifts changed both the proportion of the population living in cities and absolute city size very quickly. Friedrich Engels (p. 47) describes in horrifying detail what this revolution in urban demography meant to the impoverished urban proletariat of Manchester and other nineteenth-century industrial cities. His analysis is extremely relevant in assessing prospects for Ecumenopolis (Doxiadis, p. 459) as advanced industrial societies and eventually the world reach the end of the urbanization process, with the habitable portions of the globe perhaps becoming a single world city.

Davis's careful distinctions of possible sources of urbanization are essential. He concludes that in Europe urbanization occurred because of rural–urban migration; not because of other possible factors such as differential birth and mortality rates.

Davis believes that urbanization follows an attenuated S curve in which cities urbanize very slowly at the long bottom of the S, shoot up at the middle of the S, and then level off at the top of the S. He considers that advanced industrialized countries are now reaching the top part of an S curve, many rapidly urbanizing Third-World countries are at the steep middle of the S, and other emerging countries are still moving along the long, slowly rising bottom of the S.

Davis concludes that there will be an end to urbanization – but not necessarily to absolute population growth, the physical size of cities or the absolute number of people they might contain.

Davis found that the rural population in Third-World countries today continues to grow as these countries urbanize, unlike European cities in the nineteenth century where industrialization led to depopulation of rural areas. His vision of Third-World societies unable to sustain their populations helps to explain Saskia Sassen's description of growing poverty and inequality worldwide and the growth of large, poorly paid immigrant labor forces in the largest cities in the developed world (pp. 70, 300).

Research and scholarly debate continues on the nature and causes of world urbanization. Historians continue to shed light on the growth of cities, but, because the records from which they work are often fragmentary and incomplete, not everyone agrees with Davis or any other standard account. Debate continues on the relative importance of war, plague, medical advances, trade, technology, religion, and ideology on urban growth. And debate is even more intense in the normative area – about what, if anything, governments should do about population growth and urbanization. Davis stresses the impact of overall population growth – which he sees as excessive – on world urbanization and implies that family planning is essential if cities are to meet human needs. But many governments reject family planning on religious or policy grounds.

Davis's other writings include many articles and studies on demographics and natural resources and two anthologies: *Cities: Their Origin, Growth and Human Impact* (San Francisco: W. H. Freeman, 1973) and (with Mikhail S. Bernstram), *Resources, Environment and Population: Present Knowledge, Future Options* (New York: Population Council, and Oxford: Oxford University Press, 1991).

Data on world urbanization are given by Tertius Chandler and Gerald Fox, *Three Thousand Years of Urban Growth* (New York: Academic Press, 1974). Further insight on demography and urbanization can be found in World Bank, *World Development Report: Infrastructure for Development* (Oxford: Oxford University Press, 1994) and William Alonso, "The Population Factor in Urban Growth" in Arthur P. Solomon (ed.), *The Prospective City* (Cambridge, Mass.: MIT Press, 1980). Lester R. Brown and Jodi L. Jacobson provide a summary of recent world population studies and reflections on the future in *The Future of Urbanization: Facing the Ecological and Economic Constraints* (New York: Worldwatch Paper, May 1987).

KINGSLEY DAVIS, "The Urbanization of the Human Population"

Scientific American (1965)*

Urbanized societies, in which a majority of the people live crowded together in towns and cities, represent a new and fundamental step in man's social evolution. Although cities themselves first appeared some 5,500 years ago, they were small and surrounded by an overwhelming majority of rural people; moreover, they relapsed easily to village or small-town status. The urbanized societies of today, in contrast, not only have urban agglomerations of a size never before attained but also have a high proportion of their population concentrated in such agglomerations. In 1960, for example, nearly 52 million Americans lived in only 16 urbanized areas. Together these areas covered less land than one of the smaller counties (Cochise) of Arizona. According to one definition used by the U.S. Bureau of the Census, 96 million people – 53 percent of the nation's population – were concentrated in 213 urbanized areas that together occupied only 0.7 percent of the nation's land. Another definition used by the bureau puts the urban population at about 70 percent. The large and dense agglomerations comprising the urban population involve a degree of human contact and of social complexity never before known. They exceed in size the communities of any other large animal;

they suggest the behavior of communal insects rather than of mammals.

Neither the recency nor the speed of this evolutionary development is widely appreciated. Before 1850 no society could be described as predominantly urbanized, and by 1900 only one – Great Britain – could be so regarded. Today, only 65 years later, all industrial nations are highly urbanized, and in the world as a whole the process of urbanization is accelerating rapidly.

Some years ago my associates and I at Columbia University undertook to document the progress of urbanization by compiling data on the world's cities and the proportion of human beings living in them; in recent years the work has been continued in our center – International Population and Urban Research – at the University of California at Berkeley. The data obtained in these investigations ... show the historical trend in terms of one index of urbanization: the proportion of the population living in cities of 100,000 or larger. Statistics of this kind are only approximations of reality, but they are accurate enough to demonstrate how urbanization has accelerated. Between 1850 and 1950 the index changed at a much higher rate than from 1800 to 1850, but the rate of change from 1950 to 1960 was twice that of the preceding 50 years! If the pace of increase that obtained between 1950 and 1960 were to remain the same, by 1990 the fraction of the world's people living in cities of 100,000 or larger would be more than half. Using another index of urbanization – the proportion of the world's population living in urban places of all sizes – we found that by 1960 the figure had already reached 33 percent.

Clearly the world as a whole is not fully urbanized, but it soon will be. This change in human life is so recent that even the most urbanized countries still exhibit the rural origins of their institutions. Its full implications for man's organic and social evolution can only be surmised.

In discussing the trend – and its implications insofar as they can be perceived – I shall use the term "urbanization" in a particular way. It refers here to the proportion of the total population concentrated in urban settlements, or else to a rise in this proportion. A common mistake is to think of urbanization as simply the growth of cities. Since the total population is composed of both the urban population and the rural, however, the "proportion urban" is a function of both of them. Accordingly, cities can grow without any urbanization, provided that the rural population grows at an equal or a greater rate.

Historically, urbanization and the growth of cities have occurred together, which accounts for the confusion. As the reader will soon see, it is necessary to distinguish the two trends. In the most advanced countries today, for example, urban populations are still growing, but their proportion of the total population is tending to remain stable or to diminish. In other words, the process of urbanization – the switch from a spread-out pattern of human settlement to one of concentration in urban centers – is a change that has a beginning and an end, but the growth of cities has no inherent limit. Such growth could continue even after everyone was living in cities, through sheer excess of births over deaths.

The difference between a rural village and an urban community is of course one of degree; a precise operational distinction is somewhat arbitrary, and it varies from one nation to another. Since data are available for communities of various sizes, a dividing line can be chosen at will. One convenient index of urbanization, for example, is the proportion of people living in places of 100,000 or more. In the following analysis I shall depend on two indexes: the one just mentioned and the proportion of population classed as "urban" in the official statistics of each country. In practice the two indexes are highly correlated; therefore either one can be used as an index of urbanization.

Actually the hardest problem is not that of determining the "floor" of the urban category but of ascertaining the boundary of places that are clearly urban by any definition. How far east is the boundary of Los Angeles? Where along the Hooghly River does Calcutta leave off and the countryside begin? In the past the population of cities and towns has usually been given as the number of people living within the political boundaries. Thus the population of New York is frequently given as around eight million, this being the population of the city proper. The error in such a figure was not large before World War I, but since then, particularly in the advanced countries, urban populations have been spilling over the narrow political boundaries at a tremendous rate. In 1960 the New York–Northeastern New Jersey urbanized area, as delineated by the Bureau of the Census, had more than 14 million people. That delineation showed it to be the largest city in the world and nearly twice as large as New York City proper.

As a result of the outward spread of urbanites, counts made on the basis of political boundaries alone underestimate the city populations and exaggerate the rural. For this reason our office delineated the metropolitan areas of as many countries as possible for dates around 1950. These areas included the central, or political, cities and the zones around them that are receiving the spillover.

This reassessment raised the estimated proportion of the world's population in cities of 100,000 or larger from 15.1 percent to 16.7 percent. As of 1960 we have used wherever possible the "urban agglomeration" data now furnished to the United Nations by many countries. The U.S., for example, provides data for "urbanized areas," meaning cities of 50,000 or larger and the built-up agglomerations around them.

... My concern is with the degree of urbanization in whole societies. It is curious that thousands of years elapsed between the first appearance of small cities and the emergence of urbanized societies in the nineteenth century. It is also curious that the region where urbanized societies arose – northwestern Europe – was not the one that had given rise to the major cities of the past; on the contrary, it was a region where urbanization had been at an extremely low ebb. Indeed, the societies of northwestern Europe in medieval times were so rural that it is hard for modern minds to comprehend them. Perhaps it was the nonurban character of these societies that erased the parasitic nature of towns and eventually provided a new basis for a revolutionary degree of urbanization.

At any rate, two seemingly adverse conditions may have presaged the age to come: one the low productivity of medieval agriculture in both per-acre and per-man terms, the other the feudal social system. The first meant that towns could not prosper on the basis of local agriculture alone but had to trade and to manufacture something to trade. The second meant that they could not gain political dominance over their hinterlands and thus become warring city-states. Hence they specialized in commerce and manufacture and evolved local institutions suited to this role. Craftsmen were housed in the towns, because there the merchants could regulate quality and cost. Competition among towns stimulated specialization and technological innovation. The need for literacy, accounting skills and geographical knowledge caused the towns to invest in secular education.

Although the medieval towns remained small and never embraced more than a minor fraction of each region's population, the close connection between industry and commerce that they fostered, together with their emphasis on technique, set the stage for the ultimate breakthrough in urbanization. This breakthrough came only with the enormous growth in productivity caused by the use of inanimate energy and machinery. How difficult it was to achieve the transition is agonizingly apparent from statistics showing that even with the conquest of the New World the growth of urbanization during three postmedieval centuries in Europe was barely perceptible. I have assembled population estimates at two or more dates for 33 towns and cities in the sixteenth century, 46 in the seventeenth and 61 in the eighteenth. The average rate of growth during the three centuries was less than 0.6 percent per year. Estimates of the growth of Europe's population as a whole between 1650 and 1800 work out to slightly more than 0.4 percent. The advantage of the towns was evidently very slight. Taking only the cities of 100,000 or more inhabitants, one finds that in 1600 their combined population was 1.6 percent of the estimated population of Europe; in 1700, 1.9 percent; and in 1800, 2.2 percent. On the eve of the industrial revolution Europe was still an overwhelmingly agrarian region.

With industrialization, however, the transformation was striking. By 1801 nearly a tenth of the people of England and Wales were living in cities of 100,000 or larger. This proportion doubled in 40 years and doubled again in another 60 years. By 1900 Britain was an urbanized society. In general, the later each country became industrialized, the faster was its urbanization. The change from a population with 10 percent of its members in cities of 100,000 or larger to one in which 30 percent lived in such cities took about 79 years in England and Wales, 66 in the U.S., 48 in Germany, 36 in Japan and 26 in Australia. The close association between economic development and urbanization has persisted: ... in 199 countries around 1960 the proportion of the population living in cities varied sharply with per capita income.

Clearly, modern urbanization is best understood in terms of its connection with economic growth, and its implications are best perceived in its latest manifestations in advanced countries. What becomes apparent as one examines the trend in these countries is that urbanization is a finite process, a cycle through which nations go in their transition from agrarian to industrial society. The intensive urbanization of most of the advanced countries began within the past hundred years; in the underdeveloped countries it got under way more recently. In some of the advanced countries its end is now in sight. The fact that it will end, however, does not mean that either economic development or the growth of cities will necessarily end.

The typical cycle of urbanization can be represented by a curve in the shape of an attenuated S. Starting from the bottom of the S, the first bend tends to come early and to be followed by a long attenuation. In the United Kingdom, for instance, the swiftest rise in the proportion of people living in cities of 100,000 or larger occurred from 1811 to 1851. In the U.S. it occurred from 1820 to 1890, in Greece from 1879 to 1921. As the proportion climbs above 50 percent the curve begins to flatten out; it falters, or even declines, when the proportion urban has reached about 75 percent. In the United Kingdom, one of the world's most urban countries, the proportion was slightly higher in

1926 (78.7 percent) than in 1961 (78.3 percent).

At the end of the curve some ambiguity appears. As a society becomes advanced enough to be highly urbanized it can also afford considerable suburbanization and fringe development. In a sense the slowing down of urbanization is thus more apparent than real: an increasing proportion of urbanites simply live in the country and are classified as rural. Many countries now try to compensate for this ambiguity by enlarging the boundaries of urban places; they did so in numerous censuses taken around 1960. Whether in these cases the old classification of urban or the new one is erroneous depends on how one looks at it; at a very advanced stage the entire concept of urbanization becomes ambiguous.

The end of urbanization cannot be unraveled without going into the ways in which economic development governs urbanization. Here the first question is: where do the urbanites come from? The possible answers are few: the proportion of people in cities can rise because rural settlements grow larger and are reclassified as towns or cities; because the excess of births over deaths is greater in the city than in the country, or because people move from the country to the city.

The first factor has usually had only slight influence. The second has apparently never been the case. Indeed, a chief obstacle to the growth of cities in the past has been their excessive mortality. London's water in the middle of the nineteenth century came mainly from wells and rivers that drained cesspools, graveyards and tidal areas. The city was regularly ravaged by cholera. Tables for 1841 show an expectation of life of about 36 years for London and 26 for Liverpool and Manchester, as compared to 41 for England and Wales as a whole. After 1850, mainly as a result of sanitary measures and some improvement in nutrition and housing, city health improved, but as late as the period 1901–1910 the death rate of the urban counties in England and Wales, as modified to make the age structure comparable, was 33 percent higher than the death rate of the rural counties. As Bernard Benjamin, a chief statistician of the British General Register Office, has remarked:

"Living in the town involved not only a higher risk of epidemic and crowd diseases . . . but also a higher risk of degenerative disease – the harder wear and tear of factory employment and urban discomfort." By 1950, however, virtually the entire differential had been wiped out.

As for birth rates, during rapid urbanization in the past they were notably lower in cities than in rural areas. In fact, the gap tended to widen somewhat as urbanization proceeded in the latter half of the nineteenth century and the first quarter of the twentieth. In 1800 urban women in the U.S. had 36 percent fewer children than rural women did; in 1840, 38 percent and in 1930, 41 percent. Thereafter the difference diminished.

With mortality in the cities higher and birth rates lower, and with reclassification a minor factor, the only real source for the growth in the proportion of people in urban areas during the industrial transition was rural–urban migration. This source had to be plentiful enough not only to overcome the substantial disadvantage of the cities in natural increase but also, above that, to furnish a big margin of growth in their populations. If, for example, the cities had a death rate a third higher and a birth rate a third lower than the rural rates (as was typical in the latter half of the nineteenth century), they would require each year perhaps 40 to 45 migrants from elsewhere per 1,000 of their population to maintain a growth rate of 3 percent per year. Such a rate of migration could easily be maintained as long as the rural portion of the population was large, but when this condition ceased to obtain, the maintenance of the same urban rate meant an increasing drain on the countryside.

Why did the rural–urban migration occur? The reason was that the rise in technological enhancement of human productivity, together with certain constant factors, rewarded urban concentration. One of the constant factors was that agriculture uses land as its prime instrument of production and hence spreads out people who are engaged in it, whereas manufacturing, commerce and services use land only as a site. Moreover, the demand for agricultural products is less elastic than the demand for services and manufactures. As productivity grows, services and manufactures can absorb

more manpower by paying higher wages. Since nonagricultural activities can use land simply as a site, they can locate near one another (in towns and cities) and thus minimize the fraction of space inevitably involved in the division of labor. At the same time, as agricultural technology is improved, capital costs in farming rise and manpower becomes not only less needed but also economically more burdensome. A substantial portion of the agricultural population is therefore sufficiently disadvantaged, in relative terms, to be attracted by higher wages in other sectors.

In this light one sees why a large *flow* of people from farms to cities was generated in every country that passed through the industrial revolution. One also sees why, with an even higher proportion of people already in cities and with the inability of city people to replace themselves by reproduction, the drain eventually became so heavy that in many nations the rural population began to decline in absolute as well as relative terms. In Sweden it declined after 1920, in England and Wales after 1861, in Belgium after 1910.

Realizing that urbanization is transitional and finite, one comes on another fact – a fact that throws light on the circumstances in which urbanization comes to an end. A basic feature of the transition is the profound switch from agricultural to nonagricultural employment. This change is associated with urbanization but not identical with it. The difference emerges particularly in the later stages. Then the availability of automobiles, radios, motion pictures and electricity, as well as the reduction of the workweek and the workday, mitigate the disadvantages of living in the country. Concurrently the expanding size of cities makes them more difficult to live in. The population classed as "rural" is accordingly enlarged, both from cities and from true farms. For these reasons the "rural" population in some industrial countries never did fall in absolute size. In all the industrial countries, however, the population dependent on agriculture – which the reader will recognize as a more functional definition of the nonurban population than mere rural residence – decreased in absolute as well as relative terms. In the U.S., for example, the net migration from farms totaled more than 27 million between 1920 and 1959 and thus averaged approximately 700,000 a year. As a result the farm population declined from 32.5 million in 1916 to 20.5 million in 1960, in spite of the large excess of births in farm families. In 1964, by a stricter American definition classifying as "farm families" only those families actually earning their living from agriculture, the farm population was down to 12.9 million. This number represented 6.8 percent of the nation's population; the comparable figure for 1880 was 44 percent. In Great Britain the number of males occupied in agriculture was, at its peak, 1.8 million, in 1851; by 1961 it had fallen to 0.5 million.

In the later stages of the cycle, then, urbanization in the industrial countries tends to cease. Hence the connection between economic development and the growth of cities also ceases. The change is explained by two circumstances. First, there is no longer enough farm population to furnish a significant migration to the cities. (What can 12.9 million American farmers contribute to the growth of the 100 million people already in urbanized areas?) Second, the rural nonfarm population, nourished by refugees from the expanding cities, begins to increase as fast as the city population. The effort of census bureaus to count fringe residents as urban simply pushes the definition of "urban" away from the notion of dense settlement and in the direction of the term "nonfarm." As the urban population becomes more "rural," which is to say less densely settled, the advanced industrial peoples are for a time able to enjoy the amenities of urban life without the excessive crowding of the past.

Here, however, one again encounters the fact that a cessation of urbanization does not necessarily mean a cessation of city growth. An example is provided by New Zealand. Between 1945 and 1961 the proportion of New Zealand's population classed as urban – that is, the ratio between urban and rural residents – changed hardly at all (from 61.3 percent to 63.6 percent) but the urban population increased by 50 percent. In Japan between 1940 and 1950 urbanization actually decreased slightly, but the urban population increased by 13 percent.

The point to be kept in mind is that once urbanization ceases, city growth becomes a function of general population growth. Enough farm-to-city migration may still occur to redress the difference in natural increase. The reproductive rate of urbanites tends, however, to increase when they live at lower densities, and the reproductive rate of "urbanized" farmers tends to decrease; hence little migration is required to make the urban increase equal the national increase.

I now turn to the currently underdeveloped countries. With the advanced nations having slackened their rate of urbanization, it is the others – representing three-fourths of humanity – that are mainly responsible for the rapid urbanization now characterizing the world as a whole. In fact, between 1950 and 1960 the proportion of the population in cities of 100,000 or more rose about a third faster in the underdeveloped regions than in the developed ones. Among the underdeveloped regions the pace was slow in eastern and southern Europe but in the rest of the underdeveloped world the proportion in cities rose twice as fast as it did in the industrialized countries, even though the latter countries in many cases broadened their definitions of urban places to include more suburban and fringe residents.

Because of the characteristic pattern of urbanization, the current rates of urbanization in underdeveloped countries could be expected to exceed those now existing in countries far advanced in the cycle. On discovering that this is the case one is tempted to say that the underdeveloped regions are now in the typical stage of urbanization associated with early economic development. This notion, however, is erroneous. In their urbanization the underdeveloped countries are definitely not recreating past history. Indeed, the best grasp of their present situation comes from analyzing how their course differs from the previous pattern of development.

The first thing to note is that today's underdeveloped countries are urbanizing not only more rapidly than the industrial nations are now but also more rapidly than the industrial nations did in the heyday of their urban growth. The difference, however, is not large. In 40 underdeveloped countries for which we have data in recent decades, the average gain in the proportion of the population urban was 20 percent per decade; in 16 industrial countries, during the decades of their most rapid urbanization (mainly in the nineteenth century), the average gain per decade was 15 percent.

This finding that urbanization is proceeding only a little faster in underdeveloped countries than it did historically in the advanced nations may be questioned by the reader. It seemingly belies the widespread impression that cities throughout the nonindustrial parts of the world are bursting with people. There is, however, no contradiction. One must recall the basic distinction between a change in the proportion of the population urban, which is a ratio, and the absolute growth of cities. The popular impression is correct: the cities in underdeveloped areas are growing at a disconcerting rate. They are far outstripping the city boom of the industrializing era in the nineteenth century. If they continue their recent rate of growth, they will double their population every 15 years.

In 34 underdeveloped countries for which we have data relating to the 1940s and 1950s, the average annual gain in the urban population was 4.5 percent. The figure is remarkably similar for the various regions: 4.7 percent in seven countries of Africa, 4.7 percent in 15 countries of Asia and 4.3 percent in 12 countries of Latin America. In contrast, in nine European countries during their period of fastest urban population growth (mostly in the latter half of the nineteenth century) the average gain per year was 2.1 percent. Even the frontier industrial countries – the U.S., Australia–New Zealand, Canada and Argentina – which received huge numbers of immigrants had a smaller population growth in towns and cities: 4.2 percent per year. In Japan and the U.S.S.R. the rate was respectively 5.4 and 4.3 percent per year, but their economic growth began only recently.

How is it possible that the contrast in growth between today's underdeveloped countries and yesterday's industrializing countries is sharper with respect to the absolute urban population than with respect to the urban share of the total population? The answer lies in another profound difference between the two sets of coun-tries – a difference in total population growth, rural as well as urban. Contemporary underdeveloped populations have been growing since 1940 more than twice as fast as industrialized populations, and their increase far exceeds the growth of the latter at the peak of their expansion. The only rivals in an earlier day were the frontier nations, which had the help of great streams of immigrants. Today the underdeveloped nations – already densely settled, tragically impoverished and with gloomy economic prospects – are multiplying their people by sheer biological increase at a rate that is unprecedented. It is this population boom that is overwhelmingly responsible for the rapid inflation of city populations in such countries. Contrary to popular opinion both inside and outside those countries, the main factor is not rural–urban migration.

This point can be demonstrated easily by a calculation that has the effect of eliminating the influence of general population growth on urban growth. The calculation involves assuming that the total population of a given country remained constant over a period of time but that the percentage urban changed as it did historically. In this manner one obtains the growth of the absolute urban population that would have occurred if rural–urban migration were the only factor affecting it. As an example, Costa Rica had in 1927 a total population of 471,500, of which 88,600, or 18.8 percent, was urban. By 1963 the country's total population was 1,325,200 and the urban population was 456,600, or 34.5 percent. If the total population had remained at 471,500 but the percentage urban had still risen from 18.8 to 34.5, the absolute urban population in 1963 would have been only 162,700. That is the growth that would have occurred in the urban population if rural–urban migration had been the only factor. In actuality the urban population rose to 456,600. In other words, only 20 percent of the rapid growth of Costa Rica's towns and cities was attributable to urbanization per se; 44 percent was attributable solely to the country's general population increase, the remainder to the joint operation of both factors. Similarly, in Mexico between 1940 and 1960, 50 percent of the urban population increase was attributable to national multiplication alone and only 22 percent to urbanization alone.

The past performance of the advanced countries presents a sharp contrast. In Switzerland between 1850 and 1888, when the proportion urban resembled that in Costa Rica recently, general population growth alone accounted for only 19 percent of the increase of town and city people, and rural–urban migration alone accounted for 69 percent. In France between 1846 and 1911 only 21 percent of the growth in the absolute urban population was due to general growth alone.

The conclusion to which this contrast points is that one anxiety of governments in the underdeveloped nations is misplaced. Impressed by the mushrooming in their cities of shantytowns filled with ragged peasants, they attribute the fantastically fast city growth to rural–urban migration. Actually this migration now does little more than make up for the small difference in the birth rate between city and countryside. In the history of the industrial nations, as we have seen, the sizable difference between urban and rural birth rates and death rates required that cities, if they were to grow, had to have an enormous influx of people from farms and villages. Today in the underdeveloped countries the towns and cities have only a slight disadvantage in fertility, and their old disadvantage in mortality not only has been wiped out but also in many cases has been reversed. During the nineteenth century the urbanizing nations were learning how to keep crowded populations in cities from dying like flies. Now the lesson has been learned, and it is being applied to cities even in countries just emerging from tribalism. In fact, a disproportionate share of public health funds goes into cities. As a result, throughout the nonindustrial world people in cities are multiplying as never before, and rural–urban migration is playing a much lesser role.

The trends just described have an important implication for the rural population. Given the explosive overall population growth in underdeveloped countries, it follows that if the rural population is not to pile up on the land and reach an economically absurd density, a high rate of rural–urban migration must be maintained. Indeed, the exodus from rural areas

should be higher than in the past. But this high rate of internal movement is not taking place, and there is some doubt that it could conceivably do so.

To elaborate, I shall return to my earlier point that in the evolution of industrialized countries the rural citizenry often declined in absolute as well as relative terms. The rural population of France – 26.8 million in 1846 – was down to 20.8 million by 1926 and 17.2 million by 1962, notwithstanding a gain in the nation's total population during this period. Sweden's rural population dropped from 4.3 million in 1910 to 3.5 million in 1960. Since the category "rural" includes an increasing portion of urbanites living in fringe areas, the historical drop was more drastic and consistent specifically in the farm population. In the U.S., although the "rural" population never quite ceased to grow, the farm contingent began its long descent shortly after the turn of the century; today it is less than two-fifths of what it was in 1910.

This transformation is not occurring in contemporary underdeveloped countries. In spite of the enormous growth of their cities, their rural populations – and their more narrowly defined agricultural populations – are growing at a rate that in many cases exceeds the rise of even the urban population during the evolution of the now advanced countries. The poor countries thus confront a grave dilemma. If they do not substantially step up the exodus from rural areas, these areas will be swamped with underemployed farmers. If they do step up the exodus, the cities will grow at a disastrous rate.

The rapid growth of cities in the advanced countries, painful though it was, had the effect of solving a problem – the problem of the rural population. The growth of cities enabled agricultural holdings to be consolidated, allowed increased capitalization and in general resulted in greater efficiency. Now, however, the underdeveloped countries are experiencing an even more rapid urban growth – and are suffering from urban problems – but urbanization is not solving their rural ills.

A case in point is Venezuela. Its capital, Caracas, jumped from a population of 359,000 in 1941 to 1,507,000 in 1963; other Venezuelan towns and cities equaled or exceeded this growth. Is this rapid rise denuding the country-side of people? No, the Venezuelan farm population increased in the decade 1951–1961 by 11 percent. The only thing that declined was the amount of cultivated land. As a result the agricultural population density became worse. In 1950 there were some 64 males engaged in agriculture per square mile of cultivated land; in 1961 there were 78. (Compare this with 4.8 males occupied in agriculture per square mile of cultivated land in Canada, 6.8 in the U.S. and 15.6 in Argentina.) With each male occupied in agriculture there are of course dependants. Approximately 225 persons in Venezuela are trying to live from each square mile of cultivated land. Most of the growth of cities in Venezuela is attributable to overall population growth. If the general population had not grown at all, and internal migration had been large enough to produce the actual shift in the proportion in cities, the increase in urban population would have been only 28 percent of what it was and the rural population would have been reduced by 57 percent.

The story of Venezuela is being repeated virtually everywhere in the underdeveloped world. It is not only Caracas that has thousands of squatters living in self-constructed junk houses on land that does not belong to them. By whatever name they are called, the squatters are to be found in all major cities in the poorer countries. They live in broad gullies beneath the main plain in San Salvador and on the hillsides of Rio de Janeiro and Bogotá. They tend to occupy with implacable determination parks, school grounds and vacant lots. Amman, the capital of Jordan, grew from 12,000 in 1958 to 247,000 in 1961. A good part of it is slums, and urban amenities are lacking most of the time for most of the people. Greater Baghdad now has an estimated 850,000 people; its slums, like those in many other underdeveloped countries, are in two zones: the central part of the city and the outlying areas. Here are the *sarifa* areas, characterized by self-built reed huts; these areas account for about 45 percent of the housing in the entire city and are devoid of amenities, including even latrines. In addition to such urban problems, all the countries struggling for higher living levels find their rural population growing too and piling up on already crowded land. I have characterized urbanization as a transformation that, unlike economic development, is finally accomplished and comes to an end. At the 1950–1960 rate the term "urbanized world" will be applicable well before the end of the century. One should scarcely expect, however, that mankind will complete its urbanization without major complications. One sign of trouble ahead turns on the distinction I made at the start between urbanization and city growth per se. Around the globe today city growth is disproportionate to urbanization. The discrepancy is paradoxical in the industrial nations and worse than paradoxical in the nonindustrial.

It is in this respect that the nonindustrial nations, which still make up the great majority of nations, are far from repeating past history. In the nineteenth and early twentieth centuries the growth of cities arose from and contributed to economic advancement. Cities took surplus manpower from the countryside and put it to work producing goods and services that in turn helped to modernize agriculture. But today in underdeveloped countries, as in present-day advanced nations, city growth has become increasingly unhinged from economic development and hence from rural–urban migration. It derives in greater degree from overall population growth, and this growth in nonindustrial lands has become unprecedented because of modern health techniques combined with high birth rates.

The speed of world population growth is twice what it was before 1940, and the swiftest increase has shifted from the advanced to the backward nations. In the latter countries, consequently, it is virtually impossible to create city services fast enough to take care of the huge, never-ending cohorts of babies and peasants swelling the urban masses. It is even harder to expand agricultural land and capital fast enough to accommodate the enormous natural increase on farms. The problem is not urbanization, not rural–urban migration, but human multiplication. It is a problem that is new in both its scale and its setting, and runaway city growth is only one of its painful expressions.

As long as the human population expands, cities will expand too, regardless of whether urbanization increases or declines. This means that some individual cities will reach a size that will make nineteenth-century metropolises look like small towns. If the New York urbanized area should continue to grow only as fast as the nation's population (according to medium projections of the latter by the Bureau of the Census), it would reach 21 million by 1985 and 30 million by 2010. I have calculated that if India's population should grow as the U.N. projections indicate it will, the largest city in India in the year 2000 will have between 36 and 66 million inhabitants.

What is the implication of such giant agglomerations for human density? In 1950 the New York–Northeastern New Jersey urbanized area had an average density of 9,810 persons per square mile. With 30 million people in the year 2010, the density would be 24,000 per square mile. Although this level is exceeded now in parts of New York City (which averages about 25,000 per square mile) and many other cities, it is a high density to be spread over such a big area; it would cover, remember, the suburban areas to which people moved to escape high density. Actually, however, the density of the New York urbanized region is dropping, not increasing, as the population grows. The reason is that the territory covered by the urban agglomeration is growing faster than the population: it grew by 51 percent from 1950 to 1960, whereas the population rose by 15 percent.

If, then, one projects the rise in population and the rise in territory for the New York urbanized region one finds the density problem solved. It is not solved for long, though, because New York is not the only city in the region that is expanding. So are Philadelphia, Trenton, Hartford, New Haven and so on. By 1960 a huge stretch of territory about 600 miles long and 30 to 100 miles wide along the eastern seaboard contained some 37 million people. (I am speaking of a longer section of the seaboard than the Boston-to-Washington conurbation referred to by some other authors.) Since the whole area is becoming one big polynucleated city, its population cannot long expand without a rise in density. Thus persistent human multiplication promises to frustrate the ceaseless search for space – for ample residential lots, wide-open suburban school grounds, sprawling shopping centers, one-floor factories, broad freeways.

How people feel about giant agglomerations is best indicated by their headlong effort to escape them. The bigger the city, the higher the cost of space; yet the more the level of living rises, the more people are willing to pay for low-density living. Nevertheless, as urbanized areas expand and collide, it seems probable that life in low-density surroundings will become too dear for the great majority.

One can of course imagine that cities may cease to grow and may even shrink in size while the population in general continues to multiply. Even this dream, however, would not permanently solve the problem of space. It would eventually obliterate the distinction between urban and rural, but at the expense of the rural.

It seems plain that the only way to stop urban crowding and to solve most of the urban problems besetting both the developed and the underdeveloped nations is to reduce the overall rate of population growth. Policies designed to do this have as yet little intelligence and power behind them. Urban planners continue to treat population growth as something to be planned for, not something to be itself planned. Any talk about applying brakes to city growth is therefore purely speculative, overshadowed as it is by the reality of uncontrolled population increase.

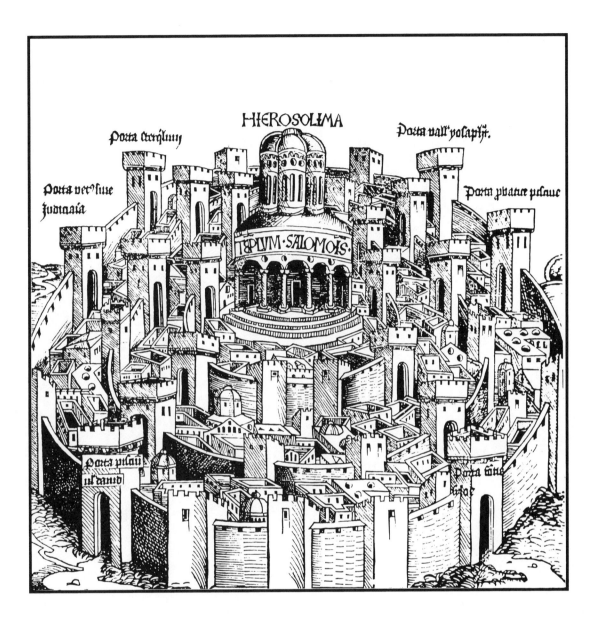

PART 1

*T*he Evolution of Cities

PART ONE

INTRODUCTION

Cities are civilization. In the nineteenth century, the standard categories of anthropology proclaimed that mankind arose from nomadic savagery through village-based barbarism to true civilization only when the first cities were established. City life alone gave rise to writing, to the authority of the state, and to complex economies based on equally complex social systems. Twentieth-century researchers adopted a new system of terminology for the evolution of humanity – from paleolithic, through neolithic, to urban and later industrial and postindustrial stages of development – but the central place of cities as the incubators and sustainers of advanced culture remained the same. The culture of cities and our notions of human civilization itself are virtually indistinguishable.

Mankind's rise to urban civilization took tens of thousands of years, but ever since the first true cities arose – most probably in Mesopotamia sometime between 4000 and 3000 B.C.E. – the influence of city-based cultures and the steady spread and increase of urban populations around the world have been the central facts of human history. In his seminal essay "The Urbanization of the Human Population" (1965) which forms the prologue to this book, Kingsley Davis makes the point that "urbanization" and "the growth of cities" are not the same thing. "Urbanization," as Davis defines it, is the *increase in the proportion* of a population that is urban as opposed to rural. That such an increase could take place without the growth of cities *per se* (for example, by the death of vast numbers of the rural population) or that city populations could grow without an increase in urbanization (as when the total population, urban and rural, increases at a similar rate) are important concepts that underlie the history of urban life. This definition of urbanization helps to explain, for example, how immigration from the countryside to the city has repeatedly been a key factor in the history of urban development, as it continues to be today.

A graph illustrating the history of the urbanization process worldwide – starting at zero before the emergence of the first cities five or six thousand years ago and rising to some 50 percent or more worldwide today – would show a steady upward drift that begins to accelerate rapidly during and after the period of the Industrial Revolution. The chart line of urbanization, however, must not be confused with urban history. The culture of cities in its historical dimension does not proceed smoothly ever onward and upward but by a series of fits and starts. In some respects, urban history is cumulative, revealing significant continuities from the earliest period to the present. But in other respects, urban history is emphatically punctuated by a series of radical discontinuities, and it is precisely these breaks with the past, these fundamental paradigm shifts, that reveal the texture, subtlety, and complex human meaning of the history of urban evolution.

The first stage of urban history is what the Australian archaeologist V. Gordon Childe called "the Urban Revolution," that momentous shift from simple tribal communities and village-based agricultural production to the complex social, economic, and political systems that characterized the earliest cities of Mesopotamia, Egypt, and the Indus Valley. True, the earliest cities – in the ancient Near East and elsewhere – grew out of accumulated neolithic knowledge, and certain extensive neolithic communities (such as Catal Huyuk in Anatolia) pre-date the Mesopotamian cities by several millennia and may be regarded as at least protourban. For Childe, however, the development of writing was a crucial cultural element of true urbanism, and the emergence of the cities of the ancient Near East, where writing began, constituted the second of a series of massive transformations that gave shape to the whole of human evolutionary development. Although the successive stages overlapped, each of his three "revolutions" – the agricultural, the urban, and the industrial – totally changed the world as it had been before.

In certain important respects, all the ancient cities are remarkably similar. Most are walled – except in Egypt, where the surrounding deserts may have been regarded as sufficient defenses – and all contain a distinct citadel precinct, separately walled, encompassing a temple, a palace, and the central granary. Most of the earliest cities also boasted some sort of pyramid or ziggurat. And, as Karl Wittfogel pointed out in *Oriental Despotism* (1957), almost all were located along major rivers and based their power (and that of their rulers) on the control of massive irrigation systems serving the surrounding countryside.

Thus, both the physical structure and socioeconomic complexity of the earliest cities are clearly unlike anything that had come before. Whereas the neolithic village had been ruled by a council of elders, the cities were mostly ruled by totalitarian god-kings and their attendant priests who formed a class totally apart from the rest of the citizenry. And whereas neolithic communities may have built earthen enclosures as ceremonial centers for ritual pageantry and hill forts for refuge and defense, the ancient cities – from Ur and Babylon on the Euphrates to Teotihuacan and Tenochtitlan in the Valley of Mexico – transformed these institutions into elaborate structures so massive that their remains are still visible today.

Although the growth of cities on the Mesopotamian model may be said to have "spread" to the Nile Delta and to the Indus Valley as a result of direct cultural contact, Paul Wheatley, in *The Pivot of the Four Quarters* (1971), argues that no such diffusionist explanation for the rise of cities outside of the ancient Near East is truly convincing. The ancient cities of Shang and Chou China – like the earliest cities of sub-Saharan Africa, Southeast Asia, and Mesoamerica – arose quite independently of the Mesopotamian example. What is remarkable is how similar ancient cities everywhere were in terms of social structure, economic function, political order, and architectural monumentality.

The cities of ancient Greece, on the other hand, developed on a very different model. Perhaps because they arose in narrow mountain valleys rather than on broad alluvial plains, the Grecian cities that emerged around 1200 B.C.E. and developed into an astonishing cultural efflorescence by 500 B.C.E. were small (sometimes with a population of only a few thousand), economically self-contained, and almost village-like in their social and political institutions. It was the concept of urban citizenship and self-government that was the distinctive contribution of the Greeks to the evolution of urban civilization. Greek democracy was by no means perfect. Women, slaves, and foreigners were all excluded from the rights and responsibilities of citizenship. But the cultural, artistic, and intellectual consequences of the democratic principle were extraordinary. "Within a couple of centuries," writes Lewis Mumford in *The City in History* (1961), "the Greeks discovered more about the nature and potentialities of man than the Egyptians or the Sumerians seem to have discovered in as many millennia."

If cities are civilization, they are also the cultural instrumentality by which humanity has attempted, since neolithic times, to achieve a higher, more inclusive concept of community. At the core of the Greek contribution to the history of urban civilization was the concept of the "polis."

Sometimes translated as "city-state," at other times identified as the collective citizenry of a Greek city, the polis – as described so brilliantly by H. D. F. Kitto in *The Greeks* (1951) – was both a community and a *sense* of community that helped to define the Greek citizen's relationship to his city, to his fellow citizens, to the world at large, and to himself. In *The Politics*, Aristotle called man the *"zoon politikon"* – the "political animal" or, more properly, "the animal that belongs to a polis" – and described the ideal city-state as one small enough for a single citizen's voice to be heard by all his assembled fellow citizens. For the Greek citizen, social life was lived in the agora or public marketplace, and contact with rural nature was immediately at hand. In that sense, the polis was a reincarnation, in an urban context, of the face-to-face human relationships that characterized the preurban community of the neolithic village.

Marking another sharp break in the history of urban life, the city of Rome began as a cluster of villages along the Tiber in central Italy, emerged as a powerful republic similar to the earlier Greek cities, but then exploded into a giant metropolis and a city of world empire. Rome's contributions to civilization were considerable. Its roads, aqueducts, and sewers set new standards of engineering excellence. Its systems of military and colonial administration spread a common law, and established a common peace, throughout a large and populous area that extended from Persia to the borders of Scotland. Roman imperial expansion also spread Roman literature, philosophy, and art, establishing the basis for a widespread cultural hegemony. And Rome planted colonial towns wherever its legions marched, often leaving traces of an original *castrum* laid out along the cardinal points of the compass at the center of later medieval cities.

But if the administrative and infrastructural accomplishments of the Romans were impressive, their record in the field of social development is more problematic. In the place of the Greek conception of community and participation in the life of the polis, the Romans erected a citizenship of imperial privilege rooted in a rigid social hierarchy of patricians, clients, and plebeians. Beginning with Augustus, the Roman emperors proclaimed themselves gods, staged extravagant spectacles to awe the cowed populace, and ruled by "bread and circuses." Rome, at a population of one million, became a kind of parasite on the entire Mediterranean world, and both city and empire eventually fell of their own weight.

For much of the medieval period that followed the fall of the Roman Empire in the West, Europe was a cultural backwater. In the early Middle Ages, self-contained monastery communities kept the larger world at bay, many provincial towns retreated inside the walls of the Roman amphitheaters, and the population of Rome itself dwindled to a few thousand while that of Chang'an in China reached one million and Teotihuacan in the Valley of Mexico reached 200,000. Raided by Vikings from the north and invaded by North African Arabs on its southern flank, most of Europe had reverted to rural conditions, and serfdom became widespread under a system of warlord feudalism. Meanwhile, the cities of Islam – Samarra and Baghdad and Moorish Cordova – were the real centers of power in what had been the Roman Empire. And other urban centers – the Khmer civilization at Angkor, Luoyang in Sung and Ch'in China, Great Zimbabwe in Africa – surpassed Europe's cities in wealth and power.

After about the year 1000 c.e., however, Europe began to revive, and the late medieval cities became true centers of commerce, culture, and community. As Henri Pirenne argues in *Medieval Cities* (1925), it was the economic function of the great trading towns that led inevitably to their growing power and political independence. Having used their wealth to win from the barons the right to self-government, the medieval towns became islands of freedom in a sea of feudal obligation.

The defensive walls of the medieval city provided a clear demarkation line between the urban and the rural, and the small size of most towns allowed for an easy reciprocity between urban industry and commerce, on the one hand, and agricultural pursuits on the other. Within the town walls, the guilds provided for the organization of economic and social life, while the church saw to the citizens' spiritual needs and established a framework for social ritual and communal unity. Cathedrals, guildhouses, charitable institutions, universities, and colorful marketplaces were all characteristic medieval institutions. Together, they established the perfect stage for what Lewis Mumford called "the urban drama." "Once the unity of this social order was broken," he wrote, "everything about it was set in confusion ... and the city became a battleground for conflicting cultures, dissonant ways of life."

The slow decay of medieval urban unity began with the Renaissance and the rise of nation-state monarchies. The new national rulers built their royal palaces – such as Louis XIV's Versailles – outside of the traditional urban centers. Their interventions into the existing urban fabric included building broad boulevards and open squares fit for the display of baroque pomp and power. The Enlightenment and the Age of Revolutions brought down the divine right of kings and reestablished the political power of the urban commercial interests. In the end, it was capitalism and capitalist industrialism that destroyed the last vestiges of the medieval city by separating the church from its social role and reducing the marketplace to its purely economic functions. The capitalist city – especially the city of the Industrial Revolution – created an entirely new urban paradigm and established the physical, social, economic, and political preconditions of all that was to follow. With the Industrial Revolution, we see the emergence of the modern city.

The political and economic consequences of the Renaissance had helped to spread European domination worldwide through extensive projects of exploration, discovery, and imperialist expansion. The forces of industrialization helped to complete that process of world domination by dividing the world between the advanced industrialized nations – originally Europe and North America – and the underdeveloped, nonindustrialized nations. It also created a new social order based on property-owning capitalists and propertyless proletarians. And the cities, especially the new industrial centers, became dismal conurbations of factories and slums such as the world had never before seen.

One of the earliest and most acute observers of the new urban-industrial order was Friedrich Engels, himself the son of a major German industrialist. In *The Condition of the Working Class in England* (1845), Engels detailed the unrelenting squalor and misery that characterized the working-class districts of Manchester and the strategies employed by the capitalist bourgeoisie to protect themselves from the physical and social horror that was the source of their wealth. One key to that overall strategy was middle-class flight to the suburbs. Suburbanization – with its consequent segregation by social class – became one of the continuing features of the modern city and one of the sources of its ongoing social disharmony and class conflict.

In multiethnic societies, racial divisions compounded class distinctions to create an even further crisis of community in the form of racially segregated neighborhoods that have remained as symbols of inequality and oppression to this very day. *The Philadelphia Negro* (1899) by W. E. B. Dubois specifically describes the African-American district of Philadelphia, Pennsylvania, as it developed in the years following the American Civil War, but the social and cultural dynamic of housing segregation and racial discrimination in the workplace that Dubois describes can be applied to ghetto and barrio experiences throughout the United States and to Third-World immigrant communities worldwide. And in the years since Dubois first surveyed the life of the racially segregated ghetto community, conditions have in some ways gotten steadily worse: so much so that the persistence of racial segregation, and the emergence of an "underclass" population radically disconnected from the rest of the urban community, seem to threaten the social stability of some of the largest, wealthiest cities in the world.

Meanwhile, middle-class suburbia has grown in size and influence to the point where it is no longer just an appendage to the city. Instead, it now actually defines many cities, leaving the old inner cores to the poorest elements of the urban population and in need of regular renewal and redevelopment. Although the first modern suburbs were built along interurban railroad lines, the newer suburbs – especially those developments built after World War II – were automobile-based and created the "sprawl" that has characterized more and more cities worldwide. The new tract-home developments have spawned a vast literature, much of it criticizing suburbia as a cultural wasteland and as a segregated sanctuary of class privilege. But one of the best analyses of contemporary suburbia, Herbert Gans's *The Levittowners* (1967), is also one of the most sympathetic. Gans experienced at first hand the Long Island, New York, tract-home suburbia built by developer Arthur Levitt and describes a family-oriented community of skilled workers and midlevel managers – that is, a true *middle* class, not an upper-middle-class elite.

Suburbia has become so widespread, and so dominant a force in the definition of contemporary urban culture and society, that some analysts are ready to write off the old urban inner cores completely and to declare cities obsolete. Others, such as Saskia Sassen, take a contrary view and argue that the newly emerging global economy makes certain urban centers more relevant and influential than ever. In *Cities in a World Economy* (1994), she argues that the global marketplace frees certain favored cities from the political constraints of the old nation-state economies and allows them to serve as worldwide command and control centers, internally characterized by the uneasy side-by-side coexistence of corporate power and service-sector marginality.

What the future holds for urban civilization is infinitely debatable. Will central cities disappear? Will "edge cities" take over the primary urban functions? Will the urbanization process itself reverse direction and lead to counterurbanization and a general dispersal of the human population? No one knows for certain, but it increasingly appears that urban history is on the cusp of a new major transformation. Looming on the horizon is a new discontinuity, tentatively described as postmodernism, which promises to be a major new stage in the history of cities, in the history of civilization, and in the evolution of the human community.

V. GORDON CHILDE

"The Urban Revolution"

from *Man Makes Himself* (1951)

Editors' introduction   V. Gordon Childe (1892–1957) is arguably the single most influential archaeologist of the twentieth century. Born in Australia, Childe won a scholarship to Queen's College, Oxford, returned to Australia where he briefly pursued a career in left-wing politics, then returned to Great Britain as Professor of Archaeology at the University of Edinburgh and, later, Director of the Institute of Archaeology at the University of London.

Childe's most important book – the one which revolutionized the world of archaeological research by laying out an entirely new theoretical framework for understanding the phases of human development throughout history and prehistory – was *Man Makes Himself* (1936). In that pioneering work, Childe threw out the "three age system" (Stone Age, Bronze Age, Iron Age) that had been left over from nineteenth-century conceptions of human historical development and substituted a series of four stages (paleolithic, neolithic, urban, industrial) punctuated by three "revolutions" (or, as we might term them today, "paradigm shifts"). According to Childe, the first revolution – from Old Stone Age hunter-gatherer cultures to settled agriculture – was the Neolithic Revolution. The second – the movement from neolithic agriculture to complex, hierarchical systems of manufacturing and trade that began during the fourth and third millennia B.C.E. – was the Urban Revolution. And the third major shift in the record of human cultural and historical development – the only truly new development since the rise of cities – was the Industrial Revolution of the eighteenth and nineteenth centuries.

Childe's work continues to figure prominently in ongoing debates about when, where, and why the first cities arose and in the antecedent debate about what a city is. Not everyone has accepted Childe's notion that the shift from neolithic to urban was a total break with the past. Evidence of ancient earthworks, wells, irrigation systems, and even continental trade networks have been traced back as far as 10,000 years in a number of areas in both the Old World and the New. Archaeologist James Mellaart has argued that evidence from the great neolithic communities of Catal Huyuk and Hacilar in ancient Turkey – which predate the earliest Mesopotamian cities by some thousands of years – calls the entire Childe theory into question. Still, it is clear that in most locations agriculture generally predated the rise of the first cities by not just thousands, but tens of thousands of years, and that the full elaboration of those cultural institutions we associate with urban life emerged only with the rise of the Mesopotamian cities.

Nor does everyone agree with Childe's definition of a city. Archaeologists excavating older, smaller, less culturally advanced settlements than the Mesopotamian cities Childe studied often argue that these settlements were urban enough to qualify as true cities. Scholars working in South and Central America point out that many of the cultural features Childe believed essential to the definition of a city

– including the wheel, writing, and the plow – did not exist in large and culturally advanced Amerindian settlements which appear truly urban in other respects. Many modern scholars question the deterministic Marxist categories Childe employed.

In the selection from *Man Makes Himself* reprinted here, Childe details the constituent elements of the Urban Revolution that accompanied the initial rise of complex civilizations in Mesopotamia and elsewhere in the ancient Near East. Childe felt that the major factors motivating the transformation were rooted in the material base of the society – its means of production and its available physical and technological resources. Thus, the economic division of labor, the elaboration of sociopolitical hierarchies, and even the emergence of basic religious and intellectual patterns of thought characteristic of urban civilizations all rested on the underlying need to increase food production through massive irrigation systems and to protect the communities themselves through the erection of massive walls and fortifications.

Although he stresses the importance of writing as an element of any truly urban society, Childe has been faulted for his apparent disregard of the primacy of non-material aspects of culture. His system has very little room for what Lewis Mumford (p. 184) called "the urban drama" or what Jane Jacobs (p. 104) called the "street ballet." As a Marxist, Childe believed that the intellectual "superstructure" of society grew out of its material base, not the other way around. Still, no one has ever called Childe's vision limited or ideologically cramped. On the contrary, he provided an expansive macrohistorical foundation upon which generations of others have built.

A tireless researcher and writer, Childe produced a veritable stream of books, many of which are still classics: *The Dawn of European Civilization* (New York: Knopf, 6th edn. 1958/1925), *The Most Ancient East* (New York: Grove Press, 1957/1928), *What Happened in History* (Harmondsworth: Penguin, 1942), *Social Evolution* (London: Watts, 1951), and many more. At the age of 65, Childe, feeling he had no more to contribute, retired from active scholarship and committed suicide.

Other important works treating the rise of the earliest cities are C. Leonard Wooley, *The Sumerians* (Oxford: Oxford University Press, 1928) and *Ur of the Chaldees* (Oxford: Oxford University Press, 1929); Mortimer Wheeler, *Civilizations of the Indus Valley and Beyond* (London: Thames & Hudson, 1966); Barry J. Kemp, *Ancient Egypt: Anatomy of a Civilization* (London: Routledge, 1989); and Karl Wittfogel, *Oriental Despotism* (New Haven, Conn.: Yale University Press, 1957). For the rise of cities elsewhere, consult Basil Davidson, *The Lost Cities of Africa* (Boston: Little, Brown, 1959); Sylvanus G. Morely and George W. Brainerd, *The Ancient Maya* (Stanford: Stanford University Press, 1956); Jacques Soustelle, *The Daily Life of the Aztecs* (New York: Macmillan, 1962); Paul Wheatley, *The Pivot of the Four Quarters: A Preliminary Inquiry into the Origins and Character of the Ancient Chinese City* (Chicago: Aldine; 1971); James Mellaart, *Earliest Civilizations of the Near East* (New York: McGraw-Hill, 1965) and *Catal Huyuk* (New York: McGraw-Hill, 1967); and Richard E. W. Adams, *Prehistoric Mesoamerica* (Norman: University of Oklahoma Press, 1991).

V. GORDON CHILDE, "The Urban Revolution"

from *Man Makes Himself* (1951)

By 4000 B.C. the great tract of semi-arid lands around the East Mediterranean and eastward to India was populated by a multiplicity of communities. Among them a diversity of economies, appropriate to the variety of local conditions, must be imagined: hunters and fishers, hoe-cultivators, nomadic pastoralists, and settled farmers. And on their fringe we can add other tribes spreading out into the distant wilderness. Among them these diverse communities had augmented man's cultural capital by the discoveries and inventions indicated in the last chapter. They had severally accumulated an imposing body of scientific knowledge (topographical, geological, astronomical, chemical, zoological, and botanical), of practical craftlore on agriculture, mechanics, metallurgy, and architecture, and of magical beliefs that might also enshrine scientific truths. As a result of the commerce and movements of peoples just hinted at, such science, techniques, and beliefs were being widely diffused; knowledge and skill were being pooled. And at the same time the exclusiveness of local groups was being broken down, the rigidity of social institutions was being relaxed, self-sufficing communities were sacrificing their economic independence.

The last-named development progressed faster than elsewhere in the great riverine depressions, in the Nile Valley, on the alluvial plains between the Tigris and Euphrates, and on those bordering the Indus and its tributaries in Sindh and Punjab. There a generous and unfailing water supply and a fertile soil annually renewed by floods ensured a reliable and super-abundant supply of food and permitted the population to expand. On the other hand, both the original draining of the marshes and jungles fringing the rivers and the subsequent maintenance of drainage channels and protective dykes imposed exceptionally heavy demands for sustained and disciplined effort upon the communities profiting by these advantages. And ... irrigation placed in the communities' hand an effective means of enforcing discipline.

And, despite the abundance of foodstuffs, alluvial valleys are exceptionally poor in other raw materials essential to civilized life. The Nile Valley lacked timber for building, freestone, ores, and magic stones. Sumer was still worse off. The only native timber was supplied by the date-palm, quarries of building stone were remoter and less accessible than in Egypt; not only was copper ore lacking, but flint, of which the Nile cliffs furnished an excellent supply, was equally hard to obtain. Indeed, on the alluvial plains and marshes even hard pebbles, suitable for making axeheads, were rarities. From the very first the Sumerians had to import Armenian obsidian or other exotic stones for cutting tools. Sindh and Punjab suffered from the same shortage of essential raw materials as Sumer.

And so on the large alluvial plains and riverside flatlands the need for extensive public works to drain and irrigate the land and to protect the settlement would tend to consolidate social organization and to centralize the economic system. At the same time, the inhabitants of Egypt, Sumer, and the Indus basin were forced to organize some regular system of trade or barter to secure supplies of essential raw materials. The fertility of lands gave their inhabitants the means for satisfying their need of imports. But economic self-sufficiency had to be sacrificed and a completely new economic structure created. The surplus of home-grown products must not only suffice to exchange for exotic materials; it must also support a body of merchants and transport workers engaged in obtaining these and a body of specialized craftsmen to work the precious imports to the best advantage. And soon soldiers would be needed to protect the convoys and back up the merchants by force, scribes to keep records of transactions growing ever more complex, and State officials to reconcile conflicting interests.

And so by 3000 B.C. the archaeologist's picture of Egypt, Mesopotamia, and the Indus valley no longer focuses attention on communities of simple farmers, but on states embracing various professions and classes. The foreground is occupied by priests, princes, scribes, and officials and an army of specialized craftsmen, professional soldiers, and miscellaneous laborers, all withdrawn from the primary task of food-production. The most striking objects now unearthed are no longer the tools of agriculture and the chase and other products of domestic industry, but temple furniture, weapons, wheel-made pots . . ., jewelry, and other manufactures turned out on a large scale by skilled artisans. As monuments we have instead of huts and farmhouses, monumental tombs, temples, palaces, and workshops. And in them we find all manner of exotic substances, not as rarities, but regularly imported and used in everyday life.

Evidently the change in the archaeologists' material reflects a transformation in the economy that produced the material. Evidently too the transformation should be accompanied by a rise in the population. Priests, officials, merchants, artisans, and soldiers should represent new classes that, as classes, could find no livelihood in a self-sufficing food-producing community, still less in a band of hunters. And the archaeological evidence alone suffices to confirm that expectation. The new cities are spatially larger and can accommodate a much denser population than the agricultural villages that have been absorbed in them or that still subsist beside them. Mohenjo-daro in Sindh, for example, spread over a square mile of land; it was a close agglomeration of two-storied houses neatly arranged along broad streets or narrow alleys. Again, the urban cemeteries attest not only an increase of wealth, but also multiplication of people. On the Nile we have not only village graveyards continuing from prehistoric times, but also large cemeteries of monumental tombs reserved for royalties and officials. The so-called "royal cemetery" at Ur was probably used by only a fraction of the citizen body, and on the most generous estimate for not more than three centuries (most authorities would reduce this figure by half). Yet it comprised over 700 interments still recognizable when discovered – a vastly larger number than found in any purely prehistoric cemetery.

The change from self-sufficing food-production to an economy based also on specialized manufacture and external trade did accordingly promote a marked expansion of the population. It had such an effect on vital statistics as to earn the title of revolution . . .

In the economic sphere the results of the second revolution in Egypt, Mesopotamia, and India were similar, but only in an abstract way. Concretely its results were strikingly different in each area. The details not only of the economic structures but also of the political and religious systems reposing thereon diverge conspicuously. This divergence extends down to the simplest archaeological objects. In each region smiths were working the same chemical substances by analogous simple processes into tools and weapons to serve common human needs. But their products – axes, knives, daggers, and spear heads – assume quite distinct forms on the Nile, on the Euphrates, and on the Indus. There is no less contrast between Indian, Sumerian, and Egyptian pottery, though the potter's craft was common to the three regions. And like contrasts can be followed in every aspect of man's activity. An abstract account of the revolution in general cannot therefore take the place of a description of its course in the several regions.

In Mesopotamia the archaeologist can watch the several stages of the revolution at a number of different sites in the south, in Sumer, at Eridu Ur, Erech, Lagash, Larsa, Shurup-pak; the later stages can also be observed in the north, in Akkad, at Kish, Jemdet Nasr, Opis, Eshnunna, and Mari. In Sumer at each site the economic systems at the start and at the end are not only similar, but identical; and ultimately this identity proves to be founded on a common language, religion, and social organization. The events revealed by the excavations at Erech may accordingly be taken as illustrating what was happening at other sites.

Erech began as a village of neolithic farmers. The decay and renewal of successive villages . . . gradually formed a mound or *tell* that slowly rose above the level of the marshy plain. The first fifty feet of this artificial hill consist entirely of the ruins of reed huts or mud-brick houses. The simple relics collected from them illustrate . . . an increasing use of metal, the introduction of the potter's wheel, and so on. The village is growing in size and wealth, but it remains a village.

But then, instead of the walls and hearths of

modest huts, appear the foundations of a truly monumental building – a temple or group of temples. And close by rises an artificial mountain, the prototype of the "ziggurat" or staged tower that was an indispensable part of an historical Sumerian temple. This first ziggurat was built entirely of hand-formed lumps of mud with layers of bitumen between them. But it towered more than thirty-five feet above the then existing surface of the ground – the street-level of the contemporary settlement – and its top measured over 1,000 yards square. The mountain's steeply-sloping sides were relieved by buttresses alternating with recesses, and were further adorned and consolidated by thousands of little pottery tumblers. These had been pushed side by side in close-packed rows into the mud of the ziggurat while it was still wet. They served to consolidate the faces while they were drying, and eventually stood out forming decorative patterns of round dimples when the monument was complete.

On the mountain-top was a tiny shrine with white-washed walls of mud brick and a staircase by which the deity might descend from the heavens. At the foot were more imposing temples.

The erection of the artificial mountain and of the temples, the collection and transportation of the materials, the manufacture of the thousands of pots and bricks required a large and disciplined force of laborers and craftsmen. While these were withdrawn from food-production they must have been supported, if not paid, from some common store of surplus food. Whose? Presumably it was already controlled by the power, we may perhaps say already "deity," to whose honor and glory the buildings were dedicated. The fertility of the land and the pious superstitions of its cultivators must have endowed its divine lord with riches at least in surplus foodstuffs.

But the erection of such a monument required more than laborers and their food. The whole was carefully planned: the artificial mountain was laid out with its corners to the cardinal points. A centralized directing force was requisite. The god being but a fictitious projection of the communal will, that force must have been supplied by his servants. Natu-

rally enough the imaginary god has found earthly representatives and interpreters glad to administer and to enlarge his terrestrial possessions in exchange for a modest share of his income. The wizards and magicians, guessed at in neolithic villages, have emerged as a corporation of priests sanctified with divine authority and emancipated from any mundane labors in field or pasture. These interpret the divine will to the toiling masses or, in other words, twist the magic ceremonies, by which society would compel natural forces, into ever more complicated rites for conciliating the power that now personifies these. And in this process of invention there are revealed the plans of temples, just as historical kings relate that the plan for a temple has been revealed to them in a dream.

We may assume then that, as in the earliest historical period, a corporation of priests already corresponds to this first of temples. And, as in all written documents, these priests must have provided the administrators of the god's treasury. But the administration of the rich treasures of the temple would impose quite a new task on the persons engaged. What those tasks were, written documents will soon reveal: it may be anticipated that some means had to be devised for keeping track of the various offerings and of their utilization, lest the deity should demand of his priest accounts of his stewardship. And, in fact, in the ziggurat-shrine the excavators found a tablet bearing the impression of a seal and hollows that are certainly numerals. It is the world's oldest account tablet, the immediate forerunner of a long series of Sumerian temple accounts.

Thus the first temple at Erech reveals a community, raised to the dignity of a city, disposing of a surplus of real wealth accumulated in the hands of a deity and administered by a corporation of priests. It implies an organized force of workers, specialized industries, and some rudimentary system of commerce and transportation. And at this crucial moment the beginnings at least of accountancy and even writing emerge. And, of course, Erech did not stand alone; the sites of the other great Sumerian cities have yielded remains of the same cultural stage and of a like absolute antiquity. And from this point the development of urban civilization can be traced continuously till the moment when the full light of written history dawns upon it and within it. The story is one of accumulating wealth, of improving technical skill, of increasing specialization of labor, and of expanding trade.

The temple at Erech fell into disrepair, and was rebuilt at least four times. Each successive temple is grander than its predecessor. The pots hammered into the walls of the first ziggurat are replaced by cones of baked clay, the ends of which are painted black, red, and white. These are stuck into the mud-brick walls so as to make mosaic patterns. By the beginning of the historical period inlays of mother-of-pearl and carnelian on black bitumen replace the mosaic of clay cones. The inner walls of the sanctuary are decorated at first with figures of animals molded in clay. Later these are replaced by friezes of plaques cut out of stone or shell and mounted in bitumen. At the dawn of history large-size groups of animals in copper, cast or beaten up over a core of bitumen, replace the molded clay figures.

The stage represented by the third principal phase of rebuilding at Erech is equally well known in Akkad (northern Babylonia), particularly at Jemdet Nasr. By this time increase of wealth, a profounder knowledge of applied chemistry and geology, and more regular and extended commerce are disclosed by the importation and utilization of lead, silver, and lapis lazuli. Increased technical skill is indicated by the manufacture of articles in glazed paste and of light war-chariots. And now the account tablets are regularly inscribed with symbols and numerals. The symbols are mainly pictures, but include already conventional signs that are hardly recognizable as likenesses of concrete objects, but must already possess a conventional meaning. There are different numeral signs for units, tens, and sixties or hundreds. The tablets already apply simple arithmetical formulas – reckoning, for instance, the area of a field as the product of two adjacent sides.

The growth of the god's revenues, and the consequent increase in the complexity of accountancy, have compelled the priestly administrators to devise systems of writing and numeral notation intelligible to their colleagues and successors in the permanent corporation of temple officers. To simplify and abbreviate their labors they have had to discover and formulate rules of reckoning and "laws" of geometry.

By the next phase, well after 3000 B.C., the "royal cemetery" of Ur brilliantly illustrates the culmination of the process. Goldsmiths can now make wire and solder; they produce delicate chains and elaborate ornaments in granulation and filigree work. The coppersmith is master of the hammer and of casting, and is probably employing the *cire perdue* process. And so he can provide his fellow craftsmen with a variety of delicate and specialized tools: axes, adzes, chisels, gouges, drills, knives, saws, nails, clamps, needles, and so on. Jewelers can now pierce the hardest stones and engrave them for seals. Sculptors are beginning to carve vases and statuettes out of limestone and even basalt. The carpenter, besides boats, chariots, and couches, fashions harps and lyres. Naturally there are professional musicians to play upon them; these actually take their places in the tomb beside their royal masters.

All this luxury and refinement means more than accumulated wealth and intensified specialization. It reposes on an enriched craft-lore and new discoveries in applied science. The fine castings of the Sumerian smiths could not have been achieved with pure copper. They are hardly conceivable unless the alloy of copper with tin that we term bronze had been discovered, and actual analyses have demonstrated the employment of this alloy. This does not in itself vindicate for the Sumerians the credit of the discovery; bronze was also used in India about the same date. It presumably began as an accidental alloy resulting from smelting a copper ore containing tin as a natural impurity or from chance mixtures of copper and tin ores. But it is only in an urban industry using "copper" drawn from a variety of different sources that comparison would reveal the superiority of the "copper" from one district or ore. That observation must be the first step to the isolation of the impurity to which that superiority was due, and so to the deliberate preparation of the alloy. Bronze can have been discovered only by deliberate comparison and experimentation.

Other evidence of experimentation is afforded by a small dagger of iron belonging to the same period. It had been made, not from meteoric iron or natural telluric iron, but from metal reduced from its ore. It may have been the result of an isolated experiment, and there is no evidence that the discovery was followed up. It was not till about 1300 B.C. that iron came into regular industrial use, and then not in Mesopotamia, but elsewhere in Asia Minor. Yet another discovery of the period was clear glass. Glazed stones and faience had been known to the prehistoric Egyptians, and the art of their manufacture had been introduced into Mesopotamia before 3000 B.C. But some time after that date we have examples of clear glass. This may rank as a Sumerian discovery resulting from experiments with the other glazes, all of which depend upon the properties of alkaline silicates.

The employment on such a vast scale of imported substances foreign to the alluvial plain implies that the commercial relations foreshadowed in earlier periods had been extended and made more regular. Some of the copper was brought from Oman south of the Persian Gulf. Silver and lead probably came from the Taurus Mountains in Asia Minor, attested as a great exporting center soon after 2500 B.C. Large shells were derived from the Persian Gulf and the Arabian Sea. Timber must have been brought from mountains that catch the rain from the Zagros, or perhaps even from Lebanon on the Mediterranean coast. Lapis is believed to have been derived from Afghanistan.

And trade did not stop short at raw materials. The second revolution was already being accomplished in Egypt and India; the cities of Sumer were in commercial relations with others on the Nile and the Indus. Commodities manufactured by the specialized industries of one urban center were traded to the bazaars of another. In several Mesopotamian cities stray seals, beads, and even pots have turned up that are not Sumerian in character, but are, on the other hand, common in contemporary cities in Sindh and Punjab. They afford conclusive proof of international trade linking the Tigris with the Indus 1,200 miles away. They reveal a picture of caravans regularly crossing the rugged ranges and salt deserts that separate the two valleys, or

of fleets of dhows sailing along the waterless coasts of the Arabian Sea between the rivers' mouths.

Now that sort of commerce in the Orient is not, and never can have been, a mere transportation of bales of merchandise from place to place. At the termini and at stations on the way the caravans and merchant dhows must make prolonged halts. Representatives, probably colonists from the exporting country, must receive the goods at their destination and arrange a return load, entertaining the travelers in the meantime. Just as there are permanent colonies of British merchants in Oporto, Stamboul, and Shanghai, so we may imagine colonies of Indian merchants settled at Ur and Kish. Trade under such conditions is very really a means of intercourse, a channel by which ideas can be diffused on an international scale.

Again, it is not only goods – the concrete embodiments of new inventions – but also men – artisans and inventors – that are transported by the caravans. In the Orient skilled labor is surprisingly mobile, and it is so traditionally. Craftsmen gravitate to centers where they can profitably employ their skill. And this must be true of antiquity. The new class of expert craftsmen, created by the second revolution, had been liberated from the tasks of primary food-production, and so from attachment to the soil. They were perhaps at the same time released from tribal bonds and not yet firmly attached to the nascent local states. So they could move whithersoever profitable employment offered. Or, were they slaves, they would be sent as commodities to where their skill would fetch the highest price for their persons. In any case, this mobility explains the rapid diffusion of technical processes.

Such were the stages of the second revolution in Mesopotamia and such its industrial and economic consequences for man's material culture. The several stages are undoubtedly moments in an organic process of economic accumulation and of scientific and technical advancement. But this continuity need not apply to the ethnological and political domains. There are, indeed, indications that accumulation and advancement were interrupted or promoted by the advent of new peoples, perhaps by conquests and invasions.

[...]

Soon after 3000 B.C. the earliest written texts give us a picture of the social and economic organization of Sumer and Akkad. The land is divided up among fifteen or twenty city states, each politically autonomous, but all enjoying a common material culture, a common religion, and a common language, and all largely interdependent economically. The center of each city was the sacred *temenos* or citadel containing the temples of the city god and other deities. We may, if we like, infer that the god is a personification of magic forces; dramatic representations of the death and rebirth of vegetation, of sowing and harvest, may once have been performed as magic rites designed to compel the germination of the crops. In time the actors who symbolized the grain and its magic fertility would be taken as playing the role of a deity who controlled the magic forces. The magic force which man had sought to compel would be personified as a god who must be helped and conciliated. Before history begins, society has projected its collective will, its corporate hopes and fears, into this fictitious person whom it reveres as Lord of its territory.

In any case, each god has an earthly dwelling, the city temple, a material estate, and human servants, the priestly corporation. The oldest decipherable documents from Mesopotamia are, in fact, the accounts of the temple revenues kept by the priests. They reveal the temple as not only the center of the city's religious life, but also the nucleus of capital accumulation. The temple functions as the great bank; the god is the chief capitalist of the land. The early temple archives record the god's loans of seed or plow animals to cultivators, the fields he has let to tenants, wages paid to brewers, boat-builders, spinners, and other employees, advances of grain or bullion to traveling merchants. The god is the richest member of the community. His wealth is available to the community from whose piety he, in fact, derived it. But the same piety required that the borrower should not only pay back the loan, but also add a little thank-offering. The god's ministers were doubt-

less careful to remind you of your duty, and even stipulated in advance what decency demanded you to offer. Such thank-offerings would today be called interest, and the temple's tariff might be styled usurious by the impious.

This economic system that made the god a great capitalist and landlord, his temple into a city bank, evidently goes back to remote prehistoric times. The figured gypsum tablet from the oldest temple at Erech, the tablets from Jemdet Nasr with their picture-writing, are undoubtedly precursors of the temple accounts that can now be read. The latter accordingly justify the description of Sumer's economic development already deduced. They will form the basis of the analysis of the second revolution's scientific consequences ...

But by 3000 B.C. there is already emerging beside the deity in every city a temporal potentate. He styles himself humbly the god's "vicegerent," but also boldly "king." Perhaps he had once impersonated the god in those sacred dramas imagined above as a factor in the genesis of godhead. Indeed, he still takes the part of the god in some acts of the drama. But he has emancipated himself from the fate of the original actor – to be consigned to the tomb as the seed is to the earth. And he has certainly usurped a substantial share of the god's temporal power over men. He even oppresses his subjects according to quite early documents. The State has, indeed, "arisen out of Society, places itself above it, and separates itself from it."

Nevertheless, the king fulfilled essential economic functions in the development of Sumerian society. He was possessed of the material power of a civil ruler and a military commander. One use of this power may have been to see that "the antagonisms," generated by the revolution, "classes with conflicting interests, did not consume themselves and society in sterile struggle." But of that the records are silent. They do mention the use of the State's power to supplement the work of "private enterprise" in providing for the economic needs of the country. Early kings boast of their economic activities – of cutting canals, of building temples, of importing timber from Syria, and copper and granite from Oman. They are sometimes depicted on monuments in the garb of brick layers or masons and of architects receiving the plan of a temple from its god.

Doubtless the royal power accelerated the accumulation of capital in foodstuffs and real wealth. Courtiers, ministers, musicians, and men-at-arms were supported by the surplus thus extorted. And the army was fulfilling an economic function in guarding the city, its canals, its irrigated fields and pastures against the incursions of starveling nomads from the surrounding steppes or wild tribes from the mountains. In the end it would create a political order more compatible with economic realities than the system of city-states.

Lower Mesopotamia is a geographical unit, dependent for life on the waters of its twin rivers, for a civilized life on the importation of the same exotic substances from common sources. Precisely because they were dependent on the waters of the same rivers, disputes about lands and water rights were liable to arise between the several autonomous cities. Just because all relied on the same foreign trade to bring them the same necessities for industry, commercial rivalries were inevitable amongst sovereign states; the contradiction between an economic system that ought to be unitary and political separatism was made manifest in interminable dynastic wars. Our earliest documents after the temple accounts, in fact, record wars between adjacent cities and treaties that temporarily ended them. The ambition of any city dynast was to obtain hegemony over his neighbors.

But no permanent result was obtained by these internecine conflicts till 2500 (or later) B.C. Then the Semitic ruler of Agade or Akkad whom we term Sargon established an empire over all Babylonia which lasted with intervals of revolt for nearly a century. His feat was subsequently imitated, more or less successfully, by kings of Ur and of other cities. But only a little after (or before) 1800 B.C. was Babylonia made a political reality, a unified nation with a common capital, a common code of written law, a common calendar, and a permanent system of government by Hammurabi, king of Babylon. Then at last the city-state was absorbed into the territorial state that corresponded on the whole to the realities of economic needs.

In Egypt it seems as if political unification coincided with the accomplishment of the second economic revolution. The Nile Valley is geographically even more a natural economic unit than is the plain of the Tigris and Euphrates, and so the natural factors tending to unity were more efficient. At the same time, the contrast between the narrow valley of Upper Egypt and the open Delta, Lower Egypt, is fundamental. Historically the unification of Egypt means the union of these two lands in a single kingdom. That event preceded Sargon's unification of Babylonia by some five centuries, so that the second revolution in the two regions is approximately contemporary.

[...]

The revolutions just described occurred almost simultaneously in Egypt and Sumer, and probably in India too. In each case the revolution was based on the same scientific discoveries, and resulted in the addition to the population of the same new classes. It is hard to believe in the independence of these events, especially when the proofs of long-standing intercourse between the areas be recalled. And this intercourse became closer than ever at the moment of the revolution or just after it. Just about the time of Egypt's unification, devices that may reasonably be regarded as Mesopotamian in origin – cylinder seals, certain artistic motives, crenelated brick architecture, a new type of boat – appear on the Nile for the first time. Soon after the revolution Indian manufactures were being imported into Sumer.

Some sort of diffusion had evidently been going on. Yet no theory of one-sided dependence is compatible with the contrasts revealed by closer scrutiny. Urban civilization was not simply transplanted from one center to another, but was in each an organic growth rooted in the local soil. If we want a modern analogy, the establishment of mechanized industry and factory production by European capitalists in Africa or India will not serve. We must think rather of the rise of that system of production in the countries on both sides of the Atlantic. America, Britain, France, the Low Countries shared a common scientific, cultural, and mercantile tradition long before the

Industrial Revolution. Despite wars and customs barriers, the interchange of goods, ideas, and persons went on continuously. England, indeed, was in the van of the Revolution itself, but the other countries did not merely copy her mechanical inventions or economic organization; they had been experimenting along the same lines, and made independent contributions when the time came. The establishment in China or even Russia of factories and railways modeled on Western lines and staffed with European and American managers and technicians was quite a different process.

And so Egypt, Sumer, and India had not been isolated or independent before the revolution. All shared more or less a common cultural tradition to which each had been contributing. And it had been maintained and enriched by a continuous intercourse involving an interchange of goods, ideas, and craftsmen. That is the explanation of the observed parallelism.

But once the new economy had been established in the three primary centers, it spread thence to secondary centers, much like Western capitalism spread to colonies and economic dependencies. First on the borders of Egypt, Babylonia, and the Indus valley – in Crete and the Greek islands, Syria, Assyria, Iran, and Baluchistan – then further afield, on the Greek mainland, the Anatolian plateau, south Russia, we see villages converted into cities and self-sufficing food-producers turning to industrial specialization and external trade. And the process is repeated in ever-widening circles around each secondary and tertiary center.

[...]

Between 3000 and 2000 B.C. bronze-using civilizations were established in Crete, on the Greek mainland, at Troy on the Dardanelles, in the Kuban basin north of the Caucasus, on the plateau of Asia Minor, in Palestine and Syria, in Iran, and in Baluchistan. Each of these civilizations has a character of its own, but all exhibit so many concrete features of agreement with the products of Egypt, Sumer, or the Indus basin or of one of the secondary centers that their indebtedness to earlier foci of civilization is indisputable.

These secondary and tertiary civilizations are not original, but result from the adoption of traditions, ideas, and processes received by diffusion from older centers. In most cases the mechanism of this transmission is lost. The foregoing pages should reveal that effective mechanisms of diffusion were at work. The second revolution, once established, had to spread. And every village, converted into a city by the spread, became at once a new center of infection. Before 1500 B.C. the new industrial structure was reaching Spain, Britain, and Germany. In less than five centuries more it had penetrated to Scandinavia and Siberia.

But in this process of diffusion culture was degraded. People who have learned a new technique are apt to apply it clumsily; proficiency requires generations of practice and of discipline. Again, the higher civilization is not adopted in its entirety; the recipient people feel the need of, and can assimilate, only a few items in the new cultural equipment. It is possible, for instance, to learn enough metallurgy and to get enough ore for armaments without learning to write or establishing such a commercial organization as should make writing indispensable. There thus arise different grades of civilization, varying degrees of approximation to the standards set by the primary centers. And these grades tend to be arranged in zones about the primary centers.

By 2500 B.C. the Minoans of Crete were dwelling in cities and living by industry and commerce. So intent are they, indeed, on profiting by the surplus wealth of Egypt and Syria that they will build a city even on a tiny island with no cultivable land, provided it offer a convenient harbor. They had borrowed various items of the necessary technical equipment from Egypt or Sumer, directly or through Syria. They had early adopted the seal as a device for labeling their jars of oil and bales of merchandise. But the early native seals are rather crude products. Eventually they devised a rather clumsy pictographic script to assist them in their accountancy. They could smelt and work metals, and they employed the Sumerian type of axe-head with a hole for the shaft. But early Minoan metal tools look very clumsy beside the original models. Wheeled wagons were employed at first, but not the potter's wheel.

The Helladic people of mainland Greece had begun to live in cities rather later than the Cretans, and were less dependent on trade and manufactures. They made no seals of their own, presumably because trade was on too small a scale for the device to be needed. Naturally they did not know how to write. Stone was still effectively competing with copper as tool material, and metal weapons were poor imitations of the Minoan. Finally, the barbarians living north of the Balkans in what was to become the Austro-Hungarian Empire were only just beginning to use metal for weapons and ornaments, and occasionally for tools, by 2000 B.C. But they continued to live in small and nearly self-sufficing village communities. Of course they had no use for writing, or even for seals. Metallurgy they had learned from Greece and Troy, but they were far behind their masters. And their neighbors to the north were still neolithic!

H. D. F. KITTO

"The Polis"

from *The Greeks* (1951)

Editors' introduction   At its peak ancient Athens had only about as many residents as Peoria, Illinois (1990 population 113,504) – not a city which leaps out as a great center of world civilization. But writing of his beloved Greece, British classicist H. D. F. Kitto reminds us not to commit the vulgar error of confusing size with significance. During its golden age, Athens and the 700 or so other tiny settlements of ancient Greece made a monumental contribution to human culture. What the Greeks achieved in philosophy, literature, drama, poetry, art, logic, mathematics, sculpture, and architecture has exercised a profound influence on Western civilization.

A Greek invention of enduring interest to urbanists is the polis. Since we have not got the thing which the Greeks called "the polis," Kitto notes, we do not possess an equivalent word. City-state comes closest.

The classical Greek polis came of age in the fifth century B.C.E. – about halfway between the emergence of the great Mesopotamian cities Childe describes above and the present time.

The physical form of the polis stressed public space. Private houses were low and turned away from the street. In contrast public temples, theaters, stadiums, and the agora (a combined market-place and public forum) received more attention. In the larger poleis, like Athens, these public buildings were spacious and often beautifully constructed of marble. Even in the smaller ones the community devoted many of its resources to them.

If the physical form of the polis was often stunning, it was the social organization of the polis that remains of particular fascination. The polis represents a form of community which still serves as a model today. In the following selection Kitto depicts the polis as the framework within which the citizen could realize his spiritual, moral, and intellectual capacities – a living community, almost an extended family. While the Greeks were very private in many ways, Kitto notes that their public life was essentially communistic.

Not that the polis supported development of every resident: women and slaves were not citizens and did not participate in much of the life of the polis. Foreigners could attend plays in the Greek theater, but were barred from many institutions reserved to the (free, non-foreign, male) citizens.

Kitto expresses a nostalgia for human qualities of life in the polis which appear threatened today. Compare the vision of polis as a supportive, humanistic, structure for human fulfillment with the vision of large modern cities as centers of alienation and anomie depicted by Louis Wirth (p. 190), or ghettos housing the Black underclass as described by William Julius Wilson (p. 226). Note the connections between humanistic values Kitto felt that the polis nurtured and J. B. Jackson's "almost perfect town" (p. 82) and the return to human-scale community Peter Calthorpe advocates in "Pedestrian Pockets" (p. 469). Compare the positive values Kitto describes in the polis as well as the status and gender barriers with Dolores Hayden's vision of a non-sexist city (p. 143).

In the debate about why the polis arose in Greece when it did, Kitto rejects deterministic answers. Geographical and economic determinists argue that the mountainous terrain required little, separate city-states. Kitto attributes the rise of the polis to the character of the Greeks rather than these external factors.

For accounts of Greek city planning see R. E. Wycherley, *How the Greeks Built Cities*, 2nd edn. (London: Macmillan, 1963) and *The Stones of Athens* (Princeton: Princeton University Press, 1978); and Spiro Kostof, "Polis and Akropolis," Chapter 7 of *A History of Architecture* (New York: Oxford University Press, 1980). Lewis Mumford agrees with Kitto that "it is art, culture, and political purpose, not numbers, that define a city." See his chapters "The Emergence of the Polis" and "Citizen versus Ideal City" in *The City in History* (New York: Harcourt Brace Jovanovich, 1961) as well as his comments in "What Is a City?" (p. 184).

H. D. F. Kitto, "The Polis"

from *The Greeks* (1951)

"Polis" is the Greek word which we translate "city-state". It is a bad translation, because the normal polis was not much like a city, and was very much more than a state. But translation, like politics, is the art of the possible; since we have not got the thing which the Greeks called "the polis", we do not possess an equivalent word. From now on, we will avoid the misleading term "city-state", and use the Greek word instead ... We will first inquire how this political system arose, then we will try to reconstitute the word "polis" and recover its real meaning by watching it in action. It may be a long task, but all the time we shall be improving our acquaintance with the Greeks. Without a clear conception what the polis was, and what it meant to the Greek, it is quite impossible to understand properly Greek history, the Greek mind, or the Greek achievement.

First then, what was the polis? ...

... In Crete ... we find over fifty quite independent poleis, fifty small "states" ... What is true of Crete is true of Greece in general, or at least of those parts which play any considerable part in Greek history...

It is important to realize their size. The modern reader picks up a translation of Plato's *Republic* or Aristotle's *Politics*; he finds Plato ordaining that his ideal city shall have 5,000 citizens, and Aristotle that each citizen should be able to know all the others by sight; and he smiles, perhaps, at such philosophic fantasies. But Plato and Aristotle are not fantasts. Plato is imagining a polis on the normal Hellenic scale; indeed he implies that many existing Greek poleis are too small – for many had less than 5,000 citizens. Aristotle says, in his amusing way ... that a polis of ten citizens would be impossible, because it could not be self-sufficient, and that a polis of a hundred thousand would be absurd, because it could not govern itself properly ... Aristotle speaks of a hundred thousand citizens; if we allow each to have a wife and four children, and then add a liberal number of slaves and resident aliens, we shall arrive at something like a million – the population of Birmingham; and to Aristotle an independent "state" as populous as Birmingham is a lecture-room joke ...

In fact, only three poleis had more than 20,000 citizens: Syracuse and Acragas (Girgenti) in Sicily, and Athens. At the outbreak of the Peloponnesian War the population of Attica was probably about 350,000, half Athenian (men, women and children), about a tenth resident aliens, and the rest slaves. Sparta, or Lacedaemon, had a much smaller citizen-body, though it was larger in area. The Spartans had conquered and annexed Messenia, and possessed 3,200 square miles of territory. By Greek standards this was an enormous area: it would take a good walker two days to cross it. The important commercial city of Corinth had a territory of 330 square miles ... The island of Ceos, which is about as big as Bute, was divided into four poleis. It had therefore four armies, four governments, possibly four different calendars, and, it may be, four different currencies and systems of measures – though this is less likely. Mycenae was in historical times a shrunken relic of Agamemnon's capital, but still independent. She sent an army to help the Greek cause against Persia at the battle of Plataea; the army consisted of eighty men. Even by Greek standards this was small, but we do not hear that any jokes were made about an army sharing a cab.

To think on this scale is difficult for us, who regard a state of ten million as small, and are accustomed to states which, like the U.S.A. and the U.S.S.R., are so big that they have to be referred to by their initials; but when the adjustable reader has become accustomed to the scale, he will not commit the vulgar error of confusing size with significance ...

But before we deal with the nature of the polis, the reader might like to know how it happened that the relatively spacious pattern of pre-Dorian Greece became such a mosaic of small fragments. The Classical scholar too would like to know; there are no records, so that all we can do is to suggest plausible reasons. There are historical, geographical and economic reasons; and when these have been duly set forth, we may conclude perhaps that the most important reason of all is simply that this is the way in which the Greeks preferred to live.

[Here Kitto describes the evolution of the Greek acropolis from a fortified hilltop strongpoint built for protection against Dorian invaders to a place of assembly, religion, and commerce.]

At this point we may invoke the very sociable habits of the Greeks, ancient or modern. The English farmer likes to build his house on his land, and to come into town when he has to. What little leisure he has he likes to spend on the very satisfying occupation of looking over a gate. The Greek prefers to live in the town or village, to walk out to his work, and to spend his rather ampler leisure talking in the town or village square. Therefore the market becomes a market-town, naturally beneath the acropolis. This became the center of the communal life of the people – and we shall see presently how important that was.

But why did not such towns form larger units? This is the important question.

There is an economic point. The physical barriers which Greece has so abundantly made the transport of goods difficult, except by sea, and the sea was not yet used with any confidence. Moreover, the variety of which we spoke earlier enabled quite a small area to be reasonably self-sufficient for a people who made such small material demands on life as the Greek. Both of these facts tend in the same direction; there was in Greece no great economic interdependence, no reciprocal pull between the different parts of the country, strong enough to counteract the desire of the Greek to live in small communities.

There is a geographical point. It is sometimes asserted that this system of independent poleis was imposed on Greece by the physical character of the country. The theory is attractive, especially to those who like to have one majestic explanation of any phenomenon, but it does not seem to be true. It is of course obvious that the physical subdivision of the country helped; the system could not have existed, for example, in Egypt, a country which depends entirely on the proper management of the Nile flood, and therefore must have a central government. But there are countries cut up quite as much as Greece – Scotland, for instance – which have never developed the polis-system; and conversely there were in Greece many neighbouring poleis, such as Corinth and Sicyon, which remained independent of each other although between them there was no physical barrier that would seriously incommode a modern cyclist. Moreover, it was precisely the most mountainous parts of Greece that never developed poleis, or not until later days – Arcadia and Aetolia, for example, which had something like a canton-system. The polis flourished in those parts where communications were relatively easy. So that we are still looking for our explanation.

Economics and geography helped, but the real explanation is the character of the Greeks ... As it will take some time to deal with this, we may first clear out of the way an important historical point. How did it come about that so preposterous a system was able to last for more than twenty minutes?

The ironies of history are many and bitter, but at least this must be put to the credit of the gods, that they arranged for the Greeks to have the Eastern Mediterranean almost to themselves long enough to work out what was almost a laboratory-experiment to test how far, and in what conditions, human nature is capable of creating and sustaining a civilization ... this lively and intelligent Greek people was for some centuries allowed to live under the apparently absurd system which suited and developed its genius instead of becoming absorbed in the dull mass of a large empire, which would have smothered its spiritual growth ... no history of Greece can be intelligible until one has understood what the polis meant to the Greek; and when we have understood that, we shall also understand why the Greeks developed it, and so obstinately tried to maintain it. Let us then examine the word in action.

It meant at first that which was later called the Acropolis, the stronghold of the whole community and the centre of its public life ... "polis" very soon meant either the citadel or the whole people which, as it were, "used" this citadel. So we read in Thucydides, "Epidamnus is a polis on the right as you sail into the Ionian gulf." This is not like saying "Bristol is a city on the right as you sail up the Bristol Channel", for Bristol is not an independent state which might be at war with Gloucester, but only an urban area with a purely local administration. Thucydides' words imply that there is a town – though possibly a very small one – called Epidamnus, which is the political centre of the Epidamnians, who live in the territory of which the town is the centre – not the "capital" – and are Epidamnians whether they live in the town or in one of the villages in this territory.

Sometimes the territory and the town have different names. Thus, Attica is the territory occupied by the Athenian people; it comprised Athens – the "polis" in the narrower sense – the Piraeus, and many villages; but the people collectively were Athenians, not Attics, and a citizen was an Athenian in whatever part of Attica he might live.

In this sense "polis" is our "state" ... The actual business of governing might be entrusted to a monarch, acting in the name of all according to traditional usages, or to the heads of certain noble families, or to a council of citizens owning so much property, or to all the citizens. All these and many modifications of them, were natural forms of "polity"; all were sharply distinguished by the Greek from Oriental monarchy, in which the monarch is irresponsible, not holding his powers in trust by the grace of god, but being himself a god. If there were irresponsible government there was no polis ...

... [T]he size of the polis made it possible for a member to appeal to all his fellow citizens in person, and this he naturally did if he thought that another member of the polis had injured him. It was the common assumption of the Greeks that the polis took its origin in the desire for Justice. Individuals are lawless, but the polis will see to it that wrongs are redressed. But not by an elaborate machinery of state-justice, for such a machine could not be operated except by individuals, who may be as unjust as the original wrongdoer. The injured party will be sure of obtaining Justice only if he can declare his wrongs to the whole polis. The word therefore now means "people" in actual distinction from state.

[...]

... Demosthenes the orator talks of a man who, literally, "avoids the city" – a translation which might lead the unwary to suppose that he lived in something corresponding to the Lake District, or Purley. But the phrase "avoids the polis" tells us nothing about his domicile; it means that he took no part in public life – and was therefore something of an oddity. The affairs of the community did not interest him.

We have now learned enough about the word polis to realize that there is no possible English rendering of such a common phrase as, "It is everyone's duty to help the polis." We cannot say "help the state", for that arouses no enthusiasm; it is "the state" that takes half our incomes from us. Not "the community", for with us "the community" is too big and too various to be grasped except theoretically. One's village, one's trade union, one's class, are entities that mean something to us at once, but "work for the community", though an admirable sentiment, is to most of us vague and flabby. In the years before the war, what did most parts of Great Britain know about the depressed areas? How much do bankers, miners and farmworkers understand each other? But the "polis" every Greek knew; there it was, complete, before his eyes. He could see the fields which gave it its sustenance – or did not, if the crops failed; he could see how agriculture, trade and industry dovetailed into one another; he knew the frontiers, where they were strong and where weak; if any malcontents were planning a *coup*, it was difficult for them to conceal the fact. The entire life of the polis, and the relation between its parts, were much easier to grasp, because of the small scale of things. Therefore to say "It is everyone's duty to help the polis" was not to express a fine sentiment but to speak the plainest and most urgent common sense. Public affairs had an immediacy and a concreteness which they cannot possibly have for us.

[...]

Pericles' Funeral Speech, recorded or re-created by Thucydides, will illustrate this immediacy, and will also take our conception of the polis a little further. Each year, Thucydides tells us, if citizens had died in war – and they had, more often than not – a funeral oration was delivered by "a man chosen by the polis". Today, that would be someone nominated by the Prime Minister, or the British Academy, or the BBC [British Broadcasting Corporation]. In Athens it meant that someone was chosen by the Assembly who had often spoken to that Assembly; and on this occasion Pericles spoke from a specially high platform, that his voice might reach as many as possible. Let us consider two phrases that Pericles used in that speech.

He is comparing the Athenian polis with the Spartan, and makes the point that the Spartans admit foreign visitors only grudgingly, and from time to time expel all strangers, "while we make our polis common to all". "Polis" here is not the political unit; there is no question of naturalizing foreigners – which the Greeks did rarely, simply because the polis was so intimate a union. Pericles means here: "We throw open to all our common cultural life", as is shown by the words that follow, difficult though they are to translate: "nor do we deny them any instruction or spectacle" – words that are almost meaningless until we realize that the drama, tragic and comic, the performance of choral hymns, public recitals of Homer, games, were all necessary and normal parts of "political" life. This is the sort of thing Pericles has in mind when he speaks of "instruction and spectacle", and of "making the polis open to all".

But we must go further than this. A perusal of the speech will show that in praising the Athenian polis Pericles is praising more than a state, a nation, or a people: he is praising a way of life; he means no less when, a little later, he calls Athens the "school of Hellas". – And what of that? Do not we praise "the English way of life"? The difference is this; we expect our State to be quite indifferent to "the English way of life" – indeed, the idea that the State should actively try to promote it would fill most of us with alarm. The Greeks thought of the polis as an active, formative thing, training the minds and characters of the citizens; we think of it as a piece of machinery for the production of safety and convenience. The training in virtue, which the medieval state left to the Church, and the polis made its own concern, the modern state leaves to God knows what.

"Polis", then, originally "citadel", may mean as much as "the whole communal life of the people, political, cultural, moral" – even "economic", for how else are we to understand another phrase in this same speech, "the produce of the whole world comes to us, because of the magnitude of our polis"? This must mean "our national wealth".

Religion too was bound up with the polis – though not every form of religion. The Olympian gods were indeed worshipped by Greeks everywhere, but each polis had, if not its own gods, at least its own particular cults of these gods ... But beyond these Olympians, each polis had its minor local deities, "heroes" and nymphs, each worshipped with his immemorial rite, and scarcely imagined to exist outside the particular locality where the rite was performed. So ... there is a sense in which it is true to say that the polis is an independent religious, as well as political, unit ...

[...]

... Aristotle made a remark which we most inadequately translate "Man is a political animal." What Aristotle really said is "Man is a creature who lives in a polis"; and what he goes on to demonstrate, in his *Politics*, is that the polis is the only framework within which man can fully realize his spiritual, moral and intellectual capacities.

Such are some of the implications of this word ... The polis was a living community, based on kinship, real or assumed – a kind of extended family, turning as much as possible of life into family life, and of course having its family quarrels, which were the more bitter because they were family quarrels.

This it is that explains not only the polis but also much of what the Greek made and thought, that he was essentially social. In the winning of his livelihood he was essentially individualist: in the filling of his life he was essentially "communist". Religion, art, games, the discussion of things – all these were needs of life that could be fully satisfied only through the polis – not, as with us, through voluntary associations of like-minded people, or through entrepreneurs appealing to individuals. (This partly explains the difference between Greek drama and the modern cinema.) Moreover, he wanted to play his own part in running the affairs of the community. When we realize how many of the necessary, interesting and exciting activities of life the Greek enjoyed through the polis, all of them in the open air, within sight of the same acropolis, with the same ring of mountains or of sea visibly enclosing the life of every member of the state – then it becomes possible to understand Greek history, to understand that in spite of the promptings of common sense the Greek could not bring himself to sacrifice the polis, with its vivid and comprehensive life, to a wider but less interesting unity ...

[...]

HENRI PIRENNE

"City Origins" and "Cities and European Civilization"

from *Medieval Cities* (1925)

Editors' introduction   The Greek polis influenced Roman ideas of city building and society. Monumental marble public buildings, orthogonal streets, inward-turning private residences, and theaters and stadiums of Roman cities were all influenced by the Greeks. But Rome achieved a population of a million people – a size so large that Aristotle had given it as an absurd example of a size inconceivable to imagine for a polis. Unlike the society of fragmented city-states Kitto described, Roman traders carried goods all over the Roman empire from present-day Iran to Scotland. Both the social structure and the physical form of Roman cities took on an imperial character as centers of military and political power which increasingly differentiated them from the Greek polis.

Between the death of the Roman emperor Justinian in 565 C.E. and the renaissance of the eleventh century, European cities' functions changed totally from what they had been during the Roman Empire and the cities withered in size to tiny shadows of their former selves. Then, beginning in the eleventh century, they began to grow in size and change in function. Their populations began the slow ascent of the shallow part of Kingsley Davis's S curve.

Exactly what happened and why during the period of medieval cities has provoked much scholarly debate. Even more interesting and controversial is the reemergence of cities and their contribution to European history from the eleventh century onward. Why did cities begin to reemerge in the eleventh century?

In the following selection, Belgian historian Henri Pirenne emphasizes the role of trade in both the decline of cities at the end of the Roman Empire and their subsequent reemergence in the eleventh century. Pirenne argues that the Barbarian invaders were absorbed into the Roman culture they overthrew, often without physically destroying Roman cities or even Roman social institutions. Generally the barbarians wanted to enjoy, not destroy, the Roman cities. Far more damaging to the Roman system of cities, according to Pirenne, was the Islamic conquest of the Mediterranean, which choked off long-distance trade routes. As trade stagnated, cities in Europe lost their economic reason for existing and withered. Regions became autarkic – self-contained. By the time of Charlemagne (742–814 C.E.) the largest settlements established by Rome had shrunk to tiny religious places. Defense and administrative functions were added somewhat later so that medieval cities blended religion, defense, and administration.

Just as lack of trade atrophied and transmuted post-Roman cities, Pirenne argues that it was trade which revived cities during the eleventh century. Merchants emerged as a separate class – independent from the clergy, the landed aristocracy, or the vast submerged population of serfs. They often lived and traded in suburbs below the walls of medieval cities built on hills. The word suburb itself is derived from the Latin "below the town." More important, the emerging merchant class was free of many of the political, legal, and social restrictions which kept medieval society so changeless.

As the merchants grew in numbers and influence, Pirenne argues, they revolutionized the social structure of cities. Cities took on new life. The old stagnant class structure loosened up. The cities produced and exchanged new goods. New, distinctively urban forms of thought and culture emerged. And urban culture in turn revolutionized social relations and thought throughout the countryside.

Contrast Childe's views on the role of agricultural production in the origins of Mesopotamian cities (p. 22) and Kitto's emphasis on the importance of defense and religion to the emergence of the Greek polis with what Pirenne has to say about economics and trade in the reemergence of cities in Europe. Compare Pirenne's views on the emergence of a free middle class and the positive contributions of capitalism to European culture with Engels's devastating description of Manchester, England, during the full flowering of early capitalism (p. 47). Compare Pirenne's views on the essentially economic function of cities to Mumford's view of the city as stage for human culture (p. 184).

Pirenne's thesis is fully developed in *Medieval Cities* (Princeton, N.J.: Princeton University Press, 1925). For overviews of European medieval cities see Paul M. Hohenberg and Lynn Hollen Lees, *The Making of Urban Europe 1000–1950* (Cambridge: Mass.: Harvard University Press, 1985), and Chapters 4 and 5, "Medieval Towns" and "The Renaissance: Italy Sets a Pattern," in A. E. J. Morris, *History of Urban Form before the Industrial Revolution* (Harlow: Longman Scientific and Technical, 1994).

Henri Pirenne, "City Origins" and "Cities and European Civilization"
from *Medieval Cities* (1925)

CITY ORIGINS

An interesting question is whether or not cities existed in the midst of that essentially agricultural civilization into which western Europe had developed in the course of the ninth century. The answer depends on the meaning given to the word "city." If by it is meant a locality the population of which, instead of living by working the soil, devotes itself to commercial activity, the answer will have to be "No." The answer will also be in the negative if we understand by "city" a community endowed with legal personality and possessing laws and institutions peculiar to itself. On the other hand, if we think of a city as a center of administration and as a fortress, it is clear that the Carolingian period knew nearly as many cities as the centuries which followed it must have known. That is merely another way of saying that the cities which were then to be found were without two of the fundamental attributes of the cities of the Middle Ages and of modern times: a middle-class population and a communal organization.

Primitive though it may be, every stable society feels the need of providing its members with centers of assembly, or meeting places. Observance of religious rites, maintenance of markets, and political and judicial gatherings necessarily bring about the designation of localities intended for the assembly of those who wish to or who must participate therein.

Military needs have a still more positive effect. Populations have to prepare refuges where will be found momentary protection from the enemy in case of invasion. War is as old as humanity, and the construction of fortresses almost as old as war. The first buildings erected by man seem, indeed, to have been protecting walls ... Their plan and their construction depended naturally upon the conformation of the terrain and upon the building materials at hand. But the general arrangement of them was everywhere the same. It consisted of a space, square or circular in shape, surrounded by ramparts made of trunks of trees, or mud or blocks of stone, protected by a moat and entered by gates. In short, it was an enclosure. And it is an interesting fact that the words which in modern English and in modern Russian (town and *gorod*) designate a city, originally designated an enclosure.

In ordinary times, these enclosures remained empty. The people resorted to them only on the occasion of religious or civic ceremonies, or when war constrained them to seek refuge there with their herds. But, little by little with the march of civilization, their intermittent animation became a continuous animation. Temples arose; magistrates or chieftains established their residence; merchants and artisans came to settle. What first had been only an occasional center of assembly became a city, the administrative, religious, political, and economic center of all the territory of the tribe whose name it customarily took.

This explains why, in many societies and particularly in classic antiquity, the political life of the cities was not restricted to the circumference of their walls. The city, indeed, had been built for the tribe, and every man in it, whether dwelling within or without the walls, was equally a citizen thereof. Neither Greece nor Rome knew anything analogous to the strictly local and particularist bourgeoisie of the Middle Ages. The life of the city was blended with the national life. The law of the city was, like the religion itself of the city, common to all the people whose capital it was and who constituted with it a single autonomous republic.

The municipal system, then, was identified in antiquity with the constitutional system. And when Rome extended her dominion over all the Mediterranean world, she made it the basis of the administrative system of her Empire. This system withstood, in western Europe, the Germanic invasions. Vestigial but thoroughly definite relics of it were still to be found in Gaul, in Spain, in Africa, and in Italy, long after the fifth century. Little by little, however, the increasing weakness of social organization did away with most of its characteristic features ... At the

same time the thrust of Islam in the Mediterranean, in making impossible the commerce which up to now had still sustained a certain activity in the cities, condemned them to an inevitable decline. But it did not condemn them to death. Curtailed and weakened though they were, they survived. Their social function did not altogether disappear. In the agricultural social order of the time, they retained in spite of everything a fundamental importance. It is necessary to take full count of the role they played, in order to understand what was to befall them later.

As has been stated above, the Church had based its diocesan boundaries on the boundaries of the Roman cities. Held in respect by the barbarians, it therefore continued to maintain, after their occupation of the provinces of the Empire, the municipal system upon which it had been based. The dying out of trade and the exodus of foreign merchants had no influence on the ecclesiastical organization. The cities where the bishops resided became poorer and less populous without the bishops themselves feeling the effects. On the contrary, the more that general prosperity declined, the more their power and their influence had a chance to assert itself. Endowed with a prestige which was the greater because the State had disappeared, sustained by donations from their congregations, and partners with the Carolingians in the governing of society, they were in a commanding position by virtue of, at one and the same time, their moral authority, their economic power, and their political activity.

When the Empire of Charlemagne foundered, their status, far from being adversely affected, was made still more secure. The feudal princes, who had ruined the power of the Monarchy, did not touch that of the Church, for its divine origin protected it from their attacks. They feared the bishops, who could fling at them the terrible weapon of excommunication. They revered them as the supernatural guardians of order and justice. In the midst of the anarchy of the tenth and eleventh centuries the ascendancy of the Church remained, therefore, unimpaired ...

This prestige of the bishops naturally lent to their places of residence – that is to say, to the old Roman cities – considerable importance. It is highly probable that this was what saved them. In the economy of the ninth century they no longer had any excuse for existence. In ceasing to be commercial centers they must have lost, quite evidently, the greatest part of their population. The merchants who once frequented them, or dwelt there, disappeared and with them disappeared the urban character which they had still preserved during the Merovingian era. Lay society no longer had the least use for them. Round about them the great demesnes lived their own life. There is no evidence that the State, itself constituted on a purely agricultural basis, had any cause to be interested in their fate. It is quite characteristic, and quite illuminating, that the palaces (*palatia*) of the Carolingian princes were not located in the towns. They were, without exception, in the country . . .

[. . .]

The State, on its part, in exercising administrative powers could contribute in no way to the continued existence of the Roman cities. The countries which formed the political districts of the Empire were without their chief-towns, just as the Empire itself was without a capital. The counts, to whom the supervision of them was entrusted, did not settle down in any fixed spot. They were constantly traveling about their districts in order to preside over judicial assemblies, to levy taxes, and to raise troops . . .

On the contrary, the immobility which ecclesiastical discipline enforced upon a bishop permanently held him to the city where was established the see of his particular diocese . . . Each diocese comprised the territory about the city which contained its cathedral and kept in constant touch with it . . .

[. . .]

During the last days of the Lower Empire, and still more during the Merovingian era, the power of the bishops over the city populace consistently increased. They had profited by the growing disorganization of civil society to accept, or to arrogate to themselves, an authority which the inhabitants did not take pains to dispute with them, and which the State had no interest in and, moreover, no means of denying them . . .

When the disappearance of trade, in the ninth century, annihilated the last vestiges of city life and put an end to what still remained of a municipal population, the influence of the bishops, already so extensive, became unrivalled. Henceforward the towns were entirely under their control. In them were to be found, in fact, practically only inhabitants dependent more or less directly upon the Church.

Though no precise information is available, it is, nevertheless, possible to conjecture as to the nature of this population. It was composed of the clerics of the cathedral church and of the other churches grouped nearby; of the monks of the monasteries which, especially after the ninth century, came to be established, sometimes in great numbers, in the see of the diocese; of the teachers and the students of the ecclesiastical schools; and finally, of servitors and artisans, free or serf, who were indispensable to the needs of the religious group and to the daily existence of the clerical agglomeration. Almost always there was to be found in the town a weekly market whither the peasants from round about brought their produce. Sometimes, even, an annual fair was held there. At the gates a market toll was levied on everything that came in or went out. A mint was in operation within the walls. There were also to be found there a number of keeps occupied by vassals of the bishop, by his advocate or by his castellan. To all of this must be added, finally, the granaries and the storehouses where were stored the harvests from the monastical demesnes brought in, at stated periods, by the tenant-farmers. At the great yearly festivals the congregation of the diocese poured into the town and gave it, for several days, the animation of unaccustomed bustle and stir.

All this little world accepted the bishop as both its spiritual and temporal head. Religious and secular authority were united or, to put it better, were blended in his person . . . [T]here was no longer any field in the administration of the town wherein, whether by law or by prerogative, he did not intervene as the guardian of order, peace, and the common weal. A theocratic form of government had completely replaced the municipal regimen of antiquity ...

[...]

These towns were fortresses as well as episcopal residences. In the last days of the Roman Empire they had been enclosed by walls as a protection against the barbarians. These walls were still in existence almost everywhere and the bishops busied themselves with keeping them up or with restoring them with the greater zeal in that the incursions of the Saracens and the Norsemen had given increasingly impressive proof, during the ninth century, of the need of protection. The old Roman *enceintes* continued, therefore, to protect the towns against new perils.

Their form remained, under Charlemagne, what it had been under Constantine. As a general rule, it took the shape of a rectangle surrounded by ramparts flanked by towers and communicating with the outside by gates, customarily to the number of four. The space so enclosed was very restricted and the length of its sides rarely exceeded four to five hundred yards. Moreover, it was far from being entirely built up; between the houses cultivated fields and gardens were to be found. The outskirts (*suburbium*), which in the Merovingian era still extended beyond the walls, had disappeared ...

[...]

In the midst of the insecurity and the disorders which imparted so lugubrious a character to the second half of the ninth century, it therefore fell to the towns to fulfill a true mission of protection. They were, in every sense of the word, the ramparts of a society invaded, under tribute, and terrorized. Soon, from another cause, they were not to be alone in filling that role.

[...]

[Pirenne describes the disintegration of the Frankish state into territories controlled by princes. The princes established burgs (fortresses) which complemented the towns as centers for defense against invaders, but had none of the towns' other characteristics.]

It is therefore a safe conclusion that the period which opened with the Carolingian era knew cities neither in the social sense, nor in the economic sense, nor in the legal sense of that word. The towns and burgs were merely fortified places and headquarters of administration. Their inhabitants enjoyed neither special laws nor institutions of their own, and their manner of living did not distinguish them in any way from the rest of society.

Commercial and industrial activity were completely foreign to them. In no respect were they out of key with the agricultural civilization of their times. The groups they formed were, after all, of trifling importance. It is not possible, in the lack of reliable information, to give an exact figure, but everything indicates that the population of the burgs never consisted of more than a few hundred men and that of the towns probably did not pass the figure of two to three thousand souls.

The towns and burgs played, however, an essential role in the history of cities. They were, so to speak, the stepping-stones thereto. Round about their walls cities were to take shape after the economic renaissance, whose first symptoms appeared in the course of the tenth century, had made itself manifest.

CITIES AND EUROPEAN CIVILIZATION

The birth of cities marked the beginning of a new era in the internal history of Western Europe. Until then, society had recognized only two active orders: the clergy and the nobility. In taking its place beside them, the middle class rounded the social order out or, rather, gave the finishing touch thereto. Thenceforth its composition was not to change; it had all its constituent elements, and the modifications which it was to undergo in the course of centuries were, strictly speaking, nothing more than different combinations in the alloy. Like the clergy and like the nobility, the middle class was itself a privileged order. It formed a distinct legal group and the special law it enjoyed isolated it from the mass of the rural inhabitants which continued to make up the immense majority of the population. Indeed, as has already been seen, it was obliged to preserve intact its exceptional status and to reserve to itself the benefits arising therefrom. Freedom, as the middle class conceived it, was a monopoly. Nothing was less liberal than the caste idea, which was the cause of its strength until it became, at the end of the Middle Ages, a cause of weakness. Nevertheless, to that middle class was reserved the mission of spreading the idea of liberty far and wide and of becoming, without having consciously desired to be, the means of the gradual enfranchisement of the rural classes. The sole fact of its existence was due, indeed, to have an immediate effect upon these latter and, little by little, to attenuate the contrast which at the start separated them from it. In vain it strove to keep them under its influence, to refuse them a share in its privileges, to exclude them from engaging in trade and industry. It had not the power to arrest an evolution of which it was the cause and which it could not suppress save by itself vanishing.

For the formation of the city groups disturbed at once the economic organization of the country districts. Production, as it was there carried on, had served until then merely to support the life of the peasant and supply the prestations due to his seigneur. Upon the suspension of commerce, nothing impelled him to ask of the soil a surplus which it would have been impossible for him to get rid of, since he no longer had outside markets to call upon. He was content to provide for his daily bread, certain of the morrow and longing for no amelioration of his lot, since he could not conceive the possibility of it. The small markets of the towns and the burgs were too insignificant and their demand was too regular to rouse him enough to get out of his rut and intensify his labor. But suddenly these markets sprang into new life. The number of buyers was multiplied, and all at once he had the assurance of being able to sell the produce he brought to them. It was only natural for him to have profited from an opportunity as favorable as this. It depended on himself alone to sell, if he produced enough, and forthwith he began to till the land which hitherto he had let lie fallow. His work took on a new significance; it

brought him profits, the chance of thrift and of an existence which became more comfortable as it became more active. The situation was still more favorable in that the surplus revenues from the soil belonged to him in his own right. The claims of the seigneur were fixed by demesnial custom at an immutable rate, so that the increase in the income from the land benefited only the tenant.

But the seigneur himself had a chance to profit from the new situation wherein the development of the cities placed the country districts. He had enormous reserves of uncultivated land: woods, heaths, marshes, and fens. Nothing could be simpler than to put them under cultivation and through them to profit from these new outlets which were becoming more and more exigent and remunerative as the towns grew in size and multiplied in number. The increase in population would furnish the necessary hands for the work of clearing and draining. It was enough to call for men; they would not fail to show up.

By the end of the eleventh century the movement was already manifest in its full force. Monasteries and local princes thenceforth were busy transforming the sterile parts of their demesnes into revenue-producing land. The area of cultivated land which, since the end of the Roman Empire, had not been increased, kept growing continually greater . . .

Meanwhile, on all sides, the seigneurs, both lay and ecclesiastic, were founding "new" towns. So was called a village established on virgin soil, occupants of which received plots of land in return for an annual rental. But these new towns, the number of which continued to grow in the course of the twelfth century, were at the same time towns. For in order to attract the farmers the seigneur promised them exemption from the taxes which bore down upon the serfs. In general, he reserved to himself only jurisdiction over them; he abolished in their favor the old claims which still existed in the demesnial organization . . .

Thus a new type of peasant appeared, quite different from the old. The latter had serfdom as a characteristic; the former enjoyed freedom. And this freedom, the cause of which was the economic disturbance communicated by the towns to the organization of the country districts, was itself copied after that of the cities. The inhabitants of the new towns were, strictly speaking, rural burghers. They even bore, in a good number of charters, the name of *burgenses*. They received a legal constitution and a local autonomy which was manifestly borrowed from city institutions, so much so that it may be said that the latter went beyond the circumference of their walls in order to reach the country districts and acquaint them with liberty.

And this new freedom, as it progressed, was not long in making headway even in the old demesnes, whose archaic constitution could not be maintained in the midst of a reorganized social order. Either by voluntary emancipation, or by prescription or usurpation, the seigneurs permitted it to be gradually substituted for the serfdom which had so long been the normal condition of their tenants. The form of government of the people was there changed at the same time as the form of government of the land, since both were consequences of an economic situation on the way to disappearing. Commerce now supplied all the necessaries which the demesnes had hitherto been obliged to obtain by their own efforts. It was no longer essential for each of them to produce all the commodities for which it had use. It sufficed to go get them at some nearby city...

... Trade, which was becoming more and more active, necessarily favored agricultural production, broke down the limits which had hitherto bounded it, drew it towards the towns, modernized it, and at the same time set it free. Man was therefore detached from the soil to which he had so long been enthralled, and free labor was substituted more and more generally for serf labor...

The emancipation of the rural classes was only one of the consequences provoked by the economic revival of which the towns were both the result and the instrument. It coincided with the increasing importance of liquid capital. During the demesnial era of the Middle Ages, there was no other form of wealth than that which lay in real estate. It ensured to the holder both personal liberty and social prestige. It was the guaranty of the privileged status of the clergy and the nobility. Exclusive holders of the land, they lived by the labor of their tenants whom they protected and whom they ruled. The serfdom of the masses was the necessary consequence of such a social organization. There was no alternative save to own the land and be lord, or to till it for another and be a serf.

But with the origin of the middle class there took its place in the sun a class of men whose existence was in flagrant contradiction to this traditional order of things. The land upon which they settled they not only did not cultivate but did not even own. They demonstrated and made increasingly clear the possibility of living and growing rich by the sole act of selling, or producing exchange values.

Landed capital had been everything, and now by the side of it was made plain the power of liquid capital. Heretofore money had been sterile. The great lay or ecclesiastic proprietors in whose hands was concentrated the very scant stock of currency in circulation, by means of either the land taxes which they levied upon their tenants or the alms which the congregations brought to the church, normally had no way of making it bear fruit... As a general rule cash was hoarded by its possessors and most often changed into vessels or ornaments for the church, which might be melted down in case of need. Trade, naturally, released this captive money and restored its proper function. Thanks to this, it became again the instrument of exchange and the measure of values, and since the towns were the centers of trade it necessarily flowed towards them. In circulating, its power was multiplied by the number of transactions in which it served. Its use, at the same time, became more general; payments in kind gave way more and more to payments in money.

A new motion of wealth made its appearance: that of mercantile wealth, consisting no longer in land but in money or commodities of trade measurable in money. During the course of the eleventh century, true capitalists already existed in a number of cities ... These city capitalists soon formed the habit of putting a part of their profits into land. The best means of consolidating their fortune and their credit was, in fact, the buying up of land. They devoted a part of their gains to the purchase of real estate, first of all in the same town where they dwelt and later in the country. But they changed themselves, especially, into money-lenders. The economic crisis provoked by the irruption of trade into the life of society had caused the ruin of, or at least trouble to, the landed proprietors who had not been able to adapt themselves to it. For in speeding up the circulation of money a natural result was the decreasing of its value and by that very fact the raising of all prices. The period contemporary with the formation of the cities was a period of high cost of living, as favorable to the businessmen and artisans of the middle class as it was painful to the holders of the land who did not succeed in increasing their revenues. By the end of the eleventh century many of them were obliged to have recourse to the capital of the merchants in order to keep going . . .

But more important operations were already current at this era. There was no lack of merchants rich enough to agree to loans of considerable amount . . . The kings themselves had recourse, in the course of the twelfth century, to the good services of the city financiers . . .

[. . .]

The power of liquid capital, concentrated in the cities, not only gave them an economic ascendancy but contributed also towards making them take part in political life. For as long as society had known no other power than that which derived from the possession of the land, the clergy and the nobility alone had had a share in the government . . .

But as soon as the economic revival enabled [the prince] to augment his revenues, and cash, thanks to it, began to flow to his coffers, he took immediate advantage of circumstances . . . Identical economic causes had changed simultaneously the organization of the land and the governing of the people. Just as they enabled the peasants to free themselves, and the proprietors to substitute the quit-rent for the demesnial mansus, so they enabled the princes, thanks to their salaried agents, to lay hold of the direct government of their territories. This political innovation, like the social innovations with

which it was contemporary, implied the diffusion of ready cash and the circulation of money . . .

The connections which were necessarily established between the princes and the burghers also had political consequences of the greatest import. It was necessary to take heed of those cities whose increasing wealth gave them a steadily increasing importance, and which could put on the field, in case of need, thousands of well-equipped men . . .

[. . .]

. . . [The cities'] natural tendency led them to become municipal republics. There is but little doubt but that, if they had had the power, they would have everywhere become States within the State. But they did not succeed in realizing this ideal save where the power of the State was impotent to counterbalance their efforts.

[. . .]

[The territorial government] did not treat them as mere subjects. It had too much need of them not to have regard for their interests. Its finances rested in great part upon them, and to the extent that they augmented the power of the State and therewith its expenses, it felt more and more frequently the need of going to the pocketbooks of the burghers . . . Little by little the princes formed the habit of calling the burghers into the councils of prelates and nobles with whom they conferred upon their affairs. The instances of such convocations were still rare in the twelfth century; they multiplied in the thirteenth; and in the fourteenth century the custom was definitely legalized by the institution of the Estates in which the cities obtained, after the clergy and the nobility, a place which soon became, although the third in dignity, the first in importance.

Although the middle classes, as we have just seen, had an influence of very vast import upon the social, economic, and political changes which were manifest in Western Europe in the course of the twelfth century, it does not seem at first glance that they played much of a role in the intellectual movement. It was not, in fact, until the fourteenth century that a literature and an art was brought forth from the bosom of the middle classes, animated with their spirit. Until then, science remained the exclusive monopoly of the clergy and employed no other tongue than the Latin. What literature was written in the vernacular had to do solely with the nobility, or at least expressed only the ideas and the sentiments which pertained to the nobility as a class. Architecture and sculpture produced their masterpieces only in the construction and ornamentation of the churches. The market and belfries, of which the oldest specimens date back to the beginning of the thirteenth century ... remained still faithful to the architectural style of the great religious edifices.

Upon closer inspection, however, it does not take long to discover that city life really did make its own contribution to the moral spirit of the Middle Ages. To be sure, its intellectual culture was dominated by practical considerations which, before the period of the Renaissance, kept it from putting forth any independent effort. But from the very first it showed that characteristic of being an exclusively lay culture. By the middle of the twelfth century the municipal councils were busy founding schools for the children of the burghers, which were the first lay schools since the end of antiquity. By means of them, instruction ceased to be furnished exclusively for the benefit of the novices of the monasteries and the future parish priests. Knowledge of reading and writing, being indispensable to the practice of commerce, ceased to be reserved for the members of the clergy alone. The burgher was initiated into them long before the noble, because what was for the noble only an intellectual luxury was for him a daily need ...

However, the teaching in these communal schools was limited, until the period of the Renaissance, to elementary instruction. All who wished to have more were obliged to turn to the clerical establishments. It was from these latter that came the "clerks" who, starting at the end of the twelfth century, were charged with the correspondence and the accounts of the city, as well as the publication of the manifold Acts necessitated by commercial life. All these "clerks" were, furthermore, laymen, the cities having never taken into their service, in contradistinction to the princes, members of the clergy who by virtue of the privileges they enjoyed would have escaped their jurisdiction.

The language which the municipal scribes employed was naturally, at first, Latin. But after the first years of the thirteenth century they adopted more and more generally the use of national idioms. It was by the cities that the common tongue was introduced for the first time into administrative usage. Thereby they showed an initiative which corresponded perfectly to that lay spirit of which they were the preeminent representatives in the civilization of the Middle Ages.

This lay spirit, moreover, was allied with the most intense religious fervor. If the burghers were very frequently in conflict with the ecclesiastic authorities, if the bishops thundered fulsomely against them with sentences of excommunication, and if, by way of counterattack, they sometimes gave way to decidedly pronounced anti-clerical tendencies, they were, for all of that, none the less animated by a profound and ardent faith ...

Both lay and mystic at the same time, the burghers of the Middle Ages were thus singularly well prepared for the role which they were to play in the two great future movements of ideas: the Renaissance, the child of the lay mind, and the Reformation, towards which religious mysticism was leading.

FRIEDRICH ENGELS

"The Great Towns"

from *The Condition of the Working Class in England* (1845)

Editors' introduction   It was the peculiar fate of Friedrich Engels (1820–1895) to live most of his adult life in the shadow of his better-known friend and partner Karl Marx and to be remembered in death as a fiercely bearded icon of international communism. It was, however, a more humanly accessible Engels who, full of youthful idealism at the age of only 24, came face to face with the social horrors of the Industrial Revolution when he was sent by his industrialist father to learn business management in the factories of Manchester in the north of England. The unintended consequence of that particular paternal decision was *The Condition of the Working Class in England* (1845), a book that ranks as one of the great examples of modern political and economic analysis as well as one of the greatest and earliest masterpieces of urban sociology.

In the selection titled "The Great Towns" reprinted here the method Engels employs is peripatetic. Although he summarizes the socialist theory of the origin and historic role of the industrial working class, and although he quotes from many contemporaneous sources to bolster his analysis, Engels constructs the bulk of his argument by merely walking around. Quickly growing impatient with *telling* his readers about the social misery of working-class life, Engels begins *showing* them the horrors of industrial urbanism by conducting them on a tour of Manchester's working-class districts. As in Dante's *Inferno*, the tour descends deeper and deeper into the filth, misery, and despair that constitute the greater part of the Manchester conurbation.

No one can read *The Condition of the Working Class* without acknowledging that Engels had come to know the various neighborhoods of proletarian Manchester – Old Town, Irish Town, Long Millgate, and Salford – almost intimately and that his observations were acute and objective. Of particular interest are his descriptions of the public health consequences (in terms of air and water pollution) of unrestrained overbuilding and his observation that the facades of the main thoroughfares tend to mask the horrors that lie beyond from the eyes of the factory owners and the middle-class managers who commute into the city from outlying suburbs.

The entire tradition of twentieth-century urban planning – capitalist and socialist alike – owes an enormous debt to Engels. The connection he draws between the physical decrepitude of the urban infrastructure and the alienation and despair of the urban poor remains valid to the present day. The urban parks movement and the construction of ideal company towns – Saltaire and Port Sunlight in the United Kingdom, Lowell and Pullman in the United States – as well as the more recent attempts at inner-city redevelopment all address issues first identified by Engels.

The conditions described by Engels form the basis for the social realist tradition in literature, a tradition that begins with Charles Dickens and Mrs. Gaskell in England and is continued in the works of Upton Sinclair and Theodore Dreiser in the United States. Other significant investigations of urban poverty in England include Henry Mayhew's *London Labour and the London Poor* (4 volumes, 1851–62), Charles Booth's *Conditions and Occupation of the People in East London and Hackney* (*Journal of the Royal Historical Society*, 1887), Jack London's *People of the Abyss* (New York: Macmillan, 1903), and George Orwell's *Down and Out in Paris and London* (London: Secker & Warburg, 1933). In the U.S., key works include Jacob Riis, *How the Other Half Lives* (New York: Scribners, 1903) and a whole series of reports on conditions in the African-American ghettos such as W. E. B. Dubois's *The Philadelphia Negro* (p. 57), St. Clair Drake and Horace Cayton's *Black Metropolis* (Chicago: University of Chicago Press, 1945), and William Julius Wilson's "The Black Underclass" (p. 226).

For an excellent summary of nineteenth-century urban poverty conditions, consult "The City of Dreadful Night" in Peter Hall's *Cities of Tomorrow* (Oxford: Basil Blackwell, 1988). For further information on Engels's Manchester, and its connections to an emerging social realism in fiction, consult literary historian Steven Marcus's magisterial *Engels, Manchester, and the Working Class* (New York: Random House, 1974). Also of interest is Robert Roberts's extraordinary *The Classic Slum* (Manchester: Manchester University Press, 1971), a first-person account of growing up in Salford during the early years of the twentieth century.

FRIEDRICH ENGELS, "The Great Towns"

from *The Condition of the Working Class in England* (1845)

A town, such as London, where a man may wander for hours together without reaching the beginning of the end, without meeting the slightest hint which could lead to the inference that there is open country within reach, is a strange thing. This colossal centralization, this heaping together of two and a half millions of human beings at one point, has multiplied the power of this two and a half millions a hundred-fold; has raised London to the commercial capital of the world, created the giant docks and assembled the thousand vessels that continually cover the Thames. I know nothing more imposing than the view which the Thames offers during the ascent from the sea to London Bridge. The masses of buildings, the wharves on both sides, especially from Woolwich upwards, the countless ships along both shores, crowding ever closer and closer together, until, at last, only a narrow passage remains in the middle of the river, a passage through which hundreds of steamers shoot by one another; all this is so vast, so impressive, that a man cannot collect himself, but is lost in the marvel of England's greatness before he sets foot upon English soil.

But the sacrifices which all this has cost become apparent later. After roaming the streets of the capital a day or two, making headway with difficulty through the human turmoil and the endless lines of vehicles, after visiting the slums of the metropolis, one realizes for the first time that these Londoners have been forced to sacrifice the best qualities of their human nature, to bring to pass all the marvels of civilization which crowd their city; that a hundred powers which slumbered within them have remained inactive, have been suppressed in order that a few might be developed more fully and multiply through union with those of others. The very turmoil of the streets has something repulsive, something against which human nature rebels. The hundreds of thousands of all classes and ranks crowding past each other, are they not all human beings with the same qualities and powers, and with the same interest in being happy? And have they not, in the end, to seek happiness in the same way, by the same means? And still they crowd by one another as though they had nothing in common, nothing to do with one another, and their only agreement is the tacit one, that each keep to his own side of the pavement, so as not to delay the opposing streams of the crowd, while it occurs to no man to honour another with so much as a glance. The brutal indifference, the unfeeling isolation of each in his private interest becomes the more repellent and offensive, the more these individuals are crowded together, within a limited space. And, however much one may be aware that this isolation of the individual, this narrow self-seeking is the fundamental principle of our society everywhere, it is nowhere so shamelessly barefaced, so self-conscious as just here in the crowding of the great city. The dissolution of mankind into monads, of which each one has a separate principle and a separate purpose, the world of atoms, is here carried out to its utmost extreme.

Hence it comes, too, that the social war, the war of each against all, is here openly declared. ..., people regard each other only as useful objects; each exploits the other, and the end of it all is, that the stronger treads the weaker under foot, and that the powerful few, the capitalists, seize everything for themselves, while to the weak many, the poor, scarcely a bare existence remains.

What is true of London, is true of Manchester, Birmingham, Leeds, is true of all great towns. Everywhere barbarous indifference, hard egotism on one hand, and nameless misery on the other, everywhere social warfare, every man's house in a state of siege, everywhere reciprocal plundering under the protection of the law, and all so shameless, so openly avowed that one shrinks before the consequences of our social state as they manifest themselves here undisguised, and can only wonder that the whole crazy fabric still hangs together.

Since capital, the direct or indirect control of the means of subsistence and production, is the weapon with which this social warfare is carried on, it is clear that all the disadvantages of such a state must fall upon the poor. For him no man has the slightest concern. Cast into the whirlpool, he must struggle through as well as he can. If he is so happy as to find work, i.e. if the bourgeoisie does him the favour to enrich itself by means of him, wages await him which scarcely suffice to keep body and soul together; if he can get no work he may steal, if he is not afraid of the police, or starve, in which case the police will take care that he does so in a quiet and inoffensive manner. During my residence in England, at least twenty or thirty persons have died of simple starvation under the most revolting circumstances, and a jury has rarely been found possessed of the courage to speak the plain truth in the matter. Let the testimony of the witnesses be never so clear and unequivocal, the bourgeoisie, from which the jury is selected, always finds some backdoor through which to escape the frightful verdict, death from starvation. The bourgeoisie dare not speak the truth in these cases. for it would speak its own condemnation. But indirectly, far more than directly, many have died of starvation, where long continued want of proper nourishment has called forth fatal illness, when it has produced such debility that causes which might otherwise have remained inoperative, brought on severe illness and death. The English working-men call this social murder, and accuse our whole society of perpetrating this crime perpetually. Are they wrong?

True, it is only individuals who starve, but what security has the working-man that it may not be his turn tomorrow? Who assures him employment, who vouches for it that, if for any reason or no reason his lord and master discharges him tomorrow, he can struggle along with those dependent upon him, until he may find some one else "to give him bread"? Who guarantees that willingness to work shall suffice to obtain work, that uprightness, industry, thrift, and the rest of the virtues recommended by the bourgeoisie, are really his road to happiness? No one. He knows that he has something today, and that it does not depend upon himself whether he shall have something tomorrow. He knows that every breeze that blows, every whim of his employer, every bad turn of trade may hurl him back into the fierce whirlpool from which he has temporarily saved himself, and in which it is hard and often impossible to keep his head above water. He knows that, though he may have the means of living today, it is very uncertain whether he shall tomorrow.

[...]

Manchester lies at the foot of the southern slope of a range of hills, which stretch hither from Oldham, their last peak, Kersallmoor, being at once the racecourse and the Mons Sacer of Manchester. Manchester proper lies on the left bank of the Irwell, between that stream and the two smaller ones, the Irk and the Medlock, which here empty into the Irwell. On the right bank of the Irwell, bounded by a sharp curve of the river, lies Salford, and farther westward Pendleton; northward from the Irwell lie Upper and Lower Broughton; northward of the Irk, Cheetham Hill; south of the Medlock lies Hulme; farther east Chorlton on Medlock; still farther, pretty well to the east of Manchester, Ardwick. The whole assemblage of buildings is commonly called Manchester, and contains about four hundred thousand inhabitants, rather more than less. The town itself is peculiarly built, so that a person may live in it for years, and go in and out daily without coming into contact with a working-people's quarter or even with workers; that is, so long as he confines himself to his business or to pleasure walks. This arises chiefly from the fact, that by unconscious tacit agreement, as well as with outspoken conscious determination, the working-people's quarters are sharply separated from the sections of the city reserved for the middle class; or, if this does not succeed, they are concealed with the cloak of charity. Manchester contains, at its heart, a rather extended commercial district, perhaps half a mile long and about as broad, and consisting almost wholly of offices and warehouses. Nearly the whole district is abandoned by dwellers, and is lonely and deserted at night; only watchmen and policemen traverse its narrow lanes with their dark lanterns. This district is cut through by certain main thoroughfares upon which the vast traffic concentrates, and in which the ground level is lined with brilliant shops. In these streets the upper floors are occupied, here and there, and there is a good deal of life upon them until late at night. With the exception of this commercial district, all

Manchester proper, all Salford and Hulme, a great part of Pendleton and Chorlton, two-thirds of Ardwick, and single stretches of Cheetham Hill and Broughton are all unmixed working-people's quarters, stretching like a girdle, averaging a mile and a half in breadth, around the commercial district. Outside, beyond this girdle, lives the upper and middle bourgeoisie, the middle bourgeoisie in regularly laid out streets in the vicinity of the working quarters, especially in Chorlton and the lower-lying portions of Cheetham Hill; the upper bourgeoisie in remoter villas with gardens in Chorlton and Ardwick or on the breezy heights of Cheetham Hill, Broughton and Pendleton, in free, wholesome country air, in fine, comfortable homes, passed once every half or quarter hour by omnibuses going into the city. And the finest part of the arrangement is this, that the members of this money aristocracy can take the shortest road through the middle of all the labouring districts to their places of business, without ever seeing that they are in the midst of the grimy misery that lurks to the right and the left. For the thoroughfares leading from the Exchange in all directions out of the city are lined, on both sides, with an almost unbroken series of shops, and are so kept in the hands of the middle and lower bourgeoisie, which, out of self-interest, cares for a decent and cleanly external appearance and *can* care for it. True, these shops bear some relation to the districts which lie behind them, and are more elegant in the commercial and residential quarters than when they hide grimy working-men's dwellings; but they suffice to conceal from the eyes of the wealthy men and women of strong stomachs and weak nerves the misery and grime which form the complement of their wealth. So, for instance, Deansgate, which leads from the Old Church directly southward, is lined first with mills and warehouses, then with second-rate shops and alehouses; farther south, when it leaves the commercial district, with less inviting shops, which grow dirtier and more interrupted by beerhouses and gin palaces the farther one goes, until at the southern end the appearance of the shops leaves no doubt that workers and workers only are their customers. So Market Street running south east from the Exchange; at first brilliant shops of the best sort, with counting-houses or warehouses above; in the continuation, Piccadilly, immense hotels and warehouses; in the farther continuation, London Road, in the neighbourhood of the Medlock, factories, beerhouses, shops for the humbler bourgeoisie and the working population; and from this point onward, large gardens and villas of the wealthier merchants and manufacturers. In this way any one who knows Manchester can infer the adjoining districts, from the appearance of the thoroughfare, but one is seldom in a position to catch from the street a glimpse of the real labouring districts. I know very well that this hypocritical plan is more or less common to all great cities; I know, too, that the retail dealers are forced by the nature of their business to take possession of the great highways; I know that there are more good buildings than bad ones upon such streets everywhere, and that the value of land is greater near them than in remoter districts; but at the same time I have never seen so systematic a shutting out of the working-class from the thoroughfares, so tender a concealment of everything which might affront the eye and the nerves of the bourgeoisie, as in Manchester. And yet, in other respects, Manchester is less built according to a plan, after official regulations, is more an outgrowth of accident, than any other city; and when I consider in this connection the eager assurances of the middle-class, that the working-class is doing famously, I cannot help feeling that the liberal manufacturers, the "Big Wigs" of Manchester, are not so innocent after all, in the matter of this sensitive method of construction.

I may mention just here that the mills almost all adjoin the rivers or the different canals that ramify throughout the city, before I proceed at once to describe the labouring quarters. First of all, there is the Old Town of Manchester [Figure 1], which lies between the northern boundary of the commercial district and the Irk. Here the streets, even the better ones, are narrow and winding, as Todd Street, Long Millgate, Withy Grove, and Shude Hill, the houses dirty, old, and tumble-down, and the construction of the side streets utterly horrible. Going from the Old Church to Long Millgate, the stroller has at

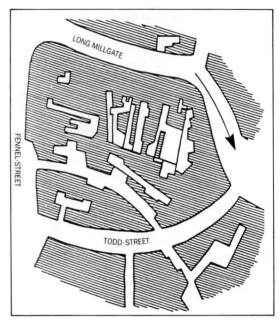

Figure 1

once a row of old-fashioned houses at the right, of which not one has kept its original level; these are remnants of the old pre-manufacturing Manchester, whose former inhabitants have removed with their descendants into better-built districts, and have left the houses, which were not good enough for them, to a working-class population strongly mixed with Irish blood. Here one is in an almost undisguised working-men's quarter, for even the shops and beerhouses hardly take the trouble to exhibit a trifling degree of cleanliness. But all this is nothing in comparison with the courts and lanes which lie behind, to which access can be gained only through covered passages in which no two human beings can pass at the same time. Of the irregular cramming together of dwellings in ways which defy all rational plan, of the tangle in which they are crowded literally one upon the other, it is impossible to convey an idea. And it is not the buildings surviving from the old times of Manchester which are to blame for this; the confusion has only recently reached its height when every scrap of space left by the old way of building has been filled up and patched over until not a foot of land is left to be further occupied.

[...]

The south bank of the Irk is here very steep and between fifteen and thirty feet high. On this declivitous hillside there are planted three rows of houses, of which the lowest rise directly out of the river, while the front walls of the highest stand on the crest of the hill in Long Millgate. Among them are mills on the river; in short, the method of construction is as crowded and disorderly here as in the lower part of Long Millgate. Right and left a multitude of covered passages lead from the main street into numerous courts, and he who turns in thither gets into a filth and disgusting grime the equal of which is not to be found – especially in the courts which lead down to the Irk and which contain unqualifiedly the most horrible dwellings which I have yet beheld. In one of these courts there stands directly at the entrance, at the end of the covered passage, a privy without a door, so dirty that the inhabitants can pass into and out of the court only by passing through foul pools of stagnant urine and excrement. This is the first court on the Irk above Ducie Bridge – in case any one should care to look into it. Below it on the river there are several tanneries which fill the whole neighbourhood with the stench of animal putrefaction. Below Ducie Bridge the only entrance to most of the houses is by means of narrow dirty stairs and over heaps of refuse and filth. The first court below Ducie Bridge, known as Allen's Court, was in such a state at the time of the cholera that the sanitary police ordered it evacuated, swept, and disinfected with chloride of lime. Dr. Kay gives a terrible description of the state of this court at that time. Since then it seems to have been partially torn away and rebuilt; at least looking down from Ducie Bridge, the passer-by sees several ruined walls and heaps of debris with some newer houses. The view from this bridge, mercifully concealed from mortals of small stature by a parapet as high as a man, is characteristic for the whole district. At the bottom flows, or rather stagnates, the Irk, a narrow, coal-black, foul-smelling stream full of debris and refuse, which it deposits on the shallower right bank. In dry weather, a long string of the most disgusting, blackish-green, slime pools are left standing on this bank, from the depths of which bubbles of miasmatic gas constantly arise and give forth a stench unendurable even on the bridge forty or fifty feet above the surface of the stream. But besides this, the stream itself is checked every few paces by high weirs, behind which slime and refuse accumulate and rot in thick masses. Above the bridge are tanneries, bonemills, and gasworks, from which all drains and refuse find their way into the Irk, which receives further the contents of all the neighbouring sewers and privies. It may be easily imagined, therefore, what sort of residue the stream deposits. Below the bridge you look upon the piles of debris, the refuse, filth, and offal from the courts on the steep left bank; here each house is packed close behind its neighbour and a piece of each is visible, all black, smoky, crumbling, ancient, with broken panes and window-frames. The background is furnished by old barrack-like factory buildings. On the lower right bank stands a long row of houses and mills; the second house being a ruin without a roof, piled with debris; the third stands so low that the lowest floor is uninhabitable, and therefore without windows or doors. Here the background embraces the pauper burial-ground, the station of the Liverpool and Leeds railway, and, in the rear of this, the Workhouse, the "Poor-Law-Bastille" of Manchester, which, like a citadel, looks threateningly down from behind its high walls and parapets on the hilltop, upon the working people's quarter below.

Above Ducie Bridge, the left bank grows more flat and the right bank steeper, but the condition of the dwellings on both banks grows worse rather than better. He who turns to the left here from the main street, Long Millgate, is lost; he wanders from one court to another, turns countless corners, passes nothing but narrow, filthy nooks and alleys, until after a few minutes he has lost all clue, and knows not whither to turn. Everywhere half or wholly ruined buildings, some of them actually uninhabited, which means a great deal here; rarely a wooden or stone floor to be seen in the houses, almost uniformly broken, ill-fitting windows and doors, and a state of filth! Everywhere heaps of debris, refuse, and offal; standing pools for gutters, and a stench which alone would make it impossible for a human being in any degree civilized to live in such a district. The newly-built extension of the Leeds railway, which crosses the Irk here, has swept away some of these courts and lanes, laying others completely open to view. Immediately under the railway bridge there stands a court, the filth and horrors of which surpass all the others by far, just because it was hitherto so shut off, so secluded that the way to it could not be found without a good deal of trouble. I should never have discovered it myself, without the breaks made by the railway, though I thought I knew this whole region thoroughly. Passing along a rough bank, among stakes and washing-lines, one penetrates into this chaos of small one-storeyed, one-roomed huts, in most of which there is no artificial floor; kitchen, living and sleeping room all in one. In such a hole, scarcely five feet long by six broad, I found two beds – and such bedsteads and beds! – which, with a staircase and chimney-place, exactly filled the room. In several others I found absolutely nothing, while the door stood open, and the inhabitants leaned against it. Everywhere before the doors refuse and offal; that any sort of pavement lay underneath could not be seen but only felt, here and there, with the feet. This whole collection of cattle-sheds for human beings was surrounded on two sides by houses and a factory, and on the third by the river, and besides the narrow stair up the bank, a narrow doorway alone led out into another almost equally ill-built, ill-kept labyrinth of dwellings.

Enough! The whole side of the Irk is built in this way, a planless, knotted chaos of houses, more or less on the verge of uninhabitableness, whose unclean interiors fully correspond with their filthy external surroundings. And how could the people be clean with no proper opportunity for satisfying the most natural and ordinary wants? Privies are so rare here that they are either filled up every day, or are too remote for most of the inhabitants to use. How can people wash when they have only the dirty Irk water at hand, while pumps and water pipes can be found in decent parts of the city alone? In truth, it cannot be charged to the account of these helots of modern society if their dwellings are not more clean than the pig-sties which are here and there to be seen among them. The landlords are not ashamed to let dwellings like

the six or seven cellars on the quay directly below Scotland Bridge, the floors of which stand at least two feet below the low-water level of the Irk that flows not six feet away from them; or like the upper floor of the corner-house on the opposite shore directly above the bridge, where the ground-floor, utterly uninhabitable, stands deprived of all fittings for doors and windows, a case by no means rare in this region, when this open ground-floor is used as a privy by the whole neighbourhood for want of other facilities!

If we leave the Irk and penetrate once more on the opposite side from Long Millgate into the midst of the working-men's dwellings, we shall come into a somewhat newer quarter, which stretches from St. Michael's Church to Withy Grove and Shude Hill. Here there is somewhat better order. In place of the chaos of buildings, we find at least long straight lanes and alleys or courts, built according to a plan and usually square. But if, in the former case, every house was built according to caprice, here each lane and court is so built, without reference to the situation of the adjoining ones. The lanes run now in this direction, now in that, while every two minutes the wanderer gets into a blind alley, or, on turning a corner, finds himself back where he started from; certainly no one who has not lived a considerable time in this labyrinth can find his way through it.

If I may use the word at all in speaking of this district, the ventilation of these streets and courts is, in consequence of this confusion, quite as imperfect as in the Irk region; and if this quarter may, nevertheless, be said to have some advantage over that of the Irk, the houses being newer and the streets occasionally having gutters, nearly every house has, on the other hand, a cellar dwelling, which is rarely found in the Irk district, by reason of the greater age and more careless construction of the houses. As for the rest the filth, debris, and offal heaps, and the pools in the streets are common to both quarters, and in the district now under discussion, another feature most injurious to the cleanliness of the inhabitants, is the multitude of pigs walking about in all the alleys, rooting into the offal heaps, or kept imprisoned in small pens. Here, as in most of the working-men's quarters of Manchester, the pork-raisers rent the courts and build pigpens in them. In almost every court one or even several such pens may be found into which the inhabitants of the court throw all refuse and offal, whence the swine grow fat; and the atmosphere, confined on all four sides, is utterly corrupted by putrefying animal and vegetable substances. Through this quarter, a broad and measurably decent street has been cut, Millers Street, and the background has been pretty successfully concealed. But if any one should be led by curiosity to pass through one of the numerous passages which lead into the courts, he will find this piggery repeated at every twenty paces.

Such is the Old Town of Manchester, and on re-reading my description, I am forced to admit that instead of being exaggerated, it is far from black enough to convey a true impression of the filth, ruin, and uninhabitableness, the defiance of all considerations of cleanliness, ventilation, and health which characterize the construction of this single district, containing at least twenty to thirty thousand inhabitants. And such a district exists in the heart of the second city of England, the first manufacturing city of the world. If any one wishes to see in how little space a human being can move, how little air – and *such* air! – he can breathe, how little of civilization he may share and yet live, it is only necessary to travel hither. True, this is the *Old* Town, and the people of Manchester emphasize the fact whenever any one mentions to them the frightful condition of this Hell upon Earth; but what does that prove? Everything which here arouses horror and indignation is of recent origin, belongs to the *industrial* epoch. The couple of hundred houses, which belong to old Manchester, have been long since abandoned by their original inhabitants; the industrial epoch alone has crammed into them the swarms of workers whom they now shelter; the industrial epoch alone has built up every spot between these old houses to win a covering for the masses whom it has conjured hither from the agricultural districts and from Ireland; the industrial epoch alone enables the owners of these cattlesheds to rent them for high prices to human beings, to plunder the poverty of the workers, to undermine the health of thousands,

in order that they *alone*, the owners, may grow rich. In the industrial epoch alone has it become possible that the worker scarcely freed from feudal servitude could be used as mere material, a mere chattel; that he must let himself be crowded into a dwelling too bad for every other, which he for his hard-earned wages buys the right to let go utterly to ruin. This manufacture has achieved, which, without these workers, this poverty, this slavery could not have lived. True, the original construction of this quarter was bad, little good could have been made out of it; but, have the landowners, has the municipality done anything to improve it when rebuilding? On the contrary, wherever a nook or corner was free, a house has been run up; where a superfluous passage remained, it has been built up; the value of land rose with the blossoming out of manufacture, and the more it rose, the more madly was the work of building up carried on, without reference to the health or comfort of the inhabitants, with sole reference to the highest possible profit on the principle that *no hole is so bad but that some poor creature must take it who can pay for nothing better.*

[. . .]

It may not be out of place to make some general observations just here as to the customary construction of working-men's quarters in Manchester. We have seen how in the Old Town pure accident determined the grouping of the houses in general. Every house is built without reference to any other, and the scraps of space between them are called courts for want of another name. In the somewhat newer portions of the same quarter, and in other working-men's quarters, dating from the early days of industrial activity, a somewhat more orderly arrangement may be found. The space between two streets is divided into more regular, usually square courts.

These courts were built in this way from the beginning, and communicate with the streets by means of covered passages. If the totally planless construction is injurious to the health of the workers by preventing ventilation, this method of shutting them up in courts surrounded on all sides by buildings is far more so. The air simply cannot escape; the chimneys of the houses are the sole drains for the imprisoned atmosphere of the courts, and they serve the purpose only so long as fire is kept burning. Moreover, the houses surrounding such courts are usually built back to back, having the rear wall in common; and this alone suffices to prevent any sufficient through ventilation. And, as the police charged with care of the streets does not trouble itself about the condition of these courts, as everything quietly lies where it is thrown, there is no cause for wonder at the filth and heaps of ashes and offal to be found here. I have been in courts, in Millers Street, at least half a foot below the level of the thoroughfare, and without the slightest drainage for the water that accumulates in them in rainy weather! More recently another different method of building was adopted, and has now become general. Workingmen's cottages are almost never built singly, but always by the dozen or score; a single contractor building up one or two streets at a time. These are then arranged as follows: One front is formed of cottages of the best class, so fortunate as to possess a back door and small court, and these command the highest rent. In the rear of these cottages runs a narrow alley, the back street, built up at both ends, into which either a narrow roadway or a covered passage leads from one side. The cottages which face this back street command least rent, and are most neglected. These have their rear walls in common with the third row of cottages which face a second street, and command less rent than the first row and more than the second. The streets are laid out somewhat as in [Figure 2].

By this method of construction, comparatively good ventilation can be obtained for the first row of cottages, and the third row is no worse off than in the former method. The middle row, on the other hand, is at least as badly ventilated as the houses in the courts, and the back street is always in the same filthy, disgusting condition as they. The contractors prefer this method because it saves them space, and furnishes the means of fleecing better-paid workers through the higher rents of the cottages in the first and third rows. These three different forms of cottage building are found all over

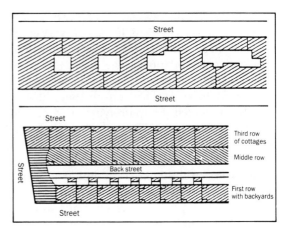

Figure 2

Manchester and throughout Lancashire and Yorkshire, often mixed up together, but usually separate enough to indicate the relative age of parts of towns. The third system, that of the back alleys, prevails largely in the great working-men's district east of St. George's Road and Ancoats Street, and is the one most often found in the other working-men's quarters of Manchester and its suburbs.

[...]

Such are the various working-people's quarters of Manchester as I had occasion to observe them personally during twenty months. If we briefly formulate the result of our wanderings, we must admit that 350,000 working-people of Manchester and its environs live, almost all of them, in wretched, damp, filthy cottages, that the streets which surround them are usually in the most miserable and filthy condition, laid out without the slightest reference to ventilation, with reference solely to the profit secured by the contractor. In a word, we must confess that in the working-men's dwellings of Manchester, no cleanliness, no convenience, and consequently no comfortable family life is possible; that in such dwellings only a physically degenerate race, robbed of all humanity, degraded, reduced morally and physically to bestiality, could feel comfortable and at home.

[...]

To sum up briefly the facts thus far cited. The great towns are chiefly inhabited by working-people, since in the best case there is one bourgeois for two workers, often for three, here and there for four; these workers have no property whatsoever of their own, and live wholly upon wages, which usually go from hand to mouth. Society, composed wholly of atoms, does not trouble itself about them; leaves them to care for themselves and their families, yet supplies them no means of doing this in an efficient and permanent manner. Every working-man, even the best, is therefore constantly exposed to loss of work and food, that is, to death by starvation, and many perish in this way. The dwellings of the workers are everywhere badly planned, badly built, and kept in the worst condition, badly ventilated, damp, and unwholesome. The inhabitants are confined to the smallest possible space, and at least one family usually sleeps in each room. The interior arrangement of the dwellings is poverty-stricken in various degrees, down to the utter absence of even the most necessary furniture. The clothing of the workers, too, is generally scanty, and that of great multitudes is in rags.

The food is, in general, bad; often almost unfit for use, and in many cases, at least at times, insufficient in quantity, so that, in extreme cases, death by starvation results. Thus the working-class of the great cities offers a graduated scale of conditions in life, in the best cases a temporarily endurable existence for hard work and good wages, good and endurable, that is, from the worker's standpoint; in the worst cases, bitter want, reaching even homelessness and death by starvation. The average is much nearer the worst case than the best. And this series does not fall into fixed classes, so that one can say, this fraction of the working-class is well off, has always been so, and remains so. If that is the case here and there, if single branches of work have in general an advantage over others, yet the condition of the workers in each branch is subject to such great fluctuations that a single working-man may be so placed as to pass through the whole range from comparative comfort to the extremest need, even to death by starvation, while almost every English working-man can tell a tale of marked changes of fortune.

W. E. B. DUBOIS

"The Negro Problems of Philadelphia," "The Question of Earning a Living," and "Color Prejudice"

from *The Philadelphia Negro* (1899)

Editors' introduction   William Edward Burghardt Dubois (1868–1963) was one of the preeminent intellectuals of his generation. As a professor, editor, author, novelist, playwright, and politician he made notable contributions in history, sociology, ethnic studies, literature, politics, and other fields.

A brilliant student, Dubois excelled at Fisk University in Nashville, Tennessee, the University of Berlin where he studied with the great sociologist Max Weber, and at Harvard University, where in 1895 he obtained the first Ph.D. degree Harvard awarded to a Negro.

Dubois defies easy classification. He was always an independent and critical thinker. During his long and varied career he was a pan-Africanist who advocated solidarity among Black Africans and Blacks elsewhere in the world; a radical pacifist who was indicted, tried, and acquitted as an unregistered foreign agent during the McCarthy era for circulating the Stockholm peace plan; a humanist who wrote novels and plays and published many of the writers of the "Harlem Renaissance"; a civil rights leader who founded the NAACP's publication *Crisis* in 1910 and served as its influential editor until 1934; a writer of children's books which taught Black pride; and a world political figure who urged UN protection for Black Americans as a nation within a nation. Dubois joined the Communist Party at age 93 and became a Ghanaian citizen in 1961 just before his death.

At the time that Dubois completed his studies Philadelphia had the largest and oldest settlement of Blacks in the northern United States. The settlement house movement was under way, and some well-intentioned Philadelphians were concerned to understand "the Negro problem" and to help the many poor Blacks in the city. Two wealthy leaders of Philadelphia society suggested a study of Negroes in the city's Black ghetto, the Seventh Ward.

Dubois was given a one-year appointment as an assistant instructor in the Sociology Department at the University of Pennsylvania. Living with his bride of three months in one room over a cafeteria in the worst part of Philadelphia's worst Black ghetto, with no contact with students and little with faculty, Dubois wrote *The Philadelphia Negro*, from which the following selection is taken. Dubois was only 31 when his monumental study was published.

While Dubois found many problems in Philadelphia's Negro community in the 1890s, there was work available for able-bodied laborers, no evidence of drug use, and little Black-on-Black violent crime. This is in marked contrast to William Julius Wilson's description of poor Black ghetto areas of Chicago in the 1980s (p. 226). Wilson describes Black ghettos in Chicago with almost no employed middle-class residents, and extremely high concentrations of single-parent families, welfare dependency, drug use, and violent crime.

Ethnographic studies by sociologists and anthropologists often shed light on variations within communities which are viewed as homogeneous by outsiders. While white Philadelphians who never visited the Seventh Ward tended to view the area as homogeneous and all African-Americans as similar, Dubois found a physical and social structure within the neighborhood: alleys peopled by criminals, loafers, and prostitutes separate from streets of the working poor and still other streets where an established group of Black middle-class home-owners lived.

In addition to *The Philadelphia Negro* (Philadelphia: University of Pennsylvania Press, 1899), from which the following selection is taken, Dubois's writings include *Suppression of the Slave Trade to the United States of America* (New York: Longmans, Green & Co., 1896), *Souls of Black Folk* (Chicago: A. C. McClurg & Co., 1903), *The Negro* (New York: Henry Holt & Co., 1915), *Black Reconstruction* (New York: Harcourt Brace, 1935), *The World and Africa* (New York: The Viking Press, 1947) and many other works.

For more by and about W. E. B. Dubois see *The Autobiography of W. E. B. Dubois* (New York: International Publishers, 1968), Francis L. Broderick, *W. E. B. Dubois* (Palo Alto, Calif.: Stanford University Press, 1959), and Walter Wilson (ed.), *The Selected Writings of W. E. B. Dubois.*

W. E. B. DUBOIS, "The Negro Problems of Philadelphia," "The Question of Earning a Living," and "Color Prejudice"

from *The Philadelphia Negro* (1899)

4. THE NEGRO PROBLEMS OF PHILADELPHIA

In Philadelphia, as elsewhere in the United States, the existence of certain peculiar social problems affecting the Negro people are plainly manifest. Here is a large group of people – perhaps forty-five thousand, a city within a city – who do not form an integral part of the larger social group. This in itself is not altogether unusual; there are other unassimilated groups: Jews, Italians, even Americans; and yet in the case of the Negroes the segregation is more conspicuous, more patent to the eye, and so intertwined with a long historic evolution, with peculiarly pressing social problems of poverty, ignorance, crime and labor, that the Negro problem far surpasses in scientific interest and social gravity most of the other race or class questions.

The student of these questions must first ask, What is the real condition of this group of human beings? Of whom is it composed, what sub-groups and classes exist, what sort of individuals are being considered? Further, the student must clearly recognize that a complete study must not confine itself to the group, but must specially notice the environment; the phys-ical environment of city, sections and houses, the far mightier social environment – the surrounding world of custom, wish, whim and thought which envelops this group and powerfully influences its social development.

[...]

The Seventh Ward starts from the historic center of Negro settlement in the city, South Seventh street and Lombard, and includes the long narrow strip, beginning at South Seventh and extending west, with South and Spruce streets as boundaries, as far as the Schuylkill River. The colored population of this ward numbered 3,621 in 1860, 4,616 in 1870, and 8,861 in 1890. It is a thickly populated district of varying character; north of it is the residence and business section of the city; south of it a middle class and workingmen's residence section; at the east end it joins Negro, Italian and Jewish slums; at the west end, the wharves of the river and an industrial section separating it from the grounds of the University of Pennsylvania and the residence section of West Philadelphia.

Starting at Seventh street and walking along Lombard, let us glance at the general character of the ward. Pausing a moment at the corner of Seventh and Lombard, we can at a glance view the worst Negro slums of the city. The houses are mostly brick, some wood, not very old, and in general uncared for rather than dilapidated. The blocks between Eighth, Pine, Sixth, and South have for many decades been the center of Negro population. Here the riots of the thirties took place, and here once was a depth of poverty and degradation almost unbelievable. Even today there are many evidences of degradation ... The alleys near, as Ratcliffe street, Middle alley, Brown's court, Barclay street, etc., are haunts of noted criminals, male and female, of gamblers and prostitutes, and at the same time of many poverty-stricken people, decent but not energetic. There is an abundance of political clubs, and nearly all the houses are practically lodging houses, with a miscellaneous and shifting population. The corners, night and day, are filled with Negro loafers – able-bodied young men and women, all cheerful, some with good natured, open faces, some with traces of crime and excess, a few pinched with poverty. They are mostly gamblers, thieves and prostitutes, and few have fixed and steady occupation of any kind. Some are stevedores, porters, laborers and laundresses. On its face this slum is noisy and dissipated, but not brutal, although now and then highway robberies and murderous assaults in other parts of the city are traced to its denizens. Nevertheless a stranger can usually walk about here day and night with little fear of being molested if he be not too inquisitive.

Passing up Lombard, beyond Eighth, the atmosphere suddenly changes, because these next two blocks have few alleys and the residences are good-sized and pleasant. Here some of the best Negro families of the ward live. Some are wealthy in a small way, nearly all are Philadelphia born, and they represent an early wave of emigration from the old slum section ...

[...]

21. THE QUESTION OF EARNING A LIVING

For a group of freedmen the question of economic survival is the most pressing of all questions; the problem as to how, under the circumstances of modern life, any group of people can earn a decent living, so as to maintain their standard of life, is not always easy to answer. But when the question is complicated by the fact that the group has a low degree of efficiency on account of previous training; is in competition with well-trained, eager and often ruthless competitors; is more or less handicapped by a somewhat wide-reaching discrimination; and finally is seeking not merely to maintain a standard of living but steadily to raise it to a higher plane – such a situation presents baffling problems to the sociologist and philanthropist.

Of the men 21 years of age and over, there were in gainful occupations, the following:

In the learned professions		61	2.0 per cent
Conducting business on their own account		207	6.5
In the skilled trades		236	7.0
Clerks, etc.		159	5.0
Laborers, better class	602		
Laborers, common class	852	1454	45.0
Servants		1079	34.0
Miscellaneous		11	0.5
		3207	100 per cent
Total male population 21 and over		3850	

Taking the occupations of women 21 years of age and over, we have:

Domestic servants	1262	37.0 per cent
Housewives and day laborers	937	27.0
Housewives	568	17.0
Day laborers, maids, etc.	297	9.0
In skilled trades	221	6.0
Conducting businesses	63	2.0
Clerks, etc.	40	1.0
Learned professions	37	1.0
	3425	100 per cent
Total female population 21 and over	3740	

47. COLOR PREJUDICE

Incidentally throughout this study the prejudice against the Negro has been again and again mentioned. It is time now to reduce this somewhat indefinite term to something tangible. Everybody speaks of the matter, everybody knows that it exists, but in just what form it shows itself or how influential it is few agree. In the Negro's mind, color prejudice in Philadelphia is that widespread feeling of dislike for his blood, which keeps him and his children out of decent employment, from certain public conveniences and amusements, from hiring houses in many sections, and in general, from being recognized as a man. Negroes regard this prejudice as the chief cause of their present unfortunate condition. On the other hand most white people are quite unconscious of any such powerful and vindictive feeling; they regard color prejudice as the easily explicable feeling that intimate social intercourse with a lower race is not only undesirable but impractical if our present standards of culture are to be maintained, and although they are aware that some people feel the aversion more intensely than others, they cannot see how such a feeling has much influence on the real situation or alters the social condition of the mass of Negroes.

As a matter of fact, color prejudice in this city is something between these two extreme views: it is not today responsible for all, or perhaps the greater part of the Negro problems, or of the disabilities under which the race labors; on the other hand it is a far more powerful social force than most Philadelphians realize. The practical results of the attitude of most of the inhabitants of Philadelphia towards persons of Negro descent are as follows:

1. As to getting work:
   No matter how well trained a Negro may be, or how fitted for work of any kind, he cannot in the ordinary course of competition hope to be much more than a menial servant.

   He cannot get clerical or supervisory work to do save in exceptional cases.

   He cannot teach save in a few of the remaining Negro schools.

   He cannot become a mechanic except for small transient jobs, and cannot join a trades union.

   A Negro woman has but three careers open to her in this city: domestic service, sewing, or married life.

2. As to keeping work:
   The Negro suffers in competition more severely than white men.

   Change in fashion is causing him to be replaced by whites in the better-paid positions of domestic service.

   Whim and accident will cause him to lose a hard-earned place more quickly than the same things would affect a white man.

   Being few in number compared with the whites the crime or carelessness of a few of his race is easily imputed to all, and the reputation of the good, industrious, and reliable suffer thereby.

   Because Negro workmen may not often work side by side with white workmen, the individual black workman is rated not only by his own efficiency, but by the efficiency of a whole group of black fellow workmen which may often be low.

   Because of these difficulties which virtually increase competition in his case, he is forced to take lower wages for the same work than white workmen.

3. As to entering new lines of work:
   Men are used to seeing Negroes in inferior positions; when, therefore, by any chance a Negro gets in a better position, most men immediately conclude that he is not fitted for it, even before he has a chance to show his fitness.

If, therefore, he set up a store, men will not patronize him.

If he is put into public position men will complain.

If he gain a position in the commercial world, men will quietly secure his dismissal or see that a white man succeeds him.

4. As to his expenditure:

The comparative smallness of the patronage of the Negro, and the dislike of other customers, makes it usual to increase the charges or difficulties in certain directions in which a Negro must spend money.

He must pay more house-rent for worse houses than most white people pay.

He is sometimes liable to insult or reluctant service in some restaurants, hotels and stores, at public resorts, theatres and places of recreation; and at nearly all barber shops.

5. As to his children:

The Negro finds it extremely difficult to rear children in such an atmosphere and not have them either cringing or impudent: if he impresses upon them patience with their lot, they may grow up satisfied with their condition; if he inspires them with ambition to rise, they may grow to despise their own people, hate the whites, and become embittered with the world.

His children are discriminated against, often in public schools.

They are advised when seeking employment to become waiters and maids.

They are liable to species of insult and temptation peculiarly trying to children.

6. As to social intercourse:

In all walks of life the Negro is liable to meet some objection to his presence or some discourteous treatment; and the ties of friendship or memory seldom are strong enough to hold across the color line.

If an invitation is issued to the public for any occasion, the Negro can never know whether he would be welcomed or not; if he goes he is liable to have his feelings hurt and get into unpleasant altercation; if he stays away, he is blamed for indifference.

If he meet a lifelong white friend on the street, he is in a dilemma; if he does not greet the friend he is put down as boorish and impolite; if he does greet the friend he is liable to be flatly snubbed.

If by chance he is introduced to a white woman or man, he expects to be ignored on the next meeting, and usually is.

White friends may call on him, but he is scarcely expected to call on them, save for strictly business matters.

If he gain the affections of a white woman and marry her he may invariably expect that slurs will be thrown on her reputation and on his, and that both his and her race will shun their company. When he dies he cannot be buried beside white corpses.

7. The result:

Any one of these things happening now and then would not be remarkable or call for especial comment; but when one group of people suffer all these little differences of treatment and discriminations and insults continually, the result is either discouragement, or bitterness, or oversensitiveness, or recklessness. And a people feeling thus cannot do their best.

Presumably the first impulse of the average Philadelphian would be emphatically to deny any such marked and blighting discrimination as the above against a group of citizens in this metropolis. Every one knows that in the past color prejudice in the city was deep and passionate; living men can remember when a Negro could not sit in a street car or walk many streets in peace. These times have passed, however, and many imagine discrimination against the Negro has passed with them. Careful inquiry will convince any such one of his error. To be sure a colored man to-day can walk the streets of Philadelphia without personal insult; he can go to theatres, parks and some places of amusement without meeting more than stares and discourtesy; he can be accommodated at most hotels and restaurants, although his treatment in some would not be pleasant. All this is a vast advance and augurs much for the future. And yet all that has been said of the remaining discrimination is but too true.

During the investigation of 1896 there was collected a number of actual cases, which may illustrate the discriminations spoken of. So far as possible these have been sifted and only those which seem undoubtedly true have been selected:

I. As to getting work

It is hardly necessary to dwell upon the situation of the Negro in regard to work in the higher walks of life: the white boy may start in the lawyer's office and work himself into a lucrative practice; he may serve a physician as office boy or enter a hospital in a minor position, and have his talent alone between him and affluence and fame; if he is bright in school, he may make his mark in a university, become a tutor with some time and much inspiration for study, and eventually fill a professor's chair. All these careers are at the very outset closed to the Negro on account of his color; what lawyer would give even a minor case to a Negro assistant? What university would appoint a promising young Negro as tutor? Thus the young white man starts in life knowing that within some limits and barring accidents, talent and application will tell. The young Negro starts knowing that on all sides his advance is made difficult if not wholly shut off by his color. Let us come, however, to ordinary occupations which concern more nearly the mass of Negroes. Philadelphia is a great industrial and business center with thousands of foremen, managers and clerks – the lieutenants of industry who direct its progress. They are paid for thinking and for skill to direct, and naturally such positions are coveted because they are well paid, well thought-of and carry some authority. To such positions Negro boys and girls may not aspire no matter what their qualifications. Even as teachers and ordinary clerks and stenographers they find almost no openings. Let us note some actual instances:

A young woman who graduated with credit from the Girls Normal School in 1892 has taught in the kindergarten, acted as substitute, and waited in vain for a permanent position. Once she was allowed to substitute in a school with white teachers; the principal commended her work, but when the permanent appointment was made a white woman got it.

A girl who graduated from a Pennsylvania high school and from a business college sought work in the city as a stenographer and typewriter. A prominent lawyer undertook to find her a position; he went to friends and said, "Here is a girl that does excellent work and is of good character; can you not give her work?" Several immediately answered yes. "But," said the lawyer, "I will be perfectly frank with you and tell you she is colored;" and not in the whole city could he find a man willing to

employ her. It happened, however, that the girl was so light in complexion that few not knowing would have suspected her descent. The lawyer therefore gave her temporary work in his own office until she found a position outside the city. "But," said he, "to this day I have not dared to tell my clerks that they worked beside a Negress." Another woman graduated from the high school and the Palmer College of Shorthand, but all over the city has met with nothing but refusal of work.

Several graduates in pharmacy have sought three years' required apprenticeship in the city and in only one case did one succeed, although they offered to work for nothing. One young pharmacist came from Massachusetts and for weeks sought in vain for work here at any price; "I wouldn't have a darky to clean out my store, much less to stand behind the counter," answered one druggist.

A colored man answered an advertisement for a clerk in the suburbs. "What do you suppose we'd want of a nigger?" was the plain answer. A graduate of the University of Pennsylvania in mechanical engineering, well recommended, obtained work in the city, through an advertisement, on account of his excellent record. He worked a few hours and then was discharged because he was found to be colored. He is now a waiter at the University Club, where his white fellow graduates dine. Another young man attended Spring Garden Institute and studied drawing for lithography. He had good references from the institute and elsewhere, but application at the five largest establishments in the city could secure him no work. A telegraph operator has hunted in vain for an opening, and two graduates of the Central High School have sunk to menial labor. "What's the use of an education?" asked one. Mr. A——— has elsewhere been employed as a traveling salesman. He applied for a position here by letter and was told he could have one. When they saw him they had no work for him.

Such cases could be multiplied indefinitely. But that is not necessary; one has but to note that, notwithstanding the acknowledged ability of many colored men, the Negro is conspicuously absent from all places of honor, trust, emolument, as well as from those of respectable grade in commerce and industry.

Even in the world of skilled labor the Negro is largely excluded. Many would explain the absence of Negroes from higher vocations by saying that while a few may now and then be found competent, the great mass are not fitted for that sort of work and are destined for some time to form a laboring class. In the matter of the trades, however, there can be raised no serious question of ability; for years the Negroes filled satisfactorily the trades of the city, and to-day in many parts of the South they are still prominent. And yet in Philadelphia a determined prejudice, aided by public opinion, has succeeded nearly in driving them from the field:

A———, who works at a bookbinding establishment on Front street, has learned to bind books and often does so for his friends. He is not allowed to work at the trade in the shop, however, but must remain a porter at a porter's wages.

B——— is a brushmaker; he has applied at several establishments, but they would not even examine his testimonials. They simply said: "We do not employ colored people."

C——— is a shoemaker; he tried to get work in some of the large department stores. They "had no place" for him.

D——— was a bricklayer, but experienced so much trouble in getting work that he is now a messenger.

E——— is a painter, but has found it impossible to get work because he is colored.

F——— is a telegraph line man, who formerly worked in Richmond, Va. When he applied here he was told that Negroes were not employed.

G——— is an iron puddler, who belonged to a Pittsburgh union. Here he was not recognized as a union man and could not get work except as a stevedore.

H——— was a cooper, but could get no work trials, and is now a common laborer.

I——— is a candy-maker, but has never been able to find employment in the city; he was always told the white help would not work with him.

J——— is a carpenter; he can only secure odd jobs or work where only Negroes are employed.

K——— was an upholsterer, but could get no work save in the few colored shops which had workmen; he is now a waiter on a dining car.

L——— was a first-class baker; he applied for work some time ago near Green street and was told shortly, "We don't work no niggers here."

[...]

HERBERT J. GANS

"Levittown and America"

from *The Levittowners* (1967)

Editors' introduction   Herbert J. Gans (born 1927) is the author of two of the most fascinating and influential books of urban sociology ever published. *The Urban Villagers* (New York: Free Press, 1962) is a brilliant study of the Italian-American immigrant community of Boston's West End neighborhood, and *The Levittowners* (New York: Pantheon, 1967) is Gans's analysis of post-World War II tract-home suburbia. Both are examples of the participant-observer methodology at its best. While never losing sight of objective scholarship, Gans lets the reader see and experience urban communities from the inside out.

The suburban developments of the 1940s, 1950s, and 1960s, in the U.S. and elsewhere, gave birth to a massive literature, much of it critical. Damned as automobile-dependent and socially/racially segregated, the post-World War II suburbs were called "sprawl" and stigmatized as "anti-cities" (to use Lewis Mumford's term) contributing to a stifling social conformity and cultural mediocrity. Titles such as John Keats's *The Crack in the Picture Window* (Boston: Houghton Mifflin, 1956), Richard E. Gordon, Catherine K. Gordon, and Mac Gunther's *The Split-Level Trap* (New York: Random House, 1961), Kenneth Jackson's *Crabgrass Frontier* (New York: Oxford University Press, 1985), and Mark Baldassare's *Trouble in Paradise: The Suburban Transformation of America* (New York: Columbia University Press, 1986) capture the tone of much of the commentary on the suburban way of life. And one prominent feminist critic – Dolores Hayden in *Redesigning the American Dream* (New York: Norton, 1984) – has charged that the first Levittown was built specifically for "the returning veteran, the beribboned male war hero who wanted his wife to stay home."

Given the overwhelming antisuburban bias of most of these analyses, Gans's view of Levittown is remarkable in that it steadfastly rejects the notion that there even exists an easily definable "suburban way of life," much less that suburbia represents a distinctly new kind of sociocultural place. On the contrary, Gans found the Levittowners to be much like hard-working middle-class people anywhere in the world engaged in the process of adapting their needs to new social and environmental situations. To be sure, Levittown had its problems. Gans analyzes them in some detail and makes clear that Levittown is no utopia. But neither is it a spiritual wasteland.

As a classic analysis of life in a contemporary suburban development, Gans's *The Levittowners* should be compared and contrasted to other views of suburbia (see above) and to the work of such antisuburban celebrators of inner-city neighborhoods as Jane Jacobs (p. 104). In addition, Gans was prophetic in 1967 about the probability that "yet another ring of suburban communities will spring up around American cities" in the (then) near future. Such prescience points directly to the new communities described by Joel Garreau in *Edge City* (New York: Anchor, 1992), to Robert Fishman's "technoburbs" (p. 485) and to Peter Calthorpe's plans for "Pedestrian Pockets" (p. 469). Other notable works on suburbia in general and Levittown in particular are W. D. Wetherell, *The Man Who Loved Levittown* (Pittsburgh: University of Pittsburgh Press, 1985), Barbara M. Kelly (ed.), *Suburbia Re-examined* (New York: Greenwood, 1989) and *Expanding the American Dream* (Albany: State University of New York Press, 1993).

For overviews of twentieth-century growth in England see Paul Lawless and Frank Brown, *Urban Growth and Change in Britain: An Introduction* (Harper & Row, 1986) and Ray Hudson and Allan Williams, *The United Kingdom* (Harper & Row, 1986).

HERBERT J. GANS, "Levittown and America"

from *The Levittowners* (1967)

CONFLICT, PLURALISM, AND COMMUNITY

Although a part of my study was concerned with the possibilities of change and innovation, I do not mean to suggest that Levittown is badly in need of either. The community may displease the professional city planner and the intellectual defender of cosmopolitan culture, but perhaps more than any other type of community, Levittown permits most of its residents to be what they want to be – to center their lives around the home and the family, to be among neighbors whom they can trust, to find friends to share leisure hours, and to participate in organizations that provide sociability and the opportunity to be of service to others.

That Levittown has its faults and problems is undeniable ... physical and social isolation, familial and governmental financial problems, insufficient public transportation, less than perfect provision of public services, inadequate decision-making and feedback processes, lack of representation for minorities and overrepresentation for the builder, and the entire array of familial and individual problems common to any population. Many of them can be traced back to three basic shortcomings, none distinctive to Levittown or the Levittowners.

One is the difficulty of coping with conflict. Like the rest of the country, Levittown is beset with conflict: class conflict between the lower middle class group and the smaller working and upper middle class groups; generational conflict between adults, children, adolescents, and the

elderly. The existence of conflict is no drawback, but the way conflict is handled leaves much to be desired. Levittowners, like other Americans, do not really accept the inevitability of conflict. Insisting that a consensus is possible, they only exacerbate the conflict, for each group demands that the other conform to its values and accept its priorities. When power is a valuable prize and resources are scarce, such a perspective is understandable, but in Levittown the exercise of power is not an end in itself for most people; they want it mainly to control the allocation of resources. Since resources are not so scarce, however, the classes and age groups could resolve their conflicts more constructively than they do, giving each group at least some of what it wants. If the inevitability of conflicting interests were accepted, differences might be less threatening, and this would make it easier to reach the needed compromises. I am not sanguine that this will happen, for if people think resources are scarce, they act as if they are scarce, and will not pay an extra $20 a year in taxes to implement minority demands. Even so, conditions to make viable compromises happen are more favorable in Levittown than in larger or poorer communities.

The second shortcoming, closely related to the first, is the inability to deal with pluralism. People have not recognized the diversity of American society, and they are not able to accept other life styles. Indeed, they cannot handle conflict because they cannot accept pluralism. Adults are unwilling to tolerate adolescent culture, and vice versa. Lower middle class people oppose the ways of the working class and upper middle class, and each of these groups is hostile to the other two. Perhaps the inability to cope with pluralism is greater in Levittown than elsewhere because it is a community of young families who are raising children. Children are essentially asocial and unacculturated beings, easily influenced by new ideas. As a result, their parents feel an intense need to defend familial values; to make sure that their children grow up according to parental norms and not by those of their playmates from another class. The need to shield the children from what are considered harmful influences begins on the block, but it is translated into the conflict over the school, the definitional struggles within the voluntary associations whose programs affect the socialization of children, and, ultimately, into political conflicts. Each group wants to put its cultural stamp on the organizations and institutions that are the community, for otherwise the family and its culture are not safe. In a society in which extended families are unimportant and the nuclear family cannot provide the full panoply of personnel and activities to hold children in the family culture, parents must use community institutions for this purpose, and every portion of the community therefore becomes a battleground for the defense of familial values.

This thesis must not be exaggerated, for much of the conflict is, as it has always been, between the haves and the have-nots. Even if Levittown's median income is considerably above the national average even for white families, no one feels affluent enough to let other people determine how their own income should be spent. Most of the political conflict in the community rages over how much of the family income should be given over to the community, and then, how it should be used. In fact consensus about municipal policies and expenditures exists only about the house. Because many Levittowners are first-time homeowners, they are especially eager to protect that home against loss of value, both as property and as status image. But every class has its own status image and its own status fears. Working class people do not want to be joined by lower class neighbors or to be forced to adopt middle class styles.

Lower middle class people do not want more working class neighbors or to be forced to adopt cosmopolitan styles, and upper middle class people want neither group to dominate them. These fears are not, as commonly thought, attributes of status-seeking, for few Levittowners are seeking higher status: they are fears about self-image. When people reject pluralism, they do so because accepting the viability of other ways of living suggests that their own is not as absolute as they need to believe. The outcome is the constant search for compatible people and the rejection of those who are different.

When the three class groups – not to mention their subgroupings and yet other groups with different values – must live together and share a common government, every group tries to make sure that the institutions and facilities which serve the entire community maintain its own status and culture, and no one is happy when another group wins. If working class groups can persuade the Township Committee to allocate funds for a firehouse, middle class groups unite in a temporary coalition to guarantee that a library is also established. When the upper middle class group attempts to influence school policy to shape education to its standard, lower middle class residents raise the specter of Levittown aping Brookline and Scarsdale, while working class people become fearful that the schools will neglect discipline or that taxes will rise further. Consequently, each group seeks power to prevent others from shaping the institutions that must be shared. They do not seek power as an end in itself, but only to guarantee that their priorities will be met by the community. Similarly, they do not demand lower taxes simply for economic reasons (except for those few really hard pressed) but in order to be sure that community institutions are responsible to their familial values and status needs. Obviously, power sought for these ends is hard to share, and decisions for levying and allocating public funds are difficult to compromise.

The third shortcoming of the community, then, is the failure to establish a meaningful relationship between home and community and to reconcile class-cultural diversity with government and the provision of public services.

Levittowners, like other Americans, not only see government as a parasite and public services as a useless expenditure of funds better spent privately, but they do not allow government to adapt these services to the diversity among the residents. Government is committed to the establishment of a single (and limited) set of public services, and its freedom to do otherwise is restricted by legislation and, of course, by American tradition.

Government has always been a minor supplier of services basic to everyday life, and an enemy whose encroachment on private life must be resisted. The primary source of this conception is the historic American prejudice against public services, which stems in part from the rural tradition of the individual and his family as a self-sufficient unit, but which is perpetuated by contemporary cultural values and made possible by the alliance which enables at least middle class families to live with only minimal dependence on local government. The bias against public services does not interfere with their use, however, but only with their financing and their extension and proliferation. Nor does it lead Levittowners to reject government outright, but only to channel it into a few limited functions. Among these, the primary one is the protection of the home against diversity.

Government thus becomes a defense agency, to be taken over by one group to defend itself against others in and out of the community. The idea that it could have positive functions, such as the provision of facilities to make life richer and more comfortable, is resisted, for every new governmental function is seen first as an attempt by one community group to increase its dominance over others. Of course, these attempts are rarely manifest, for the political dialogue deals mainly with substantive matters, but when Levittowners spoke against a proposal, they were reacting principally against those who proposed it rather than against its substance.

Until government can tailor its actions to the community's diversity, and until people can accept the inevitability of conflict and pluralism in order to give government that responsibility, they will prefer to spend their money for privately and commercially supplied services. Unlike city hall, the marketplace is sensitive to diversities among the customers and does not require them to engage in political conflict to get what they want. Of course not all people can choose the marketplace over city hall, but Levittowners are affluent enough to do so. Moreover, until parents have steered their children safely into their own class and culture – or have given up trying – they are likely to seek out relatively homogeneous communities and small ones, so that they have some control over government's inroads against personal and familial autonomy. This not only maintains the sovereignty of hundreds of small local governments but also contributes to the desire to own a house and a free-standing one.

LEVITTOWN AS AMERICA

The strengths and weaknesses of Levittown are those of many American communities, and the Levittowners closely resemble other young middle class Americans. They are not America, for they are not a numerical majority of the population, but they represent the major constituency of the latest and most powerful economic and political institutions in American society – the favored customers and voters whom these seek to attract and satisfy. Upper middle class Americans may spend more per capita and join more groups, but they are fewer in number than the lower middle classes. Working and lower class people are more numerous but they have less money and power; and people over 40, who still outnumber young adults, are already committed to most of the goods, affiliations, and ideas they will need in their lifetime.

Even so, Levittowners are not really members of the national society, or for that matter, of a mass society. They are not apathetic conformists ripe for takeover by a totalitarian elite or corporate merchandiser; they are not conspicuous consumers and slaves to sudden whims of cultural and political fashion; they are not even organization men or particularly other-directed personalities. Clearly, inner-directed strivers are a minority in Levittown, and tradition-directed people would not think of moving to a new community of strangers, but most people maintain a balance between inner personal goals and the social adjustment necessary to live with neighbors and friends that, I suspect, is prevalent all over lower middle class America ... Although ethnic, religious, and regional differences are eroding, the never-ending conflicts over other differences are good evidence that Levittowners are far from becoming mass men.

Although they are citizens of a national polity and their lives are shaped by national economic, social, and political forces, Levittowners deceive themselves into thinking that the community, or rather the home, is the single most influential unit in their lives. Of course, in one way they are right; it is the place where they can be most influential, for if they cannot persuade the decision-makers, they can influence family members. Home is also the site of maximal freedom, for within its walls people can do what they want more easily than anywhere else. But because they are free and influential only at home, their dependence on the national society ought to be obvious to them. This not being the case, the real problem is that Levittowners have not yet become aware of how much they are a part of the national society and economy.

In viewing their homes as the center of life, Levittowners are still using a societal model that fit the rural America of self-sufficient farmers and the feudal Europe of self-isolating extended families. Yet the critics who argue about the individual versus mass society are also anachronistic: they are still thinking of the individual artist or intellectual who must shield himself from a society which either rejects him or coopts him to produce popular culture. Both Levittowners and critics have to learn that they live in a national society characterized by pluralism and bureaucracy, and that the basic conflict is not between individual (or family) and society, but between the classes (and other interest groups) who live together in a bureaucratized political and cultural democracy. The prime challenge is how to live with bureaucracy; how to use it rather than be used by it; how to obtain individual freedom and social resources from it through political action.

Yet even though Levittowners and other lower middle class Americans continue to be home-centered, they are much more "in the world" than their parents and grandparents were. Those coming out of ethnic working class backgrounds have rejected the "amoral familism" which pits every family against every other in the struggle to survive and the ethnocentrism which made other cultures and even other neighborhoods bitter enemies. This generation trusts its neighbors, participates with them in social and civic activities and no longer sees government as inevitably corrupt. Even working class Levittowners have begun to give up the suspicion that isolated their ancestors from all but family and childhood friends. Similarly, the descendants of rural Protestant America have given up the xenophobia that turned previous generations against the Catholic and Jewish immigrants, they have almost forgotten the intolerant Puritanism which triggered attacks against pleasure and enjoyment, and they no longer fully accept the doctrine of laissez faire that justifies the defense of all individual rights and privileges against others' needs.

These and other changes have come about not because people are now better or more tolerant human beings, but because they are affluent. For the Levittowners, life is not a fight for survival any more; they have been able to move into a community in which income and status are equitably enough distributed so that neighbors are no longer treated as enemies, even if they are still criticized for social and cultural deviance. By any yardstick one chooses, Levittowners treat their fellow residents more ethically and more democratically than did their parents and grandparents. They also live a "fuller" and "richer" life. Their culture may be less subtle and sophisticated than that of the intellectual, their family life less healthy than that advocated by psychiatrists, and their politics less thoughtful and democratic than the political philosophers' – yet all of these are superior to what prevailed among the working and lower middle classes of past generations.

But beyond these changes, it is striking how little American culture among the Levittowners differs from what de Tocqueville reported in his travels through small-town middle class America a century ago. Of course, he was here before the economy needed an industrial proletariat, but the equality of men and women, the power of the child over his parents, the importance of the voluntary association, the social functions of the church, and the rejection of high culture seem to be holdovers from his time, and so is the adherence to the traditional virtues: individual honesty, thrift, religiously inspired morality, Franklinesque individualism and Victorian prudery. Some Levittowners have retained the values of rural ancestors; some have only begun to practice them as affluence enabled them to give up the values of a survival-centered culture. Still other eternal verities remain: class conflict is as alive as ever, even if the struggle is milder and the have-nots in Levittown have much more than the truly poor. Working class culture continues to flourish, even though its rough edges are wearing smooth and its extended family and public institutions are not brought to the suburbs. Affluence and better education have made a difference, but they have not made the factory worker middle class, any more than college attendance has made lower middle class people cosmopolitan.

What seems to have happened is that improvements and innovations are added to old culture patterns, giving affluent Americans a foot in several worlds. They have more knowledge and a broader outlook than their ancestors, and they enjoy the advantages of technology, but these are superimposed on old ways. While conservative critics rail about technology's dehumanization of modern man, the Levittowners who spend their days programming computers come home at night to practice the very homely and old-fashioned virtues these critics defend. For example, they have television sets, but they watch much the same popular comedies and melodramas their ancestors saw on the nineteenth century stage. The melodramas are less crude and vaudeville is more respectable; the girls dance with covered bosoms, but Ed Sullivan's program is pure vaudeville and *The Jackie Gleason Show* even retains traces of the working class music hall. The overlay of old and new is not all good, of course: the new technology has created methods of war and destruction which the old insularity allows Americans to unleash without much shame or guilt, and some Levittowners may find work less satisfying than their ancestors. But only some, for the majority's parents slaved in exhausting jobs which made them too tired to enjoy the advantages of suburbia even if they could have afforded them. On the whole, however, the Levittowners have only benefitted from the changes in society and economy that have occurred in this century, and if they were not given to outmoded models of social reality, they might feel freer about extending these benefits to less fortunate sectors of American society. But whether people's models are anachronistic or avant-garde, they are rarely willing to surrender their own powers and privileges to others.

SASKIA SASSEN

"A New Geography of Centers and Margins: Summary and Implications"

from *Cities in a World Economy* (1994)

Editors' introduction   A massive restructuring of the world economy during the past twenty years is one of the most potent forces in the continuing evolution of cities today. Banking, finance, corporate planning, and management are increasingly concentrated in powerful global cities. Manufacturing is dispersing around the globe. And the global distribution of wealth and power is in flux. This has enormous implications for the structure of the global system of cities, the functions cities perform, and the nature of social life within them. We explore these issues in greater depth in Part 4, Urban Politics, Governance, and Economics, and Part 6, The Future of the City, but a description of the cities in a global economy today is an appropriate way to end this part of the book, The Evolution of Cities.

Sociologist Saskia Sassen, a professor of urban and regional planning at Columbia University, provides insight into the way in which the rapid and profound changes in the world economy have affected the evolution of cities today. Sassen has carefully examined data on the economies and workforce characteristics of the largest global cities and the way in which they connect to other cities in the world economy. In the following selection Sassen describes the nature of the new global system of cities.

Sassen argues that global cities – where banks, corporate headquarters, and other command functions and high-level producer-service firms such as law firms and advertising agencies oriented to world markets are concentrated – have emerged as strategic sites in the world economy. Decisions made in London, New York, Tokyo, or Sydney affect jobs, wages, and the economic health of locations as remote as Kuala Lumpur, Malaysia, or Santiago, Chile.

Some writers argue that instant global telecommunications and an interconnected world economy may make place unimportant and portend the end of cities. But according to Sassen that is not what has happened so far. Her research indicates that global cities such as New York, London, and Tokyo have become more, not less, dense recently. And their wealth and power is growing, not declining. On the other hand, many cities which have historically served as manufacturing centers in Europe, North America, and Australia are in economic decline as manufacturing shifts to Asia, South and Central America and elsewhere in the Third World.

One of Sassen's most important theoretical contributions to the study of cities is her sharp questioning of the whole notion of "rich" countries and "rich" cities; places central to the world economy and those which exist at the margin. Sassen argues that cities at the center of the world economy are increasingly both rich and poor and that many Third-World cities – while subordinate to global command centers – are also stratified by income.

Sassen's work is central to debates about the effects of global economic restructuring on cities. As already indicated, some writers on information technology stress the decentralizing effects communications technology has had and will likely have in the future. They disagree with Sassen's assessment that command functions will be increasingly centralized. Marxist and neo-Marxist writers such as David Harvey, Doreen Massey, Richard Walker, and Michael Storper see the changes in the global system of cities as the inevitable result of current capitalist development, though they do not agree among themselves on how capitalist processes are unfolding. Their views are explored further in Mike Savage and Alan Warde's discussion of uneven development (p. 312).

This selection is from Saskia Sassen, *Cities in a Global Economy* (Thousand Oaks, Calif.: Pine Forge Press, 1994). Other books by Saskia Sassen include *The Mobility of Labor and Capital: A Study in International Investment and Labor Flows* (New York: Cambridge University Press, 1988) and *The Global City* (Princeton, N.J.: Princeton University Press, 1991).

Neil Peirce's *Citistates* (Washington, D.C.: Seven Locks Press, 1993) describes how a number of U.S. regions are managing their transformations in relation to the world economy.

For a study of the dual city phenomenon see Manuel Castells and John Mollenkopf, *Dual City: Restructuring New York* (New York: Russell Sage Foundation, 1991). On the informal economy see Alejandro Portes, Manuel Castells, and L. Benton (eds.), *The Informal Economy: Studies in Advanced and Less Developed Countries* (Baltimore: Johns Hopkins University Press, 1989).

There is a large literature on the spatial dimensions of global economic restructuring in the late twentieth century. Some important studies include Georges Benko and Mick Dunford (eds.), *Industrial Change and Regional Development: The Transformation of New Industrial Spaces* (London: Pinter; New York: Belhaven Press, 1991), Richard V. Cardew, John V. Langdale, and David C. Rich (eds.), *Why Cities Change: Urban Development and Economic Change in Sydney* (Sydney: Allen & Unwin, 1982), Paul C. Cheshire and Dennis G. Hay, *Urban Problems in Western Europe* (London: Unwin Hyman, 1989), Daniel Drache and Meric S. Gertler (eds.), *The New Era of Global Competition: State Policy and Market Power* (Montreal: McGill-Queen's University Press, 1991), and Nick Oliver and Barry Wilkinson, *The Japanization of British Industry* (Oxford: Basil Blackwell, 1988).

SASKIA SASSEN, "A New Geography of Centers and Margins: Summary and Implications"

from *Cities in a World Economy* (1994)

Three important developments over the last 20 years laid the foundation for [the following analysis] of cities in the world economy.

1   *The territorial dispersal of economic activities, of which globalization is one form, contributes to the growth of centralized functions and operations.* We find here a new logic for agglomeration and key conditions for the renewed centrality of cities in advanced economies. Information technologies, often thought of as neutralizing geography, actually contribute to spatial concentration. They make possi-

ble the geographic dispersal and simultaneous integration of many activities. But the particular conditions under which such facilities are available have promoted centralization of the most advanced users in the most advanced telecommunications centers. We see parallel developments in cities that function as regional nodes – that is, at smaller geographic scales and lower levels of complexity than global cities.

2   *Centralized control and management over a geographically dispersed array of economic operations does not come about inevitably as*

part of a "world system." It requires the production of a vast range of highly specialized services, telecommunications infrastructure, and industrial services. Major cities are centers for the servicing and financing of international trade, investment, and headquarters operations. And in this sense they are strategic production sites for today's leading economic sectors. This function is reflected in the ascendance of these activities in their economies. Again, cities that serve as regional centers exhibit similar developments. This is the way in which the spatial effects of the growing service intensity in the organization of all industries materialize in cities.

3 *Economic globalization has contributed to a new geography of centrality and marginality.* This new geography assumes many forms and operates in many terrains, from the distribution of telecommunications facilities to the structure of the economy and of employment. Global cities become the sites of immense concentrations of economic power, while cities that were once major manufacturing centers suffer inordinate declines; highly educated workers see their incomes rise to unusually high levels, while low- or medium-skilled workers see theirs sink. Financial services produce superprofits while industrial services barely survive.

Let us look more closely now at this last and most encompassing of the propositions.

THE LOCUS OF THE PERIPHERAL

The sharpening distance between the extremes evident in all major cities of developed countries raises questions about the notion of "rich" countries and "rich" cities. It suggests that the geography of centrality and marginality, which in the past was seen in terms of the duality of highly developed and less developed countries, is now also evident within developed countries and especially within their major cities.

One line of theorization posits that the intensified inequalities . . . represent a transformation in the geography of center and periphery. They signal that peripheralization processes are occurring inside areas that were once conceived of as "core" areas – whether at the global, regional, or urban level – and that alongside the sharpening of peripheralization processes, centrality has also become sharper at all three levels.

The condition of being peripheral is installed in different geographic terrains depending on the prevailing economic dynamic. We see new forms of peripheralization at the center of major cities in developed countries not far from some of the most expensive commercial land in the world: "inner cities" are evident not only in the United States and large European cities, but also now in Tokyo. Furthermore, we can see peripheralization operating at the center in organizational terms as well. We have long known about segmented labor markets, but the manufacturing decline and the kind of devaluing of nonprofessional workers in leading industries that we see today in these cities go beyond segmentation and in fact represent an instance of peripheralization.

Furthermore, the new forms of growth evident at the urban perimeter also mean crisis: violence in the immigrant ghetto of the *banlieus* (the French term for *suburbs*), exurbanites clamoring for control over growth to protect their environment, new forms of urban governance. The regional mode of regulation in many of these cities is based on the old center/suburb model and may hence become increasingly inadequate to deal with intraperipheral conflicts – conflicts among different types of constituencies at the urban perimeter or urban region. Frankfurt, for example, is a city that cannot function without its region's towns; yet this particular urban region would not have emerged without the specific forms of growth in Frankfurt's center. Keil and Ronneberger (1993) note the ideological motivation in the call by politicians to officially recognize the region so as to strengthen Frankfurt's position in the global interurban competition. This call also provides a rationale for coherence and the idea of common interests among the many objectively disparate interests in the region: it displaces the conflicts among unequally advantaged sectors onto a project of regional competition with other regions. Regionalism then emerges as the concept for bridging the global orientation of leading sectors with the various local agendas of various constituencies in the region.

In contrast, the city discourse rather than the ideology of regionalism dominates in cities such as New York or São Paulo. The challenge is how to bridge the inner city, or the squatters at the urban perimeter, with the center. In multiracial cities, multiculturalism has emerged as one form of this bridging. A "regional" discourse is perhaps beginning to emerge, but it has until now been totally submerged under the suburbanization banner, a concept that suggests both escape from and dependence on the city. The notion of conflict within the urban periphery among diverse interests and constituencies has not really been much of a factor in the United States. The delicate point at the level of the region has rather been the articulation between the residential suburbs and the city.

CONTESTED SPACE

Large cities have emerged as strategic territories for these developments. *First, cities are the sites for concrete operations of the economy.* For our purposes we can distinguish two forms of such concrete operations: (1) in terms of economic globalization and place, cities are strategic places that concentrate command functions, global markets, and ... production sites for the advanced corporate service industries. (2) In terms of day-to-day work in the leading industrial complex, finance, and specialized services ... a large share of the jobs involved are low paid and manual, and many are held by women and immigrants. Although these types of workers and jobs are never represented as part of the global economy, they are in fact as much a part of globalization as international finance is. We see at work here a dynamic of valorization that has sharply increased the distance between the devalorized and the valorized – indeed overvalorized – sectors of the economy. These joint presences have made cities a contested terrain.

The structure of economic activity has brought about changes in the organization of work that are reflected in a pronounced shift in the job supply, with strong polarization occurring in the income distribution and occupational distribution of workers. Major growth industries show a greater incidence of jobs at the high- and low-paying ends of the scale than do the older industries now in decline. Almost half the jobs in the producer services are lower-income jobs, and the other half are in the two highest earnings classes. On the other hand, a large share of manufacturing workers were in middle-earning jobs during the postwar period of high growth in these industries in the United States and the United Kingdom.

One particular concern here was to understand how new forms of inequality actually are constituted into new social forms, such as gentrified neighborhoods, informal economies, or downgraded manufacturing sectors. To what extent these developments are connected to the consolidation of an economic complex oriented to the global market is difficult to say. Precise empirical documentation of the linkages or impacts is impossible; the effort here is focused, then, on a more general attempt to understand the consequences of both the ascendance of such an international economic complex and the general move to a service economy.

Second, the city concentrates diversity. Its spaces are inscribed with the dominant corporate culture but also with a multiplicity of other cultures and identities, notably through immigration. The slippage is evident: the dominant culture can encompass only part of the city. And while corporate power inscribes noncorporate cultures and identities with "otherness," thereby devaluing them, they are present everywhere. The immigrant communities and informal economy ... are only two instances. Diverse cultures and ethnicities are especially strong in major cities in the United States and western Europe; these also have the largest concentrations of corporate power.

We see here an interesting correspondence between great concentrations of corporate power and large concentrations of "others." It invites us to see that globalization is not only constituted in terms of capital and the new international corporate culture (international finance, telecommunications, information flows) but also in terms of people and non-corporate cultures. There is a whole infrastructure of low-wage, non-professional jobs and activities that constitutes a crucial part of the so-called corporate economy.

A focus on the work behind command functions, on production in the finance and services complex, and on marketplaces has the effect of incorporating the material facilities underlying globalization and the whole infrastructure of jobs and workers typically not seen as belonging to the corporate sector of the economy: secretaries and cleaners, the truckers who deliver the software, the variety of technicians and repair workers, and all the jobs having to do with the maintenance, painting, and renovation of the buildings where it is all housed.

This expanded focus can lead to the recognition that a multiplicity of economies is involved in constituting the so-called global information economy. It recognizes the types of activities, workers, and firms that have the "center" of the economy or that have been evicted from that center in the restructuring of the 1980s and have therefore been devalued in a system that puts too much weight on a narrow conception of the center of the economy. Globalization can, then, be seen as a process that involves multiple economies and work cultures.

... [C]ities are of great importance to the dominant economic sectors. Large cities in the highly developed world are the places where globalization processes assume concrete localized forms. These localized forms are, in good part, what globalization is about. We can then think of cities also as the place where the contradictions of the internationalization of capital either come to rest or conflict. If we consider, further, that large cities also concentrate a growing share of disadvantaged populations – immigrants in both Europe and the United States; African Americans and Latinos in the United States – then we can see that cities have become a strategic terrain for a whole series of conflicts and contradictions.

On one hand, they concentrate a disproportionate share of corporate power and are one of the key sites for the overvalorization of the corporate economy; on the other, they concentrate a disproportionate share of the disadvantaged and are one of the key sites for their devalorization. This joint presence happens in a context where (1) the internationalization of the economy has grown sharply and cities have become increasingly strategic for global capital; and (2) marginalized people have come into representation and are making claims on the city as well. This joint presence is further brought into focus by the sharpening of the distance between the two. The center now concentrates immense power, a power that rests on the capability for global control and the capability to produce superprofits. And marginality, notwithstanding weak economic and political power, has become an increasingly strong presence through the new politics of culture and identity.

If cities were irrelevant to the globalization of economic activity, the center could simply abandon them and not be bothered by all of this. Indeed, this is precisely what some politicians argue – that cities have become hopeless reservoirs for all kinds of social despair. It is interesting to note again how the dominant economic narrative argues that place no longer matters, that firms can be located anywhere thanks to telematics, that major industries now are information-based and hence not place-bound. This line of argument devalues cities at a time when they are major sites for the new cultural politics. It also allows the corporate economy to extract major concessions from city governments under the notion that firms can simply leave and relocate elsewhere, which is not quite the case for a whole complex of firms ...

In seeking to show that (1) cities are strategic to economic globalization because they are command points, global marketplaces, and production sites for the information economy; and (2) many of the devalued sectors of the urban economy actually fulfill crucial functions for the center, this book attempts to recover the importance of cities specifically in a globalized economic system and the importance of those overlooked sectors that rest largely on the labor of women, immigrants, and, in the case of large U.S. cities, African Americans and Latinos. In fact it is the intermediary sectors of the economy (such as routine office work, head-quarters that are not geared to the world markets, the variety of services demanded by the largely suburbanized middle class) and of the urban population (the middle class) that can and have left cities. The two sectors that have stayed, the center and the "other," find in the city the strategic terrain for their operations.

REFERENCE

Keil, Roger and Ronneberger, Klaus (1993) "City Turned Inside Out: Spatial Strategies and Local Politics" in H. Hitz, R. Keil, V. Lehrer, K. Ronneberger, C. Schmid, and R. Wolff (eds.), *Financial Metropoles in Restructuring: Zurich and Frankfurt en Route to Post-Fordism*. Zurich: Rotpunkt Publishers.

PART 2

*P*erspectives on Urban Form and Design

PART TWO

INTRODUCTION

The physical form and design of cities described in Part 1, The Evolution of Cities, ranged from Ur's ziggurat to the marble agora of the Greek polis and from the polluted slums of nineteenth-century Manchester to the highrises of today's global city. The size, density, spatial distribution of functions, and physical characteristics of the cities described display an astonishing variety.

This section is concerned with *urban form* – writings on the physical and social structure of cities – and with *urban design* – the way in which humans shape and structure the built environment. Part 5, Urban Planning: Visions, Theory, and Practice, picks up this material, but extends the discussion beyond the confines of planning the physical form of cities.

Scholars from many disciplines have contributed to our understanding of urban form and design.

Architects and other design professionals are particularly important in this area. Architects have contributed to the building-specific study of cities and generated theory about how to design the built environment. Urban designers are usually trained as architects with further training in urban design or planning. They usually focus on the design of sites larger than individual buildings – such as entire neighborhoods, park systems, or highway corridors. Landscape architects study and provide professional advice on the relationship of the natural environment to the built environment.

Architecture and the other design professions are related to the professional field of city planning to which we return in Part 5 below. City planners develop plans for land use, traffic circulation systems, open space, and other aspects of cities. In the early part of the twentieth century many city planners were trained as architects, but design is only a part of a planner's education today.

Sociologists and geographers have studied both the internal structure of cities – the way in which population groups and functions tend to be arrayed in city space – and systems of cities – the function of different-sized cities in a region and the way they relate to other cities in a hierarchy or system.

Archaeologists who have excavated early cities and historians who have studied the artifacts and records describing them have enriched our understanding of the physical characteristics of early cities. Scholars from these disciplines have also contributed to theory about the relationship between urban form and the culture of early cities.

Many cities have grown organically – with little or no explicit overall plan or centrally controlled regulation. Other cities display a mix of organic growth and development planned at different periods in their history. The old crooked streets and irregular lots that constitute most of Boston, Massachusetts, contrast with the regularity of Back Bay where a swampy area was filled in and developed according to a plan during the nineteenth century. Disorderly districts of London which have evolved since the Middle Ages contrast with the area rebuilt after the great fire of 1666.

Only a few entire cities, such as Australia's capital city Canberra, have been built according to a consistent master plan.

Despite the fact that so much of most cities has grown with little or no formal planning or professional design until recently, little scholarly attention was devoted to studying popular design. Harvard landscape architecture professor J. B. Jackson pioneered the study of *vernacular* landscapes – the environments built by common people without trained architects, planners, or other professionals. Jackson is fascinated with the physical form of barns, fences, billboards, and grain silos; pioneer settlements with stumps in the field and muddy roads; dying former railroad towns where the train no longer stops; and humble mobile homes in rural New Mexico. Jackson was one of the first to argue that vernacular architecture provides important understanding of the culture and values of the people who have built the built environment. A careful study of barns reveals a great deal about the world view of the builders and their relationship to the world. Today, largely as a result of Jackson's influence, there is a large literature describing and analyzing the function and cultural meaning of Las Vegas casinos, White Tower hamburger stands, suburban tract homes, billboards, and other vernacular architecture.

Mike Davis, the author of *City of Quartz*, includes material in the tradition of the vernacular architecture writers, but with powerful social commentary. The objects in the built environment Davis describes include surveillance cameras, barrel-shaped park benches designed to keep people from sleeping on them, overhead sprinklers to douse the homeless, windowless concrete walls facing streets, and gated communities. All these artifacts provide a disturbing glimpse of Los Angeles culture.

Like J. B. Jackson, sociologist Ernest Burgess believes that there are discernible patterns in cities which have evolved organically. His 1925 essay "Growth of the City" represents another strand in the study of urban form: the search for regular patterns within cities. Burgess was a "social ecologist" writing from a theoretical perspective based on the belief that there were patterns in cities similar to those in the natural world. Just as a forest might have an area of moss near a stream bed giving way to vines and then to juniper bushes, social ecologists argue that there will be areas of the city devoted to vice, to absorption of new immigrants, to stable working-class communities, and to the leisure pursuits of the rich. As one type of plant or animal community invades the space of another and eventually replaces it, social ecologists saw the evolution of cities in terms of invasion and succession; constant change among groups and uses.

Sociologists inspired by Burgess, land economists, and many geographers have studied city form. Burgess's "concentric zone" theory in this section is just one of a number of theories which seek to describe theoretically the internal structure of cities. It is often juxtaposed with a theory developed by real estate economist Homer Hoyt in the 1930s postulating an organization of cities in *sectors* radiating out along transportation corridors and with an essay by geographers Chauncy Harris and Edward Ullman in the 1940s concluding that most cities have *multiple nuclei* rather than either concentric zone or sectoral organization. Burgess was writing about the way in which a single city is organized. A related topic in the study of urban form concerns *systems of cities*. *Central place theory* focuses on how cities within an entire region relate to each other. As computerized statistical analysis and geographical information systems for analyzing and mapping data rapidly increase our ability to understand urban form the debates about the internal structure of cities and systems of cities continue.

Scholars like Jackson who study vernacular landscape and Burgess, other social ecologists, and central place theorists who search for underlying patterns in the organization of urban space are in the urban studies tradition. They seek to understand how cities change because of the inherent interest of the topic. Architects, urban designers, and city planners also study the form and design of cities – in order to learn how to design better cities. The selections in this section by architect Christopher Alexander, urban designer Kevin Lynch, sociologist William Whyte, and city planners Allan Jacobs and Donald Appleyard are examples of writings on urban design.

Architects, planners, and urban designers have many different approaches and disagree among themselves concerning what makes for good design or even how to engage in the process of design. Nonetheless there are some commonalities in the writings that follow.

Many urban designers begin with intensive observation. William Whyte and his students spent hundreds of hours watching people use parks, filming them, analyzing the films, and quantifying behavior in order to reach principles for good park design. Kevin Lynch and his students surveyed people to see how they perceived their cities and asked them to draw maps in order to learn what parts were and were not clear to them. Other of the writers on city design in this section spend much of their time surveying, sketching, counting, mapping, photographing, measuring, or simply walking and looking.

Urban designers may disagree on what makes for a good design, but they share a belief in the value of design itself – consciously thinking about physical relationships in the creation of urban space. Design is usually expressed through drawings – generated by hand or computer.

Urban designers often criticize how badly the built environment fits human needs. Ugly, impersonal, dirty, dangerous, dysfunctional, race- and gender-segregated areas dominate many large cities today. Designers may have different priorities with respect to the value of improving traffic flow versus making pedestrian-friendly streets, economically revitalizing an area or retaining historic buildings, protecting the natural environment or keeping the city up with the global economy, but urban design is never value free.

Architecture may not *determine* human behavior, but implicit in the following selections is the notion that bad design can numb the human spirit and good design can have powerful, positive influences on human beings. Of the many values designers seek to build into their designs perhaps none is more important than fostering community and human interaction. To architectural critic Jane Jacobs, traffic engineering should be only one consideration in designing a street. A street designed so that people can see their children from house windows and will want to congregate on the front door stoops will be much more user-friendly and much safer than one which moves traffic efficiently, but is inhospitable to neighborhood life and insensitive to the potential for street life to reduce urban crime. Jacobs stresses the importance of designing streets to promote safety, particularly for women. And a safer environment will make community possible. Another example of connecting urban design and theory about community is in Dolores Hayden's writings. From her critique of gender, family, and work roles, Hayden generates a design-related theory of what a nonsexist city could be like which proposes a whole new form of community. In Hayden's utopia there would be much greater gender equality and much more community interaction. This would find its physical expression in retrofitting existing suburbia by knocking down fences to create common public and play space and pooling use of tools and appliances or in building new communities with much more common space.

Urban design cannot proceed without concern for the natural environment. In most cities everywhere in the world city building has meant loss of open space and agricultural land, filling of wetlands and destruction of aquifers, the destruction of native plants and wildlife, air and water pollution. Beginning in the late 1960s environmental concerns have become much more prevalent throughout the world. An important consideration in city design is how to fit the built environment harmoniously with the natural environment.

Landscape architects play a significant role in designing the fit between the natural and the built environment. So do environmental professionals trained to undertake analyses on the interface between the natural sciences and design. Ian McHarg is exemplary of theorists and professionals who seek to understand how to design "with" rather than against nature; to build *sustainable* cities that are not using up the natural resources which make them liveable. His *Design with Nature* was both an appeal to include the value of the natural environment and an early discussion of how to understand environmental impacts and design to avoid or minimize them. Professionals today devote a great deal of time to environmental impact analysis – studying the impact a proposed development will have on the natural environment and developing less environmentally damaging alternatives to reduce the negative environmental impacts which may occur. While we have taken some important steps towards designing with nature, we still have a long way to go.

JOHN BRINCKERHOFF JACKSON

"The Almost Perfect Town"

Landscape (1952)

Editors' introduction   John Brinckerhoff Jackson (born 1909) can best be described as a historian of landscapes as physical, cultural, and conceptual artifacts. To Jackson, the landscape is neither wilderness nor rural nature "out there," but the totality of natural and built environments that simultaneously surround and infuse all forms of human activity.

Jackson taught for many years in schools of landscape architecture at Harvard and the University of California, Berkeley. He was the founder of the influential journal *Landscape* and its editor from 1951 to 1968. As such, he may be regarded as an heir to the nineteenth-century French and English landscape gardening traditions and to the pioneering work of Frederick Law Olmsted (p. 338) and the American parks movement. What sets him clearly apart from those traditional roots, however, is that, for Jackson, the urban landscape is not just a city's parks, public gardens, official buildings, and tree-lined boulevards, but its highways, its shopping malls, its run-down warehouse districts, its standard-built two-bedroom houses, and its slums as well. Jackson sees these many elements of the built landscape not just as physical objects, but as social constructs full of meaning and moral implication. It is hardly surprising, then, that J. B. Jackson's approximate version of urban utopia is the commonplace, vernacular, Main Street environment of a typical American small town.

In "The Almost Perfect Town" Jackson describes a semimythical Optimo City that is located in the American Southwest but could just as easily be found almost anywhere in North America, Europe, Australia, and even parts of Asia and Africa beyond the margins of the great metropolitan regions. It is important that Optimo is a small place. Jackson observes that the "world of Optimo City is still complete" precisely because "the ties between country and town have not yet been broken." It is also important that Optimo has a history, however slender, that can be read in its architecture, in the layout of its streets, and in its traditional rivalry with Apache Center twenty miles away.

Jackson uses his loving, elegiac description of Optimo City as a way of criticizing certain recent developments in city planning that threaten to destroy local communities in the name of economic progress. He compares Optimo's unexceptional Courthouse Square to the Spanish plazas and the great public squares of the baroque era in that they all serve as socially unifying communal centers. And he notes with dismay that some of Optimo's business leaders want to tear the courthouse down to build a parking lot and to replace it with the typical "bureaucrat modernism" of so many contemporary civic centers. Jackson would like to preserve positive features of small towns that Peter Calthorpe (p. 469) and other architects associated with "the new urbanism" seek to recapture in "Pedestrian Pockets" and related neotraditional designs.

In one sense, Jackson's Optimo City is an imaginative utopia with strong ties to both Ebenezer Howard's Garden City and Frank Lloyd Wright's Broadacre. But Optimo, however mythical and idealized, is also a present, observable reality, and in that sense, ironically, Jackson's "almost perfect town" most nearly resembles the almost perfect community that Jane Jacobs describes in her evocations of Greenwich Village (p. 104).

Among the best of J. B. Jackson's book-length studies and collections of essays are *Landscapes* (Amherst: University of Massachusetts Press, 1970), *American Space* (New York: Norton, 1972), *Discovering the Vernacular Landscape* (New Haven, Conn.: Yale University Press, 1984), *The Necessity for Ruins, and Other Topics* (Amherst: University of Massachusetts Press, 1980), and *A Sense of Place, A Sense of Time* (New Haven, Conn.: Yale University Press, 1994). Also, consult the journal *Landscape* for additional writings by J. B. Jackson himself and for a continuing outpouring of articles exploring the meaning of landscape by academics and the architects, urban planners, and landscape designers Jackson inspired.

For an excellent account of the evolution of urban form, including vernacular as well as more professional architecture, in Europe from the earliest times through the Industrial Revolution see A. E. J. Morris, *History of Urban Form before the Industrial Revolution* (New York: John Wiley & Sons, 1994). Morris also includes chapters on the evolution of urban form in Islamic cities of the Middle East and the United States, and brief appendices on the evolution of urban form in China, Japan, India, and Indonesia.

JOHN BRINCKERHOFF JACKSON, "The Almost Perfect Town"

Landscape (1952)

Optimo City (pop. 10,783, alt. 2,100 ft.), situated on a small rise overlooking the N. branch of the Apache River, is a farm and ranch center served by a spur of the S.P. County seat of Sheridan Co. Optimo City (originally established in 1843 as Ft. Gaffney). It was the scene of a bloody encounter with a party of marauding Indians in 1857. (See marker on courthouse lawn.) It is the location of a state Insane Asylum, of a sorghum processing plant and an overall factory. Annual County Fair and Cowboy Roundup Sept. 4. The highway now passes through a rolling countryside devoted to grain crops and cattle raising.

Thus would the state guide dispose of Optimo City and hasten on to a more spirited topic if Optimo City as such existed. Optimo City, however, is not one town, it is a hundred or more towns, all very much alike, scattered across the United States from the Alleghenies to the Pacific, most numerous west of the Mississippi and south of the Platte. When, for instance, you travel through Texas and Oklahoma and New Mexico and even parts of Kansas and Missouri, Optimo City is the blur of filling stations and motels you occasionally pass; the solitary traffic light, the glimpse up a side street of an elephantine courthouse surrounded by elms and sycamores, the brief congestion of mud-spattered pickup trucks that slows you down before you hit the open road once more. And fifty miles farther on Optimo City's identical twin appears on the horizon, and a half dozen more Optimos beyond that until at last, with some relief, you reach the metropolis with its new housing developments and factories and the cluster of downtown skyscrapers.

Optimo City, then, is actually a very familiar feature of the American landscape. But since you have never stopped there except to buy gas, it might be well to know it a little better. What is there to see? Not a great deal, yet more than you would at first suspect.

Optimo, being after all an imaginary average small town, has to have had an average small-town history, or at least a Western version of that average. The original Fort Gaffney (named

the tractor (like the glimpse of a deer or a fox driven out of the hills by a heavy winter) restores for a moment a feeling for an old kinship that seemed to have been destroyed forever. But this is what makes Optimo, the hundreds of Optimos throughout America, so valuable; the ties between country and town have not yet been broken. Limited though it may well be in many ways, the world of Optimo City is still complete.

The center of this world is Courthouse Square, with the courthouse, ponderous, barbaric, and imposing, in the center of that. The building and its woebegone little park not only interrupts the vistas of Main and Sheridan – it was intended to do this – it also interrupts the flow of traffic in all four directions. A sluggish eddy of vehicles and pedestrians is the result, Optimo's animate existence slowed and intensified. The houses on the four sides of the square are of the same vintage (and the same general architecture) as the monument in their midst: mid-nineteenth-century brick or stone; cornices like the brims of hats, fancy dripstones over the arched windows like eyebrows; painted blood-red or mustard-yellow or white; identical except for the six-story Gaffney Hotel and the classicism of the First National Bank.

Every house has a tin roof porch extending over the sidewalk, a sort of permanent awning which protects passersby and incidentally conceals the motley of store windows and signs. To walk around the square and down Sheridan Street under a succession of these galleries or metal awnings, crossing the strips of bright sunlight between the roofs of different height, is one of the delights of Optimo – one of its amenities in the English use of that word. You begin to understand why the Courthouse Square is such a popular part of town.

SATURDAY NIGHTS – BRIGHT LIGHTS

Saturday, of course, is the best day for seeing the full tide of human existence in Sheridan County. The rows of parked pickups are like cattle in a feed lot; the sidewalks in front of Slymaker's Mercantile, the Ranch Cafe, Sears, the drugstore, resound to the mincing steps of cowboy boots; farmers and ranchers, thumbs in their pants pockets, gather in groups to lament the drought (there is always a drought) and those men in Washington, while their wives go from store to movie house to store. Radios, jukeboxes, the bell in the courthouse tower; the teenagers doing "shave-and-a-haircut; bay rum" on the horns of their parents' cars as they drive round and round the square. The smell of hot coffee, beer, popcorn, exhaust, alfalfa, cow manure. A man is trying to sell a truckload of grapefruit so that he can buy a truckload of cinderblocks to sell somewhere else. Dogs; 10-year-old cowboys firing cap pistols at each other. The air is full of pigeons, floating candy wrappers, the flat strong accent erroneously called Texan.

All these people are here in the center of Optimo for many reasons – for sociability first of all, for news, for the spending and making of money; for relaxation. "Jim Guthrie and wife were in town last week, visiting friends and transacting business," is the way the *Sheridan Sentinel* describes it; and almost all of Jim Guthrie's business takes place in the square. That is one of the peculiarities of Optimo and one of the reasons why the square as an institution is so important. For it is around the square that the oldest and most essential urban (or county) services are established. Here are the firms under local control and ownership, those devoted almost exclusively to the interest of the surrounding countryside. Upstairs are the lawyers, doctors, dentists, insurance firms, the public stenographer, the Farm Bureau. Downstairs are the bank, the prescription drugstore, the newspaper office, and of course Slymaker's Mercantile and the Ranch Cafe.

INFLUENCE OF THE COURTHOUSE

Why have the chain stores not invaded this part of town in greater force? Some have already got a foothold, but most of them are at the far end of Sheridan or even out on the Federal Highway. The presence of the courthouse is partly responsible. The traditional services want to be as near the courthouse as they can, and real-estate values are high. The courthouse itself attracts so many out-of-town visitors that the problem of parking is acute. The only solution that occurs to the enlightened minds of the Chamber of Commerce is to tear the courthouse down, use the place for parking, and build a new one somewhere else. They have already had an architect draw a sketch of a new courthouse to go at the far end of Main Street: a chaste concrete cube with vertical motifs between the windows – a fine specimen of bureaucrat modernism. But the trouble is, where to get the money for a new courthouse when the old one is still quite evidently adequate and in constant use?

If you enter the courthouse you will be amazed by two things: the horrifying architecture of the place, and the variety of functions it fills. Courthouse means of course courtrooms, and there are two of those. Then there is the office of the County Treasurer, the Road Commissioner, the School Board, the Agricultural Agent, the Extension Agent, Sanitary Inspector, and usually a group of Federal agencies as well – PMA, Soil Conservation, FHA and so on. Finally the Red Cross, the Boy Scouts, and the District Nurse. No doubt many of these offices are tiresome examples of government interference in private matters; just the same, they are for better or worse part of almost every farmer's and rancher's business, and the courthouse, in spite of all the talk about county consolidation, is a more important place than ever.

As it is, the ugly old building has conferred upon Optimo a blessing which many larger and richer American towns can envy: a center for civic activity and a symbol for civic pride – something as different from the modern "civic center" as day is from night. Contrast the array of classic edifices, lost in the midst of waste space, the meaningless pomp of flagpoles and war memorials and dribbling fountains of any American city from San Francisco to Washington with the animation and harmony and the almost domestic intimacy of Optimo Courthouse Square, and you have a pretty good measure of what is wrong with much American city planning: civic consciousness has been divorced from everyday life, put in a special zone all by itself. Optimo City has its zones; but they are organically related to one another.

Doubtless the time will never come that the square is studied as a work of art. Why should it be? The craftsmanship in the details, the architecture of the building, the notions of urbanism in the layout of the square itself are all on a very countrified level. Still, such a square as this has dignity and even charm. The charm is perhaps antiquarian – a bit of rural America of seventy-five years ago; the dignity is something else again. It derives from the function of the courthouse and the square, and from its peculiarly national character.

COMMUNAL CENTER

The practice of erecting a public building in the center of an open place is in fact pretty well confined to America – more specifically to nineteenth-century America. The vast open areas favored by eighteenth-century European planners were usually kept free of construction, and public buildings – churches and palaces and law-courts – were located to face these squares; to command them, as it were. But they were not allowed to interfere with the original open effect. Even the plans of eighteenth-century American cities, such as Philadelphia and Reading and Savannah and Washington, always left the square or public place intact. Spanish America, of course, provides the best illustrations of all; the plaza, nine times out of ten, is surrounded by public buildings, but it is left free. Yet almost every American town laid out after (say) 1820 deliberately planted a public building in the center of its square. Sometimes it was a school, sometimes a city hall, more often a courthouse, and it was always approachable from all four sides and always as conspicuous as possible.

Why? Why did these pioneer city fathers go counter to the taste of the past in this matter? One guess is as good as another. Perhaps they were so proud of their representative institutions that they wanted to give their public buildings the best location available. Perhaps frontier America was following an aesthetic movement, already at that date strong in Europe, that held that an open space was improved when it contained some prominent free-standing object – an obelisk or a statue or a triumphal arch. However that may have been, the pioneer Americans went Europe one better, and put the largest building in town right in the center of the square.

Thus the square ceased to be thought of in nineteenth-century America as a vacant space; it became a container or (if you prefer) a frame. A frame, so it happened, not merely for the courthouse, but for all activity of a communal sort. Few aesthetic experiments have ever produced such brilliantly practical results. A society which had long since ceased to rally around the individual leader and his residence and which was rapidly tiring of rallying around the meetinghouse or church all at once found a new symbol: local representative government, or the courthouse. A good deal of flagwaving resulted – as European travelers have always told us – and a good deal of very poor "representational" architecture; but Optimo acquired something to be proud of, something to moderate that American tendency to think of every town as existing entirely for money-making purposes.

SYMBOL OF INDEPENDENCE

At this juncture the protesting voice of the Chamber of Commerce is heard. "One moment. Before you finish with our courthouse you had better hear the other side of the question. If the courthouse were torn down we would not only have more parking space – sorely needed in Optimo – we would also get funds for widening Main Street into a four-lane highway. If Main Street were widened Optimo could attract many new businesses catering to tourists and other transients – restaurants and motels and garages and all sorts of drive-in establishments. In the last ten years" (continues the Chamber of Commerce) "Optimo has grown by twelve hundred. Twelve hundred! At that rate we'll still be a small town of less than twenty thousand in 1999. But if we had new businesses we'd grow fast and have better schools and a new hospital, and the young people wouldn't move to the cities. Or do you expect Optimo to go on depending on a few hundred tight-fisted farmers

and ranchers for its livelihood?" The voice, now shaking with emotion, adds something about "eliminating" South Main by means of an embankment and a clover leaf and picnic grounds for tourists under the cottonwoods where the Latinos still reside.

These suggestions are very sensible ones on the whole. Translate them into more general terms and what they amount to is this: if we want to get ahead, the best thing to do is break with our own past, become as independent as possible of our immediate environment and at the same time become almost completely dependent for our well-being on some remote outside resource. Whatever you may think of such a program, you cannot very well deny that it has been successful for a large number of American towns. Think of the hayseed communities which have suddenly found themselves next to an oil field or a large factory or an Army installation, and which have cashed in on their good fortune by transforming themselves overnight, turning their backs on their former sources of income, and tripling their population in a few years! It is true that these towns put all their eggs in one basket, that they are totally at the mercy of some large enterprise quite beyond their control. But think of the freedom from local environment; think of the excitement and the money! Given the same circumstances – and the Southwest is full of surprises still – why should Optimo not do the same?

A COMMON DESTINY

Because there are many different kinds of towns just as there are many different kinds of men, a development which is good for one kind can be death on another. Apache Center (to use that abject community as an example), with its stockyards and its one paved street and its very limited responsibility to the county, as a community might well become a boom-town and no one would be worse off. Optimo seems to have a different destiny. For almost a hundred years – a long time in this part of the world – it has been identified with the surrounding landscape and been an essential part of it. Whatever wealth it possesses has come from the farms and ranches, not from the overall factory or from tourists. The bankers and merchants will tell you, of course, that without their ceaseless efforts and their vision the countryside could never have existed; the farmers and ranchers consider Optimo's prosperity and importance entirely their own creation. Both parties are right to the extent that the town is part of the landscape – one might even say part of every farm, since much farm business takes place in the town itself.

Now if Optimo suddenly became a year-round tourist resort, or the overall capital of the Southwest; what would happen to that relationship, do you suppose? It would vanish. The farmers and ranchers would soon find themselves crowded out, and would go elsewhere for those services and benefits which they now enjoy in Optimo. And as for Optimo itself, it would soon achieve the flow of traffic, the new store fronts, the housing developments, the payrolls and bank accounts it cannot help dreaming about; and in the same process achieve a total social and physical dislocation, and a loss of a sense of its own identity. County Seat of Sheridan County? Yes; but much more important: Southwestern branch of the "American Cloak and Garment Corporation"; or the LITTLE TOWN WITH THE BIG WELCOME – 300 tourist beds which, when empty for one night out of three, threaten bankruptcy to half the town.

As of the present, Optimo remains pretty much as it has been for the last generation. The Federal Highway still bypasses the center (what a roadblock, symbolical as well as actual, that courthouse is!); so if you want to see Optimo, you had better turn off at the top of the hill near the watertower of the lunatic asylum – now called Fairview State Rest Home, and with the hideous high fence around it torn down. The dirt road eventually becomes North Main. The old Slymaker place is still intact. The Powell mansion, galleries and all, belongs to the American Legion, and a funeral home has taken over the Hooperson house. Then comes downtown Optimo; and then the courthouse, huge and graceless, in detail and proportion more like a monstrous birdhouse than a monument. Stop here. You'll find nothing of interest in the stores, and no architectural gems down a side street. Even if there were, no one would be able to point them out. The historical society, largely in the hands of ladies, thinks of antiquity in terms of antiques, and art as anything that looks pretty on the mantelpiece.

The weather is likely to be scorching hot and dry, with a wild ineffectual breeze in the elms and sycamores. You'll find no restaurant in town with atmosphere – no chandeliers made out of wagon wheels, no wall decorations of famous brands, no bar disguised as the Hitching Rail or the Old Corral. Under a high ceiling with a two-bladed fan in the middle, you'll eat ham hock and beans, hot bread, iced tea without lemon, and like it or go without. But as compensation of sorts at the next table there will be two ranchers eating with their hats on, and discussing the affairs, public and private, of Optimo City. To hear them talk, you'd think they owned the town.

That's about all. There's the market at the foot of South Main, the Latino shacks around the overall factory, a grove of cottonwoods, and the Apache River (North Branch) trickling down a bed ten times too big; and then the open country. You may be glad to have left Optimo behind.

Or you may have liked it, and found it pleasantly old-fashioned. Perhaps it is; but it is in no danger of dying out quite yet. As we said to begin with, there is another Optimo City fifty miles farther on. The country is covered with them. Indeed they are so numerous that it sometimes seems as if Optimo and rural America were one and indivisible.

ERNEST W. BURGESS

"The Growth of the City: An Introduction to a Research Project"

from Robert Park *et al.* (eds.), *The City* (1925)

Editors' introduction   Ernest W. Burgess (1886–1966) was a member of the famed Sociology Department at the University of Chicago that included such luminaries as Louis Wirth, author of "Urbanism as a Way of Life" (p. 190) and former newspaper reporter and social reformer Robert E. Park. Together, these scholars set out to virtually reinvent modern sociology by taking academic research to the streets and by using the city of Chicago itself as a "living laboratory" for the study of urban problems and social dynamics.

Throughout a long and productive career, Burgess addressed a whole series of issues that connected the social dynamics of the city as a whole with the lives of its citizens. He wrote extensively on issues related to marriage and the family, the relation of personality to social groups, and, in the final decades of his life, problems of the elderly. However, his most famous contribution to the study of the city was the 1925 essay reprinted here: "The Growth of the City."

Subtitled "An Introduction to a Research Project," Burgess's seminal analysis of the interrelation of the social growth and the physical expansion of modern cities served generations of other urban sociologists, geographers, and planners as a kind of "prolegomena." Seeking to describe what he called "the pulse of the community," Burgess devised a theory that was thoroughly organic, dynamic, and developmental. "In the expansion of the city," he wrote, "a process of distribution takes place which sifts and sorts and relocates individuals and groups by residence and occupation." And it was this dynamic process – "process" was one of Burgess's favorite words – that "gives form and character to the city."

Central to Burgess's analysis of urban growth was his famous model based on a series of concentric circles that divided the city into five zones. On one level, the concentric zone model was merely a map of contemporaneous Chicago with Zone I (the central business district area) designated "The Loop." On another level, the model was a theoretical diagram of a dynamic process Burgess called "succession," a term he borrowed from the science of plant ecology to describe "urban metabolism and mobility." By borrowing terminology from the natural sciences, and by drawing analogies between the urban and the natural worlds, Burgess established the study of "social ecology" as a distinct approach to understanding the underlying patterns of urban growth and development.

Following the publication of Burgess's essay, a number of urban theorists offered modifications and even refutations of the simple elegance of the concentric zone model. In 1939, real estate economist Homer Hoyt proposed a "sectoral model" for modern capitalist cities based on "wedges of activity" extending outward from the city center along transportation corridors. In 1945, geographers Chauncy Harris and Edward Ullman suggested a "multiple nuclei model," arguing that cities developed around several, not just one, center of economic activity.

Burgess's influence, however, was both widespread and long-standing, if not for the details of his model then for the spirit of its basic insight. Burgess's view may be compared to J. B. Jackson's notion that there is an underlying logic to urban form that occurs even in the absence of formal planning (p. 82). The work of dozens of urban sociologists such as William Julius Wilson's study of the urban underclass (p. 226) owes a profound debt to Burgess. And just as importantly, Burgess's sense of urban dynamism and vitality captures the essence of those more lyric conceptions of the city such as Lewis Mumford's notion of "the urban drama" (p. 184) and Jane Jacobs's "ballet of the streets" (p. 104).

Computer technology, including statistical packages and geographic information systems software, now makes it possible for present-day geographers and sociologists to summarize vast amounts of data and map the internal structure of cities in ever more sophisticated ways. Understanding of the relationship between social groups and urban form pioneered by Burgess continues to advance by leaps and bounds.

Robert E. Park (ed.), *The City* (3rd edn., rev., Chicago: University of Chicago Press, 1969) is the best introductory collection of the works of the Chicago School of urban sociology. For the works of Burgess in particular, including a comprehensive bibliography, see Leonard S. Cottrell, Jr., *et al.* (eds.), *On Community, Family and Delinquency* (Chicago: University of Chicago Press, 1973). Homer Hoyt's sectoral theory is described in *The Structure and Growth of Residential Neighborhoods in American Cities* (Washington: Federal Housing Administration, 1939); Chauncy Harris and Edward Ullman's multiple nuclei model is presented in "The Nature of Cities," *Annals of the American Academy of Political and Social Science*, vol. 242 (1945). Larry S. Bourne (ed.), *Internal Structure of the City: Readings on Urban Form, Growth and Policy* (New York and Oxford: Oxford University Press, 2nd edn. 1982) contains writings on the internal structure of the city. For a recent study of the Chicago School of Sociology and its impact see Martin Bulmer, *The Chicago School of Sociology: Institutionalization, Diversity and the Rise of Sociological Research* (Chicago: University of Chicago Press, 1984).

ERNEST W. BURGESS, "The Growth of the City: An Introduction to a Research Project"

from **Robert Park *et al.* (eds.), *The City* (1925)**

The outstanding fact of modern society is the growth of great cities. Nowhere else have the enormous changes which the machine industry has made in our social life registered themselves with such obviousness as in the cities. In the United States the transition from a rural to an urban civilization, though beginning later than in Europe, has taken place, if not more rapidly and completely, at any rate more logically in its most characteristic forms.

All the manifestations of modern life which are peculiarly urban – the skyscraper, the subway, the department store, the daily newspaper, and social work – are characteristically American. The more subtle changes in our social life, which in their cruder manifestations are termed "social problems," problems that alarm and bewilder us, such as divorce, delinquency, and social unrest, are to be found in their most acute forms in our largest American cities. The profound and "subversive" forces which have wrought these changes are measured in the physical growth and expansion of cities. That is the significance of the comparative statistics of Weber, Bucher, and other students.

These statistical studies, although dealing mainly with the effects of urban growth, brought out into clear relief certain distinctive characteristics of urban as compared with rural populations. The larger proportion of women to men in the cities than in the open country, the greater percentage of youth and middle-aged, the higher ratio of the foreign-born, the increased heterogeneity of occupation increase with the growth of the city and profoundly alter its social structure. These variations in the composition of population are indicative of all the changes going on in the social organization of the community. In fact, these changes are a part of the growth of the city and suggest the nature of the processes of growth.

The only aspect of growth adequately described by Bucher and Weber was the rather obvious process of the aggregation of urban population. Almost as overt a process, that of expansion, has been investigated from a different and very practical point of view by groups interested in city planning, zoning, and regional surveys. Even more significant than the increasing density of urban population is its correlative tendency to overflow, and so to extend over wider areas, and to incorporate these areas into a larger communal life. This paper, therefore, will treat first of the expansion of the city, and then of the less-known processes of urban metabolism and mobility which are closely related to expansion.

EXPANSION AS PHYSICAL GROWTH

The expansion of the city from the standpoint of the city plan, zoning, and regional surveys is thought of almost wholly in terms of its physical growth. Traction studies have dealt with the development of transportation in its relation to the distribution of population throughout the city. The surveys made by the Bell Telephone Company and other public utilities have attempted to forecast the direction and the rate

of growth of the city in order to anticipate the future demands for the extension of their services. In the city plan the location of parks and boulevards, the widening of traffic streets, the provision for a civic center, are all in the interest of the future control of the physical development of the city.

This expansion in area of our largest cities is now being brought forcibly to our attention by the Plan for the Study of New York and Its Environs, and by the formation of the Chicago Regional Planning Association, which extends the metropolitan district of the city to a radius of 50 miles, embracing 4,000 square miles of territory. Both are attempting to measure expansion in order to deal with the changes that accompany city growth. In England, where more than one-half of the inhabitants live in cities having a population of 100,000 and over, the lively appreciation of the bearing of urban expansion on social organization is thus expressed by C. B. Fawcett:

> One of the most important and striking developments in the growth of the urban populations of the more advanced peoples of the world during the last few decades has been the appearance of a number of vast urban aggregates, or conurbations, far larger and more numerous than the great cities of any preceding age. These have usually been formed by the simultaneous expansion of a number of neighboring towns, which have grown out toward each other until they have reached a practical coalescence in one continuous urban area. Each such conurbation still has within it many nuclei of denser town growth, most of which represent the central areas of the various towns from which it has grown, and these nuclear patches are connected by the less densely urbanized areas which began as suburbs of these towns. The latter are still usually rather less continuously occupied by buildings, and often have many open spaces.
>
> These great aggregates of town dwellers are a new feature in the distribution of man over the earth. At the present day there are from thirty to forty of them, each containing more than a million people, whereas only a hundred years ago there were, outside the great centers of population on the waterways of China, not more than two or three. Such aggregations of people are phenomena of great geographical and social importance; they give rise to new problems in the organization of the life and well-being of their inhabitants and in their varied activities. Few of them have yet developed a social consciousness at

all proportionate to their magnitude, or fully realized themselves as definite groupings of people with many common interests, emotions and thoughts.

In Europe and America the tendency of the great city to expand has been recognized in the term "the metropolitan area of the city," which far overruns its political limits, and, in the case of New York and Chicago, even state lines. The metropolitan area may be taken to include urban territory that is physically contiguous, but it is coming to be defined by that facility of transportation that enables a business man to live in a suburb of Chicago and to work in the loop, and his wife to shop at Marshall Field's and attend grand opera in the Auditorium.

EXPANSION AS A PROCESS

No study of expansion as a process has yet been made, although the materials for such a study and intimations of different aspects of the process are contained in city planning, zoning, and regional surveys. The typical processes of the expansion of the city can best be illustrated, perhaps, by a series of concentric circles, which may be numbered to designate both the successive zones of urban extension and the types of areas differentiated in the process of expansion [Figure 1].

[Figure 1] represents an ideal construction of the tendencies of any town or city to expand radially from its central business district – on the map "the Loop" (I). Encircling the downtown area there is normally an area in transition, which is being invaded by business and light manufacture (II). A third area (III) is inhabited by the workers in industries who have escaped from the area of deterioration (II) but who desire to live within easy access of their work. Beyond this zone is the "residential area" (IV) of high-class apartment buildings or of exclusive "restricted" districts of single family dwellings. Still farther, out beyond the city limits, is the commuters' zone: suburban areas, or satellite cities, within a thirty- to sixty-minute ride of the central business district.

This [figure] brings out clearly the main fact of expansion, namely, the tendency of each

inner zone to extend its area by the invasion of the next outer zone. This aspect of expansion may be called *succession*, a process which has been studied in detail in plant ecology. If this [figure] is applied to Chicago, all four of these zones were in its early history included in the circumference of the inner zone, the present business district. The present boundaries of the area of deterioration were not many years ago those of the zone now inhabited by independent wage-earners, and within the memories of thousands of Chicagoans contained the residences of the "best families." It hardly needs to be added that neither Chicago nor any other city fits perfectly into this ideal scheme. Complications are introduced by the lake front, the Chicago River, railroad lines, historical factors in the location of industry, the relative degree of the resistance of communities to invasion, etc.

Besides extension and succession, the general process of expansion in urban growth involves the antagonistic and yet complementary processes of concentration and decentralization. In all cities there is the natural tendency for local and outside transportation to converge in the central business district. In the downtown section of every large city we expect to find the department stores, the skyscraper office buildings, the railroad stations, the great hotels, the theaters, the art museum, and the city hall. Quite naturally, almost inevitably, the economic, cultural, and political life centers here. The relation of centralization to the other processes of city life may be roughly gauged by the fact that over half a million people daily enter and leave Chicago's "loop." More recently sub-business centers have grown up in outlying zones. These "satellite loops" do not, it seems, represent the "hoped for" revival of the neighborhood, but rather a telescoping of several local communities into a larger economic unity. The Chicago of yesterday, an agglomeration of country towns and immigrant colonies, is undergoing a process of reorganization into a centralized decentralized system of local communities coalescing into sub-business areas visibly or invisibly dominated by the central business district. The actual processes of what may be called centralized decentralization are now being studied in the development of the chain store, which is only one illustration of the change in the basis of the urban organization.

Expansion, as we have seen, deals with the physical growth of the city, and with the extension of the technical services that have made city life not only livable, but comfortable, even luxurious. Certain of these basic necessities of urban life are possible only through tremendous development of communal existence. Three millions of people in Chicago are dependent upon one unified water system, one giant gas company, and one huge electric light plant. Yet, like most of the other aspects of our communal urban life, this economic co-operation is an example of co-operation without a shred of

what the "spirit of co-operation" is commonly thought to signify. The great public utilities are a part of the mechanization of life in great cities, and have little or no other meaning for social organization.

Yet the processes of expansion, and especially the rate of expansion, may be studied not only in the physical growth and business development, but also in the consequent changes in the social organization and in personality types. How far is the growth of the city, in its physical and technical aspects, matched by a natural but adequate readjustment in the social organization? What, for a city, is a normal rate of expansion, a rate of expansion with which

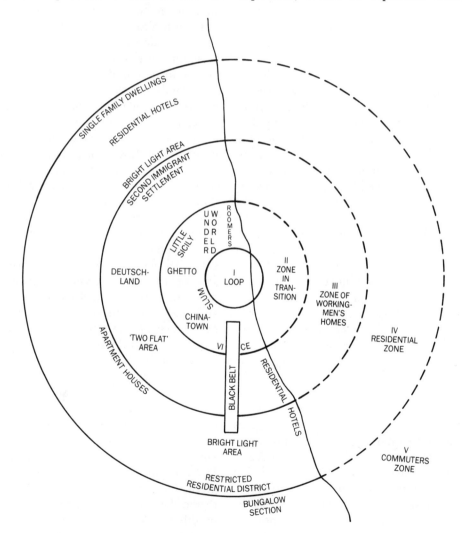

Figure 1

controlled changes in the social organization might successfully keep pace?

SOCIAL ORGANIZATION AND DISORGANIZATION AS PROCESSES OF METABOLISM

These questions may best be answered, perhaps, by thinking of urban growth as a resultant of organization and disorganization analogous to the anabolic and katabolic processes of metabolism in the body. In what way are individuals incorporated into the life of a city? By what process does a person become an organic part of his society? The natural process of acquiring culture is by birth. A person is born into a family already adjusted to a social environment – in this case the modern city. The natural rate of increase of population most favorable for assimilation may then be taken as the excess of the birth-rate over the death-rate, but is this the normal rate of city growth? Certainly, modern cities have increased and are increasing in population at a far higher rate. However, the natural rate of growth may be used to measure the disturbances of metabolism caused by any excessive increase, as those which followed the great influx of southern Negroes into northern cities since the war. In a similar way all cities show deviations in composition by age and sex from a standard population such as that of Sweden, unaffected in recent years by any great emigration or immigration. Here again, marked variations, as any great excess of males over females, or of females over males, or in the proportion of children, or of grown men or women, are symptomatic of abnormalities in social metabolism.

Normally the processes of disorganization and organization may be thought of as in reciprocal relationship to each other, and as co-operating in a moving equilibrium of social order toward an end vaguely or definitely regarded as progressive. So far as disorganization points to reorganization and makes for more efficient adjustment, disorganization must be conceived not as pathological, but as normal. Disorganization as preliminary to reorganization of attitudes and conduct is almost invari-

ably the lot of the newcomer to the city, and the discarding of the habitual, and often of what has been to him the moral, is not infrequently accompanied by sharp mental conflict and sense of personal loss. Oftener, perhaps, the change gives sooner or later a feeling of emancipation and an urge toward new goals.

In the expansion of the city a process of distribution takes place which sifts and sorts and relocates individuals and groups by residence and occupation. The resulting differentiation of the cosmopolitan American city into areas is typically all from one pattern, with only interesting minor modifications. Within the central business district or on an adjoining street is the "main stem" of "hobohemia," the teeming Rialto of the homeless migratory man of the Middle West. In the zone of deterioration encircling the central business section are always to be found the so-called "slums" and "bad lands," with their submerged regions of poverty, degradation, and disease, and their underworlds of crime and vice. Within a deteriorating area are rooming-house districts, the purgatory of "lost souls." Nearby is the Latin Quarter, where creative and rebellious spirits resort. The slums are also crowded to over flowing with immigrant colonies – the Ghetto, Little Sicily, Greek town, Chinatown – fascinatingly combining old world heritages and American adaptations. Wedging out from here is the Black Belt with its free and disorderly life. The area of deterioration, while essentially one of decay, of stationary or declining population, is also one of regeneration, as witness the mission, the settlement, the artists' colony, radical centers – all obsessed with the vision of a new and better world.

The next zone is also inhabited predominatingly by factory and shop workers, but skilled and thrifty. This is an area of second immigrant settlement, generally of the second generation. It is the region of escape from the slum, the *Deutschland* of the aspiring Ghetto family. For *Deutschland* (literally "Germany") is the name given, half in envy, half in derision, to that region beyond the Ghetto where successful neighbors appear to be imitating German Jewish standards of living. But the inhabitant of this area in turn looks to the "Promised Land" beyond, to its residential hotels, its apartment-house region, its "satellite loops," and its "bright light" areas.

This differentiation into natural economic and cultural groupings gives form and character to the city. For segregation offers the group, and thereby the individuals who compose the group, a place and a role in the total organization of city life. Segregation limits development in certain directions, but releases it in others. These areas tend to accentuate certain traits, to attract and develop their kind of individuals, and so to become further differentiated.

The division of labor in the city likewise illustrates disorganization, reorganization and increasing differentiation. The immigrant from rural communities in Europe and America seldom brings with him economic skill of any great value in our industrial, commercial, or professional life. Yet interesting occupational selection has taken place by nationality, explainable more by racial temperament or circumstance than by old-world economic background as Irish policemen, Greek ice-cream parlors, Chinese laundries, Negro porters, Belgian janitors, etc.

The facts that in Chicago one million (996,589) individuals gainfully employed reported 509 occupations, and that over 1,000 men and women in *Who's Who* gave 116 different vocations give some notion of how in the city the minute differentiation of occupation "analyzes and sifts the population, separating and classifying the diverse elements." These figures also afford some intimation of the complexity and complication of the modern industrial mechanism and the intricate segregation and isolation of divergent economic groups. Interrelated with this economic division of labor is a corresponding division into social classes and into cultural and recreational groups. From this multiplicity of groups, with their different patterns of life, the person finds his congenial social world and – what is not feasible in the narrow confines of a village – may move and live in widely separated, and perchance conflicting, worlds. Personal disorganization may be but the failure to harmonize the canons of conduct of two divergent groups.

If the phenomena of expansion and metabo-lism indicate that a moderate degree of disorganization may and does facilitate social organization, they indicate as well that rapid urban expansion is accompanied by excessive increases in disease, crime, disorder, vice, insanity and suicide, rough indexes of social disorganization. But what are the indexes of the causes, rather than of the effects, of the disordered social metabolism of the city? The excess of the actual over the natural increase of population has already been suggested as a criterion. The significance of this increase consists in the immigration into a metropolitan city like New York and Chicago of tens of thousands of persons annually. Their invasion of the city has the effect of a tidal wave inundating first the immigrant colonies, the ports of first entry, dislodging thousands of inhabitants who overflow into the next zone, and so on and on until the momentum of the wave has spent its force on the last urban zone. The whole effect is to speed up expansion, to speed up industry, to speed up the "junking" process in the area of deterioration (II). These internal movements of the population become the more significant for study. What movement is going on in the city, and how may this movement be measured? It is easier, of course, to classify movement within the city than to measure it. There is the movement from residence to residence, change of occupation, labor turnover, movement to and from work, movement for recreation and adventure. This leads to the question: what is the significant aspect of movement for the study of the changes in city life? The answer to this question leads directly to the important distinction between movement and mobility.

MOBILITY AS THE PULSE OF THE COMMUNITY

Movement, per se, is not an evidence of change or of growth. In fact, movement may be a fixed and unchanging order of motion, designed to control a constant situation, as in routine movement. Movement that is significant for growth implies a change of movement in response to a new stimulus or situation. Change of movement of this type is called *mobility*. Movement of the nature of routine finds its typical expression in work. Change of movement, or mobility, is characteristically expressed in adventure. The great city, with its "bright lights," its emporiums of novelties and bargains, its palaces of amusement, its underworld of vice and crime, its risks of life and property from accident, robbery, and homicide, has become the region of the most intense degree of adventure and danger, excitement and thrill.

Mobility, it is evident, involves change, new experience, stimulation. Stimulation induces a response of the person to those objects in his environment which afford expression for his wishes. For the person, as for the physical organism, stimulation is essential to growth. Response to stimulation is wholesome so long as it is a correlated integral reaction of the entire personality. When the reaction is segmental, that is, detached from, and uncontrolled by, the organization of personality, it tends to become disorganizing or pathological. That is why stimulation for the sake of stimulation, as in the restless pursuit of pleasure, partakes of the nature of vice.

The mobility of city life, with its increase in the number and intensity of stimulations, tends inevitably to confuse and to demoralize the person. For an essential element in the mores and in personal morality is consistency, consistency of the type that is natural in the social control of the primary group. Where mobility is the greatest, and where in consequence primary controls break down completely, as in the zone of deterioration in the modern city, there develop areas of demoralization, of promiscuity, and of vice.

In our studies of the city it is found that areas of mobility are also the regions in which are found juvenile delinquency, boys' gangs, crime, poverty, wife desertion, divorce, abandoned infants, vice.

These concrete situations show why mobility is perhaps the best index of the state of metabolism of the city. Mobility may be thought of, in more than a fanciful sense, as the "pulse of the community." Like the pulse of the human body, it is a process which reflects and is indicative of all the changes that are taking place in the community, and which is susceptible of analysis into elements which may be stated numerically.

The elements entering into mobility may be classified under two main heads: (1) the state of mutability of the person, and (2) the number and kind of contacts or stimulations in his environment. The mutability of city populations varies with sex and age composition, and the degree of detachment of the person from the family and from other groups. All these factors may be expressed numerically. The new stimulations to which a population responds can be measured in terms of change of movement or of increasing contacts. Statistics on the movement of urban population may only measure routine, but an increase at a higher ratio than the increase of population measures mobility. In 1860 the horse-car lines of New York City carried about 50,000,000 passengers; in 1890 the trolley cars (and a few surviving horse-cars) transported about 500,000,000; in 1921, the elevated, subway, surface, and electric and steam suburban lines carried a total of more than 2,500,000,000 passengers. In Chicago the total annual rides per capita on the surface and elevated lines were 164 in 1890; 215 in 1900; 320 in 1910; and 338 in 1921. In addition, the rides per capita on steam and electric suburban lines almost doubled between 1916 (23) and 1921 (41), and the increasing use of the automobile must not be overlooked. For example, the number of automobiles in Illinois increased from 131,140 in 1915 to 833,920 in 1923.

Mobility may be measured not only by these changes of movement, but also by increase of contacts. While the increase of population of Chicago in 1912–22 was less than 25 percent (23.6 percent), the increase of letters delivered to Chicagoans was double that (49.6 percent) – from 693,048,196 to 1,038,007,854. In 1912 New York had 8.8 telephones; in 1922, 16.9 per 100 inhabitants. Boston had, in 1912, 10.1 telephones; ten years later, 19.5 telephones per 100 inhabitants. In the same decade the figures for Chicago increased from 12.3 to 21.6 per 100 population. But increase of the use of the telephone is probably more significant than increase in the number of telephones. The number of telephone calls in Chicago increased from 606,131,928 in 1914 to 944,010,586 in 1922, an increase of 55.7 percent, while the population increased only 13.4 percent.

Land values, since they reflect movement, afford one of the most sensitive indexes of mobility. The highest land values in Chicago are at the point of greatest mobility in the city, at the corner of State and Madison streets, in the Loop. A traffic count showed that at the rush period 31,000 people an hour, or 210,000 men and women in sixteen and one-half hours, passed the southwest corner. For over ten years land values in the Loop have been stationary but in the same time they have doubled, quadrupled and even sextupled in the strategic corners of the "satellite loops," an accurate index of the changes which have occurred. Our investigations so far seem to indicate that variations in land values, especially where correlated with differences in rents, offer perhaps the best single measure of mobility, and so of all the changes taking place in the expansion and growth of the city.

In general outline, I have attempted to present the point of view and methods of investigation which the department of sociology is employing in its studies in the growth of the city, namely, to describe urban expansion in terms of extension, succession, and concentration; to determine how expansion disturbs metabolism when disorganization is in excess of organization; and, finally, to define mobility and to propose it as a measure both of expansion and metabolism, susceptible to precise quantitative formulation, so that it may be regarded almost literally as the pulse of the community. In a way, this statement might serve as an introduction to any one of five or six research projects under way in the department. The project, however, in which I am directly engaged is an attempt to apply these methods of investigation to a cross-section of the city – to put this area, as it were, under the microscope, and so to study in more detail and with greater control and precision the processes which have been described here in the large. For this purpose the West Side Jewish community has been selected. This community includes the so-called "Ghetto," or area of first settlement, and Lawndale, the so-called "Deutschland," or area of second settlement. This area has certain obvious advantages for this study, from the standpoint of expansion, metabolism, and mobility. It exemplifies the tendency to expansion radially from the business center of the city. It is now relatively a homogeneous cultural group. Lawndale is itself an area in flux, with the tide of migrants still flowing in from the Ghetto and a constant egress to more desirable regions of the residential zone. In this area, too, it is also possible to study how the expected outcome of this high rate of mobility in social and personal disorganization is counteracted in large measure by the efficient communal organization of the Jewish community.

KEVIN LYNCH

"The City Image and Its Elements"

from *The Image of the City* (1960)

Editors' introduction   Kevin Lynch (1918–1989) was a professor of urban studies and planning at MIT, where he taught courses in urban design. Lynch studied with Frank Lloyd Wright (p. 377), whose architectural theories and philosophical quest for harmony between human life and built forms profoundly affected his work. Drawing widely on material from psychology and the humanities, Lynch sought to understand how people perceive their environments and how design professionals can respond to the deepest human needs. Lynch's rambling, profoundly humane writings weave together a unique blend of practical design suggestions, examples drawn from his voluminous reading, and subtle theory. Lynch has had a profound effect on the teaching and practice of urban planning and urban design worldwide.

This influential chapter from *The Image of the City* presents Lynch's best-known concepts on how people perceive cities. Lynch argues that people structure their perception of cities into recurring elements such as *paths* (along which movement flows) and *edges* (which differentiate one part of the urban fabric from another). If designers understand how people perceive these elements and design to make them clear, Lynch argues, they can create more imageable, and more psychologically satisfying cities.

Many urban designers throughout the world today sketch out the elements of cities or parts of cities they are designing as paths, edges, nodes, landmarks, and districts – the perceptual categories Lynch suggested – and draw on his theories to strengthen the city image. Planners in cities as diverse as San Francisco, Cairo, Ciudad Guyana in Venezuela, and Castro's Havana have used Lynch's concepts to plan their cities.

Compare Lynch's theoretical writing with William Whyte's applied principles and standards for park and plaza design (p. 110), and Frederick Law Olmsted's vision of urban parks (p. 338). Consider how urban designers might design imageable cities in terms of Lynch's categories that are still *semi-lattices* instead of *trees* in Alexander's terminology (p. 119).

In addition to *The Image of the City* (Cambridge, Mass.: MIT Press, 1960) Lynch's books include a textbook on site-specific design: *Site Planning*, co-authored with Gary Hack (Cambridge, Mass.: MIT Press, 2nd edn. 1971); a book on historic preservation, *What Time Is This Place?* (Cambridge, Mass.: MIT Press, 1979); and his magnum opus, *Good City Form* (Cambridge, Mass.: MIT, 1991). For a biographical sketch see "Kevin Lynch" in *The Best of Planning* (Washington, D.C.: American Planning Association, 1989).

Related writings include Anthony Hiss, *The Experience of Place* (New York: Knopf, 1990), which explores how the built environment affects human consciousness. Robert Sommer's *Personal Space*

(Englewood Cliffs, N.J.: Prentice-Hall, 1969) describes how individuals react to and structure the space immediately around them.

KEVIN LYNCH, "The City Image and Its Elements"

from *The Image of the City* (1960)

There seems to be a public image of any given city which is the overlap of many individual images. Or perhaps there is a series of public images each held by some significant number of citizens. Such group images are necessary if an individual is to operate successfully within his environment and to cooperate with his fellows. Each individual picture is unique, with some content that is rarely or never communicated, yet it approximates the public image, which in different environments is more or less compelling, more or less embracing.

[...]

The contents of the city images so far studied, which are referable to physical forms, can conveniently be classified into five types of elements: paths, edges, districts, nodes, and landmarks ... These elements may be defined as follows:

1   *Paths*. Paths are the channels along which the observer customarily, occasionally, or potentially moves. They may be streets, walkways, transit lines, canals, railroads. For many people, these are the predominant elements in their image. People observe the city while moving through it, and along these paths the other environmental elements are arranged and related.

2   *Edges*. Edges are the linear elements not used or considered as paths by the observer. They are the boundaries between two phases, linear breaks in continuity: shores, railroad cuts, edges of development, walls. They are lateral references rather than coordinate axes. Such edges may be barriers, more or less penetrable, which close one region off from another;

or they may be seams, lines along which two regions are related and joined together. These edge elements, although probably not as dominant as paths, are for many people important organizing features, particularly in the role of holding together generalized areas, as in the outline of a city by water or wall.

3   *Districts*. Districts are the medium-to-large sections of the city, conceived of as having two-dimensional extent, which the observer mentally enters "inside of," and which are recognizable as having some common, identifying character. Always identifiable from the inside, they are also used for exterior reference if visible from the outside. Most people structure their city to some extent in this way, with individual differences as to whether paths or districts are the dominant elements. It seems to depend not only upon the individual but also upon the given city.

4   *Nodes*. Nodes are points, the strategic spots in a city into which an observer can enter, and which are the intensive foci to and from which he is traveling. They may be primarily junctions, places of a break in transportation, a crossing or convergence of paths, moments of shift from one structure to another. Or the nodes may be simply concentrations, which gain their importance from being the condensation of some use or physical character, as a street-corner hangout or an enclosed square. Some of these concentration nodes are the focus and epitome of a district, over which their influence radiates and of which they stand as a symbol. They may be called cores. Many nodes, of course, partake of the nature of both junctions and concentrations. The concept of node is related to the concept of path, since

junctions are typically the convergence of paths, events on the journey. It is similarly related to the concept of district, since cores are typically the intensive foci of districts, their polarizing center. In any event, some nodal points are to be found in almost every image, and in certain cases they may be the dominant feature.

5   *Landmarks*. Landmarks are another type of point-reference, but in this case the observer does not enter within them, they are external. They are usually a rather simply defined physical object: building, sign, store, or mountain. Their use involves the singling out of one element from a host of possibilities. Some landmarks are distant ones, typically seen from many angles and distances, over the tops of smaller elements, and used as radial references. They may be within the city or at such a distance that for all practical purposes they symbolize a constant direction. Such are isolated towers, golden domes, great hills. Even a mobile point, like the sun, whose motion is sufficiently slow and regular, may be employed. Other landmarks are primarily local, being visible only in restricted localities and from certain approaches. These are the innumerable signs, store fronts, trees, doorknobs, and other urban detail, which fill in the image of most observers. They are frequently used clues of identity and even of structure, and seem to be increasingly relied upon as a journey becomes more and more familiar.

[...]

PATHS

For most people interviewed, paths were the predominant city elements, although their importance varied according to the degree of familiarity with the city. People with the least knowledge of Boston tended to think of the city in terms of topography, large regions, generalized characteristics, and broad directional relationships. Subjects who knew the city better had usually mastered parts of the path structure; these people thought more in terms of

specific paths and their interrelationships. A tendency also appeared for the people who knew the city best of all to rely more upon small landmarks and less upon either regions or paths.

The potential drama and identification in the highway system should not be underestimated. One Jersey City subject, who can find little worth describing in her surroundings, suddenly lit up when she described the Holland Tunnel. Another recounted her pleasure:

> You cross Baldwin Avenue, you see all of New York in front of you, you see the terrific drop of land [the Palisades] ... and here's this open panorama of Lower Jersey City in front of you and you're going downhill, and there you know: there's the tunnel, there's the Hudson River and everything ... I always look to the right to see if I can see the ... Statue of Liberty ... Then I always look up to see the Empire State Building, see how the weather is ... I have a real feeling of happiness because I'm going someplace, and I love to go places.

[...]

Concentration of special use or activity along a street may give it prominence in the minds of observers. Washington Street in Boston is the outstanding Boston example: subjects consistently associated it with shopping and theaters ... People seemed to be sensitive to variations in the amount of activity they encountered and sometimes guided themselves largely by following the main stream of traffic. Los Angeles' Broadway was recognized by its crowds and its street cars; Washington Street in Boston was marked by a torrent of pedestrians. Other kinds of activity at ground level also seemed to make places memorable, such as construction work near South Station, or the bustle of the food markets.

Characteristic spatial qualities were able to strengthen the image of particular paths. In the simplest sense, streets that suggest extremes of either width or narrowness attracted attention...

[...]

Where major paths lacked identity, or were

easily confused one for the other, the entire city image was in difficulty ... Boston's Longfellow Bridge was not infrequently confused with the Charles River Dam, probably since both carry transit lines and terminate in traffic nodes ...

[...]

People tended to think of path destinations and origin points: they liked to know where paths came from and where they led. Paths with clear and well-known origins and destinations had stronger identities, helped tie the city together, and gave the observer a sense of his bearings whenever he crossed them. Some subjects thought of general destinations for paths, to a section of the city, for example, while others thought of specific places. One person, who made rather high demands for intelligibility upon the city environment, was troubled because he saw a set of railroad tracks, and did not know the destination of trains using them.

[...]

EDGES

Edges are the linear elements not considered as paths: they are usually, but not quite always, the boundaries between two kinds of areas. They act as lateral references. They are strong in Boston and Jersey City but weaker in Los Angeles. Those edges seem strongest which are not only visually prominent, but also continuous in form and impenetrable to cross movement. The Charles River in Boston is the best example and has all of these qualities ...

[...]

It is difficult to think of Chicago without picturing Lake Michigan. It would be interesting to see how many Chicagoans would begin to draw a map of their city by putting down something other than the line of the lake shore. Here is a magnificent example of a visible edge, gigantic in scale, that exposes an entire metropolis to view. Great buildings, parks, and tiny private beaches all come down to the water's edge, which throughout most of its length is accessible and visible to all. The contrast, the differentiation of events along the line, and the lateral breadth are all very strong. The effect is reinforced by the concentration of paths and activities along its extent. The scale is perhaps unrelievedly large and coarse, and too much open space is at times interposed between city and water, as at the Loop. Yet the facade of Chicago on the Lake is an unforgettable sight.

DISTRICTS

Districts are the relatively large city areas which the observer can mentally go inside of, and which have some common character. They can be recognized internally, and occasionally can be used as external reference as a person goes by or toward them. Many persons interviewed took care to point out that Boston, while confusing in its path pattern even to the experienced inhabitant, has, in the number and vividness of its differentiated districts, a quality that quite makes up for it. As one person put it: "Each part of Boston is different from the other. You can tell pretty much what area you're in."

[...]

Subjects, when asked which city they felt to be a well-oriented one, mentioned several, but New York (meaning Manhattan) was unanimously cited. And this city was cited not so much for its grid, which Los Angeles has as well, but because it has a number of well-defined characteristic districts, set in an ordered frame of rivers and streets. Two Los Angeles subjects even referred to Manhattan as being "small" in comparison to their central area! Concepts of size may depend in part on how well a structure can be grasped.

[...]

Usually the typical features were imaged and recognized in a characteristic cluster, the thematic unit. The Beacon Hill image, for example, included steep narrow streets; old brick row houses of intimate scale; inset, highly maintained, white doorways; black trim; cobblestones and brick walks; quiet; and upper-class pedestrians. The resulting thematic unit was distinctive by contrast to the rest of the city and could be recognized immediately...

NODES

Nodes are the strategic foci into which the observer can enter, typically either junctions of paths, or concentrations of some characteristic. But although conceptually they are small points in the city image, they may in reality be large squares, or somewhat extended linear shapes, or even entire central districts when the city is being considered at a large enough level. Indeed, when conceiving the environment at a national or international level, then the whole city itself may become a node.

The junction, or place of a break in transportation, has compelling importance for the city observer. Because decisions must be made at junctions, people heighten their attention at such places and perceive nearby elements with more than normal clarity. This tendency was confirmed so repeatedly that elements located at junctions may automatically be assumed to derive special prominence from their location. The perceptual importance of such locations shows in another way as well. When subjects were asked where on a habitual trip they first felt a sense of arrival in downtown Boston, a large number of people singled out break-points of transportation as the key places . . .

LANDMARKS

Landmarks, the point reference considered to be external to the observer, are simple physical elements which may vary widely in scale. There seemed to be a tendency for those more familiar with a city to rely increasingly on systems of landmarks for their guides – to enjoy uniqueness and specialization, in place of the continuities used earlier.

Since the use of landmarks involves the singling out of one element from a host of possibilities, the key physical characteristic of this class is singularity, some aspect that is unique or memorable in the context. Landmarks become more easily identifiable, more likely to be chosen as significant, if they have a clear form; if they contrast with the background; and if there is some prominence of spatial location. Figure–background contrast seems to be the principal factor. The background against which an element stands out need not be limited to immediate surroundings: the grasshopper weathervane of Faneuil Hall, the gold dome of the State House, or the peak of the Los Angeles City Hall are landmarks that are unique against the background of the entire city.

[...]

JANE JACOBS

"The Uses of Sidewalks: Safety"

from *The Death and Life of Great American Cities* (1961)

Editors' introduction   Jane Jacobs (born 1916) started writing about city life and urban planning not as a trained professional but as a neighborhood activist. Dismissed as the original "little old lady in tennis shoes" and derided as a political amateur more concerned about personal safety issues than state-of-the-art planning techniques, she nonetheless struck a responsive chord with a 1960s public eager to believe the worst about arrogant city planning technocrats and just as eager to rally behind movements for neighborhood control and community resistance to bulldozer redevelopment.

The Death and Life of Great American Cities hit the world of city planning like an earthquake when it appeared in 1961. The book was nothing less than a frontal attack on the planning establishment. Urban renewal was derided as a process that only served to create instant slums. Universally accepted articles of faith – that parks were good and that crowding was bad – were openly questioned with the suggestions that parks were dangerous and that crowded neighborhood sidewalks were the safest places for children to play. In addition, the planning establishment's most revered historical traditions were ridiculed as "the Radiant Garden City Beautiful" (an artful phrase that not only airily dismissed the contributions of Le Corbusier, Ebenezer Howard, and Daniel Burnham but lumped them together as well)!

The selection from The Death and Life reprinted here presents Jane Jacobs at her very best. In "The Use of Sidewalks: Safety," she outlines her basic notions of what makes a neighborhood a community and what makes a city livable. Safety – particularly for women and children – comes from "eyes on the street," the kind of involved neighborhood surveillance of public space that modern planning practice in the CIAM–Corbusian tradition had destroyed with its insistence on superblocks and skyscraper developments. A sense of personal belonging and social cohesiveness comes from well-defined neighborhoods and narrow, crowded, multiuse streets. And, finally, basic urban vitality comes from residents' participation in an intricate "street ballet," a diurnal pattern of observable and comprehensible human activity that is possible only in places like Jacobs's own Hudson Street in her beloved Greenwich Village.

It is this last quality – her unabashed love of cities and urban life – that is Jane Jacobs's most obvious and enduring characteristic. The Death and Life was a scathing attack on the planning establishment – and, in many ways, it was a grassroots political call to arms – but it was also a loving invitation to experience the joys of city living that led many young, college-educated people to seek out neighborhoods like Greenwich Village as places to live, struggle, and raise families. In one sense, the book encouraged and justified middle-class gentrification of formerly working-class neighborhoods. In another, it found itself oddly reflected in the fantasy-nostalgia of *Sesame Street*.

But in all ways it was committedly urban – never suburban – at a time when inner-city communities were being increasingly abandoned to the forces of poverty, decay, and neglect.

Jacobs's notion of the "street ballet" invites comparison with Lewis Mumford's idea of the "urban drama" (p. 184) and William Whyte's emphasis on the importance of public plazas (p. 110). Jacobs's community activism in resistance to elitist, top-down urban renewal places her within a long tradition that includes Paul Davidoff's "Advocacy and Pluralism in Planning" (p. 422) and "Toward an Urban Design Manifesto" by Allan Jacobs and Donald Appleyard (p. 165).

Other important works by Jane Jacobs include *The Economy of Cities* (New York: Random House, 1969) – a book that begins with a provocative chapter arguing that the rise of cities may have preceded, and even accounted for, rural agricultural development – and *Systems of Survival* (New York: Random House, 1992), a Platonic dialogue on "the moral foundations of commerce and politics."

JANE JACOBS, "The Uses of Sidewalks: Safety"

from *The Death and Life of Great American Cities* (1961)

Streets in cities serve many purposes besides carrying vehicles, and city sidewalks – the pedestrian parts of the streets – serve many purposes besides carrying pedestrians. These uses are bound up with circulation but are not identical with it and in their own right they are at least as basic as circulation to the proper workings of cities.

A city sidewalk by itself is nothing. It is an abstraction. It means something only in conjunction with the buildings and other uses that border it, or border other sidewalks very near it. The same might be said of streets, in the sense that they serve other purposes besides carrying wheeled traffic in their middles. Streets and their sidewalks, the main public places of a city, are its most vital organs. Think of a city and what comes to mind? Its streets. If a city's streets look interesting, the city looks interesting; if they look dull, the city looks dull.

More than that, and here we get down to the first problem, if a city's streets are safe from barbarism and fear, the city is thereby tolerably safe from barbarism and fear. When people say that a city, or a part of it, is dangerous or is a jungle what they mean primarily is that they do not feel safe on the sidewalks. But sidewalks and those who use them are not passive beneficiaries of safety or helpless victims of danger. Side-

walks, their bordering uses, and their users, are active participants in the drama of civilization versus barbarism in cities. To keep the city safe is a fundamental task of a city's streets and its sidewalks.

This task is totally unlike any service that sidewalks and streets in little towns or true suburbs are called upon to do. Great cities are not like towns, only larger. They are not like suburbs, only denser. They differ from towns and suburbs in basic ways, and one of these is that cities are, by definition, full of strangers. To any one person, strangers are far more common in big cities than acquaintances. More common not just in places of public assembly, but more common at a man's own doorstep. Even residents who live near each other are strangers, and must be, because of the sheer number of people in small geographical compass.

The bedrock attribute of a successful city district is that a person must feel personally safe and secure on the street among all these strangers. He must not feel automatically menaced by them. A city district that fails in this respect also does badly in other ways and lays up for itself, and for its city at large, mountain on mountain of trouble.

Today barbarism has taken over many city streets, or people fear it has, which comes to much the same thing in the end. "I live in a lovely, quiet residential area," says a friend of mine who is hunting another place to live. "The only disturbing sound at night is the occasional scream of someone being mugged." It does not take many incidents of violence on a city street, or in a city district, to make people fear the streets ... And as they fear them, they use them less, which makes the streets still more unsafe.

To be sure, there are people with hobgoblins in their heads, and such people will never feel safe no matter what the objective circumstances are. But this is a different matter from the fear that besets normally prudent, tolerant and cheerful people who show nothing more than common sense in refusing to venture after dark – or in a few places, by day – into streets where they may well be assaulted, unseen or unrescued until too late. The barbarism and the real, not imagined, insecurity that gives rise to such fears cannot be tagged a problem of the slums. The problem is most serious, in fact, in genteel-looking "quiet residential areas" like that my friend was leaving.

It cannot be tagged as a problem of older parts of cities. The problem reaches its most baffling dimensions in some examples of rebuilt parts of cities, including supposedly the best examples of rebuilding, such as middle-income projects. The police precinct captain of a nationally admired project of this kind (admired by planners and lenders) has recently admonished residents not only about hanging around outdoors after dark but has urged them never to answer their doors without knowing the caller. Life here has much in common with life for the three little pigs or the seven little kids of the nursery thrillers. The problem of sidewalk and doorstep insecurity is as serious in cities which have made conscientious efforts at rebuilding as it is in those cities that have lagged. Nor is it illuminating to tag minority groups, or the poor, or the outcast with responsibility for city danger. There are immense variations in the degree of civilization and safety found among such groups and among the city areas where they live. Some of the safest sidewalks in New York City, for example, at any time of day or night, are those along which poor people or minority groups live. And some of the most dangerous are in streets occupied by the same kinds of people. All this can also be said of other cities.

[...]

The first thing to understand is that the public peace – the sidewalk and street peace – of cities is not kept primarily by the police, necessary as police are. It is kept primarily by an intricate, almost unconscious, network of voluntary controls and standards among the people themselves, and enforced by the people themselves. In some city areas – older public housing projects and streets with very high population turnover are often conspicuous examples – the keeping of public sidewalk law and order is left almost entirely to the police and special guards. Such places are jungles. No amount of police can enforce civilization where the normal, casual enforcement of it has broken down.

The second thing to understand is that the problem of insecurity cannot be solved by spreading people out more thinly, trading the characteristics of cities for the characteristics of suburbs. If this could solve danger on the city streets, then Los Angeles should be a safe city because superficially Los Angeles is almost all suburban. It has virtually no districts compact enough to qualify as dense city areas. Yet Los Angeles cannot, any more than any other great city, evade the truth that, being a city, it is composed of strangers not all of whom are nice. Los Angeles' crime figures are flabbergasting. Among the seventeen standard metropolitan areas with populations over a million, Los Angeles stands so pre-eminent in crime that it is in a category by itself. And this is markedly true of crimes associated with personal attack, the crimes that make people fear the streets.

[...]

This is something everyone already knows: A well-used city street is apt to be a safe street. A deserted city street is apt to be unsafe. But how does this work, really? And what makes a city street well used or shunned? ... What about streets that are busy part of the time and then empty abruptly?

A city street equipped to handle strangers, and to make a safety asset, in itself, out of the presence of strangers, as the streets of successful city neighborhoods always do, must have three main qualities:

First, there must be a clear demarcation between what is public space and what is private space. Public and private spaces cannot ooze into each other as they do typically in suburban settings or in projects.

Second, there must be eyes upon the street, eyes belonging to those we might call the natural proprietors of the street. The buildings on a street equipped to handle strangers and to insure the safety of both residents and strangers must be oriented to the street. They cannot turn their backs or blank sides on it and leave it blind.

And third, the sidewalk must have users on it fairly continuously, both to add to the number of effective eyes on the street and to induce the people in buildings along the street to watch the sidewalks in sufficient numbers. Nobody enjoys sitting on a stoop or looking out a window at an empty street. Almost nobody does such a thing. Large numbers of people entertain themselves, off and on, by watching street activity.

In settlements that are smaller and simpler than big cities, controls on acceptable public behavior, if not on crime, seem to operate with greater or lesser success through a web of reputation, gossip, approval, disapproval and sanctions, all of which are powerful if people know each other and word travels. But a city's streets, which must control the behavior not only of the people of the city but also of visitors from suburbs and towns who want to have a big time away from the gossip and sanctions at home, have to operate by more direct, straightforward methods. It is a wonder cities have solved such an inherently difficult problem at all. And yet in many streets they do it magnificently.

It is futile to try to evade the issue of unsafe city streets by attempting to make some other features of a locality, say interior courtyards, or sheltered play spaces, safe instead. By definition again, the streets of a city must do most of the job of handling strangers, for this is where strangers come and go. The streets must not only defend the city against predatory strangers, they must protect the many, many peaceable and well-meaning strangers who use them, insuring their safety too as they pass through. Moreover, no normal person can spend his life in some artificial haven, and this includes children. Everyone must use the streets.

On the surface, we seem to have here some simple aims: to try to secure streets where the public space is unequivocally public, physically unmixed with private or with nothing-at-all space, so that the area needing surveillance has clear and practicable limits; and to see that these public street spaces have eyes on them as continuously as possible.

But it is not so simple to achieve these objects, especially the latter. You can't make people use streets they have no reason to use. You can't make people watch streets they do not want to watch. Safety on the streets by surveillance and mutual policing of one another sounds grim, but in real life it is not grim. The safety of the street works best, most casually, and with least frequent taint of hostility or suspicion precisely where people are using and most enjoying the city streets voluntarily and are least conscious, normally, that they are policing.

The basic requisite for such surveillance is a substantial quantity of stores and other public places sprinkled along the sidewalks of a district; enterprises and public places that are used by evening and night must be among them especially. Stores, bars and restaurants, as the chief examples, work in several different and complex ways to abet sidewalk safety.

First, they give people – both residents and strangers – concrete reasons for using the sidewalks on which these enterprises face.

Second, they draw people along the sidewalks past places which have no attractions to public use in themselves but which become traveled and peopled as routes to somewhere else; this influence does not carry very far geographically, so enterprises must be frequent in a city district if they are to populate with walkers those other stretches of street that lack public places along the sidewalk. Moreover, there should be many different kinds of enterprises, to give people reasons for crisscrossing paths.

Third, storekeepers and other small business-men are typically strong proponents of peace and order themselves; they hate broken win-dows and holdups; they hate having customers made nervous about safety. They are great street watchers and sidewalk guardians if present in sufficient numbers.

Fourth, the activity generated by people on errands, or people aiming for food or drink, is itself an attraction to still other people.

This last point, that the sight of people attracts still other people, is something that city planners and city architectural designers seem to find incomprehensible. They operate on the premise that city people seek the sight of empti-ness, obvious order and quiet. Nothing could be less true. People's love of watching activity and other people is constantly evident in cities everywhere.

[...]

Under the seeming disorder of the old city, wherever the old city is working successfully, is a marvelous order for maintaining the safety of the streets and the freedom of the city. It is a complex order. Its essence is intricacy of side-walk use, bringing with it a constant succession of eyes. This order is all composed of movement and change, and although it is life, not art, we may fancifully call it the art form of the city and liken it to the dance – not to a simple-minded precision dance with everyone kicking up at the same time, twirling in unison and bowing off en masse, but to an intricate ballet in which the individual dancers and ensembles all have dis-tinctive parts which miraculously reinforce each other and compose an orderly whole. The ballet of the good city sidewalk never repeats itself from place to place, and in any one place is always replete with new improvisations.

The stretch of Hudson Street where I live is each day the scene of an intricate sidewalk ballet. I make my own first entrance into it a little after eight when I put out the garbage can, surely a prosaic occupation, but I enjoy my part, my little clang, as the droves of junior high school students walk by the center of the stage

dropping candy wrappers. (How do they eat so much candy so early in the morning?)

While I sweep up the wrappers I watch the other rituals of morning: Mr. Halpert unlocking the laundry's handcart from its mooring to a cellar door, Joe Cornacchia's son-in-law stack-ing out the empty crates from the delicatessen, the barber bringing out his sidewalk folding chair, Mr. Goldstein arranging the coils of wire which proclaim the hardware store is open, the wife of the tenement's superintendent deposit-ing her chunky 3-year-old with a toy mandolin on the stoop, the vantage point from which he is learning the English his mother cannot speak. Now the primary children, heading for St. Luke's, dribble through to the south; the chil-dren for St. Veronica's cross, heading to the west, and the children for P.S. 41, heading toward the east. Two new entrances are being made from the wings: well-dressed and even elegant women and men with briefcases emerge from doorways and side streets ... Most of these are heading for the bus and subways, but some hover on the curbs, stopping taxis which have miraculously appeared at the right moment, for the taxis are part of a wider morning ritual: having dropped passengers from midtown in the downtown financial dis-trict, they are now bringing downtowners up to midtown. Simultaneously, numbers of women in housedresses have emerged and as they criss-cross with one another they pause for quick conversations that sound with either laughter or joint indignation; never, it seems, anything between. It is time for me to hurry to work too, and I exchange my ritual farewell with Mr. Lofaro, the short, thick-bodied, white-aproned fruit man who stands outside his doorway a little up the street, his arms folded, his feet planted, looking solid as earth itself. We nod; we each glance quickly up and down the street then look back to each other and smile. We have done this many a morning for more than ten years, and we both know what it means: All is well.

[...]

I know the deep night ballet and its seasons best from waking; long after midnight to tend a baby and, sitting in the dark, seeing the shadows and hearing the sounds of the sidewalk. Mostly it is a sound like infinitely pattering snatches of party conversation and, about three in the morning, singing, very good singing. Sometimes there is sharpness and anger or sad, sad weeping, or a flurry of search for a string of beads broken. One night, a young man came roaring along, bellowing terrible language at two girls whom he had apparently picked up and who were disappointing him. Doors opened; a wary semicircle formed around him, not too close, until the police came. Out came the heads, too, along Hudson Street, offering opinion, "Drunk ... Crazy ... A wild kid from the suburbs." (He turned out to be a wild kid from the suburbs. Sometimes, on Hudson Street, we are tempted to believe the suburbs must be a difficult place to bring up children.)

I have made the daily ballet of Hudson Street sound more frenetic than it is, because writing it telescopes it. In real life, it is not that way. In real life, to be sure, something is always going on, the ballet is never at a halt, but the general effect is peaceful and the general tenor even leisurely. People who know well such animated city streets will know how it is. I am afraid people who do not will always have it a little wrong in their heads like the old prints of rhinoceroses made from travelers' descriptions of rhinoceroses. On Hudson Street, the same as in the North End of Boston or in any other animated neighborhoods of great cities, we are not innately more competent at keeping the sidewalks safe than are the people who try to live off the hostile truce of Turf in a blind-eyed city. We are the lucky possessors of a city order that makes it relatively simple to keep the peace because there are plenty of eyes on the street. But there is nothing simple about that order itself, or the bewildering number of components that go into it. Most of those components are specialized in one way or another. They unite in their joint effect upon the sidewalk, which is not specialized in the least. That is its strength.

WILLIAM WHYTE

"The Design of Spaces"

from *City: Rediscovering the Center* (1988)

Editors' introduction   Puzzled by why some of New York's parks and plazas were well used while others were almost empty, the New York City Planning Commission asked sociologist William Whyte to study park and plaza use and help draft a comprehensive design plan for the city.

While Whyte held no regular academic position, his lucid writing on planning and design gave him great credibility. Hunter College appointed him to a one-year Distinguished Professor position and the National Geographic Society gave him the first domestic "expedition grant" they had ever made.

Whyte worked with bright young designers and planners at the New York City Planning Department, Hunter College sociology students, and other talented people he drew to "The Street Life Project." This team produced an exceptional study of how people use urban space and a set of urban design guidelines for New York which have been widely praised and used in New York and many other cities.

The Street Life Project is an excellent example of how to do urban research. Whyte formed hypotheses about how people would use urban space. Then he tested each hypothesis by filming people using many different plazas and parks in New York City and carefully analyzing the films. His results were often startling. Some initial hypotheses were validated, but even many which seem intuitively obvious were rejected or had to be modified. For example, Whyte hypothesized that the number of people using a plaza would be related to the amount of space or its shape. But Chart 1 (Whyte, Figure 1) shows that is not the case. New Yorkers used tiny Greenacre Park much more than the much larger J. C. Penney Park. One of New York's most popular parks is just a long, narrow indentation in a building. Whyte eventually concluded that the amount of *sittable* space in a park or plaza was much more important than either the total space or its shape.

Most writing on urban design ignores gender differences or is written from a male perspective with a separate section on design implications for women. Whyte is one of the few authors to notice gender and to weave its significance into the fabric of his study. He noticed that women are more discriminating than men as to where they will sit and are more sensitive to annoyances. He concluded that if a plaza has a high proportion of women it is probably a good and well-managed one.

Note the similarity between Whyte's description of Seagram's Plaza as "the best of stages" and Lewis Mumford's emphasis on the city as theater (p. 184). Notice what Mike Davis (p. 159) found designers in Los Angeles do to *keep people away* from public areas in light of Whyte's comment that "it takes real work to create a lousy place." And note the importance of good public spaces in Kitto's description of the Greek polis (p. 32): Whyte titles the concluding chapter in *City: Rediscovering the Center* "Return to the Agora."

This selection is from *City: Rediscovering the Center* (New York, Anchor Books, 1988). In other chapters Whyte explores water, wind, trees, light, steps and entrances, undesirables, walls, sun and shadows, and many other factors. Whyte produced a delightful film based on his research available from Direct Cinema Ltd. in Los Angeles under the title *Public Spaces/Human Places*.

Whyte's other writings on urban society and planning include *The Organization Man* (New York: Simon & Schuster, 1956) and *The Last Landscape* (Garden City, N.Y.: Doubleday, 1968).

There are many books concerning human aspects of design. Spiro Kostoff's monumental *The City Shaped: Urban Patterns and Meanings through History* (London: Thames & Hudson, 1991) and *The City Assembled* (London: Thames & Hudson, 1992) synthesize a vast amount of material from around the world and contain excellent illustrations. Daphne Spain's *Gendered Space* (Chapel Hill, N.C.: University of North Carolina Press, 1992) is an examination of the way in which different cultures design space in relation to gender roles. Oscar Newman's *Defensible Space* (New York: Macmillan, 1972) is a study of the way in which low-rent public housing project residents use space with suggestions to architects and planners on how to improve their security concerns. Clare Cooper and Wendy Sarkissien's *Housing as if People Mattered* (Berkeley: University of California Press, 1986) provides practical suggestions for designing housing responsive to the needs of all its residents – particularly working women and children. Allan Jacobs's *Looking at Cities* (Cambridge, Mass.: MIT Press, 1985) provides a stimulating discussion of how close observation like that which Whyte undertook can inform city planning and how to do it.

WILLIAM WHYTE, "The Design of Spaces"

from *City: Rediscovering the Center* (1988)

... Since 1961 New York City had been giving incentive bonuses to developers who would provide plazas ... Every new office building qualified for the bonus by providing a plaza or comparable space; in total, by 1972 some twenty acres of the world's most expensive open space.

Some plazas attracted lots of people ...

But on most plazas there were few people. In the middle of the lunch hour on a beautiful day the number of people sitting on plazas averaged four per thousand square feet of space – an extraordinarily low figure for so dense a center ...

... The city was being had. For the millions of dollars of extra floor space it was handing out to developers, it had every right to demand much better spaces in return.

I put the question to the chairman of the city planning commission, Donald Elliott ... He felt tougher zoning was in order. If we could find out why the good places worked and the bad

ones didn't and come up with tight guidelines, there could be a new code ...

We set to work. We began studying a cross section of spaces – in all, sixteen plazas, three small parks, and a number of odds and ends of space ...

[...]

We started by charting how people used plazas. We mounted time-lapse cameras at spots overlooking the plaza ... and recorded the dawn-to-dusk patterns. We made periodic circuits of the plazas and noted on sighting maps where people were sitting, their gender, and whether they were alone or with others ... We also interviewed people and found where they worked, how frequently they used the plaza, and what they thought of it. But mostly we watched what they did.

Most of them were young office workers from nearby buildings. Often there would be relatively few from the plaza's own building. As some secretaries confided, they would just as soon put a little distance between themselves and the boss come lunchtime. In most cases the plaza users came from a building within a three-block radius. Small parks, such as Paley and Greenacre, had a somewhat more varied mix of people – with more upper-income older people – but even here office workers predominated.

This uncomplicated demography underscores an elemental point about good spaces: supply creates demand. A good new space builds a new constituency. It gets people into new habits – such as alfresco lunches – and induces them to use new paths ...

The best-used plazas are sociable places, with a higher proportion of couples and groups than you will find in less-used places. At the plazas in New York, the proportion of people in twos or more runs about 50–62 percent; in the least-used, 25–30 percent. A high proportion is an index of selectivity. If people go to a place in a group or rendezvous there, it is most often because they decided to beforehand. Nor are these places less congenial to the individual. In absolute numbers, they attract more individuals than do the less-used spaces. If you are alone, a lively place can be the best place to be.

The best-used places also tend to have a higher than average proportion of women. The male–female ratio of a plaza reflects the composition of the work force and this varies from area to area. In midtown New York it runs about 60 percent male, 40 percent female. Women are more discriminating than men as to where they will sit, they are more sensitive to annoyances, and they spend more time casing a place. They are also more likely to dust off a ledge with their handkerchief.

The male–female ratio is one to watch. If a plaza has a markedly low proportion of women, something is wrong. Conversely, if it has a high proportion, the plaza is probably a good and well-managed one and has been chosen as such.

The rhythms of plaza life are much alike from place to place. In the morning hours, patronage will be sporadic ...

Around noon the main clientele begins to arrive. Soon activity will be near peak and will stay there until a little before two ...

Some 80 percent of the people activity on plazas comes during the lunchtime, and there is very little of any kind after five-thirty ...

During the lunch period, people will distribute themselves over space with considerable consistency, with some sectors getting heavy use day in and day out, others much less so. We also found that off-peak use often gives the best clues to people's preferences. When a place is jammed, people sit where they can; this may or may not be where they most want to. After the main crowd has left, however, the choices can be significant. Some parts of the plaza become empty; others continue to be used ...

Men show a tendency to take the front row seats and if there is a kind of gate they will be the guardians of it. Women tend to favor places slightly secluded. If there are double-sided ledges parallel to the street, the inner side will usually have a higher proportion of women; the outer, of men.

Of the men up front the most conspicuous are the girl watchers. As I have noted, they put on such a show of girl watching as to indicate that their real interest is not so much the girls as the show. It is all machismo. Even in the Wall Street area, where girl watchers are especially demonstrative you will hardly ever see one attempt to pick up a girl.

Plazas are not ideal places for striking up acquaintances. Much better is a very crowded street with lots of eating and quaffing going on. An outstanding example is the central runway of the South Street Seaport. At lunch sometimes, one can hardly move for the crush. As in musical chairs, this can lead to interesting combinations. On most plazas, however, there isn't much mixing. If there are, say, two smashing blondes on a ledge, the men nearby will usually put on an elaborate show of disregard. Look closely, however, and you will see them giving away the pose with covert glances.

Lovers are to be found on plazas, but not where you would expect them. When we first started interviewing, people would tell us to be sure to see the lovers in the rear places. But they weren't usually there. They would be out front. The most fervent embracing we've recorded on film has taken place in the most visible of locations, with the couple oblivious of the crowd. (In a long clutch, however, I have noted that one of the lovers may sneak a glance at a wristwatch.)

Certain locations become rendezvous points for groups of various kinds. The south wall of the Chase Manhattan Plaza was, for a while, a gathering point for camera bugs, the kind who are always buying new lenses and talking about them. Patterns of this sort may last no more than a season – or persist for years. A black civic leader in Cincinnati told me that when he wants to make contact, casually, with someone, he usually knows just where to look at Fountain Square . . .

Standing patterns on the plazas are fairly regular. When people stop to talk they will generally do so athwart one of the main traffic flows, as they do on streets. They also show an inclination to station themselves near objects, such as a flagpole or a piece of sculpture. They like well-defined places, such as steps or the border of a pool. What they rarely choose is the middle of a large space.

There are a number of explanations. The preference might be ascribed to some primeval instinct: you have a full view of all comers but your rear is covered. But this doesn't explain the inclination men have for lining up at the curb. Typically, they face inward, with their backs exposed to the vehicle traffic of the street.

Whatever their cause, people's movements are one of the great spectacles of a plaza. You do not see this in architectural photographs, which are usually devoid of human beings and are taken from a perspective that few people share. It is a misleading one. Looking down on a bare plaza, one sees a display of geometry, done almost in monochrome. Down at eye level the scene comes alive with movement and color – people walking quickly, walking slowly, skipping up steps, weaving in and out on crossing patterns, accelerating and retarding to match the moves of others. Even if the paving and the walls are gray, there will be vivid splashes of color – in winter especially, thanks to women's fondness for red coats and colored umbrellas.

There is a beauty that is beguiling to watch, and one senses that the players are quite aware of this themselves. You can see this in the way they arrange themselves on ledges and steps.

They often do so with a grace that they must appreciate themselves. With its brown-gray setting, Seagram is the best of stages – in the rain, too, when an umbrella or two puts spots of color in the right places, like Corot's red dots.

Let us turn to the factors that make for such places. The most basic one is so obvious it is often overlooked: people. To draw them, a space should tap a strong flow of them. This means location, and, as the old adage has it, location and location. The space should be in the heart of downtown, close to the 100 percent corner – preferably right on top of it.

Because land is cheaper further out, there is a temptation to pick sites away from the center. There may also be some land for the asking – some underused spaces, for example, left over from an ill-advised civic center campus of urban renewal days. They will be poor bargains. A space that is only a few blocks too far might as well be ten blocks for all the people who will venture to walk to it.

People *ought* to walk to it, perhaps; the exercise would do them good. But they don't. Even within the core of downtown the effective radius of a good place is about three blocks. About 80 percent of the users will have come from a place within that area. This does indicate a laziness on the part of pedestrians and this may change a bit, just as the insistence on close-in parking may. But there is a good side to the constrained radius. Since usage is so highly localized, the addition of other good open spaces will not saturate demand. They will increase it.

Given a fine location, it is difficult to design a space that will not attract people. What is remarkable is how often this has been accomplished. Our initial study made it clear that while location is a prerequisite for success, it in no way assures it. Some of the worst plazas are in the best spots . . .

All of the plazas and small parks that we studied had good locations; most were on the major avenues, some on attractive side-streets. All were close to bus-stops or subway stations and had strong pedestrian flows on the sidewalks beside them. Yet when we rated them according to the number of people sitting at peak time, there was a wide range: from 160 people at 77 Water Street to 17 at 280 Park Avenue.

How come? The first factor we studied was the sun. We thought it might well be the critical one, and our first time-lapse studies seemed to bear this out. Subsequent studies did not. As I will note later they show that sun was important but did not explain the differences in popularity of plazas.

Nor did aesthetics... The elegance and purity of a complex's design, we had to conclude, had little relationship to the usage of the spaces around it.

[...]

Another factor we considered was the shape of spaces. Members of the commission's urban design group believed this was very important and hoped our findings would support tight criteria for proportions and placement. They were particularly anxious to rule out strip plazas: long, narrow spaces that were little more than enlarged sidewalks, and empty of people more times than not...

Our data did not support such criteria. While it was true that most strip plazas were little used, it did not follow that their shape was the reason. Some squarish plazas were little used too, and, conversely, several of the most heavily used spaces were in fact long, narrow strips. One of the five most popular sitting places in New York is essentially an indentation in a building, long and narrow. Our research did not prove shape unimportant or designers' instincts misguided. As with the sun, however, it proved that other factors were more critical.

If not the shape of the space, what about the *amount* of it? Some conservationists believed this would be the key factor. In their view, people seek open space as a relief from over-crowding and it would follow that places with the greatest sense of space and light and air would draw the best. If we ranked plazas by the amount of space they provided, there surely would be a positive correlation between space and people.

Once again we found no clear relationship. Several of the smallest spaces had the largest number of people, and several of the largest spaces had the least number of people...

What about the amount of *sittable* space?

Here we began to get close. As we tallied the number of linear feet of sitting space, we could see that the plazas with the most tended to be among the most popular ...

... No matter how many other variables we checked, one basic point kept coming through. We at last recognized that it was the major one.

People tend to sit most where there are places to sit.

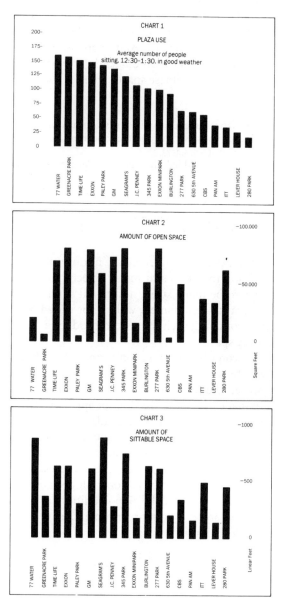

Figure 1

This may not strike the reader as an intellectual bombshell, and now that I look back on our study I wonder why it was not more apparent to us from the beginning ... Whatever the attractions of a space, it cannot induce people to come and sit if there is no place to sit.

INTEGRAL SEATING

The most basic kind of seating is the kind that is built into a place, such as steps and ledges. Half the battle is seeing to it that these features are usable by people. And there is a battle. Another force has been diligently at work finding ways to deny these spaces. Here are some of the ways:

> Horizontal metal strip with sawtooth points.
> Jagged rocks set in concrete (Southbridge House, New York City).
> Spikes imbedded in ledges (Peachtree Plaza Hotel).
> Railing placed to hit you in small of back (GM Plaza, New York City).
> Canted ledges of slippery marble (Celanese Building, New York City).

It takes real work to create a lousy place. In addition to spikes and metal objects, there are steps to be made steep, additional surveillance cameras to be mounted, walls to be raised high. Just *not* doing such things can produce a lot of sitting space.

It won't be the most comfortable kind but it will have the great advantage of enlarging choice. The more sittable the inherent features are made, the more freedom people have to sit up front, in the back, to the side, in the sun, or out of it. This means designing ledges and parapets and other flat surfaces so they can do double duty as seating, tables, and shelves. Since most building sites have some slope in them, there are bound to be opportunities for such features, and it is no more trouble to leave them sittable than not.

[...]

SITTING HEIGHT

One guideline we thought would be easy to establish was for sitting heights. It seemed obvious enough that somewhere around sixteen to seventeen inches would probably be the optimum. But how much higher or lower could a surface be and still be sittable? Thanks to slopes, several of the most popular ledges provided a range of continuously variable heights. The front ledge at Seagram, for example started at seven inches at one corner and rose to forty-four inches at the other. Here was an opportunity for a definitive study, we thought; by recording over time how many people sat at what heights, we would get a statistical measure of preferences.

We didn't ... We had to conclude that people will sit almost anywhere between a height of one foot and three, and this was the range that was to be specified in the zoning. People will sit lower or higher, of course, but there are apt to be special conditions – a wall too high for most adults to mount but just right for teenagers.

A dimension that is truly important is the human backside. It is a dimension many architects ignore. Rarely will you find a ledge or bench that is deep enough to be sittable on both sides ... Most frustrating are the ledges just deep enough to tempt people to sit on both sides, but too shallow to let them do so comfortably. At peak times people may sit on both sides but they won't be comfortable doing it. They will be sitting on the forward edge, awkwardly.

Thus to another of our startling findings: ledges and spaces two backsides deep seat more people than those that are not as deep ...

[...]

Steps work for the same reason. They afford an infinity of possible groupings, and the excellent sight lines make all the seating great for watching the theatre of the street ...

[...]

Circulation and sitting, in sum, are not antithetical but complementary. I stress this because a good many planners think that the two should be kept separate. More to the point, so do some zoning codes. New York's called for "pedestrian circulation areas" separate from "activity areas" for sitting. People ignore such boundaries.

We felt that pedestrian circulation through and within plazas should be encouraged. Plazas that are sunken or elevated tend to attract low flows, and for that reason the zoning specifies that plazas be not more than three feet below street level or above it. The easier the flow between street and plaza the more likely they are to come in and tarry and sit.

This is true of the handicapped also. If a place is planned with their needs in mind, the place is apt to function more easily for everyone. Drinking fountains that are low enough for wheelchair users are low enough for children. Walkways that are made easier for the handicapped by ramps, handrails, and steps of gentle pitch are easier for all. The guidelines make such amenities mandatory ... For the benefit of the handicapped, it is required that at least 5 percent of the seating spaces have backrests. These are not segregated for the handicapped. No facilities are segregated. The idea is to make all of the place useful for everyone.

BENCHES

Benches are design artifacts the purpose of which is to punctuate architectural photographs. They are most often sited in modular form, spaced equidistant from one another in a symmetry that is pleasing in plan view. They are not very good, however, for sitting. There are usually too few of them; they are too short and too narrow; they are isolated from other benches and from what action there is to look at.

[...]

Watch how benches fill up. The first arrival will usually take the end of a bench, not the middle. The next arrival will take the end of another bench. Subsequent arrivals head for whatever end spots are not taken. Only when there are few other places left will people sit in the middle of the bench, and some will elect to stand.

Since it's the ends of the benches that do most of the work, it could be argued that benches ought to be shortened so they're all end and no middle. But the unused middles are functional for *not* being used. They provide buffer space. They also provide choice, and if it is the least popular choice, that does not negate its utility.

[...]

CHAIRS

We come now to a wonderful invention: the movable chair. Having a back, it is comfortable, and even more so if it has armrests as well. But the big asset is movability. Chairs enlarge choice: to move into the sun, out of it; to move closer to someone, further away from another.

The possibility of choice is as important as the exercise of it. If you know you can move if you want to, you can feel all the more comfortable staying put. This is why, perhaps, people so often approach a chair and then, before sitting on it, move the chair a few inches this way or that, finally ending up with the chair just about where it was in the first place. These moves are functional. They are a declaration of one's free will to oneself, and rather satisfying. In this one small matter you are the master of your fate.

Small moves can say things to other people. If a newcomer chooses a chair next to a couple in a crowded situation, he may make several moves with the chair. He is conveying a message: Sorry about the closeness, but it can't be helped and I am going to respect your privacy as you will mine. A reciprocal shift of a chair may signal acknowledgment.

Chair arranging by groups is a ritual worth watching. In a group of three or four women, one may be dominant and direct the sitting, including the fetching of an extra chair. More times, the members of the group work it out themselves, often with false starts and second choices. The chair arranging can take quite a bit of time on occasion – it is itself a form of recreation – but people enjoy it. Watching these exercises in civility is one of the pleasures of a good place.

Fixed individual seats deny choice. They may

be good to look at, and in the form of stools, metal love seats, granite cubes, and the like, they make interesting decorative elements. That is their primary function. For sitting, however, they are inflexible and socially uncomfortable.

[...]

Where space is at a premium – in theatres, stadia – fixed seats are a necessity. In open spaces, however, they are uncalled for; there is so much space around them that the compression makes for awkward sitting ... On one campus a group of metal love seats was cemented to the paving with epoxy glue; in short order they were wrenched out of position by students. The designer is unrepentant. His love seats have won several design awards.

[...]

A salute to grass is in order. It is a wonderfully adaptable substance, and while it is not the most comfortable seating, it is fine for napping, sunbathing, picnicking, and Frisbee throwing. Like movable chairs, it also has the great advantage of offering people the widest possible choice of sitting arrangements. There are an infinity of possible groupings, but you will note that the most frequent has people self-positioned at oblique angles from each other.

Grass offers a psychological benefit as well. A patch of green is a refreshing counter to granite and concrete, and when people are asked what they would like to see in a park, trees and grass usually are at the top of the list ...

RELATIONSHIP TO THE STREET

Let us turn to a more difficult consideration. With the kind of amenities we have been discussing, there are second chances. If the designers have goofed on seating, more and better seating can be provided. If they have been too stingy with trees, more trees can be planted. If there is no food, a food cart can be put in – possibly a small pavilion or gazebo. If there is no water feature, a benefactor might be persuaded to donate a small pool or fountain.

Thanks to such retrofitting, spaces regarded as hopeless dogs have been given new life.

What is most difficult to change, however, is what is most important: the location of the space and its relationship to the street. The real estate people are right about location, location, location. For a space to function truly well it must be central to the constituency it is to serve – and if not in physical distance, in visual accessibility...

The street functions as part of the plaza or square; indeed, it is often hard to tell where the street leaves off and the plaza begins. The social life of the spaces flows back and forth between them. And the most vital space of all is often the street corner. Watch one long enough and you will see how important it is to the life of the large spaces. There will be people in 100 percent conversations or prolonged goodbyes. If there is a food vendor at the corner, like Gus at Seagram, people will be clustered around him, and there will be a brisk traffic between corner and plaza.

It is a great show, and one of the best ways to make the most of it is, simply, not to wall off the plaza from it. Frederick Law Olmsted spoke of an "interior park" and an "outer park," and he argued that the latter – the surrounding streets – was vital to the enjoyment of the former. He thought it an abomination to separate the two with walls or, worse yet, with a spiked iron fence. "In expression and association," he said, "it is in the most distinct contradiction and discord with all the sentiment of a park. It belongs to a jail or to the residence of a despot who dreads assassination."

But walls are still being put up, usually in the mistaken notion that they will make the space feel safer. They do not ... they make a space feel isolated and gloomy. Lesser defensive measures can work almost as much damage. The front rows of a space – whether ledges or steps or benches – are the best of sitting places, yet they are often modified against human use. At the General Motors Building on Fifth Avenue, the front ledges face out on one of the greatest of promenades. But you cannot sit on the ledges for more than a minute or so. There is a fussy little railing that catches you right in the small of your back. I do not think it was deliberately planned to do so. But it does and you cannot sit for more than a few moments before your back hurts. Another two inches of clearance for the railing and you would be comfortable. But day after day, year after year, one of the great front rows goes scarcely used, for want of two inches. Canted ledges, especially ones of polished marble, are another nullifying feature. You can almost sit on them if you keep pressing down on your heel hard enough.

[...]

A good space beckons people in, and the progression from street to interior is critical in this respect. Ideally, the transition should be such that it's hard to tell where one ends and the other begins. You shouldn't have to make a considered decision to enter; it should be almost instinctive...

[...]

CHRISTOPHER ALEXANDER

"A City Is Not a Tree"

Architectural Forum (1965)

Editors' introduction   Many design professionals admire and attempt to incorporate into their designs for the built environment elements reflecting underlying human psychological and spiritual needs and cultural values. But none has broken so completely with conventional architectural practice and sought more deeply to make his designs reflect these fundamental values than Austrian-born, British-trained, U.S.-based architect/planner Christopher Alexander.

Alexander is a self-proclaimed iconoclast, deliberately distancing himself from virtually all the major mainstream currents of twentieth-century architectural and planning thought. It is notable that the eight "treelike" plans he singles out for attack in the following selection represent a diverse set of the most respected and famous twentieth-century plans from Le Corbusier's plan for the new town of Chandigarh, India, based on his principles for a contemporary city (p. 368), to Paolo Soleri's visionary megastructure of Mesa City in the Arizona desert (p. 454).

Since publication of his provocative early attack on the sterility of formal "treelike" city plans in the following selection, Alexander has been engaged in a lifelong search to decipher the deep structures underlying human needs and to define recurring patterns for a new paradigm of architecture. The following selection is clear that a city should *not* be designed with a neatly branching treelike organization dividing functions from each other. Alexander condemns tidy city plans which lay out discretely bounded neighborhoods, zone one area for housing and another for business, or establish areas just for universities or cultural facilities. He sees human activity as much more complex and overlapping than that.

Alexander's approach to describing how cities *should* be designed in this selection may trouble readers who seek clear, rational guidelines. He takes the position that not enough is yet known about how to design non-treelike cities to provide definite answers. Like an artist or a Zen master instructing an apprentice, Alexander closes this selection with provocative analogies, examples, and metaphors. He suggests how an individual might pursue the quest for good design, but he does not offer a stock set of the answers.

During the past three decades Alexander and his colleagues and students at the Center for Environmental Structure at the University of California, Berkeley have conducted a series of "experiments" working to understand and demonstrate how to design cities which are not "trees." Alexander's writings since "A City Is Not a Tree" provide an abundance of specific principles and examples as well as many more unanswered questions and lines for exploration.

While Alexander is fascinated with physical form, his approach begins with an interactive process working with clients to understand their most fundamental needs. Profoundly respectful of the ideas of clients, Alexander's projects incorporate rammed earth and chicken wire into housing for Mexicali slum dwellers and Zen architectural details into a Japanese school. He and his followers seek architecture which is "alive"; architecture that possesses "the quality without a name."

Consider the relevance of J. B. Jackson's description of how the informal vernacular architecture of small U.S. towns meets human needs (p. 82) to Alexander's conviction that built environments that grow organically contain important lessons for planners. Alexander shares architectural critic Jane Jacobs's love of apparently chaotic, jumbled urban neighborhoods. Like Jacobs he sees a complex order and rationality behind an apparently disorderly facade. Consider Alexander's concept of a semi-lattice structure in relation to Jacobs's argument for designing streets to provide play space for children, security, and areas for human interaction as well as space for cars to drive (p. 104). A casual observer might consider the resulting street a confused and disorderly one. She might not see how it meets multiple, complex human needs. Alexander would like to help architects and planners design streets which achieve the positive qualities of lively streets in New York's Greenwich Village or Boston's West End before urban renewal tidied up (and deadened) the streetscape. Note also the similarity to British architect/planner Raymond Unwin's respect for natural cities and for urban forms shaped by the ideas of their residents (p. 355).

Alexander's theories are developed in a series of books published by Oxford University Press in New York: *The Oregon Experiment* (1975), *A Pattern Language* (1977), *The Timeless Way of Building* (1979), *The Linz Cafe* (1981), *The Production of Houses* (1985), and *A New Theory of Urban Design* (1987). An overview of his work by Ingrid F. King is "Christopher Alexander and Contemporary Architecture" in *Architecture and Urbanism* (August 1993).

CHRISTOPHER ALEXANDER, "A City Is Not a Tree"
Architectural Forum (1965)

The tree of my title is not a green tree with leaves. It is the name for a pattern of thought. The semi-lattice is the name for another, more complex, pattern of thought.

In order to relate these abstract patterns to the nature of the city, I must first make a simple distinction. I want to call those cities which have arisen more or less spontaneously over many, many years *natural cities*. And I shall call those cities and parts of cities which have been deliberately created by designers and planners *artificial cities*. Siena, Liverpool, Kyoto, Manhattan are examples of natural cities. Levittown, Chandigarh, and the British New Towns are examples of artificial cities.

It is more and more widely recognized today that there is some essential ingredient missing from artificial cities. When compared with ancient cities that have acquired the patina of life, our modern attempts to create cities artificially are, from a human point of view, entirely unsuccessful.

Architects themselves admit more and more freely that they really like living in old buildings more than new ones. The non-art-loving public at large, instead of being grateful to architects for what they do, regards the onset of modern buildings and modern cities everywhere as an inevitable, rather sad piece of the larger fact that the world is going to the dogs.

It is much too easy to say that these opinions represent only people's unwillingness to forget the past, and their determination to be traditional. For myself, I trust this conservatism. Americans are usually willing to move with the times. Their growing reluctance to accept the modern city evidently expresses a longing for some real thing, something which for the moment escapes our grasp.

The prospect that we may be turning the world into a place peopled only by little glass and concrete boxes has alarmed many architects too. To combat the glass box future, many valiant protests and designs have been put forward, all hoping to recreate in modern form the various characteristics of the natural city which seem to give it life. But so far these designs have only remade the old. They have not been able to create the new.

"Outrage," the *Architectural Review*'s campaign against the way in which new construction and telegraph poles are wrecking the English town, based its remedies, essentially, on the idea that the spatial sequence of buildings and open spaces must be controlled if scale is to be preserved – an idea that really derives from Camillo Sitte's book about ancient squares and piazzas.

Another kind of remedy, in protest against the monotony of Levittown, tries to recapture the richness of shape found in the houses of a natural old town. Llewelyn Davies's village at Rushbrooke in England is an example – each cottage is slightly different from its neighbor, the roofs jut in and out at picturesque angles.

A third suggested remedy is to get high density back into the city. The idea seems to be that if the whole metropolis could only be like Grand Central Station, with lots and lots of layers and tunnels all over the place, and enough people milling around in them, maybe it would be human again.

Another very brilliant critic of the deadness which is everywhere is Jane Jacobs. Her criticisms are excellent. But when you read her concrete proposals for what we should do instead, you get the idea that she wants the great modern city to be a sort of mixture between Greenwich Village and some Italian hill town, full of short blocks and people sitting in the street.

The problem the designers have tried to face is real. It is vital that we discover the property of old towns which gave them life and get it back into our own artificial cities. But we cannot do this merely by remaking English villages, Italian piazzas, and Grand Central Stations. Too many designers today seem to be yearning for the physical and plastic characteristics of the past, instead of searching for the abstract ordering principle which the towns of the past happened to have, and which our modern conceptions of the city have not yet found.

What is the inner nature, the ordering principle, which distinguishes the artificial city from the natural city?

You will have guessed from my title what I believe this ordering principle to be. I believe that a natural city has the organization of a semi-lattice; but that when we organize a city artificially, we organize it as a tree.

Both the tree and the semi-lattice are ways of thinking about how a large collection of many small systems goes to make up a large and complex system. More generally, they are both names for structures of sets.

In order to define such structures, let me first define the concept of a set. A set is a collection of elements which for some reason we think of as belonging together. Since, as designers, we are concerned with the physical living city and its physical backbone, we most naturally restrict ourselves to considering sets which are collections of material elements such as people, blades of grass, cars, bricks, molecules, houses, gardens, water pipes, the water molecules that run in them, etc.

When the elements of a set belong together because they cooperate or work together somehow, we call the set of elements a system.

For example, in Berkeley at the corner of Hearst and Euclid, there is a drugstore, and outside the drugstore a traffic light. In the entrance to the drugstore there is a newsrack where the day's papers are displayed. When the light is red, people who are waiting to cross the street stand idly by the light; and since they have nothing to do, they look at the papers displayed on the newsrack which they can see from where they stand. Some of them just read the headlines, others actually buy a paper while they wait.

This effect makes the newsrack and the traffic light interdependent; the newsrack, the newspapers on it, the money going from people's pockets to the dime slot, the people who stop at the light and read papers, the traffic light, the electric impulses which make the lights change, and the sidewalk which the people stand on form a system – they all work together.

From the designer's point of view, the physically unchanging part of this system is of special interest. The newsrack, the traffic light, and the sidewalk between them, related as they are, form the fixed part of the system. It is the unchanging receptacle in which the changing parts of the system – people, newspapers, money, and electrical impulses – can work together. I define this fixed part as a unit of the city. It derives its coherence as a unit both from the forces which hold its own elements together, and from the dynamic coherence of the larger living system which includes it as a fixed invariant part.

Of the many, many fixed concrete subsets of the city which are the receptacles for its systems, and can therefore be thought of as significant physical units, we usually single out a few for special consideration. In fact, I claim that whatever picture of the city someone has is defined precisely by the subsets he sees as units.

Now, a collection of subsets which goes to make up such a picture is not merely an amorphous collection. Automatically, merely because relationships are established among the subsets once the subsets are chosen, the collection has a definite structure.

To understand this structure, let us think abstractly for a moment, using numbers as symbols. Instead of talking about the real sets of millions of real particles which occur in the city, let us consider a simpler structure made of just half a dozen elements. Label these elements 1, 2, 3, 4, 5, 6. Not including the full set [1, 2, 3, 4, 5, 6], the empty set [–], and the one-element sets [1], [2], [3], [4], [5], [6], there are 56 different subsets we can pick from six elements.

Suppose we now pick out certain of these 56 sets (just as we pick out certain sets and call them units when we form our picture of the city). Let us say, for example, that we pick the following subsets: [123], [34], [45], [234], [345], [12345], [3456].

What are the possible relationships among these sets? Some sets will be entirely part of larger sets, as [34] is part of [345] and [3456]. Some of the sets will overlap, like [123] and [234]. Some of the sets will be disjoint – that is,

contain no elements in common, like [123] and [45].

We can see these relationships displayed in two ways. In diagram A [Figure 1] each set chosen to be a unit has a line drawn round it. In diagram B the chosen sets are arranged in order of ascending magnitude, so that whenever one set contains another (as [345] contains [34]), there is a vertical path leading from one to the other. For the sake of clarity and visual economy, it is usual to draw lines only between sets which have no further sets and lines between them; thus the line between [34] and [345], and the line between [345] and [3456], make it unnecessary to draw a line between [34] and [3456].

As we see from these two representations, the choice of subsets alone endows the collection of subsets as a whole with an overall structure. This is the structure which we are concerned with here. When the structure meets certain conditions it is called a semi-lattice. When it meets other more restrictive conditions, it is called a tree.

The semi-lattice axiom goes like this: *A collection of sets forms a semi-lattice if and only if, when two overlapping sets belong to the collection, then the set of elements common to both also belongs to the collection.*

The structure illustrated in diagrams A and B is a semi-lattice. It satisfies the axiom since, for instance, [234] and [345] both belong to the collection, and their common part, [34], also belongs to it. (As far as the city is concerned, this axiom states merely that wherever two units overlap, the area of overlap is itself a recognizable entity and hence a unit also. In the case of the drugstore example, one unit consists of the newsrack, sidewalk, and traffic light. Another unit consists of the drug store itself, with its entry and the newsrack. The two units overlap in the newsrack. Clearly this area of overlap is itself a recognizable unit, and so satisfies the axiom above which defines the characteristics of a semi-lattice.)

The tree axiom states: *A collection of sets forms a tree if and only if, for any two sets that belong to the collection, either one is wholly contained in the other, or else they are wholly disjoint.*

The structure illustrated in diagrams C and D is a tree. Since this axiom excludes the possibility of overlapping sets, there is no way in which the semi-lattice axiom can be violated, so that every tree is a trivially simple semi-lattice.

However, in this paper we are not so much concerned with the fact that a tree happens to be a semi-lattice, but with the difference between trees and those more general semi-lattices which are *not* trees because they *do* contain overlapping units. We are concerned with the difference between structures in which no overlap occurs, and those structures in which overlap does occur.

It is not merely the overlap which makes the distinction between the two important. Still more important is the fact that the semi-lattice is potentially a much more complex and subtle structure than a tree. We may see just how much more complex a semi-lattice can be than a tree

in the following fact: a tree based on 20 elements can contain at most 19 further subsets of the 20, while a semi-lattice based on the same 20 elements can contain more than 1,000,000 different subsets.

This enormously greater variety is an index of the great structural complexity a semi-lattice can have when compared with the structural simplicity of a tree. It is this lack of structural complexity, characteristic of trees, which is crippling our conceptions of the city.

To demonstrate, let us look at some modern conceptions of the city, each of which I shall show to be essentially a tree. It will perhaps be useful, while we look at these plans, to have a little ditty in our minds:

Big fleas have little fleas
Upon their back to bite 'em,
Little fleas have lesser fleas,
And so ad infinitum.

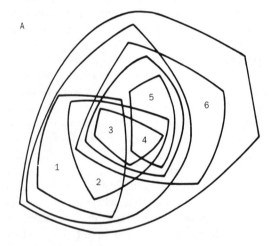

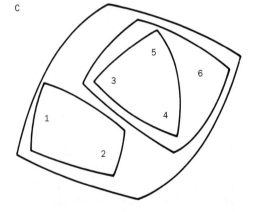

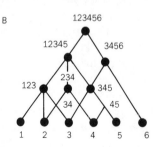

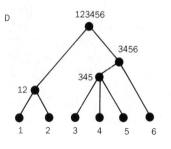

Figure 1

This rhyme expresses perfectly and succinctly the structural principle of the tree.

[Alexander discusses Columbia, Maryland, and seven other city plans by famous architects and planners: Greenbelt, Maryland (Clarence Stein), Greater London (Abercrombie and Forshaw), Tokyo (Kenzo Tange), Mesa City (Paolo Soleri), Chandigarh (Le Corbusier), Brasilia (Lucio Costa), and Communitas (Paul and Percival Goodman).]

The most beautiful example of all I have kept until last, because it symbolizes the problem perfectly. It appears in Hilberseimer's book called *The Nature of Cities*. He describes the fact that certain Roman towns had their origin as military camps, and then shows a picture of a modern military encampment as a kind of archetypal form for the city. It is not possible to have a structure which is a clearer tree.

The symbol is apt, for, of course, the organization of the army was created precisely in order to create discipline and rigidity. When a city is endowed with a tree structure, this is what happens to the city and its people. Hilberseimer's own scheme for the commercial area of a city is based on the army camp archetype.

Each of these structures, then, is a tree. Each unit in each tree that I have described, moreover, is the fixed, unchanging residue of some system in the living city (just as a house is the residue of the interactions between the members of a family, their emotions, and their belongings; and a freeway is the residue of movement and commercial exchange).

However, in every city there are thousands, even millions, of times as many more systems at work whose physical residue does not appear as a unit in these tree structures. In the worst cases, the units which do appear fail to correspond to any living reality; and the real systems, whose existence actually makes the city live, have been provided with no physical receptacle.

[...]

In a traditional society, if we ask a man to name his best friends and then ask each of these in turn to name their best friends, they will all name each other so that they form a closed group. A village is made of a number of separate closed groups of this kind.

But today's social structure is utterly different. If we ask a man to name his friends and then ask them in turn to name their friends, they will all name different people, very likely unknown to the first person; these people would again name others, and so on outwards. There are virtually no closed groups of people in modern society. The reality of today's social structure is thick with overlap – the systems

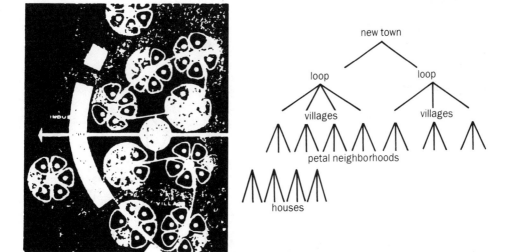

Figure 2 Columbia, Maryland, Community Research and Development Inc.: Neighborhoods, in clusters of five, form "villages." Transportation joins the villages into a new town. The organization is a tree.

of friends and acquaintances form a semi-lattice, not a tree (Figure 3).

In the natural city, even the house on a long street (not in some little cluster) is a more accurate acknowledgement of the fact that your friends live not next door, but far away, and can only be reached by bus or automobile. In this respect Manhattan has more overlap in it than Greenbelt. And though one can argue that in Greenbelt too, friends are only minutes away by car, one must then ask: since certain groups *have* been emphasized by the physical units of the physical structure, why are just these the most irrelevant ones?

In the second part of this paper, I shall further demonstrate why the living city cannot be properly contained in a receptacle which is a tree – that indeed, its very life stems from the fact that it is not a tree.

Finally, I shall try to show that it is the process of thought itself which works in a treelike way, so that whenever a city is "thought out" instead of "grown," it is bound to get a treelike structure.

In the first part of this article, we saw that the units of which an artificial city is made up are organized to form a tree. So that we get a really clear understanding of what this means, and shall better see its implications, let us define a tree once again.

Whenever we have a tree structure, it means that within this structure no piece of any unit is ever connected to other units, except through the medium of that unit as a whole.

The enormity of this restriction is difficult to grasp. It is a little as though the members of a family were not free to make friends outside the family, except when the family as a whole made a friendship.

In simplicity of structure the tree is comparable to the compulsive desire for neatness and order that insists the candlesticks on a mantlepiece be perfectly straight and perfectly symmetrical about the center. The semi-lattice, by comparison, is the structure of a complex fabric; it is the structure of living things; of great paintings and symphonies.

It must be emphasized, lest the orderly mind shrink in horror from anything that is not clearly articulated and categorized in tree form, that the idea of overlap, ambiguity, multiplicity of aspect, and the semi-lattice, are not less orderly than the rigid tree, but more so. They represent a thicker, tougher, more subtle and

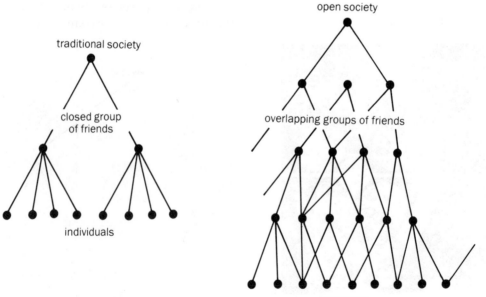

Figure 3

more complex view of structure.

Let us now look at the ways in which the natural, when unconstrained by artificial conceptions, shows itself to be a semi-lattice.

A major aspect of the city's social structure which a tree can never mirror properly is illustrated by Ruth Glass's redevelopment plan for Middlesborough, a city of 200,000 which she recommends be broken down into 29 separate neighborhoods. After picking her 29 neighborhoods by determining where the sharpest discontinuities of building type, income, and job type occur, she asks herself the question: "If we examine some of the social systems which actually exist for the people in such a neighborhood, do the physical units defined by these various social systems all define the same spatial neighborhood?" Her own answer to this question is *no*.

Each of the social systems she examines is a nodal system. It is made of some sort of central node, plus the people who use this center. Specifically she takes elementary schools, secondary schools, youth clubs, adult clubs, post offices, greengrocers', and grocers' selling sugar. Each of these centers draws its users from a certain spatial area or spatial unit. This spatial unit is the physical residue of the social system as a whole, and is therefore a unit in the terms of this paper. The units corresponding to different kinds of centers for the single neighborhood of Waterloo Road are shown in Figure 4. The hard outline is the boundary of the so-called neighborhood itself. The white circle stands for the youth club, and the small solid rings stand for areas where its members live. The ringed spot is the adult club, and the homes of its members form the unit marked by dashed boundaries. The white square is the post office and the dotted line marks the unit which contains its users. The secondary school is marked by the spot with a black triangle in it. Together with its pupils, it forms the system marked by the dot-dashed line.

As you can see at once, the different units do not coincide. Yet neither are they disjoint. They overlap.

We cannot get an adequate picture of what Middlesborough is, or of what it ought to be, in terms of 29 large and conveniently integral

chunks called neighborhoods. When we describe the city in terms of neighborhoods, we implicitly assume that the smaller elements within any one of these neighborhoods belong together so tightly that they interact with elements in other neighborhoods only through the medium of the neighborhood to which they themselves belong. Ruth Glass herself shows clearly that this is not the case.

Below [Figure 5] are two pictures of the Waterloo neighborhood. For the sake of argument I have broken it into a number of small areas. [The left-hand diagram] shows how these pieces stick together in fact, and [the right-hand diagram] shows how the redevelopment plan pretends they stick together.

There is nothing in the nature of the various

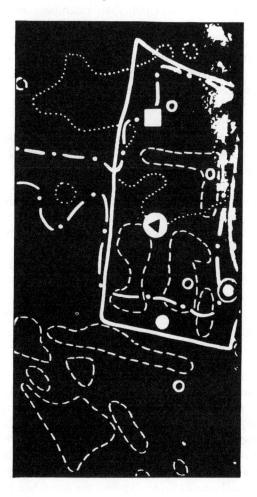

Figure 4

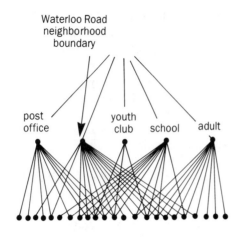
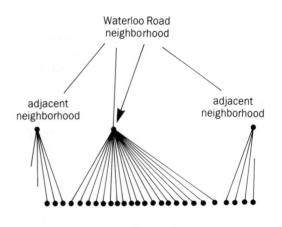
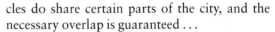

Figure 5

centers which says that their catchment areas should be the same. Their natures are different. Therefore the units they define are different. The natural city of Middlesborough was faithful to the semi-lattice structure they have. Only in the artificial tree conception of the city are their natural, proper, and necessary overlaps destroyed.

Take the separation of pedestrians from moving vehicles, a tree concept proposed by Le Corbusier, Louis Kahn, and many others. At a very crude level of thought this is obviously a good idea. It is dangerous to have 60-mile-an-hour cars in contact with little children toddling. But it is not *always* a good idea. There are times when the ecology of a situation actually demands the opposite. Imagine yourself coming out of a Fifth Avenue store; you have been shopping all afternoon; your arms are full of parcels; you need a drink; your wife is limping. Thank God for taxis.

Yet the urban taxi can function only because pedestrians and vehicles are not strictly separated. The prowling taxi needs a fast stream of traffic so that it can cover a large area to be sure of finding a passenger. The pedestrian needs to be able to hail the taxi from any point in the pedestrian world, and to be able to get out to any part of the pedestrian world to which he wants to go. The system which contains the taxicabs needs to overlap both the fast vehicular traffic system and the system of pedestrian circulation. In Manhattan pedestrians and vehi-

cles do share certain parts of the city, and the necessary overlap is guaranteed . . .

Another favorite concept of the CIAM theorists and others is the separation of recreation from everything else. This has crystallized in our real cities in the form of playgrounds. The playground, asphalted and fenced in, is nothing but a pictorial acknowledgment of the fact that "play" exists as an isolated concept in our minds. It has nothing to do with the life of play itself. Few self-respecting children will even play in a playground.

Play itself, the play that children practice, goes on somewhere different every day. One day it may be indoors, another day in a friendly gas station, another day down by the river, another day in a derelict building, another day on a construction site which has been abandoned for the weekend. Each of these play activities, and the objects it requires, forms a system. It is not true that these systems exist in isolation, cut off from the other systems in the city. The different systems overlap one another, and they overlap many other systems besides. The units, the physical places recognized as play places, must do the same.

In a natural city this is what happens. Play takes place in a thousand places – it fills the interstices of adult life. As they play, children become full of their surroundings. How can a child become filled with his surroundings in a fenced enclosure? He cannot.

A similar kind of mistake occurs in trees like

that of Goodman's Communitas, or Soleri's Mesa City, which separate the university from the rest of the city. Again, this has actually been realized in common American form of the isolated campus.

What is the reason for drawing a line in the city so that everything within the boundary is university, and everything outside is non-university? It is conceptually clear. But does it correspond to the realities of university life? Certainly it is not the structure which occurs in non-artificial university cities.

Take Cambridge University, for instance. At certain points Trinity Street is physically almost indistinguishable from Trinity College. One pedestrian crossover in the street is literally part of the college. The buildings on the street, though they contain stores and coffee shops and banks at ground level, contain undergraduates' rooms in their upper stories. In many cases the actual fabric of the street buildings melts into the fabric of the old college buildings so that one cannot be altered without the other.

There will always be many systems of activity where university life and city life overlap: pub-crawling, coffee-drinking, the movies, walking from place to place. In some cases whole departments may be actively involved in the life of the city's inhabitants (the hospital-cum-medical school is an example). In Cambridge, a natural city where university and city have grown together gradually, the physical units overlap because they are the physical residues of city systems and university systems which overlap (Figure 6).

Let us look next at the hierarchy of urban cores, realized in Brasilia, Chandigarh, the MARS plan for London, and, most recently, in the Manhattan Lincoln Center, where various performing arts serving the population of greater New York have been gathered together to form just one core.

Does a concert hall ask to be next to an Opera House? Can the two feed on one another? Will anybody ever visit them both, gluttonously, in a single evening, or even buy tickets from one after going to a concert in the other? In Vienna, London, Paris, each of the performing arts has found its own place, because all are not mixed randomly. Each has

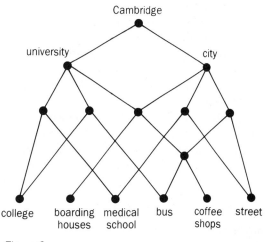

Figure 6

created its own familiar section of the city. In Manhattan itself, Carnegie Hall and the Metropolitan Opera House were not built side by side. Each found its own place, and now creates its own atmosphere. The influence of each overlaps the parts of the city which have been made unique to it.

The only reason that these functions have all been brought together in the Lincoln Center is that the concept of performing art links them to one another.

But this tree, and the idea of a single hierarchy of urban cores which is its parent, do not illuminate the relations between art and city life. They are merely born of the mania every simple-minded person has for putting things with the same name into the same basket.

The total separation of work from housing, started by Tony Garnier in his industrial city, then incorporated in the 1929 Athens Charter, is now found in every artificial city and accepted everywhere where zoning is enforced. Is this a sound principle? It is easy to see how bad conditions at the beginning of the century prompted planners to try to get the dirty factories out of residential areas. But the separation misses a variety of systems which require, for their sustenance, little parts of both.

Jane Jacobs describes the growth of backyard industries in Brooklyn. A man who wants to start a small business needs space, which he is very likely to have in his own backyard. He also needs to establish connections with larger going enterprises and with their customers. This means that the system of backyard industry needs to belong both to the residential zone, and to the industrial zone – these zones need to overlap. In Brooklyn they do . . . In a city which is a tree, they can't.

Finally, let us examine the subdivision of the city into isolated communities. As we have seen in the Abercrombie plan for London, this is itself a tree structure. The individual community in a greater city has no reality as a functioning unit. In London, as in any great city, almost no one manages to find work which suits him near his home. People in one community work in a factory which is very likely to be in another community.

There are, therefore, many hundreds of thousands of worker–workplace systems, each consisting of a man plus the factory he works in, which cut across the boundaries defined by Abercrombie's tree. The existence of these units, and their overlapping nature, indicates that the living systems of London form a semi-lattice. Only in the planner's mind has it become a tree.

The fact that we have so far failed to give this any physical expression has a vital consequence. As things are, whenever the worker and his workplace belong to separately administered municipalities, the community which contains the workplace collects huge taxes and has relatively little on which to spend the tax revenue. The community where the worker lives, if it is mainly residential, collects only little in the way of taxes, and yet has great additional burdens on its purse in the shape of schools, hospitals, etc. Clearly, to resolve this inequity, the worker–workplace systems must be anchored in physically recognizable units of the city which can then be taxed.

[. . .]

Now, why is it that so many designers have conceived cities as trees when the natural structure is in every case a semi-lattice? Have they done so deliberately, in the belief that a tree structure will serve the people of the city better? Or have they done it because they cannot help it, because they are trapped by a mental habit, perhaps even trapped by the way the mind works; because they cannot encompass the complexity of a semi-lattice in any convenient mental form; because the mind has an overwhelming predisposition to see trees wherever it looks and cannot escape the tree conception?

I shall try to convince you that it is for this second reason that trees are being proposed and built as cities – that it is because designers, limited as they must be by the capacity of the mind to form intuitively accessible structures, cannot achieve the complexity of the semi-lattice in a single mental act.

Let me begin with an example.

Suppose I ask you to remember the following four objects: an orange, a watermelon, a football, and a tennis ball. How will you keep them in your mind, in your mind's eyes? However you do it, you will do it by grouping them. Some of you will take the two fruits together, the orange and the watermelon, and the two sports balls together, the football and the tennis ball. Those of you who tend to think in terms of physical shape may group them differently, taking the two small spheres together – the orange and the tennis ball – and the two larger and more egg-shaped objects – the watermelon and the football. Some of you will be aware of both.

Let us make a diagram of these groupings (Figure 7).

Either grouping taken by itself is a tree structure. The two together are a semi-lattice. Now let us try to visualize these groupings in the mind's eye. I think you will find that you cannot visualize all four sets simultaneously – because they overlap. You can visualize one pair of sets and then the other, and you can alternate between the two pairs extremely fast, so fast that you may deceive yourself into thinking you can visualize them all together. But in truth, you cannot conceive all four sets at once in a single mental act. You cannot bring the semi-lattice structure into a visualizable form for a single mental act. In a single mental act you can only visualize a tree.

This is the problem we face as designers. While we are not, perhaps, necessarily occupied with the problem of total visualization as a single mental act the principle is still the same.

The tree is accessible mentally, and easy to deal with. The semi-lattice is hard to keep before the mind's eye, and therefore hard to deal with.

It is known today that grouping and categorization are among the most primitive psychological processes. Modern psychology treats thought as a process of fitting new situations into existing slots and pigeonholes in the mind. Just as you cannot put a physical thing into more than one physical pigeonhole at once, so, by analogy, the processes of thought prevent you from putting a mental construct into more than one mental category at once. Study of the origin of these processes suggests that they stem essentially from the organism's need to read the complexity of its environment by establishing barriers between the different events which it encounters.

It is for this reason – because the mind's first function is to reduce the ambiguity and overlap in a confusing situation, and because to this end it is endowed with a basic intolerance for ambiguity – that structures like the city, which do require overlapping sets within them, are nevertheless persistently conceived as trees.

[...]

You are no doubt wondering, by now, what a city looks like which is a semi-lattice, but not a tree. I must confess that I cannot yet show you plans or sketches. It is not enough merely to make a demonstration of overlap – the overlap must be the right overlap. This is doubly important, because it is so tempting to make plans in which overlap occurs for its own sake. This is essentially what the high-density "life-filled" city plans of recent years do. But overlap alone does not give structure. It can also give chaos. A garbage can is full of overlap. To have structure, you must have

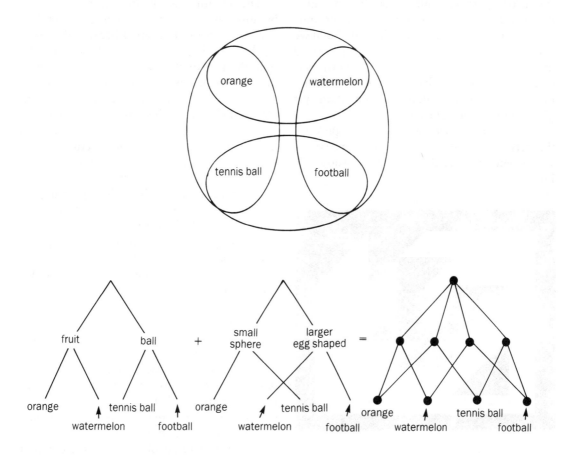

Figure 7

the right overlap, and this is for us almost certainly different from the old overlap which we observe in historic cities. As the relationships between functions change, so the systems which need to overlap in order to receive these relationships must also change. The re-creation of old kinds of overlap will be inappropriate, and chaotic instead of structured.

The work of trying to understand just what overlap the modern city requires, and trying to put this required overlap into physical and plastic terms, is still going on. Until the work is complete, there is no point in presenting facile sketches of ill thought out structure.

However, I can perhaps make the physical consequences of overlap more comprehensible by means of an image. The painting illustrated is a ... work by Simon Nicholson (Figure 8). The fascination of this painting lies in the fact that although it is constructed of rather few simple triangular elements, these elements unite in many different ways to form the larger units of the painting – in such a way, indeed, that if we make a complete inventory of the perceived units in the painting, we find that each triangle enters into four or five completely different kinds of unit, none contained in the others, yet all overlapping in that triangle.

Thus, if we number the triangles and pick out the sets of triangles which appear as strong visual units, we get the semi-lattice shown in Figure 9.

Figure 8

[Triangles] 3 and 5 form a unit because they work together as a rectangle; 2 and 4 because they form a parallelogram; 5 and 6 because they are both dark and pointing the same way; 6 and 7 because one is the ghost of the other shifted sideways; 4 and 7 because they are symmetrical with one another; 4 and 6 because they form another rectangle; 4 and 5 because they form a sort of Z; 2 and 3 because they form a rather thinner kind of Z; 1 and 7 because they are at opposite corners; 1 and 2 because they are a rectangle; 3 and 4 because they point the same way as 5 and 6, and form a sort of off-center reflection; 3 and 6 because they enclose 4 and 5; 1 and 5 because they enclose 2, 3, and 4. I have only listed the units of two triangles. The larger units are even more complex. The white is more complex still, and is not even included in the diagram because it is harder to be sure of its elementary pieces.

The painting is significant, not so much because it has overlap in it (many paintings have overlap in them), but rather because this painting has nothing else in it except overlap. It is only the fact of the overlap, and the resulting multiplicity of aspects which the forms present, that makes the painting fascinating. It seems almost as though the painter had made an explicit attempt, as I have done, to single out overlap as a vital generator of structures.

All the artificial cities I have described have the structure of a tree rather than the semi-lattice structure of the Nicholson painting. Yet it is the painting, and other images like it, which must be our vehicles for thought. And when we wish to be precise, the semi-lattice, being part of a large branch of modern mathematics, is a powerful way of exploring the structure of these images. It is the semi-lattice we must look for, not the tree.

When we think in terms of trees we are trading the humanity and richness of the living city for the conceptual simplicity which benefits only designers, planners, administrators and developers. Every time a piece of a city is torn out, and a tree made to replace the semi-lattice that was there before, the city takes a further step toward dissociation.

In any organized object, extreme compartmentalization and the dissociation of internal

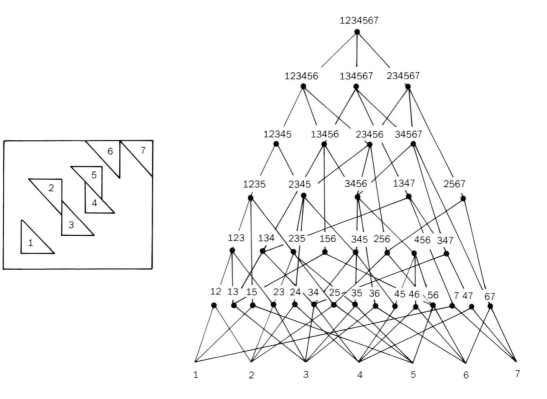

Figure 9

elements are the first signs of coming destruction. In a society, dissociation is anarchy. In a person, dissociation is the mark of schizophrenia and impending suicide. An ominous example of a city-wide dissociation is the separation of retired people from the rest of urban life, caused by the growth of desert cities for the old such as Sun City, Arizona. This separation is possible only under the influence of tree-like thought.

It not only takes from the young the company of those who have lived long, but, worse, causes the same rift inside each individual life. As you will pass into Sun City, and into old age, your ties with your own past will be unacknowledged, lost, and therefore broken. Your youth will no longer be alive in your old age – the two will be dissociated, your own life will be cut in two.

For the human mind, the tree is the easiest vehicle for complex thoughts. But the city is not, cannot, and must not be a tree. The city is a receptacle for life. If the receptacle severs the overlap of the strands of life within it, because it is a tree, it will be like a bowl full of razor blades on edge, ready to cut up whatever is entrusted to it. In such a receptacle life will be cut to pieces. If we make cities which are trees, they will cut our life within to pieces.

IAN McHARG

"Nature in the Metropolis"

from *Design with Nature* (1969)

Editors' introduction   When it appeared in 1969, Ian McHarg's *Design with Nature* was the right book at the right time. A strong worldwide environmental movement had taken hold in the late 1960s, and ecologically oriented activists and professionals were searching for a book that was both visionary and practical, a work that combined their passion to protect the natural environment with sound scholarship and practical advice. McHarg's vision, scholarship, and technique all resonated, and continue to resonate, with a large audience.

McHarg is a professor of landscape architecture and regional planning at the University of Pennsylvania. Growing up near Glasgow, Scotland, during the Great Depression of the 1930s, McHarg was overwhelmed by the contrast between much of urban Glasgow ("despondent, dreary beyond description, grimy, gritty, squalid, enduringly ugly and dispiriting") and the exhilaration and joy he felt rambling among the wheat and barley fields, meadows and marshes, and hawthorn hedges of the adjacent Scottish countryside. Resolving as a teenager to become a landscape architect, McHarg eventually studied landscape architecture and city planning at Harvard and became a practitioner and professor of landscape architecture and planning with the intention of bringing some of the natural beauty he had experienced in the Scottish countryside into cities which could otherwise be industrial wastelands.

McHarg has an ability to combine technical detail with broad basic principles for designing the built environment harmoniously with nature and good old-fashioned common sense. Even the most elementary principles he lays out were routinely ignored at the time he wrote *Design with Nature*. It makes sense to spare the best agricultural soil of a region from development, locate factories where prevailing winds will not blow pollutants into cities, make sure aquifers do not get contaminated so that the drinking water for an entire region is unsafe, and leave grass to protect shorefront sand dunes from erosion when new developments are being built in sensitive coastal areas. In some cases humans have been so inattentive to the natural environment that they ignored even these basic principles. In other cases competing economic values have led developers to develop unwisely even when they knew of the risks that ignoring the natural environment could have. Careful planning and the deployment of technical expertise can flesh out exactly what is needed to make these principles work, but deciding to abide by the basic principles is plain common sense.

Since publication of *Design with Nature*, an entire field of environmental impact analysis and planning has developed. Thousands of planners have read McHarg and incorporated his approach into their environmental impact statements, studies, and plans. Physical city and regional planning of all kinds incorporates environmental values to a much greater extent than before *Design with Nature*. McHarg can take satisfaction from the fact that the worst abuses he discusses now occur much less frequently. But much remains to be done.

Environmental planning promises to remain a battleground in the twenty-first century. Private economic interests often have much to gain – at least individually and in the short term – from practices which may be environmentally damaging to the public interest in the long run. Political structures are often too pliable to heed sound planning advice even when it is offered. And there are real trade-offs between environmental values and society's need for economic growth, affordable housing, and efficient transit. Communities of color are particularly vulnerable. Toxic dumpsites and polluting factories are often located in neighborhoods insufficiently politically powerful to protect themselves. Today, the environmental justice movement is blending McHarg's principles with concerns from the civil rights and antipoverty movements. Many communities of color are mobilizing to make sure contaminated sites are cleaned up and kept from being used as dumping grounds in the future.

McHarg builds on the ideas of his countryman, Patrick Geddes (p. 361), who emphasized the importance of surveying the physical environment as a first step in comprehensive planning. He shares with Frederick Law Olmsted (p. 338) a profound belief in the power of nature to elevate the human spirit. Like his colleague and friend Lewis Mumford (p. 184), who wrote a laudatory introduction to *Design with Nature*, McHarg is an unabashed regionalist, convinced that cities must be planned in relation to their natural regions. He is among the first planners to draw on ecological theory to stress the interconnectedness of natural systems and the value to urban areas of often ignored resources such as wetlands, marshes, airsheds, and aquifers.

This selection is taken from *Design with Nature* (Garden City, NY: Doubleday, 1969). Books describing environmental planning include William Marsh, *Landscape Planning: Environmental Applications* (New York: Wiley, 1983), Leonard Ortolano, *Environmental Planning and Decision Making* (New York: Wiley, 1984), and W. E. Westman, *Ecology, Impact Assessment, and Environmental Planning* (New York: Wiley, 1985). For a retrospective of the life and work of Ian McHarg see *Ian McHarg, A Quest for Life: An Autobiography of Ian McHarg* (New York: Wiley, 1995). Also of interest are Mark Sagoff, *The Economy of the Earth* (Cambridge: Cambridge University Press, 1988), and T. O'Riordan, *Environmentalism* (London: Pion, 2nd edn. 1981).

IAN McHARG, "Nature in the Metropolis"

from *Design With Nature* (1969)

[...]

Some years ago I was asked to advise on which lands in the Philadelphia metropolitan region should be selected for open space. It became clear at the onset that the solution could only be obscured by limiting open space to the arena for organized sweating; it seemed more productive to consider the place of nature in the metropolis. In order to conclude on this place it appeared reasonable to suggest that nature performed work for man without his investment and that such work did represent a value. It also seemed reasonable to conclude that certain areas and natural processes were inhospitable to man – earthquake areas, hurricane paths, floodplains and the like – and that those should be prohibited or regulated to ensure public safety. This might seem a reasonable and prudent approach, but let us recognize that it is a rare one.

Consider that if you are required to design a flight of steps or a sidewalk there are clear and stringent regulations; there are constraints against the sale of cigarettes and alcohol to minors; society reacts sternly to the sale or use of narcotics; and there are strong laws to deter assault, rape and murder. And we should be thankful indeed for these protections. But there is no comparable concern, reflected in law, that ensures that your house is not built on a floodplain, on unconsolidated sediments, in an earthquake zone, hurricane path, fire-prone forest, or in areas liable to subsidence or mudslides.

While great efforts are made to ensure that you do not break an ankle, there are few deterrents to arrest the dumping of poisons into the sources of public water supply or their injection into groundwater resources. You are clearly protected from assault by fist, knife or gun, but not from the equally dangerous threats of hydrocarbons, lead, nitrous oxides, ozone or carbon monoxide in the atmosphere. There is no protection from the assaults of noise, glare and stress. So while a handrail may be provided for your safety and convenience by a considerate government, you may drown in a floodplain, suffer loss of life and property from inundation of coastal areas, or from an earthquake or hurricane; the damage or loss of life could be due to criminal negligence at worst and unpardonable ignorance at best, without the protection of governmental regulation or of laws.

It clearly should be otherwise; there is a need for simple regulations which ensure that society protects the values of natural processes and is itself protected. Conceivably such lands wherein exist these intrinsic values and constraints would provide the source of open space for metropolitan areas. If so, they would satisfy a double purpose: ensuring the operation of vital natural processes and employing lands unsuited to development in ways that would leave them unharmed by these often violent processes. Presumably, too, development would occur in areas that were intrinsically suitable, where dangers were absent and natural processes unharmed.

The formulation of these regulations requires no new science; we need move no nearer to the threshold of knowledge than the late nineteenth century. We can initially describe the major natural processes and their interactions and thereafter establish the degree to which these are permissive or prohibitive to certain land uses. This done, it will remain with the government and the courts to ensure our protection through the proper exercise of police power.

Before we move to this objective it is necessary to observe that there are two other views. They must be examined if only to be dismissed. The first is the economist's view of nature as a generally uniform commodity – appraised in terms of time, distance, cost of land and development and allocated in terms of acres per unit of population. Nature, of course, is not uniform but varies as a function of historical geology, climate, physiography, soils, plants, animals and – consequently – intrinsic resources and land uses. Lakes, rivers, oceans and mountains are not where the economist might want them to be, but are where they are for clear and comprehensible reasons. Nature is *intrinsically* variable.

The geometric planner offers another alternative, that the city be ringed with a green circle in which green activities – agriculture, institutions and the like – are preserved or even introduced. Such greenbelts, where enforced by law, do ensure the perpetuation of open space and in the absence of an alternative they are successful – but it appears that nature outside the belt is no different from that within, that the greenbelt need not be the most suitable location for the green activities of agriculture or recreation. The ecological method would suggest that the lands reserved for open space in the metropolitan region be derived from natural-process lands, intrinsically suitable for "green" purposes: that is the place of nature in the metropolis.

A single drop of water in the uplands of a watershed may appear and reappear as cloud, precipitation, surface water in creek and river, lake and pond or groundwater; it can participate in plant and animal metabolism, transpiration, condensation, decomposition, combustion, respiration and evaporation. This same drop of water may appear in considerations of climate and microclimate, water supply, flood, drought and erosion control, industry, commerce, agriculture, forestry, recreation, scenic beauty, in cloud, snow, stream, river and sea. We conclude that nature is a single interacting system and that changes to any part will affect the operation of the whole.

If we use water as an indicator of the interaction of natural processes, we see that the forests felled in the uplands may have an identical effect upon the incidence of flood that is accomplished by filling estuarine marshes. Pollution of groundwater may affect surface water resources and vice versa; urbanization will affect the rate of runoff, erosion and sedimentation, causing water turbidity, diminution of aquatic organisms, and a reduction in natural water purification. These, in turn, will result in channel dredging costs, increased water treatment costs and, possibly, flood damages and drought costs.

So we can say that terrestrial processes require water and that freshwater processes are indissoluble from the land. It then follows that land management will affect water, water management will affect land processes. We cannot follow the path of every drop of water, but we can select certain identifiable aspects: precipitation and runoff, surface water in streams and rivers, marshes and floodplains, groundwater resources in aquifers and the most critical phase of these – aquifer recharge. We can now formulate some simple propositions. Simple they are indeed – almost to the point of idiocy – but they are novelties of high sophistication to the planning process and the bulk of local governmental agencies.

Water quality and quantity are related to both land and water management. Floods are natural phenomena and reveal cyclical frequencies; healthy water bodies reduce organic matter and this varies with seasons, turbidity, dissolved oxygen, alkalinity, temperature, and the biotic population; erosion and sedimentation are natural but are accelerated by almost all human adaptations – on a uniform soil, normally the greater the slope, the more the erosion. Groundwater and surface water are interacting – in periods of low precipitation the water in rivers and streams is usually groundwater; soils vary

in their productivity for agriculture as a function of texture, organic matter, chemical composition, elevation, slope, and exposure. Marshes are flood storage areas, often aquifer recharges, the homes of wildfowl and both spawning and breeding grounds; the hinterland of a city is the source of the clean air that replaces the pollutants discharged by the city. The rural hinterland also contributes to a more temperate summer climate. Can we use this information to discriminate between lands that should remain in their natural condition, lands that are permissive to certain uses but not to others and those lands that are most tolerant to urbanization – free from danger, undamaging to other values?

But, first can we afford the indulgence of reserving natural-process lands and regulating development on them in order to capture their value? Indeed we can: land is abundant. According to the French urban geographer Jean Gottman, perhaps only 1.8 percent of the United States is urbanized today. Even within metropolitan regions, there is plenty of land. In the Philadelphia Standard Metropolitan Statistical Area, 3,500 square miles – less than 20 percent – is urbanized today and even should the population increase to 6,000,000, there would remain at that time 70 percent or 2,300 square miles of open land.

If so, wherein lies the problem? Simply in the form of growth. Urbanization proceeds by increasing the density within and extending the periphery, always at the expense of open space. As a result – unlike other facilities – open space is most abundant where people are scarcest. This growth, we have seen, is totally unresponsive to natural processes and their values. Optimally, one would wish for two systems within the metropolitan region – one the pattern of natural processes preserved in open space, the other the pattern of urban development. If these were interfused, one could satisfy the provision of open space for the population. The present method of growth continuously preempts the edge, causing the open space to recede from the population center. Geometrically, a solution is not unthinkable. If the entire area of the Philadelphia region were represented in a circle it would have a radius of 33 miles. Present urbanization can be encircled by a 15-mile radius. If all the existing and proposed urbanization for a six-million population and one acre of open space for every thirty persons is encircled, then the radius is 20 miles – only five miles more than the present.

But rather than propose a blanket standard of open space, we wish to find discrete aspects of natural processes that carry their own values and prohibitions: it is from these that open space should be selected, it is these that should provide the pattern, not only of metropolitan open space, but also the positive pattern of development. Later on we shall see that there are consistencies in land morphology, soils, stream patterns, plant association, wildlife habitats, and even land use, and that these can well be examined through the concept of the physiographic region. It is premature to employ this concept now. It is enough for the moment to insist that nature performs work for man – in many cases this is best done in a natural condition – further that certain areas are intrinsically suitable for certain uses while others are less so. We can begin with this simple proposition. Moreover, we can codify it. If we select eight dominant aspects of natural process and rank them in an order of both value and intolerance to human use and then reverse the order, it will be seen as a gross hierarchy of urban suitability.

However, there is an obvious conflict in this hierarchy. The flat land, so often selected for urbanization, is often as suitable for agriculture: this category will have to be looked at more carefully. So prime agricultural land will be identified as intolerant to urbanization and constituting a high social value; all other flat land will be assumed to have a low value in the natural-process scale and a high value for urban suitability.

Within the metropolitan region natural features will vary, but it is possible to select certain of these that exist throughout and determine the degree to which they allow or discourage contemplated land uses. While these terms are relative, optimally development should occur on valuable or perilous natural-process land only when superior values are created or compensation can be awarded.

A complete study would involve identifying natural processes that performed work for man, those which offered protection or were hostile, those which were unique or especially precious and those values which were vulnerable. In the first category fall natural water purification, atmospheric pollution dispersal, climatic amelioration, water storage, flood, drought and erosion control, topsoil accumulation, forest and wildlife inventory increase. Areas that provided protection or were dangerous would include the estuarine marshes and the floodplains, among others. The important areas of geological, ecological and historic interest would represent the next category, while beach dunes, spawning and breeding grounds and water catchment areas would be included in the vulnerable areas.

No such elaborate examination has been attempted in this study. However, eight natural processes have been identified and these have been mapped and measured. Each one has been described with an eye to permissiveness and prohibition to certain land uses. It is from this analysis that the place of nature in the metropolis will be derived.

Natural-process value: degree of intolerance	Intrinsic suitability for urban use
Surface water	Flat land
Marshes	Forests, woodlands
Floodplains	Steep slopes
Aquifer recharge areas	Aquifers
Aquifers	Aquifer recharge areas
Steep slopes	Floodplains
Forests, woodlands	Marshes
Flat land	Surface water

Surface water (5,671 linear miles)

In principle, only land uses that are inseparable from waterfront locations should occupy them; and even these should be limited to those which do not diminish the present or prospective value of surface water for supply, recreation or amenity. Demands for industrial waterfront locations in the region are extravagantly predicted as 50 linear miles. Thus, even if this demand is satisfied, five thousand miles could remain in a natural condition.

Land uses consonant with this principle would include port and harbor facilities, marinas, water and sewage treatment plants, water-related and, in certain cases, water-using industries. In the category of land uses that would not damage these water resources fall agriculture, forestry, recreation, institutional and residential open space.

Marshes (173,984 acres; 8.09 percent)

In principle, land-use policy for marshes should reflect the roles of flood and water storage, wildlife habitat and fish spawning grounds. Land uses that do not diminish the operation of the primary roles include recreation, certain types of agriculture (notably cranberry bogs) and isolated urban development.

Floodplains (339,706 acres; 15.8 percent)

Increasingly, the 50-year, or 2 percent, probability floodplain is being accepted as that area from which all development should be excluded save for functions which are unharmed by flooding or for uses that are inseparable from floodplains.

In the former category fall agriculture, forestry, recreation, institutional open space and open space for housing. In the category of land uses inseparable from floodplains are ports and harbors, marinas, water-related industry and – under certain circumstances – water-using industry.

Aquifers (181,792 acres; 8.3 percent)

An aquifer is a water-bearing stratum of rock, gravel or sand, a definition so general as to encompass enormous areas of land. In the region under study, the great deposits of porous material in the coastal plain are immediately distinguishable from all other aquifers in the region because of their extent and capacity. This may well be the single most important unexploited resource in the region. The aquifer parallel to Philadelphia in New Jersey has an estimated yield of one billion gallons per day. Clearly this valuable resource should not only be protected, but managed. Development that includes the disposal of toxic wastes, biological discharges or sewage should be prohibited. The use of injection wells, by which pollutants are disposed into aquifers, should be discontinued.

Development using sewers is clearly more satisfactory than septic tanks where aquifers can be contaminated, but it is well to recognize that even sewers leak significant quantities of material and are thus a hazard.

Land-use prescription is more difficult for aquifers than for any other category as these vary with respect to yield and quality, yet it is clear that agriculture, forestry, recreation and low-density development pose no danger to this resource while industry and urbanization in general do.

All prospective land uses should simply be examined against the degree to which they imperil the aquifer; those which do should be prohibited. It is important to recognize that aquifers may be managed effectively by the impoundment of rivers and streams that transect them.

Like many other cities, Philadelphia derives its water supply from major rivers which are foul. This water is elaborately disinfected and is potable. In contrast to the prevailing view that one should select dirty water for human consumption and make it safe by superchlorination, it seems preferable to select pure water in the first place. Such water is abundant in the existing aquifers; it must be protected from the fate of the rivers.

Aquifer recharge areas (118,896 acres;
6 percent)

As the name implies, such areas are the points of interchange between surface water and aquifers. In any system there are likely to be critical interchanges. It is the movement of ground to surface water that contributes water to rivers and streams in periods of low flow. Obviously the point of interchange is also a location where the normally polluted rivers may contaminate the relatively clean – and in many cases, pure – water resources in aquifers. These points of interchange are then critical for the management and protection of groundwater resources.

In the Philadelphia region the interchange between the Delaware River and its tributaries with the adjacent aquifers is the location of greatest importance. The Delaware is foul – frequently it has been observed to lack any dissolved oxygen and was then septic. However, a thick layer of silt, almost thirty feet deep, acts as a gasket and reduces the passage of the polluted river to the adjacent aquifer. It is where an aquifer is overlaid with porous material that percolation from the ground surface will recharge it.

These two considerations, then, should regulate management of these areas. By the careful separation of polluted rivers from the aquifer and by the impoundment of clean streams that transect it, the aquifer can be managed and recharged. By regulating land uses on those permeable surfaces that contribute to aquifer recharge, normal percolation will be allowed to continue.

Steep lands

Steep lands, and the ridges which they constitute, are central to the problems of flood control and erosion. Slopes in excess of 12° are not recommended for cultivation by the Soil Conservation Service. The same source suggests that, for reasons of erosion, these lands are unsuitable for development. The recommendations of the Soil Conservation Service are that steep slopes should be in forest and that their cultivation be abandoned.

The role of erosion control and diminution of the velocity of runoff is the principal problem here. Land uses compatible with this role would be mainly forestry and recreation, with low-density housing permitted on occasion.

Prime agricultural land (248,816 acres;
11.7 percent)

Prime agricultural soils represent the highest level of agricultural productivity; they are uniquely suitable for intensive cultivation with no conservation hazards. It is extremely difficult to defend agricultural lands when their cash value can be multiplied tenfold by employment for relatively cheap housing. Yet the farm is the basic factory – the farmer is the country's best landscape gardener and maintenance work force, the custodian of much scenic beauty. Mere market values of farmlands do not reflect the long-term value or the irreplaceable nature of these living soils. An omnibus protection of all farmland is difficult to defend; but protection of the best soils in a metropolitan area would appear not only defensible, but clearly desirable.

Jean Gottman has recommended that "the very good soils are not extensive enough in Megalopolis to be wastefully abandoned to non-agricultural uses." The soils Gottman had in mind are identical to the prime agricultural soils in the metropolitan area.

The farmer, displaced from excellent soils by urbanization, often moves to another site on inferior soils. Excellent soils lost to agriculture for building can finally only be replaced by bringing inferior soils into production. This requires capital investment. "Land that is not considered cropland today will become cropland tomorrow, but at the price of much investment."

In the Philadelphia Standard Metropolitan Statistical Area, by 1980 only 30 percent of the land area will be urbanized; 70 percent will remain open. Prime agricultural lands represent only 11.7 percent of the area. Therefore, given a choice prime soils should not be developed.

In principle, USDA Category 1 soils should be exempted from development (save by those functions that do not diminish their productive potential). This would suggest retirement of prime soils into forest or their utilization as open space – for institutions, for recreation or in development for housing at densities no higher than one house per 25 acres.

Forests and woodlands

The natural vegetative cover for most of this region is forest. Where present, it improves microclimate and it exercises a major balancing effect upon the water regimen, diminishing erosion, sedimentation, flood and drought. The scenic role of woodlands is apparent, as is their provision of a habitat for game; their recreational potential is among the highest of all categories. In addition, the forest is a low-maintenance, self-perpetuating landscape.

Forests can be employed for timber production, water management, wildlife habitats, as airsheds, recreation or for any combination of these uses. In addition, they can absorb development in concentrations to be determined by the demands of the natural process they are required to satisfy.

The resolution of atmospheric pollution depends mainly upon the reduction of pollution sources. While discussion of the subject increases in intensity, remedy shows no parallel acceleration, and it may be timely to consider one fact which, if recognized, can at least enhance the future possibility of solution. The city creates the filthy air. Clean air comes from the countryside. If we can identify the major wind directions, particularly those associated with inversion conditions, and ensure that pollution source industries are not located in these critical sectors of the urban hinterland, we will at least not exacerbate the situation.

The central phase of air pollution is linked to temperature inversion, during which the air near the ground does not rise to be replaced by in-moving air. Under inversion, characterized by clear nights with little wind, the earth is cooled by long-wave radiation and the air near the ground is cooled by the ground. During such temperature inversions with stable surface air layers, air movement is limited; in cities, pollution becomes increasingly concentrated. In Philadelphia "significant" inversions occur one night in three. Parallel and related to inversion is the incidence of high pollution levels, which occurred on twenty-four "episodes" of from two to five days' duration between 1957 and 1959. Inversions, then, are common, as are "high" levels of pollution. The danger attends their conjunction and persistence. Relief, other than elimination of pollution sources, is a function of wind movement to disperse pollution over cities and, secondly, the necessity that in-moving air be cleaner than the air it replaces.

The concentration of pollution sources in Philadelphia covers an area 15 miles by 10 miles with the long axis running approximately northeast. Let us assume sulfur dioxide to be the indicator of pollution (830 tons per day produced), an air height of 500 feet as the effective dimension and an air volume of approximately 15 cubic miles to be replaced by a wind speed of 4 m.p.h., selected as a critical speed. Then one cubic mile of ventilation is provided per mile of wind speed and it is seen to require $3\frac{3}{4}$ hours for wind movement to ventilate the long axis, $2\frac{1}{2}$ hours to ventilate the cross-axis. Thus, the tributary to ensure clean air on the long axis is 15 miles beyond the pollution area, 10 miles beyond for the cross-axis. The wind rose for Philadelphia during inversions shows that wind movements are preponderantly northwest, west, and southwest, contributing 51.2 percent of wind movements; the other five cardinal and intercardinal points represent the remainder.

This very approximate examination suggests that airsheds should extend from 10 to 15 miles beyond the urban air pollution sources in those wind directions to be anticipated during inversion. The width of these belts should correspond to the dimension of the pollution core and, in very approximate terms, would probably be from three to five miles. *Such areas, described as airshed, should be prohibited to pollution source industries.*

Under the heading of atmosphere the subject of climate and microclimate was raised. In the study area the major problem is summer heat and humidity. Relief of this condition responds to wind movements. Thus, a hinterland with more equable temperatures, particularly a lower summer temperature, is of importance to climate amelioration for the city. As we have seen, areas that are in vegetative cover, notably forests, are distinctly cooler than cities in summer – a margin of 10°F is not uncommon. Air movements over such areas moving into the city will bring cooler air. Relief from humidity also results mainly from air movements. These correspond to the directions important for relief of inversion. We can then say that the areas selected as urban airsheds are likely to be those selected as appropriate for amelioration of the urban microclimate. However, to clear air pollution by airsheds, it is important only that pollution sources be prohibited or limited. To relieve summer heat and humidity, it is essential that these airsheds be substantially in vegetative cover, preferably forested.

The satisfaction of these two requirements, in the creation of urban airsheds as responses to atmospheric pollution control and microclimate control, would create fingers of open space penetrating from the rural hinterland radially into the city. This is perhaps the broadest conception of natural process in metropolitan growth and metropolitan open-space distribution. Clearly, this proposal directs growth into the interstices between the airshed corridors and suggests that metropolitan open space exist within them.

Human adaptations entail both benefits and costs, but natural processes are generally not attributed values; nor is there a generalized accounting system, reflecting total costs and benefits. Natural processes are unitary whereas human interventions tend to be fragmentary and incremental. The effect of filling the estuarine marshes or felling the upland forests is not perceived as related to the water regimen – to flood or drought – nor are both activities seen to be similar in their effect. The construction of outlying suburbs and siltation of river channels are not normally understood to be related – nor is waste disposal into rivers perceived to be connected with the pollution of distant wells.

Several factors can be observed. Normal urban growth tends to be incremental and unrelated to natural processes on the site. But the aggregate consequences of such development are not calculated nor are they allocated as

costs to the individual developments. While benefits do accrue to certain developments that are deleterious to natural processes at large (for example, clear felling of forests or conversion of farmland into subdivisions), these benefits are *particular* (related, say, to that landowner who chooses to fell trees or sterilize soil), while the results and costs are general. Thus, costs and benefits are likely to be attributed to large numbers of different and unrelated persons, corporations and levels of government. It is unlikely that long-term benefits accrue from disdain of natural process; it is quite certain and provable that substantial costs *do* result from this disdain. Finally, in general, any benefits that do occur – usually economic – tend to accrue to the private sector, while remedies and long-range costs are usually the responsibility of the public domain.

The purpose of this exploration is to show that natural process, unitary in character, must be so considered in the planning process: that changes to parts of the system affect the entire system, that natural processes do represent values and that these values should be incorporated into a single accounting system. It is unfortunate that the information we have on cost–benefit ratios of specific interventions to natural process is inadequate. However, certain generalized relationships have been shown and presumptions advanced as the basis for judgment. It seems clear that laws pertaining to land use and development need to be elaborated to reflect the public costs and consequences of private action. Present land-use regulations neither recognize natural processes – the public good in terms of flood, drought, water quality, agriculture, amenity or recreational potential – nor allocate responsibility to the acts of landowner or developer.

We have seen that land is abundant, even within a metropolitan region confronting accelerated growth. There is, then, at least hypothetically, the opportunity for choice as to the location of development and open space.

The hypothesis, central to this study, is that the distribution of open space must respond to natural process. This conception should hold true for any metropolitan area, irrespective of location. In this particular case study, directed to the Philadelphia Metropolitan Region, an attempt has been made to focus on the fundamental natural processes that show the greatest relevance to the problem of determining the form of metropolitan growth and open space.

The problem lies not in absolute area but in distribution. We seek a concept that can provide an interfusion of open space and population. The low attributed value of open space ensures that it is transformed into urban use within the urban area and at the perimeter. Customary urbanization excludes interfusion and consumes peripheral open space.

Yet as the area of a circle grows with the square of the radius, large open-space increments can exist within the urban perimeter without major increase to the radius or to the time distance from city center to urban fringe.

This case study reveals the application of the ecological view to the problem of selecting open space in a metropolitan region. For the moment, it is enough to observe that this view could considerably enhance the present mode of planning, which disregards natural processes all but completely and which, in selecting open space, is motivated more by standards of acres per thousand for organized sweating than by a concern for the place and face of nature in the metropolis.

DOLORES HAYDEN

"What Would a Non-sexist City Be Like? Speculations on Housing, Urban Design, and Human Work"

from Catharine R. Stimpson *et al.* (eds.),
***Women and the American City* (1981) (first published 1980)**

Editors' introduction   Dolores Hayden is a professor of architecture, urbanism, and American studies at Yale University where she teaches courses on American urban history and urban design. A social historian and architect, Hayden has proposed ways to make the built environment and society more responsive to the needs of women – particularly working women with children. She is also committed to new ways of building cities for a more egalitarian society, with more community interaction, which are more responsive to both social and environmental concerns, and reflect a concern for public history, cultural diversity, and urban preservation.

This and other of Hayden's writings have struck a deeply responsive chord with a spectrum of architects and planners who want to design new forms of housing to better fit contemporary family structure and needs as well as feminists favoring changes in American gender and work roles. Like other of Hayden's writings it is grounded in the *ideas* of earlier feminist writers, provides evidence that changes can work based on *actual projects* which have been tried, and forcefully states Hayden's own feminist and egalitarian *values*.

Note the similarities between Hayden's forceful scholarly writing and British Garden City architect/ planner Raymond Unwin's 1909 proposals for cooperation in site planning and shared workspace (p. 355). Contrast Hayden's scathing critique of what is wrong with suburbia with Herbert Gans's generally positive assessment of Levittown (p. 64), the quintessential suburb.

Dolores Hayden's work has inspired many young architects and planners to create buildings, neighborhoods, and cities better adapted to families which do not consist of an employed husband, nonworking wife, and children; where men and women can more easily share both childrearing and work outside the home; and where diverse households can interact in mutually helpful and personally satisfying ways.

Dolores Hayden's main books include *Seven American Utopias: The Architecture of Communitarian Socialism: 1780–1975* (Cambridge, Mass.: MIT Press, 1976), *The Grand Domestic Revolution: A History of Feminist Designs for American Houses, Neighborhoods and Cities* (Cambridge, Mass.: MIT Press, 1981), *Redesigning the American Dream: The Future of Housing, Work, and Family Life* (New York: W. W. Norton, 1984) and the *Power of Place: Urban Landscapes as Public History* (Cambridge, Mass.: MIT Press, 1995).

Other accounts of new forms of housing built with more shared space include Kathryn McCamant and Charles Durrett, *Cohousing* (Berkeley: Ten Speed Press, 2nd edn. 1992), and Steven Barton and Carol Silverman, *Common Interest Communities* (Berkeley: Institute of Governmental Studies, 1994). Writings about women and cities include Catharine Stimpson (ed.), *Women and the American City* (Chicago: University of Chicago Press, 1980) from which this selection is reprinted, Caroline Andrew and Beth Moore Milroy (eds.), *Life Spaces: Gender, Household, Employment* (Vancouver: University of British Columbia Press, 1988), Leslie Kanes Weisman, *Discrimination by Design* (Urbana and Chicago: University of Illinois Press, 1992), and Clara Greed's *Women and Planning: Creating Gendered Realities* (London: Routledge, 1993). Leonie Sandercock and Ann Forsyth's bibliography on gender issues in planning theory (p. 408) contains a further bibliography of related writings.

DOLORES HAYDEN, "What Would a Non-sexist City Be Like? Speculations on Housing, Urban Design, and Human Work"

from Catharine R. Stimpson *et al.* (eds.), *Women and the American City* (1981) (first published 1980)

"A woman's place is in the home" has been one of the most important principles of architectural design and urban planning in the United States for the last century. An implicit rather than explicit principle for the conservative and male-dominated design professions, it will not be found stated in large type in textbooks on land use. It has generated much less debate than the other organizing principles of the contemporary American city in an era of monopoly capitalism, which include the ravaging pressure of private land development, the fetishistic dependence on millions of private automobiles, and the wasteful use of energy.[1] However, women have rejected this dogma and entered the paid labor force in larger and larger numbers. Dwellings, neighborhoods, and cities designed for homebound women constrain women physically, socially, and economically. Acute frustration occurs when women defy these constraints to spend all or part of the work day in the paid labor force. I contend that the only remedy for this situation is to develop a new paradigm of the home, the neighborhood, and the city; to begin to describe the physical, social, and economic design of a human settlement that would support, rather than restrict, the activities of employed women and their families. It is essential to recognize such needs in order to begin both the rehabilitation of the existing housing stock and the construction of new housing to meet the needs of a new and growing majority of Americans – working women and their families.

When speaking of the American city in the last quarter of the twentieth century, a false distinction between "city" and "suburb" must be avoided. The urban region, organized to separate homes and workplaces, must be seen as a whole. In such urban regions, more than half of the population resides in the sprawling suburban areas, or "bedroom communities." The greatest part of the built environment in the United States consists of "suburban sprawl": single-family homes grouped in class-segregated areas, crisscrossed by freeways and served by shopping malls and commercial strip developments. Over 50 million small homes are on the ground. About two-thirds of American families "own" their homes on long mortgages; this includes over 77 percent of all AFL-CIO members.[2] White, male skilled workers are far more likely to be homeowners than members of minority groups and women, long denied equal credit or equal access to housing. Workers commute to jobs either in the center or elsewhere in the suburban ring. In metropolitan areas studied in 1975 and 1976, the journey to work, by public transit or private car, averaged about nine miles each way. Over 100 million privately owned cars filled two- and three-car garages (which would be considered magnificent housing by themselves in many developing countries). The United States, with 13 percent of the world's population, uses 41 percent of the world's passenger cars in support of the housing and transportation patterns described.[3]

The roots of this American settlement form lie in the environmental and economic policies of the past. In the late nineteenth century, millions of immigrant families lived in the crowded, filthy slums of American industrial cities and despaired of achieving reasonable living conditions. However, many militant strikes and demonstrations between the 1890s and 1920s made some employers reconsider plant locations and housing issues in their search for industrial order.[4] "Good homes make contented workers" was the slogan of the Industrial Housing Associates in 1919. These consultants and many others helped major corporations plan better housing for white, male skilled workers and their families in order to eliminate industrial conflict. "Happy workers invariably mean bigger profits, while unhappy workers are never a good investment," they chirruped.[5] Men were to receive "family wages," and become home "owners" responsible for regular mortgage payments, while their wives became home "managers" taking care of spouse and children. The male worker would return from his day in the factory or office to a private domestic environment, secluded from the tense world of work in an industrial city characterized by environmental pollution, social degradation, and personal alienation. He would enter a serene dwelling whose physical and emotional maintenance would be the duty of his wife. Thus the private suburban house was the stage set for the effective sexual division of labor. It was the commodity par excellence, a spur for male paid labor and a container for female unpaid labor. It made gender appear a more important self-definition than class, and consumption more involving than production. In a brilliant discussion of the "patriarch as wage slave," Stuart Ewen has shown how capitalism and anti-feminism fused in campaigns for homeownership and mass consumption: the patriarch whose home was his "castle" was to work year in and year out to provide the wages to support this private environment.[6]

Although this strategy was first boosted by corporations interested in a docile labor force, it soon appealed to corporations that wished to move from World War I defense industries into peacetime production of domestic appliances for millions of families. The development of the advertising industry, documented by Ewen, supported this ideal of mass consumption and promoted the private suburban dwelling, which maximized appliance purchases.[7] The occupants of the isolated household were suggestible. They bought the house itself, a car, stove, refrigerator, vacuum cleaner, washer, carpets. Christine Frederick, explaining it in 1929 as *Selling Mrs. Consumer*, promoted homeownership and easier consumer credit and advised marketing managers on how to manipulate American women.[8] By 1931 the Hoover Commission on Home Ownership and Home Building established the private, single-family home as a national goal, but a decade and a half of depression and war postponed its achievement. Architects designed houses for Mr. and Mrs. Bliss in a competition sponsored by General Electric in 1935; winners accommodated dozens of electrical appliances in their designs with no critique of the energy costs involved.[9] In the late 1940s the single-family home was boosted by FHA and VA mortgages, and the construction of isolated, overprivatized, energy-consuming dwellings became commonplace. "I'll Buy That Dream" made the postwar hit parade.[10]

Mrs. Consumer moved the economy to new heights in the 1950s. Women who stayed at home experienced what Betty Friedan called the "feminine mystique" and Peter Filene renamed the "domestic mystique."[11] While the family occupied its private physical space, the mass media and social science experts invaded its psychological space more effectively than ever before.[12] With the increase in spatial privacy came pressure for conformity in consumption. Consumption was expensive. More and more married women joined the paid labor force, as the suggestible housewife needed to be both a frantic consumer and a paid worker to keep up with the family's bills. Just as the mass of white male workers had achieved the "dream houses" in suburbia where fantasies of patriarchal authority and consumption could be acted out, their spouses entered the world of paid employment. By 1975, the two-worker family accounted for 39 percent of American households. Another 13 percent were single-parent families, usually headed by women. Seven out of ten employed women were in the work force because of financial need. Over 50 percent of all children between the ages of one and seventeen had employed mothers.[13]

How does a conventional home serve the employed woman and her family? Badly. Whether it is in a suburban, exurban, or inner-city neighborhood, whether it is a split-level ranch house, a modern masterpiece of concrete and glass, or an old brick tenement, the house or apartment is almost invariably organized around the same set of spaces: kitchen, dining room, living room, bedrooms, garage or parking area. These spaces require someone to undertake private cooking, cleaning, child care, and usually private transportation if adults and children are to exist within it. Because of residential zoning practices, the typical dwelling will usually be physically removed from any shared community space – no commercial or communal day-care facilities, or laundry facilities, for example, are likely to be part of the dwelling's spatial domain. In many cases these facilities would be illegal if placed across property lines. They could also be illegal if located on residentially zoned sites. In some cases sharing such a private dwelling with other individuals (either relatives or those unrelated by blood) is also against the law.[14]

Within the private spaces of the dwelling, material culture works against the needs of the employed woman as much as zoning does, because the home is a box to be filled with commodities. Appliances are usually single-purpose, and often inefficient, energy-consuming machines, lined up in a room where the domestic work is done in isolation from the rest of the family. Rugs and carpets that need vacuuming, curtains that need laundering, and miscellaneous goods that need maintenance fill up the domestic spaces, often decorated in "colonial," "Mediterranean," "French Provincial," or other eclectic styles purveyed by discount and department stores to cheer up that bare box of an isolated house. Employed mothers usually are expected to, and almost invariably do, spend more time in private housework and child care than employed men; often they are expected to, and usually do, spend more time on commuting per mile traveled than men, because of their reliance on public transportation. One study found that 70 percent of adults without access to cars are female.[15] Their residential neighborhoods are not likely to provide much support for their work activities. A "good" neighborhood is usually defined in terms of conventional shopping, schools, and perhaps public transit, rather than additional social services for the working parent, such as day care or evening clinics.

While two-worker families with both parents energetically cooperating can overcome some of the problems of existing housing patterns, households in crisis, such as subjects of wife and child battering, for example, are particularly vulnerable to its inadequacies. According to Colleen McGrath, every thirty seconds a woman is being battered somewhere in the United States. Most of these batterings occur in kitchens and bedrooms. The relationship between household isolation and battering, or between unpaid domestic labor and battering, can only be guessed, at this time, but there is no doubt that America's houses and households are literally shaking with domestic violence.[16] In addition, millions of angry and upset women are treated with tranquilizers in the private home – one drug company advertises to doctors: "You can't change her environment but you can change her mood."[17]

The woman who does leave the isolated, single-family house or apartment finds very few real housing alternatives available to her.[18] The typical divorced or battered woman currently seeks housing, employment, and child care simultaneously. She finds that matching her complex family requirements with the various available offerings by landlords, employers, and social services is impossible. One environment that unites housing, services, and jobs could resolve many difficulties, but the existing system of government services, intended to stabilize households and neighborhoods by ensuring the minimum conditions for a decent home life to all Americans, almost always assumes that the traditional household with a male worker and an unpaid homemaker is the goal to be achieved or simulated. In the face of massive demographic changes, programs such as public housing, AFDC, and food stamps still attempt to support an ideal family living in an isolated house or apartment, with a full-time homemaker cooking meals and minding children many hours of the day.

By recognizing the need for a different kind of environment, far more efficient use can be made of funds now used for subsidies to individual households. Even for women with greater financial resources, the need for better housing and services is obvious. Currently, more affluent women's problems as workers have been considered "private" problems – the lack of good day care, their lack of time. The aids to overcome an environment without child care, public transportation, or food service have been "private," commercially profitable solutions: maids and baby-sitters by the hour; franchise day care or extended television viewing; fast food service; easier credit for purchasing an automobile, a washer, or a microwave oven. Not only do these commercial solutions obscure the failure of American housing policies; they also generate bad conditions for other working women. Commercial day-care and fast-food franchises are the source of low-paying nonunion jobs without security. In this respect they resemble the use of private household workers by bourgeois women, who may never ask how their private maid or child-care worker arranges care for her own children. They also resemble the insidious effects of the use of television in the home as a substitute for developmental child care in the neighborhood. The logistical problems which all employed women face are not private problems, and they do not succumb to market solutions.

The problem is paradoxical: women cannot improve their status in the home unless their overall economic position in society is altered; women cannot improve their status in the paid labor force unless their domestic responsibilities are altered. Therefore, a program to achieve economic and environmental justice for women requires, by definition, a solution that overcomes the traditional divisions between the household and the market economy, the private dwelling and the workplace. One must transform the economic situation of the traditional homemaker, whose skilled labor has been unpaid but economically and socially necessary to society; one must also transform the domestic situation of the employed woman. If architects and urban designers were to recognize all employed women and their families as a constituency for new approaches to planning and design and were to reject all previous assumptions about "woman's place" in the home, what could we do? Is it possible to build non-sexist neighborhoods and design non-sexist cities? What would they be like?

Some countries have begun to develop new approaches to the needs of employed women. The Cuban Family Code of 1974 requires men to share housework and child care within the private home. The degree of its enforcement is uncertain, but in principle it aims at men's sharing what was formerly "women's work," which is essential to equality. The Family Code, however, does not remove work from the house, and relies upon private negotiation between husband and wife for its day-to-day enforcement. Men feign incompetence, espe-

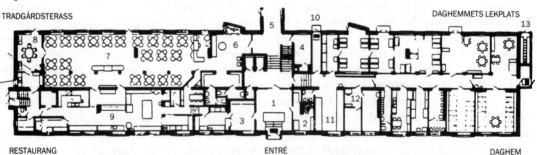

Figure 1 Sven Ivar Lind, Marieberg collective house, Stockholm, 1944, plan of entrance (*entré*), restaurant (*restaurang*), and day nursery (*deghem*): (1) entrance hall, (2) doorman's office, (3) restaurant delivery room, (4) real estate office, (5) connecting walkway to Swedberg House, (6) restaurant anteroom, (7) main dining room, (8) small dining room, (9) restaurant kitchen, (10) to day nursery's baby carriage room, (11) day nursery's baby carriage room, (12) office for day nursery's directress, (13) to Wennerberg House's cycle garage

cially in the area of cooking, with tactics familiar to any reader of Patricia Mainardi's essay, "The Politics of Housework," and the sexual stereotyping of paid jobs for women outside the home, in day-care centers for example, has not been successfully challenged.[19]

Another experimental approach involves the development of special housing facilities for employed women and their families. The builder Otto Fick first introduced such a program in Copenhagen in 1903. In later years it was encouraged in Sweden by Alva Myrdal and by the architects Sven Ivar Lind and Sven Markelius. Called "service houses" or "collective houses," such projects (Figures 1 and 2) provide child care and cooked food along with housing for employed women and their families.[20] Like a few similar projects in the USSR in the 1920s, they aim at offering services, either on a commercial basis or subsidized by the state, to replace formerly private "women's work"

performed in the household. The Scandinavian solution does not sufficiently challenge male exclusion from domestic work, nor does it deal with households' changing needs over the life cycle, but it recognizes that it is important for environmental design to change.

Some additional projects in Europe extend the scope of the service house to include the provision of services for the larger community or society. In the Steilshoop Project, in Hamburg, Germany, in the early 1970s, a group of parents and single people designed public housing with supporting services (Figure 3).[21] The project included a number of former mental patients as residents and therefore served as a halfway house for them, in addition to providing support services for the public-housing tenants who organized it. It suggests the extent to which current American residential stereotypes can be broken down – the sick, the aged, the unmarried can be integrated into new types of

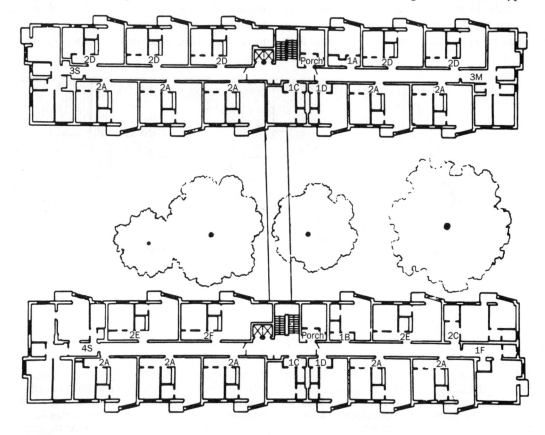

Figure 2 Plan of residential floors. Type 2A contains two rooms, bath, and kitchenette. Types 1C and 4D are efficiency units with bath and kitchenette. Type 4S includes four rooms with bath and full kitchen

households and housing complexes, rather than segregated in separate projects.

Another recent project was created in London by Nina West Homes, a development group established in 1972, which has built or renovated over sixty-three units of housing on six sites for single parents. Children's play areas or day-care centers are integrated with the dwellings; in their Fiona House project the housing is designed to facilitate shared baby-sitting, and the day-care center is open to the neighborhood residents for a fee (Figure 4). Thus the single parents can find jobs as day-care workers and help the neighborhood's working parents as well.[22] What is most exciting here is the hint that home and work can be reunited on one site for some of the residents, and home and child-care services are reunited on one site for all of them.

In the United States, we have an even longer history of agitation for housing to reflect women's needs. In the late nineteenth century and early twentieth century there were dozens of projects by feminists, domestic scientists, and architects attempting to develop community services for private homes. By the late 1920s, few such experiments were still functioning.[23] In general, feminists of that era failed to recognize the problem of exploiting other women workers when providing services for those who could afford them. They also often failed to see men as responsible parents and workers in their attempts to socialize "women's" work. But feminist leaders had a very strong sense of the possibilities of neighborly cooperation among families and of the economic importance of "women's" work.

In addition, the United States has a long tradition of experimental utopian socialist communities building model towns, as well as the example of many communes and collectives established in the 1960s and 1970s which attempted to broaden conventional definitions of household and family.[24] While some communal groups, especially religious ones, have often demanded acceptance of a traditional sexual division of labor, others have attempted to make nurturing activities a responsibility of

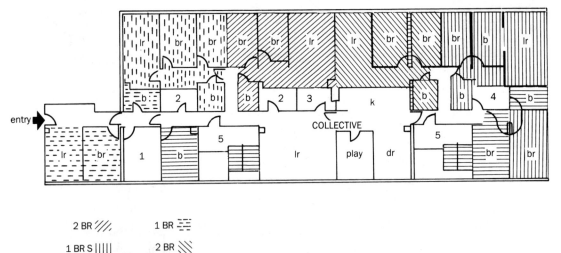

Figure 3 "Urbanes Wohnen" (urban living) Steilshoop, north of Hamburg, public housing for 206 tenants, designed by the tenant association in collaboration with Rolf Spille, 1970–3. Instead of 72 conventional units, they built 20 multifamily units and 2 studios. Twenty-six mental patients were included in the project, of whom 24 recovered. Partial floor plan. Units include private bedrooms (br), living rooms (lr), and some studios (s). They share a collective living room, kitchen, dining room, and playroom. Each private apartment can be closed off from the collective space and each is different. Key: (1) storage room, (2) closets, (3) wine cellar, (4) *buanderie*, (5) fire stairs

both women and men. It is important to draw on the examples of successful projects of all kinds, in seeking an image of a non-sexist settlement. Most employed women are not interested in taking themselves and their families to live in communal families, nor are they interested in having state bureaucracies run family life. They desire, not an end to private life altogether, but community services to support the private household. They also desire solutions that reinforce their economic independence and maximize their personal choices about child rearing and sociability.

What, then, would be the outline of a program for change in the United States? The task of reorganizing both home and work can only

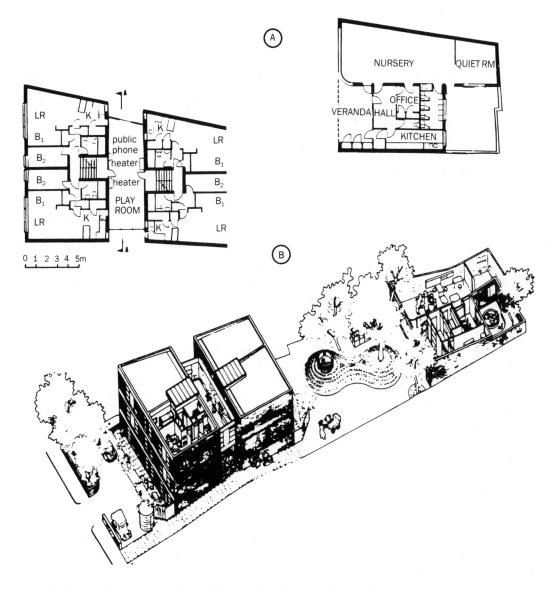

Figure 4 A, Fiona House, second-floor plan, main building, showing corridor used as a playroom, with kitchen windows opening into it; first-floor plan, rear building, showing nursery school. B, Axonometric drawing, Fiona House, Nina West Homes, London, 1972, designed by Sylvester Bone. Twelve two-bedroom units for divorced or separated mothers with additional outdoor play space and neighborhood nursery school facility. Flats can be linked by intercom system to provide an audio substitute for babysitting

be accomplished by organizations of home-makers, women and men dedicated to making changes in the ways that Americans deal with private life and public responsibilities. They must be small, participatory organizations with members who can work together effectively. I propose calling such groups HOMES (Home-makers Organization for a More Egalitarian Society). Existing feminist groups, especially those providing shelters for battered wives and children, may wish to form HOMES to take over existing housing projects and develop services for residents as an extension of those offered by feminist counselors in the shelter. Existing organizations supporting cooperative ownership of housing may wish to form HOMES to extend their housing efforts in a feminist direction. A program broad enough to transform housework, housing, and residential neighborhoods must: (1) involve both men and women in the unpaid labor associated with housekeeping and child care on an equal basis; (2) involve both men and women in the paid labor force on an equal basis; (3) eliminate residential segregation by class, race, and age; (4) eliminate all federal, state, and local programs and laws that offer implicit or explicit reinforcement of the unpaid role of the female homemaker; (5) minimize unpaid domestic labor and wasteful energy consumption; (6) maximize real choices for households concerning recreation and sociability. While many partial reforms can support these goals, an incremental strategy cannot achieve them. I believe that the establishment of experimental residential centers, which in their architectural design and economic organization transcend traditional definitions of home, neighborhood, city, and workplace, will be necessary to make changes on this scale. These centers could be created through renovation of existing neighborhoods or through new construction.

Suppose forty households in a U.S. metropolitan area formed a HOMES group and that those households, in their composition, represented the social structure of the American population as a whole. Those forty households would include: seven single parents and their fourteen children (15 percent); sixteen two-worker couples and their twenty-four children (40 percent); thirteen one-worker couples and their twenty-six children (35 percent); and four single residents, some of them "displaced home-makers" (10 percent). The residents would include sixty-nine adults and sixty-four children. There would need to be forty private dwelling units, ranging in size from efficiency to three bedrooms, all with private, fenced outdoor space. In addition to the private housing, the group would provide the following collective spaces and activities: (1) a day-care center with landscaped outdoor space, providing day care for forty children and after-school activities for sixty-four children; (2) a laundromat providing laundry service; (3) a kitchen providing lunches for the day-care center, take-out evening meals, and "meals-on-wheels" for elderly people in the neighborhood; (4) a grocery depot, connected to a local food cooperative; (5) a garage with two vans providing dial-a-ride service and meals-on-wheels; (6) a garden (or allotments) where some food can be grown; (7) a home help office providing helpers for the elderly, the sick, and employed parents whose children are sick. The use of all these collective services should be voluntary; they would exist in addition to private dwelling units and private gardens.

To provide all of the above services, thirty-seven workers would be necessary: twenty day-care workers; three food-service workers; one grocery-depot worker; five home helpers; two drivers of service vehicles; two laundry workers; one maintenance worker; one gardener; two administrative staff. Some of these may be part-time workers, some full-time. Day care, food services, and elderly services could be organized as producers' cooperatives, and other workers could be employed by the housing cooperative as discussed below.

Because HOMES is not intended as an experiment in isolated community buildings but as an experiment in meeting employed women's needs in an urban area, its services should be available to the neighborhood in which the experiment is located. This will increase demand for the services and insure that the jobs are real ones. In addition, although residents of HOMES should have priority for the jobs, there will be many who choose outside work. So some local residents may take jobs within the experiment.

In creating and filling these jobs it will be important to avoid traditional sex stereotyping that would result from hiring only men as drivers, for example, or only women as food-service workers. Every effort should be made to break down separate categories of paid work for women and men, just as efforts should be made to recruit men who accept an equal share of domestic responsibilities as residents. A version of the Cuban Family Code should become part of the organization's platform.

Similarly, HOMES must not create a two-class society with residents outside the project making more money than residents in HOMES jobs that utilize some of their existing domestic skills. The HOMES jobs should be paid according to egalitarian rather than sex-stereotyped attitudes about skills and hours. These jobs must be all classified as skilled work rather than as unskilled or semiskilled at present, and offer full social security and health benefits, including adequate maternity leave, whether workers are part-time or full-time.

Many federal Housing and Urban Development programs support the construction of nonprofit, low- and moderate-cost housing, including section 106b, section 202, and section 8. In addition, HUD section 213 funds are available to provide mortgage insurance for the conversion of existing housing of five or more units to housing cooperatives. HEW programs also fund special facilities such as day-care centers or meals-on-wheels for the elderly. In addition, HUD and HEW offer funds for demonstration projects which meet community needs in new ways.[25] Many trade unions, churches, and tenant cooperative organizations are active as nonprofit housing developers. A limited-equity housing cooperative offers the best basis for economic organization and control of both physical design and social policy by the residents.

Many knowledgeable nonprofit developers could aid community groups wishing to organize such projects, as could architects experienced in the design of housing cooperatives. What has not been attempted is the reintegration of work activities and collective services into housing cooperatives on a large enough

scale to make a real difference to employed women. Feminists in trade unions where a majority of members are women may wish to consider building cooperative housing with services for their members. Other trade unions may wish to consider investing in such projects. Feminists in the co-op movement must make strong, clear demands to get such services from existing housing cooperatives, rather than simply go along with plans for conventional housing organized on a cooperative economic basis. Feminists outside the cooperative movement will find that cooperative organizational forms offer many possibilities for supporting their housing activities and other services to women. In addition, the recently established national Consumer Cooperative Bank has funds to support projects of all kinds that can be tied to cooperative housing.

In many areas, the rehabilitation of existing housing may be more desirable than new construction. The suburban housing stock in the United States must be dealt with effectively. A little bit of it is of architectural quality sufficient to deserve preservation; most of it can be aesthetically improved by the physical evidence of more intense social activity. To replace empty front lawns without sidewalks, neighbors can create blocks where single units are converted to multiple units; interior land is pooled to create a parklike setting at the center of the block; front and side lawns are fenced to make private outdoor spaces; pedestrian paths and sidewalks are created to link all units with the central open space; and some private porches, garages, tool sheds, utility rooms, and family rooms are converted to community facilities such as children's play areas, dial-a-ride garages, and laundries.

Figure 5A shows a typical bleak suburban block of thirteen houses, constructed by speculators at different times, where about four acres are divided into plots of one-fourth to one-half acre each. Thirteen driveways are used by twenty-six cars; ten garden sheds, ten swings, thirteen lawn mowers, thirteen outdoor dining tables, begin to suggest the wasteful duplication of existing amenities. Yet despite the available land there are no transitions between public streets and these private homes.

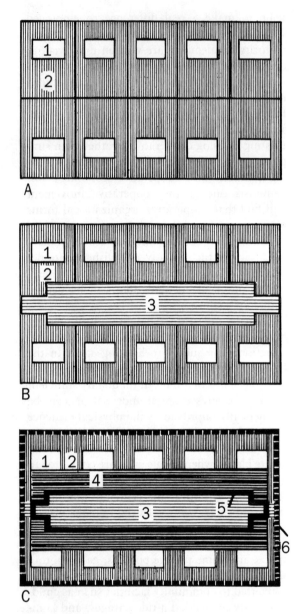

Figure 5 Diagram showing some of the possibilities of reorganizing a typical suburban block through rezoning, rebuilding, and landscaping. A, Ten single-family houses (1) on ten private lots (2); B, the same houses (1) with smaller private lots (2) after a backyard rehabilitation program has created a new village green (3) at the heart of the block; C, the same houses (1) and many small private gardens (2) with a new village green (3) surrounded by a zone for new services and accessory apartments (4) connected by a new sidewalk or arcade (5) and surrounded by a new border of street trees (6). In C, (4) can include space for such activities as day care, elderly care, laundry, and food service as well as housing, while (3) can accommodate a children's play area, vegetable or flower gardens, and outdoor seating. (5) may be a sidewalk, a vine-covered trellis, or a formal arcade. The narrow ends of the block can be emphasized as collective entrances with gates (to which residents have keys), leading to new accessory apartments entered from the arcade or sidewalk. In the densest possible situations, (3) may be alley and parking lot, if existing street parking and public transit are not adequate

Space is either strictly private or strictly public. Figure 6A shows a typical one-family house of 1,400 square feet on this block. With three bedrooms and den, two-and-a-half baths, laundry room, two porches, and a two-car garage, it was constructed in the 1950s at the height of the "feminine mystique."

To convert this whole block and the housing on it to more efficient and sociable uses, one has to define a zone of greater activity at the heart of the block, taking a total of one and one half to two acres for collective use (Figure 5B). Essentially, this means turning the block inside out. The Radburn plan, developed by Henry Wright and Clarence Stein in the late 1920s, delineated this principle very clearly as correct land use in "the motor age," with cars segregated from residents' green spaces, especially spaces for children. In Radburn, New Jersey, and in the Baldwin Hills district of Los Angeles, California, Wright and Stein achieved remarkably luxurious results (at a density of about seven units to the acre) by this method, since their multiple-unit housing always bordered a lush parkland without any automobile traffic. The Baldwin Hills project demonstrates this success most dramatically, but a revitalized suburban block with lots as small as one-fourth acre can be reorganized to yield something of this same effect.[26] In this case, social amenities are added to aesthetic ones as the interior park is designed to accommodate community day care, a garden for growing vegetables, some picnic tables, a playground where swings and slides are grouped, a grocery depot connected to a larger neighborhood food cooperative, and a dial-a-ride garage.

Large single-family houses can be remodeled quite easily to become duplexes and triplexes, despite the "open plans" of the 1950s and 1960s popularized by many developers. The house in Figure 6A becomes, in Figure 6B, a triplex, with a two-bedroom unit (linked to a community garage); a one-bedroom unit; and an efficiency unit (for a single person or elderly person). All three units are shown with private enclosed gardens. The three units share a front porch and entry hall. There is still enough land to give about two-fifths of the original lot to the community. Particularly striking is the way in which existing spaces such as back porches or garages lend themselves to conversion to social areas or community services. Three former private garages out of thirteen might be given over to collective uses – one as a central office for the whole block, one as a grocery depot, and one as a dial-a-ride garage. Is it possible to have only twenty cars (in ten garages) and two vans for twenty-six units in a rehabilitated block? Assuming that some residents switch from outside employment to working within the block, and that for all residents, neighborhood shopping trips are cut in half by the presence of day care, groceries, laundry, and cooked food on the block, as well as aided by the presence of some new collective transportation, this might be done.

What about neighbors who are not interested in such a scheme? Depending on the configuration of lots, it is possible to begin such a plan with as few as three or four houses. In Berkeley, California, where neighbors on Derby Street joined their backyards and created a cooperative day-care center, one absentee landlord refused to join – his entire property is fenced in and the community space flows around it without difficulty. Of course, present zoning laws must be changed, or variances obtained, for the conversion of single-family houses into duplexes and triplexes and the introduction of any sort of commercial activities into a residential block. However, a community group that is able to organize or acquire at least five units could become a HUD housing cooperative, with a nonprofit corporation owning all land and with producers' cooperatives running the small community services. With a coherent plan for an entire block, variances could be obtained much more easily than on a lot-by-lot basis. One can also imagine organizations that run halfway houses – for ex-mental patients, or runaway teenagers, or battered women – integrating their activities into such a block plan, with an entire building for their activities. Such groups often find it difficult to achieve the supportive neighborhood context such a block organization would offer.

I believe that attacking the conventional division between public and private space should become a socialist and feminist priority in the 1980s. Women must transform the sexual division of domestic labor, the privatized economic basis of domestic work, and the spatial separation of homes and workplaces in the built environment if they are to be equal members of society. The experiments I propose are an attempt to unite the best features of past and present reforms in our own society and others, with some of the existing social services available in the United States today. I would like to see several demonstration HOMES begun, some involving new construction following the program I have laid out, others involving the rehabilitation of suburban blocks. If the first few experimental projects are successful, homemakers across the United States will want to obtain day-care, food, and laundry services at a reasonable price, as well as better wages, more flexible working conditions, and more suitable housing. When all homemakers recognize that they are struggling against both gender stereotypes and wage discrimination, when they see that social, economic, and environmental changes are necessary to overcome these conditions, they will no longer tolerate housing and cities, designed around the principles of another era, that proclaim that "a woman's place is in the home."

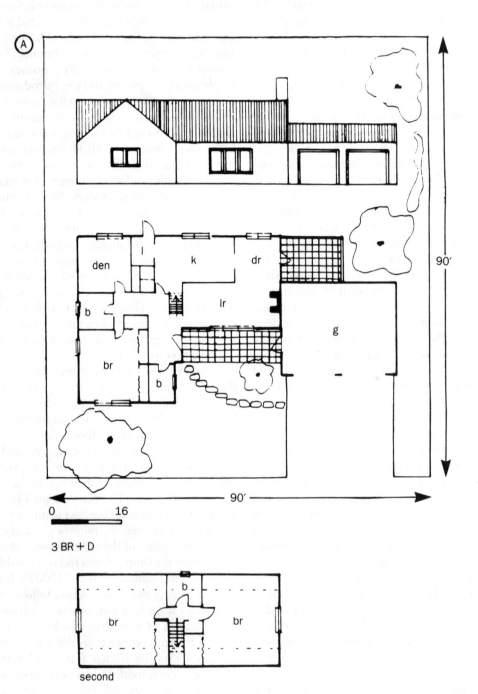

Figure 6A Suburban single-family house, plan, three bedrooms plus den

NOTES

This paper comprised part of the text of a talk for the conference "Planning and Designing a Non-Sexist Society," University of California, Los Angeles, April 21, 1979. I would like to thank Catharine Stimpson, Peter Marris, S. M. Miller, Kevin Lynch, Jeremy Brecher, and David Thompson for extensive written comments on drafts of this paper.

1. There is an extensive Marxist literature on the importance of spatial design to the economic development of the capitalist city, including Henri Lefebre, *La Production de l'espace* (Paris: Editions Anthropos, 1974); Manuel Castells, *The Urban Question* (Cambridge, Mass.: M.I.T. Press, 1977); David Harvey, *Social Justice and the City* (London: Edward Arnold, 1974); and David Gordon, "Capitalist Development and

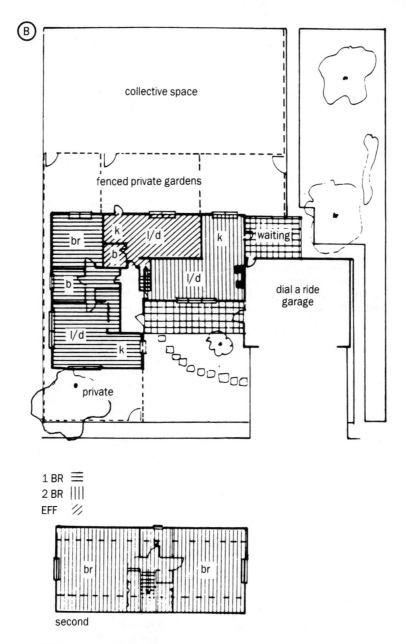

Figure 6B Proposed HOMES revitalization, same house converted to three units (two bedroom, one bedroom, and efficiency), plus dial-a-ride garage and collective outdoor space

the History of American Cities," in *Marxism and the Metropolis*, ed. William K. Tabb and Larry Sawyers (New York: Oxford University Press, 1978). None of this work deals adequately with the situation of women as workers and homemakers, nor with the unique spatial inequalities they experience. Nevertheless, it is important to combine the economic and historical analysis of these scholars with the empirical research of non-Marxist feminist urban critics and sociologists who have examined women's experience of conventional housing, such as Gerda Wekerle, "A Woman's Place Is in the City" (paper for the Lincoln Institute of Land Policy, Cambridge, Mass., 1978); and Suzanne Keller, "Women in a Planned Community" (paper for the Lincoln Institute of Land Policy, Cambridge, Mass., 1978). Only then can one begin to provide a socialist-feminist critique of the spatial design of the American city. It is also essential to develop research on housing similar to Sheila B. Kamerman, "Work and Family in Industrialized Societies," *Signs: Journal of Women in Culture and Society* 4, no. 4 (Summer 1979): 632–50, which reviews patterns of women's employment, maternity provisions, and child-care policies in Hungary, East Germany, West Germany, France, Sweden, and the United States. A comparable study of housing and related services for employed women could be the basis for more elaborate proposals for change. Many attempts to refine socialist and feminist economic theory concerning housework are discussed in an excellent article by Ellen Malos, "Housework and the Politics of Women's Liberation," *Socialist Review* 37 (January–February 1978): 41–47. A most significant theoretical piece is Movimento di Lotta Femminile, "Programmatic Manifesto for the Struggle of Housewives in the Neighborhood," *Socialist Revolution* 9 (May–June 1972): 85–90.

2. *Survey of AFL-CIO Members Housing 1975* (Washington, D.C.: AFL-CIO, 1975), p. 16. I am indebted to Allan Heskin for this reference.

3. *Transit Fact Book*, 1977–78 ed. (Washington, D.C.: American Public Transit Association, 1978), p. 29); *Motor Vehicle Facts and Figures* (Detroit, Mich.: Motor Vehicle Manufacturers Association, 1977), pp. 29, 31, 53.

4. Gordon, pp. 48–50, discusses suburban relocation of plants and housing.

5. Industrial Housing Associates, "Good Homes Make Contented Workers," 1919, Edith Elmer Wood Papers, Avery Library, Columbia University. Also see Barbara Ehrenreich and Deirdre English, "The Manufacture of Housework," *Socialist Revolution* 5 (1975): 16. They quote an unidentified corporate official (ca. 1920): "Get them to invest their savings in homes and own them. Then they won't leave and they won't strike. It ties them down so they have a stake in our prosperity."

6. Stuart Ewen, *Captains of Consciousness: Advertising and the Social Roots of the Consumer Culture* (New York: McGraw-Hill Book Co., 1976).

7. Richard Walker, "Suburbanization in Passage," unpublished draft paper (Berkeley: University of California, Berkeley, Department of Geography, 1977).

8. Christine Frederick, *Selling Mrs. Consumer* (New York: Business Bourse, 1929).

9. Carol Barkin, "Home, Mom, and Pie-in-the-Sky" (M. Arch. thesis, University of California, Los Angeles, 1979), pp. 120–24, gives the details of this competition; Ruth Schwartz Cowan, in an unpublished lecture at M.I.T. in 1977, explained GE's choice of an energy-consuming design for its refrigerator in the 1920s, because this would increase demand for its generating equipment by municipalities.

10. Peter Filene, *Him/Her/Self: Sex Roles in Modern America* (New York: Harcourt Brace Jovanovich, 1974), p. 189.

11. Betty Friedan, *The Feminine Mystique* (1963; New York: W. W. Norton & Co., 1974), p. 307, somewhat hysterically calls the home a "comfortable concentration camp"; Filene, p. 194, suggests that men are victimized by ideal homes too, thus "domestic" mystique.

12. Eli Zaretsky, *Capitalism, the Family, and Personal Life* (New York: Harper & Row, 1976), develops Friedman's earlier argument in a more systematic way. This phenomenon is misunderstood by Christopher Lasch, *Haven in a Heartless World* (New York: Alfred A. Knopf, 1977), who seems to favor a return to the sanctity of the patriarchal home.

13. Rosalyn Baxandall, Linda Gordon, and Susan Reverby, eds., *America's Working Women: A Documentary History, 1600 to the Present* (New York: Vintage Books, 1976). For more detail, see Louise Kapp Howe, *Pink Collar Workers: Inside the World of Woman's Work* (New York: Avon Books, 1977).

14. Recent zoning fights on the commune issue have occurred in Santa Monica, Calif.; Wendy Schuman, "The Return of Togetherness," *New York Times* (March 20, 1977), reports frequent illegal down zoning by two-family groups in one-family residences in the New York area.

15. Study by D. Foley, cited in Wekerle (see n. 1 above).

16. Colleen McGrath, "The Crisis of Domestic Order," *Socialist Review* 9 (January–February 1979): 12, 23.

17. Research by Malcolm MacEwen, cited in *Associate Collegiate Schools of Architecture Newsletter* (March 1973), p. 6.

18. See, for example, Carol A. Brown, "Spatial

Inequalities and Divorced Mothers" (paper delivered at the annual meeting of the American Sociological Association, San Francisco, 1978); Susan Anderson-Khleif, research report for HUD on single-parent families and their housing, summarized in "Housing for Single Parents," *Research Report, MIT-Harvard Joint Center for Urban Studies* (April 1979), pp. 3–4.

19. Patricia Mainardi, "The Politics of Housework," in *Sisterhood Is Powerful*, ed. Robin Morgan (New York: Vintage Books, 1970). My discussion of the Cuban Family Code is based on a visit to Cuba in 1978; a general review is Carollee Bengelsdorf and Alice Hageman, "Emerging from Underdevelopment: Women and Work in Cuba," in *Capitalist Patriarchy and the Case for Socialist Feminism*, ed. Z. Eisenstein (New York: Monthly Review Press, 1979). Also see Geoffrey E. Fox, "Honor, Shame and Women's Liberation in Cuba: Views of Working-Class Emigré Men," in *Female and Male in Latin America*, ed. A. Pescatello (Pittsburgh: University of Pittsburgh Press, 1973).

20. Erwin Muhlestein, "Kollektives Wohnen gestern und heute," *Architese* 14 (1975): 3–23.

21. This project relies on the "support structures" concept of John Habraken to provide flexible interior partitions and fixed mechanical core and structure.

22. "Bridge over Troubled Water," *Architects' Journal* (September 27, 1972), pp. 680–84; personal interview with Nina West, 1978.

23. Dolores Hayden, A *"Grand Domestic Revolution": Feminism, Socialism and the American Home, 1870–1930* (Cambridge, Mass.: M.I.T. Press, 1980); "Two Utopian Feminists and Their Compaigns for Kitchenless Houses," *Signs: Journal of Women in Culture and Society* 4, no. 2 (Winter 1979): 274–90; "Melusina Fay Peirce and Cooperative Housekeeping," *International Journal of Urban and Regional Research* 2 (1978): 401–20; "Challenging the American Domestic Ideal," and "Catharine Beecher and the Politics of Housework," in *Women in American Architecture*, ed. S. Torre (New York: Whitney Library of Design, 1977), pp. 22–39, 40–49; "Charlotte Perkins Gilman: Domestic Evolution or Domestic Revolution," *Radical History Review*, vol. 21 (Winter 1979–80), in press.

24. Dolores Hayden, *Seven American Utopias: The Architecture of Communitarian Socialism, 1790–1975* (Cambridge, Mass.: M.I.T. Press, 1976), discusses historical examples and includes a discussion of communes of the 1960s and 1970s, "Edge City, Heart City, Drop City: Communal Building Today," pp. 320–47.

25. I am indebted to Geraldine Kennedy and Sally Kratz, whose unpublished papers, "Toward Financing Cooperative Housing," and "Social Assistance Programs Whose Funds Could Be Redirected to Collective Services," were prepared for my UCLA graduate seminar in spring 1979.

26. See also the successful experience of Zurich, described in Hans Wirz, "Back Yard Rehab: Urban Microcosm Rediscovered," *Urban Innovation Abroad* 3 (July 1979): 2–3.

MIKE DAVIS

"Fortress L.A."

from *City of Quartz: Excavating the Future in Los Angeles* (1990)

Editors' introduction   It has been said that Mike Davis is to contemporary Los Angeles what Friedrich Engels was to mid-nineteenth-century Manchester. Engels was a kind of explorer, reporting to an educated, middle-class audience about the horrors of the industrial city and the miserable lives of the new proletarian class of modern capitalism. Similarly, Davis, 150 years later, explores the dark side of the postmodern metropolis and reports on the hopelessness and despair of the postindustrial "underclass" (largely defined by race, gender, and ethnicity) to an audience largely comprising young, disaffected intellectuals and academics. Clearly, the parallels are striking. Indeed, Davis may be the heir to Engels simply because the contemporary metropolis – characterized by wealth and homelessness and divided against itself along the fault lines that separate suburban enclaves from inner-city slums – is the heir to the geographical and social-class divisions of the cities of the Industrial Revolution.

Mike Davis, who is a native southern Californian and who teaches urban theory at the Southern California Institute of Architecture, is an insightful and acerbic social critic who makes his social-class sympathies and anti-Establishment bias perfectly clear on every page of *City of Quartz: Excavating the Future in Los Angeles* (London: Verso, 1992), which one admirer praised as a "visionary rant."

In *The Condition of the Working Class in England* (p. 47), Engels noted the boulevards that intersected the city of Manchester and how the facades of those broad thoroughfares served to mask and disguise the noisome hovels of the poor that lay beyond the view of the middle-class commuter. Davis, employing an eclectic "culture studies" methodology, makes a similar but even subtler point about contemporary Los Angeles. Not only do the freeways allow middle-class suburbanites to navigate the city as a whole without encountering the lives of the residents of the inner-city neighborhoods, but the city itself has become, in the semiotic culture of postmodernism, a vast and continuous system of signs that we read and obey on (mostly) a subconscious level. "Today's upscale, pseudo-public spaces," he writes, ". . . are full of invisible signs warning off the underclass 'Other.' Although architectural critics are usually oblivious to how the built environment contributes to segregation, pariah groups – whether poor Latino families, young Black men, or elderly homeless white females – read the meaning immediately."

Another similarity between Engels and Davis is that both men, as they proceeded to "read the streets" of their respective paradigm cities, seemed to reach the limits of language's ability to describe the physical and psychological conditions being reported. Engels adopted the strategy of social science, compiling a mountain of personal observations, journalistic reports, and official survey data to create a virtual catalog of social horror. Davis, on the other hand, relies on a more emotional, even histrionic, strategy. His overheated rhetorical excesses often seem to overwhelm rational discourse.

Still, Davis's critique of the contemporary urban social order, however enraged, has a kind of compelling validity quite independent of the received canons of intellectual discourse. Indeed, Davis turned out to be a prophet: the ghettos and barrios of Southcentral Los Angeles erupted into open rebellion in the Rodney King riots two years after the publication of *City of Quartz*.

Whereas Engels saw massive social dislocations and systematically set about to fashion a theory of revolutionary socialism in response to the observed reality, Davis offers no similarly optimistic solution. In a sense, Davis *personalizes* the horrors of the contemporary city, and his voice is one of desperation and despair offering no obvious way out of the current impasse. Unfortunately, many would say that the tone of that voice is an undeniably accurate echo of what we hear all around us today.

Davis's insights regarding the underclass "other" suggest comparisons with such classic analysts of ghettoization as Dubois (p. 57), Anthony Downs (p. 500), and William Julius Wilson (p. 226), but it is difficult to compare Davis with social policy and planning professionals – whether a conservative like Charles Murray (p. 233) or progressives like Allan Jacobs and Donald Appleyeard (p. 165) – whose focus is on influencing the existing system by working within it.

As a chronicler of southern California, Davis continues a strong muckraking tradition begun by Carey McWilliams in *Factories in the Field* (Boston: Little, Brown, 1946), *Southern California: An Island on the Land* (Santa Barbara: Peregrine Smith, 1946) and other works. For a more centrist view, see Kevin Starr, *Inventing the Dream* (New York: Oxford, 1985) and *Material Dreams* (New York: Oxford, 1990). Also useful is Sam Bass Warner's *The Urban Wilderness* (New York: Harper & Row, 1972). For another Marxist postmodernist discussion of the culture of contemporary urbanism with European examples consult British geographer David Harvey's *The Urban Experience* (Oxford: Basil Blackwell, 1989).

MIKE DAVIS, "Fortress L.A."

from *City of Quartz: Excavating the Future in Los Angeles* (1990)

The carefully manicured lawns of Los Angeles' Westside sprout forests of ominous little signs warning: "Armed Response!" Even richer neighborhoods in the canyons and hillsides isolate themselves behind walls guarded by gun-toting private police and state-of-the-art electronic surveillance. Downtown, a publicly subsidized "urban renaissance" has raised the nation's largest corporate citadel, segregated from the poor neighborhoods around it by a monumental architectural glacis. In Hollywood, celebrity architect Frank Gehry, renowned for his "humanism," apotheosizes the siege look in a library designed to resemble a foreign-legion fort. In the Westlake district and the San Fernando Valley the Los Angeles

Police barricade streets and seal off poor neighborhoods as part of their "war on drugs." In Watts, developer Alexander Haagen demonstrates his strategy for recolonizing inner-city retail markets: a panopticon shopping mall surrounded by staked metal fences and a substation of the LAPD in a central surveillance tower. Finally, on the horizon of the next millennium, an ex-chief of police crusades for an anti-crime "giant eye" – a geo-synchronous law enforcement satellite – while other cops discreetly tend versions of "Garden Plot," a hoary but still viable 1960s plan for a law-and-order armageddon.

Welcome to post-liberal Los Angeles, where the defense of luxury lifestyles is translated into a proliferation of new repressions in space and movement, undergirded by the ubiquitous "armed response." This obsession with physical security systems, and, collaterally, with the architectural policing of social boundaries, has become a zeitgeist of urban restructuring, a master narrative in the emerging built environment of the 1990s. Yet contemporary urban theory, whether debating the role of electronic technologies in precipitating "postmodern space," or discussing the dispersion of urban functions across poly-centered metropolitan "galaxies," has been strangely silent about the militarization of city life so grimly visible at the street level. Hollywood's pop apocalypses and pulp science fiction have been more realistic, and politically perceptive, in representing the programmed hardening of the urban surface in the wake of the social polarizations of the Reagan era. Images of carceral inner cities (*Escape from New York*, *Running Man*), high-tech police death squads (*Blade Runner*), sentient buildings (*Die Hard*), urban bantustans (*They Live!*), Vietnam-like street wars (*Colors*), and so on, only extrapolate from actually existing trends.

Such dystopian visions grasp the extent to which today's pharaonic scales of residential and commercial security supplant residual hopes for urban reform and social integration. The dire predictions of Richard Nixon's 1969 National Commission on the Causes and Prevention of Violence have been tragically fulfilled: we live in "fortress cities" brutally divided between "fortified cells" of affluent society and "places of terror" where the police battle the criminalized poor. The "Second Civil War" that began in the long hot summers of the 1960s has been institutionalized into the very structure of urban space. The old liberal paradigm of social control, attempting to balance repression with reform, has long been superseded by a rhetoric of social warfare that calculates the interests of the urban poor and the middle classes as a zero-sum game. In cities like Los Angeles, on the bad edge of postmodernity, one observes an unprecedented tendency to merge urban design, architecture and the police apparatus into a single, comprehensive security effort.

This epochal coalescence has far-reaching consequences for the social relations of the built environment. In the first place, the market provision of "security" generates its own paranoid demand. "Security" becomes a positional good defined by income access to private "protective services" and membership in some hardened residential enclave or restricted suburb. As a prestige symbol – and sometimes as the decisive borderline between the merely well-off and the "truly rich" – "security" has less to do with personal safety than with the degree of personal insulation, in residential, work, consumption and travel environments, from "unsavory" groups and individuals, even crowds in general.

Secondly, as William Whyte has observed of social intercourse in New York, "fear proves itself." The social perception of threat becomes a function of the security mobilization itself, not crime rates. Where there is an actual rising arc of street violence, as in Southcentral Los Angeles or Downtown Washington D.C., most of the carnage is self-contained within ethnic or class boundaries. Yet white middle-class imagination, absent from any firsthand knowledge of inner-city conditions, magnifies the perceived threat through a demonological lens. Surveys show that Milwaukee suburbanites are just as worried about violent crime as inner-city Washingtonians, despite a twentyfold difference in relative levels of mayhem. The media, whose function in this arena is to bury and obscure the daily economic violence of the city, ceaselessly throw up spectres of criminal underclasses and psychotic stalkers. Sensationalized accounts of killer youth gangs high on crack and shrilly racist evocations of marauding Willie Hortons foment the moral panics that reinforce and justify urban apartheid.

Moreover, the neo-military syntax of contemporary architecture insinuates violence and conjures imaginary dangers. In many instances the semiotics of so-called "defensible space" are just about as subtle as a swaggering white cop. Today's upscale, pseudo-public spaces – sumptuary malls, office centers, culture acropolises, and so on – are full of invisible signs warning off the underclass "Other." Although architectural critics are usually oblivious to how the built environment contributes to segregation, pariah groups – whether poor Latino families, young Black men, or elderly homeless white females – read the meaning immediately.

THE DESTRUCTION OF PUBLIC SPACE

The universal and ineluctable consequence of this crusade to secure the city is the destruction of accessible public space. The contemporary opprobrium attached to the term "street person" is in itself a harrowing index of the devaluation of public spaces. To reduce contact with untouchables, urban redevelopment has converted once vital pedestrian streets into traffic sewers and transformed public parks into temporary receptacles for the homeless and wretched. The American city, as many critics have recognized, is being systematically turned inside out – or, rather, outside in. The valorized spaces of the new megastructures and super-malls are concentrated in the center, street frontage is denuded, public activity is sorted into strictly functional compartments, and circulation is internalized in corridors under the gaze of private police.

The privatization of the architectural public realm, moreover, is shadowed by parallel restructurings of electronic space, as heavily policed, pay-access "information orders," elite databases and subscription cable services appropriate parts of the invisible agora. Both processes, of course, mirror the deregulation of the economy and the recession of non-market entitlements. The decline of urban liberalism has been accompanied by the death of what might be called the "Olmstedian vision" of public space. Frederick Law Olmsted, it will be recalled, was North America's Haussmann, as well as the Father of Central Park. In the wake of Manhattan's "Commune" of 1863, the great Draft Riot, he conceived public landscapes and parks as social safety-valves, mixing classes and ethnicities in common (bourgeois) recreations and enjoyments. As Manfredo Tafuri has shown in his well-known study of Rockefeller Center, the same principle animated the construction of the canonical urban spaces of the La Guardia–Roosevelt era.

This reformist vision of public space – as the emollient of class struggle, if not the bedrock of the American *polis* – is now as obsolete as Keynesian nostrums of full employment. In regard to the "mixing" of classes, contemporary urban America is more like Victorian England than Walt Whitman's or La Guardia's New York. In Los Angeles, once-upon-a-time a demi-paradise of free beaches, luxurious parks, and "cruising strips," genuinely democratic space is all but extinct. The Oz-like archipelago of Westside pleasure domes – a continuum of tony malls, arts centers and gourmet strips – is reciprocally dependent upon the social imprisonment of the third-world service proletariat who live in increasingly repressive ghettoes and barrios. In a city of several million yearning immigrants, public amenities are radically shrinking, parks are becoming derelict and beaches more segregated, libraries and playgrounds are closing, youth congregations of ordinary kinds are banned, and the streets are becoming more desolate and dangerous.

Unsurprisingly, as in other American cities, municipal policy has taken its lead from the security offensive and the middle-class demand for increased spatial and social insulation. De facto disinvestment in traditional public space and recreation has supported the shift of fiscal resources to corporate-defined redevelopment priorities. A pliant city government – in this case ironically professing to represent a bi-racial coalition of liberal whites and Blacks – has collaborated in the massive privatization of public space and the subsidization of new, racist enclaves (benignly described as "urban villages"). Yet most current, giddy discussions of the "postmodern" scene in Los Angeles neglect entirely these overbearing aspects of counter-urbanization and counter-insurgency. A triumphal gloss – "urban renaissance," "city of the future," and so on – is laid over the brutalization of inner-city neighborhoods and the increasing South Africanization of its spatial relations. Even as the walls have come down in Eastern Europe, they are being erected all over Los Angeles.

The observations that follow take as their thesis the existence of this new class war (sometimes a continuation of the race war of the

1960s) at the level of the built environment. Although this is not a comprehensive account, which would require a thorough analysis of economic and political dynamics, these images and instances are meant to convince the reader that urban form is indeed following a repressive function in the political furrows of the Reagan–Bush era. Los Angeles, in its usual prefigurative mode, offers an especially disquieting catalogue of the emergent liaisons between architecture and the American police state.

THE FORBIDDEN CITY

The first militarist of space in Los Angeles was General Otis of the *Times*. Declaring himself at war with labor, he infused his surroundings with an unrelentingly bellicose air:

> He called his home in Los Angeles the Bivouac. Another house was known as the Outpost. The *Times* was known as the Fortress. The staff of the paper was the Phalanx. The *Times* building itself was more fortress than newspaper plant, there were turrets, battlements, sentry boxes. Inside he stored fifty rifles.

A great, menacing bronze eagle was the *Times*'s crown; a small, functional cannon was installed on the hood of Otis's touring car to intimidate onlookers. Not surprisingly, this overwrought display of aggression produced a response in kind. On 1 October 1910 the heavily fortified *Times* headquarters – citadel of the open shop on the West Coast – was destroyed in a catastrophic explosion blamed on union saboteurs.

Eighty years later, the spirit of General Otis has returned to subtly pervade Los Angeles' new "postmodern" Downtown: the emerging Pacific Rim financial complex which cascades, in rows of skyscrapers, from Bunker Hill southward along the Figueroa corridor. Redeveloped with public tax increments under the aegis of the powerful and largely unaccountable Community Redevelopment Agency (CRA), the Downtown project is one of the largest postwar urban designs in North America. Site assemblage and clearing on a vast scale, with little mobilized opposition, have resurrected land values, upon which big developers and off-shore capital

(increasingly Japanese) have planted a series of billion-dollar, block-square megastructures: Crocker Center, the Bonaventure Hotel and Shopping Mall, the World Trade Center, the Broadway Plaza, Arco Center, CitiCorp Plaza, California Plaza, and so on. With historical landscapes erased, with megastructures and superblocks as primary components, and with an increasingly dense and self-contained circulation system, the new financial district is best conceived as a single, demonically self-referential hyperstructure, a Miesian skyscape raised to dementia.

Like similar megalomaniac complexes, tethered to fragmented and desolated Downtowns (for instance, the Renaissance Center in Detroit, the Peachtree and Omni Centers in Atlanta, and so on), Bunker Hill and the Figueroa corridor have provoked a storm of liberal objections against their abuse of scale and composition, their denigration of street landscape, and their confiscation of so much of the vital life activity of the center, now sequestered within subterranean concourses or privatized malls. Sam Hall Kaplan, the crusty urban critic of the *Times*, has been indefatigable in denouncing the anti-pedestrian bias of the new corporate citadel, with its fascist obliteration of street frontage. In his view the superimposition of "hermetically sealed fortresses" and airdropped "pieces of suburbia" has "dammed the rivers of life" Downtown.

Yet Kaplan's vigorous defense of pedestrian democracy remains grounded in hackneyed liberal complaints about "bland design" and "elitist planning practices." Like most architectural critics, he rails against the oversights of urban design without recognizing the dimension of foresight, of explicit repressive intention, which has its roots in Los Angeles' ancient history of class and race warfare. Indeed, when Downtown's new "Gold Coast" is viewed en bloc from the standpoint of its interactions with other social areas and landscapes in the central city, the "fortress effect" emerges, not as an inadvertent failure of design, but as deliberate socio-spatial strategy.

The goals of this strategy may be summarized as a double repression: to raze all association with Downtown's past and to prevent any articulation with the non-Anglo urbanity of its future. Everywhere on the perimeter of redevelopment this strategy takes the form of a brutal architectural edge or glacis that defines the new Downtown as a citadel vis-à-vis the rest of the central city. Los Angeles is unusual amongst major urban renewal centers in preserving, however negligently, most of its circa 1900–30 Beaux Arts commercial core. At immense public cost, the corporate headquarters and financial district was shifted from the old Broadway–Spring corridor six blocks west to the greenfield site created by destroying the Bunker Hill residential neighborhood. To emphasize the "security" of the new Downtown, virtually all the traditional pedestrian links to the old center, including the famous Angels' Flight funicular railroad, were removed.

The logic of this entire operation is revealing. In other cities developers might have attempted to articulate the new skyscape and the old, exploiting the latter's extraordinary inventory of theaters and historic buildings to create a gentrified history – a gaslight district, Faneuil Market or Ghirardelli Square – as a support to middle-class residential colonization. But Los Angeles' redevelopers viewed property values in the old Broadway core as irreversibly eroded by the area's very centrality to public transport, and especially by its heavy use by Black and Mexican poor. In the wake of the Watts rebellion, and the perceived Black threat to crucial nodes of white power (spelled out in lurid detail in the McCone Commission Report), resegregated spatial security became the paramount concern. The Los Angeles Police Department abetted the flight of business from Broadway to the fortified redoubts of Bunker Hill by spreading scare literature typifying Black teenagers as dangerous gang members.

As a result, redevelopment massively reproduced spatial apartheid. The moat of the Harbor Freeway and the regraded palisades of Bunker Hill cut off the new financial core from the poor immigrant neighborhoods that surround it on every side. Along the base of California Plaza, Hill Street became a local

Berlin Wall separating the publicly subsidized luxury of Bunker Hill from the lifeworld of Broadway, now reclaimed by Latino immigrants as their primary shopping and entertainment street. Because politically connected speculators are now redeveloping the northern end of the Broadway corridor (sometimes known as "Bunker Hill East"), the CRA is promising to restore pedestrian linkages to the Hill in the 1990s, including the Angels' Flight incline railroad. This, of course, only dramatizes the current bias against accessibility – that is to say, against any spatial interaction between old and new, poor and rich, except in the framework of gentrification or recolonization. Although a few white-collars venture into the Grand Central Market – a popular emporium of tropical produce and fresh foods – Latino shoppers or Saturday strollers never circulate in the Gucci precincts above Hill Street. The occasional appearance of a destitute street nomad in Broadway Plaza or in front of the Museum of Contemporary Art sets off a quiet panic; video cameras turn on their mounts and security guards adjust their belts.

Photographs of the old Downtown in its prime show mixed crowds of Anglo, Black and Latino pedestrians of different ages and classes. The contemporary Downtown "renaissance" is designed to make such heterogeneity virtually impossible. It is intended not just to "kill the street" as Kaplan fears, but to "kill the crowd," to eliminate that democratic admixture on the pavements and in the parks that Olmsted believed was America's antidote to European class polarizations. The Downtown hyperstructure – like some Buckminster Fuller post-Holocaust fantasy – is programmed to ensure a seamless continuum of middle-class work, consumption and recreation, without unwonted exposure to Downtown's working-class street environments. Indeed the totalitarian semiotics of ramparts and battlements, reflective glass and elevated pedways, rebukes any affinity or sympathy between different architectural or human orders. As in Otis's fortress *Times* building, this is the archisemiotics of class war.

ALLAN JACOBS and DONALD APPLEYARD

"Toward an Urban Design Manifesto"

Journal of the American Planning Association (1987)

Editors' introduction   Allan Jacobs and Donald Appleyard deplore many of the same aspects of the current urban environment that Mike Davis attacks: vast anonymous areas developed by giant public and private developers; dangerous, polluted, noisy, anonymous living environments; fortress-like buildings which present windowless facades to the street; cities as symbols of inequality. But "Toward an Urban Design Manifesto" moves beyond critique to set out goals for urban life and advance ideas for how the urban fabric of cities might be conserved or created anew to encourage a liveable urban environment.

Allan Jacobs is a professor of city and regional planning at the University of California, Berkeley, where Donald Appleyard also taught until his death shortly before this selection was published. Both worked closely with Kevin Lynch, whose *Image of the City* (p. 99) and other writings strongly influenced their work.

Jacobs has alternated between careers as a practicing city planner (in Pittsburgh, Philadelphia, New Delhi, and San Francisco) and academic teaching at the University of Pennsylvania and for the past decade and a half at the University of California, Berkeley's Department of City and Regional Planning. While he was San Francisco's Director of City Planning, Jacobs enlisted Donald Appleyard to work on studies of street livability in San Francisco and help the department develop an award-winning citywide urban design plan.

Jacobs and Appleyard title their piece a "manifesto" and model it on the celebrated Charter of Athens adopted by the International Congress of Modern Architecture (CIAM) – an organization which advanced the ideas for building contemporary cities based on Le Corbusier's principles (p. 368).

Jacobs and Appleyard do not like the vast clearance projects, highways, and high-rise buildings surrounded by enormous open space that have resulted from the CIAM's design ideology. They acknowledge that the Garden City ideas of Ebenezer Howard (p. 346) as implemented by Raymond Unwin (p. 355) have produced some pleasant communities, but dismiss these garden cities as more like suburbs than true *cities*. Their manifesto suggests an approach far more subtle and humane than the CIAM for development and more truly urban than Howard and Unwin's approach.

Jacobs and Appleyard's manifesto is grounded in both a command of academic theories and their own practical experience in city design. In this manifesto they propose urban development at densities higher than Howard proposed or Unwin implemented in Garden City designs, high enough to qualify as truly urban. But they would not endorse urban densities nearly as great as the CIAM theorists, particularly in megastructures surrounded by open space.

While Jacobs and Appleyard favor *reasonable* standards for decibel levels and street widths, they oppose excessive engineering standards that destroy the texture of urban life. They value pedestrians and public space. And, unlike the elitist CIAM theorists, they argue that participatory planning is essential.

In *Making City Planning Work* (Chicago: Planner's Press, 1976), Allan Jacobs alternates chapters describing the practical aspects of a city planning director's job with case studies on the San Francisco Urban Design Plan and other successful and not so successful projects he undertook during his tenure as city planning director of San Francisco. *Looking at Cities* (Cambridge, Mass.: MIT Press, 1985) grew out of a class he taught at Berkeley in which he had students take him to an unfamiliar neighborhood, leave him to look carefully at it, and then compare what he found out from looking with what they learned from examining data and reports on the same area. The resulting book reminds professionals to open their eyes and experience the areas they are planning, and outlines a methodology for reading clues in the built environment that can help with urban planning. Jacobs's most recent book is *Great Streets* (Princeton, N.J.: Princeton University Press, 1994), which summarizes a decade of observation and close study of notable streets throughout the world.

Donald Appleyard's *The View from the Road*, coauthored with Kevin Lynch and John Myer (Cambridge, Mass.: MIT Press, 1963), and *Liveable Streets* (Berkeley: University of California Press, 1981) show how ideas expressed in this urban design manifesto can be translated into action in street design.

For an overview of urban design see Jonathon Barnett, *An Introduction to Urban Design* (New York: Harper & Row, 1982). Other works on urban design include Edmund N. Bacon's *Design of Cities* (New York: Penguin Books, 1976), Vincent Scully's *American Architecture and Urbanism* (New York: Praeger, 1969), and Gordon Cullen's *Townscape* (New York: Penguin Books, 1976).

ALLAN JACOBS and DONALD APPLEYARD, "Toward an Urban Design Manifesto"

Journal of the American Planning Association (1987)

We think it's time for a new urban design manifesto. Almost 50 years have passed since Le Corbusier and the International Congress of Modern Architecture (CIAM) produced the Charter of Athens, and it is more than 20 years since the first Urban Design Conference, still in the CIAM tradition, was held (at Harvard in 1957). Since then the precepts of CIAM have been attacked by sociologists, planners, Jane Jacobs, and more recently by architects themselves. But it is still a strong influence, and we will take it as our starting point. Make no mistake: the charter was, simply, a manifesto – a public declaration that spelled out the ills of industrial cities as they existed in the 1930s and laid down physical requirements necessary to establish healthy, humane, and beautiful urban

environments for people. It could not help but deal with social, economic, and political phenomena, but its basic subject matter was the physical design of cities. Its authors were (mostly) socially concerned architects, determined that their art and craft be responsive to social realities as well as to improving the lot of man. It would be a mistake to write them off as simply elitist designers and physical determinists.

So the charter decried the medium-size (up to six storys) high-density buildings with high land coverage that were associated so closely with slums. Similarly, buildings that faced streets were found to be detrimental to healthy living. The seemingly limitless horizontal expansion of urban areas devoured the countryside, and suburbs were viewed as symbols of terrible waste. Solutions could be found in the demolition of unsanitary housing, the provision of green areas in every residential district, and new high-rise, high-density buildings set in open space. Housing was to be removed from its traditional relationship facing streets, and the whole circulation system was to be revised to meet the needs of emerging mechanization (the automobile). Work areas should be close to but separate from residential areas. To achieve the new city, large land holdings, preferably owned by the public, should replace multiple small parcels (so that projects could be properly designed and developed).

Now thousands of housing estates and redevelopment projects in socialist and capitalist countries the world over, whether built on previously undeveloped land or developed as replacements for old urban areas, attest to the acceptance of the charter's dictums. The design notions it embraced have become part of a world design language, not just the intellectual property of an enlightened few, even though the principles have been devalued in many developments.

Of course, the Charter of Athens has not been the only major urban philosophy of this century to influence the development of urban areas. Ebenezer Howard, too, was responding to the ills of the nineteenth-century industrial city, and the Garden City movement has been at least as powerful as the Charter of Athens. New towns policies, where they exist, are rooted in Howard's thought. But you don't have to look to new towns to see the influence of Howard, Olmsted, Wright, and Stein. The superblock notion, if nothing else, pervades large housing projects around the world, in central cities as well as suburbs. The notion of buildings in a park is as common to garden city designs as it is to charter-inspired development. Indeed, the two movements have a great deal in common: superblocks, separate paths for people and cars, interior common spaces, housing divorced from streets, and central ownership of land. The garden city-inspired communities place greater emphasis on private outdoor space. The most significant difference, at least as they have evolved, is in density and building type: the

garden city people preferred to accommodate people in row houses, garden apartments, and maisonettes, while Corbusier and the CIAM designers went for high-rise buildings and, inevitably, people living in flats and at significantly higher densities.

We are less than enthralled with what either the Charter of Athens or the Garden City movement has produced in the way of urban environments. The emphasis of CIAM was on buildings and what goes on within buildings that happen to sit in space, not on the public life that takes place constantly in public spaces. The orientation is often inward. Buildings tend to be islands, big or small. They could be placed anywhere. From the outside perspective, the building, like the work of art it was intended to be, sits where it can be seen and admired in full. And because it is large it is best seen from a distance (at a scale consistent with a moving auto). Diversity, spontaneity, and surprise are absent, at least for the person on foot. On the other hand, we find little joy or magic or spirit in the charter cities. They are not urban, to us, except according to some definition one might find in a census. Most garden cities, safe and healthy and even gracious as they may be, remind us more of suburbs than of cities. But they weren't trying to be cities. The emphasis has always been on "garden" as much as or more than on "city."

Both movements represent overly strong design reactions to the physical decay and social inequities of industrial cities. In responding so strongly, albeit understandably, to crowded, lightless, airless, "utilitiless," congested buildings and cities that housed so many people, the utopians did not inquire what was good about those places, either socially or physically. Did not those physical environments reflect (and maybe even foster) values that were likely to be meaningful to people individually and collectively, such as publicness and community? Without knowing it, maybe these strong reactions to urban ills ended up by throwing the baby out with the bathwater.

In the meantime we have had a lot of experience with city building and rebuilding. New spokespeople with new urban visions have emerged. As more CIAM-style buildings were built people became more disenchanted. Many began to look through picturesque lenses back to the old preindustrial cities. From a concentration on the city as a kind of sculpture garden, the townscape movement, led by the *Architectural Review*, emphasized "urban experience." This phenomenological view of the city was espoused by Rasmussen, Kepes, and ultimately Kevin Lynch and Jane Jacobs. It identified a whole new vocabulary of urban form – one that depended on the sights, sounds, feels, and smells of the city, its materials and textures, floor surfaces, facades, style, signs, lights, seating, trees, sun, and shade all potential amenities for the attentive observer and user. This has permanently humanized the vocabulary of urban design, and we enthusiastically subscribe to most of its tenets, though some in the townscape movement ignored the social meanings and implications of what they were doing.

The 1960s saw the birth of community design and an active concern for the social groups affected, usually negatively, by urban design. Designers were the "soft cops," and many professionals left the design field for social or planning vocations, finding the physical environment to have no redeeming social value. But at the beginning of the 1980s the mood in the design professions is conservative. There is a withdrawal from social engagement back to formalism. Supported by semiology and other abstract themes, much of architecture has become a dilettantish and narcissistic pursuit, a chic component of the high art consumer culture, increasingly remote from most people's everyday lives, finding its ultimate manifestation in the art gallery and the art book. City planning is too immersed in the administration and survival of housing, environmental, and energy programs and in responding to budget cuts and community demands to have any clear sense of direction with regard to city form.

While all these professional ideologies have been working themselves out, massive economic, technological, and social changes have taken place in our cities. The scale of capitalism has continued to increase, as has the scale of bureaucracy, and the automobile has virtually destroyed cities as they once were.

In formulating a new manifesto, we react against other phenomena than did the leaders of CIAM 50 years ago. The automobile cities of California and the Southwest present utterly different problems from those of nineteenth-century European cities, as do the CIAM-influenced housing developments around European, Latin American, and Russian cities and the rash of squatter settlements around the fast-growing cities of the Third World. What are these problems?

PROBLEMS FOR MODERN URBAN DESIGN

Poor living environments

While housing conditions in most advanced countries have improved in terms of such fundamentals as light, air, and space, the surroundings of homes are still frequently dangerous, polluted, noisy, anonymous wastelands. Travel around such cities has become more and more fatiguing and stressful.

Giantism and loss of control

The urban environment is increasingly in the hands of the large-scale developers and public agencies. The elements of the city grow inexorably in size, massive transportation systems are segregated for single travel modes, and vast districts and complexes are created that make people feel irrelevant.

People, therefore, have less sense of control over their homes, neighborhoods, and cities than when they lived in slower-growing locally based communities. Such giantism can be found as readily in the housing projects of socialist cities as in the office buildings and commercial developments of capitalist cities.

Large-scale privatization and the loss of public life

Cities, especially American cities, have become privatized, partly because of the consumer society's emphasis on the individual and the private sector, creating Galbraith's "private affluence and public squalor," but escalated greatly by the spread of the automobile. Crime in the streets is both a cause and a consequence of this trend, which has resulted in a new form of city: one of closed, defended islands with blank and windowless facades surrounded by wastelands of parking lots and fast-moving traffic. As public transit systems have declined, the number of places in American cities where people of different social groups actually meet each other has dwindled. The public environment of many American cities has become an empty desert, leaving public life dependent for its survival solely on planned formal occasions, mostly in protected internal locations.

Centrifugal fragmentation

Advanced industrial societies took work out of the home, and then out of the neighborhood, while the automobile and the growing scale of commerce have taken shopping out of the local community. Fear has led social groups to flee from each other into homogeneous social enclaves. Communities themselves have become lower in density and increasingly homogeneous. Thus the city has spread out and separated to form extensive monocultures and specialized destinations reachable often only by long journeys – a fragile and extravagant urban system dependent on cheap, available gasoline, and an effective contributor to the isolation of social groups from each other.

Destruction of valued places

The quest for profit and prestige and the relentless exploitation of places that attract the public have led to the destruction of much of our heritage, of historic places that no longer turn a profit, of natural amenities that become overused. In many cases, as in San Francisco, the very value of the place threatens its destruction as hungry tourists and entrepreneurs flock to see and profit from it.

Placelessness

Cities are becoming meaningless places beyond their citizens' grasp. We no longer know the origins of the world around us. We rarely know where the materials and products come from, who owns what, who is behind what, what was intended. We live in cities where things happen without warning and without our participation. It is an alien world for most people. It is little surprise that most withdraw from community involvement to enjoy their own private and limited worlds.

Injustice

Cities are symbols of inequality. In most cities the discrepancy between the environments of the rich and the environments of the poor is striking. In many instances the environments of the rich, by occupying and dominating the prevailing patterns of transportation and access, make the environments of the poor relatively worse. This discrepancy may be less visible in the low-density modern city, where the display of affluence is more hidden than in the old city; but the discrepancy remains.

Rootless professionalism

Finally, design professionals today are often part of the problem. In too many cases, we design for places and people we do not know and grant them very little power or acknowledgment. Too many professionals are more part of a universal professional culture than part of the local cultures for whom we produce our plans and products. We carry our "bag of tricks" around the world and bring them out wherever we land. This floating professional culture has only the most superficial conception of particular place. Rootless, it is more susceptible to changes in professional fashion and theory than to local events. There is too little inquiry, too much proposing. Quick surveys are made, instant solutions devised, and the rest of the time is spent persuading the clients. Limits on time and budgets drive us on, but so do lack of understanding and the placeless culture. Moreover, we designers are often unconscious of our own roots, which influence our preferences in hidden ways.

At the same time, the planning profession's retreat into trendism, under the positivist influence of social science, has left it virtually unable to resist the social pressures of capitalist economy and consumer sovereignty. Planners have lost their beliefs. Although we believe citizen participation is essential to urban planning, professionals also must have a sense of what we believe is right, even though we may be vetoed.

GOALS FOR URBAN LIFE

We propose, therefore, a number of goals that we deem essential for the future of a good urban environment: livability; identity and control; access to opportunity, imagination, and joy; authenticity and meaning; open communities and public life; self-reliance; and justice.

Livability

A city should be a place where everyone can live in relative comfort. Most people want a kind of sanctuary for their living environment, a place where they can bring up children, have privacy, sleep, eat, relax, and restore themselves. This means a well-managed environment relatively devoid of nuisance, overcrowding, noise, danger, air pollution, dirt, trash, and other unwelcome intrusions.

Identity and control

People should feel that some part of the environment belongs to them, individually and collectively, some part for which they care and are responsible, whether they own it or not. The urban environment should be an environment that encourages people to express themselves, to become involved, to decide what they want and act on it. Like a seminar where everybody has something to contribute to communal discussion, the urban environment should encourage

participation. Urbanites may not always want this. Many like the anonymity of the city, but we are not convinced that the freedom of anonymity is a desirable freedom. It would be much better if people were sure enough of themselves to stand up and be counted. Environments should therefore be designed for those who use them or are affected by them, rather than for those who own them. This should reduce alienation and anonymity (even if people want them); it should increase people's sense of identity and rootedness and encourage more care and responsibility for the physical environment of cities.

Respect for the existing environment, both nature and city, is one fundamental difference we have with the CIAM movement. Urban design has too often assumed that new is better than old. But the new is justified only if it is better than what exists. Conservation encourages identity and control and, usually, a better sense of community, since old environments are more usually part of a common heritage.

Access to opportunity, imagination, and joy

People should find the city a place where they can break from traditional molds, extend their experience, meet new people, learn other viewpoints, have fun. At a functional level, people should have access to alternative housing and job choices; at another level, they should find the city an enlightening cultural experience. A city should have magical places where fantasy is possible, a counter to and an escape from the mundaneness of everyday work and living. Architects and planners take cities and themselves too seriously; the result too often is deadliness and boredom, no imagination, no humor, alienating places. But people need an escape from the seriousness and meaning of the everyday. The city has always been a place of excitement; it is theater, a stage upon which citizens can display themselves and see others. It has magic, or should have, and that depends on a certain sensuous, hedonistic mood, on signs, on night lights, on fantasy, color, and other imagery. There can be parts of the city where belief can be suspended, just as in the experience of fiction. It may be that such places have to be framed so that people know how to act. Until now such fantasy and experiment have been attempted mostly by commercial facilities, at rather low levels of quality and aspiration, seldom deeply experimental. One should not have to travel as far as the Himalayas or the South Sea Islands to stretch one's experience. Such challenges could be nearer home. There should be a place for community utopias; for historic, natural, and anthropological evocations of the modern city, for encounters with the truly exotic.

Authenticity and meaning

People should be able to understand their city (or other people's cities), its basic layout, public functions, and institutions; they should be aware of its opportunities. An authentic city is one where the origins of things and places are clear. All this means an urban environment should reveal its significant meanings; it should not be dominated only by one type of group, the powerful; neither should publicly important places be hidden. The city should symbolize the moral issues of society and educate its citizens to an awareness of them.

That does not mean everything has to be laid out as on a supermarket shelf. A city should present itself as a readable story, in an engaging and, if necessary, provocative way, for people are indifferent to the obvious, overwhelmed by complexity. A city's offerings should be revealed or they will be missed. This can affect the forms of the city, its signage, and other public information and education programs.

Livability, identity, authenticity, and opportunity are characteristics of the urban environment that should serve the individual and small social unit, but the city has to serve some higher social goals as well. It is these we especially wish to emphasize here.

Community and public life

Cities should encourage participation of their citizens in community and public life. In the face of giantism and fragmentation, public life, especially life in public places, has been seriously eroded. The neighborhood movement, by bringing thousands, probably millions of people out of their closed private lives into active participation in their local communities, has begun to counter that trend, but this movement has had its limitations. It can be purely defensive, parochial, and self-serving. A city should be more than a warring collection of interest groups, classes, and neighborhoods; it should breed a commitment to a larger whole, to tolerance, justice, law, and democracy. The structure of the city should invite and encourage public life, not only through its institutions, but directly and symbolically through its public spaces. The public environment, unlike the neighborhood, by definition should be open to all members of the community. It is where people of different kinds meet. No one should be excluded unless they threaten the balance of that life.

Urban self-reliance

Increasingly cities will have to become more self-sustaining in their uses of energy and other scarce resources. "Soft energy paths" in particular not only will reduce dependence and exploitation across regions and countries but also will help reestablish a stronger sense of local and regional identity, authenticity, and meaning.

An environment for all

Good environments should be accessible to all. Every citizen is entitled to some minimal level of environmental livability and minimal levels of identity, control, and opportunity. Good urban design must be for the poor as well as the rich. Indeed, it is more needed by the poor.

We look toward a society that is truly pluralistic, one where power is more evenly distributed among social groups than it is today in virtually any country, but where the different values and cultures of interest- and place-based groups are acknowledged and negotiated in a just public arena.

These goals for the urban environment are both individual and collective, and as such they are frequently in conflict. The more a city promises for the individual, the less it seems to have a public life; the more the city is built for public entities, the less the individual seems to count. The good urban environment is one that somehow balances these goals, allowing individual and group identity while maintaining a public concern, encouraging pleasure while maintaining responsibility, remaining open to outsiders while sustaining a strong sense of localism.

AN URBAN FABRIC FOR AN URBAN LIFE

We have some ideas, at least, for how the fabric or texture of cities might be conserved or created to encourage a livable urban environment. We emphasize the structural qualities of the good urban environment – qualities we hope will be successful in creating urban experiences that are consonant with our goals.

Do not misread this. We are not describing all the qualities of a city. We are not dealing with major transportation systems, open space, the natural environment, the structure of the large-scale city, or even the structure of neighborhoods, but only the grain of the good city.

There are five physical characteristics that must be present if there is to be a positive response to the goals and values we believe are central to urban life. They must be designed, they must exist, as prerequisites of a sound urban environment. All five must be present, not just one or two. There are other physical characteristics that are important, but these five are essential: livable streets and neighborhoods; some minimum density of residential development as well as intensity of land use; an integration of activities – living, working, shopping – in some reasonable proximity to each other; a manmade environment, particularly buildings, that defines public space (as opposed to buildings that, for the most part, sit in space); and many, many separate, distinct buildings with complex arrangements and relationships (as opposed to few, large buildings).

Let us explain, keeping in mind that all five of

the characteristics must be present. People, we have said, should be able to live in reasonable (though not excessive) safety, cleanliness, and security. That means livable streets and neighborhoods: with adequate sunlight, clean air, trees, vegetation, gardens, open space, pleasantly scaled and designed buildings; without offensive noise; with cleanliness and physical safety. Many of these characteristics can be designed into the physical fabric of the city.

The reader will say, "Well of course, but what does that mean?" Usually it has meant specific standards and requirements, such as sun angles, decibel levels, lane widths, and distances between buildings. Many researchers have been trying to define the qualities of a livable environment. It depends on a wide array of attributes, some structural, some quite small details. There is no single right answer. We applaud these efforts and have participated in them ourselves. Nevertheless, desires for livability and individual comfort by themselves have led to fragmentation of the city. Livability standards, whether for urban or for suburban developments, have often been excessive.

Our approach to the details of this inclusive physical characteristic would center on the words "reasonable, though not excessive ..." Too often, for example, the requirement of adequate sunlight has resulted in buildings and people inordinately far from each other, beyond what demonstrable need for light would dictate. Safety concerns have been the justifications for ever wider streets and wide, sweeping curves rather than narrow ways and sharp corners. Buildings are removed from streets because of noise considerations when there might be other ways to deal with this concern. So although livable streets and neighborhoods are a primary requirement for any good urban fabric – whether for existing, denser cities or for new development – the quest for livable neighborhoods, if pursued obsessively, can destroy the urban qualities we seek to achieve.

A *minimum density* is needed. By density we mean the number of people (sometimes expressed in terms of housing units) living on an area of land, or the number of people using an area of land.

Cities are not farms. A city is people living

and working and doing the things they do in relatively close proximity to each other.

We are impressed with the importance of density as a perceived phenomenon and therefore relative to the beholder and agree that, for many purposes, perceived density is more important than an "objective" measurement of people per unit of land. We agree, too, that physical phenomena can be manipulated so as to render perceptions of greater or lesser density. Nevertheless, a narrow, winding street, with a lot of signs and a small enclosed open space at the end, with no people, does not make a city. Cities are more than stage sets. Some minimum number of people living and using a given area of land is required if there is to be human exchange, public life and action, diversity and community.

Density of people alone will account for the presence or absence of certain uses and services we find important to urban life. We suspect, for example, that the number and diversity of small stores and services – for instance, groceries, bars, bakeries, laundries and cleaners, coffee shops, secondhand stores, and the like – to be found in a city or area is in part a function of density. That is, that such businesses are more likely to exist, and in greater variety, in an area where people live in greater proximity to each other ("higher" density). The viability of mass transit, we know, depends partly on the density of residential areas and partly on the size and intensity of activity at commercial and service destinations. And more use of transit, in turn, reduces parking demands and permits increases in density. There must be a critical mass of people, and they must spend a lot of their time in reasonably close proximity to each other, including when they are at home, if there is to be an urban life. The goal of local control and community identity is associated with density as well. The notion of an optimum density is elusive and is easily confused with the health and livability of urban areas, with lifestyles, with housing types, with the size of area being considered (the building site or the neighborhood or the city), and with the economics of development. A density that might be best for child rearing might be less than adequate to support public transit. Most recently, energy

efficiency has emerged as a concern associated with density, the notion being that conservation will demand more compact living arrangements.

Our conclusion, based largely on our experience and on the literature, is that a minimum net density (people or living units divided by the size of the building site, excluding public streets) of about 15 dwelling units (30–60 people) per acre of land is necessary to support city life. By way of illustration, that is the density produced with generous town houses (or row houses). It would permit parcel sizes up to 25 feet wide by about 115 feet deep. But other building types and lot sizes also would produce that density. Some areas could be developed with lower densities, but not very many. We don't think you get cities at 6 dwellings to the acre, let alone on half-acre lots. On the other hand, it is possible to go as high as 48 dwelling units per acre (96 to 192 people) for a very large part of the city and still provide for a spacious and gracious urban life. Much of San Francisco, for example, is developed with three-story buildings (one unit per floor) above a parking story, on parcels that measure 25 feet by 100 or 125 feet. At those densities, with that kind of housing, there can be private or shared gardens for most people, no common hallways are required, and people can have direct access to the ground. Public streets and walks adequate to handle pedestrian and vehicular traffic generated by these densities can be accommodated in rights-of-way that are 50 feet wide or less. Higher densities, for parts of the city, to suit particular needs and lifestyles, would be both possible and desirable. We are not sure what the upper limits would be but suspect that as the numbers get much higher than 200 people per net residential acre, for larger parts of the city, the concessions to less desirable living environments mount rapidly.

Beyond residential density, there must be a minimum intensity of people using an area for it to be urban, as we are defining that word. We aren't sure what the numbers are or even how best to measure this kind of intensity. We are speaking here, particularly, of the public or "meeting" areas of our city. We are confident that our lowest residential densities will provide most meeting areas with life and human exchange, but are not sure if they will generate enough activity for the most intense central districts.

There must be an *integration of activities* – living, working, and shopping as well as public, spiritual, and recreational activities – reasonably near each other.

The best urban places have some mixtures of uses. The mixture responds to the values of publicness and diversity that encourage local community identity. Excitement, spirit, sense, stimulation, and exchange are more likely when there is a mixture of activities than when there is not. There are many examples that we all know. It is the mix, not just the density of people and uses, that brings life to an area, the life of people going about a full range of normal activities without having to get into an automobile.

We are not saying that every area of the city should have a full mix of all uses. That would be impossible. The ultimate in mixture would be for each building to have a range of uses from living, to working, to shopping, to recreation. We are not calling for a return to the medieval city. There is a lot to be said for the notion of "living sanctuaries," which consist almost wholly of housing. But we think these should be relatively small, of a few blocks, and they should be close and easily accessible (by foot) to areas where people meet to shop or work or recreate or do public business. And except for a few of the most intensely developed office blocks of a central business district or a heavy industrial area, the meeting areas should have housing within them. Stores should be mixed with offices. If we envision the urban landscape as a fabric, then it would be a salt-and-pepper fabric of many colors, each color for a separate use or a combination. Of course, some areas would be much more heavily one color than another, and some would be an even mix of colors. Some areas, if you squinted your eyes, or if you got so close as to see only a small part of the fabric, would read as one color, a red or a brown or a green. But by and large there would be few if any distinct patterns, where one color stopped and another started. It would not be patchwork quilt, or an even-colored fabric. The fabric would be mixed.

In an urban environment, *buildings* (and other objects that people place in the environment) *should be arranged in such a way as to define and even enclose public space, rather than sit in space*. It is not enough to have high densities and an integration of activities to have cities. A tall enough building with enough people living (or even working) in it, sited on a large parcel, can easily produce the densities we have talked about and can have internally mixed uses, like most "mixed use" projects. But that building and its neighbors will be unrelated objects sitting in space if they are far enough apart, and the mixed uses might be only privately available. In large measure that is what the Charter of Athens, the garden cities, and standard suburban development produce.

Buildings close to each other along a street, regardless of whether the street is straight, or curved, or angled, tend to define space if the street is not too wide in relation to the buildings. The same is true of a plaza or a square. As the spaces between buildings become larger (in relation to the size of the buildings, up to a point), the buildings tend more and more to sit in space. They become focal points for few or many people, depending on their size and activity. Except where they are monuments or centers for public activities (a stadium or meeting hall), where they represent public gathering spots, buildings in space tend to be private and inwardly oriented. People come to them and go from them in any direction. That is not so for the defined outdoor environment. Avoiding the temptation to ascribe all kinds of psychological values to defined spaces (such as intimacy, belonging, protection – values that are difficult to prove and that may differ for different people), it is enough to observe that spaces surrounded by buildings are more likely to bring people together and thereby promote public interaction. The space can be linear (like streets) or in the form of plazas of myriad shapes. Moreover, interest and interplay among uses is enhanced. To be sure, such arrangements direct people and limit their freedom – they cannot move in just any direction from any point – but presumably there are enough choices (even avenues of escape) left open, and the gain is in greater potential for sense stimulation, excitement, surprise, and focus. Over and over again we seek out and return to defined ways and spaces as symbolic of urban life emphasizing the public space more than the private building.

It is important for us to emphasize *public places* and a *public* way system. We have observed that the central value of urban life is that of publicness, of people from different groups meeting each other and of people acting in concert, albeit with debate. The most important public places must be for *pedestrians*, for no public life can take place between people in automobiles. Most public space has been taken over by the automobile, for travel or parking. We must fight to restore more for the pedestrian. Pedestrian malls are not simply to benefit the local merchants. They have an essential public value. People of different kinds meet each other directly. The level of communication may be only visual, but that itself is educational and can encourage tolerance. The revival of street activities, street vending, and street theater in American cities may be the precursor of a more flourishing public environment, if the automobile can be held back.

There also must be symbolic, public meeting places, accessible to all and publicly controlled. Further, in order to communicate, to get from place to place, to interact, to exchange ideas and goods, there must be a healthy public circulation system. It cannot be privately controlled. Public circulation systems should be seen as significant cultural settings where the city's finest products and artifacts can be displayed, as in the piazzas of medieval and renaissance cities.

Finally, *many different buildings and spaces with complex arrangements and relationships* are required. The often elusive notion of human scale is associated with this requirement – a notion that is not just an architect's concept but one that other people understand as well.

Diversity, the possibility of intimacy and confrontation with the unexpected, stimulation, are all more likely with many buildings than with few taking up the same ground areas.

For a long time we have been led to believe that large land holdings were necessary to design healthy, efficient, aesthetically pleasing urban environments. The slums of the industrial city were associated, at least in part, with all those small, overbuilt parcels. Socialist and capitalist ideologies alike called for land assembly to permit integrated, socially and economically useful developments. What the socialist countries would do via public ownership the capitalists would achieve through redevelopment and new fiscal mechanisms that rewarded large holdings. Architects of both ideological persuasions promulgated or were easily convinced of the wisdom of land assembly. It's not hard to figure out why. The results, whether by big business or big government, are more often than not inward-oriented, easily controlled or controllable, sterile, large-building projects, with fewer entrances, fewer windows, less diversity, less innovation, and less individual expression than the urban fabric that existed previously or that can be achieved with many actors and many buildings. Attempts to break up facades or otherwise to articulate separate activities in large buildings are seldom as successful as when smaller properties are developed singly.

Health, safety, and efficiency can be achieved with many smaller buildings, individually designed and developed. Reasonable public controls can see to that. And, of course, smaller buildings are a lot more likely if parcel sizes are small than if they are large. With smaller buildings and parcels, more entrances must be located on the public spaces, more windows and a finer scale of design diversity emerge. A more public, lively city is produced. It implies more, smaller groups getting pieces of the public action, taking part, having a stake. Other stipulations may be necessary to keep public frontages alive, free from the deadening effects of offices and banks, but small buildings will help this more than large ones. There need to be large buildings, too, covering large areas of land, but they will be the exception, not the rule, and should not be in the centers of public activity.

ALL THESE QUALITIES . . . AND OTHERS

A good city must have all those qualities. Density without livability could return us to the slums of the nineteenth century. Public places without small-scale, fine-grain development would give us vast, overscale cities. As an urban fabric, however, those qualities stand a good chance of meeting many of the goals we outlined. They directly attend to the issue of livability though they are aimed especially at encouraging public places and a public life. Their effects on personal and group identity are less clear, though the small-scale city is more likely to support identity than the large-scale city. Opportunity and imagination should be encouraged by a diverse and densely settled urban structure. This structure also should create a setting that is more meaningful to the individual inhabitant and small group than the giant environments now being produced. There is no guarantee that this urban structure will be a more just one than those presently existing. In supporting the small against the large, however, more justice for the powerless may be encouraged.

Still, an urban fabric of this kind cannot by itself meet all these goals. Other physical characteristics are important to the design of urban environments. Open space, to provide access to nature as well as relief from the built environment, is one. So are definitions, boundaries if you will, that give location and identity to neighborhoods (or districts) and to the city itself. There are other characteristics as well: public buildings, educational environments, places set aside for nurturing the spirit, and more. We still have work to do.

MANY PARTICIPANTS

While we have concentrated on defining physical characteristics of a good city fabric, the process of creating it is crucial. As important as many buildings and spaces are *many participants* in the building process. It is through this involvement in the creation and management of their city that citizens are most likely to identify with it and, conversely, to enhance their own sense of identity and control.

AN ESSENTIAL BEGINNING

The five characteristics we have noted are essential to achieving the values central to urban life. They need much further definition and testing. We have to know more about what configurations create public space: about maximum densities, about how small a community can be and still be urban (some very small Swiss villages fit the bill, and everyone knows some favorite examples), about what is perceived as big and what small under different circumstances, about landscape material as a space definer, and a lot more. When we know more we will be still further along toward a new urban design manifesto.

We know that any ideal community, including the kind that can come from this manifesto, will not always be comfortable for every person. Some people don't like cities and aren't about to. Those who do will not be enthralled with all of what we propose.

Our urban vision is rooted partly in the realities of earlier, older urban places that many people, including many utopian designers, have rejected, often for good reasons. So our utopia will not satisfy all people. That's all right. We *like* cities. Given a choice of the kind of community we would like to live in – the sort of choice earlier city dwellers seldom had – we would choose to live in an urban, public community that embraces the goals and displays the physical characteristics we have outlined. Moreover, we think it responds to what people want and that it will promote the good urban life.

PART 3

*U*rban Society and Culture

PART THREE

INTRODUCTION

As Shakespeare wrote – and as urbanists ever since have never tired of quoting – "the city is the people." Urban history expresses the progressive evolution of the city as an institution. Urban form and design describe the physical appearance and infrastructural layout of cities. But it is the people of the city – their individual aspirations and collective struggles, their day-to-day lives and their moments of heightened awareness – that constitute the core subject of urban studies and planning.

In Part 2 of this book, Urban Form and Design, we saw that the physical shape and arrangement of cities reflect the culture of the societies from which they spring. Sensitive urban theorists respect the vernacular landscape (J. B. Jackson), remind us that "a city is not a tree" (Alexander), and take account of human psychology and perception in designing the built environment (Whyte, Lynch, Jacobs, and Appleyard). Clearly, then, there is a reciprocity between the physical and social environments of cities.

In turning to the people of the cities themselves, we move to an even deeper level of reciprocity: the subtle and ever-shifting interplay between society, community, and culture. This section addresses how being urban affects social structure and how social structure, in turn, affects individual human interactions. It asks what human culture is in an urban context and how it fragments or evolves in different social contexts. It analyzes what urban community is and speculates about what it could be. Taken together, these questions form a bridge to the next three parts of the book, which discuss how cities work politically and economically, how they are planned, and what they might be like in the future.

In studying the people of the city, the key methodology is sociology, the "science of society" that arose alongside the emergence of the modern industrial city itself. Urban sociology has always been allied with urban anthropology, and in recent years new formulations – social studies, social theory, social relations, culture studies – have joined the discipline either as adjuncts or rivals. But the basic sociological vision remains central to all investigations of people in cities. And as Harvard sociologist Talcott Parsons once reportedly remarked, putting the word urban before the word sociology was like putting the word horse before the word doctor!

There is no better person with whom to begin a section on urban society and culture than Lewis Mumford, one of the great public intellectuals of the twentieth century. Mumford never lost sight of the human dimension of cities. For over sixty years he sparred with those who argued that cities arose and prospered for purely economic reasons or that cities were best defined in terms of size and density. Not so!, thundered Mumford: cities are expressions of the human spirit and cities exist to contribute to the ever-evolving human personality. This perspective comes through loud and clear in "What Is a City?" To Mumford, defining a city in terms of population size, or density, or attributes of the built environment is inadequate. Rather, the human side of cities is their very essence, and city streets are a stage on which life's drama is played out. Like William Whyte

(p. 110), Mumford delighted in city life. For him, cities reflect and enlarge the human spirit, and creating better, more human cities will enrich civilization itself.

Mumford, of course, was not alone in focusing on the connections between urban life and the human personality. In "Urbanism as a Way of Life," Louis Wirth asked the fundamental question "What does it mean to be urban?" and discovered that an urban "way of life" resulted in an "urban type" of character and personality. Wirth was one of a gifted group of sociologists at the University of Chicago who, in the 1920s and 1930s, developed a pioneering body of urban sociological theory that still shapes the field of urban sociology today. Studying rural migrants to Chicago from the peasant societies of Southern and Eastern Europe, Wirth perceived that the whole way of life in modern cities was fundamentally different from the way of life in rural cultures. In "Urbanism as a Way of Life," he attempts to abstract the essential characteristics of urban as opposed to rural life and to find the sources of the widely perceived urban characteristics of brusqueness and impersonality. As the face-to-face transactions of static rural village life are replaced by the distanced and mediated transactions of a large city, human personalities are transformed, and the new urbanites respond to each other and to society as a whole in entirely different ways than they did in their rural folk communities. While Wirth's is a *theoretical* study, it is important to remember that his theories were generated by empirical studies he and his colleagues were conducting in Chicago during the early decades of the twentieth century.

One of the ways that the modern urbanite differs from his rural counterpart is in his deep immersion in an almost overpowering consumer economy and culture of mindless materialism. This is the focus of Paul and Percival Goodman's *Communitas*, a critique of modern urban life just as rooted in empirical observations as Wirth's work but more aligned with what would today be called culture studies or critical theory. The Goodmans agree that cities should express the best in human culture but feel that today's cities rarely achieve that goal, and "The City of Efficient Consumption" is a clear, if decidedly tongue-in-cheek, statement of their attack on the spiritually empty, profit-driven consumer society. The spatial arrangement of the Goodman's model city parodies the importance of materialist values to middle-class urban society by locating the university as the gateway to the central, mall-like consumerist urban core. In the years since the Goodmans wrote, urban reality has seemed to approach, and even surpass, what was once merely social satire.

Whereas the Goodmans concentrate on the material comforts and moral deficiencies of middle-class urban culture, a larger body of sociological investigation has focused on the urban working class, the poor, and the recently emerging underclass populations that are such an integral social element of the modern industrial city. British sociologists Michael Young and Peter Willmott, for example, studied the working-class residents of London's Bethnal Green district – one of the classic slums from the earliest days of the Industrial Revolution – and followed them as they were relocated to new housing estates far removed from their original neighborhood. What Young and Willmott discovered and reported in their influential *Family and Kinship in East London* was that Bethnal Green, for all its poverty and infrastructural shortcomings, had constituted a real community and that a genuine working-class culture had flourished that encouraged a sense of neighborliness and social solidarity. When Bethnal Greeners were moved to Greenleigh – some of them becoming home-owners in the process – the material conditions of life improved, but the old sense of community was shattered, and a distinct working-class culture – a real urban way of life – was irretrievably lost.

In North America, the urban anthropologist Oscar Lewis is another important – and controversial – scholar whose ideas about urban society and poverty have had a profound impact.

Using the anthropologist's method of detailed observation and analysis, Lewis explored the lives of poor city dwellers in Mexico, Puerto Rico, and Cuba. In *The Children of Sanchez* and several other books, Lewis provides a detailed account of how rural newcomers experience and adapt to city life. While the factual record Lewis developed provides an extraordinary depth and subtlety of understanding, it is his theories – developed from his observations – that attracted the most attention. In "The Culture of Poverty," Lewis summarizes his argument that there are a distinct set of cultural attributes associated with many of the urban poor. It follows that changing this culture may be the key to ending the "cycle of poverty" and some of the negative aspects of urban life that so many poor people experience. But is Lewis right? Many believe that traits of so diverse a group as the worldwide urban poor cannot be generalized. Is the culture of shantytown residents in Dakar really just like the culture of Jamaicans and Pakistanis in London? Still others argue that perhaps a general set of traits *can* be developed but that the traits that Lewis identified – particularly many of the negative ones such as wife-beating and early sexual activity – are both invalid and offensive to minorities.

The Black ghettos of the United States have been the subject of an enormous body of sociological research that both celebrates the distinctive culture and analyzes the social pathology of segregated, poverty-ridden inner-city communities. Beginning with W. E. B. Dubois's study *The Philadelphia Negro* (1899) (p. 57) and continuing through the work of E. Franklin Frazier (*The Negro Family in the United States*, 1939), St. Clair Drake and Horace Cayton (*Black Metropolis*, 1945), and Kenneth B. Clark (*Dark Ghetto*, 1965), African-American scholars have taken the lead in examining the social and cultural dynamics of the ghetto communities of America's northern cities.

University of Chicago sociologist William Julius Wilson is a contemporary heir of both the first-generation Chicago School researchers such as Louis Wirth and the subsequent tradition of African-American scholarship. Wilson's penetrating analysis "The Black Underclass" is here followed by "Choosing a Future" from Charles Murray's *Losing Ground*. Wilson, a Black liberal, and Murray, a white conservative, illustrate the role of ideology in shaping urban theory. Both agree that the situation of the poorest urban Blacks in the U.S. has grown worse during the last generation and that poor ghetto Blacks today, especially the youth, are in deep trouble. But they part company on why this is so ... and what to do about it. Wilson, like John Kasarda (p. 306), stresses the loss of jobs accessible to unskilled Black youth. It is this loss of jobs, Wilson argues, that has destroyed ghetto family structure and lies at the root of crime, substance abuse, and other ghetto ills. Murray looks at many of the same facts and reaches different conclusions. As he sees it, many young Black males are not "marriageable" because they lack minimum job skills, have substance abuse problems, or are in jail. Without "marriageable" males, many young Black women cannot form two-parent nuclear families, and teen pregnancies, out-of-wedlock births, and female-headed, welfare-dependent, single-parent households result.

William Julius Wilson would like to see government intervene with a universal – not race-specific – full employment program. If Blacks are employed, he reasons, family stability will return, and substance abuse and criminal behavior will drop. Charles Murray disagrees. According to him, the last thing poor Blacks need is more government assistance. After government poverty programs increased, he notes, the condition of inner-city Blacks only got worse. Murray argues that patronizing government programs sapped initiative and created perverse incentives to stay out of the labor market. Why work at a hard, dirty job when you can get almost as much, and sometimes more, doing nothing on welfare? Why stay married and work if you can split up and get federal welfare for single-parent, female-headed households? Murray's remedy: cut government welfare and social service programs. When previously-unemployed Blacks know they are making it on their own – by working long hours at hard jobs, without paternalistic government programs – they will regain self-respect and cut down on drugs and criminality. Or so the argument goes.

In exploring urban society and culture, sociologists are trained to investigate a range of measurable conditions and observable social behaviors and to analyze their findings in terms of class, race, ethnicity, and socioeconomic status. But urban culture has other dimensions that do not lend themselves so easily to quantitative analysis or narrative description. Among these are the expressions of the creative arts and the other cultural productions that emerge from urban communities everywhere. Working-class neighborhoods and inner-city ghettos do not just produce poverty and crime, after all; they also produce formal poetry and the linguistic inventiveness of street talk, rhapsodies and jazz music, paintings and graffiti. These – as much as the hustle and bustle of the street or the systole and diastole of the daily commute – are elements of what Lewis Mumford called "the urban drama."

In "The City as Image," comparative literature professor Burton Pike examines one whole body of urban artistic production – the nineteenth- and twentieth-century literary tradition of urban experience – to extract some deeper meaning about what coming to the city, and living in the city, has meant for modern humanity. As Pike sees it, the lesson that emerges from these works is one of ambiguity and contradiction. "Perhaps the central fascination of the city, both real and fictional," he writes, "is that it embodies man's contradictory feelings – pride, love, anxiety, and hatred – toward the civilization he has created and the culture to which he belongs." Mumford wrote that in "the Book of Job one beholds Jerusalem; in Plato, Sophocles, and Euripides, Athens; in Shakespeare and Marlowe, Dekker and Webster, London." What is equally clear is that Paris emerges from Monet, Vienna from Robert Musil, Chicago from Upton Sinclair and Theodore Dreiser, Berlin from Berthold Brecht and Kurt Weill, and Harlem from Langston Hughes, Countee Cullen, and Zora Neale Hurston. In the final analysis, the urban drama is not just about the abstractions of class and socioeconomic dynamics; it is about the real, everyday experience of people and their communities. These are the ultimate building blocks of the urban community.

LEWIS MUMFORD

"What Is a City?"

Architectural Record (1937)

Editors' introduction   Lewis Mumford (1895–1990) has been called America's last great public intellectual. Beginning with his first book in 1922 and continuing throughout a career that saw the publication of some twenty-five influential volumes, Mumford made signal contributions to social philosophy, American literary and cultural history, the history of technology and, preeminently, the history of cities and urban planning practice.

Mumford saw the urban experience as an integral component in the development of human culture and the human personality. He consistently argued that the physical design of cities and their economic functions were secondary to their relationship to the natural environment and to the spiritual values of human community. Mumford applied these principles to his architectural criticism for *The New Yorker* magazine in the 1920s, to his work with the Regional Planning Association of America, to his campaign against plans to build a highway through Washington Square in New York's Greenwich Village in the 1950s, and to his lifelong championing of the Garden City ideals of Ebenezer Howard.

In "What Is a City?" Mumford lays out his fundamental propositions about the planning of cities and the human potential, both individual and social, of urban life. The city, he writes, is "a theater of social action," and everything else – art, politics, education, commerce – only serve to make the "social drama . . . more richly significant, as a stage-set, well-designed, intensifies and underlines the gestures of the actors and the action of the play." It was a theme and an image to which Mumford would return over and over again: in the chapter "The Nature of the Ancient City" in his magisterial *The City in History: Its Origins, Its Transformations, and Its Prospects* (New York: Harcourt Brace, 1961), he wrote that the city is "above all things a theater" and, as if commenting on the cultural conformity of the 1950s, warned that an urban civilization that has lost its sense of dramatic dialogue "is bound to have a fatal last act."

Mumford's influence on modern urban planning theory can hardly be overstated. He wrote introductions to Ian McHarg's *Design with Nature* (p. 133) and the MIT Press edition of Howard's *Garden Cities of To-morrow* (p. 346), and his "urban drama" idea clearly resonates with an entire line of urban cultural analysts. Jane Jacobs, for example, talks about "street ballet" (p. 104). Allan Jacobs and Donald Appleyard (p. 165) urge planners to fulfill human needs for "fantasy and exoticism." And William Whyte (p. 110) says that a good urban plaza should function like a stage. The city, they write, "has always been a place of excitement; it is a theater, a stage upon which citizens can display themselves and be seen by others."

As a historian, Mumford is the antithesis of Henri Pirenne (p. 38), whom Mumford considered too much of an economic determinist despite his "excellent basic scholarship," but Mumford's emphasis on community values and the city's role in enlarging the potential of the human personality connects him with a long line of urban theorists that includes Paul and Percival Goodman (p. 199), Christopher Alexander (p. 119), and Peter Calthorpe (p. 469).

The City in History is undoubtedly Mumford's masterpiece, but an earlier version of the same material, The Culture of Cities (New York: Harcourt Brace, 1938), is still of interest. The Urban Prospect (New York: Harcourt Brace, 1968) is an outstanding collection of his essays on urban planning and culture, and The Myth of the Machine (New York: Harcourt Brace, 1967) and The Pentagon of Power (New York: Harcourt Brace, 1970) are excellent analyses of the influence of technology on human culture. The illuminating The Transformations of Man (New York: Harper, 1956) invites comparison with V. Gordon Childe's theory of the urban revolution in Man Makes Himself (p. 22). Donald L. Miller's Lewis Mumford: A Life (New York: Weidenfeld & Nicolson, 1989) is a serviceable biography. Mumford's correspondence with Patrick Geddes (p. 361) is contained in Frank G. Novak, Lewis Mumford and Patrick Geddes: The Correspondence (London: Routledge, 1995).

LEWIS MUMFORD, "What Is a City?"

Architectural Record (1937)

Most of our housing and city planning has been handicapped because those who have undertaken the work have had no clear notion of the social functions of the city. They sought to derive these functions from a cursory survey of the activities and interests of the contemporary urban scene. And they did not, apparently, suspect that there might be gross deficiencies, misdirected efforts, mistaken expenditures here that would not be set straight by merely building sanitary tenements or straightening out and widening irregular streets.

The city as a purely physical fact has been subject to numerous investigations. But what is the city as a social institution? The earlier answers to these questions, in Aristotle, Plato, and the Utopian writers from Sir Thomas More to Robert Owen, have been on the whole more satisfactory than those of the more systematic sociologists: most contemporary treatises on "urban sociology" in America throw no important light upon the problem. One of the soundest definitions of the city was that framed by John Stow, an honest observer of Elizabethan London, who said:

> Men are congregated into cities and commonwealths for honesty and utility's sake, these shortly be the commodities that do come by cities,

commonalties and corporations. First, men by this nearness of conversation are withdrawn from barbarous fixity and force, to certain mildness of manners, and to humanity and justice ... Good behavior is yet called urbanitas because it is rather found in cities than elsewhere. In sum, by often hearing, men be better persuaded in religion, and for that they live in the eyes of others, they be by example the more easily trained to justice, and by shamefastness restrained from injury.

And whereas commonwealths and kingdoms cannot have, next after God, any surer foundation than the love and good will of one man towards another, that also is closely bred and maintained in cities, where men by mutual society and companying together, do grow to alliances, commonalties, and corporations.

It is with no hope of adding much to the essential insight of this description of the urban process that I would sum up the sociological concept of the city in the following terms:

The city is a related collection of primary groups and purposive associations: the first, like family and neighborhood, are common to all communities, while the second are especially characteristic of city life. These varied groups support themselves through economic organizations that are likewise of a more or less corporate, or at least publicly regulated, character; and they are all housed in permanent structures, within a relatively limited area. The essential physical means of a city's existence are the fixed site, the durable shelter, the permanent facilities for assembly, interchange, and storage; the essential social means are the social division of labor, which serves not merely the economic life but the cultural processes. The city in its complete sense, then, is a geographic plexus, an economic organization, an institutional process, a theater of social action, and an aesthetic symbol of collective unity. The city fosters art and is art; the city creates the theater and *is* the theater. It is in the city, the city as theater, that man's more purposive activities are focused, and work out, through conflicting and cooperating personalities, events, groups, into more significant culminations.

Without the social drama that comes into existence through the focusing and intensification of group activity there is not a single function performed in the city that could not be performed – and has not in fact been performed – in the open country. The physical organization of the city may deflate this drama or make it frustrate; or it may, through the deliberate efforts of art, politics, and education, make the drama more richly significant, as a stage-set, well-designed, intensifies and underlines the gestures of the actors and the action of the play. It is not for nothing that men have dwelt so often on the beauty or the ugliness of cities: these attributes qualify men's social activities. And if there is a deep reluctance on the part of the true city dweller to leave his cramped quarters for the physically more benign environment of a suburb – even a model garden suburb! – his instincts are usually justified: in its various and many-sided life, in its very opportunities for social disharmony and conflict, the city creates drama; the suburb lacks it.

One may describe the city, in its social aspect, as a special framework directed toward the creation of differentiated opportunities for a common life and a significant collective drama. As indirect forms of association, with the aid of signs and symbols and specialized organizations, supplement direct face-to-face intercourse, the personalities of the citizens themselves become many-faceted: they reflect their specialized interests, their more intensively

trained aptitudes, their finer discriminations and selections: the personality no longer presents a more or less unbroken traditional face to reality as a whole. Here lies the possibility of personal disintegration; and here lies the need for reintegration through wider participation in a concrete and visible collective whole. What men cannot imagine as a vague formless society, they can live through and experience as citizens in a city. Their unified plans and buildings become a symbol of their social relatedness; and when the physical environment itself becomes disordered and incoherent, the social functions that it harbors become more difficult to express.

One further conclusion follows from this concept of the city: social facts are primary, and the physical organization of a city, its industries and its markets, its lines of communication and traffic, must be subservient to its social needs. Whereas in the development of the city during the last century we expanded the physical plant recklessly and treated the essential social nucleus, the organs of government and education and social service, as mere afterthought, today we must treat the social nucleus as the essential element in every valid city plan: the spotting and inter-relationship of schools, libraries, theaters, community centers is the first task in defining the urban neighborhood and laying down the outlines of an integrated city.

In giving this sociological answer to the question: What is a City? one has likewise provided the clue to a number of important other questions. Above all, one has the criterion for a clear decision as to what is the desirable size of a city – or may a city perhaps continue to grow until a single continuous urban area might cover half the American continent, with the rest of the world tributary to this mass? From the standpoint of the purely physical organization of urban utilities – which is almost the only matter upon which metropolitan planners in the past have concentrated – this latter process might indeed go on indefinitely. But if the city is a theater of social activity, and if its needs are defined by the opportunities it offers to differentiated social groups, acting through a specific nucleus of civic institutes and associations, definite limitations on size follow from this fact.

In one of Le Corbusier's early schemes for an ideal city, he chose three million as the number to be accommodated: the number was roughly the size of the urban aggregate of Paris, but that hardly explains why it should have been taken as a norm for a more rational type of city development. If the size of an urban unit, however, is a function of its productive organization and its opportunities for active social intercourse and culture, certain definite facts emerge as to adequate ratio of population to the process to be served. Thus, at the present level of culture in America, a million people are needed to support a university. Many factors may enter which will change the size of both the university and the population base; nevertheless one can say provisionally that if a million people are needed to provide a sufficient number of students for a university, then two million people should have two universities. One can also say that, other things being equal, five million people will not provide a more effective university than one million people would. The alternative to recognizing these ratios is to keep on overcrowding and overbuilding a few existing institutions, thereby limiting, rather than expanding, their genuine educational facilities.

What is important is not an absolute figure as to population or area: although in certain aspects of life, such as the size of city that is capable of reproducing itself through natural fertility, one can already lay down such figures. What is more important is to *express size always as a function of the social relationships to be served* ... There is an optimum numerical size, beyond which each further increment of inhabitants creates difficulties out of all proportion to the benefits. There is also an optimum area of expansion, beyond which further urban growth tends to paralyze rather than to further important social relationships. Rapid means of transportation have given a regional area with a radius of from forty to a hundred miles, the unity that London and Hampstead had before the coming of the underground railroad. But the activities of small children are still bounded by a walking distance of about a quarter of a mile; and for men to congregate freely and frequently in neighborhoods the maximum distance means nothing, although it may properly define the area served for a selective minority by a university, a central reference library, or a completely equipped hospital. The area of potential urban settlement has been vastly increased by the motor car and the airplane; but the necessity for solid contiguous growth, for the purposes of intercourse, has in turn been lessened by the telephone and the radio. In the Middle Ages a distance of less than a half a mile from the city's center usually defined its utmost limits. The block-by-block accretion of the big city, along its corridor avenues, is in all important respects a denial of the vastly improved type of urban grouping that our fresh inventions have brought in. For all occasional types of intercourse, the region is the unit of social life but the region cannot function effectively, as a well-knit unit, if the entire area is densely filled with people – since their very presence will clog its arteries of traffic and congest its social facilities.

Limitations on size, density, and area are absolutely necessary to effective social intercourse; and they are therefore the most important instruments of rational economic and civic planning. The unwillingness in the past to establish such limits has been due mainly to two facts: the assumption that all upward changes in magnitude were signs of progress and automatically "good for business," and the belief that such limitations were essentially arbitrary, in that they proposed to "decrease economic opportunity" – that is, opportunity for profiting by congestion – and to halt the inevitable course of change. Both these objections are superstitious.

Limitations on height are now common in American cities; drastic limitations on density are the rule in all municipal housing estates in England: that which could not be done has been done. Such limitations do not obviously limit the population itself: they merely give the planner and administrator the opportunity to multiply the number of centers in which the population is housed, instead of permitting a few existing centers to aggrandize themselves on a monopolistic pattern. These limitations are necessary to break up the functionless, hypertrophied urban masses of the past. Under this mode of planning, the planner proposes to replace the "mononucleated city," as Professor Warren Thompson has called it, with a new type of "polynucleated city," in which a cluster of communities, adequately spaced and bounded, shall do duty for the badly organized mass city. Twenty such cities, in a region whose environment and whose resources were adequately planned, would have all the benefits of a metropolis that held a million people, without its ponderous disabilities: its capital frozen into unprofitable utilities, and its land values congealed at levels that stand in the way of effective adaptation to new needs.

Mark the change that is in process today. The emerging sources of power, transport, and communication do not follow the old highway network at all. Giant power strides over the hills, ignoring the limitations of wheeled vehicles; the airplane, even more liberated, flies over swamps and mountains, and terminates its journey, not on an avenue, but in a field. Even the highway for fast motor transportation abandons the pattern of the horse-and-buggy era. The new highways, like those of New Jersey and Westchester, to mention only examples drawn locally, are based more or less on a system definitively formulated by Benton MacKaye in his various papers on the Townless Highway. The most complete plans form an independent highway network, isolated both from the adjacent countryside and the towns that they bypass: as free from communal encroachments as the railroad system. In such a network no single center will, like the metropolis of old, become the focal point of all regional advantages: on the contrary, the "whole region" becomes open for settlement.

Even without intelligent public control, the likelihood is that within the next generation this dissociation and decentralization of urban facilities will go even farther. The Townless Highway begets the Highwayless Town in which the needs of close and continuous human association on all levels will be uppermost. This is just the opposite of the earlier mechanocentric picture of Roadtown, as pictured by Edgar Chambless and the Spanish projectors of the Linear City. For the highwayless town is based upon the notion of effective zoning of functions

through initial public design, rather than by blind legal ordinances. It is a town in which the various functional parts of the structure are isolated topographically as urban islands, appropriately designed for their specific use with no attempt to provide a uniform plan of the same general pattern for the industrial, the commercial, the domestic, and the civic parts.

The first systematic sketch of this type of town was made by Messrs. Wright and Stein in their design for Radburn in 1929; a new type of plan that was repeated on a limited scale – and apparently in complete independence – by planners in Köln and Hamburg at about the same time. Because of restrictions on design that favored a conventional type of suburban house and stale architectural forms, the implications of this new type of planning were not carried very far in Radburn. But in outline the main relationships are clear: the differentiation of foot traffic from wheeled traffic in independent systems, the insulation of residence quarters from through roads; the discontinuous street pattern; the polarization of social life in specially spotted civic nuclei, beginning in the neighborhood with the school and the playground and the swimming pool. This type of planning was carried to a logical conclusion in perhaps the most functional and most socially intelligent of all Le Corbusier's many urban plans: that for Nemours in North Africa, in 1934.

Through these convergent efforts, the principles of the polynucleated city have been well established. Such plans must result in a fuller opportunity for the primary group, with all its habits of frequent direct meeting and face-to-face intercourse: they must also result in a more complicated pattern and a more comprehensive life for the region, for this geographic area can only now, for the first time, be treated as an instantaneous whole for all the functions of social existence. Instead of trusting to the mere massing of population to produce the necessary social concentration and social drama, we must now seek these results through deliberate local nucleation and a finer regional articulation. The words are jargon; but the importance of their meaning should not be missed. To embody these new possibilities in city life, which come to us not merely through better technical organization but through acuter sociological understanding, and to dramatize the activities themselves in appropriate individual and urban structures, forms the task of the coming generation.

LOUIS WIRTH

"Urbanism as a Way of Life"

American Journal of Sociology (1938)

Editors' introduction   Louis Wirth (1897–1952) was a member of the famed "Chicago School" of urban sociology that included such academic luminaries as Ernest W. Burgess (author of "The Growth of the City," p. 90) and former newspaper reporter and social reformer Robert E. Park. Together, these scholars at the University of Chicago set out virtually to reinvent modern sociology by taking academic research to the streets and by using the city of Chicago itself as a "living laboratory" for the study of urban problems and social processes.

Wirth's major contribution to urban sociology was the formulation of nothing less fundamental than a meaningful and logically coherent "sociological definition" of urban life. As he lays it out in the magnificent synthesis that is his 1938 essay "Urbanism as a Way of Life," a "sociologically significant definition of the city" looks beyond the mere physical structure of the city, or its economic product, or its characteristic cultural institutions – however important all these may be – to discover those underlying "elements of urbanism which mark it as a distinctive mode of human group life."

Wirth argues that three key characteristics of cities – large population size, social heterogeneity, and population density – contribute to the development of a peculiarly "urban way of life" and, indeed, a distinct "urban personality." For centuries – at least as far back as Aesop's fable of the city mouse and the country mouse – casual observers have noted sharp personality differences between urban and rural people and between nature-based and machine-based styles of living. Wirth attempts to explain those differences in terms of the functional responses of urban dwellers to the characteristic environmental conditions of modern urban society. If, for example, city people are regarded as rather more socially tolerant than rural people – and, at the same time, more impersonal and seemingly less friendly – these are merely adaptations to the experience of living in large, dense, socially diverse urban environments.

Although some see Wirth's explanation of the sociology of urban life as nothing more than the social scientific verification of the obvious, others have argued that there is actually no such thing as an "urban personality" or an "urban way of life." Herbert Gans, for example, argues that both inner-city "urban villagers" and suburbanites tend to maintain their preexisting cultures and personalities (p. 64). Wirth's work, however, led to the development of a whole school of urban social ecology – see Brian Berry and John Kasarda (eds.), *Contemporary Urban Ecology* (New York: Macmillan, 1977) for recent contributions to the field – and Wirth's basic ideas about personality and adaption to urban conditions informs the full range of more recent urban planning theorists and practitioners who attempt to create and nurture a sense of community in the urban environment – from Raymond Unwin (p. 355) to Allan Jacobs and Donald Appleyard (p. 165).

LOUIS WIRTH, "Urbanism as a Way of Life"

American Journal of Sociology (1938)

THE CITY AND CONTEMPORARY CIVILIZATION

Just as the beginning of Western civilization is marked by the permanent settlement of formerly nomadic peoples in the Mediterranean basin, so the beginning of what is distinctively modern in our civilization is best signalized by the growth of great cities. Nowhere has mankind been farther removed from organic nature than under the conditions of life characteristic of great cities ... The city and the country may be regarded as two poles in reference to one or the other of which all human settlements tend to arrange themselves. In viewing urban-industrial and rural-folk society as ideal types of communities, we may obtain a perspective for the analysis of the basic models of human association as they appear in contemporary civilization.

A SOCIOLOGICAL DEFINITION OF THE CITY

Despite the preponderant significance of the city in our civilization, however, our knowledge of the nature of urbanism and the process of urbanization is meager. Many attempts have indeed been made to isolate the distinguishing characteristics of urban life. Geographers, historians, economists, and political scientists have incorporated the points of view of their respective disciplines into diverse definitions of the city. While it is in no sense intended to supersede these, the formulation of a sociological approach to the city may incidentally serve to call attention to the interrelations between them by emphasizing the peculiar characteristics of the city as a particular form of human association. A sociologically significant definition of the city seeks to select those elements of urbanism which mark it as a distinctive mode of human group life.

[...]

While urbanism, or that complex of traits which makes up the characteristic mode of life in cities, and urbanization, which denotes the development and extensions of these factors, are thus not exclusively found in settlements which are cities in the physical and demographic sense, they do, nevertheless, find their most pronounced expression in such areas, especially in metropolitan cities. In formulating a definition of the city it is necessary to exercise caution in order to avoid identifying urbanism as a way of life with any specific locally or historically conditioned cultural influences which, while they may significantly affect the specific character of the community, are not the essential determinants of its character as a city.

It is particularly important to call attention to the danger of confusing urbanism with industrialism and modern capitalism. The rise of cities in the modern world is undoubtedly not independent of the emergence of modern power-driven machine technology, mass production, and capitalistic enterprise. But different as the cities of earlier epochs may have been by virtue of their development in a preindustrial and precapitalistic order from the great cities of today, they were, nevertheless, cities.

For sociological purposes a city may be defined as a relatively large, dense, and permanent settlement of socially heterogeneous individuals. On the basis of the postulates which this minimal definition suggests, a theory of urbanism may be formulated in the light of existing knowledge concerning social groups.

A THEORY OF URBANISM

In the rich literature on the city we look in vain for a theory of urbanism presenting in a systematic fashion the available knowledge concerning the city as a social entity. We do indeed have excellent formulations of theories on such special problems as the growth of the city viewed as a historical trend and as a recurrent process, and we have a wealth of literature presenting insights of sociological relevance and empirical studies offering detailed information on a variety of particular aspects of urban life. But despite the multiplication of research and textbooks on the city, we do not as yet have a comprehensive body of competent hypotheses which may be derived from a set of postulates implicitly contained in a sociological definition of the city, and from our general sociological knowledge which may be substantiated through empirical research. The closest approximations to a systematic theory of urbanism that we have are to be found in a penetrating essay, "Die Stadt," by Max Weber, and a memorable paper by Robert E. Park titled "The City: Suggestions for the Investigation of Human Behavior in the Urban Environment." But even these excellent contributions are far from constituting an ordered and coherent framework of theory upon which research might profitably proceed.

In the pages that follow, we shall seek to set forth a limited number of identifying characteristics of the city. Given these characteristics we shall then indicate what consequences or further characteristics follow from them in the light of general sociological theory and empirical research. We hope in this manner to arrive at the essential propositions comprising a theory of urbanism. Some of these propositions can be supported by a considerable body of already available research materials; others may be accepted as hypotheses for which a certain amount of presumptive evidence exists, but for which more ample and exact verification would be required. At least such a procedure will, it is hoped, show what in the way of systematic knowledge of the city we now have and what are the crucial and fruitful hypotheses for future research.

[...]

There are a number of sociological propositions concerning the relationship between (a) numbers of population, (b) density of settlement, (c) heterogeneity of inhabitants and group life, which can be formulated on the basis of observation and research.

SIZE OF THE POPULATION AGGREGATE

Ever since Aristotle's *Politics*, it has been recognized that increasing the number of inhabitants in a settlement beyond a certain limit will affect the relationships between them and the character of the city. Large numbers involve, as has been pointed out, a greater range of individual variation. Furthermore, the greater the number of individuals participating in a process of interaction, the greater is the potential differentiation between them. The personal traits, the occupations, the cultural life, and the ideas of the members of an urban community may, therefore, be expected to range between more widely separated poles than those of rural inhabitants.

That such variations should give rise to the spatial segregation of individuals according to color, ethnic heritage, economic and social status, tastes and preferences, may readily be inferred. The bonds of kinship, of neighborliness, and the sentiments arising out of living together for generations under a common folk tradition are likely to be absent or, at best, relatively weak in an aggregate the members of which have such diverse origins and backgrounds. Under such circumstances competition and formal control mechanisms furnish the substitutes for the bonds of solidarity that are relied upon to hold a folk society together.

[...]

The multiplication of persons in a state of interaction under conditions which make their contact as full personalities impossible produces that segmentalization of human relationships which has sometimes been seized upon by students of the mental life of the cities as an explanation for the "schizoid" character of urban personality. This is not to say that the urban inhabitants have fewer acquaintances than rural inhabitants, for the reverse may actually be true; it means rather that in relation to the number of people whom they see and with whom they rub elbows in the course of daily life, they know a smaller proportion, and of these they have less intensive knowledge.

Characteristically, urbanites meet one

another in highly segmental roles. They are, to be sure, dependent upon more people for the satisfactions of their life-needs than are rural people and thus are associated with a greater number of organized groups, but they are less dependent upon particular persons, and their dependence upon others is confined to a highly fractionalized aspect of the other's round of activity. This is essentially what is meant by saying that the city is characterized by secondary rather than primary contacts. The contacts of the city may indeed be face to face, but they are nevertheless impersonal, superficial, transitory, and segmental. The reserve, the indifference, and the blasé outlook which urbanites manifest in their relationships may thus be regarded as devices for immunizing themselves against the personal claims and expectations of others.

The superficiality, the anonymity, and the transitory character of urban social relations make intelligible, also, the sophistication and the rationality generally ascribed to city-dwellers. Our acquaintances tend to stand in a relationship of utility to us in the sense that the role which each one plays in our life is overwhelmingly regarded as a means for the achievement of our own ends. Whereas, therefore, the individual gains, on the one hand, a certain degree of emancipation or freedom from the personal and emotional controls of intimate groups, he loses, on the other hand, the spontaneous self-expression, the morale, and the sense of participation that comes with living in an integrated society. This constitutes essentially the state of anomie or the social void to which Durkheim alludes in attempting to account for the various forms of social disorganization in technological society.

The segmental character and utilitarian accent of interpersonal relations in the city find their institutional expression in the proliferation of specialized tasks which we see in their most developed form in the professions. The operations of the pecuniary nexus lead to predatory relationships, which tend to obstruct the efficient functioning of the social order unless checked by professional codes and occupational etiquette. The premium put upon utility and efficiency suggests the adaptability of the corporate device for the organization of enterprises in which individuals can engage only in groups. The advantage that the corporation has over the individual entrepreneur and the partnership in the urban-industrial world derives not only from the possibility it affords of centralizing the resources of thousands of individuals or from the legal privilege of limited liability and perpetual succession, but from the fact that the corporation has no soul.

[...]

DENSITY

As in the case of numbers, so in the case of concentration in limited space certain consequences of relevance in sociological analysis of the city emerge. Of these only a few can be indicated.

As Darwin pointed out for flora and fauna and as Durkheim noted in the case of human societies, an increase in numbers when area is held constant (i.e. an increase in density) tends to produce differentiation and specialization, since only in this way can the area support increased numbers. Density thus reinforces the effect of numbers in diversifying men and their activities and in increasing the complexity of the social structure.

On the subjective side, as Simmel has suggested, the close physical contact of numerous individuals necessarily produces a shift in the mediums through which we orient ourselves to the urban milieu, especially to our fellow-men. Typically, our physical contacts are close but our social contacts are distant. The urban world puts a premium on visual recognition. We see the uniform which denotes the role of the functionaries and are oblivious to the personal eccentricities that are hidden behind the uniform. We tend to acquire and develop a sensitivity to a world of artifacts and become progressively farther removed from the world of nature.

We are exposed to glaring contrasts between splendor and squalor, between riches and poverty, intelligence and ignorance, order and chaos. The competition for space is great, so that each area generally tends to be put to the use which yields the greatest economic return. Place of work tends to become dissociated from place of residence, for the proximity of industrial and commercial establishments makes an area both economically and socially undesirable for residential purposes.

Density, land values, rentals, accessibility, healthfulness, prestige, aesthetic consideration, absence of nuisances such as noise, smoke, and dirt determine the desirability of various areas of the city as places of settlement for different sections of the population ... The different parts of the city thus acquire specialized functions. The city consequently tends to resemble a mosaic of social worlds in which the transition from one to the other is abrupt. The juxtaposition of divergent personalities and modes of life tends to produce a relativistic perspective and a sense of toleration of differences which may be regarded as prerequisites for rationality and which lead toward the secularization of life.

The close living together and working together of individuals who have no sentimental and emotional ties foster a spirit of competition, aggrandizement, and mutual exploitation. To counteract irresponsibility and potential disorder, formal controls tend to be resorted to. Without rigid adherence to predictable routines a large, compact society would scarcely be able to maintain itself. The clock and the traffic signal are symbolic of the basis of our social order in the urban world. Frequent close physical contact, coupled with great social distance, accentuates the reserve of unattached individuals toward one another and, unless compensated for by other opportunities for response, gives rise to loneliness. The necessary frequent movement of great numbers of individuals in a congested habitat gives occasion to friction and irritation. Nervous tensions which derive from such personal frustrations are accentuated by the rapid tempo and the complicated technology under which life in dense areas must be lived.

HETEROGENEITY

The social interaction among such a variety of personality types in the urban milieu tends to break down the rigidity of caste lines and to complicate the class structure, and thus induces a more ramified and differentiated framework of social stratification than is found in more integrated societies. The heightened mobility of the individual, which brings him within the range of stimulation by a great number of diverse individuals and subjects him to fluctuating status in the differentiated social groups that compose the social structure of the city, tends toward the acceptance of instability and insecurity in the world at large as a norm. This fact helps to account, too, for the sophistication and cosmopolitanism of the urbanite. No single group has the undivided allegiance of the individual. The groups with which he is affiliated do not lend themselves readily to a simple hierarchical arrangement. By virtue of his different interests arising out of different aspects of social life, the individual acquires membership in widely divergent groups, each of which functions only with reference to a single segment of his personality. Nor do these groups easily permit of a concentric arrangement so that the narrower ones fall within the circumference of the more inclusive ones, as is more likely to be the case in the rural community or in primitive societies. Rather the groups with which the person typically is affiliated are tangential to each other or intersect in highly variable fashion.

Partly as a result of the physical footlooseness of the population and partly as a result of their social mobility, the turnover in group membership generally is rapid. Place of residence, place and character of employment, income and interests fluctuate, and the task of holding organizations together and maintaining and promoting intimate and lasting acquaintanceship between the members is difficult. This applies strikingly to the local areas within the city into which persons become segregated more by virtue of differences in race, language, income, and social status, than through choice or positive attraction to people like themselves. Overwhelmingly the city-dweller is not a homeowner, and since a transitory habitat does not generate binding traditions and sentiments, only rarely is he truly a neighbor. There is little opportunity for the individual to obtain a conception of the city as a whole or to survey his place in the total scheme. Consequently he finds it difficult to determine what is to his own "best interests" and to decide between the issues and leaders presented to him by the agencies of mass suggestion. Individuals who are thus detached from the organized bodies which integrate society comprise the fluid masses that make collective behavior in the urban community so unpredictable and hence so problematical.

Although the city, through the recruitment of variant types to perform its diverse tasks and the accentuation of their uniqueness through competition and the premium upon eccentricity, novelty, efficient performance, and inventiveness, produces a highly differentiated population, it also exercises a leveling influence. Wherever large numbers of differently constituted individuals congregate, the process of depersonalization also enters ... Individuality under these circumstances must be replaced by categories. When large numbers have to make common use of facilities and institutions, an arrangement must be made to adjust the facilities and institutions to the needs of the average person rather than to those of particular individuals. The services of the public utilities, of the recreational, educational, and cultural institutions, must be adjusted to mass requirements. Similarly, the cultural institutions, such as the schools, the movies, the radio, and the newspapers, by virtue of their mass clientele, must necessarily operate as leveling influences. The political process as it appears in urban life could not be understood without taking account of the mass appeals made through modern propaganda techniques. If the individual would participate at all in the social, political, and economic life of the city, he must subordinate some of his individuality to the demands of the larger community and in that measure immerse himself in mass movements.

THE RELATION BETWEEN A THEORY OF URBANISM AND SOCIOLOGICAL RESEARCH

By means of a body of theory such as that illustratively sketched above, the complicated and many-sided phenomena of urbanism may be analyzed in terms of a limited number of basic categories. The sociological approach to the city thus acquires an essential unity and coherence enabling the empirical investigator not merely to focus more distinctly upon the problems and processes that properly fall in his province but also to treat his subject matter in a more integrated and systematic fashion. A few typical findings of empirical research in the field of urbanism, with special reference to the United States, may be indicated to substantiate the theoretical propositions set forth in the preceding pages, and some of the crucial problems for further study may be outlined.

On the basis of the three variables, number, density of settlement, and degree of heterogeneity, of the urban population, it appears possible to explain the characteristics of urban life and to account for the differences between cities of various sizes and types.

Urbanism as a characteristic mode of life may be approached empirically from three interrelated perspectives: (1) as a physical structure comprising a population base, a technology, and an ecological order; (2) as a system of social organization involving a characteristic social structure, a series of social institutions, and a typical pattern of social relationships; and (3) as a set of attitudes and ideas, and a constellation of personalities engaging in typical forms of collective behavior and subject to characteristic mechanisms of social control.

URBANISM IN ECOLOGICAL PERSPECTIVE

Since in the case of physical structure and ecological processes we are able to operate with fairly objective indices, it becomes possible to arrive at quite precise and generally quantitative results. The dominance of the city over its hinterland becomes explicable through the functional characteristics of the city which derive in large measure from the effect of numbers and density. Many of the technical facilities and the skills and organizations to which urban life gives rise can grow and prosper only in cities where the demand is sufficiently great. The nature and scope of the services rendered by these organizations and institutions and the advantage which they enjoy over the less developed facilities of smaller towns enhances the dominance of the city and the dependence of ever wider regions upon the central metropolis.

The urban population composition shows the operation of selective and differentiating factors. Cities contain a larger proportion of persons in the prime of life than rural areas which contain more old and very young people. In this, as in so many other respects, the larger the city the more this specific characteristic of urbanism is apparent. With the exception of the largest cities, which have attracted the bulk of the foreign-born males, and a few other special types of cities, women predominate numerically over men. The heterogeneity of the urban population is further indicated along racial and ethnic lines. The foreign born and their children constitute nearly two-thirds of all the inhabitants of cities of one million and over. Their proportion in the urban population declines as the size of the city decreases, until in the rural areas they comprise only about one-sixth of the total population. The larger cities similarly have attracted more Negroes and other racial groups than have the smaller communities. Considering that age, sex, race, and ethnic origin are associated with other factors such as occupation and interest, it becomes clear that one major characteristic of the urban-dweller is his dissimilarity from his fellows. Never before have such large masses of people of diverse traits as we find in our cities been thrown together into such close physical contact as in the great cities of America. Cities generally, and American cities in particular, comprise a motley of peoples and cultures, of highly differentiated modes of life between which there often is only the faintest communication, the greatest indifference and the broadest tolerance, occasionally bitter strife, but always the sharpest contrast.

The failure of the urban population to reproduce itself appears to be a biological consequence of a combination of factors in the complex of urban life, and the decline in the birth-rate generally may be regarded as one of the most significant signs of the urbanization of the Western world. While the proportion of deaths in cities is slightly greater than in the country, the outstanding difference between the failure of present-day cities to maintain their population and that of cities of the past is that in former times it was due to the exceedingly high death-rates in cities, whereas today, since cities have become more livable from a health standpoint, it is due to low birth-rates. These biological characteristics of the urban population are significant sociologically, not merely because they reflect the urban mode of existence but also because they condition the growth and future dominance of cities and their basic social organization. Since cities are the consumers rather than the producers of men, the value of human life and the social estimation of the personality will not be unaffected by the balance between births and deaths. The pattern of land use, of land values, rentals, and ownership, the nature and functioning of the physical structures, of housing, of transportation and communication facilities, of public utilities – these and many other phases of the physical mechanism of the city are not isolated phenomena unrelated to the city as a social entity, but are affected by and affect the urban mode of life.

URBANISM AS A FORM OF SOCIAL ORGANIZATION

The distinctive features of the urban mode of life have often been described sociologically as consisting of the substitution of secondary for primary contacts, the weakening of bonds of kinship, and the declining social significance of the family, the disappearance of the neighborhood, and the undermining of the traditional basis of social solidarity. All these phenomena can be substantially verified through objective indices. Thus, for instance, the low and declining urban reproduction rates suggest that the city is not conducive to the traditional type of family life, including the rearing of children and the maintenance of the home as the locus of a whole round of vital activities. The transfer of industrial, educational, and recreational activities to specialized institutions outside the home has deprived the family of some of its most characteristic historical functions. In cities mothers are more likely to be employed, lodgers are more frequently part of the household, marriage tends to be postponed, and the proportion of single and unattached people is greater. Families are smaller and more frequently without children than in the country. The family as a unit of social life is emancipated from the larger kinship group characteristic of the country, and the individual members pursue their own diverging interests in their vocational, educational, religious, recreational, and political life.

[...]

On the whole, the city discourages an economic life in which the individual in time of crisis has a basis of subsistence to fall back upon, and it discourages self-employment. While incomes of city people are on the average higher than those of country people, the cost of living seems to be higher in the larger cities. Home ownership involves greater burdens and is rarer. Rents are higher and absorb a large proportion of the income. Although the urban-dweller has the benefit of many communal services, he spends a large proportion of his income for such items as recreation and advancement and a smaller proportion for food. What the communal services do not furnish the urbanite must purchase, and there is virtually no human need which has remained unexploited by commercialism. Catering to thrills and furnishing means of escape from drudgery, monotony, and routine thus become one of the major functions of urban recreation, which at its best furnishes means for creative self-expression and spontaneous group association, but which more typically in the urban world results in passive spectatorism on the one hand, or sensational record-smashing feats on the other.

Being reduced to a stage of virtual impotence as an individual, the urbanite is bound to exert himself by joining with others of similar interest into organized groups to obtain his ends. This results in the enormous multiplication of voluntary organizations directed toward as great a variety of objectives as there are human needs and interests. While on the one hand the traditional ties of human association are weakened, urban existence involves a much greater degree of interdependence between man and man and a more complicated, fragile, and volatile form of mutual interrelations over many phases of which the individual as such can exert scarcely any control. Frequently there is only the most tenuous relationship between the economic position or other basic factors that determine the individual's existence in the urban world and the voluntary groups with which he is affiliated. While in a primitive and in a rural society it is generally possible to predict on the basis of a few known factors who will belong to what and who will associate with whom in almost every relationship of life, in the city we can only project the general pattern of group formation and affiliation, and this pattern will display many incongruities and contradictions.

URBAN PERSONALITY AND COLLECTIVE BEHAVIOR

It is largely through the activities of the voluntary groups, be their objectives economic, political, educational, religious, recreational, or cultural, that the urbanite expresses and develops his personality, acquires status, and is able to carry on the round of activities that constitute his life-career. It may easily be inferred, however, that the organizational framework which these highly differentiated functions call into being does not of itself insure the consistency and integrity of the personalities whose interests it enlists. Personal disorganization, mental breakdown, suicide, delinquency, crime, corruption, and disorder might be expected under these circumstances to be more prevalent in the urban than in the rural community. This has been confirmed in so far as comparable indices are available; but the mechanisms underlying these phenomena require further analysis.

Since for most group purposes it is impossible in the city to appeal individually to the large number of discrete and differentiated individuals, and since it is only through the organizations to which men belong that their interests and resources can be enlisted for a collective cause, it may be inferred that social control in the city should typically proceed through formally organized groups. It follows, too, that the masses of men in the city are subject to manipulation by symbols and stereotypes managed by individuals working from afar or operating invisibly behind the scenes through their control of the instruments of communication. Self-government either in the economic, the political, or the cultural realm is under these circumstances reduced to a mere figure of speech or, at best, is subject to the unstable equilibrium of pressure groups. In view of the ineffectiveness of actual kinship ties we create fictional kinship groups. In the face of the disappearance of the territorial unit as a basis of social solidarity we create interest units. Meanwhile the city as a community resolves itself into a series of tenuous segmental relationships superimposed upon a territorial base with a definite center but without a definite periphery and upon a division of labor which far transcends the immediate locality and is world-wide in scope. The larger the number of persons in a state of interaction with one another the lower is the level of communication and the greater is the tendency for communication to proceed on an elementary level, i.e. on the basis of those things which are assumed to be common or to be of interest to all.

It is obviously, therefore, to the emerging trends in the communication system and to the production and distribution technology that has come into existence with modern civilization that we must look for the symptoms which will indicate the probable future development of urbanism as a mode of social life. The direction of the ongoing changes in urbanism will for good or ill transform not only the city but the world. Some of the more basic of these factors and processes and the possibilities of their direction and control invite further detailed study.

It is only insofar as the sociologist has a clear conception of the city as a social entity and a workable theory of urbanism that he can hope to develop a unified body of reliable knowledge, which what passes as "urban sociology" is certainly not at the present time. By taking his point of departure from a theory of urbanism such as that sketched in the foregoing pages to be elaborated, tested, and revised in the light of further analysis and empirical research, it is to be hoped that the criteria of relevance and validity of factual data can be determined. The miscellaneous assortment of disconnected information which has hitherto found its way into sociological treatises on the city may thus be sifted and incorporated into a coherent body of knowledge. Incidentally, only by means of some such theory will the sociologists escape the futile practice of voicing in the name of sociological science a variety of often unsupportable judgments concerning such problems as poverty, housing, city-planning, sanitation, municipal administration, policing, marketing, transportation, and other technical issues. While the sociologist cannot solve any of these practical problems – at least not by himself – he may, if he discovers his proper function, have an important contribution to make to their comprehension and solution. The prospects for doing this are brightest through a general, theoretical, rather than through an *ad hoc* approach.

PAUL GOODMAN and PERCIVAL GOODMAN

"A City of Efficient Consumption"

from *Communitas: Means of Livelihood and Ways of Life* (1947)

Editors' introduction Novelist, poet, philosopher, social critic, political activist, gestalt psychologist, and avatar of sexual liberation, Paul Goodman (1911–1972) helped to define the counterculture of the 1960s by excoriating hypocrisy wherever he found it and by advocating a combination of anarchist libertarianism and small-group communitarianism. His brother Percival (1904–1989) was a practicing architect who also taught at the New School for Social Research and the Columbia University School of Architecture and Planning.

Both of the Goodman brothers enjoyed distinguished careers. With the publication of a whole series of books that examined the alienation of contemporary culture and dissected the conformist tendencies of American culture, Paul became nothing less than a guru for rebellious youth. Percival began his architectural career by winning the Prix de Paris in 1925, and during the 1970s he published pioneering work that called for the integration of the principles of ecology and economics in the design of new communities. But the crowning achievement of both brothers was the collaboration that produced *Communitas: Means of Livelihood and Ways of Life* (Chicago: University of Chicago Press, 1947).

Reissued as a best-selling paperback in 1960, *Communitas* combined Percival's fine sense of design and proportion with brother Paul's messianic voice and penetrating social criticism, and instantly became something of a cult classic to a whole generation of young planners and social activists. The book is divided into two parts. The first, "A Manual of Modern Plans," brilliantly reviews the conceptual history of the principal urban planning traditions of the twentieth century – from Ebenezer Howard's Garden Cities proposals (p. 345) and Le Corbusier's Towers in the Park (p. 368) to Frank Lloyd Wright's Broadacre City (p. 377) and the Soviet regional plan for Baku. The second section, "Three Community Paradigms," presents a series of utopian options for our own urban futures, each of which proposes answers to the central questions of the book: "How to make a selection of modern technology? How to use our surplus? How to find the right relation between means and ends?"

Of the three proposed community paradigms, one suggests "planned security with minimum regulation," a minimalist state affording a maximum degree of personal liberty but weak community structures and social amenities. Another, probably the Goodman brothers' own favored approach, proposes an integrated "new community" based on "the elimination of the difference between production and consumption." And the third, here reprinted, is "a city of efficient consumption," a *tour de force* profile of 1950s-style American consumerism that combines architectural criticism, urban planning analysis, and an almost Swiftean sense of social satire.

Of Paul Goodman's many books, perhaps the best are *Growing Up Absurd: Problems of Youth in the Organized System* (New York: Random House, 1960) and *The Community of Scholars* (New York: Random House, 1962). For a full exposition of Percival Goodman's environmental design theories combining principles of economy and ecology, consult *The Double E* (New York: Doubleday, 1977). As with the case of Patrick Geddes (p. 361), however, the work of the Goodmans is almost unclassifiable. Their conceptual starting point, however, connects them with almost every urban planner and with almost every theorist of the influence of urban spatial arrangements on urban social life (for example, Ernest W. Burgess, p. 90). "Of the man-made things," Paul and Percival Goodman write, "the works of engineering and architecture and town plan are the heaviest and biggest part of what we experience." All too often, we "do not realize that somebody once drew some lines on a piece of paper who might have drawn otherwise" and that "now, as engineer and architect once drew, people have to walk and live."

The Goodmans' "city of efficient consumption" is obviously meant ironically, and many have compared it to Thorstein Veblen's tongue-in-cheek analysis of "conspicuous consumption" in *The Theory of the Leisure Class* (1899). But not everyone gets the joke. Christopher Alexander (p. 119) criticizes the plan's concentric ring diagram as being a classic "tree."

PAUL GOODMAN and PERCIVAL GOODMAN, "A City of Efficient Consumption"

from *Communitas: Means of Livelihood and Ways of Life* (1947)

THE METROPOLIS AS A DEPARTMENT STORE

We must have a big community. For it is mass production that provides the maximum quantity of goods. Yet, for a productivity expanding by the reinvestment of capital, the most efficient technical use of machinery is self-defeating: the product is standard and once it has been universally distributed, there is no more demand. (For instance, a great watch manufacturer has said, in a private remark, that in a year he could give everybody in the world a cheap durable watch and shut up shop.) One solution is to build obsolescence into the product; this, it is alleged, is being done in some industries, but it is morally repugnant. More morally tolerable, and psychologically exciting, is to have a variety of styles and changing fads. So we require a combination of mass production, variety of style, and changing fads. This means a big population: let us say, to mass-produce requires a large market (100,000), and if there are 50 styles of each kind, we come to 5 million.

But why must the big population be concentrated in metropoles? First, of course, on purely technical grounds, for efficient distribution and servicing under conditions of mass production. (Under conditions of a quasi-domestic industry, the situation is otherwise.) We must refer here to the well-known fact that, during the last 70 years, although the percentage of farmers has steadily dwindled, the percentage of workers in manufacturing has hardly increased; the great gain has been in the workers in "services." A part of these are teachers, doctors, social workers – groups playing a major role in any consumption economy; but the greater part are in transport, city services, etc. These have only an indirect role in production, and therefore countervene our principle of the simplest relation of means and ends.

[...]

To minimize non-productive and non-consumptive services we must have (1) concentration of production and market, and (2) planning of the city to minimize services.

We can come to the same conclusion of big cities by moral and psychological considerations. There is the possibility, as we shall presently show, of making machine production a way of life and immediate satisfaction; but when, as in the case we are now discussing, the tendency of production is toward quantity and sale on a profitable market, the possibility of satisfaction in the work vanishes. The ideal of work then becomes, as we see in the current demands of labor unions, pleasant and hygienic working conditions, short hours at the task, and high wages to spend away from it. The workman wants to hasten away wealthy, unimpaired in health and spirits, from the job that means nothing to the home, the market, the city, where are all good things. This tendency is universal; it does not depend on machine industry; for we see that the farm youth, once it is acquainted with the allures of city life and city money, flocks to the city year after year in 50 percent of its strength.

[...]

The goods must be on display; this is possible only in a big city. And the chief motivation to get those goods for oneself is not individual, the satisfaction of instinct and need; it is social. It is imitation and emulation, and these produce a lively demand. At first, perhaps, it is "mass comforts" that satisfy city folk – these show that one belongs; but then it is luxuries, for these give what Veblen used to call the "imputation of superiority," by which a man who is not in close touch with his own easygoing nature can affirm himself as an individual, show he has style and taste, and is better. All this can take place only in a big city.

Aristotle said long ago, "The appetite of man is infinite" – it is infinitely suggestible.

The heart of the city of expanding effective demand is the department store. This has been seen by many social critics, such as Charlie Chaplin, Lewis Mumford, and Lee Simonson. Here all things are available according to desire, and are on display in order to suggest the desire.

The streets are the corridors of the department store.

Figure 1

Then let us sum up this preliminary program for the city [Figure 1]:

1   A population of several million as the least economic (regional) unit.
2   Production and market concentrated to minimize distribution services.
3   The city concentrated to minimize city services.
4   Work and life to center around the market.
5   Morality of imitation and emulation.
6   Decoration is display.
7   Close by the open country, for full flight.

[...]

THE CENTER: THEORY OF METROPOLITAN STREETS AND HOUSES

Our proposal to place the entire work and market center under one roof, as one immense container, once seemed extreme and sensational; today it is not unusual and reflection will show that it is logical.

In existing great cities, which have large buildings and congested downtown centers, there are always three simultaneous systems of streets: the through highways (skyways, freeways, etc.); the old city-streets (avenues and side streets); and the corridors of the large buildings. The through highways, coming more and more to be elevated or tunneled, carry the main stream of traffic uptown and to places outside the city. It is wrongly thought that by increasing these highways and so facilitating approach to the center, the traffic congestion can be thinned out; but in the end all the highways must pour their cars into the city-streets, for it is these streets that join building to building, and it is at a particular building, and not at downtown as a whole, that the motorist wants to arrive. Once he has arrived at the building, however, he is quite willing to leave his car (if there were a place to leave it) and go indoors and use the corridors and elevators of the building to bring him to the office or department where he has business.

Under these conditions, of motor traffic and increasingly large buildings, the city-streets become pointless: they are useless for traveling and unfit for walking and window shopping. At the same time they cover 35 percent of the ground space and require the most costly and elaborate of the city services: paving, traffic control, cleaning, snow removal, etc. For servicing, they are neither properly in the open (so that snow, for example, could be simply pushed aside) nor yet are they indoors (protected). These streets, then, serve as the perfect example of the intermediaries that waste away the social wealth and health.

So we make of the many large buildings one immense container. The intermediary streets vanish. They have merged with the internal corridors, which are now transfigured and assume the functions of promenade and display which the street performed so badly – in summer too hot, in winter too cold. (What we propose is no different from the arcades or souks of hot North African countries.) And the through driveways now carry out their function to the end, bringing passengers and goods directly to stations in the container, without two speeds and without double loading for trucks and trains. This makes simple sense.

Let us look at it from the opposite term of the relation, the building arrived at. The concept of a self-contained "house" has two extremes: at the one extreme is the private house on its land, with which it maintains a productive relation; at the other is the large building, containing many activities within its walls. In between we can trace a continuous series from the allotment garden to the two-family and semi-detached house to the tenement and the skyscraper. Each point of this series answers best to particular conditions. But the pell-mell of buildings, large and small, in a congested downtown district loses every function whatsoever: the streets are no longer an environment; the buildings must be lighted and ventilated in disregard of them; the real environment is increasingly distant; yet because of the crowding and competition for street space, and the need to have a dim illumination left for the streets, the interiors cannot expand to their proper spaciousness. Therefore we proceed to the extreme of merging the buildings.

The gain in concentration is enormous, amounting to several hundred percent. Even more remarkable is the saving in construction and servicing: in the entire downtown district there is now only one exterior wall and rigid roof to lose heat and cold. Lighting, ventilation, cleaning, and so forth can be handled on a uniform system.

In a market economy, the concentration of display and convenience creates social wealth. We have the spaciousness and brilliance of a great department store.

The center, then, is the container of the work, the public pleasures, and the market. Its population, at the busy hours, is about two and a half million. It is zoned as follows. The materials and products of light manufacturing go via the freight routes in the basement or the cargo planes that alight on the roof: the heart of industry is about in the middle. Business and administrative offices are in the upper and outer regions. The lower stories – most immediately available to the citizens who come by bus or car – house the stores and popular entertainments. In the outer envelope and in projecting spokes, with natural light and a good natural view, are the hotels and restaurants, opening out, on the ground floor, into the park of the university. Convenient to all is the roof airport and the basement levels of parking and transit.

ADVERTISING

In planning and decoration the center is a department store. Everywhere, in every corridor, as at a permanent fair, are on display the products that make it worthwhile to get up in the morning to go to work, and to work efficiently in order to have at the same time the most money and the most leisure.

The genius of this fair is advertising. Advertising has learned to associate with the idea of commodities the deepest and most various instincts of the soul. Poetry and painting are advantageous to sales; the songs of musicians are bound inextricably to soaps and wines. The scientific curiosity of men is piqued by industrial exhibits. The sentiments of brotherhood and ambition both make it imperative to buy something; sexual desire even more so. Also, the fear of loneliness or sexual failure make it impossible to omit to buy something. Mother love is a great promoter of sales. In this manner the integral man is involved in the economy.

Once upon a time advertising was a means of informing the public that such and such a commodity was for sale and where it could be got. Later, advertising became competitive, persuasion to buy such and such a brand rather than any other brand. But in our time, among the largest companies – and especially among those who have something to sell that is, perhaps, not absolutely necessary – the competitive use of advertising is no longer the chief use;

indeed these companies ("partial monopolies") confine themselves to the same amount and type of advertising in order not to compete to the death. But the chief use of advertising, in which the rivals cooperate, is to suggest to a wider public the need for the product which is not, perhaps, absolutely necessary. It is this new departure in advertising that gives one confidence in the economic feasibility of an expanding productivity. But such advertising must be given the right atmosphere in which to breathe.

THE UNIVERSITY

The next zone is the university, extending in a mile-wide ring around the center: this consists of theaters, opera houses, museums, libraries, lecture halls and laboratories of liberal arts and sciences, and everything that belongs to these. It is the region of the things created by man or discovered in nature, and not consumed in the enjoyment.

This region, as we witness in our great cities and their universities, is the field of a deadly internecine strife: between those who would integrate these classical creations and discov-

Figure 2

eries very closely into the culture of the center, and those who fear that this integration corrupts everything into hogwash. Thus, there is a great museum in New York City which alternates the exhibition of severe modern classics of painting with the exhibition of advertising posters. The problem comes up as a problem of location: whether, for instance, to locate among the humanities of the university such popular humanities as higher merchandising, or to locate these in the center as trade schools. There is no question, also, that the classics of art and science do enter into the nexus of exchange (e.g. paperbound books), and could be made to do so even more. On the other hand, such books are not consumed in the enjoyment, they do not have an expanding production, and to exploit them is penny-wise, pound-foolish. Careless popularization of the classics injures the solid economic value of illustrated weeklies. Humane education is necessary to keep things going at all, but too much of it makes people too simple.

Provision is made in the park for thrashing out these and similar problems. There are outdoor cafes and places for dancing, accessible to the transients from the hotels as they emerge from the center.

Within the center, style and decoration present no difficulty. They are whatever is fashionable this season. To illustrate them for our purposes we need merely imitate what is highly correct in the spring of 1960 (taken from *The New Yorker* magazine). Such imitation would not be good decoration, for decoration requires an intuitive popular sympathy, hard to keep up year after year unless one is in the business, but it would be like good decoration.

But the style of the university is a different matter, and a thorny problem. What is the "future" style of something that is only an analytic model? Therefore we cannot show any illustration of the elevation.

NEIGHBORHOODS

In modern community plans that take any account at all of amenity there is always an ideal of neighborhood, neighborhood blocks, as opposed to the endless addition of the city gridiron or of isolated dwellings in the suburbs. This is because it returns to the human scale and face-to-face acquaintance. And in the city of efficient consumption, too, the neighborhood is the primary unit of emulation and invidious imputation.

We demonstrate this as follows. It is in the end unsatisfactory and indelicate to emulate, or to impute economic inferiority to, one's family and friends; on the other hand, to do so with total strangers is pointless. Therefore, at least for domestic display, the unit of emulation and so forth must be the neighborhood. Residents of one's neighborhood take notice, judge one's clothes, see that the lawn is clipped; they are not so well known that one is embarrassed to show off to them; they do not know us well enough to see through us.

The neighborhood must be a mixture of classes. Each class must be well enough represented to fortify each family's security and to allow for the more subtle forms of imputation that are practiced among persons invited to one another's homes. But the juxtaposition of different classes is necessary in order to practice the grosser forms of emulation, which keep people on their toes. (For intraclass emulation is more likely to keep people on each other's toes, considering that we make a personal as well as economic judgment of our friends.) In our fortunate city, there is no danger to the juxtaposition of even extreme classes, since all have goods and need not despair of getting more.

We need, then, a neighborhood of a certain size, perhaps a few thousand. So we typically arrange the residences in neighborhood blocks of about 4,000 population, in a continuous apartment house around an open space of up to ten acres. Each block has its shops, tennis courts, nurseries, elementary schools, where the neighbors may commune and vie. It is not desirable for these neighborhoods to generate important local differences, for all must take their standards from the mass-produced peculiarities on sale at the center. This residential population is composed largely, up to 40 percent, of older persons. This is the inevitable result of two trends: increased longevity under improved medicine and the flight of young families to the suburbs. Our city has the maximum of medicine, urbanism and wealth.

Correspondingly, we have the perfection of a valetudinarian environment: protected from the elements, air-conditioned, with smooth transportation, rapid service, all arranged not to excite the weak heart or demand agility from unsteady feet. The neighborhoods contain clinics, hospitals, and nursing homes.

It is an environment of space, food, sunlight, games, and quiet entertainment, whose standard requirements, largely biological and psychological, are agreed on by everybody.

[. . .]

OPEN COUNTRY

The last zone is the open country. This appears suddenly, not straggling into being amid outlying homes, factories, and cultivated fields, as if marking the exhaustion of the energies of the city, but full of the ambivalent energy of society, as nightmare and waking are parts of the same life. For a dream (but which is the dream, the city or the woods?) is not a temperate expression of the repressed desires of the day, but a strange flowering of them, often too rich to bear. In this vacationland there is exchanged for the existence where everything is done for you, the existence where nothing is done for you. You have, who venture there, the causality of your own hands, and the gifts of nature.

These conditions are hard for city folk and they are finally moderated – after, say, 50 miles, three-quarters of an hour by car or 15 minutes by helicopter – into the imitation wildness of state parks and the bathos of adult camps.

Perhaps in this moderate and forgetful forest can be initiated the procreation which is impossible to initiate by urban standards.

Children are here conveniently disposed of in camps during the summer season.

It seems wise to locate in the open region the age of adolescence, and its junior colleges. Here is space for its unconventional moods and violent play. This group, more than any other, wants to be alone with its contemporaries in small communities; it is impatient of the old and young, meaning anybody five years older or two years younger.

As civilization becomes more complex and demanding, the problem of psychological initiation into culture becomes more pressing. Now the small child, brought up in the metropolis, remembers, rather unconsciously than consciously, the elegance of his mother at home – still elegance to him, even when it is contrived of cheap cosmetics. But the adolescent, given to rebellion, is encouraged, by a more animal existence in the open country. And we know that as his longings settle into habitual desires, it is the environment of adult achievement that seems attractive to him; he has been away from it, and "nothing increases relish like a fast." In hundredfold strength the impressions of childhood have him in grip. Then the university, the school of adults both young and old, glorifies the values of the city in its popular humanities, and in its pure humanities it provides the symbols of reasonable sublimation for those who come by destiny to see through the machinery.

Such then are the four zones of the city.

POLITICS

There is no direct political initiative to make either central or neighborhood policy. For the expanding economy exists more and more in its nice interrelationships and is run by a corporation of technologists, merchandisers, and semi-economists as directors. Periodic elections are like other sales campaigns, to choose one or another brand name of a basically identical commodity.

An existence of this kind, apparently so repugnant to craftsmen, farmers, artists, or any others who want a say in what they lend their hands to, is nevertheless satisfactory to the mass of our countrymen, so it must express deep and universal impulses. These probably center around what Morris Cohen used to call the first principle of politics, inertia; that is, that people do not want to take the trouble to decide political issues because, presumably, they have more important things on their minds.

But in fact the most powerful influence that people exercise, and would exert even more powerfully in a city of efficient consumption, is the economic choice to buy or not to buy a product and to be employed in this or that factory or office. We are not speaking of such strenuous efforts as boycotts or strikes, but of the delicate pressures of the market, which in a market of luxuries and a production of full employment profoundly affect particular brands, without disturbing the system as a whole. In our society even great captains of industry and princes of merchandise who, one would have thought, would have freedom to do it their own way, cannot step out of line. A famous manufacturer, for instance, is said to have believed in the transmigration of souls, but he was not allowed by his public relations department to proselytize to this belief because it might seem odd to potential customers. Everybody who has a penny can influence society by his choice, and everybody has, in principle, a penny.

Thus, there is direct social initiative neither from above nor below. This explains the simply unbearable quality of facade or "front" in American public thought: nobody speaks for himself, it is always an Organization (limited liability) that speaks.

CARNIVAL

But now comes – what is proper to great cities – a season of carnival, when the boundaries are overridden between zone and zone, and the social order is loosed to the equalities and inequalities of nature. "A holiday," said Freud, "is a permitted, rather than a proscribed, excess; it is the solemn violation of a prohibition."

Yet it is not necessary to imagine any astonishing antics and ceremonies of carnival; for as society becomes more extensively and intensively organized in its means of livelihood, any simple gesture occurring in the ways of life is already astounding, just as in Imperial Germany to walk across the grass was a revolutionary act. By day-to-day acquiescence and cooperation, people put on the habit of some society or other – whether a society of consuming goods or some other makes no difference, so long as there are real satisfactions. Meantime, submerged impulses of excess and destruction gather force and periodically explode in wild public holidays or gigantic wars. (There is also occasional private collapse.)

The carnival, to describe it systematically, would be simply the negation of all the schedules and careful zoning that are full of satisfaction in their affirmation. No one can resist a thrill when a blizzard piles up in the streets and the traffic stops dead. The rumor of a hurricane brings out our child souls and much community spirit.

Describing the Saturnalia of the Roman Empire, an old writer gives the following particulars: "During its continuance, the utmost liberty prevailed: all was mirth and festivity; friends made presents to each other; schools were closed; the Senate did not sit; no war was proclaimed, no criminal executed; slaves were permitted to jest with their masters, and were even waited on at table by them. This last circumstance was probably founded on the original equality between master and slave, the latter having been, in the early times of Rome, usually a captive taken in the war or an insolvent debtor, and consequently originally the equal of his master ... According to some, the Saturnalia was emblematic of the freedom enjoyed in the golden age, when Saturn ruled over Italy."

During the carnival in the city of efficient consumption a peculiar incident sometimes occurs. At one of the automatic cafeterias in the center where, on the insertion of a coin, coffee and cream pour from twin faucets and neatly fill a cup to the brim, this machine breaks down – all nature conspiring in the season of joy – and the coffee and cream keep flowing and do not stop, superabounding, overflowing the cup, splashing onto the floor; many cups can be filled from the same source. (This is not so absurd, it happened to our mother once in Minneapolis.) Then gathers a crowd and a cheer goes up as they indulge in inefficient consumption.

Installment debts are forgiven. And with the pressure of installment payments removed, people swing to the opposite extreme and don't work at all: they fail to provide even for the day's necessities and begin to eat up the capital investment. They consume the reserve piled up on the market. The economy apparently ceases to expand (but its shelves are merely being cleared for new fashions).

In the factories, basketball courts are rigged up, emblematic of the sit-down strikes that occurred in America in 1935.

The people are not really idle, but only economically so. They are feverishly preparing and launching immense floats: works of imperishable form – there is a classic tradition of the forms – but made of the most perishable materials possible, papier-mâché, soap, ice. These floats, after parading through the streets, are destroyed without residue: the paper is pushed into bonfires, toasts a moment, and leaps up in a puff of flame, through which the deathless form seems to shine one last moment after its matter has vanished. The soap is deluged by hoses and dissolves in lather and iridescent bubbles; and the forms of ice are left to melt slowly away in the brilliant darts of the sun.

At home people engage in rudimentary domestic industry and in the imitation of self-sufficient family economy. It is customary for each family to engage in a little agriculture in the closet and grow mushrooms, the *fungus impudicus* that springs up in the night like the phallus. Women devote themselves to the home – manufacture of a kind of spaghetti or noodles, and from all the windows in the residential neighborhoods can be seen, hanging from poles and drying in the sun, such fringes of spaghetti or noodles. Wood fires are lit from sticks of furniture going out of fashion, and meals are prepared of noodles or spaghetti with mushroom sauce.

It is during this week that there is the highest hope of engendering children, not to have to rely exclusively on the immigration of the tribes beyond the forest.

From the forest invade mummers in the guise of wolves and bears. These wolves and bears (students from the junior colleges) prowl and dance among the monuments of urbanism. They sniff along the superhighways by moonlight, and they browse among the deserted rows of seats in cinemas, where candy is left for them to eat. By their antics, they express astonishment at these places.

Thus, finally, can be observed the dread sight that poets, ancient and modern, have seen in visions: of wolves prowling by moonlight in the deserted streets of cities. So now – when the coffee and cream have soured among the legs of the tables, and the shelves are bare; when only the smoke is arising from the pyres and the bubbles have collapsed, and there are puddles where stood the statues of ice; and when the city folk are asleep, gorged with their meal and with love; the streets are deserted; now by moonlight come these wolves, rapidly up the wrong side of the streets and prowling in empty theaters where perhaps the picture (that the operator neglected to turn off) is still flickering on the screen, to no audience.

Next day, however, when the carnival is over and the rubbish is efficiently cleared away by the post-carnival squad, it can be seen that our city has suffered no loss. The shelves have been cleared for the springtime fashions; debtors have been given new heart to borrow again; and plenty of worn-out chattels have been cleaned out of the closets and burnt.

MICHAEL YOUNG and PETER WILLMOTT

"Kinship and Community" and "Keeping Themselves to Themselves"

from *Family and Kinship in East London* (1957)

Editors' introduction   In the decades following World War II, working-class populations in the United States, Europe, and elsewhere faced new challenges and dislocations almost as significant as those that accompanied the Industrial Revolution itself. As major cities grew and underwent the process of urban renewal, overcrowded working-class and lower-middle-class districts were often "redeveloped" and the residents relocated to new urban or suburban neighborhoods.

In *Family and Kinship in East London* (1957), sociologists Michael Young and Peter Willmott examine the relocation of working-class residents of the Bethnal Green neighborhood to new housing estates such as Greenleigh in order to discover just how strong – or, indeed, fragile – are the bonds of working-class culture and community in the face of such action. Peter Hall has written that Young and Willmott's conclusions – that "by exporting people from London to overspill estates the planners were destroying a uniquely rich pattern of working-class folk-life" – were "enormously influential" in both academic and urban policy-making circles.

Both Michael Young and Peter Willmott are among the most distinguished and respected urban sociologists in the world. Willmott (born 1923) is a senior fellow of the Policy Studies Institute and the author of numerous books and monographs on housing policy, urban subcultures, and community development issues. Young (Lord Young of Dartington, born 1915) has written extensively on a variety of theoretical issues in the fields of educational policy and social science research and is the author of *The Rise of the Meritocracy, 1870–2033* (1958), one of the most remarkable and prescient exercises in social forecasting ever produced.

In focusing their researches on the Bethnal Green neighborhood, Young and Willmott chose one of the most famous working-class slums in all of Great Britain. In the nineteenth century, Friedrich Engels, Henry Mayhew, and Charles Booth all reported on this district, and in the twentieth century Bethnal Green figured prominently in both Jack London's *People of the Abyss* (1903) and George Orwell's *Down and Out in Paris and London* (1933). What Young and Willmott discovered was that the narrow kinship-based culture of Bethnal Green was in fact a community-building and community-maintaining force. Family connections led to wider community connections, and, when residents were moved "socially upward" into new housing estates outside the old neighborhood, the culture of friendliness and familiarity was replaced by distrust, social privacy, and materialism.

In addition to *The Rise of the Meritocracy* (mentioned above), Michael Young's books include *Forecasting and the Social Sciences* (London: Social Science Research Council, 1965), *The Rhythms of Society* (London: Routledge, 1988) and *The Metronomic Society* (Cambridge, Mass.: Harvard University Press, 1988).

Peter Willmott's work includes *The Evolution of a Community* (London: Routledge & Kegan Paul,

1963), *Adolescent Boys of East London* (London: Routledge & Kegan Paul, 1966), *Policing and the Community* (London: Policy Studies Institute, 1987), and *Polarisation and Social Housing* (London: Policy Studies Institute, 1988).

For other perspectives on the effect of population relocation on urban culture and community in a variety of other contexts, see Herbert Gans, *The Urban Villagers* (New York: Free Press, 1962), Joan Aldous, "Urbanization, the Extended Family, and Kinship Ties in West Africa" (*Social Forces*, vol. 61, October 1962), Chester Hartman, *The Transformation of San Francisco* (Totowa, N.J.: Rowman & Allenheld, 1984), and Mike Savage *et al.*, *Property, Bureaucracy and Culture* (London: Routledge, 1992).

MICHAEL YOUNG and PETER WILLMOTT, "Kinship and Community" and "Keeping Themselves to Themselves"

from *Family and Kinship in East London* (1957)

KINSHIP AND COMMUNITY

We have ... moved successively outwards from the married couple to the extended family, from the extended family to the kinship network, and from there to certain of the relations between the family and the outside world. We shall now turn from the economic to the social, and consider whether, outside the workplace, people in this particular local community unrelated either by marriage or blood are related in any other way.

Since family life is so embracing in Bethnal Green, one might perhaps expect it would be all-embracing. The attachment to relatives would then be at the expense of attachment to others. But in practice this is not what seems to happen. Far from the family excluding ties to outsiders, it acts as an important means of promoting them. When a person has relatives in the borough, as most people do, each of these relatives is a go-between with other people in the district. His brother's friends are his acquaintances, if not his friends; his grandmother's neighbours so well known as almost to be his own. The kindred are, if we understand their function aright, a bridge between the individual and the community: this will be the main theme of the chapter.

The function of the kindred can only be understood when it is realized that long-

standing residence is the usual thing. Fifty-three per cent of the people in the general sample were born in Bethnal Green, and over half those not born locally had lived in the borough for more than 15 years. Most people have therefore had time to get to know plenty of other local inhabitants. They share the same background. The people they see when they go out for a walk are people they played with as children. "I've always known Frank and Barney," said Mr. Sykes, "We was kids together. We knew each other from so high. We were all in the same street." They are the people they went to school with. "It's friendly here," according to Mrs. Warner. "You can't hardly ever go out without meeting someone you know. Often it's someone you were at school with." They are the people they knew at the youth club, fellow-members of a teen-age gang or boxing opponents. They have the associations of a lifetime in common. If they are brought up from childhood with someone, they may not necessarily like him, but they certainly "know" him. If they live in the same street for long they cannot help getting to know people whom they see every day, talk to and hear about in endless conversation. Long residence by itself does something to create a sense of community with other people in the district. Even an unmarried orphan would have local acquaintances if he were established in this way. But unmarried orphans being rare, as a rule a person has relatives also living in the district, and as a result his own range of contacts is greatly enlarged. His relatives are also established. Their playmates and their school-friends, their work-mates and their pub-companions are people whom he knows as well. Likewise, his friends and acquaintances also have their families in the district, so that when he gets to know any individual person, he is also likely to know at least some of their relatives.

[...]

Home and street

We should make it clear that we are talking mainly about what happens *outside* the home. Most people meet their acquaintances in the street, at the market, at the pub or at work. They do not usually invite them into their own houses. We asked people whether they visited, or were visited by, friends in one or other home at least once a month. "Friend" was here defined as anyone other than a relative. Out of the 90 men and women in the marriage sample, 84 exchanged visits with relatives, and only 32 with friends. Those exchanging the most visits with relatives also did so with friends; those most sociable inside the family were also the most sociable outside. But the majority neither had, nor were, guests.

Several people said they had possessed many more friends when they were single. Marriage and children made the difference.

> "Since we've had the children I've got no more friends outside the family I mean."

> "I don't see my best friend much. She's married too, and she's always round her Mum's like I'm always round mine."

> "Since we've had the baby, I've got no men friends – outside the family, that is."

The general attitude was summed up by Mr. Jefferys:

> "I've got plenty of friends around here. I've always got on well with people, but I don't invite anyone here. I've got friends at work and friends at sport and friends I have a drink with. I know all the

people around here, and I'm not invited into anyone else's home either. It doesn't seem right somehow. Your home's your own."

Where every front door opens on to street or staircase, and houses are crowded on top of one another, such an attitude helps to preserve some privacy against the press of people.

The streets are known as "turnings", and adjoining ones as "back-doubles". Surrounded by their human associations, the words had a glow to them. "In our turning *we*," they would say, "do this, that or the other." "I've lived in this turning for 50 years," said one old man proudly, "and here I intend to stay."

Sometimes a person's relatives are in the same turning, more often in another nearby turning, and this helps to account for the attachment which people feel to the precinct, as distinct from the street, in which they live. A previous observer remarked:

> "There is further localism within the borough. People are apt to look for their friends and their club within a close range. The social settlements draw nearly all their members from within a third of a mile, while tradition dictates which way borderline streets face for their social life. The main streets are very real social barriers, and to some residents the Cambridge Heath Road resembles the Grand Canyon."

In Bethnal Green the one-time villages which have as elsewhere been physically submerged and their boundaries usually obliterated – Mumford talks of London as a "federation of historic communities" – live on in people's minds. Bow is one, Cambridge Heath another, Old Bethnal Green Road another, the Brick Lane area, once just outside the environs of the City, another. "I reckon it's nice – this part of Bethnal Green I'm talking about," remarked Mr. Townsend, "I'm not talking of Brick Lane or that end. Here we're by Victoria Park." "It's all right on this side of the canal," said Mrs. Gould, who lives in Bow; "I wouldn't like to live on the other side of the canal. It's different there." Another man, in a letter asking for help in getting another home, wrote, "I am not particular where you send me, the further the better. I do not mind if it is as far as Old Ford as I have left my wife and wish to keep as far away as possible." Old Ford is five minutes' walk from his wife. Other researchers have reported how difficult it was to get people to move even in the war. "Many stories were told of families who would rather camp in the kitchens of their uninhabitable blitzed houses or sleep in public shelters than accept accommodation in another area of the Borough."

[...]

When there is such localism within the borough it is not surprising that for a few people places beyond Bethnal Green are another world. One woman had never been outside the borough except for an odd visit to the "Other End", as the West End of London is known locally. Another never left the borough except for the usual day-trip once a year to Southend. Yet another said, "I only went out once when we went to Canvey just before the war. I felt very strange and lonely when I went there. I've never been out of Bethnal Green since except once to go to Southend for the day." Many of the most rooted people do not talk about fares but about "riding fares", and while we do not know the origin of the term, in context it sometimes suggested that to pay a fare to travel anywhere was something outlandish and even a little daring. One man said that his aged mother was in an Old People's Home "over the water". "Over the water" meant over the Thames, a mile or two away in Southwark.

In Bethnal Green the person who says he "knows everyone" is, of course, exaggerating, but pardonably so. He does, with various degrees of intimacy, know many people outside (but often through) his family, and it is this which makes it, in the view of many informants, a "friendly place". Bethnal Green, or at any rate the precinct, is, it appears, a community which has some sense of being one. There is a sense of community, that is a feeling of solidarity between people who occupy the common territory, which springs from the fact that people and their families have lived there a long time. We cannot do better than put it in our informants' own words.

"Well, you're born into it, aren't you. You grow up here. I don't think I'd like to live anywhere else. Both my husband and me were born here and have lived here all our lives."

"You asking me what I think of Bethnal Green is like asking a countryman what he thinks of the country. You understand what I mean? Well, I've always lived here, I'm contented. I suppose when you've always lived here you like it."

[...]

Kinship and residence: in conclusion

We started this chapter by enquiring – in the lives of Bethnal Greeners is kinship all? Is there any room for others than relatives? The answer is tentative. We did not ask in our interviews as closely or systematically about non-relatives as about relatives. But we are left with the impression that the kindred, far from being a barrier, are in fact a doorway to the community. Some people do, no doubt, enclose themselves completely within the family; many do not willingly admit any but family to the privacy of their homes; most have no friend who takes pride of place over close relatives. But in general, it seems, relatives do not compete with friends, rather act as intermediaries with them. We said in the Introduction that each of the relatives in a person's family of origin is a link with yet another family, and so on in a widening network, "each family of marriage being knitted to each family of origin and each family of origin to each family of marriage by a member that they have in common". Our present proposition is that each of the relatives in the families of origin, and indeed in the network as a whole, is a link not only with other families but with people outside the family as well.

In itself this is only a formal proposition, just as the original proposition was formal. To say that there is a "link" (a clumsy metaphorical term, we admit) is not to say anything about its character. We have to enquire what actually happens between the family and the outside world, that is, into the nature of the "links", just as we have to enquire what actually animates the formal structure of the family. Our belief is that in Bethnal Green the links, with a mother who lives in the next street and hence with her friends, acquaintances and enemies, are more continuously effective because of the proximity to her and of the length of time for which proximity has existed.

[...]

In this old-established district the relatives are a vital means of connecting people with their community. We do not suggest that family is the only doorway to friendship; by taking account of the associations of school and work we have tried to keep a balance between kinship and the rest. Certainly, many friends of whom informants spoke were made by them quite independently, at school, at work or in the Army. But here the family does more than anything else to make the local society a familiar society, filled with people who are not strangers. This has its disadvantages. If you know other people's business, they know yours. Feuds may be all the more bitter for being contained in such small space. But there are advantages too. For many people, familiarity breeds content. Bethnal Greeners are not lonely people; whenever they go for a walk in the street, for a drink in the pub, or for a row on the lake in Victoria Park, they know the faces in the crowd.

[...]

We have stressed the bearing of residence, in its time dimension, upon family ties and upon the friendliness of unrelated people. But have we not, here as elsewhere, perhaps overdone its importance? The best way to test our impressions is to watch what happens when people change their residence. We cannot, as research sometimes can, induce an experimental change and observe the results. We cannot select a sample of people and persuade them to move for the sake of our strange mission. The best we can do is to follow ex-Bethnal Greeners who have recently moved out of the borough to a housing estate and select from the migrants a sample similar to the people upon whom we have focused so far. In the next chapters we follow some couples from Bethnal Green to Greenleigh.

KEEPING THEMSELVES TO THEMSELVES

[This section describes former residents of Bethnal Green after their relocation to the new housing estate of Greenleigh.] People's relatives are no longer neighbours sharing the intimacies of daily life. Their new neighbours are strangers, drawn from every part of the East End, and they are, as we have seen, treated with reserve. In point of services, neighbours do not make up for kin.

Our informants were so eager to talk about their neighbours, and generally about their attitude to other residents on the estate, that we feel bound to report them. They frequently complained of the unfriendliness of the place, which they found all the more mysterious because it was so different from Bethnal Green. Why should Greenleigh be considered unfriendly? This chapter tries to explain.

The prevailing attitude is expressed by Mr. Morrow: "You can't get away from it, they're not so friendly down here. It's not 'Hello, Joe,' 'Hello, mate'. They pass you with a side-glance as though they don't know you." And by Mr. Adams: "We all come from the slums, not Park Lane, but they don't mix. In Bethnal Green you always used to have a little laugh on the doorstep. There's none of that in Greenleigh. You're English, but you feel like a foreigner here, I don't know why. Up there you'd lived for years, and you knew how to deal with the people there. People here are different." And by Mr. Prince. "The neighbours round here are very quiet. They all keep themselves to themselves. They all come from the East End but they all seem to change when they come down here."

[...]

This attitude is supported by reference to the skirmishes and back-biting which have resulted from being "too friendly" in the past. "It's better if you just talk to neighbours and don't get too friendly," concludes Mr. Sandeman from his past experience. "You stop friends if you don't get to know them too well. When you get to know them you're always getting little troubles breaking out. I've had too much of that and so I'm not getting too friendly now."

Mr. Young told his wife, "When I walk into these four walls, I always tell her 'Don't make too many friends. They turn out to be enemies.'" And one experience had turned Mr. Yule into a recluse. "We don't mix very well in this part of the estate. At first I used to lend every Tom, Dick or Harry all my tools or lawn mower or anything. Then I had £20 pinched from my wallet. Now we don't want to know anyone – we keep ourselves to ourselves. There's a good old saying – the Englishman's home is his castle. It's very true."

Usually the troubles are shadowy affairs which have happened to people other than oneself. "We're friendly," says Mr. Wild in the usual style, "but we don't get too involved, because we've found that causes gossip and trouble. We've seen it happen with other people, so we don't want it to happen to us. Now we keep ourselves to ourselves." Whatever the justification, the result is the same. People do not treat others either as enemies or friends. They are wary, though polite. They pass the time of day in the road. They have an occasional word over the fence or a chat at the garden gate. They nod to each other in the shops. Neighbours even borrow and lend little things to each other, and when this accommodation is refused, it is a sign that acquaintance has turned into enmity. Mrs. Chortle has broken off trading as well as diplomatic relations with one of her neighbours. "These people are very dirty," she said, "and I've told them I don't want to borrow or lend." So has Mrs. Morrow, for the different reason that "Just because they've got a couple of ha'pence more than you they don't want to know you. In Bethnal Green it was different – neighbours were more friendly."

Not that all women resent it. A few, like Mrs. Painswick, actually welcome seclusion. She had been more averse to the quarrels amongst the "rowdy, shouty" Bethnal Greeners than appreciative of the mateyness to which quarrels are the counterpart, and finds the less intense life of Greenleigh a pleasant contrast. "In London people had more squabbles. We haven't seen neighbours out here having words."

Absence of kin

When people regard others as unfriendly, the comparisons they implicitly make are with Bethnal Green. We have already discussed the reasons why people living in the borough considered that a friendly place. They and their relatives had lived there a long time, and consequently had around them a host of long-standing friends and acquaintances. At Greenleigh they neither share long residence with their fellow tenants nor as a rule have kin to serve as bridges between the family and the wider community. These two vital interlocked conditions of friendliness are missing, and their absence goes far to explain the attitude we have illustrated.

It also accounts for the astringency of the criticism. Migrants, to the United States or to housing estates, always take part of their homeland with them, our informants like everyone else. They take with them the standards of Bethnal Green, derived from a close community of kindred and neighbours. Friends, within and without the kinship network, were the unavoidable accompaniment of the kind of life they led – too much so for devotees of quiet and privacy. They grew up with their friends, they met them at auntie's, for ten years they walked down the street with them to work. They are used to friendliness, and, their standards in this regard being so high, they are all the more censorious about the other tenants of the County Council. They are harsh in their comment, where someone arriving from a less settled district, or from another and even newer housing estate, might be accustomed to the standoffishness, and, by his canons, even impressed by the good behaviour, of the same neighbours.

It would not matter quite so much people being newcomers if they had moved into an established community. The place would then already have been criss-crossed with ties of kinship and friendship, and one friend made would have been an introduction to several. But Greenleigh was built in the late 1940s on ground that had been open fields before. The nearest substantial settlement, a few miles away at Barnhurst, is the antithesis of east London, an outer suburb of privately owned houses, mainly built between the wars for the rising middle classes of the time. The distance between the estate and its neighbour is magnified by the resentment, real and imagined, of the old residents of Barnhurst at the intrusion of rough East Enders into the rides of Essex and, what is worse, living in houses not very unlike their own put up at the expense of the taxpayer. "People at Barnhurst look down on us. They treat us like dirt. They're a different class of people. They've got money." "It's not so easy for the girls to get boys down here. If people from the estate go to the dance hall at Barnhurst they all look down on them. There's a lot of class-distinction down here." These, the kind of thoughts harboured by the ex-Bethnal Greeners, do nothing to make for ease of communication between the two places. So there is no tradition into which the newcomers can enter. If Barnhurst has any influence upon Greenleigh, it is to sharpen the resentment of the estate against its environment and to stimulate the aspiration for material standards as high.

Nor would it matter quite so much if the residents of Greenleigh all had the same origin. No doubt if they all came from Bethnal Green, they would get on much better than they do: many of them would have known each other before and, anyway, at least have a background in common. As it is, they arrive from all over London, though with East Enders predominant. Such a vast common origin might be enough to bind together a group of Cockneys in the Western Desert; western Essex is too near for that. When all are from London, no one is from London: they are from one of the many districts into which the city is divided. What is then emphasized is far more their difference than their sameness. The native of Bethnal Green feels himself different from the native of Stepney or Hackney. One of our informants, who had recently moved into Bethnal Green from Hackney, a few minutes away, told us, "I honestly don't like telling people I live in Bethnal Green. I come from Hackney myself and when I was a child living in Hackney, my parents wouldn't let me come to Bethnal Green. I thought it was something terrible." These distinctions are carried over to Greenleigh, where it is no virtue in a neighbour to have come from Stepney, rather

the opposite. Mr. Abbot summed it up as follows: "You've not grown up with them. They come from different neighbourhoods, they're different sorts of people and they don't mix."

We had expected that, despite these disadvantages, people would, in the course of time, settle down and make new friendships, and our surprise was that this had not happened to a greater extent. The informants who had been on the estate longest had no higher opinion than others of the friendliness of their fellows. Four of the 18 couples who had been there six or seven years judged other people to be friendly, as did six of the 23 couples with residence for five years or less. Mr. Wild was one who commented on how long it was taking for time its wonders to perform:

> "They're all Londoners here but they get highbrow when they get here. They're not so friendly. Coming from a turning like the one where we lived, we knew everyone. We were bred and born amongst them, like one big family we were. We knew all their troubles and everything. Here they're all total strangers to each other and so they are all wary of each other. It's a question of time, I suppose. But we've been here four years and I don't see any change yet. It does seem to be taking a very long while to get friendly."

One reason it is taking so long is that the estate is so strung out – the number of people per acre at Greenleigh being only one-fifth what it is in Bethnal Green – and low density does not encourage sociability.

In Bethnal Green your pub, and your shop, is a "local". There people meet their neighbours. At Greenleigh they are put off by the distance. They don't go to the pub because it may take 20 minutes to walk, instead of one minute as in Bethnal Green. They don't go to the shops, which are grouped into specialized centres instead of being scattered in converted houses through the ordinary streets, more than they have to, again because of the distance. And they don't go so much to either because when they get there, the people are gathered from the corners of the estate, instead of being neighbours with whom they already have a point of contact. The pubs and shops of Bethnal Green serve so well as "neighbourhood centres" because there are so many of them: they provide the same small face-to-face groups with continual opportunities to meet. Where they are few and large, as at Greenleigh, they do not serve this purpose so well.

From people to house

The relatives of Bethnal Green have not, therefore, been replaced by the neighbours of Greenleigh. The newcomers are surrounded by strangers instead of kin. Their lives outside the family are no longer centred on people; their lives are centred on the house. This change from a people-centred to a house-centred existence is one of the fundamental changes resulting from the migration. It goes some way to explain the competition for status which is in itself the result of isolation from kin and the cause of estrangement from neighbours, the reason why coexistence, instead of being just a state of neutrality – a tacit agreement to live and let live – is frequently infused with so much bitterness.

When we asked what in their view had made people change since they moved from east London, time and time again our informants gave the same kind of suggestive answers – that people had become, as they put it, "toffee-nosed", "big-headed", "high and mighty", "jealous", "a cut above everybody else".

"It's like a strange land in your own country," said Mrs. Ames. "People are jealous out here. They're made to be much quieter in a high-class way, if you know what I mean. They get snobbish, and when you get snobbish you're not sociable any more."

[...]

One key to this attitude, as we have said, is the house. When they compare it with the gloomy tenement or decaying cottage, is it any wonder that they should feel they have moved up in the world? "When people moved out here it was a big change for them," said Mr. Adams. "In Bethnal Green the people were cooped up in two rooms or something like that, and when they get here they think they've bettered

themselves – and so they have bettered themselves. And they try to raise their standard of living."

A house is one bearer of status in any society – it most certainly is in a country where a semi-detached suburban house with a garden has become the signal mark of the middle classes. When the migrants compare the new with the old, is it any wonder that they should for a time feel "big-headed"? In their mind's eye the people with whom they compare themselves may be less their fellow-residents at Greenleigh with their identical houses than their old neighbours of Bethnal Green, and, compared to them, they are in this one way undeniably superior.

Mr. Berry, a milkman, was one of several who connected the "snobbishness" with the possession of a new house:

"I deliver milk all over the estate so I think I know practically everybody on this estate. And I can tell you that when they move down here – I suppose it's just that they've got a new house – they just think they're a cut above everybody else."

Mrs. Allen, although rather more tentative, was of the same mind:

"I don't like it, the atmosphere. People are not the same; I don't know if they get big-headed because they've got a house. Out here you just get a 'good morning'."

The women most appreciate their new workshop and nursery. The man's status is the status of his job; the woman's the status of her home. Since she has moved up most in the world, she is only being realistic to recognize it:

"When I was in London I had a four-roomed house on my own, but you get a few of them who come from, say, two rooms. Then they get a house. Well, they've worked hard – you must admit they've worked hard – they've got themselves a nice home, television and all that. So you find this type of person temporarily gets a bit to thinking that they are somebody. You do find it with some people, and I think you find it more amongst the women than amongst the men."

[...]

Kinship and status

In Bethnal Green people, as we said earlier, commonly belong to a close network of personal relationships. They know intimately dozens of other local people living near at hand, their school-friends, their work-mates, their pub-friends, and above all their relatives. They know them well because they have known them over a long period of time. Common family residence since childhood is the matrix of friendship. In this situation, Bethnal Greeners are not, as we see it, concerned to any marked extent with what is usually thought of as "status". It is true, of course, that people have different incomes, different kinds of jobs, different kinds of houses – in this respect there is much less uniformity than at Greenleigh – even different standards of education. But these attributes are not so important in evaluating others. It is personal characteristics which matter. The first thing they think of about Bert is not that he has a fridge and a car. They see him as bad-tempered, or a real good sport, or the man with a way with women, or one of the best boxers of the Repton Club, or the person who got married to Ada last year. In a community of long standing, status, in so far as it is determined by job and income and education, is more or less irrelevant to a person's worth. He is judged instead, if he is judged at all, more in the round, as a person with the usual mixture of all kinds of qualities, some good, some bad, many indefinable. He is more of a life-portrait than a figure on a scale.

People in Bethnal Green are less concerned with "getting on". Naturally they want to have more money and a better education for their children. The borough belongs to the same society as the estate, one in which standards and aspirations are moving upwards together. But the urge is less compulsive. They stand well with plenty of other people whether or not they have net curtains and a fine pram. Their credit with others does not depend so much on their "success" as on the subtleties of behaviour in their many face-to-face relationships. They have the security of belonging to a series of small and overlapping groups, and from their fellows they get the respect they need.

How different is Greenleigh we have already seen. Where nearly everyone is a stranger, there is no means of uncovering personality. People cannot be judged by their personal characteristics: a person can certainly see that his neighbour works in his back garden in his shirt sleeves and his wife goes down to the shops in a blue coat, with two canvas bags: but that is not much of a guide to character. Judgment must therefore rest on the trappings of the man rather than on the man himself. If people have nothing else to go by, they judge from his appearance, his house, or even his Minimotor. He is evaluated accordingly. Once the accepted standards are few, and mostly to do with wealth, they become the standards by which "status" is judged. In Bethnal Green it is not easy to give a man a single status, because he has so many; he has, in addition to the status of citizen, a low status as a scholar, high as a darts-player, low as a bargainer, and high as a story-teller. In Greenleigh, he has something much more nearly approaching one status because something much more nearly approaching one criterion is used: his possessions.

[. . .]

People at Greenleigh want to get on in the light of these simple standards, and they are liable to be more anxious about it just because they no longer belong to small local groups. Their relationships are window-to-window, not face-to-face. Their need for respect is just as strong as it ever was, but instead of being able to find satisfaction in actual living relationships, through the personal respect that accompanies almost any steady human interaction, they have to turn to the other kind of respect which is awarded, by some strange sort of common understanding, for the quantity and quality of possessions with which the person surrounds himself. Those are the rules of the game and they are, under strong pressure from the neighbours, almost universally observed. Indeed, one of the most striking things about Greenleigh is the great influence the neighbours have, all the greater because they are anonymous. Though people stay in their houses, they do in a sense belong to a strong and compelling group. They do not know their judge personally but her influence is continuously felt. One might even suggest, to generalize, that the less the personal respect received in small-group relationships, the greater is the striving for the kind of impersonal respect embodied in a status judgment. The lonely man, fearing he is looked down on, becomes the acquisitive man; possession the balm to anxiety; anxiety the spur to unfriendliness.

We took as the starting point of this chapter people's remarks, so frequent and vehement as to demand discussion, about the unfriendliness of their fellow residents. We have suggested two main explanations. Negatively, people are without the old relatives. Positively, they have a new house. In a life now house-centred instead of kinship-centred, competition for status takes the form of a struggle for material acquisition. In the absence of small groups which join one family to another, in the absence of strong personal associations which extend from one household to another, people think that they are judged, and judge others, by the material standards which are the outward and visible mark of respectability.

OSCAR LEWIS

"The Culture of Poverty"

Scientific American (1966)

Editors' introduction   Anthropologists often spend years observing communities and compile thousands of pages of field notes on kinship patterns, beliefs, rituals, child rearing, rites of passage to puberty, marriage customs, funerals, and other lifeways of the groups they are studying. Ethnographic studies using this research method provide understanding of diverse cultures that do not appear in census statistics or other quantitative studies.

Oscar Lewis (1914–1970) was one of the most influential (and controversial) urban anthropologists and one of the most thorough in his use of ethnomethodology. Unlike many anthropologists who chose to observe exotic South Sea island or Indian cultures far removed from modern urban culture, Lewis studied poor residents of Mexico City, San Juan (Puerto Rico), Havana and other cities. Returning year after year to talk for hours with each member of the Sanchez family in Mexico City, he gained an intimate familiarity with poor urban Mexican culture. His research with families in Puerto Rico and Cuba was also based on extensive field interviews.

Lewis's books mix voluminous descriptions of the lives of the people he studied with theory to explain what he saw. Lewis argued that there is a distinct *culture of poverty* – shared by residents of poor urban communities as varied as the Black ghetto of Chicago, the squatters' settlements of Mexico City, and the Bustees of Calcutta. Not all urban poor people are members of the culture. East European Jews and some lower-caste Indians may be in poverty, but because they have strong community institutions and cultural traits quite different from those shared by members of the culture of poverty Lewis would not consider them to be in the culture of poverty.

According to Lewis, while members of the culture of poverty talk about and may even claim many middle-class values, on the whole they do not live by them. While Lewis was sympathetic to the people he studied, many of the traits he identified strike middle-class readers as negative. He found many men immature, unreliable, preoccupied with their machismo, and prone to wife-beating; women to be authoritarian, promiscuous, and unable to defer present gratification; childhood to be unvalued; and all members of the culture of poverty to have strong feelings of fatalism, helplessness, dependence, and inferiority. Overall Lewis concluded that members of the culture of poverty had less sociocultural organization than most primitive peoples. He believed that children quickly absorbed the negative lessons of the culture and were unlikely to break out of it once they had been socialized to accept its premises. Accordingly, Lewis argued, the culture of poverty was transmitted from generation to generation.

Lewis's work stimulated hundreds of related studies; some supportive and many highly critical. Conservatives have emphasized Lewis's conclusion that poverty is related to *personal* traits rather than social-structural causes and drawn from this the political conclusion that efforts to eliminate poverty through changing society will not work. Liberals have emphasized the validity of his method – careful observation of the poor themselves – while often emphasizing positive aspects of the cultures of poor people they have studied such as resourcefulness in making a living and nontraditional family and support structures.

The culture of poverty debate of the 1960s and 1970s is similar to the underclass debate of the 1980s and 1990s. Compare Lewis's findings with William Julius Wilson's description of the contemporary Black underclass (p. 226) and Charles Murray's prescriptions for what is appropriate public policy towards the urban poor (p. 233).

Lewis's books include *The Children of Sanchez* (New York: Random House, 1961) and *La Vida: A Puerto Rican Family in the Culture of Poverty* (New York: Random House, 1966). Another notable and similar work of urban anthropology is Elliot Liebow's *Talley's Corner* (Boston: Little, Brown, 1967), a study of the friendships, family life, and work patterns of Black men who congregated on a street corner in Washington, D.C.

OSCAR LEWIS, "The Culture of Poverty"

Scientific American (1966)*

Poverty and the so-called war against it provide a principal theme for the domestic program of the present Administration. In the midst of a population that enjoys unexampled material well-being – with the average annual family income exceeding $7,000 – it is officially acknowledged that some 18 million families, numbering more than 50 million individuals, live below the $3,000 "poverty line." Toward the improvement of the lot of these people some $1,600 million of Federal funds are directly allocated through the Office of Economic Opportunity, and many hundreds of millions of additional dollars flow indirectly through expanded Federal expenditures in the fields of health, education, welfare and urban affairs.

Along with the increase in activity on behalf of the poor indicated by these figures there has come a parallel expansion of publication in the social sciences on the subject of poverty. The new writings advance the same two opposed evaluations of the poor that are to be found in literature, in proverbs and in popular sayings throughout recorded history. Just as the poor have been pronounced blessed, virtuous, upright, serene, independent, honest, kind and happy, so contemporary students stress their great and neglected capacity for self-help, leadership and community organization. Conversely, as the poor have been characterized as shiftless, mean, sordid, violent, evil and criminal, so other students point to the irreversibly destructive effects of poverty on individual character and emphasize the corresponding need to keep guidance and control of poverty projects in the hands of duly constituted authorities. This clash of viewpoints reflects in part the infighting for political control of the program between Federal and local officials. The confusion results also from the tendency to focus study and attention on the personality of the individual victim of poverty rather than on the slum community and family and from the consequent failure to distinguish between poverty and what I have called the culture of poverty.

The phrase is a catchy one and is used and

*Lewis, Oscar, "The Culture of Poverty", *Scientific American*, Vol. 215, No. 4 (October 1966). Reprinted with permission. Copyright © 1966 by Scientific American. All rights reserved.

misused with some frequency in the current literature. In my writings it is the label for a specific conceptual model that describes in positive terms a subculture of Western society with its own structure and rationale, a way of life handed on from generation to generation along family lines. The culture of poverty is not just a matter of deprivation or disorganization, a term signifying the absence of something. It is a culture in the traditional anthropological sense in that it provides human beings with a design for living, with a ready-made set of solutions for human problems, and so serves a significant adaptive function. This style of life transcends national boundaries and regional and rural–urban differences within nations. Wherever it occurs, its practitioners exhibit remarkable similarity in the structure of their families, in interpersonal relations, in spending habits, in their value systems and in their orientation in time.

Not nearly enough is known about this important complex of human behavior. My own concept of it has evolved as my work has progressed and remains subject to amendment by my own further work and that of others. The scarcity of literature on the culture of poverty is a measure of the gap in communication that exists between the very poor and the middle-class personnel – social scientists, social workers, teachers, physicians, priests and others – who bear the major responsibility for carrying out the antipoverty programs. Much of the behavior accepted in the culture of poverty goes counter to cherished ideals of the larger society. In writing about "multiproblem" families social scientists thus often stress their instability, their lack of order, direction and organization. Yet, as I have observed them, their behavior seems clearly patterned and reasonably predictable. I am more often struck by the inexorable repetitiousness and the iron entrenchment of their lifeways.

The concept of the culture of poverty may help to correct misapprehensions that have ascribed some behavior patterns of ethnic, national or regional groups as distinctive characteristics. For example, a high incidence of common law marriage and of households headed by women has been thought to be distinctive of Negro family life in this country and has been attributed to the Negro's historical experience of slavery. In actuality it turns out that such households express essential traits of the culture of poverty and are found among diverse peoples in many parts of the world and among peoples that have had no history of slavery. Although it is now possible to assert such generalizations, there is still much to be learned about this difficult and affecting subject. The absence of intensive anthropological studies of poor families in a wide variety of national contexts – particularly the lack of such studies in socialist countries – remains a serious handicap to the formulation of dependable cross-cultural constants of the culture of poverty.

My studies of poverty and family life have centered largely in Mexico. On occasion some of my Mexican friends have suggested delicately that I turn to a study of poverty in my own country. As a first step in this direction I am currently engaged in a study of Puerto Rican families. Over the past three years my staff and I have been assembling data on 100 representative families in four slums of Greater San Juan and some 50 families of their relatives in New York City.

Our methods combine the traditional techniques of sociology, anthropology and psychology. This includes a battery of 19 questionnaires, the administration of which requires 12 hours per informant. They cover the residence and employment history of each adult; family relations; income and expenditure; complete inventory of household and personal possessions; friendship patterns, particularly the *compradrazgo*, or godparent, relationship that serves as a kind of informal social security for the children of these families and establishes special obligations among the adults; recreational patterns; health and medical history; politics; religion; world view and "cosmopolitanism." Open-end interviews and psychological tests (such as the thematic apperception test, the Rorschach test and the sentence-completion test) are administered to a sampling of this population.

All this work serves to establish the context for close-range study of a selected few families. Because the family is a small social system, it lends itself to the holistic approach of anthropology. Whole-family studies bridge the gap between the conceptual extremes of the culture at one pole and of the individual at the other, making possible observation of both culture and personality as they are interrelated in real life. In a large metropolis such as San Juan or New York the family is the natural unit of study.

Ideally our objective is the naturalistic observation of the life of "our" families, with a minimum of intervention. Such intensive study, however, necessarily involves the establishment of deep personal ties. My assistants include two Mexicans whose families I have studied; their "Mexican's-eye view" of the Puerto Rican slum has helped to point up the similarities and differences between the Mexican and Puerto Rican subcultures. We have spent many hours attending family parties, wakes and baptisms, responding to emergency calls, taking people to the hospital, getting them out of jail, filling out applications for them, hunting apartments with them, helping them to get jobs or to get on relief. With each member of these families we conduct tape-recorded interviews, taking down their life stories and their answers to questions on a wide variety of topics. For the ordering of our material we undertake to reconstruct, by close interrogation, the history of a week or more of consecutive days in the lives of each family, and we observe and record complete days as they unfold. The first volume to issue from this study is to be published ... under the title of *La Vida: A Puerto Rican Family in the Culture of Poverty – San Juan and New York* (Random House).

There are many poor people in the world. Indeed, the poverty of the two-thirds of the world's population who live in the underdeveloped countries has been rightly called "the problem of problems." But not all of them by any means live in the culture of poverty. For this way of life to come into being and flourish it seems clear that certain preconditions must be met.

The setting is a cash economy, with wage labor and production for profit and with a persistently high rate of unemployment and underemployment, at low wages, for unskilled labor. The society fails to provide social, political and economic organization, on either a voluntary basis or by government imposition, for the low-income population. There is a bilateral kinship system centered on the nuclear progenitive family, as distinguished from the unilateral extended kinship system of lineage and clan. The dominant class asserts a set of values that prizes thrift and the accumulation of wealth and property, stresses the possibility of upward mobility and explains low economic status as the result of individual personal inadequacy and inferiority.

Where these conditions prevail the way of life that develops among some of the poor is the culture of poverty. That is why I have described it as a subculture of the Western social order. It is both an adaptation and a reaction of the poor to their marginal position in a class-stratified, highly individuated, capitalistic society. It represents an effort to cope with feelings of hopelessness and despair that arise from the realization by the members of the marginal communities in these societies of the improbability of their achieving success in terms of the prevailing values and goals. Many of the traits of the culture of poverty can be viewed as local, spontaneous attempts to meet needs not served in the case of the poor by the institutions and agencies of the larger society because the poor are not eligible for such service, cannot afford it or are ignorant and suspicious.

Once the culture of poverty has come into existence it tends to perpetuate itself. By the time slum children are 6 or 7 they have usually absorbed the basic attitudes and values of their subculture. Thereafter they are psychologically unready to take full advantage of changing conditions or improving opportunities that may develop in their lifetime.

My studies have identified some 70 traits that characterize the culture of poverty. The principal ones may be described in four dimensions of the system: the relationship between the subculture and the larger society; the nature of the slum community; the nature of the family; and the attitudes, values and character structure of the individual.

The disengagement, the nonintegration, of the poor with respect to the major institutions of society is a crucial element in the culture of poverty. It reflects the combined effect of a variety of factors including poverty, to begin with, but also segregation and discrimination, fear, suspicion and apathy and the development of alternative institutions and procedures in the slum community. The people do not belong to labor unions or political parties and make little use of banks, hospitals, department stores or museums. Such involvement as there is in the institutions of the larger society – in the jails, the army and the public welfare system – does little to suppress the traits of the culture of poverty. A relief system that barely keeps people alive perpetuates rather than eliminates poverty and the pervading sense of hopelessness.

People in a culture of poverty produce little wealth and receive little in return. Chronic unemployment and underemployment, low wages, lack of property, lack of savings, absence of food reserves in the home and chronic shortage of cash imprison the family and the individual in a vicious circle. Thus for lack of cash the slum householder makes frequent purchases of small quantities of food at higher prices. The slum economy turns inward; it shows a high incidence of pawning of personal goods, borrowing at usurious rates of interest, informal credit arrangements among neighbors, use of second-hand clothing and furniture.

There is awareness of middle-class values. People talk about them and even claim some of them as their own. On the whole, however, they do not live by them. They will declare that marriage by law, by the church or by both is the ideal form of marriage, but few will marry. For men who have no steady jobs, no property and no prospect of wealth to pass on to their children, who live in the present without expectations of the future, who want to avoid the expense and legal difficulties involved in marriage and divorce, a free union or consensual marriage makes good sense. The women, for their part, will turn down offers of marriage from men who are likely to be immature, punishing and generally unreliable. They feel that a consensual union gives them some of the freedom and flexibility men have. By not giving the fathers of their children legal status as husbands, the women have a stronger claim on the children. They also maintain exclusive rights to their own property.

Along with disengagement from the larger society, there is a hostility to the basic institutions of what are regarded as the dominant classes. There is hatred of the police, mistrust of government and of those in high positions and a cynicism that extends to the church. The culture of poverty thus holds a certain potential for protest and for entrainment in political movements aimed against the existing order.

With its poor housing and overcrowding, the community of the culture of poverty is high in gregariousness, but it has a minimum of organization beyond the nuclear and extended family. Occasionally slum dwellers come together in temporary informal groupings; neighborhood gangs that cut across slum settlements represent a considerable advance beyond the zero point of the continuum I have in mind. It is the low level of organization that gives the culture of poverty its marginal and anomalous quality in our highly organized society. Most primitive peoples have achieved a higher degree of socio-cultural organization than contemporary urban slum dwellers. This is not to say that there may not be a sense of community and *esprit de corps* in a slum neighborhood. In fact, where slums are isolated from their surroundings by enclosing walls or other physical barriers, where rents are low and residence is stable and where the population constitutes a distinct ethnic, racial or language group, the sense of community may approach that of a village. In Mexico City and San Juan such territoriality is engendered by the scarcity of low-cost housing outside of established slum areas. In South Africa it is actively enforced by the apartheid that confines rural migrants to prescribed locations.

The family in the culture of poverty does not cherish childhood as a specially prolonged and protected stage in the life cycle. Initiation into sex comes early. With the instability of consensual marriage the family tends to be mother-centered and tied more closely to the mother's extended family. The female head of the house is given to authoritarian rule. In spite of much verbal emphasis on family solidarity, sibling rivalry for the limited supply of goods and maternal affection is intense. There is little privacy.

The individual who grows up in this culture

has a strong feeling of fatalism, helplessness, dependence and inferiority. These traits, so often remarked in the current literature as characteristic of the American Negro, I found equally strong in slum dwellers of Mexico City and San Juan, who are not segregated or discriminated against as a distinct ethnic or racial group. Other traits include a high incidence of weak ego structure, orality and confusion of sexual identification, all reflecting maternal deprivation; a strong present-time orientation with relatively little disposition to defer gratification and plan for the future, and a high tolerance for psychological pathology of all kinds. There is widespread belief in male superiority and among the men a strong preoccupation with *machismo*, their masculinity.

Provincial and local in outlook, with little sense of history, these people know only their own neighborhood and their own way of life. Usually they do not have the knowledge, the vision or the ideology to see the similarities between their troubles and those of their counterparts elsewhere in the world. They are not class-conscious, although they are sensitive indeed to symbols of status.

The distinction between poverty and the culture of poverty is basic to the model described here. There are numerous examples of poor people whose way of life I would not characterize as belonging to this subculture. Many primitive and preliterate peoples that have been studied by anthropologists suffer dire poverty attributable to low technology or thin resources or both. Yet even the simplest of these peoples have a high degree of social organization and a relatively integrated, satisfying and self-sufficient culture.

In India the destitute lower-caste peoples – such as the Chamars, the leatherworkers, and the Bhangis, the sweepers – remain integrated in the larger society and have their own panchayat institutions of self-government. Their panchayats and their extended unilateral kinship systems, or clans, cut across village lines, giving them a strong sense of identity and continuity. In my studies of these peoples I found no culture of poverty to go with their poverty.

The Jews of eastern Europe were a poor urban people, often confined to ghettos. Yet they did not have many traits of the culture of poverty. They had a tradition of literacy that placed great value on learning; they formed many voluntary associations and adhered with devotion to the central community organization around the rabbi; and they had a religion that taught them they were the chosen people.

I would cite also a fourth, somewhat speculative example of poverty dissociated from the culture of poverty. On the basis of limited direct observation in one country – Cuba – and from indirect evidence, I am inclined to believe the culture of poverty does not exist in socialist countries. In 1947 I undertook a study of a slum in Havana. Recently I had an opportunity to revisit the same slum and some of the same families. The physical aspect of the place had changed little, except for a beautiful new nursery school. The people were as poor as before, but I was impressed to find much less of the feelings of despair and apathy, so symptomatic of the culture of poverty in the urban slums of the U.S. The slum was now highly organized, with block committees, educational committees, party committees. The people had found a new sense of power and importance in a doctrine that glorified the lower class as the hope of humanity, and they were armed. I was told by one Cuban official that the Castro government had practically eliminated delinquency by giving arms to the delinquents!

Evidently the Castro regime – revising Marx and Engels – did not write off the so-called lumpenproletariat as an inherently reactionary and antirevolutionary force but rather found in them a revolutionary potential and utilized it. Frantz Fanon, in his book *The Wretched of the Earth*, makes a similar evaluation of their role in the Algerian revolution: "It is within this mass of humanity, this people of the shantytowns, at the core of the lumpenproletariat, that hordes of starving men, uprooted from their tribe and from their clan, constitute one of the most spontaneous and most radically revolutionary forces of a colonized people."

It is true that I have found little revolutionary spirit or radical ideology among low-income Puerto Ricans. Most of the families I studied were politically conservative, about half of them favoring the Statehood Republican Party, which provides opposition on the right to the Popular Democratic Party that dominates the politics of the commonwealth. It seems to me, therefore, that disposition for protest among people living in the culture of poverty will vary considerably according to the national context and historical circumstances. In contrast to Algeria, the independence movement in Puerto Rico has found little popular support. In Mexico, where the cause of independence carried long ago, there is no longer any such movement to stir the dwellers in the new and old slums of the capital city.

Yet it would seem that any movement – be it religious, pacifist or revolutionary – that organizes and gives hope to the poor and effectively promotes a sense of solidarity with larger groups must effectively destroy the psychological and social core of the culture of poverty. In this connection, I suspect that the civil rights movement among American Negroes has of itself done more to improve their self-image and self-respect than such economic gains as it has won – although, without doubt, the two kinds of progress are mutually reinforcing. In the culture of poverty of the American Negro the additional disadvantage of racial discrimination has generated a potential for revolutionary protest and organization that is absent in the slums of San Juan and Mexico City and, for that matter, among the poor whites in the South.

If it is true, as I suspect, that the culture of poverty flourishes and is endemic to the free-enterprise, pre-welfare-state stage of capitalism, then it is also endemic in colonial societies. The most likely candidates for the culture of poverty would be the people who come from the lower strata of a rapidly changing society and who are already partially alienated from it. Accordingly the subculture is likely to be found where imperial conquest has smashed the native social and economic structure and held the natives, perhaps for generations, in servile status, or where feudalism is yielding to capitalism in the later evolution of a colonial economy. Landless rural workers who migrate to the cities, as in Latin America, can be expected to fall into this way of life more readily than migrants from stable peasant villages with well-organized traditional culture, as in India. It remains to be seen, however, whether the culture of poverty has not already begun to develop in the slums of Bombay and Calcutta. Compared with Latin America also the strong corporate nature of many African tribal societies may tend to inhibit or delay the formation of a full-blown culture of poverty in the new towns and cities of that continent. In South Africa the institionalization of repression and discrimination under apartheid may also have begun to promote an immunizing sense of identity and group consciousness among the African Negroes.

One must therefore keep the dynamic aspects of human institutions forward in observing and assessing the evidence for the presence, the waxing or the waning of this subculture. Measured on the dimension of relationship to the larger society, some slum dwellers may have a warmer identification with their national tradition even though they suffer deeper poverty than members of a similar community in another country. In Mexico City a high percentage of our respondents, including those with little or no formal schooling, knew of Cuauhtemoc Hidalgo, Father Morelos, Juárez, Díaz, Zapata, Carranza and Cárdenas. In San Juan the names of Ramón Power, José de Diego, Baldorioty de Castro, Ramón Betances, Nemesio Canales, Llorens Torres rang no bell; a few could tell about the late Albizu Campos. For the lower-income Puerto Rican, however, history begins with Muñoz Rivera and ends with his son Muñoz Marin.

The national context can make a big difference in the play of the crucial traits of fatalism and hopelessness. Given the advanced technology, the high level of literacy, the all-pervasive reach of the media of mass communications and the relatively high aspirations of all sectors of the population, even the poorest and most marginal communities of the U.S. must aspire to a larger future than the slum dwellers of Ecuador and Peru, where the actual possibilities are more limited and where an authoritarian social order persists in city and country. Among the 50 million U.S. citizens now more or less officially certified as poor, I would guess that about 20 percent live in a culture of poverty. The largest numbers in this group are made up of Negroes, Puerto Ricans, Mexicans, American Indians and Southern poor whites. In these figures then is some reassurance for those concerned, because it is much more difficult to undo the culture of poverty than to cure poverty itself.

Middle-class people – this would certainly include most social scientists – tend to concentrate on the negative aspects of the culture of poverty. They attach a minus sign to such traits as present-time orientation and readiness to indulge impulses. I do not intend to idealize or romanticize the culture of poverty – "it is easier to praise poverty than to live in it." Yet the positive aspects of these traits must not be overlooked. Living in the present may develop a capacity for spontaneity, for the enjoyment of the sensual, which is often blunted in the middle-class, future-oriented man. Indeed, I am often struck by the analogies that can be drawn between the mores of the very rich – of the "jet set" and "cafe society" – and the culture of the very poor. Yet it is, on the whole, a comparatively superficial culture. There is in it much pathos, suffering and emptiness. It does not provide much support or satisfaction; its pervading mistrust magnifies individual helplessness and isolation. Indeed, poverty of culture is one of the crucial traits of the culture of poverty. The concept of the culture of poverty provides a generalization that may help to unify and explain a number of phenomena hitherto viewed as peculiar to certain racial, national or regional groups. Problems we think of as being distinctively our own or distinctively Negro (or as typifying any other ethnic group) prove to be endemic in countries where there are no segregated ethnic minority groups. If it follows that the elimination of physical poverty may not by itself eliminate the culture of poverty, then an understanding of the subculture may contribute to the *design* of measures specific to that purpose.

What is the future of the culture of poverty? In considering this question one must distinguish between those countries in which it represents a relatively small segment of the population and those in which it constitutes a large one. In the U.S. the major solution proposed by social workers dealing with the "hard core" poor has been slowly to raise their level of living and incorporate them in the middle class. Wherever possible psychiatric treatment is prescribed.

In underdeveloped countries where great masses of people live in the culture of poverty, such a social-work solution does not seem feasible. The local psychiatrists have all they can do to care for their own growing middle class. In those countries the people with a culture of poverty may seek a more revolutionary solution. By creating basic structural changes in society, by redistributing wealth, by organizing the poor and giving them a sense of belonging, of power and of leadership, revolutions frequently succeed in abolishing some of the basic characteristics of the culture of poverty even when they do not succeed in curing poverty itself.

WILLIAM JULIUS WILSON

"The Black Underclass"

Wilson Quarterly (1984)

Editors' introduction   Contemporary University of Chicago sociologist William Julius Wilson, like earlier Chicago School sociologists Ernest W. Burgess (p. 90) and Louis Wirth (p. 190) writing in the 1920s and 1930s, uses careful empirical studies of Chicago to generate important urban theory. An Afro-American, Wilson has been particularly concerned about the situation of poor Blacks.

Wilson is critical of timid liberals who avoid confronting tough questions about race and poverty because they are afraid anything negative they say about Blacks will appear racist. Wilson feels the situation of Blacks, particularly poor urban Blacks, requires objective research and honest reportage. He is unwilling to let conservatives such as Charles Murray (p. 233) dominate theoretical discourse about the causes of and cures for Black poverty.

Wilson argues that there is an *urban underclass* (a term many liberals will not use) and that residents of poor Black ghettos today are caught in a tangle of pathology characterized by crime (including violent Black-on-Black crime), teenage pregnancy, out-of-wedlock births, welfare dependency, and drug use.

Wilson's research has convinced him that conditions for poor Black ghetto residents are far worse in many ways than a century ago when W. E. B. Dubois wrote *The Philadelphia Negro* (p. 57). Dubois's pioneering study found more Blacks employed and role models of upward mobility present, a higher proportion of nuclear families, less Black-on-Black violence, and much less drug use than exist in the poorest Black ghettos today.

Wilson argues that the changed structure of the U.S. economy is more responsible for the plight of poor Blacks today than is racism. A generation ago, Wilson argues, an unskilled Black man could readily find work sufficient to support himself and a family – albeit often physically hard, racially segregated, and dirty work. But in the last generation unskilled manual urban jobs have largely disappeared. Without work, Black males cannot support a family. Hence, Wilson argues, few "marriageable" Black males capable of supporting a family and a high incidence of out-of-wedlock births, family dissolution, and welfare-dependent female-headed households. With little sense of self-worth, Wilson argues, unemployed Blacks naturally turn to drug dependence and crime.

One of Wilson's most controversial contentions is that race and racism are declining in importance as causes of Black distress. Paradoxically, he argues, less racial discrimination has made matters in Black ghettos worse. According to Wilson, as upwardly mobile Blacks move out of Black ghetto areas, community leadership and positive role models disappear and pathology is concentrated.

Wilson is skeptical that race-specific policies such as affirmative action will address problems as pervasive and profound as he describes. Rather he favors universal social policies aimed at improving the lot of all poor people regardless of race: new education, training, and particularly full employment policy.

Wilson's most influential book is *The Truly Disadvantaged* (Chicago: University of Chicago Press, 1987) which incorporates and extends the analysis presented in the following selection. His other books include *The Declining Significance of Race: Blacks and Changing American Institutions* (Chicago: University of Chicago Press, 2nd edn. 1980) and *Power, Racism, and Privilege: Race Relations in Theoretical and Sociohistorical Perspective* (New York: Free Press, 1976).

For a recent overview of the literature on the underclass debate and writings by Latino scholars exploring the relevance and limitations of underclass theory for America's varied Latino communities see Joan Moore and Raquel Pinderhughes, *In the Barrios: Latinos and the Underclass Debate* (New York: Russell Sage Foundation, 1993).

Conservative explanations of and suggested public policy regarding poverty and race include Edward Banfield, *The Unheavenly City Revisited* (Boston: Little, Brown, 1974) and Charles Murray, *Losing Ground* (New York: Basic Books, 1984).

For a recent comparative examination of poverty see "The City of the Permanent Underclass," Chapter 12 of Peter Hall's *Cities of Tomorrow* (Oxford: Basil Blackwell, 1988).

WILLIAM JULIUS WILSON, "The Black Underclass"

Wilson Quarterly (1984)*

It is no secret that the social problems of urban life in the United States are, in great measure, associated with race.

While rising rates of crime, drug addiction, out-of-wedlock births, female-headed families, and welfare dependency have afflicted American society generally in recent years, the increases have been most dramatic among what has become a large and seemingly permanent black underclass inhabiting the cores of the nation's major cities.

And yet, liberal journalists, social scientists, policy-makers, and civil-rights leaders have for almost two decades been reluctant to face this fact. Often, analysts of such issues as violent crime or teenage pregnancy deliberately make no reference to race at all, unless perhaps to emphasize the deleterious consequences of racial discrimination or the institutionalized inequality of American society.

Some scholars, in an effort to avoid the appearance of "blaming the victim," or to protect their work from charges of racism, simply ignore patterns of behavior that might be construed as stigmatizing to particular racial minorities.

Such neglect is a relatively recent phenomenon. Twenty years ago, during the mid-1960s, social scientists such as Kenneth B. Clark (*Dark Ghetto*, 1965), Daniel Patrick Moynihan (*The Negro Family*, 1965), and Lee Rainwater (*Behind Ghetto Walls*, 1970) forthrightly examined the cumulative effects on inner-city blacks of racial isolation and class subordination. They vividly described aspects of ghetto life that, as Rainwater observed, "are usually forgotten or ignored in polite discussions." All of these studies attempted to show the connection between the economic and social environment into which many blacks are born and the

---

creation of patterns of behavior that, in Clark's words, frequently amounted to a "self-perpetuating pathology."

Why have scholars lately shied away from this line of research? One reason has to do with the vitriolic attacks by many black leaders against Moynihan upon publication of his report in 1965 – denunciations that generally focused on the author's unflattering depiction of the black family in the urban ghetto rather than on his proposed remedies or his historical analysis of the black family's special plight. The harsh reception accorded to *The Negro Family* undoubtedly dissuaded many social scientists from following in Moynihan's footsteps.

The "black solidarity" movement was also emerging during the mid-1960s. A new emphasis by young black scholars and intellectuals on the positive aspects of the black experience tended to crowd out older concerns. Indeed, certain forms of ghetto behavior labeled pathological in the studies of Clark *et al.* were redefined by some during the early 1970s as "functional" because, it was argued, blacks were displaying the ability to survive and in some cases flourish in an economically depressed environment. Scholars such as Andrew Billingsley (*Black Families in White America*, 1968), Joyce Ladner (*Tomorrow's Tomorrow*, 1971), and Robert Hill (*The Strengths of Black Families*, 1971) described the ghetto family as resilient and capable of adapting creatively to an oppressive, racist society.

In the end, the promising efforts of the early 1960s to distinguish the socioeconomic characteristics of different groups within the black community, and to identify the structural problems of the U.S. economy that affected minorities, were cut short by calls for "reparations" or for "black control of institutions serving the black community." In his 1977 book, *Ethnic Chauvinism*, sociologist Orlando Patterson lamented that black ethnicity had become "a form of mystification, diverting attention from the correct kinds of solutions to the terrible economic condition of the group."

Meanwhile, throughout the 1970s, ghetto life across the nation continued to deteriorate. The situation is best seen against the backdrop of the family.

In 1965, when Moynihan pointed with alarm to the relative instability of the black family, one-quarter of all such families were headed by women; 15 years later, the figure was a staggering 42 percent. (By contrast, only 12 percent of white families and 22 percent of Hispanic families in 1980 were maintained by women.) Not surprisingly, the proportion of black children living with both their father and their mother declined from nearly two-thirds in 1970 to fewer than half in 1978.

In the inner city, the trend is more pronounced. For example, of the 27,178 families with children living in Chicago Housing Authority projects in 1980, only 2,982, or 11 percent, were husband-and-wife families.

TEENAGE MOTHERS

These figures are important because even if a woman is employed full-time, she almost always is paid less than a man. If she is not employed, or employed only part-time, and has children to support, the household's situation may be desperate. In 1980, the median income of families headed by black women ($7,425) was only 40 percent of that of black families with both parents present ($18,593). Today, roughly five out of 10 black children under the age of 18 live below the poverty level; the vast majority of these kids have only a mother to come home to.

The rise in the number of female-headed black families reflects, among other things, the increasing incidence of illegitimate births. Only 15 percent of all births to black women in 1959 were out of wedlock; the proportion today is well over one-half. In the cities, the figure is invariably higher: 67 percent in Chicago in 1978, for example. Black women today bear children out of wedlock at a rate nine times that for whites. In 1982, the number of black babies born out of wedlock (328,879) nearly matched the number of illegitimate white babies (337,050). White or black, the women bearing these children are not always mature adults. Almost half of all illegitimate children born to blacks today will have a teenager for a mother.

The effect on the welfare rolls is not hard to

imagine. A 1976 study by Kristin Moore and Steven B. Cardwell of Washington's Urban Institute estimated that, nationwide, about 60 percent of the children who are born outside of marriage and are not adopted receive welfare; furthermore, "more than half of all AFDC [Aid to Families with Dependent Children] assistance in 1975 was paid to women who were or had been teenage mothers." A 1979 study by the Department of City Planning in New York found that 75 percent of all children born out of wedlock in that city during the previous 18 years were recipients of AFDC.

WHY NO PROGRESS?

I have concentrated on young, female-headed families and out-of-wedlock births among blacks because these indices have become inextricably connected with poverty and welfare dependency, as well as with other forms of social dislocation (including joblessness and crime).

As James Q. Wilson observed in *Thinking about Crime* (1975), these problems are also associated with a "critical mass" of young people, often poorly supervised. When that mass is reached, or is increased suddenly and substantially, "a self-sustaining chain reaction is set off that creates an explosive increase in the amount of crime, addiction, and welfare dependency." The effect is magnified in densely populated ghetto neighborhoods, and further magnified in the massive public housing projects.

Consider Robert Taylor Homes, the largest such project in Chicago. In 1980, almost 20,000 people, all black, were officially registered there, but according to one report "there are an additional 5,000 to 7,000 who are not registered with the Housing Authority." Minors made up 72 percent of the population and the mother alone was present in 90 percent of the families with children. The unemployment rate was estimated at 47 percent in 1980, and some 70 percent of the project's 4,200 official households received AFDC. Although less than 0.5 percent of Chicago's population lived in Robert Taylor Homes, 11 percent of all the city's

murders, 9 percent of its rapes, and 10 percent of its aggravated assaults were committed in the project in 1980.

Why have the social conditions of the black underclass deteriorated so rapidly?

Racial discrimination is the most frequently invoked explanation, and it is undeniable that discrimination continues to aggravate the social and economic problems of poor blacks. But is discrimination really greater today than it was in 1948, when black unemployment was less than half of what it is now, and when the gap between black and white jobless rates was narrower?

As for the black family, it apparently began to fall apart not before but after the mid-twentieth century. Until publication in 1976 of Herbert Gutman's *The Black Family in Slavery and Freedom*, most scholars had believed otherwise. "Stimulated by the bitter public and academic controversy over the Moynihan report," Gutman produced data demonstrating that the black family was not significantly disrupted during slavery or even during the early years of the first migration to the urban North, beginning after the turn of the century. The problems of the modern black family, he implied, were a product of modern forces.

Those who cite racial discrimination as the root cause of poverty often fail to make a distinction between the effects of historic discrimination (that is, discrimination prior to the mid-twentieth century) and the effects of contemporary discrimination. That is why they find it so hard to explain why the economic position of the black underclass started to worsen soon after Congress enacted, and the White House began to enforce, the most sweeping civil-rights legislation since Reconstruction.

MAKING COMPARISONS

My own view is that historic discrimination is far more important than contemporary discrimination in understanding the plight of the urban underclass; that, in any event, there is more to the story than discrimination (of whichever kind).

Historic discrimination certainly helped to

create an impoverished urban black community in the first place. In his recent *A Piece of the Pie: Black and White Immigrants since 1880* (1980), Stanley Lieberson shows how, in many areas of life, including the labor market, black newcomers from the rural South were far more severely discriminated against in Northern cities than were the new white immigrants from southern, central, and eastern Europe. Skin color was part of the problem, but it was not all of it.

The disadvantage of skin color – the fact that the dominant whites preferred whites over nonwhites – is one that blacks shared with Japanese, Chinese, and others. Yet the experience of the Asians, whose treatment by whites "was of the same violent and savage character in areas where they were concentrated," but who went on to prosper in their adopted land, suggests that skin color per se was not an insurmountable obstacle. Indeed, Lieberson argues that the greater success enjoyed by Asians may well be explained largely by the different context of their contact with whites. Because changes in immigration policy cut off Asian migration to America in the late nineteenth century, the Japanese and Chinese populations did not reach large numbers and therefore did not pose as great a threat as did blacks.

Furthermore, the discontinuation of large-scale immigration from Japan and China enabled Chinese and Japanese to solidify networks of ethnic contacts and to occupy particular occupational niches in small, relatively stable communities. For blacks, the situation was different. The 1970 census recorded 22,580,000 blacks in the United States but only 435,000 Chinese and 591,000 Japanese. "Imagine," Lieberson exclaims, "22 million Japanese Americans trying to carve out initial niches through truck farming."

THE YOUTH EXPLOSION

If different population sizes accounted for a good deal of the difference in the economic success of blacks and Asians, they also helped determine the dissimilar rates of progress of urban blacks and the new European arrivals.

European immigration was curtailed during the 1920s, but black migration to the urban North continued through the 1960s. With each passing decade, Lieberson writes, there were many more blacks who were recent migrants to the North, whereas the immigrant component of the new Europeans dropped off over time. Eventually, other whites muffled their dislike of the Poles and Italians and Jews and saved their antagonism for blacks. As Lieberson notes, "The presence of blacks made it harder to discriminate against the new Europeans because the alternative was viewed less favorably."

The black migration to New York, Philadelphia, Chicago, and other Northern cities – the continual replenishment of black populations there by poor newcomers – predictably skewed the age profile of the urban black community and kept it relatively young. The number of central-city black youths aged 16–19 increased by almost 75 percent from 1960 to 1969. Young black adults (ages 20–24) increased in number by two-thirds during the same period, three times the increase for young white adults. In the nation's inner cities in 1977, the median age for whites was 30.3, that for blacks 23.9. The importance of this jump in the number of young minorities in the ghetto, many of them lacking one or more parent, cannot be overemphasized.

Age correlates with many things. For example, the higher the median age of a group, the higher its income; the lower the median age, the higher the unemployment rate and the higher the crime rate. (More than half of those arrested in 1980 for violent and property crimes in American cities were under 21.) The younger a woman is, the more likely she is to bear a child out of wedlock, head up a new household, and depend on welfare. In short, much of what has gone awry in the ghetto is due in part to the sheer increase in the number of black youths. As James Q. Wilson has argued, an abrupt rise in the proportion of young people in any community will have an "exponential effect on the rate of certain social problems."

The population explosion among minority youths occurred at a time when changes in the economy were beginning to pose problems for unskilled workers. Urban minorities have been particularly vulnerable to the structural economic changes of the past two decades: the shift from goods-producing to service-providing industries, the increasing polarization of the labor market into low-wage and high-wage sectors, technological innovations, and the relocation of manufacturing industries out of the central cities. During the 1970s, Chicago lost more than 200,000 jobs, mostly in manufacturing, where many inner-city blacks had traditionally found employment. New York City lost 600,000 jobs during the same period, even though the number of white-collar professional, managerial, and clerical jobs increased in Manhattan. Today, as John D. Kasarda has noted, the nation's cities are being transformed into "centers of administration, information exchange, and service provision." Finding work now requires more than a willing spirit and a strong back.

BEYOND RACE

Roughly 60 percent of the unemployed blacks in the United States reside within the central cities. Their situation, already more difficult than that of any other major ethnic group in the country, continues to worsen. Not only are there more blacks without jobs every year; many, especially young males, are dropping out of the labor force entirely. The percentage of blacks who were in the labor force fell from 45.6 in 1960 to 30.8 in 1977 for those aged 16–17 and from 90.4 to 78.2 for those aged 20–24. (During the same period, the proportion of white teenagers in the labor force actually *increased*.)

More and more black youths, including many who are no longer in school, are obtaining no job experience at all. The proportion of black teenage males who have *never* held a job increased from 32.7 to 52.8 percent between 1966 and 1977; for black males under 24, the percentage grew from 9.9 to 23.3. Research shows, not surprisingly, that joblessness during youth has a harmful impact on one's future success in the job market.

There have been recent signs, though not many, that some of the inner city's ills may have begun to abate. For one, black migration to urban areas has been minimal in recent years; many cities have experienced net migration of blacks *to* the suburbs. For the first time in the twentieth century, a heavy influx from the countryside no longer swells the ranks of blacks in the cities. Increases in the urban black population during the 1970s, as demographer Philip Hauser has pointed out, were mainly due to births. This means that one of the major obstacles to black advancement in the cities has been removed. Just as the Asian and European immigrants benefited from a cessation of migration, so too should the economic prospects of urban blacks improve now that the great migration from the rural South is over. Even more significant is the slowing growth in the number of young blacks inhabiting the central cities. In metropolitan areas generally, there were 6 percent fewer blacks aged 13 or under in 1977 than there were in 1970; in the inner city, the figure was 13 percent. As the average age of the urban black community begins to rise, lawlessness, illegitimacy, and unemployment should begin to decline.

Even so, the problems of the urban black underclass will remain crippling for years to come. And I suspect that any significant reduction of joblessness, crime, welfare dependency, single-parent homes, and out-of-wedlock pregnancies would require far more comprehensive social and economic change than Americans have generally deemed appropriate or desirable. It would require a radicalism that neither the Republican nor the Democratic Party has been bold enough to espouse.

The existence of a black underclass, as I have suggested, is due far more to historic discrimination and to broad demographic and economic trends than it is to racial discrimination in the present day. For that reason, the underclass has not benefited significantly from "race specific" antidiscrimination policies, such as affirmative action, that have aided so many trained and educated blacks. If inner-city blacks are to be helped, they will be helped not by policies addressed primarily to inner-city minorities but by policies designed to benefit all of the nation's poor.

I am reminded in this connection of Bayard

Rustin's plea during the early 1960s that blacks recognize the importance of fundamental economic reform (including a system of national economic planning along with new education, manpower, and public works programs to help achieve full employment) and the need for a broad-based coalition to achieve it. Politicians and civil-rights leaders should, of course, continue to fight for an end to racial discrimination. But they must also recognize that poor minorities are profoundly affected by problems that affect other people in America as well, and that go beyond racial considerations. Unless those problems are addressed, the underclass will remain a reality of urban life.

CHARLES MURRAY

"Choosing a Future"

from *Losing Ground: American Social Policy 1950–1980* (1984)

Editors' introduction Beginning with Margaret Thatcher's administration in the U.K. and Ronald Reagan's in the U.S. during the 1980s, conservative social policies which favor shrinking national government expenditures on social programs and privatizing government functions have been in vogue in many countries in the world. Simultaneously, an influential new breed of conservative scholars has undertaken empirical research that emphasizes the failures of government programs and constructed theory which argues in favor of less government generally, and particularly less national government meddling in issues of poverty and inequality in cities.

Charles Murray's book *Losing Ground* was published in 1984, midway through Ronald Reagan's presidency. It quickly became a conservative icon. Murray juxtaposes data on massive increases in federal spending on welfare, education, job training, violence prevention, and other U.S. social programs during the late 1960s and 1970s with data on worsening situations of poor people – particularly poor urban Blacks. By comparison, Murray argues, data for the 1950s and early 1960s show the condition of poor Blacks was improving with very little in the way of government social programs.

Murray takes aim squarely at liberal social policies. He characterizes programs intended to support poor people – particularly poor Blacks – as paternalistic, a new form of unequal treatment which he feels undermines initiative and is as harmful as historic racial discrimination. Giving a teenage mother welfare to support an illegitimate child, Murray argues, undermines families and eliminates the incentive for the mother, father, or either's parents to act responsibly. It discourages the mother from taking necessary steps to lift herself out of dependency, condemning her to a life at the bottom of the social ladder. Unlike William Julius Wilson (p. 226) or John Kasarda (p. 306), Murray does not see loss of unskilled jobs accessible to Blacks as the primary reason for the underclass. To the contrary, in the following selection Murray argues that patronizing social programs that attempt to help poor Blacks through welfarism should be eliminated or changed to foster self-reliance.

This selection is from *Losing Ground: American Social Policy 1950–1980* (New York: Basic Books, 1984). Murray's other books include an extremely controversial best-selling study of race and intelligence, *The Bell Curve* (New York: Free Press, 1994) and, with Louis A. Cox, *Beyond Probation: Juvenile Corrections and the Chronic Delinquent* (Beverly Hills, Calif.: Sage Publications, 1979).

For a scathing attack on the government programs for the poor during the U.S. "war on poverty" see Daniel Patrick Moynihan, *Maximum Feasible Misunderstanding* (New York: Free Press, 1969). Conservative critiques of urban social policy include Edward Banfield, *The Unheavenly City Revisited* (Boston: Little, Brown, 1974), and E. S. Savas, *Privatizing the Public Sector* (Chatham, N.J.: Chatham House, 1982). Liberal alternatives include William Julius Wilson (p. 226), William Goldsmith and

Edward J. Blakeley, *Separate Societies: Poverty and Inequality in U.S. Cities* (Philadelphia: Temple University Press, 1992), Peter Marris, *Community Planning and Conceptions of Change* (London: Routledge & Kegan Paul, 1982), and Francis Fox Piven and Richard A. Cloward, *Regulating the Poor: The Functions of Public Welfare* (New York: Pantheon, 1971).

For discussions of Conservative Party urban policy in the U.K. see K. Ascher, *The Politics of Privatization* (London: Macmillan, 1987), D. Green, *The New Right* (London: Wheatsheaf, 1987), and Gerry Stoker, *The Politics of Local Government* (London: Macmillan, 1988). See also Timothy Barnekov, Robin Boyle, and Daniel Rich, *Privatism and Urban Policy in Britain and the United States* (Oxford: Oxford University Press, 1989), for a comparative study of conservative policies on both sides of the Atlantic.

CHARLES MURRAY, "Choosing a Future"

from *Losing Ground: American Social Policy 1950–1980* (1984)

... [I]f the behaviors of members of the underclass are founded on a rational appreciation of the rules of the game, and as long as the rules encourage dysfunctional values and behaviors, the future cannot look bright. Behaviors that work will tend to persist until they stop working. The rules will have to be changed. How might they be changed? I present three proposals: one for education, one for public welfare, and one for civil rights. The proposals of greatest theoretical interest involve education and public welfare ... I begin ... with the proposal for civil rights. It is simple, would cost no money to implement, and is urgently needed.

A PROPOSAL FOR SOCIAL POLICY AND RACE

Real reform of American social policy is out of the question until we settle the race issue. We have been dancing around it since 1964, wishing it would go away and at the same time letting it dominate, sub rosa, the formation of social policy.

The source of our difficulties has been the collision, with enormous attendant national anxiety and indecision, of two principles so much a part of the American ethos that hardly anyone, whatever his political position, can wholly embrace one and reject the other. The principles are equal treatment and a fair shake.

The principle of equal treatment demands that we all play by the same rules – which would seem to rule out any policy that gives preferential treatment to anyone. A fair shake demands that everyone have a reasonably equal chance at the brass ring – or at least a reasonably equal chance to get on the merry-go-round.

Thus hardly anyone, no matter how strictly noninterventionist, can watch with complete equanimity when a black child is deprived of a chance to develop his full potential for reasons that may be directly traced to a heritage of exploitation by whites. Neither can anyone, no matter how devoted to Affirmative Action, watch with complete equanimity when a white job applicant is turned down for a job in favor of a black who is less qualified. Something about it is fundamentally unfair – un-American – no matter how admirable the ultimate goal.

Until 1965, the principles of equal treatment and a fair shake did not compete. They created no tension. Their application to racial policy was simple: Make the nation color-blind. People were to be judged on their merits. But then the elite wisdom changed. Blacks were to be helped to catch up.

... In summarizing [the] results as they pertain to the poorest blacks, this harsh judgment is warranted: If an impartial observer from another country were shown the data on the black lower class from 1950 to 1980 but given no information about contemporaneous changes in society or public policy, that observer would infer that racial discrimination against the black poor increased drastically during the late 1960s and 1970s. No explanation except a surge in outright, virulent discrimination would as easily explain to a "blind" observer why things went so wrong.

Such an explanation is for practical purposes correct. Beginning in the last half of the 1960s, the black poor were subjected to new forms of racism with effects that outweighed the waning of the old forms of racism. Before the 1960s, we had a black underclass that was held down because blacks were systematically treated differently from whites, by whites. Now, we have a black underclass that is held down for the same generic reason – because blacks are systematically treated differently from whites, by whites.

The problem consists of a change in the nature of white condescension toward blacks. Historically, virtually all whites condescended toward virtually all blacks; there is nothing new in that. The condescension could be vicious in intent, in the form of "keeping niggers in their place." It could be benign, as in the excessive solicitousness with which whites who considered themselves enlightened tended to treat blacks.

These forms of condescension came under withering attack during the civil rights movement, to such an extent that certain manifestations of the condescension disappeared altogether in some circles. A variety of factors – among them, simply greater representation of blacks in the white professional world of work – made it easier for whites to develop relationships of authentic equality and respect with black colleagues. But from a policy standpoint, it became clear only shortly after the War on Poverty began that henceforth the black lower class was to be the object of a new condescension that would become intertwined with every aspect of social policy. Race is central to the problem of reforming social policy, not because it is intrinsically so but because the debate about what to do has been perverted by the underlying consciousness among whites that "they" – the people to be helped by social policy – are predominantly black, and blacks are owed a debt.

The result was that the intelligentsia and the policymakers, coincident with the revolution in social policy, began treating the black poor in ways that they would never consider treating people they respected. Is the black crime rate skyrocketing? Look at the black criminal's many grievances against society. Are black illegitimate birth rates five times those of whites? We must remember that blacks have a much broader view of the family than we do – aunts and grandmothers fill in. Did black labor force participation among the young plummet? We can hardly blame someone for having too much pride to work at a job sweeping floors. Are black high school graduates illiterate? The educational system is insensitive. Are their test scores a hundred points lower than others? The tests are biased. Do black youngsters lose jobs to white youngsters because their mannerisms and language make them incomprehensible to their prospective employers? The culture of the ghetto has its own validity.

That the condescension should be so deep and pervasive is monumentally ironic, for the injunction to respect the poor (after all, they are not to blame) was hammered home in the tracts of OEO [the Office of Economic Opportunity] and radical intellectuals. But condescension is the correct descriptor. Whites began to tolerate and make excuses for behavior among blacks that whites would disdain in themselves or their children.

The expression of this attitude in policy has been a few obvious steps – Affirmative Action, minority set-asides in government contracts, and the like – but the real effect was the one that I discussed in the history of the period. The white elite could not at one time cope with two reactions. They could not simultaneously feel compelled to make restitution for past wrongs to blacks and blame blacks for not taking advantage of their new opportunities. The system had to be blamed, and any deficiencies demonstrated by blacks had to be overlooked or covered up – by whites.

A central theme of this book [*Losing Ground*] has been that the consequences were disastrous for poor people of all races, but for poor blacks especially, and most emphatically for poor blacks in all-black communities – precisely that population that was the object of the most unremitting sympathy.

My proposal for dealing with the racial issue in social welfare is to repeal every bit of legislation and reverse every court decision that in any way requires, recommends, or awards differential treatment according to race, and thereby put us back onto the track that we left in 1965. We may argue about the appropriate limits of government intervention in trying to enforce the ideal, but at least it should be possible to identify the ideal: Race is not a morally admissible reason for treating one person differently from another. Period.

A PROPOSAL FOR EDUCATION

There is no such thing as an undeserving 5-year-old. Society, in the form of government intervention, is quite limited in what it can do to make up for many of the deficiencies of life that an unlucky 5-year-old experiences; it can, however, provide a good education and thereby give the child a chance at a different future.

The objective is a system that provides more effective education of the poor and disadvantaged without running afoul of the three laws of social programs. The objective is also to construct what is, in my view, a just system – one that does not sacrifice one student's interests to another's, and one that removes barriers in the way of those who want most badly to succeed and are prepared to make the greatest efforts to do so. So once again let us put ourselves in the position of bureaucrats of sweeping authority and large budgets. How shall we make things better?

We begin by installing a completely free educational system that goes from preschool to the loftiest graduate degrees, removing economic barriers entirely. Having done so, however, we find little change from the system that prevailed in 1980. Even then, kindergarten through high school were free to the student, and federal grants and loans worth $4.4 billion plus a very extensive system of private scholarships and loans were available for needy students who wanted to continue their education. By making the system entirely free, we are not making more education newly accessible to large numbers of people, nor have we done anything about the quality of education.

We then make a second and much more powerful change. For many years, the notion of a voucher system for education has enjoyed a periodic vogue. In its pure form, it would give each parent of a child of school age a voucher that the parent could use to pay for schooling at any institution to which the child could gain admittance. The school would redeem the voucher for cash from the government. The proposals for voucher systems have generally foundered on accusations that they are a tool for the middle class and would leave the disadvantaged in the lurch. My proposition is rather different: a voucher system is the single most powerful method available to us to improve the education of the poor and disadvantaged. Vouchers thus become the second component of our educational reforms.

For one large segment of the population of poor and disadvantaged, the results are immediate, unequivocal, and dramatic. I refer to children whose parents take an active role in overseeing and encouraging their children's education. Such parents have been fighting one of the saddest of the battles of the poor – doing everything they can within the home environment, only to see their influence systematically undermined as soon as their children get out the door. When we give such parents vouchers, we find that they behave very much as their affluent counterparts behave when they are deciding upon a private school. They visit prospective schools, interview teachers, and place their children in schools that are demanding of the students and accountable to the parents for results. I suggest that when we give such parents vouchers, we will observe substantial convergence of black and white test scores in a single generation. All that such parents have ever needed is an educational system that operates on the same principles they do.

This is a sufficient improvement to justify the

system, for we are in a no-lose situation with regard to the children whose parents do not play their part effectively. These children are sent to bad schools or no schools at all – just as they were in the past. How much worse can it be under the new system?

This defect in the voucher system leaves us, however, with a substantial number of students who are still getting no education through no fault of their own. Nor can we count on getting results if we round them up and dispatch them willy-nilly to the nearest accredited school. A school that can motivate and teach a child when there is backup from home cannot necessarily teach the children we are now discussing. Many of them are poor not only in money. Many have been developmentally impoverished as well, receiving very little of the early verbal and conceptual stimulation that happens as a matter of course when parents expect their children to be smart. Some arrive at the school door already believing themselves to be stupid, expecting to fail. We can be as angry as we wish at their parents, but we are still left with the job of devising a school that works for these children. What do we do – not in terms of a particular pedagogical program or curriculum, but in broad strokes?

First, whatever else, we decide to create a world that makes sense in the context of the society we want them to succeed in. The school is not an extension of the neighborhood. Within the confines of the school building and school day, we create a world that may seem as strange and irrelevant as Oz.

We do not do so with uniforms or elaborate rules or inspirational readings – the embellishments are left up to the school. Rather, we install one simple, inflexible procedure. Each course has an entrance test. Tenth-grade geometry has an entrance test; so does first-grade reading. Entrance tests for simple courses are simple; entrance tests for hard courses are hard. Their purpose is not to identify the best students, but to make sure that any student who gets in can, with an honest effort, complete the course work.

Our system does not carry with it any special teaching technique. It does, however, give the teacher full discretion over enforcing an orderly working environment. The teacher's only obligation is to teach those who want to learn.

The system is also infinitely forgiving. A student who has just flunked algebra three times running can enroll in that or any other math class for which he can pass the entrance test. He can enroll even if he has just been kicked out of three other classes for misbehavior. The question is never "What have you been in the past?" but always "What are you being as of now?"

The evolving outcomes of the system are complex. Some students begin by picking the easiest, least taxing courses, and approach them with as little motivation as their counterparts under the current system. Perhaps among this set of students are some who cannot or will not complete even the simplest courses. They drop by the wayside, failures of the system.

Among those who do complete courses, any courses, five things happen, all of them positive. First, the system is so constructed that to get into a course is in itself a small success ("I passed!"). Second, the students go into the course with a legitimate reason for believing that they can do the work; they passed a valid test that says they can. Third, they experience a success when they complete the course. Fourth, they experience – directly – a cause–effect relationship between their success in one course and their ability to get into the next course, no matter how small a step upward that next course may be. Fifth, all the while this is going on, they are likely to be observing other students no different from them – no richer, no smarter – who are moving upward faster than they are but using the same mechanism.

What of those who are disappointed, who try to get into a class and fail? Some will withdraw into themselves and be forever fearful of taking a chance on failure, as almost all do under the current system anyway. But there is a gradation to risk, and a peculiar sort of guarantee of success in our zero-transfer system. Whatever class a student finally takes, the student will have succeeded in gaining entrance to it. He will go into the classroom with official certification – based on reality – that he will be able to learn the material if he gives it an honest effort. The success–failure, cause–effect features of the system are indispensable for teaching some critical lessons:

- Effort is often rewarded with success.
- Effort is not always rewarded with success.
- Failure in one instance does not mean inability to succeed in anything else.
- Failure in one try does not mean perpetual failure.
- The better the preparation, the more likely the success.

None of these lessons is taught as well or as directly under the system prevailing in our current education of the disadvantaged. The central failing of the educational system for the poor and disadvantaged, and most especially poor and disadvantaged blacks, is not that it fails to provide meaningful ways for a student to succeed, though that is part of it. The central failing is not that ersatz success – fake curricula, fake grades, fake diplomas – sets the students up for failure when they leave the school, though that too is part of it. The central failing is that the system does not teach disadvantaged students, who see permanent failure all around them, how to fail. For students who are growing up expecting (whatever their dreams may be) ultimately to be a failure, with failure writ large, the first essential contravening lesson is that failure can come in small, digestible packages. Failure can be dealt with. It can be absorbed, analyzed, and converted to an asset.

We are now discussing a population of students – the children of what has become known as "the underclass" – that comes to the classroom with an array of disadvantages beyond simple economic poverty. I am not suggesting that, under our hypothetical system, all children of the underclass will become motivated students forthwith. Rather, some will. Perhaps it will be a small proportion; perhaps a large one. Certainly the effect interacts with the inherent abilities of the children involved. But some effect will be observed. Some children who are at the very bottom of the pile in the disadvantages they bear will act on the change in the reality of their environment. It will be an improvement over the situation in the system we have replaced, in which virtually none of them gets an education in anything except the futility of hoping.

A PROPOSAL FOR PUBLIC WELFARE

I begin with the proposition that it is within our resources to do enormous good for some people quickly. We have available to us a program that would convert a large proportion of the younger generation of hard-core unemployed into steady workers making a living wage. The same program would drastically reduce births to single teenage girls. It would reverse the trendline in the breakup of poor families. It would measurably increase the upward socio-economic mobility of poor families. These improvements would affect some millions of persons.

All these are results that have eluded the efforts of the social programs installed since 1965, yet, from everything we know, there is no real question about whether they would occur under the program I propose. A wide variety of persuasive evidence from our own culture and around the world, from experimental data and longitudinal studies, from theory and practice, suggests that the program would achieve such results.

The proposed program, our final and most ambitious thought experiment, consists of scrapping the entire federal welfare and income-support structure for working-aged persons, including AFDC [Aid to Families with Dependent Children], Medicaid, Food Stamps, Unemployment Insurance, Worker's Compensation, subsidized housing, disability insurance, and the rest. It would leave the working-aged person with no recourse whatsoever except the job market, family members, friends, and public or private locally funded services. It is the Alexandrian solution: cut the knot, for there is no way to untie it.

It is difficult to examine such a proposal dispassionately. Those who dislike paying for welfare are for it without thinking. Others reflexively imagine bread lines and people starving in the streets. But as a means of gaining fresh perspective on the problem of effective reform, let us consider what this hypothetical society might look like.

A large majority of the population is unaffected. A surprising number of the huge American middle and working classes go from birth to grave without using any social welfare benefits until they receive their first Social Security check. Another portion of the population is technically affected, but the change in income is so small or so sporadic that it makes no difference in quality of life. A third group comprises persons who have to make new arrangements and behave in different ways. Sons and daughters who fail to find work continue to live with their parents or relatives or friends. Teenaged mothers have to rely on support from their parents or the father of the child and perhaps work as well. People laid off from work have to use their own savings or borrow from others to make do until the next job is found. All these changes involve great disruption in expectations and accustomed roles.

Along with the disruptions go other changes in behavior. Some parents do not want their young adult children continuing to live off their income, and become quite insistent about their children learning skills and getting jobs. This attitude is most prevalent among single mothers who have to depend most critically on the earning power of their offspring.

Parents tend to become upset at the prospect of a daughter's bringing home a baby that must be entirely supported on an already inadequate income. Some become so upset that they spend considerable parental energy avoiding such an eventuality. Potential fathers of such babies find themselves under more pressure not to cause such a problem, or to help with its solution if it occurs.

Adolescents who were not job-ready find they are job-ready after all. It turns out that they can work for low wages and accept the discipline of the workplace if the alternative is grim enough. After a few years, many – not all, but many – find that they have acquired salable skills, or that they are at the right place at the right time, or otherwise find that the original entry-level job has gradually been transformed into a secure job paying a decent wage. A few – not a lot, but a few – find that the process leads to affluence.

Perhaps the most rightful, deserved benefit goes to the much larger population of low-income families who have been doing things right all along and have been punished for it: the young man who has taken responsibility for his wife and child even though his friends with the same choice have called him a fool; the single mother who has worked full time and forfeited her right to welfare for very little extra money; the parents who have set an example for their children even as the rules of the game have taught their children that the example is outmoded. For these millions of people, the instantaneous result is that no one makes fun of them any longer. The longer-term result will be that they regain the status that is properly theirs. They will not only be the bedrock upon which the community is founded (which they always have been), they will be recognized as such. The process whereby they regain their position is not magical, but a matter of logic. When it becomes highly dysfunctional for a person to be dependent, status will accrue to being independent, and in fairly short order. Noneconomic rewards will once again reinforce the economic rewards of being a good parent and provider.

The prospective advantages are real and extremely plausible. In fact, if a government program of the traditional sort (one that would "do" something rather than simply get out of the way) could as plausibly promise these advantages, its passage would be a foregone conclusion. Congress, yearning for programs that are not retreads of failures, would be prepared to spend billions. Negative side-effects (as long as they were the traditionally acceptable negative side-effects) would be brushed aside as trivial in return for the benefits. For let me be quite clear: I am not suggesting that we dismantle income support for the working-aged to balance the budget or punish welfare cheats. I am hypothesizing, with the advantage of powerful collateral evidence, that the lives of large numbers of poor people would be radically changed for the better.

There is, however, a fourth segment of the population yet to be considered, those who are pauperized by the withdrawal of government supports and unable to make alternate arrangements: the teenaged mother who has no one to turn to; the incapacitated or the inept who are thrown out of the house; those to whom economic conditions have brought long periods in which there is no work to be had; those with illnesses not covered by insurance. What of these situations?

The first resort is the network of local services. Poor communities in our hypothetical society are still dotted with storefront health clinics, emergency relief agencies, employment services, legal services. They depend for support on local taxes or local philanthropy, and the local taxpayers and philanthropists tend to scrutinize them rather closely. But, by the same token, they also receive considerably more resources than they formerly did. The dismantling of the federal services has poured tens of billions of dollars back into the private economy. Some of that money no doubt has been spent on Mercedes and summer homes on the Cape. But some has been spent on capital investments that generate new jobs. And some has been spent on increased local services to the poor, voluntarily or as decreed by the municipality. In many cities, the coverage provided by this network of agencies is more generous, more humane, more wisely distributed, and more effective in its results than the services formerly subsidized by the federal government.

But we must expect that a large number of people will fall between the cracks. How might we go about trying to retain the advantages of a zero-level welfare system and still address the residual needs?

As we think about the nature of the population still in need, it becomes apparent that their basic problem in the vast majority of the cases is the lack of a job, and this problem is temporary. What they need is something to tide them over while finding a new place in the economy. So our first step is to re-install the Unemployment Insurance program in more or less its previous form. Properly administered, unemployment insurance makes sense. Even if it is restored with all the defects of current practice, the negative effects of unemployment insurance alone are relatively minor. Our objective is not to wipe out chicanery or to construct a theoretically unblemished system, but to meet legitimate human needs without doing more harm than good. Unemployment insurance is one of the least harmful ways of contributing to such ends. Thus the system has been amended to take care of the victims of short-term swings in the economy.

Who is left? We are now down to the hardest of the hard core of the welfare-dependent. They have no jobs. They have been unable to find jobs (or have not tried to find jobs) for a longer period of time than the unemployment benefits cover. They have no families who will help. They have no friends who will help. For some reason, they cannot get help from local services or private charities except for the soup kitchen and a bed in the Salvation Army hall.

What will be the size of this population? We have never tried a zero-level federal welfare system under conditions of late-twentieth-century national wealth, so we cannot do more than speculate. But we may speculate. Let us ask of whom the population might consist and how they might fare.

For any category of "needy" we may name, we find ourselves driven to one of two lines of thought. Either the person is in a category that is going to be at the top of the list of services that localities vote for themselves, and at the top of the list of private services, or the person is in a category where help really is not all that essential or desirable. The burden of the conclusion is not that every single person will be taken care of, but that the extent of resources to deal with needs is likely to be very great – not based on wishful thinking, but on extrapolations from reality.

To illustrate, let us consider the plight of the stereotypical welfare mother – never married, no skills, small children, no steady help from a man. It is safe to say that, now as in the 1950s, there is no one who has less sympathy from the white middle class, which is to be the source of most of the money for the private and local services we envision. Yet this same white middle class is a soft touch for people trying to make it on their own, and a soft touch for "deserving" needy mothers – AFDC was one of the most widely popular of the New Deal welfare measures, intended as it was for widows with small children. Thus we may envision two quite different scenarios.

In one scenario, the woman is presenting the local or private service with this proposition: "Help me find a job and day-care for my children, and I will take care of the rest." In effect, she puts herself into the same category as the widow and the deserted wife – identifies herself as one of the most obviously deserving of the deserving poor. Welfare mothers who want to get into the labor force are likely to find a wide range of help. In the other scenario, she asks for an outright and indefinite cash grant – in effect, a private or local version of AFDC – so that she can stay with the children and not hold a job. In the latter case, it is very easy to imagine situations in which she will not be able to find a local service or a private philanthropy to provide the help she seeks. The question we must now ask is: What's so bad about that? If children were always better off being with their mother all day and if, by the act of giving birth, a mother acquired the inalienable right to be with the child, then her situation would be unjust to her and injurious to her children. Neither assertion can be defended, however, especially not in the 1980s, when more mothers of all classes work away from the home than ever before, and even more especially not in view of the empirical record for the children growing up under the current welfare system. Why should the mother be exempted by the system from the pressures that must affect everyone else's decision to work?

As we survey these prospects, important questions remain unresolved. The first of these is why, if federal social transfers are treacherous, should locally mandated transfers be less so? Why should a municipality be permitted to legislate its own AFDC or Food Stamp program if their results are so inherently bad?

Part of the answer lies in conceptions of freedom. I have deliberately avoided raising them – the discussion is about how to help the disadvantaged, not about how to help the advantaged cut their taxes, to which arguments for personal freedom somehow always get diverted. Nonetheless, the point is valid: Local or even state systems leave much more room than a federal system for everyone, donors and recipients alike, to exercise freedom of choice about the kind of system they live under. Laws are more easily made and changed, and people who find them unacceptable have much more latitude in going somewhere more to their liking.

But the freedom of choice argument, while

legitimate, is not necessary. We may put the advantages of local systems in terms of the Law of Imperfect Selection. A federal system must inherently employ very crude, inaccurate rules for deciding who gets what kind of help, and the results are as I outlined them in [another chapter]. At the opposite extreme – a neighbor helping a neighbor, a family member helping another family member – the law loses its validity nearly altogether. Very fine-grained judgments based on personal knowledge are being made about specific people and changing situations. In neighborhoods and small cities, the procedures can still bring much individualized information to bear on decisions. Even systems in large cities and states can do much better than a national system; a decaying industrial city in the Northeast and a booming sunbelt city of the same size can and probably should adopt much different rules about who gets what and how much.

A final and equally powerful argument for not impeding local systems is diversity. We know much more in the 1980s than we knew in the 1960s about what does not work. We have a lot to learn about what does work. Localities have been a rich source of experiments. Marva Collins in Chicago gives us an example of how a school can bring inner-city students up to national norms. Sister Falaka Fattah in Philadelphia shows us how homeless youths can be rescued from the streets. There are numberless such lessons waiting to be learned from the diversity of local efforts. By all means, let a hundred flowers bloom, and if the federal government can play a useful role in lending a hand and spreading the word of successes, so much the better.

The ultimate unresolved question about our proposal to abolish income maintenance for the working-aged is how many people will fall through the cracks. In whatever detail we try to foresee the consequences, the objection may always be raised: We cannot be sure that everyone will be taken care of in the degree to which we would wish. But this observation by no means settles the question. If one may point in objection to the child now fed by Food Stamps who would go hungry, one may also point with satisfaction to the child who would have an entirely different and better future. Hungry children should be fed; there is no argument about that. It is no less urgent that children be allowed to grow up in a system free of the forces that encourage them to remain poor and dependent. If a strategy reasonably promises to remove those forces, after so many attempts to "help the poor" have failed, it is worth thinking about.

But that rationale is too vague. Let me step outside the persona I have employed and put the issue in terms of one last intensely personal hypothetical example. Let us suppose that you, a parent, could know that tomorrow your own child would be made an orphan. You have a choice. You may put your child with an extremely poor family, so poor that your child will be badly clothed and will indeed sometimes be hungry. But you also know that the parents have worked hard all their lives, will make sure your child goes to school and studies, and will teach your child that independence is a primary value. Or you may put your child with a family with parents who have never worked, who will be incapable of overseeing your child's education – but who have plenty of food and good clothes, provided by others. If the choice about where one would put one's own child is as clear to you as it is to me, on what grounds does one justify support of a system that, indirectly but without doubt, makes the other choice for other children? The answer that "What we really want is a world where that choice is not forced upon us" is no answer. We have tried to have it that way. We failed. Everything we know about why we failed tells us that more of the same will not make the dilemma go away.

BURTON PIKE

"The City as Image"

from *The Image of the City in Modern Literature* (1981)

Editors' introduction   One way to look at urban society and culture is through the prism of the arts. Novels and short stories – as well as paintings, sculptures, musical compositions, and architectural designs – are all created out of specific urban contexts and all reflect, to one degree or another, the social, political, and economic conditions of the urban cultures that give them birth.

Burton Pike, who is a professor of comparative literature at Queens College and the Graduate Center of the City University of New York, explores the ways urban culture is reflected in literature and how what he calls "the literary city" or "the word city" expresses the underlying social psychology of the city's people. In *The Image of the City in Modern Literature* (Princeton, N.J.: Princeton University Press, 1981), he recalls Sigmund Freud's use of an urban metaphor in *Civilization and Its Discontents* to explain the workings of the unconscious and writes that "during the nineteenth century the literary city came more and more to express the isolation or exclusion of the individual from a community, and in the twentieth century to express the fragmentation of the very concept of community."

Although the city has been a constant and recurrent theme of literature since the very beginnings of urban civilization, Pike notes that the image of the city has been highly ambiguous and contradictory. "The word-city," he writes, ". . . leads a double life, evoking deep-rooted archetypal associations while its surface features reflect changing attitudes and values."

Pike's analysis of Hawthorne, Henry James, Freud, and Dostoyevsky in "The City as Image" is an excellent introduction to a consideration of the question, "How do the arts today – our novels and paintings, our films and television – reflect and express our urban culture and community?" It also opens the door to an entire body of analytical literature on the relationship of arts culture to society. For literature, Diana Spearman's *The Novel and Society* (London: Routledge & Kegan Paul, 1966) is an excellent overview, and Raymond Williams's *The Country and the City* (London: Oxford University Press, 1973) is especially insightful on the relationship of Charles Dickens to nineteenth-century London. For painting, one should consult Arnold Hauser's chapter on "Impressionism" in *The Social History of Art* (New York: Knopf, 1952) and T. J. Clark's magisterial *The Painting of Modern Life* (New York: Knopf, 1985).

For the relationship of architecture to urban life – an enormous field – one can begin with Spiro Kostof's *A History of Architecture: Settings and Rituals* (New York: Oxford University Press, 1985) and Mark Girouard's *Cities and People: A Social and Architectural History* (New Haven, Conn.: Yale University Press, 1985). In addition, David Harvey's "Monument and Myth: The Building of the Basilica of the Sacred Heart" from *The Urban Experience* (Baltimore: Johns Hopkins University Press, 1989) is a *tour de force* of Marxist cultural analysis that ties the major themes of nineteenth-century French politics to the construction of Sacré-Coeur.

For film, Hauser's *The Social History of Art* is again useful, as is Stanley J. Solomon's "Film as an Urban Art" (*Carnegie Review*, 22 April 1970) and S. M. Sherman's "How the Movies See the City" (*Landscape*, Spring 1967). And other interesting perspectives on the general relationship of arts culture to urban history and culture are Roland Barthes's "Semiology and the Urban" from M. Gottdiener and Alexandros Ph. Lagopoulos (eds.), *The City and the Sign* (New York: Columbia University Press, 1986), Vera Zolberg's *Constructing a Sociology of the Arts* (Cambridge: Cambridge University Press, 1990), and Richard Sennett's *Flesh and Stone: The Body and the City in Western Civilization* (New York: W. W. Norton, 1994).

BURTON PIKE, "The City as Image"

from *The Image of the City in Modern Literature* (1981)

> The crowd had rolled back and were now huddled together nearly at the extremity of the street, while the soldiers had advanced no more than a third of its length. The intervening space was empty – a paved solitude between lofty edifices, which threw almost a twilight shadow over it.
>
> Nathaniel Hawthorne, "The Gray Champion"

Since there has been literature, there have been cities in literature. We unthinkingly consider this phenomenon modern, but it goes back to early epic and mythic thought. We cannot imagine *Gilgamesh*, the Bible, the *Iliad*, or the *Aeneid*, without their cities, which contain so much of their energy and radiate so much of their meaning. Small settlements and villages had, then as now, some direct connection to the land around them, and provided clear and limited social functions. But cities were from the beginning something special. As centers of religious and military power, as well as of social life on a large scale, they were things apart.

The city has always been man's single most impressive and visible achievement. It is a human artifact which has become an object in the world of nature. Cities are a plural phenomenon: There are many of them, but though each has its individual history, they all seem to exemplify similar patterns. The most basic of these is the interpenetration of past and present. On the one hand there is the visible city of streets and buildings, frozen forms of energy fixed at different times in the past and around which the busy kinetic energy of the present

swirls. On the other hand there are the subconscious currents arising in the minds of the city's living inhabitants from this combination of past and present. These currents include the city's ties with the realm of the dead through its temples, cemeteries, and ceremonies as well as its old buildings, and also its functions as the seat of secular power, embodied in kings, governments, and banks. Northrop Frye, following Kierkegaard's concept of repetition as re-creation, writes that "the culture of the past is not only the memory of mankind, but our own buried life, and study of it leads to a recognition scene, a discovery in which we see, not our past lives, but the cultural form of our present life." The city is, as Joseph Rykwert characterizes it, a curious artifact "compounded of willed and random elements, imperfectly controlled." It has even been called "a state of mind."

The city has been used as a rhetorical topos throughout the history of Western culture. But it has another aspect as well, whose referent seems to be a deep-seated anxiety about man's relation to his created world. The city crystallizes those conscious and unconscious tensions which have from the beginning characterized the city in Western culture. Only such a crystallization can explain man's deep preoccupation with the city, or account for the hypnotic attraction of its destruction since Troy, Sodom and Gomorrah, and Carthage.

"Man constructs according to an archetype,"

writes Mircea Eliade. Man's city and temple, as well as the entire region he inhabits, are built on celestial models. The act of Creation was a divine act; when man creates, he repeats the divine act, and formalizes the connection through ritual. The sacred city or temple is symbolically the center of the universe, the meeting point of heaven, earth, and hell. The sacred rites of the founding of the city were repeated in regular recurrent festivals, and in its monuments. The founding of cities, even as late as those of the Roman Empire, was a matter of myth and ritual to which practical concerns were completely subordinated. "The city had to be founded by a hero," Rykwert says, and the "hero-founder had to be buried at the heart of the city; only the tomb of the hero-founder could guarantee that the city lived." The distance from this rite of the early city to Pushkin's vivified statue in *The Bronze Horseman* is not as great as one might at first suppose.

[. . .]

This book is interested in the response of the human imagination to the phenomenon of "city." From the beginning the image of the city served as the nexus of many things, all characterized by strongly ambivalent feelings: presumption (Babel), corruption (Babylon), perversion (Sodom and Gomorrah), power (Rome), destruction (Troy, Carthage), death, the plague (the City of Dis), and revelation (the heavenly Jerusalem). In Christian thought, the city came to represent both Heaven and Hell. Significantly, the early cities of the epics and the Bible have retained their metaphorical force throughout Western history, as if they stood for certain constants of feeling. Thus Proust could make an important metaphorical point by calling one of the volumes of *In Search of Lost Time* "Sodom and Gomorrah." Several centuries earlier, in 1667, John Dryden had the inspired idea of dedicating his poem "Annus Mirabilis: The Year of Wonders 1666" to "the Metropolis of Great Britain, the most renowned and late flourishing City of London." Noting in his dedication that he is perhaps the first person to dedicate a poem to a city, Dryden celebrates London for having survived a war, a plague,

and a devastating fire: "You, who are to stand a wonder to all Years and Ages, and who have built yourselves an Immortal Monument on your own Ruins. You are now a *Phoenix* in her ashes, and, as far as Humanity can approach, a great Emblem of the suffering Deity."

The city has often been celebrated as the place where the pulse of life is most strongly felt. Samuel Johnson, although well acquainted with adversity in London, never tired of praising the city in poetry, essays, and conversation. His famous epigram is a paradigm of the city's vitality: "When a man is tired of London, he is tired of life."

In modern times the real cities of Western Europe and America have generally tended to be associated with the evils of human nature; ideal cities, on the model of Revelation, have been put off to some vague future time, as in Blake's vow to build Jerusalem in England's green and pleasant land, or the alabaster cities of "America the Beautiful," which gleam (rather curiously) "undimmed by human tears."

The double view of the real city and the mythic city is not so mysterious as might first appear, for all myths are attempts to explain realities. Most basic myths are, however, attempts to account for occurrences of nature. The myth of the city must rationalize an object built by man which, because of its size and concentration of ritual and power (religious, governmental, military, financial) has displaced nature in the natural world.

The myth of the city as corruption, the myth of the city as perfection: this bifocal vision of Western culture is still very much with us. Indeed, the image of the city stands as the great reification of ambivalence, embodying a complex of contradictory forces in both the individual and the collective Western minds. The idea of the city seems to trigger conflicting impulses, positive and negative, conscious and unconscious. At a very deep level, the city seems to express our culture's restless dream about its inner conflicts and its inability to resolve them. On a more conscious level, this ambivalence expresses itself in mixed feelings of pride, guilt, love, fear, and hate toward the city. The fascination people have always felt at the destruction of a city may be partly an expression of satisfaction at the destruction of an emblem of irresolvable conflict.

If one of the writer's functions is to give voice to aspects of culture which are fragmentary perceptions, or preconscious or perhaps even unconscious feelings in the mind of the citizen, then the city is one of the most important metaphors at his command. Technically, the city is an ideal mechanism for the writer, especially the novelist; it enables him to bring together in a plausible network extremely diverse characters, situations, and actions. But this should not mislead us, as readers, into dismissing it as a mere contrivance. The image of the city is a figure with profound tones and overtones, a presence and not simply a setting. This emerges, for instance, in the peculiar opening pages of *Moby Dick*, in which Ishmael and the city dwellers of Manhattan are drawn magnetically to the edge of the water, yearning outward from their city existence – which itself is presented in strongly negative terms. *Moby Dick* is not a "city novel," and yet it begins with the image of the city. This opening passage, which arouses resonances in the characters and the reader, stands in a long tradition of the city as a figure for ambivalence in literature.

These conflicting resonances of the image are reinforced by a writer's and reader's own experiences of city life, whether real or imagined. What exactly does happen when one experiences a city in real life? The question itself makes us realize the complexity of the problems facing anthropologist, sociologist, writer, and critic. The basic problem is how to reduce a cacophony of impressions to some kind of harmony. Kevin Lynch has tried to categorize some aspects of this problem as far as empirical response is concerned. The inhabitant or visitor basically experiences the city as a labyrinth, although one with which he may be familiar. He cannot see the whole of a labyrinth at once, except from above, when it becomes a map. Therefore his impressions of it at street level at any given moment will be fragmentary and limited: rooms, buildings, streets. These impressions are primarily visual, but involve the other senses as well, together with a crowd of memories and associations. The impressions a real city makes on an observer are thus both complex and composite in a purely physical sense, even without taking into account his or his culture's pre-existing attitudes. "Observer" is a slightly awkward term to use here since it indicates a person who is, with some awareness, looking at the city from a detached viewpoint. "Observer" applies better to the writer and the narrator than to the citizen. In daily life most urbanites go about in the city concentrating on their immediate business; they swim in the urban ocean without being particularly aware of it. Susanne Langer may call architecture "the total environment made visible," but this remark would certainly nonplus Leopold Bloom.

There is a paradox in this entire situation. The city is, on the one hand, incomprehensible to its inhabitants; as a whole "it is inaccessible to the imagination unless it can be reduced and simplified." But on the other hand, "any individual citizen, by virtue of his particular choices of alternatives for action and experience, will need a vocabulary to express what he imagines the entire city to be."

[...]

Many writers for whom the image of the city is important have been urban journalists and dedicated *flaneurs*, saunterers through the streets of real cities who have paid careful attention to their impressions. Balzac, Dickens, Poe, Baudelaire, Whitman, Dostoevsky, and Zola all fit this mold exactly. But even writers who don't share with the others the peculiar and difficult problem of transposing the urban scene from personal impression to literature. For there is a gulf between the living experience of a real city and the word-city of a poem or novel. How does one make printed statements, ink on paper, into "London," "New York," or "Rome," aside from the associations evoked by the names themselves? Even the sociologist and the urban historian, whose primary obligation is fidelity to empirical reality rather than to the imagination, must, as we say, "reduce" the city to words; for them, as well as for creative writers, the process is one of metaphorization. The sociologist and historian would ideally like to establish identity between the sign and its meaning; the writer calls attention to the separation between them.

[...]

So the process by which the writer evokes the city appears to parallel the process by which the citizen seeks to encompass his experience of it. The writer's task is both to evoke and to organize many kinds and levels of response in the reader. It is not the artist who dreams, says Kenneth Burke, but rather the audience, "while the artist oversees the conditions which determine this dream." In this process of overseeing it is clear that the city evoked in words, especially in a fictional text, is toponymical rather than topographical. The name of the city and whatever physical features are labeled function within the relational context of the work; their reference to the real city outside the text may appear to be direct, but is actually indirect. One test of this is the coherence of the word-city to readers who are not the author's contemporaries or countrymen. Raskolnikov's walks through the streets of St. Petersburg in *Crime and Punishment* can be mapped, and would evoke certain associations in readers of Dostoevsky's time and place, but Dostoevsky evokes a thematically coherent city in the text itself, which makes sense a century later to readers in other countries. There are writers who do not sufficiently generalize the city in this way; for example, it is very difficult for a reader to follow Heimito von Doderer's Vienna novels without a thorough topographical and social knowledge of Vienna. Thus, however artfully the word-city may be decked out with the trimmings of a real one, they are parallel or analogous rather than identical: Dickens's London and London, England, are located in two different countries.

Writers seem to pay careful attention to this difference between reality and image. For instance, though Flaubert, Hugo, Balzac, and Dickens have been praised for the realistic urban descriptions in their novels, close examination shows that they typically create in their fictions the Paris or London of a time considerably before the actual time of writing. Through the use of the conventions governing verb tenses in narration, they give the impression of describing a present scene when they are actually inventing the picture of a past one. It is as if, by displacing the city backward in time in this fashion, they wished to insure its metaphorization, to place it as firmly as possible in the realm of the imaginary while at the same time presenting it as a "reality." The result of this procedure is not the evocation of a historically past city but a palimpsestic impression, which results in a tension between the city as past and the city as present.

To point out the discontinuity between the empirical city and its fictional counterpart is not to suggest that in using this image the writer has in mind a secret, coded meaning which the reader is challenged to decipher. That would make the city too literally symbolic, when actually it seems to function primarily as both an emblem and an archetype. As such it has more various and more diffuse associations and resonances than a symbol can generally encompass. However the city-image may function, it always brings into the text a power of its own; it might be more accurate to say that a writer harnesses this image rather than that he creates it ...

Whatever the variety of associations this word conjures up, it has one irreducible core. "City" is, by any definition, a social image. Throughout history, and literary history, it has chiefly represented the idea of community, whatever values might be attached to it in any particular context. For religion, philosophy, and literature from the time of the Greeks and the Old Testament, the image of the city was the image of a community, whether positive or negative. But then this idea began to shift its ground. "From the Renaissance onwards," writes Ian Watt, "there was a growing tendency for individual experience to replace collective tradition as the ultimate arbiter of reality." The modern form of realism began with the idea that the individual could discover the truth through his senses, and this concept led to the rise of the novel as a literary form. Whereas earlier literary forms had been characterized by making "conformity to traditional practice the major test of truth," the primary criterion of the novel was "truth to individual experience." Thus the plot of the novel "had to be acted out by particular people in particular circumstances, rather than, as had been common in the past, by general human types against a background primarily determined by the appropriate literary convention."

One of the favorite devices of the eighteenth-century novel was to play off an individual outcast against an urban community of shared values. Moll Flanders is a criminal operating on the community of bourgeois mercantile London (although her religious conversion reunites her with society on a higher level for both). The primacy of the community's shared values is still operating in Balzac, if with less conviction; Balzac's heroes and heroines are typically outsiders, like Rastignac or Lucien Chardon, whose goal in life is to get to the top of the shaky heap. But the presence of Vautrin in Balzac's world shows how the idea of an urban community as a community of shared values was losing its force. Vautrin strikes a different note from Moll Flanders'; her criminality defines the boundaries of an integral community she is operating against, his subverts the whole idea of a community which Balzac presents as essentially corrupt to begin with. And throughout the nineteenth century we find that the isolation of the individual rather than the cohesion of urban society becomes increasingly the focus of the image of the city. Dickens's extreme emphasis on portraying urban eccentrics is an indirect witness to this shift; Baudelaire's neurotic poet and Dostoevsky's underground man and Raskolnikov are direct statements of it.

This new emphasis on the isolated individual applies not only to characters in novels, but also to the stress which nineteenth- and twentieth-century writers and critics put on the concept of the narrator (or, in poetry, the speaker), whose individualized point of view is the lens through which the reader views the world of the work. Of special interest is the way in which character or narrator typically presents himself alone against the city, an isolated individual consciousness observing the urban community. It is this stance which makes Hawthorne's "paved solitude" a paradigm for the city in modern literature.

Henry James's *The American Scene* is a work of non-fiction written by a novelist. Many of its passages combine the personal reactions of a sharp-witted observer of cities with the boldness of the novelist's invention. James frequently sees the city as casting back an image of truth at a self-deluded character, as Paris does to Strether in *The Ambassadors*; in *The American Scene* the image is cast back at James himself. Summing up his impression at seeing New York again after an absence of a quarter-century, James writes that

> the skyscrapers and the league-long bridges, present and to come, marked the point where the age ... had come out. That in itself was nothing – ages do come out, as a matter of course, so far from where they have gone in. But it had done so, the latter half of the nineteenth century, in one's own more or less immediate presence; the difference, from pole to pole, was so vivid and concrete that no single shade of any one of its aspects was lost. This impact of the whole condensed past at once produced a horrible, hateful sense of personal antiquity.

In this complicated reaction to the city James makes the physical city an organism like himself, whose changes and rhythms in both time and space are, however, on a different scale and rhythm from his own. It is this discrepancy which reminds him so abruptly of his "personal antiquity" when suddenly faced with "the whole condensed past." The overall impression of the physical city to one who observes it, as James does here, is of buildings and streets deposited in sedimentary fashion over a long period, and implying a future ("present and to come").

[...]

However, the image of the city seen historically only partly explains its fascination. At a deeper level, as I have indicated, the widely varying historical cities of Western culture are the same city, a powerful archetype-emblem representing deep-rooted social and psychological constants. For this reason history and cultural psychology are intimately linked in any study of the literary city. An arresting example of this symbiotic relationship occurs in an essay which lies on the borderline between science and poetry, Freud's *Civilization and Its Discontents*. The figure of the city was a strong emblematic magnet for Freud; he is elsewhere drawn to Pompeii and London. In this late essay he uses the city of Rome as an incidental but profound and curious analogy. In seeking to illustrate the point that the primitive part of the brain still survives in the brain of modern man, Freud turns to the city as illustration. He first refers to "the history of the Eternal City," which he only then goes on to identify as Rome. It is as if this common tag for Rome ("the Eternal City") were important for him in a literal sense, standing for something which has survived through time basically unchanged; this is indeed the argument Freud goes on to develop. Traces of early stages in the development of the brain still survive in the modern brain, he argues, in the same way that traces of the history and pre-history of the "Eternal City" still survive in present-day Rome.

In a remarkable flight of the imagination, bordering on reverie, Freud asks his reader to visualize a surrealistic picture: wherever we might look in contemporary Rome we would see, simultaneously with a present building and occupying the same space, all the earlier structures which had ever stood on that one spot. As if rousing himself, he then goes on to reject his own analogy. One cannot, he says, represent mental life in pictorial (that is, spatial) terms. But the analogy has been made, and it has been made with the evocative power we might expect from a poet. Indeed, the comparison has so much force that Freud himself felt it necessary to comment further on it. As he continues his argument, he returns to the strictures of scientific discourse, but he notes in one of those asides which seem to hang in the air long after they are spoken: "The question may be raised why we chose precisely the past of a *city* to compare with the past of the mind." It is a question he does not really answer.

[...]

Freud's subject in this passage is the mind, not the city. He uses the city only as an illustration, and yet, for both author and reader, the image seems to have resonances which have nothing to do with the context. His point would be quite clear without any image at all. Freud's life provides an interesting clue to the power of this particular figure. His biographer Ernest Jones points out that Freud attached great importance to Rome, and that this city had great emotional significance for him. Jones concludes that for Freud "Rome contained two entities, one loved, the other feared and hated"; in other words, that it was for him a perfect emblem of ambivalence.

It would, however, be a mistake to stop with this personal explanation. There seems to have been in Freud's thinking an association between civilization (*Kultur*) as the highest product of the human mind, and the city as the densest – and at the same time the most rarefied – distillation of civilization. This association is unstated, but it does not appear to have been entirely unconscious on Freud's part, since he himself wonders in print why he chose a city as a metaphor. (This time he writes "a city" rather than "the Eternal City" or "Rome.") One might speculate further that the choice of Rome is both appropriate and necessary for his comparison, for Rome presents the observer with the image of a living city in the present superimposed on the impressive ruins of a ghostly past. Rome is a living community, but its life rests on the many layers of the dead, who have left visible and grandiose reminders of their former presence. Rome is also, of course, one of the main foundation stones of our culture, the *locus classicus* of Western civilization: "at once the Paradise, / The grave, the city, and the wilderness," Shelley called it in *Adonais*, the twin oxymorons underlining its ambivalence for Keats, Shelley himself, and European culture.

[...]

The word-city, then, leads a double life, evoking deep-rooted archetypal associations while its surface features reflect changing attitudes and values. Viewers of medieval paintings and woodcuts depicting cities are struck by the fact that a representation of Jerusalem, for instance, is that of a medieval city. E. H. Gombrich refers to the illustrations in Hartmann Schedel's "Nuremberg Chronicle," in which the identical woodcut of a medieval city recurs with different captions as Damascus, Ferrara, Milan, and Mantua; all that these pictures were expected to do, Gombrich writes, "was to bring home to the reader that these names stood for cities." What was to be depicted was the idea, not the concrete individualized form. Gombrich calls this "the principle of the adapted stereotype," in which the illustrator depicts an inner stereotype derived from the current culture, rather than an objective rendering of a real city.

Such an adapted stereotype occurs in Hawthorne's "The Gray Champion." In this story from *Twice-Told Tales* the city is located in the past rather than the present: Hawthorne is ostensibly writing about Boston during the colonial period. But the fine icy chill of the passage which serves as epigraph to this chapter belongs to the writer of 1837, not to the screen Boston of "1689." This single use of the image of the city contains many layers of meaning: "The crowd had rolled back and were now huddled together nearly at the extremity of the street, while the soldiers had advanced no more than a third of its length. The intervening space was empty – a paved solitude between lofty edifices, which threw almost a twilight shadow over it."

[. . .]

The metaphorical application of solitude to the city was by no means limited to America in the nineteenth century. Baudelaire, for example, was fond in his poetry of playing off the solitude of the observing poet against the city as a collective scene. Just how conscious and deliberate this was on his part can be seen in a section of *The Spleen of Paris* called "Crowds":

> Multitude, solitude: equal and convertible terms for the active and fecund poet. He who does not know how to people his solitude will not know either how to be alone in a bustling crowd.
> The poet enjoys the incomparable privilege of being able as he likes to be himself and others. Like those wandering souls which search for a

body, he can enter every person whenever he wants. For him alone, everything is empty . . .
> The solitary and pensive walker draws from this universal communion a singular sense of intoxication.

Ever the Latin linguist, Baudelaire begins by playing on the antiphonal contrast between "multitude" and "solitude," manyness and oneness, which he proceeds to equate. Using the terms to mean "togetherness" and "isolation," he throws them in the air and plays with them like a juggler. The isolated poet can through his imagination be the many as well as the one; he can be both "solitary and pensive" and partake at the same time of the "universal communion." (Baudelaire's use of the religious term is interesting, underlining as it does the integration of the individual into the sharing group in a ceremony of reconciliation.) As a poet, the individual must be isolated from the group in order to create, but through his imagination, and his poetry, he can join it. This sovereign freedom understandably produces in the poet "a singular sense of intoxication." However, this intoxication is indeed singular. The underlying tone of this passage is not that of the playful equation of opposites, but the expression of a splenetic solitude; as Walter Benjamin has pointed out, Baudelaire's attitude toward the city is predominantly negative. Henri Lefebvre, though not discussing Baudelaire specifically, has perhaps pinpointed this quirkiness more exactly in a thought about the extreme ambivalence of modern society. This ambivalence expresses itself in two contradictory obsessions, integrating and disintegrating. Lefebvre sees one of these obsessions, the compulsive need to integrate and be integrated, as a response to the other, the disintegration of the idea of community.

Clashing contradictions: perhaps the central fascination of the city, both real and fictional, is that it embodies man's contradictory feelings – pride, love, anxiety, and hatred – toward the civilization he has created and the culture to which he belongs.

PART 4

Urban Politics, Governance, and Economics

INTRODUCTION

The culture of poverty and urban underclass debates discussed in Part 3 above deal not only with issues of social structure, class, and race. They also raise questions about the kinds of *economic* activities which occur in cities, the presence or absence of work opportunities, and what local economic development and employment policies cities should pursue. As the debate between William Julius Wilson (p. 226) and Charles Murray (p. 233) described in Part 3 shows, these economic questions are intimately related to questions of urban *politics and governance*.

V. Gordon Childe emphasized the importance of ruling elites and attendant bureaucracies to the rise of the first cities in Mesopotamia (p. 22). There and in the first cities of Egypt, Mesoamerica, and Asia god-kings or ruling oligarchies organized the affairs of their cities and their subjects with an iron hand. Their power was based as much on their control of the basic economic functions and infrastructures of their cities, such as the water irrigation systems and markets, as on the military might of their armies and the religious authority of their temple priests.

From earliest times, therefore, urban political power has rested on the ability to manage and command basic economic structures and resources – including human resources of the populace itself.

But the real practice of *urban politics* only emerged in the Greek polis (p. 32). The very word politics comes from the word polis. The ancient Athenians practiced direct democracy, with every citizen taking an active role in the affairs of the government and with public officials often chosen by lot. Today's urban democracies are the intellectual heirs of the polis. At least in theory, the people themselves rule through elected representatives. As individuals the people are free to vote on the issues of the day, and as collectives – socioeconomic classes, members of territorially based neighborhood communities, ethnic groups, or ideological factions – they are able to influence the policies to be carried out by the urban regimes in power.

Is democratic self-government free from economic influence? Certainly not. During the Middle Ages in Europe, the independent urban communes were ruled by rigid economic guild structures that exercised a monopoly over the production process, the systems of market exchange, and the day-to-day administration of the city's business. During the Industrial Revolution, the manufacturing cities – and the lives of the residents – were clearly dominated by a small group of rich capitalists who organized the physical, social, and political aspects of the cities to the purposes of profit. Today, when so much of a city's democratic political discourse is carried out in the media, the ownership of the newspapers and television outlets by the richest citizens gives them disproportionate power in the councils of government. And, of course, the changing structure of the economy over time plays an even greater role in determining the shape and content of urban politics.

The interrelationship between social structure, politics, and economics helps explain why both political scientists and sociologists have produced important writings on urban political power and why the hybrid discipline of urban political economy has produced some of the best work on the economy of cities.

Urban politics has existed for some time as a distinct subfield within the social science discipline of political science. In the 1960s seminal work by political scientist Robert Dahl and sociologist Floyd Hunter began a major debate between two schools of thought. In *Who Governs?* (1961) Dahl concluded that local political power in New Haven – and by implication other cities – was fragmented. He reported that many different people from a variety of walks of life were involved in decision making by the city of New Haven and influenced the outcome of different political decisions. In sum, Dahl advanced a *pluralist model* of urban community power. In *Community Power Structure* (1963) Floyd Hunter reported conclusions almost diametrically opposed to Dahl's: that a small, interlocking elite consisting of key businessmen, members of established and socially prominent families, and other leaders sat on the boards of each other's corporations, chatted at the same social clubs, and made all the really important decisions about Atlanta. Because Hunter believed that a small elite ruled Atlanta his model of urban community power is often referred to as the *elitist* model. Because Hunter argued that the economic and social structure of Atlanta largely determined urban decision making he and similar writers are also referred to as *structuralists*. During the next three decades Dahl's and Hunter's competing models stimulated dozens of empirical community power studies and the development of a body of theory about urban political power.

John Mollenkopf, a political scientist at the Graduate School of the City University of New York, reviews the current status of the debate between the pluralists and the structuralists in the first selection in Part 4: "How to Study Urban Political Power." He notes that in the recent past Marxist and other structuralist explanations of urban political power have gained wider acceptance than pluralist explanations, which were more widely accepted in the 1960s and 1970s. Extreme structuralists even question whether the study of urban politics itself makes sense. They feel that urban outcomes are so largely determined by economic and social structures that urban politics is irrelevant.

Mollenkopf rejects the extreme structuralist interpretation. His own answer to the question he poses – how to study urban political power – is synthetic and subtle. It acknowledges the importance of structural constraints, but notes that the real world of urban politics involves many conflicting forces and leaves plenty of room for politics. Mollenkopf stresses the connection between formal political structures and processes, corporate decision making, and the exercise of power by many other institutions such as churches, unions, professional associations and neighborhood groups which form alliances with elected officials in order to get things done. Like earlier pluralists Mollenkopf marshals evidence that there is broad participation in local government and he believes that many participants do influence decisions. Mollenkopf discusses and borrows heavily from the most important new paradigm in urban politics and community power studies: regime theory.

British political scientist Gerry Stoker reviews recent regime theory, particularly the work of Clarence Stone. Stone, a political scientist, studied decision making in Atlanta, Georgia during the 1980s – the same city Hunter had studied in the 1960s. Stone concluded that "regimes" of both elected government officials and nongovernmental allies formed to get things done. He developed a regime theory to explain urban politics. Regime theorists like Stone argue that urban politics by government cannot be divorced from the broader context of all decision making – both governmental and nongovernmental – in which it is embedded.

While pluralists, structuralists, and regime theorists seek to understand the exercise of urban political power, other political scientists study how cities are – or should be – governed. British political scientist Robin Hambelton reviews trends in urban governance in England and the United States during the 1980s and develops a theoretical model to help understand trends in the 1990s. Urban governments in both the United Kingdom and North America are under pressure to change. Hambelton describes competing ideological currents to *reform* public service functions, but still keep them governmental, versus more conservative approaches wishing to completely *privatize* the functions and turn them over to the private sector. For example, one approach to an inefficient city-run garbage collection system would be to shake up the management and make it perform more efficiently. Another would be to do away with the city-run garbage collection system altogether and allow private companies to provide garbage services in the free market. Conservatives argue that competition in the free market would force garbage collection companies to be efficient. If they failed to pick up the garbage on time, were rude to customers, or their monthly bills were unintelligible customers would switch to competing companies.

Within the category of public service reform Hambelton distinguishes between approaches which would make urban government more responsive to consumers and those which provide collectivist solutions.

While Hambelton is a political scientist discussing urban governance, many of the issues he addresses are economic ones. The articles on urban economics in this part of the book provide different perspectives on how the changing world economy is affecting cities.

There are some recurring themes in the literature on the economy of cities. A starting point is that the world economy has become global and the fate of individual cities is now linked to world trends as never before. In this new global economy there has been a massive restructuring of the world economy – many cities are performing economic roles quite different from those that they were performing just a short time ago. And this economic restructuring will surely accelerate in the years to come. Two of the most significant trends in the emerging global economy are a shift of manufacturing jobs from the developed world to Third-World countries and the growth of high-tech, information management-oriented advanced service jobs in many cities within the developed world. These trends create problems of job loss and unemployment among some sectors in some cities and boomtowns elsewhere. Both types of cities imply dramatic changes in the wealth and class structure of cities.

American sociologist John Kasarda (p. 306) provides global data to show why these trends have occurred: the enormous outflow of manufacturing jobs not only from the United Kingdom, but from the U.S. and other developed countries as well. The loss of manufacturing and other low-skill urban jobs coupled with increases in the less educated minority and immigrant population of inner cities creates what Kasarda calls a "jobs–skills mismatch." New jobs in cities of the developed world are related to their new economic functions in information management. Many require advanced education in accounting, computer science, law, finance, and research and development. At the same time many young entrants to these urban labor forces are not only not completing more advanced education, but dropping out of high school.

Sociologist/planner Saskia Sassen, whose work on the changing geography of jobs was introduced in Part 1 (p. 70), explores the new economic realities more deeply here. Many of her conclusions are similar to Kasarda's, but she emphasizes that the new economic order of global cities creates a large demand for low-skilled jobs – janitors to clean the new office buildings, fast food workers to flip burgers for the new global executives, maids to look after the children of high-powered two-wage-earner households. Kasarda stresses prospects for continuing urban unemployment, whereas Sassen foresees a dual labor market with very highly paid workers in the parts of the global economy which require advanced education and very low-paid workers supporting them in a variety of new, nonmanufacturing low-skilled jobs.

The structural effects of the world economy are so great that John Mollenkopf's question – "Is urban politics worth studying at all?" – seems ever more pertinent and can easily lead one to the view that local political activity is largely an illusion. Still, urban politics has come a long way from the ancient absolutisms, and even from the polis-based systems of classic Greece where the forms of democratic self-government may have been purer and more direct, but far less inclusive. Today, the citizen of a liberal democracy can speak his or her mind and attempt to use the system to achieve his or her perceived self-interest. Even in societies that have not fully adopted democratic political norms, the "power of the people" is at least a force to be reckoned with. The power to govern is no longer based exclusively on the control of economic systems and resources, but grows out of political struggles and the clash of social forces.

The final article in Part 4 by Mike Savage and Alan Warde (p. 312) is more theoretical and more synthetic. It reviews the literature on "uneven economic development" in search of basic explanations for the phenomena Kasarda and Sassen describe. Savage and Warde draw upon works by geographers, sociologists, economists, and many researchers who are best classified as a blend of all these disciplines. Capitalist and Marxist critics agree that economic power exerts a tremendous influence over political decision making. But whereas the Marxists see the economic forces as ever-dominant – reducing urban politics to an ongoing exercise in managing the class struggle – the capitalist analysts argue that free-market systems afford everyone some degree of economic opportunity and that the bourgeois liberal democracies provide guarantees of individual liberty to all. For them, the Marxist vision of unrelenting class struggle gives way to an often overly optimistic vision of upward social mobility.

In summary, both economics and politics matter a great deal to cities. Cities are affected by the forces of global economic restructuring which they often barely comprehend and cannot control. How to equip their residents with the skills to compete in the new global economy is essential to them, and unemployment is a major problem. But the range of responses to local and world economic conditions open to cities is very broad. And here politics is crucial. What strategies of economic development to pursue, how to distribute available public revenue, the interests of which social groups or neighborhoods within which to advance are essentially political questions.

JOHN MOLLENKOPF

"How to Study Urban Political Power"

from *A Phoenix in the Ashes: The Rise and Fall of the Koch Coalition in New York City Politics* (1992)

Editors' introduction   "Is urban politics worth studying at all, or is the urban political realm so subordinate to, dependent on, and constrained by its economic and social context that factors from this domain have little independent explanatory power?" In posing this question, John Mollenkopf (born 1946) raises the fundamental issue that has dominated urban political thought since at least the period of the Industrial Revolution. Indeed, the question of whether urban residents are actually members of a self-governing political community – citizens of a modern polis – or merely the helpless pawns of larger, faceless forces is an issue as old as Aristotle's definition of man as a *zoon politikon*.

John Mollenkopf taught at Stanford University, where he was one of the founders of the Program on Urban Studies, and is now a professor of political science and Director of the Public Policy Program at the Graduate School of the City University of New York. In 1983, he published *The Contested City* (Princeton, N.J.: Princeton University Press), a pioneering study of postwar American urban politics. On the basis of the experience of Boston and San Francisco, Mollenkopf outlined the process by which federal development programs were employed to help forge powerful pro-growth political coalitions at the local level. In *A Phoenix in the Ashes* (Princeton, N.J.: Princeton University Press, 1992), he applies a similar analysis to the politics of the city of New York during the mayoralty of Edward Koch.

"How to Study Urban Political Power" is a kind of prolegomena to Mollenkopf's analysis of New York politics and to the study of urban politics generally. Analysts of city politics, he explains, fall into two camps – the pluralists and the structuralists – and the recent history of urban political theory has been a back-and-forth struggle between the contending conceptual frameworks.

To begin with, writes Mollenkopf, an extensive body of theory (both by sociologists and political scientists) argued that local decision making was dominated by entrenched elites. In opposition to this prevailing orthodoxy, a number of pluralist scholars "went into the field" where no elitist model of governance "could easily explain what they saw." Noting that almost one-quarter of the gross national product of the United States "passes through the public sector ... much of it through urban governments," pluralist political analysts tended to see urban politics "as an autonomous realm that possessed real authority and commanded important resources."

But in a kind of intellectual counterattack, a new body of structuralist theory arose out of the social upheavals of the 1960s and 1970s that argued that the pluralist dispersion of power, especially to inner-city minority communities, was mostly illusion, and that the imperatives of capitalism, in both the economic and social structural realms, repeatedly and inevitably established the basic parameters of local development policy.

After exploring the two poles of urban political theory – and providing a catalog of their principal exponents – Mollenkopf proposes a synthesis that simultaneously avoids the pitfalls of one-dimensionality and recognizes the legitimate claims of each school. "How can we develop a vocabulary for analyzing politics and state action," he asks, "that reconciles the political system's independent impact on social outcomes with its observed systemic bias in favor of capital?" And here, in a sense, he returns to his initial question – whether urban politics is worth studying at all – and answers in the affirmative.

Although the structuralists are undoubtedly correct in stressing the importance of underlying economic forces, they typically lack "a well-developed theory of the state," and thus "economy-centered theorizing" must always be tempered by "polity-centered" thinking.

The classic pluralist study of urban community power is Floyd Hunter, *Community Power Structure* (New York: Anchor, 1963). The classic structuralist study of urban community power is Robert Dahl, *Who Governs?* (New Haven, Conn.: Yale University Press, 1961). Other studies of urban politics include Douglas Yates, *The Ungovernable City* (Cambridge, Mass.: MIT Press, 1977), Ira Katznelson, *City Trenches* (New York: Pantheon Books, 1981), Paul E. Peterson, *City Limits* (Chicago: University of Chicago Press, 1981), Barbara Ferman, *Governing the Ungovernable City: Political Skill, Leadership, and the Modern Mayor* (Philadelphia, Pa.: Temple University Press, 1985), John R. Logan and Harvey L. Molotch, *Urban Fortunes: The Political Economy of Place* (Berkeley and Los Angeles: University of California Press, 1987), Timothy Barnekov, Robin Boyle, and Daniel Rich, *Privatism and Urban Policy in Britain and the United States* (Oxford: Oxford University Press, 1989), John R. Logan and Todd Swandstrom, *Beyond the City Limits: Urban Policy and Economic Restructuring in Comparative Perspective* (Philadelphia, Pa.: Temple University Press, 1990), Patrick Dunleavy and Brendan O'Leary, *Theories of the State* (London: Macmillan, 1987), Michael Harloe, C. G. Pickvance, and John Urry, *Place, Policy and Politics* (London: Unwin Hyman, 1990), and Michael Keating, *Comparative Urban Politics: Power and the City in the United States, Canada, Britain and France* (Aldershot: Edward Elgar, 1993).

JOHN MOLLENKOPF, "How to Study Urban Political Power"

from *A Phoenix in the Ashes: The Rise and Fall of the Koch Coalition in New York City Politics* (1992)

What is the appropriate way to conceptualize the organization of political power in New York City during the Koch era? The dialogue between the pluralist interpreters of urban power and their structuralist critics has produced a rich variety of answers to this question. In the early 1960s, pluralist political scientists launched an attack on the previously accepted view, established by sociologists, that socioeconomic elites dominated urban politics. The success of this assault enabled pluralists to establish their view as the norm in political science.

From the mid-1970s onward, however, a new generation of structurally oriented critics challenged the pluralist point of view. While they were able to undermine the prevailing wisdom, they did not manage to supplant it with a new one, in part because of defects in their arguments that pluralists were quick to point out. More recently, students of urban politics have attempted to synthesize the strengths of both approaches. With respect to framing the study of how the Koch administration amassed and exercised political power, the debate between pluralists and their critics focuses our attention on four interrelated questions:

1 Is urban politics worth studying at all, or is the urban political realm so subordinate to, dependent on, and constrained by its economic and social context that factors from this domain have little independent explanatory power?

2 If urban politics does have an independent impact, how should we conceptualize power relations among interests or actors?

3 In particular, what factors govern the construction of a dominant political coalition within a given set of structural constraints and opportunities?

4 In constructing such a coalition, how important is promoting private investment compared to other strategies, such as increasing social spending to incorporate potentially insurgent groups?

THE PLURALIST CONCEPTION OF THE URBAN POLITICAL ORDER

The classic pluralist studies of a generation ago, like Banfield's *Political Influence*, Dahl's *Who Governs?*, or Sayre and Kaufman's *Governing New York City*, made important theoretical and methodological advances over the so-called elitists they attacked. They did not deduce power relations from the interlocks between economic and political elites. Instead, they went into the field to examine the tangled complexity of interest alignments around actual policy decisions and disputes. Pluralist scholars showed that no model of direct control by a unified economic or status elite could easily explain what they saw.

While most pluralists did not dwell theoretically on the larger relationship between the state and the economy, they implicitly rejected the notion that some underlying structural logic subordinated local politics to the private economy. They saw politics as an autonomous realm that possessed real authority and commanded important resources. They explicitly rejected the notion that economic or social notables controlled the state in any instrumental sense. Since they argued that every "legitimate" group

commanded some important resource (if only the capacity to resist) and no one group commanded sufficient resources to control all others, pluralists argued that the bargaining among a multiplicity of groups defined the urban power structure.

In this view, coalition building was central to the definition of power. Political leaders and private interests built coalitions around specific issues, the coalitions varied from issue to issue, and they tended to be short lived. By selecting a range of different policy decisions as case studies for research, pluralists seemed to imply that urban development and social service issues had an equal importance in organizing political competition.

In the face of examples where entrenched interest groups dominated their own particular, fragmented policy areas over time to the exclusion of the public interest, the pluralist approach developed a clearly critical strand of analysis. But these scholars simply saw the dark side of the pluralist worldview without fundamentally challenging its basic assumptions or deflating the optimistic claims about system openness or responsiveness prevailing among other pluralists.

[...]

While the pluralist studies may have been convincing and accurate portraits of urban politics in the 1950s and early 1960s, the eruption of turmoil and political mobilization in the 1960s and the fiscal crisis of the 1970s soon revealed basic flaws in the pluralist analysis. Except for Robert Dahl's work, *Who Governs?*, these studies lacked a context in economic and political development. Despite obligatory opening chapters covering economic, social, and political trends, pluralist studies such as Sayre and Kaufman's did not treat the changing structure of urban economies or racial succession as problematic for the urban political order. It would, they thought, simply absorb and adapt to these changes. While Dahl provided a fine treatment of the transition from patrician dominance to what he argued were the dispersed inequalities of pluralist democracy in New Haven, he also failed to see that blacks might be led to challenge the system, not just participate in it as a minor interest. Neither Dahl nor his colleagues foresaw how economic transformation and racial succession might fundamentally challenge the previously observed "normal" patterns.

[...]

Dahl explicitly denied that economic and social inequalities would overlap and reinforce each other in the political arena. Other pluralist scholars also did not recognize the possibility that nonelite elements of the urban population would feel systematically excluded from power and would react by pressing for greater representation and more vigorously redistributive policies. As a result, the urban battles that erupted in the latter 1960s in New York City and elsewhere made their relatively tranquil picture of urban politics as a kind of market equilibrium-reaching mechanism seem anachronistic.

STRUCTURALIST CRITIQUES

As the pluralist political equilibrium unraveled on the ground, it came under increasing challenge from structuralist critics. The broad outlines of their progress may be traced from Peter Bachrach and Morton Baratz's classic essay on the "two faces of power" to Clarence Stone's work on "systemic power" to John Manley's "class analysis of pluralism." Bachrach and Baratz attacked pluralists for focusing on the "first face" of power, namely its exercise, while ignoring the second, namely the way that the relationship between the state and the underlying socioeconomic system shapes the political agenda. "Power may be, and often is," they said, "exercised by confining the scope of decision-making to relatively 'safe' issues." But while making a case for analyzing how the values embedded in institutional practices bias the rules of the game, they do not specify the mechanisms that promote some interests and issues while dampening others.

Stone advanced this line of thought by shifting the locus of analysis from decisions ("mar-

ket exchange") toward the mechanisms that create systemic or strategic advantages for some interests over others ("production"). The unequal distribution of private resources, he argues, creates a differential capacity among political actors to shape the flow of benefits from the basic rules of the game, the construction of particular agendas, and the making of specific decisions. Business, in particular, derives systemic power not only from its juridical status and economic resources but from its attractiveness as an ally for those who advance any policy change and from the shared subculture from which private and public officials both emerged.

Despite the structuralist leaning in his concept of "systemic power," Stone did not break decisively with the pluralist interplay of interests around decisions. Manley's Marxist critique does make this break. He embraced the argument that the legal and structural primacy enjoyed by private ownership of capital requires the state to reinforce the systemic inequalities that result from the drive for private profit. He attacked pluralists, even the later work of Dahl and Lindblom that concedes that business enjoys a privileged position in pluralist competition, for lacking a theory of exploitation and, hence, an objective standard of a just or equal distribution. In Manley's view, the juridical protection of private property inevitably commits the state to control workers and promote capital.

While neo-Marxist work similar to Manley's stressed the systematic subordination of the state and politics to capital accumulation and the private market, a parallel and quite nonradical strand of public choice analysis reached quite similar conclusions. Focusing on the notion that cities compete to attract well-off residents and private investment, this line of analysis ... is logically quite similar to some neo-Marxist critiques of pluralism.

NEO-MARXIST CRITIQUES

Structuralists have decisively transcended the pluralist vocabulary. They provided the social and economic context missing from pluralism and highlighted the ways that private property, market competition, wealth and income inequality, the corporate system, and the stage of capitalist development pervasively shape the terrain on which political competition occurs. They underscored the need to analyze how basic patterns of the economic, political, or cultural rules of the game bias the capacity of different interests to realize their ends through politics and the state.

Most importantly, neo-Marxist structuralists were able to empirically investigate these mechanisms, refuting the pluralist retort that "non-decisions" either must be studied just like decisions or else are unobservable ideological constructs. They have shown cases in which the systemic and cumulative inequality of political capacity undergirded, and indeed was ideologically reinforced by, a superficial pluralism. Structuralist studies may be flawed by economic determinism, but they are factually on target in observing and describing mechanisms that generate systemic, cumulative, political inequality, which has a more profound impact on outcomes than the coalition patterns studied by pluralists. Such critiques won relatively broad support among the younger generation of scholars, if not their elders. They may be subclassified into theories that stress the political logic of capital accumulation, social control, or the interplay of accumulation and legitimation. Each offers a different perspective on the central mechanisms that generate cumulative political inequality.

Theorists influenced by Marx's economic works have tended to argue that the mode of production stamps its pattern more or less directly on the organization of the state and on the dynamics of political competition. Marxists as different as David Harvey and David Gordon have both argued that the stage of capitalist development and the circuits of capital have determined urban spatial patterns, the bureaucratic state, and for Harvey even urban consciousness. While this strand of Marxist thinking made a breakthrough in orienting analysts to the importance of the process of capital accumulation, it has generally lacked a well-developed theory of the state that either identifies the instrumental mechanisms that link

state actions to the power of capital or grants the relative autonomy to the state.

This literature does stress one mechanism, however: the state's dependence on private investment for public revenues. If the mobility of capital can discipline the state and constrain political competition, then competition among polities (whether cities or nations) to attract investment leads them to grant systematic benefits for capital, a dynamic that Alford and Friedland have called "power without participation." As Harvey wrote,

> The successful urban region is one that evolves the right mix of life-styles and cultural, social, and political forms to fit with the dynamics of capital accumulation ... Urban regions racked by class struggle or ruled by class alliances that take paths antagonistic to accumulation ... at some point have to face the realities of competition for jobs, trade, money, investments, services, and so forth.

Sooner or later, the state and political competition will be subordinated to the needs of capital.

Several analysts, including Friedland and Palmer as well as Molotch and Logan, abstracted this mechanism from the larger Marxian vocabulary and made it central to their analysis of urban power. Friedland and Palmer argued that, while businesses do directly influence policy-making, such intervention is logically secondary. "The growth of locales depends on the fortunes of their firms," according to Friedland and Palmer, thus "dominant and mobile [corporate] actors set the boundaries within which debate over public policy takes place." As capital has become more mobile and less tied to specific locations, the need for business to intervene directly in politics has waned, while the structural subordination of local government to the general interests of business has waxed.

Molotch and Logan took a different tack on the same course. While conceding that the mobility of capital gives local government a powerful incentive to defer to capitalists, they argued that certain classes of business are not mobile: real estate developers, utilities, newspapers, and others with a fixed relationship to a place. Large sunk costs give these interests a powerful incentive to intervene in and dominate local politics in order to get local government to promote new investment. They saw this "growth machine" as a ubiquitous, inevitable, and at best weakly challenged feature of American cities . . .

[. . .]

While this strand of thinking argued that the multiplicity of competing local governments forces the state to reproduce and protect basic features of the advanced capitalist economy, a second, equally important school of neo-Marxist thinking stressed the way urban politics serves to dampen and regulate the conflicts inevitably generated by capitalist urbanization. Castells's work on "collective consumption" and urban social movements, Piven and Cloward's studies of urban protest, and Katznelson's studies of the absorptive capacity of local bureaucracies and the bias against class issues in urban politics represent the best of this work.

While these analysts differed over how the state coopts movements that challenge urban governments, they share the idea that this process is a central feature of urban politics in advanced capitalist societies. Not everyone, even on the left, has agreed with these contentions. Theret, Mingione, and Gottdiener have criticized the explanatory power of the notion of collective consumption, while Ceccarelli has argued that urban social movements did not turn out to be the force in west European urban politics that Castells portrayed them to be. Whatever the situation in Europe, the civil rights movement, urban unrest, and community organization clearly had a profound impact on urban politics in the United States after the 1960s, particularly in the rise of programs designed to absorb and deflect these forces.

[. . .]

PUBLIC CHOICE CRITIQUES

Neo-Marxist thinking is not the only source of structural criticism of the pluralist paradigm, however. Microeconomics, in the form of public choice theory, has contributed its own critique. Tiebout's seminal work led to Forrester's simulation of urban systems and ultimately to Paul Peterson's sophisticated "unitary" theory of urban politics. This tradition, born of the economists' distrust of state allocation of resources, has sought a functional equivalent to the marketplace in the multiplicity of local governments. They would compete, Tiebout argued, for residents of different means and desires by providing different service packages at various tax costs. An equilibrium would thus be reached in the sorting of populations across urban and suburban jurisdictions within the metropolis. This equilibrium would represent an efficient production of public goods, matching the marginal prospective resident with the jurisdiction's need to add (or subtract) residents on its own margin to provide services at the most efficient scale.

Such thinking has undergirded much of the orthodox literature on urban economics and local public finance. Urban housing, for example, has been analyzed as a function of how consumers trade off housing and commuting costs, given various levels of residential amenities. Forrester built the underlying assumptions into a model, influential for a time, that implied that whatever cities do to provide housing or social services for the poor will attract more of them, drive out the better off, and erode the tax base.

[. . .]

STRUCTURALISM RECONSIDERED

By providing the missing economic and social-structural context, these structuralist critiques achieved a considerable advance over pluralist analysis. Cities can no longer be taken as independent entities isolated from the larger economic and social forces that operate on them. Analysts can no longer ignore the impact of global and national economic restructuring on large central cities. Since cities cannot retard these global economic trends (though New York and others may propagate them), nor remake their populations at will, they clearly navigate in a sea of externally generated constraints and imperatives.

The structuralist critiques also make it clear that urban politics can no longer be considered to be unrelated to the cumulative pattern of inequality in the economy and society. They have focused attention on how the state's dependence on private investment fosters political outcomes that systematically favor business interests. Structuralists have explored specific mechanisms that produce this result, such as the invidious competition among fragmented, autonomous urban governments for investment, the segregation of local government functions into quasi-private agencies that promote investment and politically exposed agencies that absorb and deflect protest, and the organization of the channels of political representation so as to articulate interests in some ways but not others. By stressing that advanced capitalism characteristically generates urban social movements and political conflicts, some structuralists have also implied that political action can alter some of the constraints capitalism imposes on democracy.

Despite these strengths, however, structuralist perspectives also have grave flaws. The assertion that the state "must" undertake activities that favor capital tends to be functionalist. Such a standpoint begs the question of how these "imperatives" are put in place and reproduced over time, which inevitably must be through the medium of politics. As a result, structuralists may not see that political actors can fail to fulfill or to maximize their supposed imperatives. Dominant urban political coalitions have certainly done things that cost them elections and the ability to exercise power; they have persisted in increasing the tax burden on private capital and imposing exactions on private developers even after the point that they diminish further investment. Others have chosen to increase budget deficits and risk their bond ratings.

Given the right conditions, nothing is inevitable about an administration's pursuit of electoral success, private investment, well-managed social tensions, or even good bond ratings. Nothing guarantees that city government will be willing or able to fulfill the functions struc-turalists have assigned to it. As Piven and Friedland observed in rejecting a "smoothly functioning determinism," a structural analysis cannot be adequate until it specifies "the political processes through which ... systematic imperatives are translated into government policies."

Structural critiques also tend not to be disconfirmable. For example, if structuralists argue that the use of legal injunctions by the conservative Republican administrations before the New Deal illustrates how the state supports capitalism, while the New Deal's recognition and promotion of trade unions also illustrate state support for capitalism, then they are explaining everything and nothing. Put another way, structural theories tend to have a hard time explaining the real and important variation over time and across places. The basic features of capitalism are common across nations and evolve slowly, while the political outcomes that capitalism is supposed to drive are highly varied and change more quickly.

Finally, when structuralists appeal to an ultimate economic determinism, they aggravate these problems. Agency fades out of the analytic picture. To be sure, the most attractive variants of neo-Marxism sought to avoid this trap by using the concepts of the "relative autonomy of the state" and "conflicting imperatives of accumulation and legitimation" to introduce a political dimension into an otherwise inadequate economic determinism. Yet in their discomfort with granting politics a co-equal causal role, even these variants ultimately retreat to the view that politics is subordinate to economics: autonomy is after all only relative. From Gottdiener at one end of the spectrum to Peterson on the other, structuralist analysts have made no bones about calling politics analytically irrelevant in the face of the economy's ability to constrain and impel.

To summarize, for all their strengths, structuralists conceptualized the political system as ultimately subordinate to economic structure. They tended to reduce urban politics to the fulfillment of economic imperatives; even social control achieved through political means serves capitalist ends. The most promising threads of structuralist thinking examined how systemic imperatives might conflict with each other or generate system-threatening conflict, thus opening the way for political indeterminacy. Here, however, they risked moving outside and beyond a structuralist paradigm. Indeed, orthodox Marxism (or for that matter orthodox neoclassical economics) simply does not provide a good basis for building a theory of politics. To the extent that structuralist theorists held true to the logic of their argument, they underplayed the importance of politics. They did not appreciate that policies that promote private investment must be constructed in a political environment that may favor but by no means guarantees this outcome. Indeed, popular, social, and communal forces pressure the state and the political process just as strongly in different, and often opposed, directions.

This tendency to trivialize politics removes a way to explain why outcomes vary even though capitalism is constant. States may be constrained, but they are also sovereign. They exercise a monopoly on the legitimate use of force, establish the juridical basis for private property, and shape economic development in myriad ways. Economies are delicate. They depend on political order and have been deformed or smashed by political disorder. State actions may be conditioned by economic structure, but they cannot be reduced to it. Many substantially different capitalisms are possible, and politics determine which ones evolve. Just as the state is dependent on the economy, economic institutions depend on and are vulnerable to the state and its changing political circumstances.

[...]

"Polity-centered" thinking must thus augment the "economy-centered" theorizing of the structuralist critiques. This does not require an equally one-sided political determinism. Rather, it requires us to extend the lines of structuralist thinking that stress conflict among imperatives or developmental tendencies until we go beyond the limits of economic determinism. We must recognize that "state power is *sui generis*, not reducible to class power," as Block put it. Or as Manuel Castells recently reflected, "experience was right and Marxist theory was wrong" about the central theoretical importance of urban social movements and the impossibility of reducing them to a class basis.

But if we give politics an analytic weight equal to that of economic structure, how can we avoid returning to a voluntaristic pluralism? How can we develop a vocabulary for analyzing politics and state action that reconciles the political system's independent impact on social outcomes with its observed systemic bias in favor of capital? A satisfactory approach must operate at three interrelated levels: (1) how the local state's relationship to the economy and society conditions its capacity to act; (2) how the "rules of the game" of local politics shape the competition among interests and actors to construct a dominant political coalition able to exercise that capacity to act; and (3) how economic and social change and the organization of political competition shape the mobilization of these interests.

TOWARD A THEORETICAL SYNTHESIS

We can begin to build such an approach by recognizing that city government and its political leaders interact with the resident population and constituency interests in its political and electoral operating environment and with market forces and business interests in its economic operating environments. This approach emphasizes two primary interactions: first, between the leaders of city government and their political/electoral base; and second, between the leaders of city government and their economic environment. It also suggests that political entrepreneurs who seek to direct the actions of city government must contend with three distinct sets of interests: (1) public sector producer interests inside local government; (2) popular or constituency interests (which are also public sector consumer interests), especially as they are organized in the electoral system; and (3) private market interests, particularly corporations with discretion over capital investment, as they are organized in the local economy.

To be sure, these interests are highly complex in a city like New York and cannot be captured by simple dichotomies like black versus white or capitalist versus worker . . . The city's residential communities are highly heterogeneous. Terms like "minority" hide far more than they reveal; even "black" or "Latino" blur important distinctions regarding nativity and ethnicity. Business interests come in many sizes, industries, and competitive situations; even corporate elites vary greatly. Still, a focus on the relationships among state, citizenry, and marketplace provides an entry point for analyzing what determines the shape of the urban political arena.

The concept of a "dominant political coalition" gives us a focal point for this analysis. A dominant political coalition is a working alliance among different interests that can win elections for executive office and secure the cooperation it needs from other public and private power centers in order to govern. To have an opportunity to become dominant, it must first win election to the chief executive office. To remain dominant, it must use the powers of government to consolidate its electoral base, win subsequent elections, and gain support from those other wielders of public authority and private resources whose cooperation is necessary for state action to go forward. Put another way, a dominant coalition must organize working control over both its political and its private market operating environments.

This formulation improves on the pluralist approach by directing our attention toward how the relationship between politics and markets biases outcomes in favor of private market interests, as structuralist approaches have pointed out. The notion of a dominant political coalition would not sit well with pluralists, who have argued that coalitions are unstable, form or re-form according to the issue, and may be stymied by the capacity of any sizable group to resist. We posit instead that coalitions can be stable, operate across issues, and create persistent winners and losers. Challenging and supplanting such coalitions have generally been difficult, particularly for constituencies that lack resources or are particularly vulnerable to sanction. Effective challenges generally arise only at moments of crisis in periods of rapid social and economic change.

This formulation also improves on the struc-

turalist approach by according the political/electoral arena an influence equal to that of economic forces. It also points us toward how strategies to control the direction of city government are shaped by (and in turn shape) the political environment and by the public sector producer interests that have a permanent stake in its operation. It posits a scope for political choice and innovation that is lacking in the structuralist perspective.

This approach points us toward the following central questions: how do political entrepreneurs seek to organize such coalitions, what enables them to succeed in the first instance, and how do they sustain success over time? In what ways can such coalitions be bound together? What interests do dominant coalitions include and exclude and why? How do the economic and political contexts affect these binding relationships? And what tensions or conflicts undermine dominant coalitions, opening the way for power realignment?

As structuralists have shown, one part of the answer to these questions lies in the relationship of politics to the structure of economic interests. Efforts to explore this relationship may be found in Stone's studies of Atlanta, Shefter's study of New York, and my own work on pro-growth coalitions in Boston and San Francisco. Stone distinguished three levels at which to analyze the relationship between a dominant coalition and various urban interests. The least interesting is the pluralist domain of individual decisions or "command power" in which one actor induces or coerces others to follow his or her bidding. The two others are more relevant to this analysis.

Political actors wield "coalition power" when they join together to exercise the policy powers of the state to produce a steady flow of benefits to their allies, without the need for coercing or inducing specific actions. Stone showed how the Atlanta regime used public and private subcontracts to minority business enterprises to cement its political support, but he gave relatively little attention to other aspects of how the coalition tried to dominate its political operating environment.

Instead, he emphasized the "preemptive" or "systemic power" enjoyed by private interests whose command over private resources is so great as to make their support crucial to the dominant coalition. Among the mechanisms of preemptive power in Atlanta, Stone identified the unity of a well-organized downtown business community, newspaper and television support for policies that favored downtown development, the reliance of politicians on campaign contributions from developers, business control over the equity and credit that government needed to carry out its plans, and the business community's ability to provide or deny access to upward mobility for the black middle class. These systemic powers made corporate interests ideal allies for politicians seeking to achieve and sustain political dominance.

While the arrival of a black majority in the electorate, militant new black leadership, and neighborhood mobilization eventually destabilized and modified the tradition of white dominance that prevailed in Atlanta until Maynard Jackson was elected mayor in 1973, Stone argued that they did not overturn the preemptive power of corporate interests. Jackson's successor, Andrew Young, chose to abandon the fragmented and undisciplined neighborhood movement in favor of pro-growth politics with a new face, consolidated by white business support for set-asides to minority entrepreneurs.

[...]

My own study of how political entrepreneurs constructed pro-growth coalitions in Boston, San Francisco, and other large cities in the late 1950s and 1960s also advanced reasons why politicians would want to forge alliances with private sector elites. Promoting private development was an obvious way to bring together such otherwise disparate elements as a Republican corporate elite, regular Democratic party organizations, and reform-oriented rising public sector and nonprofit professionals.

These perspectives on how dominant political coalitions shape development politics and budget policy to secure business support, while convincing, remain incomplete. The "preemptive power" of business interests only explains part of how political actors construct a coalition to direct city government in the exercise of its powers. As Lincoln Steffens long ago observed, dominant coalitions needed to develop a grassroots base of legitimacy as well as support from elite interests. However much they may need corporate support, dominant coalitions must also have support from popular constituencies organized by such organizations as political parties, labor unions, and community organizations.

Mayors can lead dominant political coalitions only when they win electoral majorities and keep potential sources of electoral challenge fragmented or demobilized. The mobilization of blacks and Latinos and the neighborhood organization that began in the mid-1960s and continue today have prompted many currently dominant political coalitions to adopt policies that do not follow from a devotion to private market interests or public sector producer interests. For example, dominant coalitions must respond to mobilizations against the negative impacts of downtown growth and inadequate public services, or demands for government programs that provide upward mobility for excluded groups.

Rufus Browning, Dale Marshall, and David Tabb have argued, for example, that when insurgent liberal biracial coalitions came to power in a few of the northern California cities they studied, the coalitions shifted policies in favor of the formerly underrepresented groups that helped to elect them. Albert Karnig and Susan Welch's and Peter Eisinger's studies of the impact of black mayors reach a similar conclusion. My work on Boston and San Francisco showed that, while neighborhood protest and greater mayoral sensitivity toward neighborhood concerns did not halt the transformation of these two cities, they did produce numerous specific policy changes. In a comparative context, studies by Michael Aiken and Guido Martinotti and Edmond Preteceille suggest that left-wing local governments in Europe produced more progressive policy outputs. Castells concludes that "grassroots mobilization has been a crucial factor in the shaping of the city, as well as the decisive element in urban innovation against prevailing social interests."

[...]

In sum, the analysis of how Edward Koch and his allies constructed a new dominant political coalition in New York City must be framed in terms of three broad sets of factors. Building on the structuralists, it must understand how the local political system's interaction with private interests creates constraints and imperatives for the local state but also opportunities that astute political entrepreneurs can seize. Second, it must go beyond the structuralists by recognizing that how popular constituencies are organized in the city's political and electoral arena has an equally strong impact on the strategies pursued by coalition builders. Finally, a sound theory must be sensitive to how the organization of interests within the public sector, embodied in political practices as well as formal authority, also influenced their choices and actions ...

GERRY STOKER

"Regime Theory and Urban Politics"

from David Judge, Gerry Stoker, and Harold Wolman (eds.), *Theories of Urban Politics* (1995)

Editors' introduction Beginning in the 1980s, U.S. political scientist Clarence Stone and others observed that building and maintaining local political power involved creating "regimes" among formal government structures such as parties, local elected officials, and governmental bureaucracies and many other centers of authority in society such as businesses, labor unions, churches, neighborhood, ethnic, environmental and feminist organizations. Stone pioneered the study of how urban regimes structure a particular set of values from among both governmental and nongovernmental groups to obtain and exercise political power. Regime theory is now a dominant approach to the study of urban political power with a conceptual framework and set of theoretical statements different from earlier pluralist and structuralist writings.

Because regime theory emphasizes the variety regimes take, other writings on regime theory are often built on detailed case studies. Clarence Stone's theoretical statement of regime theory is embedded in a very detailed discussion of how the Atlanta, Georgia political regime actually worked.

In this selection Gerry Stoker, a professor of government at the University of Strathclyde in Glasgow, Scotland, steps back from detailed case studies to summarize the current state of regime theory and urban politics. As a student of comparative urban government Stoker extends regime theory to the European context and offers an insightful critique and his own views on prospects for the future.

Regime theory emphasizes the relationship between governmental and nongovernmental actors in dominant coalitions. It focuses on the way in which interests achieve results they desire through a combination of governmental and nongovernmental means. It acknowledges the importance of private business in local governance, but conflicts with more extreme structuralist theories which portray business as all-powerful. Regime theory recognizes that urban decision making is nonhierarchical and fragmented. It emphasizes the importance of politics and rejects economic determinism. To Mollenkopf's question "Is urban politics worth studying at all?" the regime theorists answer "Yes."

While the relationships between governmental and nongovernmental entities are not new, regime theory is particularly appropriate during the era when conservative national governments in the U.S. and U.K. are emphasizing private sector alternatives to local government service provision and, as Robin Hambleton (p. 283) describes, the relationship of government to other institutions is being seriously debated. As some current government functions are privatized, public–private partnerships are developed, and private and nonprofit sector organizations interact with government in more complex ways, regime theory becomes increasingly important in understanding urban politics and governance.

Regime theory is thus one important new approach to the study of urban political power. As

Mollenkopf (p. 258) describes, pluralist and structuralist approaches to understanding urban political power have been dominant in the recent past and continue to have their adherents. New formulations of pluralist and structuralist theory and hybrid neopluralist and hyperpluralist theory compete with regime theory as dominant paradigms for explaining urban political power today.

Clarence Stone's book *Regime Politics: Governing Atlanta, 1946–1988* (Lawrence: University Press of Kansas, 1989) provides the most extensive exposition of urban regime theory and a detailed case study applying regime theory to the governance of Atlanta, Georgia. Related writings include Frank R. Baumgartner and Brian D. Jones, *Agendas and Instability in American Politics* (Chicago: University of Chicago Press, 1993), Steven Elkin, *City and Regime in the American Republic* (Chicago: University of Chicago Press, 1987), and Rich DeLeon, *Left Coast City: Progressive Politics in San Francisco 1975–1991* (Lawrence: University Press of Kansas, 1992).

GERRY STOKER, "Regime Theory and Urban Politics"

from David Judge, Gerry Stoker, and Harold Wolman (eds.), *Theories of Urban Politics* (1995)

Regime theory came to the fore in the study of urban politics from the mid-1980s onwards. In contrast, then, to pluralist and elitist accounts it is a relatively new theoretical force and indeed cannot claim to be as well developed as either of those two currents. It also lacks the extent and range of empirical work surrounding pluralist and elitist studies. Yet this chapter argues that regime theory offers a distinctive approach to the study of urban politics and in particular the issue of power. It provides a framework for analysis which captures key aspects of urban governance at the end of the century. It provides a new conceptual framework and more particular theoretical statements about causal relationships and behaviour in urban politics.

Regime theory holds substantial promise for understanding the variety of responses to urban change. Its emphasis on the interdependence of governmental and non-governmental forces in meeting economic and social challenges focuses attention upon the problem of cooperation and coordination between governmental and non-governmental actors. While significant differences persist from country to country, it is clear that the need for some form of public–private cooperation exists in all advanced capitalist societies. Growing competition between cities for investment, and the role of business interests

in local decision making have increasingly shaped the urban terrain. Decentralization and shifting responsibilities within the state, increased financial constraints, and the development of privatized services utilizing both for-profit and non-profit organizations have also created additional complexities for local governments. Urban governments are increasingly working through and alongside other interests. This concern with "governance" emerges in a range of policy areas: economic development, human capital and training programmes, crime prevention, environmental protection and anti-drug campaigns. In the U.K. the word "enabling" has emerged to describe the shifting role of government (Cochrane, 1993). In the U.S. the talk is of government being "reinvented" and having a catalytic rather than a direct provision role (Osborne and Gaebler, 1992). Because of its emphasis on the way governmental and non-governmental actors work across boundaries, regime theory is especially relevant, given the shifting role of urban government.

Regime theory provides a new perspective on the issue of power. It directs attention away from a narrow focus on power as an issue of social control towards an understanding of power expressed through social production. In a complex, fragmented urban world the paradigmatic form of power is that which enables certain interests to blend their capacities to achieve common purposes. Regime analysis directs attention to the conditions under which such effective long-term coalitions emerge in order to accomplish public purposes.

In the first two sections ... the core elements of regime theory are presented. These core propositions are unfortunately for regime theory often buried within detailed case studies. An effort is made to provide a more general statement drawing in particular on the work of Clarence Stone. The differences between regime theory, elitist and pluralist interpretations are explored. In doing so the assessment made of regime theory in [Chapter 2, "Pluralism" by David Judge of Judge, Stoker, and Wolman, *Theories of Urban Politics* (London: Sage, 1995)] is challenged and a more positive judgement about its potential presented.

The next section ... explores the application of regime analysis in the urban context. One of the problems of the regime concept is that it provides a descriptive label that can be used in single-city case studies that in the United States especially have a prominent position in publishing schedules and listings. Regime terminology is used but a regime analysis is not really provided. To address this problem the most suitable case study to take is that provided by Stone of Atlanta. A brief account of Stone's regime analysis of the politics of that city is provided.

The final main section of the chapter raises a series of questions about regime theory identifying areas of criticism or where further development is required. The pioneering efforts of Stone, Elkin and others in relation to regime theory leave a number of issues unexplored. First, it is necessary to examine the understanding of power offered in regime analysis and how that understanding can be explored through empirical study. Second, regime theory needs to escape the "localist" trap and place its analysis in the context of the broader political environment. Third, regime theory lacks a coherent approach to the issue of regime continuity and change. A brief concluding section provides an overall assessment of the theory.

REGIME THEORY, PLURALISM AND NEO-PLURALISM

Stone comments that "regime theory has many antecedents" (1989a: 145). The work of Fainstein and Fainstein (1986), Jones and Bachelor (1986) and Elkin (1987) would seem particularly relevant in the context of urban politics. According to Elkin (1987: 18):

The way in which popular control operates in contemporary cities is largely a consequence of the division of labour between state and market as that is manifest in cities. This division, which stems from the corresponding arrangement of the national political economy, means that ownership of productive assets in the city is largely placed in private hands. Public officials share responsibility for the level of citizen well-being with these private controllers, but these officials cannot command economic performance, only induce it. The concern of public officials with citizen well-being stems largely from their being subject to election or appointment by those who themselves have been elected.

Regime theory takes as given a set of government institutions subject to some degree of popular control and an economy guided mainly but not exclusively by privately controlled investment decisions. A regime is a set of "arrangements by which this division of labour is bridged" (Stone, 1993: 2).

David Judge is right to argue in Chapter 2 [of *Theories of Urban Politics*] that regime theorists have taken on board the central thrust of much Marxist-inspired work of the 1970s ... namely that business control over investment decisions and resources central to societal welfare gives it a privileged position in relation to government decision making. In the words of Stone, "we must take into account these contextual forces – the facet of community decision-making I label 'systemic power'". He continues: "public officials form their alliances, make their decisions and plan their futures in a context in which strategically important resources are hierarchically arranged ... Systemic power therefore has to do with *the impact of the larger socioeconomic system on the predispositions of public officials*" (1980: 979, original emphasis).

Regime theorists argue that "politics matters". In this sense their work challenges economic determinists such as Peterson (1981) and some neo-Marxist work. The founding premise of regime theory is that urban decision makers have a relative autonomy. Systemic power is constraining but scope for the influence of political forces and activity remains. Regime theorists argue that the organization of politics leads to very inadequate forms of popular control and makes government less responsive to socioeconomically disadvantaged groups. As Elkin argues, "the roots of the city's failures are not in the necessity of earning its keep but in how that impulse gets translated into action" (1987: 98). The organization of politics does not facilitate large-scale popular participation and involvement in an effective way.

Elkin (1987: 95–7) argues that urban politics suffers not only from a systematic basis in the benefits provided to certain interests but also is undermined by failures in social intelligence. In the policy debate within cities one solution and one view about how to proceed tends to dominate. Problem solving in these circumstances is not likely to be to the benefit of citizens because desirable alternatives go unexplored.

All this suggests that regime theory stands on different ground to the "classical urban pluralism, the reigning wisdom of 30 years ago and earlier" (Stone, 1993: 1). Yet David Judge is right to suggest that regime theorists do share common ground with the revised statements of pluralists such as Dahl and Lindblom. In many respects regime theory takes as its starting point many of the concerns of "neo-pluralists" (as defined by Dunleavy and O'Leary, 1987: Ch. 6). It accepts the privileged position of business. It is concerned about the limits to effective democratic politics. It also shares the neo-pluralists' concern with the fragmentation and complexity of governmental decision making. Stone comments: "we have a special need to think about what it means politically to live under conditions of social complexity ... about the special character of power relationships in complex social systems" (1986: 77).

Thus far then regime theory shares common ground with the "neo-pluralists". Who deserves most credit for carving out this common ground

is a matter of debate. In the urban field regime writers can reasonably claim a stronger track record. Dahl and Lindblom's revised statements are of a more general nature. Pluralists in the urban world have rather developed hyperpluralist visions ... which sit rather uncomfortably alongside the thrust of "neo-pluralist" and regime arguments. For hyperpluralists (Yates, 1977; Thomas and Savitch, 1991) the number of organized interests, the weakness of government and the scale of social and economic problems lead to a process of policy instability and a fragmented and ineffective decision-making process.

Regime theory stands in contrast to hyperpluralism. It is about how in the midst of diversity and complexity a capacity to govern can emerge within a political system.

Regime theory can thus be distinguished from classical pluralism and from the dominant thrust of urban pluralism – hyperpluralist models. It has, however, as David Judge argues, "backed into" the same ground as the "neo-pluralists". If on the surface it can appear that we are all pluralists now then this phenomenon tells us more about the changing nature and diversity of pluralism than it does about how regime theorists and others are supposedly rediscovering the past wisdoms of pluralist writers.

THE CONTRIBUTION OF REGIME THEORY

What is attractive about regime theory is that it begins to address the questions which flow from the common ground it shares with "neo-pluralists".

- What are the implications of social complexity for politics?
- What does the systemic advantage of certain interests imply for the nature of urban politics?
- What forms of power dominate modern systems of urban governance?
- What role is there for democratic politics and the role of disadvantaged groups?

Regime theory moves beyond "neo-pluralism" by offering a series of distinctive answers to these questions and provides a broad framework for analysis to examine the variety of politics within cities.

In this section of the chapter the discussion concentrates on the work of Clarence Stone. His work represents the most advanced application of regime analysis. However, some of his core insights are submerged in the details of his intensive case study of Atlanta (Stone, 1989b). Moreover, it is necessary to free the regime perspective offered by Stone from its exclusive focus on the United States (cf. Stoker and Mossberger, 1994b). What is offered, then, is a general statement of the regime conceptual framework drawn largely from the original insights of Stone.

Complexity is central to the regime perspective (Stone, 1986). Institutions and actors are involved in an extremely complex web of relationships. Diverse and extensive patterns of interdependence characterize the modern urban system. Lines of causation cannot be easily traced and the policy world is full of unpredicted spillover effects and unintended consequences. Fragmentation and lack of consensus also characterize the system. "Many activities are autonomous and middle-range accommodations are worked out. In some ways the ... world is chaotic; certainly it is closely coupled, and most processes continue without active intervention by a leadership group" (Stone, 1989b: 227).

This kind of society "does not lend itself to the establishment of direct and intense control over a large domain in a wide scope of activity" (Stone, 1986: 89). Such command or social control power is limited to particular aspects or segments of society. The study of regime politics focuses on how these limited segments or domains of command power combine forces and resources for "a publicly significant result" – a policy initiative or development.

Complexity and fragmentation limits the capacity of state as an agency of authority or control. Nor can the state simply be seen as an arbiter or judge of competing societal claims. Rather "as complexity asserts itself government becomes ... more visible as a mobilizer and coordinator of resources" (Stone, 1986: 87). It is this third type of governmental activity which is particularly the target of regime analysis. As

was argued in the introduction to the chapter, it is this form of urban politics which is becoming more important.

The state can on occasion still impose its will. It can also mediate between parties. Yet authoritative action and pluralist bargaining capture "only a small part of political life in socially complex systems" (Stone, 1986: 88). Politics in complex urban systems is about establishing overarching priorities and "the issue is how to bring about enough cooperation among disparate community elements to get things done" (Stone, 1989b: 227). Politics is about government working with and alongside other institutions and interests and about how in that process certain ideas and interests prevail.

The point is that "to be effective, governments must *blend* their capacities with those of various non-governmental actors" (Stone, 1993: 6, original emphasis). In responding to social change and conflict governmental and non-governmental actors are encouraged to form regimes to facilitate action and empower themselves. Thus following Stone (1989b: 4) a regime can be defined as "an informal yet relatively stable group *with access to institutional resources* that enable it to have a sustained role in making governing decisions" (original emphasis). Participants are likely to have an institutional base – that is, they are likely to have a domain of command power. The regime, however, is formed as an informal basis for coordination and without an all-encompassing structure of command.

Regimes operate not on the basis of formal hierarchy. There is no single focus of direction and control. But neither is regime politics governed by the open-ended competitive bargaining characteristic of some pluralist visions of politics. Regimes analysts point to a third mode of coordinating social life: the network. The network approach, like regime analysis, sees effective action as flowing from the cooperative efforts of different interests and organizations. Cooperation is obtained, and subsequently sustained, through the establishment of relations premised on solidarity, loyalty, trust and mutual support rather than through hierarchy or bargaining. Under the network model organizations learn to cooperate by recognizing their mutual dependency.

Relationships within the regime then have a character that is different to the mayor-centred coalitions identified in some pluralist work, especially that of Dahl's study of New Haven (Dahl, 1961). Regime partners are trying to assemble long-running relationships rather than secure for themselves access to immediate spoils: "Governance is not the issue-by-issue process that pluralism suggests ... Politics is about the production rather than distribution of benefits ... Once formed, a relationship of cooperation becomes something of value to be protected by all of the participants" (Stone, 1993: 8–9). Politics is not then the fluid coalition building characteristic of many versions of pluralism. Regime theory focuses on efforts to build more stable and intense relationships in order that governmental and non-governmental actors can accomplish difficult and non-routine goals.

Politics is about achieving governing capacity, which has to be created and maintained. Stone (1989b) refers to power being a matter of social production rather than social control. In contrast to the old debate between pluralists and elitists which focused on the issue of "who governs?" the social production perspective is concerned with a capacity to act: "What is at issue is not so much domination and subordination as a capacity to act and accomplish goals. The power struggle concerns, not control and resistance, but gaining and fusing a capacity to act – power to, not power over" (Stone, 1989b: 229).

Unlike elite theorists, regime theory recognizes that any group is unlikely to be able to exercise comprehensive control in a complex world. Regime analysts, however, do not regard governments as likely to respond to groups on the basis of their electoral power or the intensity of their preferences as some pluralists do. Rather, governments are driven to cooperate with those who hold resources essential to achieving a range of policy goals. As Stone argues: "Instead of the power to govern being something that can be captured by an electoral victory, it is something created by bringing cooperating actors together, not as equal claim-

ants, but often as unequal contributors to a shared set of purposes" (1993: 8). Regime theorists emphasize how the structure of society privileges the participation of certain interests in coalitions. As Stone (1986: 91) comments, for actors to be effective regime partners two characteristics seem especially appropriate: first, possession of strategic knowledge of social transactions and a capacity to act on the basis of that knowledge; and second, control of resources that make one an attractive coalition partner.

The U.S.-based regime literature (see, for example, Stone and Sanders, 1987) sees two groups as the key participants in most localities: elected officials and business. Beyond this, however, there is recognition that a variety of other community interests may be drawn in based on minorities, neighbourhoods or even organized labour. Writing with a comparative perspective means that it is useful to add a fourth broad category: technical/professional officials. Such officials may well be influential participants in some U.S. coalitions but in other Western democracies, especially in Europe, their leading role is difficult to deny. These officials (for examples see Harloe et al., 1990) may be employed by elected local government, work for various non-elected local agencies or be local agents of various central or regional government departments. Knowledge joins economic position as a key resource that gives groups privileged access to decision making.

Regime theory is concerned more with the process of government–interest group mediation than with the wider relationship between government and its citizens. Regime theory views power as structured to gain certain kinds of outcomes within particular fields of governmental endeavour. The key driving force is "the internal politics of coalition building" (Stone, 1989b: 178). If capacity to govern is achieved, if things get done, then power has been successfully exercised and to a degree it is irrelevant whether the mass of the public agreed with, or even knew about, the policy initiative.

Yet regime theory gives some recognition to the role of popular politics, elections and public participation in liberal democratic politics. Opposition to policy agendas that are being pursued can be mobilized and disrupt established policy regimes (see DeLeon, 1992). Established regimes, however, can be expected to seek to incorporate certain marginal groups, to make them part of their project. People are brought in, it is suggested, less by being sold "big ideas" or "world views" and more by small-scale material incentives (Stone, 1989b: 186–91). Regimes may also practise a politics of exclusion, seeking to ensure that certain interests are not provided with access to decision making. Generally, all regimes have to develop strategies for coping with the wider political environment.

A further distinction between pluralism and regime theory is highlighted by Stone (1993). Politics from a regime perspective is not the aggregation of preferences since this neglects the prior question of how preferences are formed. In a complex differentiated world preferences are likely to emerge through action, social relationships and experience. Regime theory sees preference formation as critical whereas much pluralist work regards the matter as unproblematic. Policy preferences do not simply exist, rather in the messy, uncertain world of politics they have to be formed. From a regime perspective preferences are developed within the dynamic of the political process and as such are subject to the influence of the logic of the situation and judgements about what is possible.

The task of regime formation is about gaining a shared sense of purpose and direction. This in turn is influenced by an understanding of what is feasible and what is not. Feasibility favours linking with resource-rich actors. It also favours some goals over others whose achievement may be more intractable and problematic. The "iron law", as it were, governing regime formation is that "in order for governing coalition to be viable, it must be able to mobilize resources commensurate with its main policy agenda" (Stone, 1993: 21).

This "iron law" is then operationalized by Stone (1993) to identify four types of regime to be found in American cities. The logic of the topology is driven by the concern to demonstrate how different regimes have to match resources to the requirements of their proposed agenda. The difficulties and challenges of col-

lective action become more intense as regimes propose more radical and socially inclusive change. Maintenance regimes seek no major change but rather to preserve what is. Their core governing task of routine service delivery requires relatively straightforward relationships between government officials and non-governmental actors. A development regime in contrast needs more resources and is attempting a more complex governing task. Such regimes are concerned to take positive action to promote growth or counter decline. Middle-class progressive regimes in contrast seek environmental protection and control over growth and/or social gains from growth. Such regimes engage in a complex form of regulation as their core governing task. Finally Stone identifies lower-class opportunity expansion regimes which in order to achieve their ends require substantial mass mobilization. Such regimes face resource and coordination prerequisites that are often absent in American cities.

Regime theory, then, is ultimately a model of policy choice in the urban setting. Regime theory according to Stone "holds that public policies are shaped by three factors: (1) the composition of a community's governing coalition; (2) the nature of the relationships among members of the governing coalition, and (3) the resources that members bring to the governing coalition" (1993: 2). Regime members make their policies in the context of a socioeconomic environment which presents problems as well as opportunities. Achieving cooperation among regime partners is assumed to be problematic in a fragmented and uncertain world. The essence of the regime approach to politics is not to identify an elite partnership of governmental and non-governmental actors, but rather to explore the conditions for such a partnership to be created and maintained. The underlying issue is the extent to which a regime achieves a sustained capacity to act and influence developments in key policy areas.

THE APPLICATION OF REGIME THEORY

Urban regime has in the United States become a familiar and popular phrase. The pages of *Urban*

Affairs Quarterly and the *Journal of Urban Affairs* have throughout the 1990s seen a constant flow of references to "regimes". The phrase has entered the urban political vocabulary with a considerable force. However, there is a great danger that this very popularity has created a new descriptive catchword – a regime – in place of an explanation of the phenomenon under question (cf. Garvin, 1994). Not every study of a city that refers to its political regime constitutes a regime analysis or a contribution to regime theory. The difficulties caused by a loose use of the regime concept are illustrated by Savitch and Thomas's book *Big City Politics in Transition*. The book contains some valuable and interesting case studies of many of the major cities of the United States. In the final chapter, Savitch and Thomas (1991: 224–50) use regime terminology to draw some general conclusions. Different cities are seen to have their politics dominated by various types of governing coalition or political regime. Pluralist regimes are dominated by strong political leaders who bring together a mixed, diffuse and competitive set of private actors. Elitist regimes are run primarily by a strong cohesive business elite with weak political leaders taken along with them. Corporatist regimes combine both strong political leaders, who set their own agenda, and a unified business elite, which knows what it wants (p. 248). The final category is the hyperpluralist regime in which "neither political leaders or private actors are powerful enough to pull together the strings of the urban political economy" (p. 248). The direction of change within city politics is seen as "towards some kind of pluralist or hyperpluralist system" (p. 248).

Plainly Savitch and Thomas (1991) mean their analysis to capture broad trends. As a description of developments in various cities it has a certain value. But is it a regime analysis? First, no explanation is offered as to why certain political leaders or business elites are strong or cohesive. Indeed, the argument is somewhat circular along the lines that if political leaders are strong then that city's politics is dominated by strong political leaders. Second, no regime analysis is provided of the nature of the partnership forged between governmental or non-governmental leaders. For example, in the corporatist regime how is it that political and

business elites agree a joint agenda from their own clearly defined and strongly held positions? Third, no effective distinction is made between power exercised as social control and power as social production. Fourth, the term regime is used as a convenient descriptive label for any political system whereas in Stone's analysis a regime is a particular type of long-term stable relationship between governmental and non-governmental partners. Indeed, it is difficult to be certain whether any of the regimes identified by Savitch and Thomas could be counted as a regime in terms of Stone's definition. Finally, the identification of pluralist and in particular hyperpluralist tendencies in city politics by Savitch and Thomas overlooks the claim of regime analysis that beyond the surface of fragmented and disjointed interest group conflicts certain partnerships between government and non-governmental actors may be formed that gives its members a "preemptive occupancy of a strategic role" (Stone, 1988: 82).

Regime is a label that scholars have used for different purposes. The regime framework and theory which is the focus of attention in this chapter has at its core certain key propositions and a way of understanding urban politics. A regime analysis as defined here needs to make use of that particular framework and conceptualization. To illustrate a regime analysis in practice the obvious example to take is Stone's study of Atlanta.

Stone (1989b) provides an account of Atlanta's politics between 1946 and 1988. What is observed is a single regime which despite some elements of change retains a stable means of cooperation and a resolute commitment to an activist agenda of economic growth. The dominant policy push towards full-tilt development represents the triumph of a particular perspective and the pursuit of measures that involve extensive government spending and considerable risk. The regime has worked to maintain its overarching policy aim against significant opposition and the context of alternative policy options.

Two groups dominate the regime. The first is the downtown business elite which has operated and structured itself to have a single voice: "The banks, the utilities, the major department stores, the daily newspapers, and Coca-Cola, in particular, have a long history of acting in concert, and they draw other businesses that may be new to the Atlanta scene into the same pattern of unified public action" (Stone, 1989b: 169). The other main coalition partner is the political force represented by black mayors in the context of the emerging postwar black electoral majority in the city. Black political leaders have proved adept at mobilizing their supporters and with the help of the black clergy of Atlanta have been able to present a relatively unified front and stable political position. Ultimately it is the black middle class that manipulates this political resource for its benefit.

These two change-oriented elements came to share a commitment based on the increased opportunities presented to them by a full-tilt development strategy. Business saw the attraction of economic success and expansion. For the black middle class it was the selective incentives of high-quality housing, employment and small-business opportunities that encouraged a desire to go along. These material incentives were matched by the development of trust and co-operation between the regime partners through a series of shared civic institutions and informal exchanges. Both elements of the regime developed an attachment to their alliance.

Both partners were able to position themselves in a way that made them indispensable to the strategic decision making of the city. Business interests offered a groupwide view and selective incentives to encourage cooperation, and established a network of civic organizations to make and maintain partnership in practice. Yet business would not pursue its objectives on its own and relied on government support and therefore an alliance with black leaders and more broadly the black middle class. The active mobilization of the resources of both sides through a network of civic cooperation created a regime that was capable of pursuing a development agenda that was beneficial to both partners. The Atlanta regime was thereby imbued "with a means to achieve [a] publicly significant result that an otherwise divided and fragmented system of authority could not provide" (Stone, 1989b: 198).

CRITICISMS AND DEVELOPMENTS

This section ... reviews various criticisms of regime theory and the way in which regime analysis can be taken forward and developed.

The need for care in defining and applying the regime understanding of power

The regime framework is still evolving and perhaps suffers from the tendency of most of its main propositions to emerge inductively from observation of the urban scene. The "groundedness" of regime theory is a value that should not be overlooked but it may be helpful to state in more abstract terms its approach to community power.

The regime approach is premised on the view that power in urban politics can be observed in a variety of forms. There are at least four forms of power in operation. The first is systemic power which is available to certain interests because of their position in the socioeconomic structure. Business, for example, because of its control over investment decisions and resources crucial to societal welfare is seen as having a privileged position in policy making. So much so that it may not need to act in order for its interests and concerns to be taken into account in community decision making. This form of power "is a matter of context, of the nature of or 'logic' of the situation" (Stone, 1980: 979). A participant need not make a conscious effort to obtain a structurally advantaged position for that position to be power relevant. Further, the participant need not be aware of the particular consequences of their power position. Systemic power reflects the advantages and disadvantages conferred on certain groups in society based on their position within the socioeconomic structure.

The second form of power is less positional and more active. In regime terms the second form of power is that of command or social control. Power in this sense involves the active mobilization of resources (information, finance, reputation, knowledge) to achieve domination over other interests. "The emphasis is, therefore, on one actor's capacity to achieve compliance and the other's capacity to resist" (Stone, 1988: 88). Regime theory argues, however, that command power typically only extends over a limited domain and a restricted set of activities in most urban politics. The resources, the skill and the time to achieve command power are only likely to be available to certain interests in limited arenas. Because of the limited capacity for domination and control in urban politics a third type of power can also be observed: coalition power.

Coalition power involves actors not seeking to dominate but rather to bargain on the basis of their respective autonomous basis of strength. The bargaining depends on seeking others that share compatible goals and complementary resources and for this reason coalitional arrangements tend to be relatively unstable.

Systemic, command and coalitional power are all seen as having a role in urban politics. However, the distinctive contribution of regime theory is its emphasis on a fourth form of power. Preemptive power or the power of social production forms a crucial axis within regime theory. Power here rests on the need for leadership in a complex society and the capacity of certain interests in coalition to provide that leadership. This leadership control is not achieved through ideological indoctrination (as in Lukes's (1974) third face of power), rather it is a result of a group of interests being able to solve substantial collective action problems to put together a structure capable of performing the needed function. The act of power is to build a regime and achieve the capacity to govern. This form of power is intentional and active.

Regime theory contends that certain interests are at an advantage when it comes to building regimes: those with systemic power and those with resources associated with command power. Yet to turn that advantage to preemptive power they have to manipulate their strategic position and control over resources into an effective long-term coalition which is able "to guide the community's policy responses to social change and alter the terms on which social cooperation takes place" (Stone, 1988: 102).

What is needed is a capacity for collective action to achieve significant results. The coalition needs to be able to attract participants. It needs to succeed or at least convince people that it can succeed or is succeeding in obtaining an attractive goal. It needs to offer a range of incentives to keep partners committed to a common sense of purpose. It needs to manage its relationship with the wider political environment. Its aim is to achieve "the strength and mastery of resources to make control of the leadership responsibility difficult for anyone else. That is the act of pre-emption" (Stone, 1988: 102). A regime once established is a powerful force in urban politics. Opponents "have to go along to get along" or face the daunting task of building an effective counter-regime.

The above makes it clear that care is needed in defining the approach to power taken within regime theory. The regime analyst may be operating with four understandings of power. Regime studies require a considerable degree of care and subtlety from researchers in developing and presenting their findings. The sharpness of distinctions made in the abstract may become blurred in the detail of empirical application. Studies need to move from theory through empirical application and back to theory. For this reason the regime approach does not need a stack of case studies which discover regimes to bolster its position against pluralists and elitists. It rather needs to be able to substantiate the claim that its framework for analysing urban politics is robust and flexible enough to both describe and explain a variety of power distributions in different localities.

To make the same point in a more particular way: there is no need for a regime analysis to discover an effective and operational regime in a city. Indeed, Orr and Stoker's (1994) regime study of Detroit in the 1990s finds a city with a limited and weak-regime building capacity. It explores factors such as the nature of the potential regime partners and the weakness of civic organizations to explain how the collective action obstacles to effective city leadership were not overcome.

At the height of the community power debate in the 1950s and 1960s elitists got the result they wanted when they discovered an elite;

pluralists claimed victory when they showed there was no elite. The regime approach cannot be subject to such simple testing. Regime theory holds that causal relationships underlying policy development are very complex and so it offers a broad conceptual framework to guide analysis. Case studies test that framework by being able to demonstrate its application in practice. The test is of a capacity to explain a process rather than to predict an outcome.

The need to put regimes in context

Urban regime analysis holds that public policies are shaped by the composition, relationships and resources of the community's governing coalition. It also acknowledges the way that the socioeconomic environment frames the options open to the governing coalition and how federal grants or state-level policies are necessary to make certain options feasible. However, the focus in Stone's case study of Atlanta (Stone, 1989b) is on the internal dynamics of the governing coalition to the detriment of contextual forces. A dilemma facing all studies of community power is how to place the analysis within the context of wider processes of change. There is a problem with the regime model if it exclusively "locates causes for policy actions in agents that are too proximate to the action" (Jones, 1993: 1). The crucial challenge is to connect local and non-local sources of policy change.

Regimes exist within the broader external regional or national environment, as well as a local environment (cf. Horan, 1991). The capacity of local regimes can be substantially enhanced by their access to non-local power and resources. Equally, non-local forces can constrain or influence the direction of regimes. Regimes need to be placed in the architecture of governmental complexity. Keating (1991: 66) comments:

> The wider political context is critical in determining the terms of the relationship. The central state can be oppressive, or it can be a resource allowing localities to escape other forms of dependence ... This, in turn, depends on the weight of local elites in the national political system and their ability to

forge coalitions to extract resources on their own terms.

A crucial dimension to regime formation is the way local elites are able to manage their relationship with higher levels of government and the wider political environment.

The argument for putting regimes in context is taken a step further by Jones and Bachelor (1993) and Jones (1993). They argue that in particular eras certain policy ideas become so dominant that urban regimes become locked into that way of seeing the world. There are echoes here of Elkin's concern with the limited social intelligence that guides decision making in urban politics. These dominant policy ideas may have a dynamic that reflects national or even cross-national forces at play (Stoker and Mossberger, 1994a). Trends in economic development ideas from physical renewal to more human capital based schemes would, for example, seem to follow that pattern. Urban regimes are affected by these trends in policy ideas about what is appropriate and what is feasible. They "codify solutions and problem definitions into a solution-set that tends to dominate policy-making for a period of time" (Jones and Bachelor, 1993: 18). Regimes come to be defined as much by the solution-sets they adopt as the nature of the participants involved in the regime. Indeed, the position of some groups in terms of their ability to form a regime may be enhanced by the dominance of policy ideas and a definition of "the problem" that suggest that their participation and the kind of solutions they can offer are particularly appropriate or apt. As Harding concludes in Chapter 3 [of *Theories of Urban Politics*], a comparative framework for the analysis of urban politics needs to be much less "localist" than many of the approaches dominant in the United States. Regime theory must escape from the "localist" trap. Indeed, it needs to do so to operate successfully in the United States let alone as a framework for broader cross-national comparison.

The need to explain regime continuity and change

Regime studies need to explore the dynamics of regime change as well as regime continuity. Community power needs to be viewed within a dynamic perspective. Stone (1989b) in his study of Atlanta focuses on the forces of continuity and on how the collective action problems for those challenging the established order are considerable. Yet changes do occur in regimes. DeLeon (1992), for example, analyses a shift in San Francisco from a pro-growth to a progressive or at least a slow-growth regime. Shifts in the patterns of funding from Federal government and the arrival of a business leadership that held their position as managers and had fewer direct ties to San Francisco are seen as having weakened the grip of the pro-growth regime. These processes of continuity and change need to be located within a developing framework of regime theory. What is needed is a recognition of the impact of shifts in exogenous conditions as well as developments in the internal dynamics of coalition building.

The role of policy ideas in explaining both regime continuity and change is emphasized in the work of Jones and his colleagues referred to earlier. The stability of a regime is explained by the solution-set it adopts. Once in place, solution-sets tend to dominate policy search and sustain the regime's policy perspective, allowing some scope for incremental change. This condition of policy stasis, however, can break down and be punctured by rapid policy development and change (for a wider discussion see Baumgartner and Jones, 1993). In these circumstances "fresh policy proposals and symbolic representations of them have the capacity to attract new participants to politics, altering the existing governing arrangements" (Jones and Bachelor, 1993: 250). When the regime's favoured policy solution falls into disrepute the promotion of an attractive alternative policy more "in tune with the times" can rapidly gain supporters and generate considerable positive feedback: "that is, changes cascade in a kind of urban bandwagon that sweeps through the system" (Jones, 1993: 3).

Orr and Stoker (1994) propose a model of regime transition which gives recognition to the influence of non-local forces – reflecting broader shifts in the political and economic environment – as well as the internal dynamics of coalition building. They argue that it is useful to think of regime transition in terms of a three-stage scheme.

The first stage revolves around the questioning of the established regime. Doubts may be raised about its capacity and about the goals it is pursuing. Such questions are most likely to be raised where developments in the wider environment appear to contradict or challenge the established regime. Questions and doubts have to find some vehicle of expression among corporate, political or other potential leaders.

The second stage involves a conflict about redefining the scope and purpose of the regime. Here competing groups of elite actors may organize to seek new ways forward and a new policy direction. This is a period of much uncertainty and debate. Hostility between opposing camps may find public expression. There will be a battle for "hearts and minds" of established actors and a search for new actors to support a new way forward. Experiments and pilot initiatives may also perform the useful function of [acting as] visible flags around which the challenging forces can assemble, gathering strength and gaining in mutual understanding.

A third stage involves the institutionalization of the new regime. The institutionalization of a new regime involves the establishment of a new set of material incentives and ideological outlook. In short, a new solution-set would need to be established alongside appropriate institutional arrangements and selective incentives.

Regime transition is not likely to be a simple and straightforward process. To challenge a regime is a difficult task. To assemble an alternative regime, as has been argued throughout this chapter, reflects a considerable expression of power.

CONCLUSION

Regime theory has made a useful contribution to the study of urban politics. It provides a framework for analysis which encourages attention to be directed to important aspects of urban polities. In particular, the attempt to push urban political science beyond a narrow focus on power as an issue of social control is to be welcomed. To understand the politics of a complex urban system it is necessary to move beyond a notion of power as the ability to get another actor to do something they would not otherwise do. Politics is not restricted to acts of domination by the elite and consent or resistance from the ruled. Social control or command power, because of the cost of obtaining compliance, is likely to be restricted to limited domains of action. In a complex society the crucial act of power is the capacity to provide leadership and a mode of operation that enables significant tasks to be done. This is the power of social production. Regime theory suggests that this form of power involves actors and institutions gaining and fusing a capacity to act by blending their resources, skills and purposes into a long-term coalition: a regime. If they succeed they pre-empt the leadership role in their community and establish for themselves a near decision-making monopoly over the cutting-edge choices facing their locality.

The framework for analysis offered by regime theory and its layered conception of power provides the basis for a more subtle understanding of urban polities than that provided by hyperpluralist models ... and the growth coalition literature ... It is a theory in need of further development. It needs to avoid the trap of a narrow localism and enhance its capacity to explain regime change. Above all it needs to avoid its terminology and language being usurped to serve the needs of a multitude of atheoretical case studies of city polities.

Finally, regime theory has the capacity to travel. If some of its ethnocentric assumptions are removed it may be able to offer an effective framework for analysis in other countries ... Political scientists have in the past been reluctant to undertake such empirical tests. Yet in its concern with the blending of capacities between governmental and non-governmental actors regime theory would seem to highlight processes which are now more to the fore in the British system. It may also be possible to go further and use regime theory as a framework for cross-national comparison. Some of the groundwork for such a move has been provided already (Stoker and Mossberger, 1994b). Regime theory will need to grow and develop if it is to survive. It has succeeded in establishing a new agenda for researchers. If in ten years' time regime analysts have a track record of empirical research and theoretical development on both sides of the Atlantic then regime theory will really have come of age.

REFERENCES

Baumgartner, F. and Jones, B. (1993) *Agendas and Instability in American Politics*. Chicago: University of Chicago Press.

Cochrane, A. (1993) *Whatever Happened to Local Government?* Milton Keynes: Open University Press.

Dahl, R. (1961) *Who Governs?* New Haven, Conn.: Yale University Press.

DeLeon, R. (1992) *Left Coast City: Progressive Politics in San Francisco 1975–1991*. Lawrence: University of Kansas Press.

Dunleavy, P. and O'Leary, B. (1987) *Theories of the State*. London: Macmillan.

Elkin, S. (1987) *City and Regime in the American Republic*. Chicago: University of Chicago Press.

Fainstein, N. and Fainstein, S. (1986) "Regime Strategies, Communal Resistance and Economic Forces", in S. Fainstein, R. C. Hill, D. Judd and M. Smith (eds) *Restructuring the City: The Political Economy of Urban Redevelopment*. New York: Longman.

Garvin, J. (1994) Personal communication.

Harloe, M., Pickvance, C. and Urry, J. (eds) (1990) *Place, Policy and Politics*. London: Unwin Hyman.

Horan, C. (1991) "Beyond Governing Coalitions: Analyzing Urban Regimes in the 1990s", *Journal of Urban Affairs* 13(2).

Jones, B. (1993) "Social Power and Urban Regimes", *Urban News. Newsletter of the Urban Politics Section of the American Political Science Association* 7(3): 1–3.

Jones, B. and Bachelor, L. with Wilson, C. (1986) *The Sustaining Hand: Community Leadership and Corporate Power*. Lawrence: University of Kansas Press.

Jones, B. and Bachelor, L. (1993) *The Sustaining Hand: Community Leadership and Corporate Power* (2nd edn., revised). Lawrence: University of Kansas Press.

Keating, M. (1991) *Comparative Urban Politics: Power and the City in the United States, Canada,*

Britain, and France. Lawrence: University of Kansas Press.

Lukes, S. (1974) *Power: A Radical View*. London: Macmillan.

Orr, M. and Stoker, G. (1994) "Urban Regimes and Leadership in Detroit", *Urban Affairs Quarterly* 30(1): 48–73.

Osborne, D. and Gaebler, T. (1992) *Reinventing Government: How the Entrepreneurial Spirit Is Transforming the Public Sector*. Reading, Mass.: Addison-Wesley.

Peterson, P. (1981) *City Limits*. Chicago: University of Chicago Press.

Savitch, H. and Thomas, J. (1991) "Conclusion: End of the Millennium Big City Politics", in H. Savitch and J. Thomas (eds) *Big City Politics in Transition*. Newbury Park, Calif.: Sage.

Stoker, G. and Mossberger, K. (1994a) "The Dynamics of Cross-National Policy Borrowing: Frameworks for Analysis in the Urban Setting", paper presented at the Urban Affairs Association Annual Conference, New Orleans, 2–5 March.

Stoker, G. and Mossberger, K. (1994b) "Urban Theory in Comparative Perspective", *Government and Policy* 12: 195–212.

Stone, C. (1980) "Systemic Power in Community Decision Making: A Restatement of Stratification Theory", *American Political Science Review* 74(4): 978–90.

Stone, C. (1986) "Power and Social Complexity", in R. Waste (ed.) *Community Power: Directions for Future Research*. Newbury Park, Calif.: Sage.

Stone, C. (1988) "Pre-emptive Power: Floyd Hunter's 'Community Power Structure' Reconsidered", *American Journal of Political Science* 32: 82–104.

Stone, C. (1989a) "Paradigms, Power and Urban Leadership", in B. Jones (ed.) *Leadership and Politics*. Lawrence: University of Kansas Press.

Stone, C. (1989b) *Regime Politics: Governing Atlanta, 1946–1988*. Lawrence: University of Kansas Press.

Stone, C. (1993) "Urban Regimes and the Capacity to Govern: A Political Economy Approach", *Journal of Urban Affairs* 15(1): 1–28.

Stone, C. and Sanders, H. (eds) (1987) *The Politics of Urban Development*. Lawrence: University of Kansas Press.

Thomas, J. and Savitch, H. "Introduction: Big City Politics, Then and Now", in H. Savitch and J. Thomas (eds) *Big City Politics in Transition*. Newbury Park, Calif.: Sage.

Yates, D. (1977) *The Ungovernable City: The Politics of Urban Problems and Policy Making*. Cambridge, Mass.: MIT Press.

ROBIN HAMBLETON

"Future Directions for Urban Government in Britain and America"

Journal of Urban Affairs (1990)

Editors' introduction   How will urban government evolve as the great forces shaping urban society are played out in the twenty-first century? What roles can and should they perform in a global, high-tech society? Which of the competing ideologies about urban governance being tried and debated today will be followed in the future? The following selection addresses these important questions about the urban future.

University of Bristol professor of government Robin Hambleton is an insightful writer in the field of comparative urban government. He has studied urban governance in both the U.S. and the U.K. Here Hambleton reviews changes which occurred under the conservative Thatcher and Reagan governments, liberal alternatives which have been undertaken or proposed in both countries, and his own conceptual framework for understanding possible futures for urban governance.

The past decade and a half have been a turbulent period in the politics of both the U.S. and British local government and they presage even bigger changes to come. Local governments must face the technological and economic challenges described in other selections in this part of the book. And major ideological debates have occurred between different strands of conservative and liberal thought on the future role of urban government in a changing world.

Hambleton is careful to note differences between the more uniform centralized system of urban governance in the U.K. and the pluralism inherent in the U.S. federal system. He reminds the reader that each urban political system is embedded in its distinct political culture. Nonetheless all urban governments must respond to underlying changes: the global restructuring of capital discussed by Sassen (p. 300) and the revolution of communications technology discussed by Castells (p. 494). Hambleton emphasizes a third force: the decentralization of forms of organization and management in both the private and public sectors which cuts across national boundaries.

Conservatives like Charles Murray (p. 233) have been highly critical of public, as opposed to private, operations – branding many local government activities as wasteful, inefficient, and of little or no real use. Beginning in the 1980s conservatives in both the U.S. and the U.K. developed and have partially carried out an approach to local government which emphasizes cutting local government expenditures and privatizing government functions. With less government money available for programs, local governments on both sides of the Atlantic are doing less than they did in the 1960s and 1970s: building little or no government-assisted housing, cutting local school lunch programs, reducing welfare assistance. Some local governments have turned over former functions to the private sector. For example, some local governments have abandoned local government-operated garbage collection in favor of private garbage collection. Similarly, some local governments are selling off municipally owned housing.

Will radical conservatives be able to push this agenda further? One possibility Hambleton suggests in his Figure 1 (p. 287) is increased "market pluralism." Perhaps local government will sell off more assets, the private sector will take over more functions, and local authorities, forced to compete in the private market, will become more efficient and consumer oriented.

Another alternative is that local government will reform itself so as better to serve consumers of government services. Critics of local government argue that local government has lost public confidence because it does not deliver what the public wants. Imagine the following stereotype of public vs. private response. When a storm drain clogs, the local *public* works department does nothing for a week and then sends out a crew of six to poke a pole through the drain. By contrast a consumer-oriented private garbage collection service maintains a twenty-four-hour-a-day hotline and immediately sends special trucks out to collect excess garbage on request. If local government adopts a consumerist approach and delivers what the public wants it may develop new levels of political support. But what public? And what does it want?

Hambleton notes that governments in both the U.S. and the U.K. are now devoting more resources to "economic development" – but that in some cases these are aimed at strengthing wealth creation by local business elites and in others at redistributive policies which will economically empower the urban underclass (Wilson, p. 226).

The final and most intriguing possibility Hambleton discusses is for decentralization. Some members of the political right, left, and center support radical decentralization of financing for and provision of public services – the "pluralist collectivist" circle at the bottom of Figure 1.

Robin Hambleton is the author of *Policy Planning and Local Government* (London: Hutchinson; New York: Allanheld Osmum, 1978) and many journal articles on comparative urban politics.

Other writings on the future of local urban government include Allen Cochrane, *Whatever Happened to Local Government?* (Milton Keynes: Open University Press, 1993), David Osborne and Ted Graebler, *Reinventing Government: How the Entrepreneurial Spirit Is Transforming the Public Sector* (Reading, Mass.: Addison-Wesley, 1992), M. Goldsmith (ed.), *Essays on the Future of Local Government* (Wakefield: West Yorkshire Metropolitan Council, 1986), Gerry Stoker and John Stewart, *The Future of Local Government* (London: Macmillan, 1989), Desmond S. King and Jon Pierre (eds.), *Challenges to Local Government* (London: Sage, 1990), and Michael Clarge and John Stewart, *Choices for Local Government for the 1990s and Beyond* (Harlow: Longman, 1991).

ROBIN HAMBLETON, "Future Directions for Urban Government in Britain and America"

Journal of Urban Affairs (1990)

INTRODUCTION

The 1990s was a period of crisis and change for British local government. To a lesser degree the last decade has also been a turbulent period for American local authorities. Drawing on a recent comparative review of urban government under Thatcher and Reagan (Hambleton, 1989a), we can identify a number of similarities and contrasts. On the other hand, it is clear that there are strong parallels between the U.K. and the U.S.A.: the socioeconomic trends impacting on urban areas are similar; both the Thatcher and the Reagan administrations have reduced financial support to city governments in the name of national economic policy; and urban areas are increasingly divided, with extraordinary concentrations of deprivation and poverty in some neighborhoods. On the other hand alongside these similarities there are remarkable divergences: the Thatcher government's commitment to political centralization would be unthinkable in the United States; party politics in Britain has become highly politicized in a way which is, on the whole, foreign to American city councils; and, linked with this, attempts by local authorities to pursue radical reform programs appear to be more widespread in Britain than in the United States.

This article offers a simple conceptual framework for thinking about current and future developments in urban government in Britain and America. In particular, it tries to make sense of the various moves toward privatization, consumerism, and neighborhood decentralization. It will be suggested that the changing pressures on local government in both countries with continue, even intensify, in the 1990s.

CHANGING PRESSURES ON URBAN GOVERNMENT

Comparative government is a fascinating but treacherous field. Major political, cultural, social, economic, racial, legal, historical, and geographical differences need to be recognized. Furthermore, when the focus is local government, it is important to recognize the constitutional differences. Local government in America is a creature of each of the 50 states. There is huge variation in the form and financing of American local authorities. This contrasts sharply with the high degree of institutional and fiscal uniformity found in British local government (cf. Sharpe, 1973; Hambleton, 1978: 89–113; Lee, 1985; Magnusson, 1986).

Clearly, we should beware of drawing cross-national parallels which disregard these differences. However, having made this caveat, we can point to several trends which have little regard for national boundaries.

First, it can be argued that we are witnessing

a global restructuring of capital that has implications for all the major cities in the U.S.A. and the U.K., as well as elsewhere. Capital flight, foreign investment, multinational corporate competition, and international interdependence of production activities are all part of the globalization of economic relations (Smith, 1987). From this perspective a key current issue for city government is managing the tensions between the imperatives of transnational capital accumulation and local political forces demanding a stable economic base.

The globalization of economic relations has been accelerated by the revolutions in communication systems and microelectronics. Advances in information technology are diminishing the significance of place and leading to delocalization of the processes of production and consumption. We are witnessing "the decomposition of the processes of work and management so that different tasks can be performed in different places and assembled through signals (in the case of information) or through advanced transportation technology (standardized assembly pieces shipped away from very remote points of production)" (Castells, 1983: 6).

A second key trend which is inextricably linked to the global restructuring of capital and the delocalization of the processes of production and consumption is organizational. My colleague, Paul Hoggett, has argued that current shifts toward decentralized forms of organization and management in both the private and the public sectors can be viewed as part of a new technomanagerial paradigm (Hoggett, 1987). On this analysis the postwar boom was based upon a technological style which combined Fordist techniques of mechanized mass production with Taylorist models of management and organization. Mass production, economies of scale, fragmentation and specialization of work, and the deskilling of manual labor through removal of discretion were key features of what might be called the "Fordist" era.

Hoggett argues that the revolution in microelectronics, robotics, and information technology is leading toward the flexible, automated production of a diversified range of more custom-designed quality products. In organizational terms "the emergent technomanagerial paradigm replaces bureaucratic supervision by delegation, participation and team work organized within a subtle framework of increasingly computerized control systems" (Hoggett, 1987: 222). Fordism stressed organizational structure and strong, centralized power control. In post-Fordist organizations power is more dispersed; structures are cellular rather than pyramid-like and the units tend to regulate themselves, rather than being governed by rules and commands that flow downward (Mulgen, 1988; Peters, 1989).

A third key trend is political. The pressures toward globalization and delocalization referred to earlier are being opposed by political movements seeking more local autonomy and urban self-management. In some cases, political parties feature boldly in these campaigns; this is certainly the case in the U.K. (Blunkett and Jackson, 1987). In many cases, however, these urban social movements lie outside formal party structures (Lowe, 1986). These pressures for local autonomy are, to varying degrees, confronted by centralizing trends within nation states. In the U.K., for example, the central state has worked relentlessly to undermine local government in recent years (Hambleton, 1989a).

In summary, it can be suggested that these three sets of forces – the economic, the organizational, and the political – will dominate the development of urban government in the 1990s in both the U.S.A. and the U.K. What, in practice, might this mean for urban government?

EMERGING TENSIONS: ECONOMIC, ORGANIZATIONAL, AND POLITICAL

First, economic forces are likely to shrink the differences between urban government in the U.S. and the U.K. For example, commercial property investment now operates in a very competitive global market. City authorities in both countries can be expected to extend their knowledge of and involvement with different private sector interests in order to attract inward investment. In support of this we can note that survey evidence suggests that Amer-

ican city councils have become very heavily involved in urban economic development over the last 20 years (Robinson, 1988; Bowman, 1988). The strategies most American cities adopt are very business oriented, even though the social costs of this approach can be considerable (Cummings, 1988; Hambleton, 1988a, 1989b).

In Britain, too, there has been a rapid growth in the number of local authorities pursuing local economic development strategies (Young and Mason, 1983; Lovering, 1988). Many of these strategies have had a much more explicit social purpose than their American counterparts. Not surprisingly, there is ongoing conflict between central and local government about the nature and purpose of local economic development: is it about wealth creation or is it about helping local residents (Blunkett and Jackson, 1987: 108–42)? The general point, however, is that, while different political parties will emphasize different objectives, we can anticipate continued growth in public–private sector collaboration as city councils wrestle with economic restructuring.

The issue of organizational change is discussed in detail later. In general terms, we can, following Schon (1971), suggest that the institutions of urban government, like most social systems, are resistant to change to the point of exhibiting dynamic conservatism; that is, they fight to stay the same (Schon, 1971: 32). This is not necessarily bad. We don't want institutions that fly apart at the seams. Our organizations of urban government "need to maintain their identity, and their ability to support the self-identity of those who belong to them, but they must at the same time be capable of frequently transforming themselves" (Schon, 1971: 60). Schon rightly stresses that external pressures require constant innovation.

Again, at a general level, it can be suggested that the organizations of urban government have not paid sufficient attention to the needs of the consumer. The burgeoning, largely American, literature on consumer-oriented management suggests that superior (private or public sector) performance requires organizations to take exceptional care of their customers (Peters and Waterman, 1982; Peters and Austin, 1986).

According to this line of argument, the institutions of urban government need to launch a customer revolution. They need to become obsessed with listening to their consumers and to achieve extraordinary levels of responsiveness (Peters, 1989).

The consequences of the third key trend, political change, are more difficult to predict because developments within both the U.K. and the U.S.A. seem to point in two directions: some would seem to be widening the differences between urban government in Britain and America while others could narrow the gap. On the first point the intensification of ideological conflict in British party politics might be expected to widen the gap. A variety of political movements (emanating from the political right, left, and center) are articulating and implementing radical reform programs which seek to transform established approaches to providing and financing urban services.

These various initiatives are discussed further below. Examples are: radical right privatization and cost-cutting strategies as in the London Borough of Wandsworth (Beresford, 1987); radical left neighborhood decentralization strategies as in the London Borough of Islington (Hodge, 1987; du Parcq, 1987); and center party innovation with area-based management as in the London Borough of Tower Hamlets (Morphet, 1987). While it is possible to imagine similar programs being developed by American city councils, we would not expect to find such a strong party political emphasis in local government strategies for organizational change, notwithstanding developments in some progressive cities (Clavel, 1986).

This divergence in party politics is, however, only part of the picture. It is also possible to suggest that city politics in Britain is moving toward an American form in the sense that local politics is becoming more pluralistic. The electorate is certainly more heterogeneous than it was [around 1980]. Class is no longer the only important political cleavage. Citizens have become more assertive and more diversified and organizations based around neighborhood, ethnicity, and specific issues (such as homelessness or transport policy) are having an increasingly significant impact on local government. Urban

social movements have certainly grown in Britain in the 1980s. Various writers have shown that local politics has become much more sectional and that local interest groups have become more influential (Gyford, 1986; Stoker, 1988: 106–28). If the upsurge in interest group politics continues, it can be suggested that British urban politics could, over a period of time, become more like American city politics, which has a strong pluralistic tradition (Waste, 1987).

It would be wrong to imply that these three driving forces for change – the economic, the organizational, and the political – are independent of one another. On the contrary, it is clear that there are strong overlaps. In particular, it is clear that major business interests are capable of dominating local interest group politics by virtue of their economic power.

In summary, it can be argued that it is helpful to engage in Anglo-American comparative study of trends affecting urban government not least because it provides insights on prospects for the coming years. (Some of the wider arguments for engaging in cross-national comparative study in the field of public administration are explored by Bull and Hambleton (1989).) As explained below, some key trends point toward an Americanization of British urban government. If these trends continue into the 1990s, we can anticipate an increase in urban conflicts as party political organizations wrestle with the pressures from new social groups and take on the challenge of developing a creative relationship with powerful, often international, business interests.

The next section outlines a conceptual framework for understanding the way British urban government has evolved over the last 20 years or so. The subsequent sections expand on the key themes identified in the framework. While the focus is on Britain, the discussion attempts to highlight lessons for American cities.

UNDERSTANDING DEVELOPMENTS IN BRITAIN: A CONCEPTUAL FRAMEWORK

The framework outlined in Figure 1 was originally developed by a group of staff at the School for Advanced Urban Studies (SAUS) to help us understand the strong British movement toward various forms of neighborhood decentralization (Hambleton and Hoggett, 1987; Hambleton *et al.*, 1989). The framework can, however, be used to serve the broader purpose of introducing an international audience to some of the key currents of change running through British local government as a whole. Figure 1 represents a drastic simplification of a far more complex reality. While it has proved useful in a number of seminars and workshops run by SAUS for local

government managers and politicians, no claim is made that it provides a comprehensive map.

The framework contrasts old solutions (broadly pre-1980) with the new patterns of the 1980s and speculates about the possibilities for the 1990s. The phrase bureaucratic paternalism succinctly describes the old solutions that have become today's problems in local government. Too many local authority departments are large, hierarchical organizations structured to mass-produce services in line with the Fordist model outlined earlier. The 1980s have not only seen a

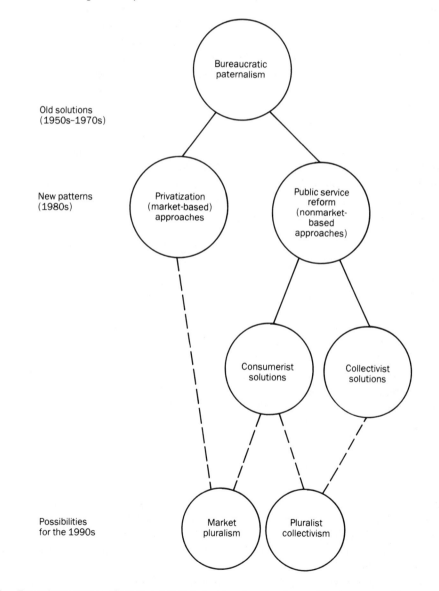

Figure 1   Emerging patterns of relationship between local authorities and their communities

crisis in these old solutions, but the emergence of two post-Fordist alternatives. The first alternative, usually associated with the radical right, seeks to challenge the very notion of collective and nonmarket provision for public need. Centering upon the strategy of privatization, it seeks to replace public provision with private provision. The second alternative aims to preserve the notion of public provision, but seeks a radical reform of the manner in which this provision is undertaken. Thus it seeks to replace the old bureaucratic paternalist model with a much more responsive and democratic model.

This latter approach to reform appears to have two central variants, the one being essentially consumerist, the other being essentially collectivist. Consumerist approaches to reform give primary emphasis to enhancing the responsiveness of local government services to individual consumers. However, many services cannot be individualized; they relate to groups of consumers or to society at large. Collective interests can only be protected through appropriate forms of political accountability. Hence, collectivist approaches place their primary emphasis on the democratization of local government service provision. Clearly, there are very close links between responsiveness and democracy.

Nevertheless, we have found it helpful to distinguish between the two approaches. The consumerist approach is essentially concerned with the reform of local government considered as an administrative system, whereas the collectivist approach seeks to reform local government considered as a political system. Looking to the future, it is important to stress the speed at which developments are occurring. With the election of the Conservatives for a third term in June 1987, new scenarios for the public sector in the 1990s and beyond have emerged. New legislation on the contracting out of public services (referred to as Compulsory Competitive Tendering or CCT), on the break-up of public sector housing, on changes to education (including provisions for schools to opt out of the state system), on alterations to the National Health Service, all points to the creation of more pluralist patterns of public service provision in the future. The key point is, what kind of pluralism will emerge?

A market-based pluralism, which gives emphasis to deregulated, private institutional forms to run schools, housing estates, hospitals, elderly persons' homes, and so on, is clearly the objective of the radical Thatcherites. An alternative pattern of pluralist collectivism is also possible. Within this scenario, provision remains public but not necessarily state. New forms of social provision (social trusts, management co-operatives, tenant management corporations, etc.) emerge accountable by contract, regulation, and inspection to local authorities. The market-based pluralism scenario envisages a proliferation of profit-seeking organizations providing for individualized consumers. Pluralist collectivism implies a growing diversity of nonprofit organizations and trusts offering a variety of ways of meeting public needs. Needless to say, American cities are replete with many examples of both kinds of organizations, and this is one of the main reasons for suggesting that an Americanization of British local government may be in train. Having provided an overall framework, we can now sketch in a few details.

There are two developing critiques of the old solutions. First, there is the political critique of massive alienating public bureaucracies. This analysis suggests that the Thatcher government has cashed in on the paternalism and inadequacies of the welfare state and that the response must be radical. One influential political leader on the left put it this way:

> We must start debating as a movement our values and the ways in which we will extend democracy, participative democracy, as well as defending what we've got; because it is partly the inadequacy of, and the alienation from, the way in which the system is worked that has enabled Thatcher to take the steps she has with such success.
>
> (Blunkett, 1986)

Second, there is the management critique of inward-looking organizational cultures. As discussed earlier, there has been a widespread failure in the private as well as the public sector to put the customer first. The critique has been developed in popular form by American management consultants in the best-seller *In Search of Excellence* (Peters and Waterman, 1982).

The key point to stress is that both the political and the managerial critiques suggest that radical rather than marginal change is needed. The next three sections highlight key features of the three main sets of responses that have emerged in Britain in the 1980s.

THE RADICAL RIGHT: EXPENDITURE CUTS AND PRIVATIZATION

Both the Thatcher and the Reagan administrations have cut central government financial support to local government. In Britain between 1979–80 and 1986–87 the government slashed the rate support grant (which resembles general revenue sharing) by £17 billion (roughly $29 billion). Similarly, the so-called policy earthquake of the Reagan Omnibus Budget Reconciliation Act (OBRA) of 1981 produced sharp declines of federal aid in the 1981–82 period. One independent study revealed that federal funding for specifically urban programs fell by $5.8 billion in fiscal 1982 from what it would have been had fiscal 1980 policy continued in effect (Peterson, 1986). In both countries then, central government has put fiscal pressure on city councils.

In Britain this has been a running saga throughout the 1980s. There has been a torrent of legislation on local government finance including the Local Government Planning and Land Act of 1980 (to punish overspending), measures to introduce rate capping (in 1984), measures to replace rates with a poll tax and new measures to reform housing finance and local authority capital spending (the 1989 Local Government and Housing Act). These various measures, which are discussed more fully elsewhere (Hambleton, 1989a), are all designed to restrain council spending.

The radical right has a philosophy which goes well beyond holding down public spending. A further key feature has been the strategy of privatizing local government (Ascher, 1987; Stoker, 1988: 173–91). Nicholas Ridley, then Secretary of State for the Environment, set out the philosophy underlying the Conservative government's policies (Ridley, 1988). He restates the view that it is essential "to constrain

the growth of local authority expenditure in order to stop it taking an ever-larger proportion of the total national product at the expense of other areas of the economy" (Ridley, 1988: 7). This view is, of course, contested. One critique offers 12 reasons why the argument is flawed (Newton and Karran, 1985: 20–35). For example, local government is one of the private sector's best customers and local government provides and maintains industrial infrastructure and services which are crucial to the success of the national economy. In other words, local government is contributing to, not taking from, other areas of the economy.

To secure better local government in the future, Ridley suggests that two of the keys to success lie in strengthening accountability and extending competition:

> To strengthen accountability we need a more direct relationship between payment for local services through local taxation and the service being provided ...
>   Competition is a spur to efficiency and value for money wherever it operates. Too much of the public sector has been insulated from it. The spread of competition in education, housing and other local services should do an enormous amount to improve standards of efficiency.
> (Ridley, 1988: 8)

On the first point, the claim of the radical right is that the new poll tax (or community charge as it is called officially) will strengthen accountability. All adult citizens will be liable and, so the argument runs, will therefore have a stronger interest than they do at present in holding their local councils to account through the ballot box. Opponents of the poll tax raise a string of objections. First, it is unfair in that, in principle, it requires everyone over 18 to pay the same, regardless of means. This leads to a substantial redistribution of income from the less well-off to the better-off. Secondly, the costs of collecting the tax from a far larger number of people are substantial. Some estimates suggest the tax will cost almost three times as much as rates to collect. Third, the compilation of the register will involve intrusion into the private lives of individuals.

Fourth, even with energetic enforcement

there will be substantial tax evasion. In particular, it will deter young people from registering to vote. These objections have not stopped the government from pressing ahead with the scheme. The tax was introduced in Scotland in April 1989 and the plans are to introduce it in England and Wales in April 1990.

The second theme of competition is hinted at in the subtitle to the Ridley pamphlet: enabling not providing. Thus, the argument runs, the role of the local authority should no longer be that of universal provider. Rather, it should be to encourage diversity and alternatives, with elements of competition between the different providers. This emphasis on competition is directly in line with New Right belief in the virtues of the market:

> As far as possible competition should prevail, or at least, every supplier should be open to competition. Neither private nor government contrivances should be allowed to obliterate or blur the commercial signaling role of the free market.
> (Green, 1987: 211–12)

More than that, the Ridley pamphlet argues that ownership should shift into private hands:

> This government goes in for private ownership, because assets in *private* hands are cared for and used efficiently, while assets in public hands have too often been allowed to decay and stagnate and become a burden on the community.
> (Ridley, 1988: 23, emphasis added)

Privatization is a term which is used rather loosely to describe a variety of policies which aim to limit the role of the public sector and increase the role of the private sector. In terms of the government's policies for local government, we can identify three main aspects. First, the sale of local authority assets has been a key feature. For example, the 1980 Housing Act gave public sector housing tenants the right to buy their houses with discounts of up to 50 percent on the market value. Over 1,000,000 council houses were sold in the period 1980–86 (Malpass and Murie, 1987: 102). More recent legislation (the Housing and Planning Act 1986) provides for the disposal of whole housing estates to private developers and the taking over of housing management by nonlocal authority agencies.

Second is the expansion of the private sector role in service provision and investment. Thus, the private sector has moved into social service provision through a rapid growth in private homes for the elderly. Financial institutions have begun to invest more heavily in urban redevelopment, encouraged by a range of financial inducements not dissimilar to the American Urban Development Action Grant approach (Boyle, 1985).

Third, and arguably of most long-term significance, is the introduction of market discipline into local authority service delivery through the introduction of Compulsory Competitive Tendering (CCT). The tendering exercise involves contracting services previously provided inhouse by the local authority. The inhouse workforce is required to compete against interested private bidders. If the local authority department submits the most competitive tender, the contract price becomes its budget and it operates as if it were an arm's-length organization servicing the local authority. If the private sector company wins, it gets the contract and the local authority department (usually known as the direct labor organization) is disbanded. The underlying driving force behind the various privatization initiatives is an ideological belief that private equals good while public equals bad (Dunleavy and Rhodes, 1986: 141).

These authors suggest that the Conservative electoral strategy is designed to intensify public–private conflicts. This approach, when coupled with a continuing series of measures to roll back the state, is seen as the main plank in a strategy to build up long-term Conservative electoral support. The importance of gut politics in explaining Conservative enthusiasm for privatization should not be underestimated but other factors are relevant (Stoker, 1988: 173–6). First, the strategy has developed at a time of financial austerity – selling off assets reduces pressure for public sector borrowing. Second, privatization creates new markets and greater opportunities for the private sector – it attempts to strengthen the operation of market forces and reduce public expectations about what the state should do and what it should be responsible for.

Opponents of privatization argue that there is no evidence to support the view that assets in private hands are better cared for and used more effectively than those in public hands. Rather, they argue that the Conservative drive toward contracting out is part of a campaign against public sector trade unionism (Ascher, 1987: 46–53). Employees in the private sector are less likely to be strongly unionized. If private contractors are able to offer a cheaper service – and this is contested – it is, so the argument runs, because they are exploiting their workers.

Much of the argument over privatization is strongly colored by ideological prejudice. It is noteworthy, therefore, that Sir John Banham, the head of the Audit Commission, the national organization set up by the Thatcher government to ensure value for money in the public sector, who is now Director General of the British Confederation for British Industry (CBI), made the following remarks at a ... national conference:

> The best local government is superb and private enterprise could never improve on it ... with Sheffield as a shining example.
> A well-managed direct labour organization is going to be fully competitive with the best of the private sector. Sheffield collects refuse rather more economically than Southend which is privatized – a fact which went down like a lead balloon in Marsham Street, the Department of the Environment headquarters. There is no excuse for lousy management and privatization is the last resort of a management that has given up.
> (Quoted in Blunkett and Jackson, 1987, 122)

PUBLIC SERVICE REFORM: CONSUMERISM

The major alternative to privatization was, as indicated in Figure 1, public service reform. This approach recognizes that a successful defense of the welfare state requires a response which goes well beyond defending existing forms of service provision to develop new ways forward which will win popular support. As explained earlier, the framework distinguishes two kinds of public service reform. In this section we are concerned with the consumerist approach.

The idea of getting closer to the consumer has enjoyed a resurgence within the private sector during the 1980s. There are many strands to this but one study of successful American companies, *In Search of Excellence*, has, as mentioned earlier, been particularly influential. The authors of this book argue that despite all the lip service given to market orientation, in many firms the customer is being either ignored or regarded as a nuisance. Their findings were summarized as follows: "The excellent companies really are close to their customers. That's it. Other companies talk about it; the excellent companies do it" (Peters and Waterman, 1982: 156).

It was not long before these private sector management ideas began to permeate through to the public sector. American local government was ahead of British local government. In 1984 a Californian handbook, *Excellence in Local Government Management*, appeared which attempted to adapt the Peters and Waterman criteria of success for use in local government – the authors were enthusiastic about the possibilities (Barbour *et al.*, 1984). British local government has now also started to address the issues which arise when a local authority wants to get closer to its consumers. The Local Government Training Board ... produced an impressive 96-page booklet, *Getting Closer to the Public*, which sets out the basic ideas and approaches, provides a framework for reviewing current practice and considers some of the staff development activities needed to bring about change (Local Government Training Board, 1987). This has been followed up with a further publication, *Learning from the Public* (Local Government Training Board, 1988).

It would be misleading to imply that these consumerist ideas are simply the latest import from the private sector into current public sector management thinking. On the contrary, the cause of consumerism has advanced steadily over some 30 years. In saying this it is important to distinguish two definitions of consumerism: the narrow and fairly familiar meaning used to describe problems associated with the consumption of high street goods and services and the broader usage applied to problems associated with the use of public sector services. As Smith (1986) argues, this wider definition has been with us at least since the founding of the British National Consumer Council in 1975 and is implicit in a number of popular radio and television programs which carry the consumer label.

What is new is the political context within which these consumerist ideas are being debated. As outlined earlier, central government is putting enormous pressure on public sector organizations via its cost cutting/privatization strategy and this is forcing rethinking. In addition to these pressures from above, the population at large has become increasingly able to voice its views regarding public service inadequacies. These different pressures have given weight to those professionals and politicians within local authorities who are alert to the inadequacies of existing service provision and wish to develop a more consumer-oriented service.

Within the fashion for consumerism, as Pollitt (1988) observes, rival conceptions are at work "ranging all the way from cosmetic, 'charm school' approaches through improved provision of information to direct consumer participation and power-sharing." He suggests that the brands of consumerism actually being implemented tend to be at the cosmetic end of the spectrum. The established power relationship between those providing and those receiving services is not usually challenged.

An influential variant on the consumerist idea is the public service orientation (Stewart and Clarke, 1987). Such an orientation sets service for the public as the key organizational value, providing motivation and purpose both for the local authority and its staff. These authors argue that service for the public can provide a shared vision for those involved with local government at a time when local authorities are under attack. Their ideas draw on the private sector thinking outlined earlier but extend beyond the mechanistic transfer of consumerist ideas from the market place to the public sector. They claim that concern for the citizen as well as the customer distinguishes the public service orientation from the concern for the customer that should mark any service organization. The emphasis is both on the customer for whom the service is provided and

on the citizen to whom the local authority is accountable.

The sorts of measures advocated in documents like *Getting Closer to the Public* (Local Government Training Board, 1987) could, if implemented with enthusiasm, lead to significant improvements in local government service delivery. There are, however, two main sets of reasons why it is necessary to go beyond the consumerist/public service approach (Hambleton and Hoggett, 1987: 23–5). The first stems from the fact that many of these ideas have been imported from the private sector where, within limits, the consumer enjoys a degree of power by virtue of personal choice. If a retailer in the market place is too expensive or sells a shoddy product, it is possible (for most of us) to shop elsewhere.

There are, of course, constraints on this consumer power. For example, poor, infirm consumers may be insufficiently mobile to take their business elsewhere. Also, it has been clear for at least 30 years that the market is able to create desires and shape consumer wants in subtle but extremely effective ways (Packard, 1957). However, allowing for these constraints, the private sector consumer has the power of choice.

Advocates of the market approach have encountered serious problems when trying to extend consumer choice within the public sector. Even when services are privatized, individual consumer choice is not enhanced. Thus, individuals cannot switch their refuse collector, their fire service, their water company, their electricity board, etc. In the public sector we have built up political structures to provide a mechanism for holding service providers (whether public servants or private contractors) accountable to the citizen. For these services, which are effectively monopolies, the consumer derives power from political control, not from the ability to exercise choice within the market place. The consumerist/public service approach fails to address the issues raised by this distinction, in particular, the imbalance of power in the server–served relationship which arises when the consumer has little or no choice.

The second major limitation of the consumerist/public service approach is that it has difficulty coping with the needs of groups of consumers. Many public services provide a collective rather than an individual benefit. Clean air, roads, street lighting, environmental quality, environmental health, police protection, and schooling are just some of the services provided and consumed on a collective basis. In a democracy, collective needs of this kind need to be addressed collectively. Conflicts of view need to be expressed and choices which take account of other people's preferences have to be made. In short, a large range of decisions which affect people's lives cannot sensibly be made by individuals operating in isolation. They must be conceived politically. This is not to imply that existing arrangements for democratic control of public service organizations are adequate. On the contrary, we need improved mechanisms for enabling different groups of consumers and citizens to influence political decisionmaking about the collective provision of services. This leads us to a discussion of public service reform strategies which center on empowering the consumer and the citizen.

EMPOWERING THE CONSUMER AND THE CITIZEN

The consumerist proposals discussed so far have concentrated on managerial rather than political change. While the public service orientation attempts to go beyond the supermarket model of consumerism by introducing the notion of concern for the citizen, it centers on improving service delivery and, as a result, does little to enhance citizenship. This is the essence of the critique offered by Rhodes, who argues that local government is about more than providing services. He suggests it is a means for emancipating the individual and creating a free society through citizen participation:

> If it seems grandiloquent to load local government with idealistic goals such as emancipation, it can be countered that a sense of mission does not lie in the sale of hamburgers with due deference to *In Search of Excellence* but in the 'nobility' of the aspiration.
>
> (Rhodes, 1987: 67)

Rhodes goes on to argue that the public service orientation should be modified to embrace a broad conception of citizenship because local government is that pre-eminent location for the integrative political experience outside Parliament.

The decentralization of services to neighborhood level is attracting considerable attention within local government in Britain. Making local authority services more accessible to the public, breaking down departmental barriers at local level, creating completely new avenues for staff development – these are the sorts of aspirations which explain the surge in support for decentralization in recent years. A growing number of local authorities have now decentralized many of their services to local level and many others are either in the process of decentralizing or are contemplating decentralizing (Hoggett and Hambleton, 1987; Hambleton, 1988b). In one sense this is not a new development. In the 1970s there was an earlier shift toward neighborhood management in both Britain and the United States (Yates, 1973; Hambleton, 1978). While these developments often improved the responsiveness of public service bureaucracies at the margin, they rarely challenged entrenched departmentalism effectively and had only modest success in raising citizen involvement (Hambleton, 1978; Ross and Stedman, 1984: 96–123). There are two main reasons why the British developments of the 1980s seem to differ from the initiatives of the 1970s; one is managerial, the other is political. First, aided by new information technology, decentralized forms of organization are rapidly developing within private sector companies across the world. These managerial innovations, which represent a shift toward the post-Fordist forms of organization referred to earlier, are now being imported into the public sector (Hoggett, 1987). Second, different forms of decentralization are proving attractive, in varying degrees, to all the major political parties in Britain. In many cases the town hall leaders who now advocate decentralization were active in community groups in the 1970s attacking remote, centralized decisionmaking. Their commitment to decentralization is often deeply held. The unifying theme of both the managerial and the political critiques of bureaucratic paternalism is the recognition of the need to desegregate and break up organizations which have become too big and complex to manage effectively.

It would be misleading, however, to suggest that the many neighborhood decentralization initiatives being taken forward in Britain have been successful in empowering the consumer and the citizen. On the contrary, the need for political change is often not seen as a primary focus of interest; decentralization is being pursued for a variety of objectives. Elsewhere I have suggested that this policy confusion can be penetrated by distinguishing five overlapping yet distinct objectives (Hambleton, 1988b). These possible objectives for decentralization are summarized in Table 1.

There is no need to discuss each of these objectives in detail here. We can note, however, that the potential objectives of decentralization are wide ranging. Some of the objectives present a fundamental challenge to familiar and well-established ways of running services while others involve comparatively minor change. Some of the five objectives are reinforcing, some are in tension if not conflict. For example, the fourth objective of increasing public support for local government links easily with the first objective of improving public services. This is difficult to achieve if the fifth objective of staff development is ignored. On the other hand, an example of possible conflict would be between the second and third objectives. A radical approach to strengthening the accountability of services to the local neighborhood could be incompatible with the pursuit of authority-wide policies concerned to even up opportunities for neglected groups.

Despite the difficulties, a number of local authorities are experimenting with new forms of local accountability and some examples are given below. These councils are not only striving for improved service responsiveness. They are concerned to encourage local political activity as a means of sustaining democracy as a whole, the advancement of citizenship, to use Rhodes's (1987) term. While there is not space to explore the literature on democracy here, we can, following the ... Widdicombe Report (1986: 45–52), note that the three main arguments for local government stem largely from democratic theory.

The first argument derives from concern with

Table 1 Possible objectives of neighborhood decentralization

---

1 Improving services
- Service delivery (convenient, one-stop, local coordination, local decisions)
- Cost effectiveness (local financial management)
- Service planning and policy (locality planning)
- The relationship between public servants and the public
2 Local accountability
- Varying degrees – authority or influence?
- To whom? (Local councilors? Consumers? Local people? A combination?)
- Community development
3 Distribution
- Priority areas?
- Different resources for different areas/groups
- Equal opportunities policy
4 Public support
- Win public support for local government
- Win support for political party
5 Staff development
- Job satisfaction
- Multidisciplinary teams
- Friendly environment
- Neighborhood loyalty
- Central support

---

political liberty: local government supports political pluralism and is able to moderate a tendency or temptation toward autocracy which is itself destructive of good government. Second, local government contributes to political education: it is a school in which democratic habits are acquired and practiced and the infrastructure of democracy laid down. The third set of arguments revolves around responsiveness: the necessity for local needs to be locally defined in order that appropriate services can be provided, the need for constant innovation, and the need to maximize public choice. These three arguments have been elaborated elsewhere (Hill, 1974; Stewart, 1983; Jones and Stewart, 1983; Gyford, 1984). Young (1986: 18) stresses that any valid theory of local government must be a political theory: "The current fashionable concern to regard local government as simply nothing more than a convenient mechanism for the delivery of public services is, in the long run, the most dangerous to its continued survival and vitality."

These three arguments in favor of local government can, with appropriate modifications, be used to support the development of various forms of neighborhood government, i.e. governmental structures below the level of the local authority. This is not to suggest that decentralization is the only way to extend local democracy. There are many ways of strengthening local political accountability and Table 2, in outlining four broad approaches, does not exhaust the possibilities. (For a full discussion of these four broad approaches, see Hambleton (1988b).)

First, there is a range of steps which can be taken to improve the existing mechanisms of local representative democracy. For example, in recent years many British local authorities have developed much better support services for politicians ranging from good secretarial help through to research support and policy advice (Thomas, 1987). A second approach is to extend representative democracy by creating new, more local settings within which representatives can decide on local issues. An increasing number of local authorities now have area or neighborhood committees which have decisionmaking powers relating to areas of the local authority. Examples are Stockport Metropolitan Borough Council, Birmingham City Council and Walsall Borough Council. The London Borough of Tower Hamlets, which is Liberal controlled, has probably gone furthest with this model. In 1984 the council scrapped most of its central committees and handed power over to new neighborhood committees (Morphet, 1987).

A third approach is to extend direct democracy. The central idea is to break with the notion that local government should always be the vehicle through which local needs are met and to invest in the voluntary sector. This approach involves decentralizing influence and power to groups rather than areas. This is important because the neighborhood does not necessarily command its inhabitants' primary loyalties. Arrangements have developed for consultation with and provision of direct funding to a range of interest groups, for example, community relations councils, ethnic minority groups, and women's groups. In addition, many councils support the involvement of user groups in the running of council services. Tenants' associations provide a long-standing example of a local government user group. In recent years new user groups have appeared, seeking some say over

Table 2 Ways of strengthening local democracy

1   Improving representative democracy: voter registration drives, open government, citizens' rights at meetings, better support to councilors.
2   Extending representative democracy: area committees based on wards or groups of wards, urban parish councils.
3   Extending direct democracy: funding of nonstatutory groups, community development, user group participation.
4   Infuse representative with direct democracy: co-option into committees, neighborhood committees of councilors and representatives from community and disadvantaged groups.

how council services are planned and delivered. This has happened particularly in the sphere of leisure and recreation where user groups are involved in running major facilities. Other groups are also emerging: for the parents of children in day nurseries, transport users' groups, parks users' groups, and so on.

A fourth way of strengthening local democracy is to infuse representative democracy with direct democracy. This approach recognizes the limitations of both representative democracy and direct democracy. Representative democracy has led to a professionalization of party politics with the result that white, middle-class, middle-aged men tend to dominate. Second, the form of involvement offered by representative democracy is passive and minimalist, a vote every three or four years. This form fits well with the paternalistic "leave it to us" approach. Third, and despite the startling amount of energy and commitment many councilors invest in local politics, elected members can only effect a fragile form of accountability from service professionals to the electorate. On the other hand, direct forms of democracy can be attacked on the grounds that they are often unrepresentative and parochial in their concerns. For example, tenants' associations are sometimes criticized for being white dominated or are accused of focusing only on the interests of tenants and disregarding the needs of those without tenancies, such as the homeless.

One interesting example of an attempt to infuse representative democracy with direct democracy is provided by the neighborhood forums in the London Borough of Islington. Each forum covers a neighborhood office catchment area, the aim being to enable administrative change and political reform to reinforce one another. No attempt is made to impose a blueprint upon all neighborhoods; councilors are involved, but it is equally important that the public and organized community groups be represented. The forums try to compensate for the lack of representation of disadvantaged groups by positively discriminating in their favor (places for these groups are guaranteed). Each forum has a budget to spend of around £60,000 per annum (roughly $100,000). It is too early to assess how the Islington neighborhood forums are working but they are a significant innovation of interest to other urban local authorities.

CONCLUSION

This article has suggested that urban government in Britain and America is confronted with a range of new pressures: economic, organizational, and political. There are, of course, major constitutional differences between the governmental structures of the two countries and there are also interesting policy divergences (Hambleton, 1989a). However, the thrust of this article has been to focus on forces which appear to be international in scope. If this analysis is broadly correct, there may be some convergence in British and American approaches to urban government in the 1990s.

Figure 1 provides a framework for understanding some of the key currents of change running through British local government. It is hoped that the framework can also serve as a useful prompt for reflecting on current trends within the United States. The framework is used to identify three main sets of responses to the perceived problems of local government:

1　The radical right strategy of cutting public spending and promoting privatization.
2　The reform of public service conceived as a management strategy for improving the responsiveness of services to the needs of consumers.
3　The reform of public service conceived as a political strategy for empowering the consumer and the citizen in order to strengthen local democracy.

There are ways in which developments in Britain contrast sharply with American experience. For example, the Thatcher government's policy of political centralization would be regarded as unacceptable in the United States (whether nationally or within one state). Yet, in other ways, we may be witnessing the Americanization of British urban government. The way city councils are responding to economic restructuring often follows American models. Urban politics in Britain is becoming more pluralistic. Class is no longer the only important political cleavage. The contracting out of public services to private companies, which is now receiving such attention in Britain, has been long-established practice in many American cities. The push toward a consumer-oriented strategy for public sector organizations owes much to American private sector management rhetoric about "getting closer to the consumer." The break-up of the public sector and the development of more plural forms of service provision is a further shift toward American models.

Set against the market, which attempts to individualize needs, is the notion of citizenship:

> The notion of the citizen implies a notion of the city, of the polis, of the public realm, of public purposes, publicly debated and determined ... To narrow the scope of public power, to take activities out of the public domain and put them into the private, is, by definition, to narrow the sphere of citizenship.
>
> (Marquand, 1989)

A large number of local authorities in Britain are attempting through a range of measures to strengthen citizenship through political participation. These strategies seek to empower the consumer and the citizen. The argument here is that none of us are merely consumers – our relationship with society is far more complex. The citizen has a stake in all services, even in those services which he or she does not consume directly. One of the most striking urban trends of the 1980s in both Britain and the United States is the growth of social divisions. Cities have become more unequal in the last ten years and serious tensions are building up. The central task for urban government in the 1990s is to respond to economic, organizational, and political pressures in a way which recovers a shared sense of values and renews the tradition of social idealism which city government has often stood for in the past.

REFERENCES

Ascher, K. (1987) *The Politics of Privatization*. London: Macmillan.

Barbour, G. P., Fletcher, T. W., and Sipel, G. A. (1984) *Excellence in Local Government Management*. Palo Alto: Center for Excellence in Local Government.

Beresford, P. (1987) *The Good Council Guide*, Policy Study 84, April. London: Centre for Policy Studies.

Blunkett, D. (1986) "Ratecap Resistance," *Marxism Today*, March.

Blunkett, D. and Jackson, K. (1987) *Democracy in Crisis: The Two Halls Respond*. London: Hogarth Press.

Bowman, A. O'M. (1988) "City Government Promotion of Economic Development," paper presented at the annual meeting of the Urban Affairs Association, St. Louis, 9–12 March.

Boyle, R. (ed.) (1985) "Symposium: Leveraging Urban Development: A Comparison of Urban Policy Directions in the United States and Britain," *Policy and Politics* 13(2): 175–210.

Bull, D. and Hambleton, R. (1989) "The Comparative Study of Public Administration: An Innovative Approach," paper presented at the 13th National Conference on Teaching Public Administration, Charlottesville, Va., 14–16 March.

Castells, M. (1983) "Crisis, Planning and the Quality of Life: Managing the New Historical Relationships between Space and Society," *Environment and Planning D: Society and Space* 1: 3–21.

Clavel, P. (1986) *The Progressive City. Planning and Participation 1969–84*. New Brunswick, N.J.: Rutgers University Press.

Cummings, S. (ed.) (1988) *Business Elites and Urban Development*. Albany: State University of New York Press.

Dunleavy, P. and Rhodes, R. (1986) "Government beyond Whitehall," in H. Drucker (ed.) *Developments in British Politics*, London: Macmillan.

du Parcq, L. (1987) "Neighbourhood Services: The Islington Experience," in P. Willmott (ed.) *Local Government Decentralization and Community*. Discussion Paper 18. London: Policy Studies Institute, 25–9.

Green, D. (1987) *The New Right*. London: Wheatsheaf.

Gyford, J. (1984) *Local Politics in Britain*, 2nd edn. London: Croom Helm.

Gyford, J. (1986) "Diversity, Sectionalism and Local Democracy," in Widdicombe Report, *The Conduct of Local Authority Business*, Research Vol. 4, Cmnd. 9801. June. London: HMSO.

Hambleton, R. (1978) *Policy Planning and Local Government*. London: Hutchinson; New York: Allanheld Osmum.

Hambleton, R. (1988a) "The New St. Louis Blues," *The Guardian*, 11 May.

Hambleton, R. (1988b) "Consumerism, Decentralisation and Local Democracy," *Public Administration* 66(Summer): 25–147.

Hambleton, R. (1989a) "Urban Government under Thatcher and Reagan," *Urban Affairs Quarterly* 24(3): 359–88.

Hambleton, R. (1989b) "Boomtown Houston?" *Local Economy* 3(4): 273–8.

Hambleton, R. and Hoggett, P. (1987) "Beyond Bureaucratic Paternalism," in P. Hoggett and R. Hambleton (eds.) *Decentralisation and Democracy: Localising Public Services*. Bristol: School for Advanced Urban Studies, University of Bristol.

Hambleton, R., Hoggett, P. and Tolan, F. (1989) "The Decentralisation of Public Services: A Research Agenda," *Local Government Studies*, January/February: 39–56.

Hill, D. M. (1974) *Democratic Theory and Local Government*. London: George Allen & Unwin.

Hodge, M. (1987) "Central/Local Conflicts: The View from Islington," in P. Hoggett and R. Hambleton (eds.) *Decentralisation and Democracy: Localising Public Services*. Bristol: School for Advanced Urban Studies, University of Bristol.

Hoggett, P. (1987) "A Farewell to Mass Production? Decentralisation as an Emergent Private and Public Sector Paradigm," in P. Hoggett and R. Hambleton (eds.) *Decentralisation and Democracy: Localising Public Services*. Bristol: School for Advanced Urban Studies, University of Bristol.

Hoggett, P. and Hambleton, R. (eds) (1987) *Decentralisation and Democracy: Localising Public Services*. Bristol: School for Advanced Urban Studies, University of Bristol.

Jones, G. and Stewart, J. D. (1983) *The Case for Local Government*. London: George Allen & Unwin.

Lee, E. C. (1985) "Reflections on Local Government and Politics in England and the United States," *Local Government Studies*, September/October: 49–67.

Local Government Training Board (1987) *Getting Closer to the Public*. Luton: LGTB.

Local Government Training Board (1988) *Learning from the Public*. Luton: LGTB.

Lovering, J. (1988) "The Local Economy and Local Economic Strategies," *Policy and Politics* 16(3): 145–57.

Lowe, S. (1986) *Urban Social Movements: The City after Castells*. London: Macmillan.

Magnusson, W. (1986) "Bourgeois Theories of Local Government," *Political Studies* 34: 1–18.

Malpass, P. and Murie, A. (1987) *Housing Policy and Practice*, 2nd edn. London: Macmillan.

Marquand, D. (1989) *The Unprincipled Society*. London: Fontana.

Morphet, J. (1987) "Local Authority Decentralisation: Tower Hamlets Goes All the Way," *Policy and Politics* 15(2): 119–26.

Mulgen, G. (1988) "The power of the weak," *Marxism Today*, December: 24–31.

Packard, V. (1957) *The Hidden Persuaders*. New York: D. McKay.

Peters, T. (1989) *Thriving on Chaos: Handbook for a Management Revolution*. London: Pan.

Peters, T. and Austin, N. (1986) *A Passion for Excellence*. London: Fontana.

Peters, T. J. and Waterman, R. H. (1982) *In Search of Excellence: Lessons from America's Best Run Companies*. New York: Harper & Row.

Peterson, G. E. (1986) "Urban Policy and the Cyclical Behavior of Cities," in G. E. Peterson and C. W. Lewis (eds.) *Reagan and the Cities*. Washington, D.C.: Urban Institute, 11–35.

Pollitt, C. (1988) "Bringing Consumers into Performance Measurement: Concepts, Consequences and Constraints," *Policy and Politics* 16(2): 77–87.

Rhodes, R. A. W. (1987) "Developing the Public Service Orientation," *Local Government Studies*, May/June: 63–73.

Ridley, M. (1988).

Robinson, C. J. (1988) "Economic Development Planning and Policy: Results of a National Survey of Large Cities," *Planning Advisory Service (PAS) Memo*. Chicago: American Planning Association.

Ross, B. H. and Stedman, M. S. (1984) *Urban Politics*, 3rd edn. Itasca, Ill.: Peacock.

Schon, D. A. (1971) *Beyond the Stable State*. London: Temple Smith.

Sharpe, L. J. (1973) "American Democracy Reconsidered. Parts 1 and 2," *British Journal of Political Science* 3: 1–28, 129–67.

Smith, M. (1986) *The Consumer Case for Socialism*, Fabian Tract 513, July. London: Fabian Society.

Smith, M. P. (1987) "Global Capital Restructuring and Local Political Crisis in U.S. Cities," in J. Henderson and M. Castells (eds.) *Global Restructuring and Territorial Development*. London: Sage.

Stewart, J. (1983) *Local Government: The Conditions of Local Choice*. London: George Allen & Unwin.

Stewart, J. and Clarke, M. (1987) "The Public Service Orientation: Issues and Dilemmas", *Public Administration* 65: 161–77.

Stoker, G. (1988) *The Politics of Local Government*. London: Macmillan.

Thomas, Sir R. (1987) *Support Services for Councillors*. Report by the Association of Councillors, 2nd edn. Croydon: Charles Knight.

Waste, R. J. (1987) *Power and Pluralism in American Cities*. New York: Greenwood Press.

Widdicombe Report (1986) *The Conduct of Local Authority Business*. Report of Committee of Inquiry on the conduct of local authority business (Chairman: David Widdicombe, QC). Cmnd. 9797. London: HMSO.

Yates, D. (1973) *Neighborhood Democracy: The Politics and Impacts of Decentralization*. Lexington, Mass.: Lexington Books.

Young, K. (1986) "The Justification of Local Government," in M. Goldsmith (ed.) *Essays on the Future of Local Government*. Wakefield: West Yorkshire Metropolitan Council.

Young, K. and Mason, C. (eds.) (1983) *Urban Economic Development: New Roles and Relationships*. London: Macmillan.

SASKIA SASSEN

"Place and Production in the Global Economy"

from *Cities in a World Economy* (1994)

Editors' introduction   One of the most important phenomena of the last decades of the twentieth century is the rise of an integrated world economy. Local economies are increasingly integrated into a single world economic system. Capital flows freely across national borders. Distance has been neutralized through telecommunications and computer technologies that allow for instantaneous transmission of information.

The emergence of a truly global economy has tremendous implications for firms and national economies, immigration, the nature of work and the whole social and economic fabric of society. As was pointed out in the reading by Saskia Sassen, "A New Geography of Centers and Margins" (p. 70), the new global economy also has profound implications for cities. In the following selection Sassen elaborates on place and production in the global economy.

Some people in some cities benefit tremendously from the emerging economic order. Some Third-World cities are experiencing a boom in manufacturing – bringing jobs, higher wages for some workers, and wealth and power to middle- and upper-class property owners reminiscent of the boom for Manchester's bourgeoisie during the Industrial Revolution 150 years earlier (p. 47). Managerial elites – experts in banking, finance, accounting, law, and other specialties in New York, London, Tokyo, and other global cities – are becoming wealthier and more powerful. But global economic changes are creating new problems for many people in many cities.

Just as the Industrial Revolution did in the nineteenth century, the emergence of an information-based global economy in the twentieth century is producing extremes of inequality. Sassen extends her argument about central and peripheral areas of the world economy and rich and poor cities. She argues that large concentrations of very-low-income Third-World immigrants now live only blocks away from the offices of wealthy business elites in global cities like New York and London. These extreme social divisions also exist in Third-World cities. There are wealthy bankers and lawyers in São Paolo, Brazil, within a stone's throw from the teeming favelas of the urban poor.

As high-powered command and information functions grow, Saskia Sassen argues that the very poor population of cities does not shrink: the new global economy requires more low-paid janitors and food service workers. Women in particular are entering the low-paid labor force of global cities in large numbers in roles such as maids, waitresses, domestics, and electronics assembly workers.

Immigrants in large cities in the developed world often participate in informal economies similar to the economies of their countries of origin. In some inner-city ethnic neighborhoods goods are bought and sold on the street, work may be performed below minimum wage, income is not reported to tax or other authorities, and there is little heed to occupational health and safety, environmental, consumer, or other laws.

Note the similarity between Engels's description of the juxtaposition of extremes of wealth and poverty in the emerging industrial city of Manchester in the mid-nineteenth century (p. 47) and Sassen's description of inequality in the emerging global cities of today.

Compare Sassen's findings to Manuel Castells and Peter Hall's work on technopoles (p. 476). Contrast Castells's view on the future role of place-boundedness in the global information economy (p. 494) with Sassen's theories.

In addition to Sassen's other writings cited in the introduction to "A New Geography of Centers and Margins" in Part 1 (p. 70), other books on global economic restructuring and cities include Jeff Henderson and Manuel Castells (eds.), *Global Restructuring and Territorial Development* (London: Sage, 1987), R. V. Knight and G. Gappert (eds.), *Cities in a Global Society*, vol. 35, *Urban Affairs Annual Reviews* (Newbury Park, Calif.: Sage, 1989), Ann Markusen, Amy Glasmeir, and Peter Hall, *High Tech America: The What, How, Where and Why of the Sunrise Industries* (London and Boston: Allen & Unwin, 1986), Robert Reich, *The Work of Nations: Preparing Ourselves for Twenty-first Century Capitalism* (New York: Knopf, 1989), and Hank Savitch, *Post-industrial Cities* (Princeton, N.J.: Princeton University Press, 1988).

For a study of the dual-city phenomenon see Manuel Castells and John Mollenkopf, *Dual City: Restructuring New York* (New York: Russell Sage Foundation, 1991). On the informal economy see Alejandro Portes, Manuel Castells, and L. Benton (eds.), *The Informal Economy: Studies in Advanced and Less Developed Countries* (Baltimore: Johns Hopkins University Press, 1989).

SASKIA SASSEN, "Place and Production in the Global Economy"

from *Cities in a World Economy* (1994)

As the end of the twentieth century approaches, massive developments in telecommunications and the ascendance of information industries have led analysts and politicians to proclaim the end of cities. Cities, they tell us, should now be obsolete as economic entities. With large-scale relocations of offices and factories to less congested and lower cost areas than central cities, the computerized workplace can be located anywhere: in a clerical "factory" in the Bahamas or in a home in the suburbs. The growth of information industries has made it possible for outputs to be transmitted around the globe instantaneously. And the globalization of economic activity suggests that place – particularly the type of place represented by cities – no longer matters.

This is but a partial account, however. These trends are indeed all taking place, but they represent only half of what is happening. Alongside the well-documented spatial dispersal of economic activities, new forms of territorial centralization of top-level management and control operations have appeared. National and global markets, as well as globally integrated operations, require central places where the work of globalization gets done. Furthermore, information industries require a vast physical infrastructure containing strategic nodes with a hyperconcentration of facilities. Finally, even the most advanced information industries have a production process.

Once this process is brought into the analysis, funny things happen; secretaries are part of it, and so are the cleaners of the buildings where the professionals do their work. An economic configuration very different from that suggested by the concept of *information economy* emerges, whereby we recover the material conditions, production sites, and placeboundedness that are also part of globalization and the information economy. A detailed examination of the activities, firms, markets, and physical infrastructure that are involved in globalization and concentrated in cities allows us to see the actual role played by cities in a global economy. Thus when telecommunications were introduced on a large scale in all advanced industries in the 1980s, we saw the central business districts of the leading cities and international business centers of the world – New York, Los Angeles, London, Tokyo, Frankfurt, São Paulo, Hong Kong, and Sydney, among others – reach their highest densities ever. This explosion in the numbers of firms locating in the downtowns of major cities during that decade goes against what should have been expected according to models emphasizing territorial dispersal; this is especially true given the high cost of locating in a major downtown area.

If telecommunications has not made cities obsolete, has it at least altered the economic function of cities in a global economy? And if this is so, what does it tell us about the importance of place, of the locale, in an era dominated by the imagery and the language of economic globalization and information flows? Is there a new and strategic role for major cities, a role linked to the formation of a truly global economic system, a role not sufficiently recognized by analysts and policymakers? And could it be that the reason this new and strategic role has not been sufficiently recognized is that economic globalization – what it actually takes to implement global markets and processes – is misunderstood?

The notion of a global economy has become deeply entrenched in political and media circles all over the world. Yet its dominant images – the instantaneous transmission of money around the globe, the information economy, the neutralization of distance through *telematics* – are partial and hence profoundly inadequate representations of what globalization and the rise of information economies actually entail for cities. Missing from this abstract model are the actual material processes, activities, and infrastructures that are central to the implementation of globalization. Both overlooking the spatial dimension of economic globalization and over-emphasizing the information dimensions have served to distort the role played by major cities

in the current phase of economic globalization.

The last 20 years have seen pronounced changes in the geography, composition, and institutional framework of economic globalization. A world economy has been in existence for several centuries, but it has been reconstituted repeatedly over time. A key starting point ... is the fact that, in each historical period, the world economy has consisted of a distinct combination of geographic areas, industries, and institutional arrangements. One of the important changes over the last 20 years has been the increase in the mobility of capital at both the national and especially the transnational level. The transnational mobility of capital brings about specific forms of articulation among different geographic areas and transformations in the role played by these areas in the world economy. This trend in turn produces several types of locations for international transactions, the most familiar of which are *export processing zones* and *offshore banking centers*. One question for us, then, is the extent to which major cities are yet another type of location for international transactions, though clearly one at a very high level of complexity.

Increased capital mobility does not only bring about changes in the geographic organization of manufacturing production and in the network of financial markets. Increased capital mobility also generates a demand for types of production needed to ensure the management, control, and servicing of this new organization of manufacturing and finance. These new types of production range from the development of telecommunications to specialized services that are key inputs for the management of a global network of factories, offices, and financial markets. The mobility of capital also includes the production of a broad array of innovations in these sectors. These types of production have their own locational patterns; they tend toward high levels of agglomeration. We will want to ask whether a focus on the *production* of these service inputs illuminates the question of place in processes of economic globalization, particularly the kind of place represented by cities.

Specialized services for firms and financial transactions, as well as the complex markets both entail, are a layer of activity that has been central to the organization of major global processes in the 1980s. To what extent is it useful to think in terms of the broader category of cities as key locations for such activities – in addition to the more narrowly defined locations represented by headquarters of transnational corporations or offshore banking centers – to further our understanding of major aspects of the organization and management of the world economy?

Much of the scholarly literature on cities has focused on internal aspects of the urban social, economic, and political systems, and it has considered cities to be part of national urban systems. International aspects typically have been considered the preserve of nation-states, not of cities. The literature on international economic activities, moreover, has traditionally focused on the activities of multinational corporations and banks and has seen the key to globalization in the power of multinational firms. Again, this conceptualization has the effect of leaving no room for a possible role by cities.

Including cities in the analysis adds two important dimensions to the internationalization. First, it breaks down the nation-state into a variety of components that may be significant in understanding international economic activity. Second, it displaces the focus from the power of large corporations over governments and economies to the range of activities and organizational implementation and maintenance of a global network of factories, service operations, and markets: these are all processes only partly encompassed by the activities of transnational corporations and banks. Third, it contributes to a focus on place and on the urban social and political order associated with these activities. Processes of economic globalization are thereby reconstituted as concrete production complexes situated in specific places containing a multiplicity of activities and interests, many unconnected to global processes. Focusing on cities allows us to specify a geography of strategic places on a global scale, as well as the microgeographies and politics unfolding within these places.

A central thesis organizing this book [*Cities in a World Economy*] is that the transformation during the last two decades in the composition of the world economy accompanying the shift to services and finance brings about a renewed importance of major cities as sites for certain types of activities and functions. In the current phase of the world economy, it is precisely the combination of the global dispersal of economic activities *and* global integration – under conditions of continued concentration of economic ownership and control – that has contributed to a strategic role for certain major cities that I call *global cities*. Some have been centers for world trade and banking for centuries, but beyond these long-standing functions, today's global cities are (1) command points in the organization of the world economy; (2) key locations and marketplaces for the leading industries of the current period, which are finance and specialized services for firms; and (3) major sites of production for these industries, including the production of innovations. Several cities also fulfill equivalent functions on the smaller geographic scales of both trans- and subnational regions.

Alongside these new global and regional hierarchies of cities is a vast territory that has become increasingly peripheral, increasingly excluded from the major economic processes that fuel economic growth in the new global economy. A multiplicity of formerly important manufacturing centers and port cities have lost functions and are in decline, not only in the less developed countries but also in the most advanced economies. This is yet another meaning of economic globalization. We can think of these developments as constituting new geographies of centrality (that cut across the old divide of poor/rich countries) and of marginality that have become increasingly evident in the less developed world and in highly developed countries as well.

The most powerful of these new geographies of centrality binds the major international financial and business centers: New York, London, Tokyo, Paris, Frankfurt, Zurich, Amsterdam, Sydney, Hong Kong, among others. But this geography now also includes cities such as São Paulo and Mexico City. The intensity of transactions among these cities, particularly through the financial markets, flows of services, and investment have increased sharply, and so have the orders of magnitude involved. At the same time, there has been a sharpening inequality in the concentration of strategic resources and activities between each of these cities and others in the same country. For instance, Paris now concentrates a larger share of leading economic sectors and wealth in France than it did 20 years ago, whereas Marseilles, once a major economic center, has lost its share and is suffering severe decline. Some national capitals, for example, have lost central economic functions and power to the new global cities, which have taken over some of the coordination functions, markets, and production processes once concentrated in national capitals or in major regional centers. São Paulo has gained immense strength as a business and financial center in Brazil over Rio de Janeiro – once the capital and most important city in the country – and over the once powerful axis represented by Rio and Brasilia, the current capital. This is one of the meanings, or consequences, of the formation of a globally integrated economic system.

What is the impact of this type of economic growth on the broader social and economic order of these cities? A vast literature on the impact of a dynamic, high-growth manufacturing sector in highly developed countries shows that it raises wages, reduces economic inequality, and contributes to the formation of a middle class. There is much less literature on the impact on the service economy, especially the rapidly growing specialized services.

Specialized services, which have become a key component of all developed economies, are not usually analyzed in terms of a production or work process. Such services are usually seen as a type of output – that is, high-level technical expertise. Thus insufficient attention has been paid to the actual array of jobs, from high paying to low paying, involved in the production of these services. A focus on production displaces the emphasis from expertise to work. Services need to be produced, and the buildings that hold the workers need to be built and cleaned. The rapid growth of the financial industry and of highly specialized services generates not only high-level technical and administrative jobs but also low-wage unskilled jobs.

Together with the new interurban inequalities mentioned above, we are also seeing new economic inequalities within cities, especially within global cities and their regional counterparts.

The new urban economy is in many ways highly problematical. This is perhaps particularly evident in global cities and their regional counterparts. The new growth sectors of specialized services and finance contain capabilities for profit making that are vastly superior to those of more traditional economic sectors. The latter are essential to the operation of the urban economy and the daily needs of residents, but their survival is threatened in a situation where finance and specialized services can earn superprofits. This sharp polarization in the profit-making capabilities of different sectors of the economy has always existed. But what we see happening today takes place on a higher order of magnitude, and it is engendering massive distortions in the operations of various markets, from housing to labor. We can see this effect, for example, in the unusually sharp increase in the beginning salaries of MBAs and in the precipitous fall in the wages of low-skilled manual workers and clerical workers.

We can see the same effect in the retreat of many real estate developers from the low- and medium-income housing market who are attracted to the rapidly expanding housing demand by the new highly paid professionals and the possibility for vast overpricing of this housing supply.

The rapid development of an international property market has made this disparity even worse. It means that real estate prices at the center of New York City are more connected to the overall real estate market in London or Frankfurt than to the overall real estate market in the city. Powerful institutional investors from Japan, for instance, find it profitable to buy and sell property in Manhattan or central London. They force prices up because of the competition and raise them even further to sell at a profit. How can a small commercial operation in New York compete with such investors and the prices they can command?

The high profit-making capability of the new growth sectors rests partly on speculative activity. The extent of this dependence on speculation can be seen in the crisis of the 1990s that followed the unusually high profits in finance and real estate in the 1980s. The real estate and financial crisis, however, seems to have left the basic dynamic of the sector untouched. The crisis can thus be seen as an adjustment to more reasonable (that is, less speculative) profit levels. The overall dynamic of polarization in profit levels in the urban economy remains in place, as do the distortions in many markets.

The typical informed view of the global economy, cities, and the new growth sectors does not incorporate these global dimensions. Elsewhere I have argued that we could think of the dominant narrative or mainstream account of economic globalization as a narrative of eviction. In the dominant account the key concepts of globalization, information economy, and telematics all suggest that place no longer matters and that the only type of worker that matters is the highly educated professional. This account favors the capability for global transmission over the concentrations of established infrastructure that make transmission possible; favors information outputs over the workers producing those outputs, from specialists to secretaries; and favors the new transnational corporate culture over the multiplicity of cultural environments, including reterritorialized immigrant cultures within which many of the "other" jobs of the global information economy take place. In brief, the dominant narrative concerns itself with the upper circuits of capital, not the lower ones.

This narrow focus has the effect of excluding from the account the place-boundedness of significant components of the global information economy; it thereby also excludes a whole array of activities and types of workers from the story of globalization that are as vital to it as international finance and global telecommunications are. By failing to include these activities and workers, it ignores the variety of cultural contexts within which they exist, a diversity as present in processes of globalization as is the new international corporate culture. When we focus on place and production, we can see that globalization is a process involving not only the corporate economy and the new transnational corporate culture but also, for example, the immigrant economies and work cultures evident in our large cities.

The new empirical trends and the new theoretical developments have made cities prominent once again in most of the social sciences. Cities have reemerged not only as objects of study but also as strategic sites for the theorization of a broad array of social, economic, and political processes central to the current era: economic globalization and international migration; the emergence of specialized services and finance as the leading growth sector in advanced economies; and new types of inequality. In this context, it is worth noting that we are also seeing the beginning of a repositioning of cities in policy arenas. Two instances in particular stand out. One is the recent programmatic effort at the World Bank to produce analyses that show how central urban economic productivity is to macroeconomic performance. The other is the explicit competition among major cities to gain access to increasingly global markets for resources and activities ranging from foreign investment, headquarters, and international institutions to tourism and conventions.

[. . .]

JOHN KASARDA

"The Jobs–Skills Mismatch"

New Perspectives Quarterly (1990)

Editors' introduction   The global restructuring of the world economy and the changing economy of world cities Saskia Sassen describes (p. 300) has powerful consequences for the economy of cities. New York, London, Tokyo and other global cities are emerging as new command centers for the world economy. Information-based and high-tech postindustrial service-sector jobs increasingly dominate the economies of the most developed cities of the world. And manufacturing jobs are shifting increasingly to cities in developing countries.

University of North Carolina sociology professor John Kasarda has studied how these economic changes affect the job prospects of people in cities of the developed world. William Julius Wilson (p. 226) draws heavily on Kasarda's analysis in understanding the new urban underclass and developing policy options for them.

In the following selection Kasarda documents the dramatic shift in manufacturing jobs from the U.S. and Western Europe to Third-World export-processing zones. Increasingly, Kasarda notes, multinational manufacturers headquartered in the developed world subcontract out the entire production process to the Third World – from tennis balls to fork-lift trucks, numerically controlled lathes and key telephone systems. Jobs requiring less than a high school degree are disappearing from many cities in the developed world. New York City lost half a million such jobs between 1970 and 1986.

In contrast, Kasarda argues, U.S. and Western European cities are increasingly hubs in a network of governmental, industrial, commercial, and cultural organizations. These roles require top managers with advanced schooling and specialized skills. Even mid- and lower-level professionals in accounting, research and development, and management need college educations.

But are the skills of the urban workforce keeping up with the changing needs? Kasarda says not, and particularly not for minority youth. Just as urban economies in the developed world require more educated workers as many as half of the African-American youth drop out of high school before graduation.

Kasarda's research feeds into wider academic and policy debates about the nature of urban economies, the changing structure of urban workforces, and appropriate government strategies. Not everyone agrees with Kasarda that the rise of a postindustrial service sector will lead to a loss of low-skilled jobs. Saskia Sassen (p. 300) argues that global cities require large numbers of low-skilled blue-collar janitors, fast food servers and domestics. Others argue that the new economy can absorb many low-skilled workers – even those without high school degrees – as pink-collar file clerks, data entry people, and photocopy machine operators.

Kasarda takes a distinct place in policy debates as well. Conservative Charles Murray (p. 233) would eliminate government social programs to force marginal workers to work in unpleasant, low-wage jobs whereas William Julius Wilson argues for universal full employment programs to provide meaningful work even for the low skilled (p. 226). Kasarda favors increased emphasis on education – including investment in college and professional education. He believes there is a "supply side" or "skills side" effect: that a country which invests in educating its workers will compete more effectively in the global economy. If potential drop-outs are kept in school and educated to the level the economy requires they will not have to be forced to accept dead-end low-wage jobs or supported by government full employment programs.

Professor Kasarda's other writings related to urbanization and the changing workforce include: *Contemporary Urban Ecology*, with Brian J. L. Berry (New York: Macmillan, 1977); *The Metropolitan Era*, co-edited with Mattei Dogan, of which volume 1 is titled *A World of Giant Cities* and volume 2 *Mega Cities* (Newbury Park, Calif.: Sage, 1988); *Job Earnings and Employment Growth Policies in the U.S.* (editor) (Norwell, Mass.: Kluwer Academic Publishers, 1990); and *Third World Cities: Problems, Policies, and Prospects* (co-edited with Allan Parnell) (Newbury Park, Calif.: Sage, 1993).

More information on the decline of low-skilled manufacturing jobs is to be found in Stephen Cohen and John Zysman, *Manufacturing Matters: The Myth of the Post-industrial Economy* (New York: Basic Books, 1987). See also Chris Hasluck, *Urban Unemployed* (Harlow: Longman, 1987) for a description of similar trends in the U.K. Works which explore the growth sectors in developed countries include Orio Giarini, *The Emerging Service Economy* (Oxford and New York: Pergamon Press, 1987), Robert Reich, *The Work of Nations: Preparing Ourselves for Twenty-first Century Capitalism* (New York: Knopf, 1991), and Ann Markusen, Amy Glasmeir, and Peter Hall, *High Tech America: The What, How, Where and Why of the Sunrise Industries* (London and Boston: Allen & Unwin, 1986).

JOHN KASARDA, "The Jobs–Skills Mismatch"

New Perspectives Quarterly (1990)

The role of industrial cities in North America and Western Europe is being radically transformed by two trends in global economic restructuring: the growth of the service economy and the shift of production toward the less-developed countries. These trends are increasing the demand for higher skills among the labor force and causing intractably high rates of urban unemployment among less-skilled workers.

Between 1965 and 1987, the proportion of Gross Domestic Product accounted for by manufacturing in the US declined from 28 percent to 20 percent, while the proportion of the GDP accounted for by services rose from 57 percent to 68 percent.

Over the same period, manufacturing in West Germany fell from 40 percent of the GDP to 33 percent, while services rose from 43 percent to 60 percent. Manufacturing shrunk from over one-third of the GDP to one-fourth in the United Kingdom while services expanded to 60 percent of the economy.

This shifting composition of economic activity translates directly into employment changes. From 1979 through 1986, the European Community lost manufacturing jobs at the rate of 2.2 percent per year. At the same time, service employment rose at the rate of 1.6 percent per year. Manufacturing job losses in the United Kingdom averaged 4.5 percent per year during this time period while those in the U.S. and West

Germany hovered around 1 percent per year.

In the past few years of this period, manufacturing employment losses have decelerated and service sector employment accelerated. The major exception to the pattern of manufacturing job loss was Japan, with annual gains of 1.1 percent through the early and mid-1980s.

By 1985, US steel industry employment was 46 percent of what it was a decade earlier. In Germany it was two-thirds of what it had been in 1974 and in the UK less than one-third.

As manufacturing jobs disappeared in Europe and North America, employment in Third World export-processing zones – where production is intended for immediate export – increased from approximately 500,000 in 1975 to almost 1.3 million in 1986. And much more export production is located outside these zones.

Increasingly, multinational manufacturers headquartered in the developed world are subcontracting out the entire production process to the Third World – from tennis balls to fork-lift trucks, numerically controlled lathes and key telephone systems. Two of the top ten exporters of telecommunication equipment are in the Third World.

SKYSCRAPERS VS. SMOKESTACKS

The social effects of the trend towards increased service employment and decreased manufacturing are most evident in the metropolitan areas, where 80.3 percent of Americans, 92.5 percent of Britons and 87.3 percent of Germans reside. Cities are increasingly shedding their function of production and becoming only centers of coordination and control. The production plant is no longer necessarily a few miles from company headquarters in a nearby industrial district; it may be on the next continent.

If US and Western European cities are to have a significant role in the global economy it will not be as production sites, but as hubs in a network of governmental, industrial, commercial and cultural organizations. They will house the headquarters of international organizations, banks and financial firms as well as the administrative headquarters of producer-service firms and Third World manufacturers.

This new urban role will require a new set of skills. The higher-level administrative functions which at least some U.S. and Western European cities could fulfill require advanced schooling and specialized skills. Even below the professional level accounting, management and R and D require relatively high levels of education. Increasingly employers in these sectors require four-year college degrees for entry-level positions. Yet at a time when increasing levels of education by workers in OECD cities are required to match emerging high-skill jobs, their educational systems seem to be faltering, particularly in the U.S. Few OECD countries are increasing university enrollments at a significant pace. In the U.S. secondary schools are not doing an adequate job at retaining students or educating the ones that remain.

Minorities who are beginning to dominate the residential bases of major U.S. cities are experiencing high-school drop-out rates in excess of 33 percent.

The undereducation problem is particularly acute among blacks in urban America and among new immigrants, particularly with respect to language skills.

The changing skill requirements coupled with the ineffectiveness of educational systems have resulted in the marginalization of these groups. Increasingly, underclass blacks and Hispanic immigrants in the U.S., and the ex-colonials, Africans and Mediterranean immigrants in Europe, are not integrated into the social or economic mainstream. Europe is coming to resemble America in the numbers of immigrants that now make up its population. In Frankfurt, for example, more than 20 percent of the residents are foreign born, mostly Turks and more recently Africans with limited educations.

NO MOBILITY WITHOUT SKILLS

The functional transformation of cities has radically affected the distribution of job opportunities based on levels of education The data are already very clear for U.S. cities. Available evidence suggests that Western Europe is following the same patterns as the U.S. with a 10- to 15-year lag.

All major cities had consistent employment losses in industries with the lowest skill requirements. By far the heaviest job losses occurred after 1970 when growth in urban underclass populations accelerated in the American industrial North.

New York City, for instance, lost only 9,000 jobs between 1953 and 1970 in those industries in which the educational level of the average jobholder was less than high-school completion. But it lost more than half a million jobs in these industries between 1970 and 1986. Philadelphia, Baltimore and St. Louis have also lost substantial numbers of jobs since 1970 in industries typically requiring less than college education. The four cities that accounted for the lion's share of the increase in concentrated poverty populations during the 1970s – New York, Chicago, Philadelphia and Detroit – also experienced the lion's share of declines in jobs held by high-school drop-outs and by those with only a high-school degree. Particularly affected were those large numbers of urban blacks who had not completed high school, especially younger ones. For city black youth school drop-out rates ranged from 30 to 50 percent during the 1970s and early 1980s.

The educational disparities between black residents and skill levels needed for jobs in America's urban areas are dramatic. Despite their educational gains black urban labor remains highly concentrated in the less-than-high-school education category where city employment has most rapidly declined since 1970. Blacks are greatly underrepresented in the college-graduate categories where urban employment is rapidly rising. The structural mismatch between city jobs and the low level of education attained by black labor helps explain why policies based primarily on urban economic development have had limited success in reducing urban black joblessness. The fact is that most blacks simply lack the education to participate in the new growth sectors of the urban economy. While newly created urban jobs taken by college graduates have skyrocketed, the percentage of urban black males who have completed college remains extremely small. For those who are out of work the disparity at the higher-education end is even greater. Decline in

manufacturing jobs is by no means the only pertinent indicator of losses in traditional blue-collar employment but it corresponds to other indicators of the capacity of cities to sustain large numbers of residents with limited educational attainment. Further, between 1970 and 1980 there were dramatic drops across all cities in the percentage of poorly educated black males who worked full time and a leap in the percentage not working at all. By 1980 fewer than half of the out-of-school black males in each city had full-time jobs. Conversely, the percentage not working at all rose in Baltimore from 24.7 to 45.0; in New York from 28.2 to 43.9; in Philadelphia from 26.7 to 50.6; in St. Louis from 31.8 to 48.4; and in Washington D.C. from 23.4 to 42.1.

Clearly the loss of low-education-requisite jobs in traditional city industries accelerated black joblessness.

In sum, education–job opportunity mismatches are particularly acute in those cities where declines in traditional blue-collar industries and the growth of information-processing industries have been most substantial since 1970.

So different are the skills used and the education required in these growing, as opposed to declining, urban industrial sectors that adaptation by the poorly educated is exceedingly difficult. This difficulty is concretely represented in the exceptionally high jobless rates of those central-city residents who have not completed high school regardless of race and rapid rises since 1970 in jobless rates of residents who are poorly educated even though they may have obtained a high-school diploma.

SOCIAL DISTRESS

U.S., U.K. and West German cities are undergoing functional transformations from being centers of goods processing to centers of information processing. The data for the U.S. show that the education levels associated with urban jobs have risen faster than that of the labor pool – particularly the minority labor pool – to be found in those cities. The result is a labor–job mismatch which stymies social progress. The situation in the U.K. and Germany appears to be analogous. The national and urban economies are losing manufacturing jobs while the service sector takes on new importance. Many Europeans, both native and immigrant, are poorly prepared educationally for the new roles cities can play. Despite a diversity of ethnic groups the minority populations are on the whole less well prepared. This relative lack of education is reflected in higher unemployment rates. At the same time the minority portion of the work force is growing.

These minority populations in the U.S. and Europe were attracted by the economic opportunities cities had to offer. A dynamic of family reunification and chain migration was set in motion that resulted in increasing minority populations even after the opportunities had dwindled. The result has been high unemployment and social distress in our urban centers.

[*Note*: The balance of this article is in the form of questions and answers. NPQ indicates a question by *New Perspectives Quarterly*, the journal in which this article originally appeared]:

NPQ: A recent report issued by former Secretary of Labor Ray Marshall and former U.S. Trade Representative Bill Brock suggests that our low-achieving students are just what a low-wage economy demands. They say the U.S. employs one and a half times as many janitors, nearly twice as many secretaries, and five times as many clerks as all the lawyers, accountants, investment bankers, stockbrokers and computer programmers combined. If that is the case is there really a jobs–skills mismatch?

John D. Kasarda: The basic fact is that there is an overall decline of all types of blue-collar jobs in American cities. This is certainly true of manufacturing. But even within the growing service sector the occupational mix is shifting away from blue-collar jobs such as in food and drink establishments to white-collar information-processing jobs which require more than a high-school education. Typically, a high-school degree is no longer considered training enough to be an effective secretary.

Within the manufacturing sector itself there is a sharp decline in production workers and an increase in administrative employees.

In 1988 there were some 80 million people working in all service-producing industries. Eight million of those jobs were executive and managerial; almost 12 million were professional specialty jobs such as computer operators or engineers; another 3 million were health and science technicians of some sort; almost 11 million were in marketing and sales; almost 18 million were in administrative support occupations – supervisors, stenographers, managers, and secretaries. All told there were some 52 million jobs each requiring a higher-education component.

By contrast only 17 million low-skill jobs such as nurses, aides or janitors, or hamburger flippers exist in the American economy.

According to the Bureau of Labor Statistics 90 percent of job growth by the year 2000 will be in the service-producing sector with approximately two-thirds of that growth in higher-education white-collar occupations. Administrative support services alone are expected to add nearly 20 million jobs. Moreover, in this new advanced industrial era interpersonal skills are as important as technical skills in obtaining and holding onto a job. If lack of technical skills traps urban youngsters either in the multi-problem environment of the underclass or in stagnant or declining working-poor jobs they are unlikely to be able to improve those interpersonal skills either.

NPQ: It has always been the role of the schools to provide the technical skills. But are they equipped and should they be expected to provide interpersonal skills? Isn't that the role of the parents?

Kasarda: Yes. The need to forge interpersonal skills particularly at the growing margins of the mainstream is another problem dumped on the schools. It is an unreasonable burden for them, reflecting the basic reality that what we face in this country is not an education crisis but a social crisis. All the failures of the family and community that other primary groups once took care of – mom and dad, relatives, close friends, neighbors – are being dumped on the public schools. In many cases a youngster reaching the first grade is already a basket case. The testimony of inner-city teachers on this subject is instructive: "I am a professional; I can handle two or three disruptive children but I cannot handle five or six. Then the other 20 suffer." Needless to add, then no one gets the technical skills that the school is supposed to provide.

NPQ: What are the consequences of our educational system not producing enough skilled workers?

Kasarda: If we produce people who can do little more than wash cars and press cash register buttons at McDonald's it will be very difficult to compete in the international arena. With low skills come low wages. But no matter how low, a livable wage in America can't compete with the pittances that hundreds of millions will work for in the desperate Third World.

America can't compete on wages so it has to compete on quality. And that requires a highly skilled work force.

NPQ: Will such a highly skilled work force actually drive a higher-wage, higher-value-added economy?

Kasarda: Yes, I do believe there is a supply-side or skill-side effect. The greater the skills workers have, the greater the value they can add to production. The history of economic growth is that skills are always utilized to improve a product's quality or create something new.

The pool of scientific skills after all is what gave birth to the semiconductor industry.

MIKE SAVAGE and ALAN WARDE

"Cities and Uneven Economic Development"

from *Urban Sociology, Capitalism, and Modernity* (1993)

Editors' introduction   As the global economy becomes more and more interconnected, the economic functions of different cities in the world become ever more dramatically different from each other. Some Third-World cities like Timbuktu have economies based on trade or primitive manufacturing, operating as they have for centuries. Other Third-World cities like Bangkok, Thailand, have booming economies manufacturing computers, phone systems, televisions and fax machines. Some cities in the developed world like New York and London have emerged as economically potent centers for manipulation of information, technological innovation, and global financial command functions while once prosperous cities in England's Midlands and North and the U.S. Midwest are in steep economic decline.

What explains this "uneven" economic development of cities? This question has intrigued many economists, geographers, and sociologists. Can world cities be classified into clearly distinct *types* based on their economic function? Is there a regular progression from preindustrial to postindustrial status which cities move through over time? Are there structural aspects of advanced capitalism which explain what is occurring? In the following section, sociologists Mike Savage and Alan Warde review the literature on uneven economic development.

There have been many attempts to classify cities into categories based on their economic function. The authors of this selection identify five types – Third-World cities, global cities, older industrial cities, new industrial districts, and cities in socialist countries. While such broad categories may be helpful, the authors are quick to note that such a topology is neither exhaustive nor are its categories mutually exclusive. There are many kinds of "Third-World cities." São Paulo, Brazil, is very different from Kathmandu, Nepal. In Glasgow, Scotland, old dockyard activity remains, but billions of dollars of new high-tech investment has come to "Silicon Glen" on the city's outskirts. Among urbanists who seek to classify cities on the basis of their economic function there are continuing debates about what the categories should be. Should Glasgow be considered an older industrial city, a new industrial district or what? Because cities' economies are so diverse, many urbanists do not think that meaningful systems to classify cities based on their economic functions can be developed at all.

Another controversial approach is to look at the evolution of cities' economies through time. We know from V. Gordon Childe (p. 22) that Ur and other Mesopotamian cities had revolutionized the economies of their regions by 3500 B.C.E., from Pirenne (p. 38) that by the eleventh century some medieval European cities had evolved elaborate preindustrial economies based on the revival of trade, from Engels (p. 47) that by the mid-nineteenth century Manchester had become an industrial city with enormous disparities of wealth, and from Saskia Sassen (p. 70) that some global cities now base their economies on managing information and global financial services. Savage and Warde discuss theorists who have looked carefully at the stages in the evolution (perhaps devolution) of industrial cities. For example, Peter Hall – whose writings on urban theory and high-tech cities appear elsewhere in this anthology (pp. 383, 476) – describes a series of stages through which declining U.S. industrial cities appear to move. Among evolutionary theorists there is no firm agreement on what the "stages" of evolution are. For example, contrast Savage and Warde's description of an eleven-thousand-year stage of "primordial urbanization" before 4000 B.C.E., followed by an epoch of preindustrial "definitive urbanization" which lasted until 1700 C.E., and a second epoch of industrial "definitive urbanization" after 1700 with evolutionary typologies developed by V. Gordon Childe (pp. 22, 361) or Patrick Geddes (p. 361).

A third approach to the question of "uneven economic development" stresses the international division of labor – particularly the movement of manufacturing from developed countries to the Third World. Good descriptive work has been done on changes at the local level both in cities in developed countries which are exporting their manufacturing bases and in Third-World countries where the manufacturing is going. Theorists have used this empirical research to build theory as to why the changes are occurring.

One of the most important wellsprings of theory about the changing economy of cities is Marxist theory. As Peter Hall describes in his study of "The City of Theory" (p. 383), Marxist and neo-Marxist urban theory experienced a resurgence during the 1970s and 1980s. British geographer David Harvey applies Marxist theory to explain the current evolution of city economies. And other theorists in the U.K., U.S., continental Europe and elsewhere are employing Marxist insights to uneven development today.

Other writings on uneven economic development include Folker Froebel, Jürgen Heinrichs and Otto Kreye, *The New International Division of Labor: Structural Unemployment in Industrialized Countries and Industrialization in Developing Countries* (Cambridge: Cambridge University Press, 1980), David Harvey, *The Urbanization of Capital* (Oxford: Basil Blackwell, 1985), Doreen Massey, *Spatial Divisions of Labor* (London: Macmillan, 1984) and Michael Smith and Joe Feagin, *The Capitalist City: Global Restructuring and Territorial Development* (London: Sage, 1987). A recent anthology of writings on "post-Fordism" is Ash Amin (ed.), *Post-Fordism: A Reader* (Oxford: Basil Blackwell, 1995).

MIKE SAVAGE and ALAN WARDE, "Cities and Uneven Economic Development"

from *Urban Sociology, Capitalism, and Modernity* (1993)

... There is no consensus as to how capitalism operates as an economic system, and in particular how it operates over space, between places, and hence how it affects urban development. This chapter clarifies differing views of the relationship between economic systems and urban development, in order to assess their value in placing cities in their context. It is structured around the way different writers emphasize the temporal or spatial dimensions of urban differentiation and uneven spatial development.

In Section 3.1 we consider approaches, largely non-Marxist, which adopt a temporal focus, where cities are related to particular stages of historical development, but are rarely analysed in terms of their spatial relation to each other. The principal axiom is that cities evolve in line with broader economic development. This evolutionary perspective is typical of the early urban economists, such as Alfred Weber, Jane Jacobs, Peter Hall and others. The problem with such accounts is that they tend to assume that there is only one type of urban development, which all cities from whatever culture follow, and hence they ignore the diversity and specificity of cities.

This leads to the work of urban geographers who have concentrated their research on the analysis of urban differentiation. Section 3.2 examines Marxist theories of uneven development whose focus is a spatial one, where cities are seen as occupying specific places within a worldwide capitalist economic system. Within this broad perspective we evaluate four rather different ways in which such differentiation is explained. The first version is the "New International Division of Labour Theory", which can be seen as the most important contemporary application of Wallerstein's "World Systems Theory". One of the problems with world systems theory is its ahistorical analysis, its inattention to the significance of social conflict on uneven development, and its tendency to ignore dynamic and changing forms of uneven development. Then we consider another Marxist account, that associated with the early work of David Harvey, which is explicitly concerned with the historical specificity of differing processes (or "circuits") of capital accumulation, and with the significance of social struggle. In Section 3.2.3 we contrast Harvey's account with that offered by Doreen Massey, which places greater importance on industrial restructuring and has produced a well-documented account of contemporary urban change in Britain and other advanced industrial countries. Both Harvey and Massey incline towards a certain economic reductionism. Finally, in Section 3.2.4 we examine the accounts derived from the "Regulation School", which has become increasingly influential in urban studies.

3.1 EVOLUTIONARY THEORIES OF CITIES

In the work of Simmel and the Chicago School cities represented the new and the modern, epitomes of the emergent economic and social order produced by industrial capitalism. Implicitly they drew upon an evolutionary model of economic change. The city of Chicago, in particular, was taken as representative of the modern industrial city, and attempts to apply the concentric ring model (developed by Burgess and modified by others) to other industrial cities were legion. Within this frame of thought the city was seen as the product of the elaborate division of labour characteristic of modern industrial society. Cities owed their economic role to their pivotal place in this new industrial order as centres of commerce, sites of production, and bases for the most specialized economic activities. In this line of reasoning the city was the most advanced manifestation of an evolutionary process of economic change, "the workshops of civilization" in Park's words (see Harvey, 1973: 195).

Evolutionary approaches to urban development argued that the industrial city was the culmination of a long evolutionary process, stretching back to the earliest historical periods. Lampard (1965) distinguished two urban epochs in human history. These were, first, "primordial urbanization" where settlements first emerged in the years between 15000 B.C. and 4000 B.C., as a collective form of organization additional to the usual migratory agricultural activities. The importance of the second period of "definitive urbanization", which began in Mesopotamia after 4000 B.C., was that cities developed as fixed sites, in which "by means of its capacity to generate, store, and utilise social saving, the definitive city artefact is capable of transplanting itself out of its native uterine environments" (Lampard, 1965: 523). This period of "definitive urbanization" is itself split into two epochs, before and after 1700 A.D. In the first of these, cities were centres for a hinterland and existed in a stable hierarchy, in which hamlets formed a hinterland for villages, villages for towns, towns for cities, and cities for capital cities. Urban expansion was limited since cities were essentially parasitic on a limited agricultural economy. After 1700, the industrial city emerged as a dynamic force, able to increase in size because of the ability of economic producers based in cities to sever their dependency on agriculture.

The industrial city was hence seen as the locus of the new industrial society and as ushering in a new period in history when urban growth could continue at a vastly expanded level. Yet since the 1930s the industrial societies which cities were seen to embody have themselves been transformed by deindustrialization: manufacturing industries in many urban heartlands have collapsed; service industries have arisen; and industrial production has developed in new, rural, areas, appearing to cut the apparently close connection between cities and industry on which the evolutionary ideas were based.

Attempts to apply evolutionary lines of thinking have persisted into the present day and have taken a new turn as industrial economies have changed. A good example is the work of Peter Hall, who has developed the evolutionary model of the city to encompass deindustrialization as well as industrialization (see Hall and Hay, 1980; Hall, 1988). Hall begins by arguing that the urban system has been massively transformed in recent decades. Drawing upon American evidence he argues that four linked processes have undermined the centrality of the large, industrial urban conurbation which characterized earlier periods of industrial capitalism. These are:

1   suburbanization, where urban growth takes place in suburban rather than central urban areas;
2   deurbanization, where the urban population reduces relative to the population of rural and non-urban areas;
3   the contraction of the largest cities; and
4   the rise of new regions and the decline of old.

Hall explains this transformation by distinguishing six evolutionary stages through which cities go as industrial economies change and decline. His emphasis is upon the way in which, as regions industrialize, cities develop in size and concentration. After a period of time, however, any industrial area begins to stagnate as innovation occurs elsewhere. Hence cities

begin to decline. Because this process of industrial growth and fall is inevitable, all cities pass through the same six-stage cycle.

The six stages Hall specifies are divided into two groups. The first three stages occur during industrialization, the last three when deindustrialization begins to take effect in any given region:

1   The stage of "centralization during loss" happens during early industrialization. People migrate from the country to the city, leading to a growing urban population, but the overall population in any region is in net decline as more people leave the region overall.
2   As industrialization continues, the overall proportion of people living in cities within regions increases.
3   "Relative centralization" occurs when the city stretches over its boundaries and begins to develop suburbs. Nevertheless the proportion of urban dwellers continues to grow. This is the type of city which was the focus of the Chicago School studies, where there were large and dense urban populations and suburbs had begun to emerge.

Hall's argument, however, is that urban evolution has now continued beyond this, and a process of urban decline marks a new stage from that studied by the Chicago writers:

4   Suburbs begin to grow faster than the urban core, so that "relative decentralization" occurs as people move to the outer reaches of cities.
5   Starting about 1900 in the largest European cities (but generally much more recently) "absolute decentralization" occurs as people begin to move out of the inner city as it becomes increasingly specialized around office and commercial functions.
6   The entire city begins to decline as people begin to move out to the rural areas as deindustrialization proceeds.

This process of "counter-urbanization" has been much debated since the 1960s (Fielding, 1982). The period of industrial urban expansion, which earlier writers had expected to continue unabated, gives way, in Hall's view, to a situation of urban decline.

Hall is wary about applying his evolutionary model. It is derived from research in the U.S.A. chronicling the decline of large cities from the 1960s. In Western Europe there are different patterns, and "the different countries' urban systems ... display marked differences from one another" (Hall, 1988: 116). In Britain and Germany the largest cities were declining in population by the 1970s as Hall would have expected. However in France, Italy and the Benelux countries they were not.

Although many cities are seeing significant population loss, there are a number of difficulties with an evolutionary model such as Hall's. First, there is a problem with the way that Hall, in common with other writers referring to the phenomenon of "counter-urbanization", characterizes the decline of cities in the current period. There is no doubt that in many parts of the developed world population and employment are moving from central urban locations, but whether this should be seen as testifying to the decline of cities rather than their further expansion into new areas is a moot point. If fixed boundaries are drawn round a city at any one point in time it is always possible that when the population within these boundaries decreases this may be interpreted as urban decline. In reality, however, the city may be expanding outside these boundaries and increasing in significance. Scott, for instance, emphasizes the continuing urbanization process in capitalist societies (Scott, 1988a: 63).

Second, there is a problem about generalizing from Hall's study of urban trends in twentieth-century Western Europe. It could be argued that contemporary cities are becoming increasingly differentiated according to their role in the world economy, which makes it unhelpful to generalize about a single evolutionary path for all. Five prominent urban types stand out – Third World cities, global cities, declining industrial cities, new industrial districts, and socialist cities – all of which have a different character.

Third World cities are themselves heterogeneous, but tend to possess a number of distinctive features. They are "over-urbanized" (Timberlake, 1987). This means that they tend to be extremely large relative to the population of the particular country – a result of the fact that inward capitalist investment often focuses upon these capital city sites, a phenomenon described as "urban bias". They also tend to be "dualistic", with major divisions between the

formal and informal economy, between city and country, and between social groups. This dualistic format is related, in many cases, to the colonial legacy of "urban apartheid" (Abu-Lughod, 1980; King, 1990), where colonial rulers lived in separate parts of the city and were subject to a different jurisdiction from that applying to native dwellers.

"*Global cities*" (or world cities) are ones which increasingly depend on multinational financial services and are linked to the circulation and realization of wealth. They are frequently the location of corporate headquarters of major multinational enterprises and are the sites of what Massey (1988) refers to as "control functions", whence the control and management of corporate enterprise is directed. London, New York, Frankfurt and Tokyo are examples of this type of city. They tend to be large and centralized (with a distinct urban core specializing in international financial services), and contain both an elite group of workers and lower-paid servicing workers (Kasarda, 1988).

Older industrial cities, now in precipitate decline following the collapse of urban manufacturing, constitute the third type. Britain has many of the most dramatic examples – Glasgow, Liverpool (a trading rather than industrial city) and Bradford being especially prominent. Other noted examples have been found in the North-East and Mid-West of America (Detroit, Buffalo, Cleveland), and in Germany (Essen, Duisberg). These cities are characterized by decay and dereliction, high levels of unemployment, poor housing conditions and so forth.

"*New industrial districts*" have recently been given a great deal of attention. These are distinctively new urban developments (colonial cities, global cities, and older industrial cities being adaptations of older urban forms), which are not organized around an urban core with a suburban hinterland, but are more decentralized and cover a larger area. Here much development takes place round neighbourhood centres, and around the major transport networks, in the form of out-of-town shopping malls, employment centres and suburban housing. Examples include the Los Angeles area of the U.S.A., and parts of the Home Counties in South-East England.

Cities in socialist countries have also experienced dynamics very different from those in the capitalist world. They have tended to grow more slowly than their capitalist counterparts. Many socialist regimes have been explicitly anti-urban (Forbes and Thrift, 1987). The immediate post-revolutionary period tended to freeze, and in some cases reduce, urban population growth. These cities have been subject to greater planning and zoning.

The foregoing topology is not exhaustive. Many urban centres fall into several of these categories. The point is that it is impossible to see one form of city as archetypal of the current economic and social order in the way in which Chicago was taken as an exemplar of industrial capitalism in the early twentieth century. It is not true that all cities experience the same logic of development, but rather that some cities obtain distinct roles in the world economy, and once established they become differentiated from other cities occupying different roles within the same environment.

At the heart of the analysis is the fact that cities exist within a wider world system. The dynamics of this world system affect the way that cities develop and decline. A recognition of this belies a linear historical view of urban differentiation – where different urban forms are reflections of the specific period which any given city has reached in an evolutionary urban cycle – implying instead that spatial dynamics of the world system profoundly shape urban form. It is to a greater consideration of these processes that we now turn.

3.2 COMPETING THEORIES OF UNEVEN DEVELOPMENT

We have shown that evolutionary views fail to recognize the specificity of cities and the distinct roles they perform in a wider world economy. Let us consider in greater detail how these differences are sustained by spatial processes of uneven development. Various theories address this issue. Many are of Marxist provenance, emerging from the revived intellectual reputation of Marxist analysis in the social sciences in

the 1970s. The effect was to focus attention on the specifically capitalist mechanisms operating to create the geography of economic life. Thus, rather than beginning from the nature of industrialism, as did much orthodox economic sociology and geography in the post-war period, the central concerns were ones of capitalist accumulation, competition, exploitation and restructuring. When applied to the area of urban studies this constituted a more rigorous and detailed approach to the economic bases of urban systems.

Theories of uneven development, however, are bedevilled by a number of problems. Since these problems recur many times in the following pages it is worth listing them briefly:

1 Spatial analyses of uneven development may be ahistorical, failing fully to deal with its historically specific forms.
2 These theories may present static approaches, where the explanatory weight of the theory is geared to explaining how uneven development between places is sustained. It then becomes difficult to explain why some places are able to change their economic standing, possibly against the odds, the theory being insufficiently attuned to specificity.
3 Theories may be unable to register the significance of human agency in affecting processes of uneven development, particularly in the form of social conflict.
4 Such theories may be over-determinist, trying to explain more about the character of places or cities than can usefully be derived from the process of uneven development itself.

3.2.1 The new international division of labour thesis

One of the earliest and most original of the new accounts of the contemporary spatial division of labour was presented by Frobel, Heinrichs and Kreye in their *New International Division of Labour* (NIDL), first published in German in 1977. Their concern was with the growing internationalization of production since 1945 and its effects on the world economic system. Their main point was that manufacturing production processes which had once been undertaken in core countries in Western Europe were increasingly located in the Third World, which as peripheral countries within the world economy had previously concentrated on agricultural produce and raw materials for export to the advanced countries. Whereas in the 1950s Western Europe imported scarcely any manufactured goods, by 1975 much of the production in certain industrial sectors, like textiles and electrical goods, was carried out overseas, financed and controlled by metropolitan companies.

> The development of the world economy has increasingly created conditions in which the survival of more and more companies can only be assured through the relocation of production to new industrial sites, where labour-power is cheap to buy, abundant and well-disciplined; in short, through the transnational reorganization of production.
>
> (Frobel et al., 1980: 15)

This process seemed to mark a new phase in the relationships between core and periphery which Wallerstein (1974) had observed. The prime reason for the emergence of the NIDL, according to Frobel et al., was the change in the labour process as levels of skill involved in manufacturing production were reduced sharply. In such circumstances, a vast pool of unemployed or underemployed unskilled labour could be exploited on a world scale. The terms of employment of unskilled labour in Third World countries were especially favourable to capital: wages are much lower, working conditions poorer, trade unions weaker, labour forces easier to discipline, etc., than in the West. The improvement in methods of communication and transport made it possible to exploit these new reserves of labour. Other factors such as tax concessions to multinationals, absence of pollution control, and the absence of health and safety legislation enhance the attractiveness of these locations. Also, certain other conditions have to be fulfilled to make overseas sites acceptable: transport costs, which depend on the size and weight of the product; the political ability of overseas political regimes; property law; the corruptibility of officials, etc. (see Frobel et al., 1980: 145–7 for a list). But, where such conditions are met, it becomes profitable to transfer machinery to sites outside Europe to take advantage of favourable labour conditions.

The ramifications of this new international division of labour were thought very considerable, both for metropolitan and peripheral countries. One was the changing industrial structure in metropolitan countries, especially the decline of manufacturing employment. Deindustrialization, as the process was first known, had implications also for levels and types of occupational opportunity, with fewer skilled and unskilled manufacturing jobs available at home.

The NIDL thesis was intellectually of enormous importance. It brought to scholarly attention a new form of internationalization of the capitalist economy, explained recent changes in patterns of employment and indicated how multinational and transnational corporations could exploit spatial differences in labour markets in conjunction with a new technical division of labour within particular industrial sectors. It offered a relatively simple explanation of the phenomenon of deindustrialization. Derived in part from the neo-Marxist world-systems theory of Wallerstein, it did not depend on any particularly sophisticated economic theory. As Frobel et al. express their premises:

> The determining force, the prime mover, behind capitalist development is therefore the valorization and accumulation process of capital, and not, for example, any alleged tendency towards the extension and deepening of the wage labour/ capital relation or the "unfolding" of the productive forces.
>
> (Frobel et al., 1980: 25)

From that point of view the dynamic was mostly one of profit-seeking and minimizing labour costs in deskilled production processes.

What is of particular concern to us is the implication of the NIDL for urban systems. The NIDL thesis can be used, in some ways, to explain the differentiation of cities in different parts of the world. Rather than see cities inevitably decline as an evolutionary concomitant of deindustrialization, as Hall suggests, the NIDL thesis is able to explain the differential fate of cities in various parts of the globe. At one level, the prime position of Western capital cities could be explained by their coordinating role in the new international division of labour. At another level the growth of large cities, such as Mexico City, in the periphery could also be explained by the role they played as sites for the new decentralized production.

Other important work has focused upon the impacts of NIDL on Western cities and urban systems. The collection of essays by Smith and Feagin entitled *The Capitalist City* (1987) perhaps offers the best access to work in this vein. In some old manufacturing towns, such as Buffalo, New York, the removal of production to peripheral locations has led to the collapse of employment (Perry, 1987). In Buffalo employment in manufacturing fell from 200,000 in the 1950s to 100,000 by the early 1980s. In other, often neighbouring, cities, economic expansion – particularly in the service sector – has followed the consolidation of new controlling activities in the NIDL.

It is perhaps because the NIDL thesis is so closely specified in terms of *manufacturing* that it has been applied most often by U.S. and British scholars for it is in the U.S.A. and U.K. that deindustrialization has been most severe as old manufacturing towns have been affected detrimentally. There the very force of a description of a changing local economic situation and its obvious impact upon employment opportunities, living standards and social relations is sufficient to demonstrate the effects of corporate restructuring in a global economy. However, since many countries have not deindustrialized, and since most formal economic activity is in the service sector in all Western societies, the overall impact of economic transformations on cities is not fully grasped.

[Here Savage and Warde discuss criticisms of the NIDL thesis.]

There are three main problems with the NIDL thesis as a tool by which to analyse urban change. First, it is economistic, since it is incapable of systematically analysing anything other than economic change. As a result it gave few insights into changes internal to any particular city, and can only indicate the broad views of a city's general prosperity. It thus says little about process such as suburbanization, social segregation or housing provision.

Second, it ignores human agency; in particular there was an assumption that jobs, not people, were mobile, and hence that deskilled work would be moved to peripheral locations. This simplistic assumption precludes the possibility that unskilled labour may migrate to existing urban centres, or to growing urban areas in developed countries. The migration of Hispanic workers to the south-west U.S.A., for instance, has been of major significance in the development of the Californian economy, pointing to the variety of possible strategies which firms can use to find suitable labour for jobs. The decisions of particular firms are not structural necessities, but are partly choices in the light of a number of alternatives.

Finally, it has problems explaining why some cities were able to carve out particular places for themselves in the NIDL and others were not. In other words, it is insufficiently attuned to the way in which urban actors can create a role for a particular place in the NIDL. Why are some manufacturing cities better able than others to readjust to the NIDL and change the basis of their local economies? Lancaster, in the U.K., for instance, deindustrialized much earlier and faster than would be expected given its economic base in the 1950s (Murgatroyd and Urry, 1985). The role of corporate actors and local political forces in affecting any city's economic position, even given the broad economic changes sketched out by the NIDL thesis, is largely ignored. While persuasive descriptions of local economic change could be offered, the roles of the state and politics were always included as historically contingent responses. The theoretical link between the activities of the capitalist corporation and the political apparatuses of national or local state was absent. Explicitly considered links occurred usually only if the local state had fiscal problems because major employers were closing down their operations. This would encourage them to offer incentives to private firms either to persuade them to stay or to attract new inward investment. Similarly, at the level of local popular resistance, although urban social movements, community groups, etc. were perceived as organizing opposition (e.g. Fainstein, 1987), there was no *theoretical* basis for appreciating their significance. These limits were indeed partly recognized by Smith and Tardanico (1987) in their attempts to improve the understanding of the reproduction of labour power within this school of thought. Failings in this respect are partly the result of exaggerating the mobility of capital. The NIDL thesis would lead one to expect much higher levels of geographical mobility among firms than actually occurs, partly, as the "Californian School" considered below would contend, because they underestimate the importance of economic networks and the benefits of agglomeration.

3.2.2 David Harvey, the second circuit of capital and urbanization

In the 1970s David Harvey attempted an ambitious theoretical approach to the analysis of uneven development, derived from a new appreciation of Marx's economic theory and its implications for urban growth. In many ways it offered a powerful contrast to the NIDL thesis, since it tried to build a theory which is historically sensitive, aware of urban specificity, and deliberately emphasizing the importance of social conflict for urban development.

Harvey's starting-point was to develop Marx's own analysis of capital accumulation and draw out the implications for the urban structure. This primarily involved an examination of landed property and its role in capital accumulation, a subject about which Marx said relatively little. In Harvey's early work (1973) he specified the distinctive nature of land as a commodity in capitalist society: while it is something which can be bought and sold – like any other commodity – it has a number of peculiarities. The most important of these are that it is spatially fixed, since land cannot be transported; it is necessary to human life, since we all need to live somewhere; it allows assets and improvements to be stored; and it is relatively permanent, since improvements to land (e.g. buildings) tend to survive considerable periods of time, longer than the time it takes for clothes to wear out or food to be eaten, for instance!

Much of Harvey's work can be seen as an exploration of the implications of the specific character of capital investment in land rather than in other areas. He emphasized that such investment is both highly significant for the functioning of the capitalist economy – since a great deal of capital is usually tied up in the built environment – and also that such investment leaves a relatively enduring physical legacy. The resulting built form can help to aid capital accumulation, if it is a profitable avenue for investment, but can also be a barrier to it, when its enduring qualities render it outdated and anachronistic in a relatively short period of time. Much of Harvey's work can be seen as an elaboration of this idea of the double-edged nature of property for capital accumulation.

Harvey, in later work (1977, 1982), developed his analysis of the precise role of land for capital accumulation by examining the three circuits of capital. The primary circuit – the production of commodities within manufacturing – is the one to which Marx gives greatest attention. Harvey emphasized how the accumulation of profit by the exploitation of labour within capitalist enterprises runs into severe contradictions, most notably when goods are overproduced without adequate money in the economy to purchase them. As a result of this, profits may fall and capital lie idle. It is this crisis of overaccumulation that causes capital to be switched into the "second circuit" – where capital is fixed in the built environment money is moved from the primary circuit to the secondary – so long as a supportive framework for this transition exists, as when a state encourages such investment. The tertiary circuit of capital involves scientific knowledge and expenditures to reproduce labour power. Expenditure in this circuit is often the result of social struggle rather than being a direct opportunity for capital to find new avenues for accumulation.

Harvey's analysis illuminated urban processes in two ways. First, it conceptualized the significance of investment in the built environment in relation to other economic processes, suggesting links between urban restructuring and economic restructuring. Harvey's principal example attributed the growth of suburbs in America after the Second World War to the switching of capital out of the primary circuit, where cases of overaccumulation were emerging. The changing structure of the capitalist city was thus related to broader trends in the capitalist economy. The property boom of the early 1970s in the U.S.A. and Britain, which saw the development of office blocks in many urban centres, owed much to similar pressures.

The built environment, however, is not simply a means of resolving crises in capital accumulation: it can, in turn, cause further crises. As capital is invested in the built environment and hence the economy is more generally "cooled down", new opportunities for capital accumulation in the primary circuit open up again: capital moves back into this circuit, capital of the secondary circuit is devalued and it becomes a less attractive avenue for investment. Once constructed, the existing built environment is no longer as efficient as new building and may prove a barrier to effective capital accumulation, so causing capital investment to move to newer and more advanced sites. One result is that the built environment concerned is abandoned or downgraded such that capital moves elsewhere to restore profitability.

Harvey's model of the urban process under capitalism is hence the very opposite of the evolutionary view we discussed above. For Harvey investment in the urban form offers a temporary solution to crises in capitalism, but then in turn it becomes a problem which needs to be addressed by switching capital investment elsewhere. Cities – and other spatial units – hence grow and decline in an almost cyclical way. Yet Harvey is also attuned to the social and political struggles that can attempt to "fix" the role of a particular city, against particular economic forces. Struggles by social groups threatened by the removal of capital can prevent capital flight and ensure the survival of an urban infrastructure. The miners' strike in Britain in 1984–85 is an example of a failed attempt to fix investment to particular traditional coal-mining areas. In other cases "growth coalitions" may succeed in attracting investment. Ultimately, it is a matter of political struggle as to the way that the tendencies within capitalism to make *and* break places work out in practice . . .

Harvey also helped to draw attention to the social and political role of the bourgeoisie – landlords – who had a particular stake within any one place. Capitalists owning land are committed to keeping their investment in a specific place. They often play a crucial role in defending local economies and engage in civic "boosterism" to encourage the economic prosperity of their place, which will enhance property prices and the value of their land. This theme has been developed by American writers such as Gottdiener (1985) and Logan and Molotch (1987), who identify the central role of landed interests in affecting urban fortunes.

The strengths of Harvey's account are several. First, it is possible to use his ideas to explore the *variety* of urban processes in the contemporary world. Whilst his discussion of the tendencies of capital to move between circuits very usefully explores the bases of switches of investment in the built environment, he is also cognizant of the role of political struggle. Thus, he is able to show how social and political forces in a particular city may act to modify or even thwart attempts by capitalists to disinvest. His stress on the way in which the built environment is at different times a help and a hindrance for capital accumulation, and thus how dramatic changes can occur to the same city within relatively short time-spans, makes sense of dramatic episodes of contemporary urban change. His theory of uneven development allows historical specificity and recognizes the role of human agency.

Harvey's analysis is not without problems, however. The major one is that his work is empirically largely unsubstantiated, for little research has actually used Harvey's insights to shed light on processes of urban change. The main exception to this concerns studies of suburbanization and gentrification . . . Harvey's own case studies, such as that of Paris in the nineteenth century, seem to lapse all too quickly into detailed historical accounts.

One reason why Harvey's work remains weakly developed empirically emanates from some underlying theoretical weaknesses in his approach. His arguments can be seen as circular. Decisions to invest in the built environment can be seen as resulting from a crisis in the primary circuit which causes a shift of capital to the secondary circuit. How do we know that there is a crisis in the primary circuit? Because capital is being switched into the secondary circuit. In other words, it can be difficult to distinguish the evidence for the causes of urban change from evidence about urban changes themselves. Harvey's theory can be used to explain anything that happens. His more recent work, possibly aware of such a problem, has therefore become more concerned with analysing the dynamics of capitalist economies, and in the 1980s he turned to "Regulation School" Marxism, discussed below in section 3.2.4.

More specifically, it is possible to question Harvey's rather static conception of the built environment. In his view once the built environment has been produced it is relatively unchangeable, and hence can be a drag on capital accumulation in the future. There are clear examples of this: elaborate motorway systems, for instance, may appear to offer solutions both to overaccumulation problems and to the general economic problems associated with traffic congestion in one year, but shortly afterwards they pose more problems as they attract more traffic than they are designed for. Yet other forms of built environment are arguably more flexible and are less of a constraint once built. Residential and office buildings, for instance, can be used by different people in varying ways, and the extent to which a given built environment is a constraint to future users would appear to be an empirical matter (see also Saunders, 1986: 253ff.).

Third, one of the attractions of Harvey's view is his insistence on the role of social and political struggle in shaping urban processes. This has been developed, in different ways, by other writers, such as Manuel Castells (1983) and American writers on growth coalitions and the like (Logan and Molotch, 1987). The problem with Harvey's account, however, is a certain reductionism to social class relations which diverts attention from the significance of other social groups and actors. This is in sharp contrast with Castells, who emphasizes that urban struggles are rarely based purely on class lines, but are organized around such issues as gender, ethnicity or neighbourhood. This is not to say that Harvey (1985a, b) fails to recognize the complexity of class relations, for he refers to

intra-class conflicts, divisions within the capitalist class and the way in which regional class alliances can form as members of the working class and bourgeoisie ally together to defend their stake in particular areas. However, he still says nothing about the social significance of groups other than classes.

Finally, there is also a certain tension in Harvey's work between his emphasis upon the dynamics of capital accumulation and his stress on social conflict as forces behind urban development. Ultimately, he sees struggle as caused by the contradictory nature of the relation between classes. Hence, his references to the significance of social conflict for urban development do not, in the end, make serious concession to the argument that social groups, by their own efforts, have important historical effects. Although he tries to resist the implications of his position (see, e.g., Harvey, 1982: 450), in the final instance his position is economically determinist.

3.2.3 Industrial restructuring and class struggle

The relationship between social conflict and capitalist restructuring lies at the heart of a third account of uneven development, pioneered by Doreen Massey. Sometimes called the "restructuring" approach (see Bagguley *et al.*, 1990), it led to a large amount of empirical research, particularly in the U.K., concerning the relationship between economic restructuring, urban and regional change, and political conflict.

Massey's approach differs from those discussed above in being concerned less with the abstract logic of capital accumulation, and more with how the strategies adopted by enterprises to survive and prosper in the world capitalist economy affect patterns of spatial inequality. She examines the ways in which organizations restructure in response to changes in their economic environment and the spatial consequences. Whilst the other theories operate at a macro-level, Massey's work occupies a middle ground, providing conceptual guidance as to how specific places are affected by differing types of restructuring.

In her earlier work with Richard Meegan (Massey and Meegan, 1979, 1982), it was argued that firms in different sectors of the economy responded to international economic pressures by adopting different strategies. The most important of these were rationalization (the closure of specific units of production and centralization of production in other sites), intensification (making employees work harder), and investment and technical change (involving capital investment and better productivity). These strategies make for uneven development, for some areas lose employment as production is rationalized away from them, whilst others gain employment because they are subject to fresh investment. Spatial differentiation is also linked to the way in which firms deal with resistance to their restructuring strategies. One repeatedly used strategy is to shed skilled workers in one location and replace them, when necessary, with unskilled people somewhere else. Thus, workplaces in the inner cities, often employing union-organized skilled workers, might be closed down and the production process, with perhaps new technology, shifted to, or expanded in, other areas where new, unskilled, often inexperienced, and often female labour will be engaged. There are plenty of examples of this in Britain: rural regions like East Anglia and North Wales have been fastest growing in terms of manufacturing employment in the past twenty years. Again, car production in the U.S.A. has been moved out of Detroit and Chicago to sites further south where labour is more docile. For Massey, labour becomes locally (or perhaps more correctly, regionally) specialized as workers with specific skills congregate together.

In her best-known work, *Spatial Divisions of Labor* (1984), Massey developed and systematized this argument by showing how, as firms restructured, they tended to specialize activities in those areas where the cheapest and most pliable labour force could be found. Research and development work, along with the administrative functions of head office, was located in those areas where professional and managerial workers were plentiful and near the corridors of power. As a result, she argued, Britain could increasingly be seen as a country divided between a prosperous South-East, where the "control functions" of large organizations were concentrated, and the depressed peripheral regions, where employment tended to be concentrated in branch plants and largely involved unskilled workers. This polarization marked a new spatial division of labour and was a major change from the older patterns where differing parts of Britain had semi-autonomous regional economies, typically based on a specific product (textiles in north-west England, shipbuilding in north-east England, and so on), and in which skilled, unskilled and managerial workers were employed in smaller, less spatially desegregated firms.

The logic of Massey's account is that capital has come to use spatial differentiation in the competitive search for profit, as it invests in those areas where it can draw upon a suitable labour force. Spatial advantage is most readily obtained by discriminating among available labour forces. This acknowledges that capital is nowadays highly mobile, and certainly more mobile than labour, thus implying that many constraints on industrial location which pertained in earlier epochs have been overcome.

Unlike the NIDL theorists and David Harvey, Massey avoids a purely economistic account, and finds a way of explaining how the social character of specific places impacts on processes of restructuring. The social qualities of labour are significant in repelling or attracting capital and hence, Massey argues, it is important to consider how local work cultures are formed and how they facilitate types of militancy or passivity. In the U.K., for instance, industrial employment in the Home Counties expanded in the 1980s partly because firms chose to locate to areas without trade-union traditions where workers might be more compliant. Trade-union membership has become much more dispersed recently, indicating the demise of densely unionized towns and regions. As their populations have declined, some of the larger industrial cities have lost some bases for labour militancy.

Massey's work avoids many of the problems we have identified in other research. Her account is historically sensitive, and she is not committed to a static view of uneven development where the fortunes of places are fixed into core or peripheral status from the beginning of world capitalism. Most importantly of all, she is explicitly concerned to elaborate on the way that social conflict and local forms of agency impact on forms of economic restructuring and uneven development. It was in developing this insight that research focused in the 1980s, as attention turned to detailed consideration of the way that economic restructuring was both affected by, and in turn impacted upon, local social relations and local cultures. The promise was to find tighter connections between economic restructuring and social and cultural changes within particular places (see Cooke, 1989a; Bagguley *et al.*, 1990). The principal way in which Massey has been taken up in U.K. studies has been through a series of "locality studies" including a programme of research into the Changing Urban and Regional System (CURS) (e.g. Cooke, 1986, 1989b). This research programme attempted to explore in greater detail both how the social complexion of various places affected forms of economic restructuring, and also how restructuring impacted on these "localities". This research strategy entailed detailed localized inquiry, taking the distinctive features of different places seriously and trying to describe and explain differentiation. The promise of such an approach is a better understanding of social and economic activity in its material context, connecting together general forces and specific outcomes.

Massey's framework offered a sophisticated attempt to theorize urban differentiation as the interplay between the restructuring strategies of firms and the social and cultural characteristics of particular local areas. It appeared to resolve many of the weaknesses of other research, and in particular it laid a path from theoretical formalism to a detailed research programme. This programme expanded on Massey's ideas in a number of ways. Important among these was the successful application of her analysis, which was based primarily on restructuring in manufacturing, to the restructuring of "service" employment, for instance in the health services. Bagguley *et al.* (1990) and Pinch (1989) were able to show that even in the British health service, not organized on a profit-making basis,

many of the restructuring strategies discussed by Massey, and others, were in operation, causing serious job loss. Even though it had been traditionally supposed that service industries were much less spatially mobile than manufacturing firms since they had to be situated closer to their market, they were shown to be subject to processes of the spatial separation of functions very similar to those analysed by Massey (see, for example, Marshall *et al.*, 1988).

[Here Savage and Warde discuss critiques of Massey's theories.]

So far restructuring theory has offered a series of major insights into processes of economic restructuring, but was limited in its attempts to explain social and cultural processes.

3.2.4 Regulation Marxism and the California School

The final approach to uneven development and urban differentiation which we consider is associated with the Regulation School, in particular through its impact on neo-Marxist geographers such as Allen Scott, Michael Storper, Richard Walker, and the more recent work of David Harvey. As with work inspired by Massey, one of the main attractions of this theoretical current is its ability to support a wide-ranging research programme. Also in common with Massey this approach is historically sensitive and attuned to urban specificity.

Regulation School theory is descended from French structural Marxism of the 1970s (see Jessop, 1990, for an overview). Its principal figures, Aglietta, Lipietz, Boyer, and others, have employed a distinctive set of theoretically generated concepts – regime of accumulation, mode of regulation, Fordism – to explore relationships between capital, labour and the state. The main starting-point for these writers is the argument that nation-states play a crucial role in regulating capital accumulation, and they see the differing ways in which capitalism is regulated as historically specific "regimes of accumulation". Much of their work is thus an historically grounded attempt to consider the implications of the contemporary shift from one "regime of accumulation" – Fordism – to another "regime of accumulation" – neo-Fordism, or post-Fordism.

The Italian Marxist, Gramsci, apparently coined the phrase "Fordism" to characterize the mass-production methods pioneered by Henry Ford in the inter-war years of the twentieth century, and some of their effects on social and family life in Italy. The concept re-entered contemporary social and economic thought through the writings of the Regulation School, which referred to a complete era in capitalist development as Fordist. Their argument is that Fordism was the dominant mode of industrial organization in the mid-twentieth century and that it constituted a distinctive "regime of accumulation". The regime of accumulation is based on a specific "mode of regulation" (whence the name of the School), where regulation refers to things like the forms of the state, the nature of intervention, welfare arrangements, legal forms, and so forth. In addition, for the Regulation School, phases of capitalist development are determined both by the mode of production and consumption. The Fordist era was characterized by mass production and mass consumption. However, they argued that in the 1980s this regime was gradually giving way to a neo- or post-Fordist one with less demand for mass-produced goods and in which competitive pressures required much more flexible methods of production.

The concept of post-Fordism, like many other concepts, is primarily constructed as a negative ideal-type, identifying characteristics that were not present in a preceding, and better understood, institutional setting. The model of Fordism is relatively well-established, and many commentators would think of Fordist arrangements as characterizing the leading manufacturing firms from the 1930s through to the 1970s. The Fordist firm is one characterized by scientific management, economies of scale, mass production and technical control. Post-Fordist production arrangements are associated with the declining size of production units, small-batch production, customized products, flexible working practices, greater worker discretion and more responsible autonomy.

Critics of regulation theory see it as bearing many of the alleged defects of its structuralist predecessors: functionalist, economist, reductionist, excessively abstract, ignoring individual action and underemphasizing social struggles. Nevertheless, the technical vocabulary of the Regulation School is frequently slipped into discussions of new flexible forms of production, though often in a highly eclectic way (e.g. *Society and Space*, 1988). Quite often the concepts are invoked without regard to the theoretical scheme from which they were derived. Nevertheless, the notions of Fordism, post-Fordism and flexibility have been widely taken up to analyse new patterns of spatial inequality. David Harvey's book *The Condition of Postmodernity* (1989) is an important example.

In *The Condition of Postmodernity* Harvey dissects the demise of the post-war settlement. His account is based on the proposition that

> the contrasts between present political-economic practices and those of the post-war boom period are sufficiently strong to make the hypothesis of a shift from Fordism to what might be called a "flexible" regime of accumulation a telling way to characterize recent history.
>
> (Harvey, 1989: 1)

Fordism was the regime of accumulation that supported the "long boom" after 1945 and was epitomized by the operations of the Ford motor company which produced cheap automobiles using assembly-line techniques while paying their (generally very bored) workers comparatively high wages.

> What was special about Ford (and what ultimately separates Fordism from Taylorism) was his vision, his explicit recognition that mass production meant mass consumption, a new system of the reproduction of labour power, a new politics of labour control and management, a new aesthetics and psychology, in short, a new kind of rationalized, modernist, and populist democratic society.
>
> (Harvey, 1989: 15–16)

For Harvey, consistent with other exponents of Regulation Theory, observes: "Post-war Fordism has to be seen, therefore, less as a mere system of mass production and more as a total way of life" (ibid.: 135). The post-war settlement generally worked well, productivity rose, wealth increased, and the gains were in part redistributed through the mechanism of the welfare state and social democratic political policies – a particular mode of regulation. Not everyone was satisfied or contented: there were many workers on poor wages, poverty was not eliminated even in the core countries; immigrants into Europe, of whom there were many, were particularly disprivileged; and the effects on the Third World were far from positive. Nor was it a permanent solution: it began to show signs of difficulty in the mid-1960s, and the early 1970s, which saw not only the end of a stable international financial system, but also oil-price rises and inflation; and the beginning of fresh recession effectively ended an era. For Harvey, 1973 was the turning-point, a change that he sees associated with the emergence of post-modernism as an aesthetic . . .

Harvey interprets this in terms of a transition to a regime of flexible accumulation. He observes changes in the labour market with a growing disparity between core and peripheral workers; changes in industrial organization, especially the emergence of subcontracting, but also of homeworking, sweat-shops, and the use of women's domestic labour. Small-batch production entails a move away from the economies of scale that Fordism offered. New products – particularly responding to quickly changing fashions – require constant innovation from capital. This also has cultural consequences:

> The relatively stable aesthetic of Fordist modernism has given way to all the ferment, instability and fleeting qualities of a post-modernist aesthetic that celebrates difference, ephemerality, spectacle, fashion, and the commodification of cultural forms.
>
> (Harvey, 1989: 156)

Employment in service industries increased. The dialectic between monopolization and competition in capitalist economy works out in a new way, with tighter organization through access to, and control over, information and a complete rejigging of the financial system since the mid-1970s. This is a result partly of new information technology and its rapid transmission, partly of new opportunities for capital gains and partly of powers beyond the control of nation-states. Moreover, Harvey discerns changes in attitudes and norms, seeing the emergence of a "rampant individualism" associated with entrepreneurialism.

Harvey explains the shift in terms of his older stress on the logic of over-accumulation, but sees the 1970s as a particular configuration of conditions. He develops a distinctive analysis in terms of "time–space compression". In the world of new information technology the circulation-time of capital is reduced. Effectively the size of the globe shrinks as it becomes possible to trade stocks and shares throughout 24 hours – when the London Exchange is closed either New York or Tokyo will be open, and vice versa. The capacity of firms to use different spaces for different purposes is another aspect of time–space compression. Economically we live in a smaller world.

Harvey uses his analysis to explain the use of what he terms "the condition of 'post-modernity'" . . . Harvey does not, in this book, consider in detail the urban transformations brought about by the new form of flexible accumulation. Whilst Harvey might have strengthened his analysis of the contemporary transformation of capitalism, he has not applied his framework to uneven development and urban change in any detail.

It is in this field that the geographers of the "California School" have made greater strides. They might be seen as attempting to prove a theoretical account of the dramatic development of the California urban conglomerations of Los Angeles and (to a lesser extent) San Francisco. Los Angeles is perhaps the most discussed city of the late-twentieth-century world (Davis, 1990; Soja, 1989; Jameson, 1984, etc.): for the School, Los Angeles is to the 1980s and 1990s what Chicago was to the early twentieth century, a particularly stark example of the urbanizing processes which are to be found throughout much of the world economy. They see the rise of the California economy as tied to the decline of the old industrial regions of the north-east of the U.S.A. (the "Rust Belt") and the fact that new industries, such as electronics and defence, are located in California, while contracting ones, like shipbuilding, are in the Rust Belt. They concentrate on the experience of recently grown industrial sectors and argue that establishments in these sectors are tending to cluster in "new industrial districts". They provide evidence for a variety of sectors – for example, motion pictures (Christopherson and Storper, 1986), animated pictures (Scott, 1988b), printed-circuit fabrication (Scott, 1988b) – where factories tend to cluster together in the same district of a large metropolitan area. The reason for this is to obtain economies of scope rather than the economies of scale that were the objective of Fordist mass production.

Although the Californians deploy Marxist concepts (particularly of regulation theory), the core of their current position is a theory of the firm associated with the economist Oliver Williamson (for a summary see Williamson, 1990), who has developed the theory of "transaction cost analysis". Very simply, their theory distinguishes those situations under which firms find it best to internalize contributory activities (such as marketing, or research, or various production functions), and those where it is best to externalize them, by using subcontractors or buying services on the market. Scott (1988b) pursues the spatial implications of this contrast, observing that when firms externalize their activities they tend to congregate close to the other firms involved in their production network, leading to agglomeration economies and the emergence of New Industrial Districts. Alternatively, if activities are internalized, firms may be able to separate functions spatially onto different sites. Massey's account of the spatial separation of production functions will apply only to such cases.

These writers largely accept the empirical trends identified as flexible accumulation in Piore and Sabel's (1984) analysis of the Third Italy, and argue that they testify to the rise of new industries, based on external linkages. Firms tend to be smaller and to subcontract activities, leading to vertical disintegration. The development of new products encourages the concentration of small firms that can share expert knowledge, for which purposes social networks, often based on face-to-face interaction, are ideal. New industrial districts tend to contain firms in advanced innovative sectors, attracting and retaining workers with appropriate knowledge and expertise. In some versions strong priority is accorded to technological developments (e.g. Storper and Walker, 1989) where the development of new products is deemed conducive to external links between firms as, for instance, new companies cluster round the innovating enterprise.

Much of the work of the California School is directed purely towards explaining industrial location and tends to avoid any wider discussion of its effects on urban development. An exception to this is Scott's (1988a) *Metropolis: From the Division of Labor to Urban Form*. Having outlined the process whereby firms reorganize, compelled by the benefits of vertical disintegration, he makes a series of claims about the way in which the concentration of workers' residences near to the "neo-Marshallian" industrial districts in which they work has effects on social segregation, ethnic differentiation and community formation.

Beginning from the premise of the spatial separation of home and workplace in capitalist economies, Scott (1988a: 217–30) argues that the employment relation is a key determinant of residential location. He uses data to show that although there are other cross-cutting bases of residential segregation, occupation is primary, universal and constant in large cities of the advanced capitalist societies. Blue-collar and white-collar workers live in different zones of the city. The reasons for this are several: blue-collar workers, who travel shorter distances to work, will concentrate around workplaces; state practices of zoning segregate social groups; and there are group preferences as regards housing that are mediated by cost. However, Scott goes beyond these factors to try to make out a case that

> neighborhoods are the privileged locales within which social reproduction of the determinate forms of life engendered in the capitalist city goes on ... Here, I use the term reproduction in its double sense to mean both generational replacement and the maintenance of stable subjective/ ideological accommodations with workaday life.
>
> (Scott, 1988a: 223)

The significance of this is threefold. First,

neighbourhoods are sites for educating and socializing children, and families tend to choose them on the basis of their educational facilities with a view to ensuring that children get an education appropriate to their anticipated class position. Parents try to prevent their children becoming downwardly mobile and choose schools accordingly. Second, neighbourhoods signify social prestige and status, and social groups differentiate themselves by adopting particular behavioural and cultural traits that are reinforced and sanctioned in local communities. Third, neighbourhoods are places where inter-family social networks develop. Sometimes in poor neighbourhoods a network is protection against the insecurities of employment, in others it constitutes the source of information by which new jobs are found. On this third basis the concentration of ethnic groups can also be explained, Scott claims, because they tend to have access only to limited niches in the labour market: "ethnicity in the American metropolis is thus pre-eminently a contingent outcome of local labor market pressures and needs" (Scott, 1988a: 226). Ultimately industrial location gives rise to cities and neighbourhoods composed of people who work in the industries, and the social homogeneity of these neighbourhoods becomes self-reinforcing over time.

Scott's account is not entirely convincing simply because firm reorganization and labour market are insufficient as basic mechanisms to generate the complete range of social effects. The Californians, unlike Harvey and certainly Massey, say very little about social conflict and its impact on economic restructuring and social change. Their analysis is conducted at the level of economic theory and even at that level it is probably too narrow. The Californians take little notice of trends in the service industries and their role in employment, since they see services as largely dependent on manufacturing production (see Sayer and Walker, 1992). If urbanization is connected only to industrialization, as it is by Scott, then we have a limited grasp on the impact of most economic activity.

One final problem with the Californian account, and another sense in which it may be seen as unduly economistic, is that it almost entirely ignores the state. Here again this may be the result of focusing attention on one country, the U.S.A., where the federal government in particular is relatively non-interventionist in regional planning. Nevertheless the state does many things short of direct intervention that set the framework for business activity. This criticism is developed by Feagin and Smith (1987) and Gottdiener (1989).

3.3 CONCLUSION

In the past decade, theories of uneven development have become increasingly sophisticated and aware of the problems raised at the beginning of [this extract]. Accounts have grown more sensitive historically and have identified explicitly how different places may be affected in diverse ways by uneven development. It has been demonstrated that urban development is not some evolutionary process through which all cities pass. Rather these new theories have demonstrated the instability of urban fortunes and the reasons why cities rise and fall, fall and rise. Causes include the dynamics of the world capitalist economy which allow the relocation of industry across the globe; the cycles of investment and disinvestment in the built environment; forms of corporate restructuring; and the dynamics of product innovation. As a result, particular cities cannot be deemed emblematic of a form of social organization, in the way that the city of Chicago stood for industrial capitalism. Instead we should recognize the inherent impermanence of the economic foundations of cities and the multiple roles of cities in a world capitalist economy.

Jointly, these theories succeeded in analysing the economic foundations of urban change and identifying a series of forces which derive specifically from mechanisms of the capitalist organization of production. As such they have proved an important corrective to the previous neglect by urban sociology of such matters. Individually, each seems to have identified some characteristic recent strategies and processes of the global economy. Their disagreements stem partly from concentrating on different nations and different industrial sectors, though there are more fundamental theoretical sources of dispute too.

Theories of uneven development have been far less successful at explaining the sources of intra-urban change and social change within cities. Once they move away from delineating the economic position of particular places, and begin to refer to the impact of uneven development on their urban structure, social order and cultural patterns, they begin to falter. Although Harvey sought to capture the importance of social conflict for urban development, Massey sought to show how economic restructuring is related to local social and political change and Scott sought to try to demonstrate how neighbourhoods are produced by industrial location, their solutions are at best partial.

Theories of uneven development need to be supplemented by a much fuller analysis of the social, cultural and political processes which shape and are themselves shaped by cities. Much might be gained by uniting some aspects of classical urban sociology with the enhanced understanding of capitalist spatial development. Subsequent chapters examine material inequality, sociation, the cultural specificity of place and the nature of political conflict in the contemporary city, all themes that have featured prominently in urban sociology. Typically, though, they were explored through analysis of the nature of modernity, rather than of capitalism. What is required is better specification of the relationship between capitalist dynamics and the social conditions of modernity. A principal connection is through the analysis of the inequalities constantly generated by the mechanisms of accumulation which are reproduced, modulated or transformed in the course of the mundane practices of daily life captured by analyses of the experience of modernity.

REFERENCES

Abu-Lughod, J. (1980) *Urban Apartheid: A Study of Rabat*. Cambridge, Mass.: MIT Press.
Bagguley, P., Mark-Lawson, J., Shapiro, D., Urry, J., Walby, S. and Warde, A. (1990) *Restructuring: Place, Class and Gender*. London: Sage.
Castells, M. (1983) *The City and the Grassroots*. London: Edward Arnold.
Christopher, S. and Storper, M. (1986) 'The City as Studio: The World as Back Lot: The Impact of Vertical Disintegration on the Location of the Modern Picture Industry', *Environment and Planning D: Society and Space* 4(3): 305–20.
Cooke, P. (ed.) (1986) *Global Restructuring, Local Response*. London: ESRC.
Cooke, P. (1989a) "Locality, Economic Restructuring and World Development" in P. Cooke (ed.) *Localities*. London: Unwin Hyman, 1–44.
Cooke, P. (ed.) (1989b) *Localities*. London: Unwin Hyman.
Davis, M. (1990) *City of Quartz: Excavating the Future in Los Angeles*. London: Verso.
Fainstein, S. (1987) "Local Mobilisation and Economic Discontent" in M. P. Smith and J. R. Feagin (eds) *The Capitalist City*. Oxford: Basil Blackwell, 323–42.
Feagin, J. R. and Smith, M. P. (1987) "Cities and the New International Division of Labour: An Overview" in M. P. Smith and J. R. Feagin (eds) *The Capitalist City*. Oxford: Basil Blackwell, 3–36.
Fielding, A. J. (1982) *Counter Urbanisation*. London: Methuen.
Forbes, D. and Thrift, N. (1987) *The Socialist Third World*. Oxford: Basil Blackwell.
Frobel, F., Heinrichs, J. and Kreye, K. (1980) *The New International Division of Labour: Structural Unemployment in Industrial Countries and Industrialisation in Developing Countries*. Cambridge: Cambridge University Press.
Gottdiener, M. (1985) *The Social Production of Urban Space*. Austin: University of Texas Press.
Hall, P. (1988) "Urban Growth in Western Europe" in M. Dogan and J. D. Kasarda (eds) *The Metropolis Era*, vol. 1. New York: Sage, 111–27.
Hall, P. and Hay, P. (1980) *Growth Centers in European Urban Systems*. Berkeley: University of California Press.
Harvey, D. (1973) *Social Justice and the City*. London: Edward Arnold.
Harvey, D. (1977) "Labour, Capital and Class Struggle around the Built Environment in Advanced Capitalist Societies", *Politics and Society* 6: 265–95.
Harvey, D. (1982) *The Limits to Capital*. Oxford: Basil Blackwell.
Harvey, D. (1985a) *The Urbanisation of Capital*. Oxford: Basil Blackwell.
Harvey, D. (1985b) *Consciousness and the Urban Experience*. Oxford: Basil Blackwell.
Harvey, D. (1989) *The Condition of Postmodernity*. Oxford: Basil Blackwell.
Jameson, F. (1984) "Postmodernism, or the Cultural Logic of Late Capitalism", *New Left Review* 146: 53–92.
Jessop, B. (1990) "Regulation Theories in Retrospect and Prospect", *Economy and Society* 19(2): 153–216.
Kasarda, J. (1988) "Economic Restructuring and the

American Urban Dilemma", in M. Dogan and J. Kasarda (eds) *The Metropolis Era*. Newbury Park, Calif.: Sage, 56–84.

King, A. (1990) *World Cities*. London: Routledge.

Lampard, E. (1965) "Historical Aspects of Urbanisation" in P. M. Hauser and L. F. Schnore (eds) *The Study of Urbanization*. New York: Wiley, 519–54.

Logan, J. and Molotch, H. (1987) *Urban Fortunes: The Political Economy of Place*. Berkeley: University of California Press.

Marshall, G., Rose, G., Newby, H. and Vogler, C. (1988) *Social Class in Britain*. London: Unwin Hyman.

Massey, D. (1984) *Spatial Divisions of Labour*. London: Macmillan.

Massey, D. (1988) "Uneven Redevelopment: Social Change and Spatial Divisions of Labour" in D. Massey and J. Allen (eds) *Uneven Redevelopment*. London: Hodder & Stoughton.

Massey, D. and Meegan, R. (1979) "The Geography of Industrial Reorganisation", *Progress in Planning* 10: 159–237.

Massey, D. and Meegan, R. (1982) *The Anatomy of Job Loss: The How, Why and Where of Employment Decline*. London: Macmillan.

Murgatroyd, L. and Urry, J. (1985) "The Class and Gender Restructuring of Lancaster" in L. Murgatroyd, M. Savage, D. Shapiro, J. Urry, S. Walby and A. Warde, *Localities, Class and Gender*. London: Pion, 30–53.

Perry, D. C. (1987) "The Politics of Dependency in Deindustrialising America: The Case of Buffalo, New York" in M. P. Smith and J. R. Feagin (eds), *The Capitalist City*. Oxford: Basil Blackwell.

Pinch, S. (1989) "The Restructuring Thesis and the Study of Public Services", *Environment and Planning A* 21(7): 905–26.

Piore, M. and Sabel, C. (1984) *The Second Industrial Divide: Possibilities for Prosperity*. New York: Basic Books.

Saunders, P. (1986) *Social Theory and the Urban Question*, 2nd edn. London: Hutchinson.

Sayer, A. and Walker, R. (1992) *The New Social Economy: Reworking the Division of Labour*. Oxford: Basil Blackwell.

Scott, A. J. (1988a) *Metropolis: From the Division of Labor to Urban Form*. Berkeley: University of California Press.

Scott, A. J. (1988b) *New Industrial Spaces: Flexible Production, Organization and Regional Development in North America and Western Europe*. London: Pion.

Smith, M. P. and Feagin, J. (eds) (1987) *The Capitalist City: Global Restructuring and Community Politics*. Oxford: Basil Blackwell.

Smith, M. P. and Tardanico, R. (1987) "Urban Theory Reconsidered: Production, Reproduction and Collective Action" in M. P. Smith and J. R. Feagin (eds) *The Capitalist City*. Oxford: Basil Blackwell, 87–112.

Soja, E. (1989) *Postmodern Geographies*. London: Verso.

Storper, M. and Walker, R. (1989) *The Capitalist Imperative: Territory, Technology and Industrial Growth*. Oxford: Basil Blackwell.

Timberlake, M. (1987) "World Systems Theory and Comparative Urbanisation" in M. P. Smith and J. Feagin (eds) *The Capitalist City*. Oxford: Basil Blackwell, 37–65.

Wallerstein, I. (1974) *The Modern World System*, vol. 1. New York: Academic Press.

Williamson, O. E. (1990) "The Firm as a Nexus of Treaties: An Introduction" in M. Aoki, B. Gustafsson and O. Williamson (eds) *The Firm as a Nexus of Treaties*. London: Sage, 1–25.

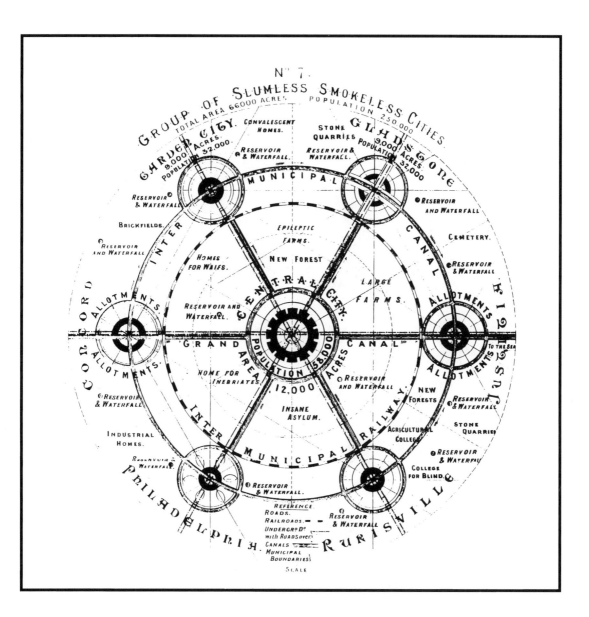

PART 5

*U*rban Planning: Visions, Theory, and Practice

PART FIVE

INTRODUCTION

The effects of urban planning are perhaps the greatest – and, at the same time, the most invisible – influences on human life and culture. In the words of Paul and Percival Goodman, the coauthors of *Communitas* (p. 199), we hardly realize as we go about the daily round of our lives "that somebody once drew some lines on a piece of paper who might have drawn otherwise" and that "now, as engineer and architect once drew, people have to walk and live."

When the Sumerian kings built the walls of Eridu and Uruk, they engaged in acts of urban planning and thus determined how their people would "walk and live." The walls provided safety and protection for the people of the city and also defined the new political unity of the city-state. Similarly, the associated roads, bridges, irrigation systems, and prepared centers for market and ceremonial functions all served a dual function in that they met the practical needs of the urban population in general and fulfilled the power aspirations of the urban elites in particular.

Whether in China, or in India, or in Mesoamerica, ancient urban planning followed a similar pattern of imposing human order on the natural environment to achieve both social and political purposes. And when the Greeks and the Romans and the Renaissance princes spread their empires by planting colonial cities, most often laid out in a strict rectilinear form, they were extending both the imperial reach of their cultures and the political power of their ruling classes.

The origins of modern urban planning are complex. On one level, modern planning is a direct extension of the ancient model: imposing order on nature for the health, safety, and amenity of the urban masses and for the political benefit of the urban elites. On another level, however, modern planning is far more complex than anything that had ever gone on before. Modern planning operates, by and large, in a politically and economically pluralistic environment, making every alteration of the physical arrangements of the city a complex negotiation between competing interests. And the practice of modern urban planning also takes place at a stage of human development when the planner's defining goal is no longer merely to impose human order on nature, but to continuously impose order on the city itself.

Urban planning today involves many actors. Local governments, acting within a legal framework established by national or subnational governments, are responsible for preparing plans to guide the future of their land use, infrastructure, transportation systems, parks and open space, housing, and other physical (and sometimes social and economic) development. Larger governmental units such as states, provinces, or even countries may undertake large-scale regional plans for highways, water supply, or the development of the region itself.

Large local governments may employ dozens or even hundreds of professionally trained planners to carry out this planning work and even many small and moderate-sized towns employ city planners and have some kind of explicit plan for their future. In addition to staff whose formal education is in city (or town) planning, planning staffs are likely to include architects and urban designers, engineers, quantitative analysts, economists, transportation experts, environmental professionals and others. City plans are grounded in analysis of local conditions and contain visions of desirable futures. They vary greatly in sophistication, comprehensiveness, time frame planned for, and format. Plans developed for the London County Council or the Los Angeles City Planning Commission run to many volumes built on mountains of data and sophisticated analysis. The town plan for a provincial market town may contain a commonsense description of the town's situation and some practical suggestions worked out by the residents.

All of these goals and functions of planning – both the ancient holdovers and the modern elaborations – are present in the first planning responses to the urban conditions associated with the Industrial Revolution. As described by Friedrich Engels (p. 47) and many other contemporary observers, the cities of the new industrialism were characterized by horrendous overcrowding and ubiquitous misery and despair. There were daily threats to the public health and safety, not just for the impoverished working class but for the capitalist middle class as well.

These conditions gave rise to movements for housing reform, to great advances in the technologies of water supply and sewage disposal, to the emergence of middle-class suburbs, and to the construction of model "company towns" by various industrial firms in both Europe and America. And in the urban parks movement – especially in the work of Frederick Law Olmsted – the Industrial Revolution gave rise to something very like comprehensive urban planning practice.

Projects like Central Park in New York represented a transplantation and democratization of European landscape gardening traditions, to be sure, but Olmsted's goal was not merely to bring nature into the city. Rather, Olmsted repeatedly appealed to the political and economic leadership of American cities to create parks that would achieve a whole range of public benefits: they would contribute to the public health by serving as the "lungs" of the city; they would be practical and necessary additions to the physical infrastructure of the metropolis, providing a general recreation ground; their ponds and reservoirs would serve as adjuncts to municipal water-supply systems; and they would soften and tame human nature, by providing wholesome alternatives to the vulgar street amusements that daily tempted poor and working-class youth.

Olmsted was a visionary and a reformer, but he was also a successful businessman and a canny political operative capable of offering his clients useful strategic advice on how to fund and build constituencies in favor of large municipal projects. Somewhat less practical, but even more visionary, were a group of architects, planners, and activists who may be termed, collectively, the utopian modernists. Three of these – Ebenezer Howard, Le Corbusier, and Frank Lloyd Wright – define the mainstream of that utopian tradition. Not one of them had his utopian vision realized in its entirety, but each had an enormous influence on the way contemporary cities, and city life, developed in the twentieth century.

Ebenezer Howard prided himself on being "the inventor of the Garden City idea," and his tireless devotion to the project of decongesting the modern metropolis by building small, self-contained, greenbelted cities in the rural countryside is one of the marvels of modern urban planning history. Howard originally wanted his Garden Cities to be cooperatively owned. He wanted the surrounding greenbelt to be much larger than the built-up part of the city itself. And he wanted his cities to be economically independent, not commuter suburbs. In the process of actually building Letchworth and Welwyn (pronounced "Wellin") – the two Garden Cities constructed before his death in 1924 – Howard had to compromise many of his original goals. Building lots and businesses were privately owned; the greenbelt became more of a park than an extensive rural buffer zone; and neither of the original Garden Cities ever became a fully independent economic entity. Still, the Garden City experiment gave rise to a larger movement of town planning, and disciples of Howard – including the prophet of regionalism Patrick Geddes (p. 361), the architect-planner Raymond Unwin (p. 355), and Lewis Mumford (p. 184) – spread his ideas and his example worldwide.

Charles-Edouard Jeanneret, better known as Le Corbusier, was another utopian visionary who never saw his ideal plans fully developed but who was enormously influential nonetheless. Le Corbusier wanted his "Contemporary City of Three Million" to be a series of exquisite towers, geometrically arranged in a surrounding park, and he spent years looking for governmental and industrial sponsors for his plan. Many "Corbusian" high-rise urban developments have been built throughout the world, of course. Indeed, the "International Style" of modern architecture which he pioneered has become a global standard. But in almost every case, the surrounding park has been compromised away in the process of realization. In case after case, the tower in the park has become the tower without the park or, even worse, the tower in the parking lot!

Frank Lloyd Wright, the originator of the visionary "Broadacre City" plan, suffered an almost identical fate. Wright called for a city composed of family homesteads – one full acre per person – and the withering away of the dense and crowded traditional cities. The private automobile, he thought, would virtually abolish distance and allow for a new kind of community based on individualism and self-reliance. What actually became of Wright's Broadacre was sprawl suburbia. One acre per person became one-eighth acre per family (or less); the core cities refused to wither away; the automobile became a new form of dependency, rather than a technology of liberation; and the family-oriented suburban community became problematic at best, an object of ridicule at worst.

The utopian visionaries were more than just planners, if they can be said to be planners at all. Even Ebenezer Howard, the most moderate of the group, was a dreamer. Together, the utopian modernists concerned themselves with great philosophical issues such as the connection between Mankind and Nature, the relationship of city plan to moral reform, and role of urban design and technologies to the evolutionary transformation of society. It would be left to more practical men and women – the actual members of the urban planning profession as it developed in the twentieth century – to address the real-world problems of ever-changing cities and metropolitan regions. If the utopian modernists established the lofty goals, the professional planners attended to the details.

At different times, the actual details of the urban planning process have been collected into influential guides, handbooks, and textbooks that have attained more or less official status as definitive statements of professional practice. In the nineteenth century, such volumes often focused on questions of infrastructural engineering: proper road construction techniques, water supply facilities, and the provision of efficient drainage for sewage disposal and public health. During the early twentieth century, emerging issues were the management of municipal bureaucracies and the professionalization of urban administration. And in the years immediately after World War II, standard guides concentrated on "urban blight," massive inner-city redevelopment strategies, and regional highway systems. In a sense, each such statement of official planning practice was a mirror of both the specific challenges facing the cities of the day and the way people projected their social and cultural concerns on the urban environment.

Today, a number of standard references embody official urban planning practice in various regions and localities around the world. *The Practice of Local Government Planning*, edited by Frank So and Judith Getzels (p. 398), published by the International City Management Association and known as "the green book," is among the reference books most widely used by practicing city planners in the U.S. An examination of its various chapters reveals both the high degree of sophistication that the modern planning profession has achieved and the extent to which urban planning has become an indispensable tool for societal evolution in the late twentieth century.

The introduction to the ICMA green book, included in this section, describes the full spectrum of planning methodologies that a modern planner must deal with every day – from the multivolume general plan or strategic plan, to complex systems plans for utility infrastructures, to the detailed site plan for specific developments. It also provides a step-by-step outline of the complex urban planning process, a field pioneered by Geddes, from initial surveys and goal setting through final implementation and evaluation. And it details a wide range of planning environments – from the decaying downtowns of older cities to the new "high-growth suburban centers" – that reflects the startling diversity of towns, cities, and metropolitan regions today. Most importantly, So and Getzels describe how the modern planner must be a "jack-of-all-trades," combining a knowledge of law, municipal finance, economic development, ecology, aesthetics, sociology, and, above all, "the changing world of politics."

Modern urban planning practice emerged over time both from day-to-day in-the-field experience and from an evolving body of planning theory. Peter Hall's "The City of Theory" recounts how that body of theory began as an attempt to create stable cities "geared to a static world" only to be overwhelmed, beginning in the 1950s, as "the pace of urban development and urban change began to accelerate to an almost superheated level." Hall also shows how planning developed from an early-twentieth-century "golden age" when the planner was "free from political interference" and "serenely sure of his technical capacities" to a late-twentieth-century world in which urban planning was seen as operating within a larger political environment over which planning agencies and the planning profession had little control.

From the turbulent 1960s onwards, the primacy of politics has been a constant focus of planning theory and practice. In cities throughout America and Europe, local community activists began to protest redevelopment projects and to demand a greater voice in the formation of urban planning decisions that affected their lives. These local activists were soon joined by young, idealistic planning professionals, the "advocate planners" described by Paul Davidoff in "Advocacy and Pluralism in Planning" (p. 422). Not every exercise in advocacy planning worked according to plan. Community groups profited from the expertise of their new allies, but differing long-range objectives, charges of careerism, and other suspicions sometimes got in the way of forging effective partnerships across the gulfs of class and race. But a new understanding of the planner's role clearly did emerge from the conflicts surrounding the planning process and its implementation. As John Forester makes clear in "Planning in the Face of Conflict" (p. 434), planners have had to add a facility for negotiating, mediating, conflict resolving, and diplomacy to their professional skills base.

Today, the practice of urban planning remains deeply imbedded in the local municipal political process and in a larger – indeed, increasingly global – political economy of advanced capitalism. As has always been the case, planners simultaneously serve the practical needs of the urban masses and the political aspirations of the urban elites. But the world is rapidly changing. The forces of both globalism and nationality, economic centralization and community decentralization, pull the planner in different directions. And the emergence of major new conceptual forces – such as the impact of feminism on the planning profession that Leonie Sandercock and Ann Forsyth describe (p. 408) – suggests that the dynamic process of change that has been a constant in the history of planning will continue long into the urban future.

FREDERICK LAW OLMSTED

"Public Parks and the Enlargement of Towns"

American Social Science Association (1870)

Editors' introduction   Frederick Law Olmsted (1822–1903) has been called "America's great pioneer landscape architect," and, during his lifetime, he was widely recognized as one of the most influential public figures in the nation. Along with his business partner, the English-born architect Calvert Vaux, he originated and dominated the urban parks movement, pioneered the development of planned suburbs, and laid out scores of public and private institutions. If Central Park in New York remains his best known masterpiece, the designs for Riverside, Illinois (outside Chicago), the Boston park system, the Capitol grounds in Washington, D.C., the 1893 World's Fair, and the campus of Stanford University in California are equally impressive contributions to the built environment.

Olmsted began his career practicing and writing about farming, then turned his talents to journalism and, in the 1850s, published a series of books describing the society and economy of the slave states of the American South (collected into one volume as *The Cotton Kingdom* in 1861). With this background, it is hardly surprising that Olmsted thoroughly imbued his art of landscape architecture with a wide variety of social and political, as well as cultural, concerns.

"Public Parks and the Enlargement of Towns" was originally presented as an address to the American Social Science Association, meeting at the Lowell Institute, Boston, in 1870. In it, Olmsted provides a number of specific guidelines for parks and parkways and suggests ways to overcome political resistance to public funding for parks and planned urban growth. Most importantly, however, he lays out the political and philosophical case for public parks in terms of three great moral imperatives: first, the need to improve public health by sanitation measures and the use of trees to combat air and water pollution; second, the need to combat urban vice and social degeneration, particularly among the children of the urban poor; and third, the need to advance the cause of civilization by the provision of urban amenities that would be democratically available to all.

Both as a practitioner and as a theorist, Olmsted anticipated many of the principal concerns of urban planning – both infrastructural and social – down to the present day. Indeed, behind the somewhat convoluted Victorianisms of his prose lies a strikingly modern mind. In the design of the Garden City (p. 346), Ebenezer Howard borrowed directly from Olmsted, and even plans so fundamentally different as those of Frank Lloyd Wright (p. 377) and Le Corbusier (p. 368) owe a debt to Olmsted insofar as they recognize and address the central problem of the relationship between nature and the built urban environment. And as the father of modern landscape architecture, Olmsted's work and thought invite comparison with all those, including Ian McHarg (p. 133) and J. B. Jackson (p. 82), who came after him in the profession, either as practitioners or critics.

Two excellent biographies of Olmsted are Laura Wood Roper's *FLO: A Biography of Frederick Law Olmsted* (Baltimore: Johns Hopkins, 1973) and Elizabeth Stevenson's *Park Maker: A Life of Frederick Law Olmsted* (New York: Macmillan, 1977). Galen Cranz's *The Politics of Park Design: A History of*

Urban Parks in America (Cambridge, Mass.: MIT Press, 1982) is a superb overview which places Olmsted's planning and landscape design achievements in the context of a larger movement for urban social reform.

FREDERICK LAW OLMSTED, "Public Parks and the Enlargement of Towns"

American Social Science Association (1870)

We have reason to believe, then, that towns which of late have been increasing rapidly on account of their commercial advantages, are likely to be still more attractive to population in the future; that there will in consequence soon be larger towns than any the world has yet known, and that the further progress of civilization is to depend mainly upon the influences by which men's minds and characters will be affected while living in large towns.

Now, knowing that the average length of the life of mankind in towns has been much less than in the country, and that the average amount of disease and misery and of vice and crime has been much greater in towns, this would be a very dark prospect for civilization, if it were not that modern Science has beyond all question determined many of the causes of the special evils by which men are afflicted in towns, and placed means in our hands for guarding against them. It has shown, for example, that under ordinary circumstances, in the interior parts of large and closely built towns, a given quantity of air contains considerably less of the elements which we require to receive through the lungs than the air of the country or even of the outer and more open parts of a town, and that instead of them it carries into the lungs highly corrupt and irritating matters, the action of which tends strongly to vitiate all our sources of vigor – how strongly may perhaps be indicated in the shortest way by the statement that even metallic plates and statues corrode and wear away under the atmosphere influences which prevail in the midst of large towns, more rapidly than in the country.

The irritation and waste of the physical powers which result from the same cause, doubtless indirectly affect and very seriously affect the mind and the moral strength; but there is a general impression that a class of men are bred in towns whose peculiarities are not perhaps adequately accounted for in this way. We may understand these better if we consider that whenever we walk through the denser part of a town, to merely avoid collision with those we meet and pass upon the sidewalks, we have constantly to watch, to foresee, and to guard against their movements. This involves a consideration of their intentions, a calculation of their strength and weakness, which is not so much for their benefit as our own. Our minds are thus brought into close dealings with other minds without any friendly flowing toward them, but rather a drawing from them. Much of the intercourse between men when engaged in the pursuits of commerce has the same tendency – a tendency to regard others in a hard if not always hardening way. Each detail of observation and of the process of thought required in this kind of intercourse or contact of minds is so slight and so common in the experience of towns-people that they are seldom conscious of it. It certainly involves some expenditure nevertheless. People from the country are even conscious of the effect on their nerves and minds of the street contact – often complaining that they feel confused by it; and if we had no relief from it at all during our waking hours, we should all be conscious of suffering from it. It is upon our opportunities of relief from it, therefore, that not only our comfort in town life, but our ability to maintain a temperate, good-natured, and healthy state of mind, depends. This is one of many ways in which it happens that men who have been brought up, as the saying is, in the streets, who have been most directly and completely affected by town influences, so generally show, along with a remarkable quickness of apprehension, a peculiarly hard sort of selfishness. Every day of their lives they have seen thousands of their fellow-men, have met them face to face, have brushed against them, and yet have had no experience of anything in common with them.

[. . .]

It is practically certain that the Boston of to-day is the mere nucleus of the Boston that is to be. It is practically certain that it is to extend over many miles of country now thoroughly rural in character, in parts of which farmers are now laying out roads with a view to shortening the teaming distance between their wood-lots and a railway station, being governed in their courses by old property lines, which were first run simply with reference to the equitable division of heritages, and in other parts of which, perhaps, some wild speculators are having streets staked off from plans which they have formed with a rule and pencil in a broker's office, with a view, chiefly, to the impressions they would make when seen by other speculators on a lithographed map. And by this manner of planning, unless views of duty or of interest prevail that are not yet common, if Boston continues to grow at its present rate even for but a few generations longer, and then simply holds its own until it shall be as old as the Boston in Lincolnshire now is, more men, women, and children are to be seriously affected in health and morals than are now living on this Continent.

Is this a small matter – a mere matter of taste; a sentimental speculation?

It must be within the observation of most of us that where, in the city, wheel-ways originally twenty feet wide were with great difficulty and cost enlarged to thirty, the present width is already less nearly adequate to the present business than the former was to the former business; obstructions are more frequent, movements are slower and oftener arrested, and the liability to collision is greater. The same is true of sidewalks. Trees thus have been cut down,

porches, bow-windows, and other encroachments removed, but every year the walk is less sufficient for the comfortable passing of those who wish to use it.

It is certain that as the distance from the interior to the circumference of towns shall increase with the enlargement of their population, the less sufficient relatively to the service to be performed will be any given space between buildings.

In like manner every evil to which men are specially liable when living in towns, is likely to be aggravated in the future, unless means are devised and adapted in advance to prevent it.

Let us proceed, then, to the question of means, and with a seriousness in some degree befitting a question, upon our dealing with which we know the misery or happiness of many millions of our fellow-beings will depend.

We will for the present set before our minds the two sources of wear and corruption which we have seen to be remediable and therefore preventible. We may admit that commerce requires that in some parts of a town there shall be an arrangement of buildings, and a character of streets and of traffic in them which will establish conditions of corruption and of irritation, physical and mental. But commerce does not require the same conditions to be maintained in all parts of a town.

Air is disinfected by sunlight and foliage. Foliage also acts mechanically to purify the air by screening it. Opportunity and inducement to escape at frequent intervals from the confined and vitiated air of the commercial quarter, and to supply the lungs with air screened and purified by trees, and recently acted upon by sunlight, together with opportunity and inducement to escape from conditions requiring vigilance, wariness, and activity toward other men, – if these could be supplied economically, our problem would be solved.

In the old days of walled towns all tradesmen lived under the roof of their shops, and their children and apprentices and servants sat together with them in the evening about the kitchen fire. But now that the dwelling is built by itself and there is greater room, the inmates have a parlor to spend their evening in; they spread carpets on the floor to gain in quiet, and hang drapery in their windows and papers on their walls to gain in seclusion and beauty. Now that our towns are built without walls, and we can have all the room that we like, is there any good reason why we should not make some similar difference between parts which are likely to be dwelt in, and those which will be required exclusively for commerce?

Would trees, for seclusion and shade and beauty, be out of place, for instance, by the side of certain of our streets? It will, perhaps, appear to you that it is hardly necessary to ask such a question, as throughout the United States trees are commonly planted at the sides of streets. Unfortunately they are seldom so planted as to have fairly settled the question of the desirableness of systematically maintaining trees under these circumstances. In the first place, the streets are planned, wherever they are, essentially alike. Trees are planted in the space assigned for sidewalks, where at first, while they are saplings and the vicinity is rural or suburban, they are not much in the way, but where, as they grow larger, and the vicinity becomes urban, they take up more and more space, while space is more and more required for passage. That is not all. Thousands and tens of thousands are planted every year in a manner and under conditions as nearly certain as possible either to kill them outright, or to so lessen their vitality as to prevent their natural and beautiful development, and to cause premature decrepitude. Often, too, as their lower limbs are found inconvenient, no space having been provided for trees in laying out the street, they are deformed by butcherly amputations. If by rare good fortune they are suffered to become beautiful, they still stand subject to be condemned to death at any time, as obstructions in the highway.

What I would ask is, whether we might not with economy make special provision in some of our streets – in a twentieth or a fiftieth part, if you please, of all – for trees to remain as a permanent furniture of the city? I mean, to make a place for them in which they would have room to grow naturally and gracefully. Even if the distance between the houses should have to be made half as much again as it is required to be in our commercial streets, could not the

space be afforded? Out of town space is not costly when measures to secure it are taken early. The assessments for benefit where such streets were provided for, would, in nearly all cases, defray the cost of the land required. The strips of ground required for the trees, six, twelve, twenty feet wide, would cost nothing for paving or flagging.

The change both of scene and of air which would be obtained by people engaged for the most part in the necessarily confined interior commercial parts of the town, on passing into a street of this character after the trees have become stately and graceful, would be worth a good deal. If such streets were made still broader in some parts, with spacious malls, the advantage would be increased. If each of them were given the proper capacity, and laid out with laterals and connections in suitable directions to serve as a convenient trunk line of communication between two large districts of the town or the business centre and the suburbs, a very great number of people might thus be placed every day under influences counteracting those with which we desire to contend.

These, however, would be merely very simple improvements upon arrangements which are in common use in every considerable town. Their advantages would be incidental to the general uses of streets as they are. But people are willing very often to seek recreations as well as receive it by the way. Provisions may indeed be made expressly for public recreations, with certainty that if convenient they will be resorted to.

We come then to the question: what accommodations for recreation can we provide which shall be so agreeable and so accessible as to be efficiently attractive to the great body of citizens, and which, while giving decided gratification, shall also cause those who resort to them for pleasure to subject themselves, for the time being, to conditions strongly counteractive to the special, enervating conditions of the town?

In the study of this question all forms of recreation may, in the first place, be conveniently arranged under two general heads. One will include all of which the predominating influence is to stimulate exertion of any part or parts needing it; the other, all which cause us to receive pleasure without conscious exertion.

Games chiefly of mental skill, as chess, or athletic sports, as baseball, are examples of means of recreation of the first class, which may be termed that of *exertive* recreation; music and the fine arts generally of the second or *receptive* division.

Considering the first by itself, much consideration will be needed in determining what classes of exercises may be advantageously provided for. In the Bois de Boulogne there is a race-course; in the Bois de Vincennes a ground for artillery target-practice. Military parades are held in Hyde Park. A few cricket clubs are accommodated in most of the London parks, and swimming is permitted in the lakes at certain hours. In the New York Park, on the other hand, none of these exercises are provided for or permitted, except that the boys of the public schools are given the use on holidays of certain large spaces for ball playing. It is considered that the advantage to individuals which would be gained in providing for them would not compensate for the general inconvenience and expense they would cause.

I do not propose to discuss this part of the subject at present, as it is only necessary to my immediate purpose to point out that if recreations requiring large spaces to be given up to the use of a comparatively small number, are not considered essential, numerous small grounds so distributed through a large town that some one of them could be easily reached by a short walk from every house, would be more desirable than a single area of great extent, however rich in landscape attractions it might be. Especially would this be the case if the numerous local grounds were connected and supplemented by a series of trunk-roads or boulevards such as has already been suggested.

Proceeding to the consideration of receptive recreations, it is necessary to ask you to adopt and bear in mind a further subdivision, under two heads, according to the degree in which the average enjoyment is greater when a large congregation assembles for a purpose of receptive recreation, or when the number coming together is small and the circumstances are favorable to the exercise of personal friendliness.

The first I shall term *gregarious*; the second, *neighborly*. Remembering that the immediate matter in hand is a study of fitting accommodations, you will, I trust, see the practical necessity of this classification.

Purely gregarious recreation seems to be generally looked upon in New England society as childish and savage, because, I suppose, there is so little of what we call intellectual gratification in it. We are inclined to engage in it indirectly, furtively, and with complication. Yet there are certain forms of recreation, a large share of the attraction of which must, I think, lie in the gratification of the gregarious inclination, and which, with those who can afford to indulge in them, are so popular as to establish the importance of the requirement.

If I ask myself where I have experienced the most complete gratification of this instinct in public and out of doors, among trees, I find that it has been in the promenade of the Champs-Élysées. As closely following it I should name other promenades of Europe, and our own upon the New York parks. I have studiously watched the latter for several years. I have several times seen fifty thousand people participating in them; and the more I have seen of them, the more highly have I been led to estimate their value as means of counteracting the evils of town life.

Consider that the New York Park and the Brooklyn Park are the only places in those associated cities where, in this eighteen hundred and seventieth year after Christ, you will find a body of Christians coming together, and with an evident glee in the prospect of coming together, all classes largely represented, with a common purpose, not at all intellectual, competitive with none, disposing to jealousy and spiritual or intellectual pride toward none, each individual adding by his mere presence to the pleasure of all others, all helping to the greater happiness of each. You may thus often see vast numbers of persons brought closely together, poor and rich, young and old, Jew and Gentile. I have seen a hundred thousand thus congregated, and I assure you that though there have been not a few that seemed a little dazed, as if they did not quite understand it, and were, perhaps, a little ashamed of it, I have looked studiously but vainly among them for a single face completely unsympathetic with the prevailing expression of good nature and light-heartedness.

Is it doubtful that it does men good to come together in this way in pure air and under the light of heaven, or that it must have an influence directly counteractive to that of the ordinary hard, hustling working hours of town life?

You will agree with me, I am sure, that it is not, and that opportunity, convenient, attractive opportunity, for such congregation, is a very good thing to provide for, in planning the extension of a town.

[...]

Think that the ordinary state of things to many is at this beginning of the town. The public is reading just now a little book in which some of your streets of which you are not proud are described. Go into one of those red cross streets any fine evening next summer, and ask how it is with their residents. Oftentimes you will see half a dozen sitting together on the door-steps or, all in a row, on the curb-stones, with their feet in the gutter; driven out of doors by the closeness within; mothers among them anxiously regarding their children who are dodging about at their play, among the noisy wheels on the pavement.

Again, consider how often you see young men in knots of perhaps half a dozen in lounging attitudes rudely obstructing the sidewalks, chiefly led in their little conversation by the suggestions given to their minds by what or whom they may see passing in the street, men, women, or children, whom they do not know and for whom they have no respect or sympathy. There is nothing among them or about them which is adapted to bring into play a spark of admiration, of delicacy, manliness, or tenderness. You see them presently descend in search of physical comfort to a brilliantly lighted basement, where they find others of their sort, see, hear, smell, drink, and eat all manner of vile things.

Whether on the curb-stones or in the dram-shops, these young men are all under the influence of the same impulse which some satisfy about the tea-table with neighbors and wives

and mothers and children, and all things clean and wholesome, softening, and refining.

If the great city to arise here is to be laid out little by little, and chiefly to suit the views of land-owners, acting only individually, and thinking only of how what they do is to affect the value in the next week or the next year of the few lots that each may hold at the time, the opportunities of so obeying this inclination as at the same time to give the lungs a bath of pure sunny air, to give the mind a suggestion of rest from the devouring eagerness and intellectual strife of town life, will always be few to any, to many will amount to nothing.

But is it possible to make public provision for recreation of this class, essentially domestic and secluded as it is?

It is a question which can, of course, be conclusively answered only from experience. And from experience in some slight degree I shall answer it. There is one large American town, in which it may happen that a man of any class shall say to his wife, when he is going out in the morning: "My dear, when the children come home from school, put some bread and butter and salad in a basket, and go to the spring under the chestnut-tree where we found the Johnsons last week. I will join you there as soon as I can get away from the office. We will walk to the dairy-man's cottage and get some tea, and some fresh milk for the children, and take our supper by the brook-side"; and this shall be no joke, but the most refreshing earnest.

There will be room enough in the Brooklyn Park, when it is finished, for several thousand little family and neighborly parties to bivouac at frequent intervals through the summer, without discommoding one another, or interfering with any other purpose, to say nothing of those who can be drawn out to make a day of it, as many thousand were last year. And although the arrangements for the purpose were yet very incomplete, and but little ground was at all prepared for such use, besides these small parties, consisting of one or two families, there came also, in companies of from thirty to a hundred and fifty, somewhere near twenty thousand children with their parents, Sunday-school teachers, or other guides and friends, who spent the best part of a day under the trees and on the turf, in recreations of which the predominating element was of this neighborly receptive class. Often they would bring a fiddle, flute, and harp, or other music. Tables, seats, shade, turf, swings, cool spring-water, and a pleasing rural prospect, stretching off half a mile or more each way, unbroken by a carriage road or the slightest evidence of the vicinity of the town, were supplied them without charge and bread and milk and ice-cream at moderate fixed charges. In all my life I have never seen such joyous collections of people. I have, in fact, more than once observed tears of gratitude in the eyes of poor women, as they watched their children thus enjoying themselves.

The whole cost of such neighborly festivals, even when they include excursions by rail from the distant parts of the town, does not exceed for each person, on an average, a quarter of a dollar; and when the arrangements are complete, I see no reason why thousands should not come every day where hundreds come now to use them; and if so, who can measure the value, generation after generation, of such provisions for recreation to the over-wrought, much-confined people of the great town that is to be?

For this purpose neither of the forms of ground we have heretofore considered are at all suitable. We want a ground to which people may easily go after their day's work is done, and where they may stroll for an hour, seeing, hearing, and feeling nothing of the bustle and jar of the streets, where they shall, in effect, find the city put far away from them. We want the greatest possible contrast with the streets and the shops and the rooms of the town which will be consistent with convenience and the preservation of good order and neatness. We want, especially, the greatest possible contrast with the restraining and confining conditions of the town, those conditions which compel us to walk circumspectly, watchfully, jealously, which compel us to look closely upon others without sympathy. Practically, what we most want is a simple, broad, open space of clean greensward, with sufficient play of surface and a sufficient number of trees about it to supply a variety of light and shade. This we want as a central feature. We want depth of wood enough about it not only for comfort in hot weather, but to completely shut out the city from our landscapes.

The word *park*, in town nomenclature, should, I think, be reserved for grounds of the character and purpose thus described.

[...]

A park fairly well managed near a large town, will surely become a new center of that town. With the determination of location, size, and boundaries should therefore be associated the duty of arranging new trunk routes of communication between it and the distant parts of the town existing and forecasted.

These may be either narrow informal elongations of the park, varying say from two to five hundred feet in width, and radiating irregularly from it, or if, unfortunately, the town is already laid out in the unhappy way that New York and Brooklyn, San Francisco and Chicago, are, and, I am glad to say, Boston is not, on a plan made long years ago by a man who never saw a spring-carriage, and who had a conscientious dread of the Graces, then we must probably adopt formal Park-ways. They should be so planned and constructed as never to be noisy and seldom crowded, and so also that the straightforward movement of pleasure-car carriages need never be obstructed, unless at absolutely necessary crossings, by slow-going heavy vehicles used for commercial purposes. If possible, also, they should be branched or reticulated with other ways of a similar class, so that no part of the town should finally be many minutes' walk from some one of them; and they should be made interesting by a process of planting and decoration, so that in necessarily passing through them, whether in going to or from the park, or to and from business, some substantial recreative advantage may be incidentally gained. It is a common error to regard a park as something to be produced complete in itself, as a picture to be painted on canvas. It should rather be planned as one to be done in fresco, with constant consideration of exterior objects, some of them quite at a distance and even existing as yet only in the imagination of the painter.

I have thus barely indicated a few of the

points from which we may perceive our duty to apply the means in our hands to ends far distant, with reference to this problem of public recreations. Large operations of construction may not soon be desirable, but I hope you will agree with me that there is little room for question, that reserves of ground for the purposes I have referred to should be fixed upon as soon as possible, before the difficulty of arranging them, which arises from private building, shall be greatly more formidable than now.

EBENEZER HOWARD

"Author's Introduction" and "The Town–Country Magnet"

from *Garden Cities of To-morrow* (1898)

Editors' introduction A stenographer by trade, Ebenezer Howard (1850–1928) was a quiet, modest, even self-effacing man – "a man without credentials or connections," as one biographer put it – who nevertheless managed to change the world.

Born in London, Howard early experienced the pollution, congestion, and social dislocations of the modern industrial metropolis. After a year in America (as a homesteader in Nebraska!), he returned to England in 1876 and became involved in a number of political movements and discussion groups addressing what was then termed "the Social Question." Influenced by a number of radical theorists and visionaries (including the social reformer Robert Owen, the utopian novelist Edward Bellamy, and the "single tax" advocate Henry George), Howard published *To-morrow: a Peaceful Path to Real Reform* in 1898 (now better known under its 1902 title, *Garden Cities of To-morrow*) and methodically set about convincing people of the beauty and utility of "the Garden City idea."

Although Howard's plan may seem quaintly Victorian to the modern reader, the ideas he put forth were nothing short of revolutionary at the time. Indeed, Howard's ideas of urban decentralization, zoning for different uses, the integration of nature into cities, greenbelting, and the development of self-contained "New Town" communities outside crowded central cities illustrated in the figure at the beginning of Part 5 may be said to have laid the groundwork for the entire tradition of modern city planning. And, unlike many other utopian dreamers, Howard lived to see his plans (if in a somewhat compromised form) actually put into action. In his own lifetime, the garden cities of Letchworth and Welwyn were built in England. Later, the Garden City idea spread to continental Europe, to America by way of the New Deal, and to much of the rest of the world.

Howard's argument begins with a protest against urban overcrowding, the one issue upon which, he writes, "men of all parties" are "wellnigh universally agreed." He then explains why "the people continue to stream into the already over-crowded cities" by reference to "the town magnet," that combination of jobs and amenities that characterizes the modern metropolis. Arrayed against this urban magnetic force is "the country magnet," the appealing features of the more natural, but increasingly desolate, rural districts. Finally, Howard describes his own plan, a new kind of human community based on "the town–country magnet," which is the best of both worlds. As detailed in his famous concentric-ring diagram (which, he is careful to warn, is "a diagram only," not an actual site plan), the center of Garden City is to be a central park containing important public buildings and surrounded by a "Crystal Palace" ring of retail stores. The entire city of approximately 1,000 acres is to be encircled by a permanent agricultural greenbelt of some 5,000 acres, and the new cities are to be connected with central "Social Cities" (and each other) by a system of railroad lines.

Howard's ideas about the evils of overcrowding are similar to those of Friedrich Engels (p. 47), and his solution to the problem invites comparison with those of Le Corbusier (p. 368) and Frank Lloyd Wright (p. 377). Direct followers of Howard include Raymond Unwin (p. 355), Patrick Geddes (p. 361), and Lewis Mumford (p. 184), all of whom helped to spread the Garden City idea throughout Europe and America. More recently, Peter Calthorpe (p. 469) has effectively reinvented the Garden City idea in California in the form of greenbelted, suburban "Pedestrian Pockets" linked to central cities (and each other) by a network of light-rail transportation systems.

Garden Cities of To-morrow remains a readable and relevant book. Currently out of print, it is available in most libraries in an MIT Press edition that includes a preface by F. J. Osborn and an introductory essay by Lewis Mumford. A biography of Ebenezer Howard is Robert Bevers, *The Garden City Utopia: A Critical Biography of Ebenezer Howard* (London: Macmillan, 1987). Excellent accounts of Howard and the Garden City movement may be found in Robert Fishman's *Urban Utopias in the Twentieth Century* (New York: Basic Books, 1977) and Peter Hall's *Cities of Tomorrow* (Oxford: Basil Blackwell, 1988).

EBENEZER HOWARD, "Author's Introduction" and "The Town—Country Magnet"

from *Garden Cities of To-morrow* (1898)

AUTHOR'S INTRODUCTION

In these days of strong party feeling and of keenly contested social and religious issues, it might perhaps be thought difficult to find a single question having a vital bearing upon national life and well-being on which all persons, no matter of what political party, or of what shade of sociological opinion, would be found to be fully and entirely agreed ...

[...]

There is, however, a question in regard to which one can scarcely find any difference of opinion ... It is wellnigh universally agreed by men of all parties, not only in England, but all over Europe and America and our colonies, that it is deeply to be deplored that the people should continue to stream into the already over-crowded cities, and should thus further deplete the country districts.

All ... are agreed on the pressing nature of this problem, all are bent on its solution, and though it would doubtless be quite Utopian to expect a similar agreement as to the value of any remedy that may be proposed, it is at least of immense importance that, on a subject thus universally regarded as of supreme importance, we have such a consensus of opinion at the outset. This will be the more remarkable and the more hopeful sign when it is shown, as I believe will be conclusively shown in this work, that the answer to this, one of the most pressing questions of the day, makes of comparatively easy solution many other problems which have hitherto taxed the ingenuity of the greatest thinkers and reformers of our time. Yes, the key to the problem how to restore the people to the land – that beautiful land of ours, with its canopy of sky, the air that blows upon it, the sun that warms it, the rain and dew that moisten it – the very embodiment of Divine love for man – is indeed a *Master Key*, for it is the key to a portal through which, even when scarce ajar, will be seen to pour a flood of light on the problems of intemperance, of excessive toil, of restless anxiety, of grinding poverty – the true limits of Governmental interference, ay, and even the relations of man to the Supreme Power.

It may perhaps be thought that the first step to be taken towards the solution of this question – how to restore the people to the land – would involve a careful consideration of the very numerous causes which have hitherto led to their aggregation in large cities. Were this the case, a very prolonged enquiry would be necessary at the outset. Fortunately, alike for writer and for reader, such an analysis is not, however, here requisite, and for a very simple reason, which may be stated thus: Whatever may have been the causes which have operated in the past, and are operating now, to draw the people into the cities, those causes may all be summed up as "attractions"; and it is obvious, therefore, that no remedy can possibly be effective which will not present to the people, or at least to considerable portions of them, greater "attractions" than our cities now possess, so that the force of the old "attractions" shall be overcome by the force of new "attractions" which are to be created. Each city may be regarded as a magnet, each person as a needle; and, so viewed, it is at once seen that nothing short of the discovery of a method for constructing magnets of yet greater power than our cities possess can be effective for redistributing the population in a spontaneous and healthy manner.

So presented, the problem may appear at first sight to be difficult, if not impossible, of solution. "What", some may be disposed to ask, "can possibly be done to make the country more attractive to a workaday people than the town – to make wages, or at least the standard of physical comfort, higher in the country than in the town; to secure in the country equal possibilities of social intercourse, and to make the prospects of advancement for the average man or woman equal, not to say superior, to those enjoyed in our large cities?" The issue one constantly finds presented in a form very similar to that. The subject is treated continually in the public press, and in all forms of discussion, as though men, or at least working men, had not now, and never could have, any choice or alternative, but either, on the one hand, to stifle their love for human society – at least in wider relations than can be found in a straggling village – or, on the other hand, to forgo almost entirely all the keen and pure delights of the country. The question is universally considered as though it were now, and for ever must remain, quite impossible for working people to live in the country and yet be engaged in pursuits other than agricultural; as though crowded, unhealthy cities were the last word of economic science; and as if our present form of industry, in which sharp lines divide agricultural from industrial pursuits, were necessarily an enduring one. This fallacy is the very common one of ignoring altogether the possibility of alternatives other than those presented to the mind. There are in reality not only, as is so constantly assumed, two alternatives – town life and country life – but a third alternative, in which all the advantages of the most energetic and active town life, with all the beauty and delight of the country, may be secured in perfect combination; and the certainty of being able to live this life will be the magnet which will produce the effect for which we are all striving – the spontaneous movement of the people from our crowded cities to the bosom of our kindly mother earth, at once the source of life, of happiness, of wealth, and of power. The town and the country may, therefore, be regarded as two magnets, each striving to draw the people to itself – a rivalry which a new form of life, partaking of the nature of both, comes to take part in. This may be illustrated by a diagram (Figure 1) of "The Three Magnets", in which the chief advantages of the Town and of the Country are set forth with their corresponding drawbacks, while the advantages of the Town–Country are seen to be free from the disadvantages of either.

The Town magnet, it will be seen, offers, as compared with the Country magnet, the advantages of high wages, opportunities for employment, tempting prospects of advancement, but these are largely counterbalanced by high rents and prices. Its social opportunities and its places of amusement are very alluring, but excessive hours of toil, distance from work, and the "isolation of crowds" tend greatly to reduce the value of these good things. The well-lit streets are a great attraction, especially in winter, but the sunlight is being more and more shut out, while the air is so vitiated that the fine public buildings, like the sparrows, rapidly become covered with soot, and the very statues are in despair. Palatial edifices and fearful slums are the strange, complementary features of modern cities.

The Country magnet declares herself to be the source of all beauty and wealth; but the Town magnet mockingly reminds her that she is very dull for lack of society, and very sparing of her gifts for lack of capital. There are in the country beautiful vistas, lordly parks, violet-scented woods, fresh air, sounds of rippling water; but too often one sees those threatening words, "Trespassers will be prosecuted". Rents, if estimated by the acre, are certainly low, but such low rents are the natural fruit of low wages rather than a cause of substantial comfort; while long hours and lack of amusements forbid the bright sunshine and the pure air to gladden the hearts of the people. The one industry, agriculture, suffers frequently from excessive rainfalls; but this wondrous harvest of the clouds is seldom properly in-gathered, so that, in times of drought, there is frequently, even for drinking purposes, a most insufficient supply. Even the natural healthfulness of the country is largely lost for lack of proper drainage and other sanitary conditions, while, in parts almost deserted by the people, the few who remain are yet frequently huddled together as if in rivalry with the slums of our cities.

But neither the Town magnet nor the Country magnet represents the full plan and purpose of nature. Human society and the beauty of nature are meant to be enjoyed together. The two magnets must be made one. As man and woman by their varied gifts and faculties supplement each other, so should town and country. The town is the symbol of society – of mutual help and friendly co-operation, of fatherhood, motherhood, brotherhood, sisterhood, of wide relations between man and man – of broad, expanding sympathies – of science,

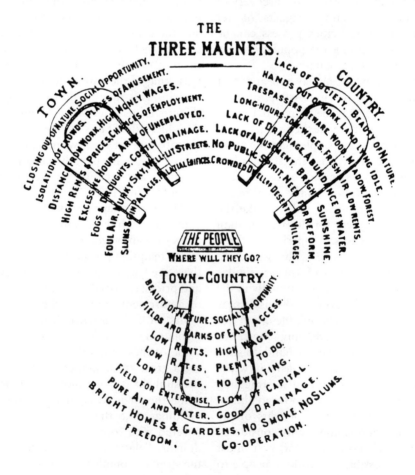

Figure 1

art, culture, religion. And the country! The country is the symbol of God's love and care for man. All that we are and all that we have comes from it. Our bodies are formed of it; to it they return. We are fed by it, clothed by it, and by it are we warmed and sheltered. On its bosom we rest. Its beauty is the inspiration of art, of music, of poetry. Its forces propel all the wheels of industry. It is the source of all health, all wealth, all knowledge. But its fullness of joy and wisdom has not revealed itself to man. Nor can it ever, so long as this unholy, unnatural separation of society and nature endures. Town and country *must be married*, and out of this joyous union will spring a new hope, a new life, a new civilization. It is the purpose of this work to show how a first step can be taken in this direction by the construction of a Town–Country magnet; and I hope to convince the reader that this is practicable, here and now, and that on principles which are the very soundest, whether viewed from the ethical or the economic standpoint.

I will undertake, then, to show how in "Town–Country" equal, nay better, opportunities of social intercourse may be enjoyed than are enjoyed in any crowded city, while yet the beauties of nature may encompass and enfold each dweller therein; how higher wages are compatible with reduced rents and rates; how abundant opportunities for employment and bright prospects of advancement may be secured for all; how capital may be attracted and wealth created; how the most admirable sanitary conditions may be ensured; how beautiful homes and gardens may be seen on every hand; how the bounds of freedom may be widened, and yet all the best results of concert and co-operation gathered in by a happy people.

The construction of such a magnet, could it be effected, followed, as it would be, by the construction of many more, would certainly afford a solution of the burning question set before us by Sir John Gorst, "how to back the tide of migration of the people into the towns, and to get them back upon the land".

[...]

THE TOWN–COUNTRY MAGNET

The reader is asked to imagine an estate embracing an area of 6,000 acres, which is at present purely agricultural, and has been obtained by purchase in the open market at a cost of £40 an acre, or £240,000. The purchase money is supposed to have been raised on mortgage debentures, bearing interest at an average rate not exceeding 4 per cent. The estate is legally vested in the names of four gentlemen of responsible position and of undoubted probity and honour, who hold it in trust, first, as a security for the debenture-holders, and, secondly, in trust for the people of Garden City, the Town–Country magnet, which it is intended to build thereon. One essential feature of the plan is that all ground rents, which are to be based upon the annual value of the land, shall be paid to the trustees, who, after providing for interest and sinking fund, will hand the balance to the Central Council of the new municipality, to be employed by such Council in the creation and maintenance of all necessary public works – roads, schools, parks, etc. The objects of this land purchase may be stated in various ways, but it is sufficient here to say that some of the chief objects are these: To find for our industrial population work at wages of *higher purchasing power*, and to secure healthier surroundings and more regular employment. To enterprising manufacturers, co-operative societies, architects, engineers, builders, and mechanicians of all kinds, as well as to many engaged in various professions, it is intended to offer a means of securing new and better employment for their capital and talents, while to the agriculturists at present on the estate as well as to those who may migrate thither, it is designed to open a new market for their produce close to their doors. Its object is, in short, to raise the standard of health and comfort of all true workers of whatever grade – the means by which these objects are to be achieved being a healthy, natural, and economic combination of town and country life, and this on land owned by the municipality.

Garden City, which is to be built near the centre of the 6,000 acres, covers an area of 1,000 acres, or a sixth part of the 6,000 acres, and might be of circular form, 1,240 yards (or nearly three-quarters of a mile) from centre to circumference. (Figure 2 is a ground plan of the whole municipal area, showing the town in the centre; and Figure 3, which represents one section or ward of the town, will be useful in following the description of the town itself – *a description which is, however, merely suggestive, and will probably be much departed from …*)

Six magnificent boulevards – each 120 feet wide – traverse the city from centre to circumference, dividing it into six equal parts or wards. In the centre is a circular space containing about five and a half acres, laid out as a beautiful and well-watered garden; and, surrounding this garden, each standing in its own ample grounds, are the larger public buildings – town hall, principal concert and lecture hall, theatre, library, museum, picture-gallery, and hospital.

The rest of the large space encircled by the "Crystal Palace" is a public park, containing 145 acres, which includes ample recreation grounds within very easy access of all the people.

Running all round the Central Park (except where it is intersected by the boulevards) is a wide glass arcade called the "Crystal Palace", opening on to the park. This building is in wet weather one of the favourite resorts of the people, whilst the knowledge that its bright shelter is ever close at hand tempts people into Central Park, even in the most doubtful of weathers. Here manufactured goods are exposed for sale, and here most of that class of shopping which requires the joy of deliberation and selection is done. The space enclosed by the Crystal Palace is, however, a good deal larger than is required for these purposes, and a considerable part of it is used as a Winter Garden – the whole forming a permanent exhibition of a most attractive character, whilst its circular form brings it near to every dweller in the town – the furthest removed inhabitant being within 600 yards.

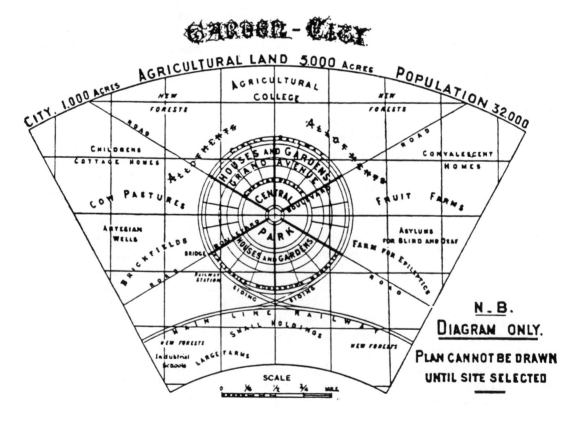

Figure 2

Passing out of the Crystal Palace on our way to the outer ring of the town, we cross Fifth Avenue – lined, as are all the roads of the town, with trees – fronting which, and looking on to the Crystal Palace, we find a ring of very excellently built houses, each standing in its own ample grounds; and, as we continue our walk, we observe that the houses are for the most part built either in concentric rings, facing the various avenues (as the circular roads are termed), or fronting the boulevards and roads which all converge to the centre of the town. Asking the friend who accompanies us on our journey what the population of this little city may be, we are told about 30,000 in the city itself, and about 2,000 in the agricultural estate, and that there are in the town 5,500 building lots of an *average* size of 20 feet × 130 feet – the minimum space allotted for the purpose being 20 × 100. Noticing the very varied architecture and design which the houses and groups of houses display – some having common gardens

and co-operative kitchens – we learn that general observance of street line or harmonious departure from it are the chief points as to house building, over which the municipal authorities exercise control, for, though proper sanitary arrangements are strictly enforced, the fullest measure of individual taste and preference is encouraged.

Walking still toward the outskirts of the town, we come upon "Grand Avenue". This avenue is fully entitled to the name it bears, for it is 420 feet wide, and, forming a belt of green upwards of three miles long, divides that part of the town which lies outside Central Park into two belts. It really constitutes an additional park of 115 acres – a park which is within 240 yards of the furthest removed inhabitant. In this splendid avenue six sites, each of four acres, are occupied by public schools and their surrounding playgrounds and gardens, while other sites are reserved for churches, of such denominations as the religious beliefs of the people may

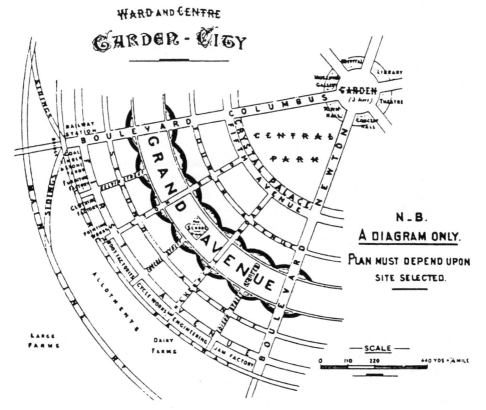

Figure 3

determine, to be erected and maintained out of the funds of the worshippers and their friends. We observe that the houses fronting on Grand Avenue have departed (at least in one of the wards – that of which Figure 3 is a representation) – from the general plan of concentric rings, and, in order to ensure a longer line of frontage on Grand Avenue, are arranged in crescents – thus also to the eye yet further enlarging the already splendid width of Grand Avenue.

On the outer ring of the town are factories, warehouses, dairies, markets, coal yards, timber yards, etc., all fronting on the circle railway, which encompasses the whole town, and which has sidings connecting it with a main line of railway which passes through the estate. This arrangement enables goods to be loaded direct into trucks from the warehouses and work shops, and so sent by railway to distant markets, or to be taken direct from the trucks into the warehouses or factories; thus not only effecting a very great saving in regard to packing and cartage, and reducing to a minimum loss from breakage, but also, by reducing the traffic on the roads of the town, lessening to a very marked extent the cost of their maintenance. The smoke fiend is kept well within bounds in Garden City; for all machinery is driven by electric energy, with the result that the cost of electricity for lighting and other purposes is greatly reduced.

The refuse of the town is utilized on the agricultural portions of the estate, which are held by various individuals in large farms, small holdings, allotments, cow pastures, etc.; the natural competition of these various methods of agriculture, tested by the willingness of occupiers to offer the highest rent to the municipality, tending to bring about the best system of husbandry, or, what is more probable, the best systems adapted for various purposes. Thus it is easily conceivable that it may prove advantageous to grow wheat in very large fields, involving united action under a capitalist farmer, or by a body of co-operators; while the cultivation of vegetables, fruits, and flowers, which requires closer and more personal care, and more of the artistic and inventive faculty, may possibly be best dealt with by individuals, or by small groups of individuals having a common belief in the efficacy and value of certain dressings, methods of culture, or artificial and natural surroundings.

This plan, or, if the reader be pleased to so term it, this absence of plan, avoids the dangers of stagnation or dead level, and, though encouraging individual initiative, permits of the fullest co-operation, while the increased rents which follow from this form of competition are common or municipal property, and by far the larger part of them are expended in permanent improvements.

While the town proper, with its population engaged in various trades, callings, and professions, and with a store or depot in each ward, offers the most natural market to the people engaged on the agricultural estate, inasmuch as to the extent to which the townspeople demand their produce they escape altogether any railway rates and charges; yet the farmers and others are not by any means limited to the town as their only market, but have the fullest right to dispose of their produce to whomsoever they please. Here, as in every feature of the experiment, it will be seen that it is not the area of rights which is contracted, but the area of choice which is enlarged.

This principle of freedom holds good with regard to manufacturers and others who have established themselves in the town. These manage their affairs in their own way, subject, of course, to the general law of the land, and subject to the provision of sufficient space for workmen and reasonable sanitary conditions. Even in regard to such matters as water, lighting, and telephonic communication – which a municipality, if efficient and honest, is certainly the best and most natural body to supply – no rigid or absolute monopoly is sought; and if any private corporation or any body of individuals proved itself capable of supplying on more advantageous terms, either the whole town or a section of it, with these or any commodities the supply of which was taken up by the corporation, this would be allowed. No really sound system of *action* is in more need of artificial support than is any sound system of *thought*. The area of municipal and corporate action is probably destined to become greatly enlarged; but, if it is to be so, it will be because the people possess faith in such action, and that faith can be best shown by a wide extension of the area of freedom.

Dotted about the estate are seen various charitable and philanthropic institutions. These are not under the control of the municipality, but are supported and managed by various public-spirited people who have been invited by the municipality to establish these institutions in an open healthy district, and on land let to them at a pepper-corn rent, it occurring to the authorities that they can the better afford to be thus generous, as the spending power of these institutions greatly benefits the whole community. Besides, as those persons who migrate to the town are among its most energetic and resourceful members, it is but just and right that their more helpless brethren should be able to enjoy the benefits of an experiment which is designed for humanity at large.

RAYMOND UNWIN

"Of Cooperation in Site Planning, and How Common Enjoyment Benefits the Individual"

from *Town Planning in Practice* (1909)

Editors' introduction   Raymond Unwin (1863–1940) was the most influential British city planner of the first half of the twentieth century. He worked through practical city plans to implement Ebenezer Howard's vision of Garden Cities (p. 346). Design ideas he and his cousin and lifelong collaborator, Barry Parker, developed have been incorporated into thousands of developments throughout the world.

Shortly after *Garden Cities of To-morrow* was published, Howard and his disciples formed a company to buy land and build Garden Cities. After secret negotiations, they bought a site at Letchworth, 34 miles from London, in 1903 and hired Unwin and Parker to design a Garden City for 30,000 people. Despite formidable problems, Letchworth was eventually built following Unwin's plan as a quite successful garden city. City planners, social reformers, architects, and others from all over the world drew inspiration from the Parker–Unwin plan for Letchworth. Until his death in 1940, Unwin remained a much-admired city planner whose ideas continued to shape both theoretical discourse and the practice of city planning in the U.K. and the world.

Unwin combined practical skills from his education as an engineer, a reverence for medieval architecture developed by sketching city sites in England and on the Continent, and a passionate belief in Fabian socialist ideas about better housing for the working class and more collective decision making.

Unwin–Parker designs contain curving streets and narrow roads. They reduce overcrowding through residential densities lower than was common at the time – though greater than in many contemporary suburbs today. The plans devote much land to gardens and open space, and contain village greens, greenbelts, and landscaped pedestrian paths. They seek to increase human interaction through cul-de-sacs, quadrangle courtyards reminiscent of monastery cloisters, and community centers. The designs always include features adapted to children, including child-sized benches and community sandboxes. Houses are sited to afford sunlight and views, and the plans pay attention to architectural detail from the city scale through the smallest aspect of individual buildings. In Letchworth and elsewhere, Unwin and Parker devoted as much space to modest "workman's cottages" as politically possible.

The following selection from Unwin's 1909 textbook on city planning reflects the influence of his study of medieval communities, his attention to comprehensive planning of an entire site from "the big interests and the main lines" down to "building details," and concern for essential elements including squares, gardens, open space, and children's space, and his Fabian socialist predilection for greater collective "cooperation." Note similarities between Howard and Unwin's humanistic approach to cities as places where humans may realize their full potential and Kitto's description of the Greek conception of the polis (p. 32). Consider the similarities between Unwin's attack on the wastefulness of individual household appliances, cooking, and day care and Dolores Hayden's ideas for redesigning suburbs and collective use of household appliances (p. 143). Note Unwin's underlying emphasis on physical planning and design as vehicles for unifying and improving society and its similarities to the ideas of urban designers Christopher Alexander (p. 119), Allan Jacobs and Donald Appleyard (p. 165), and William Whyte (p. 110).

The most complete statement of Unwin's ideas is *Town Planning in Practice* (Princeton, N.J.: Princeton University Press, 1993. Reprint of the 1909 original). Accounts of his life and work are in Walter L. Creese, *The Legacy of Raymond Unwin: A Human Pattern for Planning* (Cambridge, Mass.: MIT Press, 1967) and Frank Jackson, *Sir Raymond Unwin: Architect, Planner and Visionary* (London: Zwemmer, 1985).

RAYMOND UNWIN, "Of Cooperation in Site Planning, and How Common Enjoyment Benefits the Individual"

from *Town Planning in Practice* (1909)

The consideration of site planning can hardly have failed to emphasize still further what appeared so evident when considering the question of town planning, namely, that the features which we deplore in the present condition of our residential areas have been largely due to the excessively individualistic character of their development. We have referred in an earlier chapter to the fact that towns and suburbs are the expression of something in the lives of those who build them. The fact that our town populations have been too much mere aggregations of struggling units, having little orderly relationship one with the other, and little of corporate life, has naturally expressed itself in our street plans and in the arrangement of sites. The absence of any attempt to develop with a view to making the best of the whole site or the benefit of everybody dwelling on it and of any unity and harmony in the total effect produced, are but too evident.

In feudal days there existed a definite relationship between the different classes and individuals of society, which expressed itself in the character of the villages and towns in which dwelt those communities of interdependent people. The order may have been primitive in its nature, unduly despotic in character, and detrimental to the development of the full powers

and liberties of the individual, but at least it was an order. Hitherto the growth of democracy, which has destroyed the old feudal structure of society, has but left the individual in the helpless isolation of his freedom. But there is growing up a new sense of the rights and duties of the community as distinct from those of the individual. It is coming to be more and more widely realized that a new order and relationship in society are required to take the place of the old, that the mere setting free of the individual is only the commencement of the work of reconstruction, and not the end. The town planning movement and the powers conferred by legislation on municipalities are strong evidence of the growth of this spirit of association. To no one can this growth appeal more strongly than to the architect, who must realize that his efforts to improve the design of individual buildings will be of comparatively little value until opportunity is again afforded of bringing them into true relationship one with the other, and of giving in each case proper weight and consideration to the total effect. In the planning of our towns in future there will be opportunity for the common life and welfare to be considered first; how are we to secure that consideration for the commonweal shall also come first in the planning of our sites and buildings? To some extent the planning of sites and buildings will, no doubt, be taken in hand by the community, as organized in its municipality; but there seems no need to wait until the development of corporate life and feeling has reached the stage at which it would seem natural for the community to carry out for itself through its own officials the entire development of its towns and homes; it may be better that smaller bodies, more responsive to the initiative of individual pioneers, should deal with the more detailed work. There is a wide field for the activities of companies, associations, and co-operative societies, and for what the Germans call Societies of Public Utility, to develop suburban areas and sites, on lines which shall place first the good of the whole of their community. The way has been shown to some extent by individuals. [Unwin discusses some notable examples of cooperative planning.] The first Garden City at Letchworth and the Hampstead Garden Suburb Trust are examples of companies banded together for the purpose of experimenting on a larger scale in the development of new towns and suburbs, while the various Co-partnership Tenants' Societies are proving the value of co-operation in the development of the sites themselves, and in the building of the houses upon them. Many estates have, of course, been developed in the past by co-operative societies with a view to housing their members, and in a sense they are co-operatively developed. Too often, however, co-operation has ceased with the purchase of the estate, and the development has been carried out very much on the old lines without a full realization of the opportunities which co-operation offers. It is the importance of these opportunities which I wish to emphasize, and to illustrate to some extent from the work of those Co-partnership Tenants' Societies. In some cases, as in the Garden City at Letchworth and the Garden Suburb at Hampstead, the roads and the laying out of the land have been carried out by parent bodies, and the Tenant Societies have developed co-operatively the sites thus prepared. In other cases, as at Ealing, Manchester, Birmingham, Leicester, etc., they have taken up sites of 50 to 100 acres and have undertaken the construction of the subsidiary roads themselves.

Consider how different is the position of the site planner when designing for one of these co-operative societies from his position when planning an area to be let in plots to individuals or speculative builders. In the latter case his first consideration must be the dividing up of the land into well-marked individual plots, avoiding any joint usage or other complications – in fact, securing first of all the absolute separation of each holding from its neighbour. He cannot well provide sites even for minor public buildings, for these will be chosen on individual lines and only after the need for them has arisen. But in working for a co-operative body, such as the Tenants' Society, where the houses when built remain the property of the association, the site planner can approach the problem from a quite different point of view; he at once begins to think of the good of the whole. Just as in the other case he was bound to concentrate his attention on making individual "sell-able" plots, now he can concentrate it on the creation of a village community; he can consider the needs of such a community, how far they will be met by outside opportunities already existing or likely to be developed, and how far they will need to be met on the area of the site. The shops, schools, institutes, and places of worship can all be considered, and the most suitable sites for each reserved. Some *place* can be arranged around which many of these buildings can be grouped and a centre point to the plan be thus secured. The designer can then proceed to lay out the buildings as a whole, considering first their main lines and arrangement, with a view to creating a good total effect, and to preserving and developing any fine views or other advantages the site may offer. It is not necessary for him to think of the absolute isolation of his buildings; this point, instead of being his first consideration, becomes his last thought. The whole of the land remaining in one ownership, there is no difficulty in the common enjoyment of footpaths, greens, or other open spaces; hence he is able to consider the grouping of his buildings with much greater freedom. Where, as may often happen in connection with such co-operative societies, the architect who plans the site also plans the buildings, a most complete opportunity is given for making the best of the site.

Only under some such circumstances is it possible to work up the whole scheme in the right order, taking first the big interests and the main lines, following on with the buildings in their masses and their grouping, working down to the individual buildings themselves, and finally to the details of their arrangement, placing the best rooms where it has been planned to give the best aspect and the best outlook; designing bay windows to take advantage of views which have been kept open, giving special attention and care to those elevations which will most prominently come into the picture, and, indeed, welding the plan of the site, the buildings, and the gardens, more and more into one complete whole.

With a co-operative society it is safe to count also on the common enjoyment of much of the garden space. It is, indeed, possible, even where houses are sold to individuals, to arrange some degree of associated use of gardens, as has often been done in the centres of squares; but difficult problems, both legal and practical, are always raised by such schemes, which do not arise where the whole of the site is owned co-operatively. Where this is the case it becomes possible to group the houses around greens, to provide playgrounds for the children, bowling greens, croquet or tennis lawns or ornamental gardens for the elders, or allotment gardens for those who wish for more ground than the individual plot affords. It becomes possible also to carry out some consistent treatment of garden land, such as the creation of an orchard; for by a consistent planting of fruit-trees in an orderly manner in a series of gardens, much of the beauty and effect of an orchard may be produced. In this way it seems possible to hope that with co-operation there may be introduced into our town suburbs and villages that sense of being the outward expression of an orderly community of people, having intimate relations one with the other, which undoubtedly is given in old English villages, and which has been the cause of much of the beauty which we find there.

The growth of co-operation among cottage dwellers which will, no doubt, spring from the development of the Tenants' Co-partnership and other Societies of Public Utility which are undertaking, and no doubt in future will increasingly undertake, the erection of dwellings, will lead to a need for something in the way of common rooms, baths, washhouses, recreation-rooms, reading-rooms, and possibly eventually common kitchens and dining-halls. These will give to the architect the opportunity of introducing central features in his cottage group designs, like the dining-halls, chapels, and libraries that we associate with colleges and almshouses.

However much we may strive to improve the individual cottage, to extend its accommodation, and enlarge its share of garden or public ground, it must for a long time, and probably for ever, remain true that the conveniences and luxuries with which the few rich are able to surround themselves cannot be multiplied so that they can be added to every house. It is possible, however, and indeed easy, by co-operation to provide for all a reasonable *share* of these same conveniences and luxuries; and if we once overcome the excessive prejudice which shuts up the individual family and all its domestic activities within the precincts of its own cottage, there is hardly any limit to be set to the advantages which co-operation may introduce. Nothing can be more wasteful, alike of first capital cost, cost of maintenance, and cost of labour, than the way in which hundreds and thousands of little inefficient coppers are lit on Monday morning, in small, badly-equipped sculleries, to carry out insignificant quantities of washing. Here, at least, one would think it possible to take a step in the direction of co-operation. Where cottages are built in groups round a quadrangle, how simple it would be to provide one centre where a small, well-arranged laundry could be placed, with proper facilities for heating water, plenty of fixed tubs with taps to fill and empty them, and with properly heated drying-rooms. By two or three hours' use of such a laundry each housewife could carry out her weekly wash more expeditiously and more cheaply than she could do it at home. Perhaps some play-room would need to be attached in which the children could be within reach of their mothers, during the hour or two they would be at work in the laundry. The distance to the laundry from any of the cottages using it must not be too great, and it would be better if it were accessible without passing through the street. In connection with this laundry there might be an arrangement by which, at any time, a hot bath could be obtained at a minimum charge. Where houses are built in continuous rows it would be easy from such a centre to distribute hot water to all of them, thus effecting a great saving in fuel, boilers, and plumbing systems in the separate houses. Such an arrangement has been carried out by the Liverpool Corporation in some of their dwellings. In many other simple ways co-operation may provide for the needs of the individual tenants. Cloisters or covered play-places for the children; public rooms of reasonable size, in which the individual may entertain a number of guests, too many for the small accommodation his cottage affords; reading-room, and library at once suggest themselves as obvious and easily managed projects. More difficult, perhaps, is the question of the common kitchen and dining-hall, and yet it is probably quite as uneconomical, in every sense of the word, for forty housewives to heat up forty ovens and cook forty scrappy dinners, as to do the weekly washing in the usual way. Among the middle class the difficulty of obtaining efficient domestic service is forcing large numbers of people to give up the privacy of family life altogether and to live in boarding-houses and hotels; but by co-operation it is quite possible to combine all the valuable elements of private family life with the advantages of a more varied diet, less engrossing domestic labour and care, and a greater degree of social intercourse, which are the features that attract so many people to the life of the boarding-house and hotel – a kind of life which is unsatisfactory owing to its entire destruction of family life, just as the individual house is unsatisfactory owing to its oppression of the individual by all the necessary details of that life.

This, however, is carrying us beyond the scope of the present subject. We should need a volume in order adequately to discuss the advantages and the difficulties of co-operative living. Along certain directions it is clearly possible, even with the present prejudices, to secure by co-operation very great advantages to the individual; but such a form of life can only be developed tentatively, and the subject is considered here mainly as it affects town planning and architecture. One cannot but feel that for successful work to be produced in this field there must be some form of social life, some system of social relationships, which must find expression, and may be the means of introducing harmony into the work. We see that in the great periods of architecture there have been definite organizations of society, definite relationships, the interdependence of different clearly defined classes, and the association of large bodies of people, held together either by a common religion, a common patriotism, or by the rules of a common handicraft guild. Many of these uniting forces have been weakened or lost in modern times. One naturally looks around to see in what way the unit members of society, who have secured their freedom from so many of the old restraints and guiding influences, are likely in the future to be drawn and bound together. These units are undoubtedly realizing very strongly in the present day how limited is the life which it is possible for them to obtain for themselves under conditions of greater freedom from restraint and organization. They are seeking more and more to procure an extension of opportunities through the State, the municipality, and other existing institutions, and through numberless voluntary unions and associations. It seems, therefore, likely that we may with some confidence predict that co-operation will recover for society some organized form, which will find expression in our architecture and the planning of our towns and cities.

How far this more crystalline structure of society will be due to the direct effort of the whole body, acting through the medium of its State, municipal, and parochial organizations, and how far it will spring from independent, voluntary societies, only time can show. Experience alone can prove how far our present municipal organizations can advantageously carry the work of town planning, laying out of sites, making of streets, and building of houses. Obvious advantages would be found if the whole of the people living in a limited area could co-operate for its development, for the laying out of their city and the building of their houses. The possibilities are greater and the convenience of the whole community can be more thoroughly considered, the wider the area covered by the unit of association. On the other hand, effective oversight of expenditure and details and effective adaptability to new ideas are apt to decrease in proportion as the magnitude of the unit of organization increases. The problem may well be worked out from both ends. The municipalities will find how far they can wisely go, working from the town-planning end; while the smaller societies, beginning with co-operative building, will find by experience how far they can extend their sphere of operations without losing touch with the individual needs. They will prove, also, how far the interests of separate societies will come into conflict, and will need to be harmonized by some federation, controlling in the interests of a wider whole.

The whole question is more one of convenience and form of organization than one of principle. By the present haphazard system we entrust the satisfaction of the community's needs to the individual, who generally acts only when, and in so far as, that satisfaction falls in with his own inclination, and his own limited view of his personal interest. The real opposition of principle lies between this and the organization on co-operative lines of the spontaneous ministering of the community to its own requirements. The form in which this associated effort will organize itself is of secondary importance. The essential thing is that it shall be as little artificial as possible, that it shall be a spontaneous growth following the traditional lines of development; for in so far as it is the natural outcome of the past and present life of the community will its foundation be firm and its future assured.

PATRICK GEDDES

"City Survey for Town Planning Purposes, of Municipalities and Government"

from *Cities in Evolution* (1915)

Editors' introduction   Patrick Geddes (1854–1932) was an eccentric, even enigmatic, Scot who rarely published but who nonetheless became one of the most widely influential urban theorists and urban planning practitioners of the twentieth century. In Peter Hall's phrase, Geddes was "an unclassifiable polymath." Trained as a biological scientist, he was a professor of botany at University College, Dundee, in Scotland; self-trained as a sociologist and historian, he was later a professor of sociology and civics at the University of Bombay.

Through a network of close friendships with such notables as the anarchist philosopher Peter Kropotkin, Ebenezer Howard in England, and Lewis Mumford in the U.S., Geddes was instrumental in the process of spreading Garden City ideas and town planning practices throughout the world. He coined the term "conurbation" to describe the emergent urban agglomerations that Constantin Doxiadis sees becoming "Ecumenopolis" (p. 459). He pioneered modern conceptions of environmentalism by insisting that planning be regional in scope and firmly rooted in local geography (a very radical idea at a time when urban planning was dominated by the primarily aesthetic notions of the City Beautiful movement). And he was an early advocate of community empowerment, having carried out an "unslumming" project in the Old Town district of Edinburgh that began with the distribution of whitewash and flower boxes to the slum residents themselves.

Geddes published *Cities in Evolution* in 1915. In it, he presented a macrohistorical view of urban evolution from village, to civilization, and to eventual decadence. In reference to the then current state of urban affairs, he wrote: "slum, semi-slum, and super-slum, to this has come the Evolution of Cities." His visionary proposal was for the systematic planning of entire regions and for regarding each city's unique regional environment as the basis for a total reconstruction of social and political life.

In the selection here reprinted, Geddes calls for the completion of a complex city survey of local and regional conditions (including physical, social, cultural, and even historical investigations) that must precede any actual planning efforts by local government boards (LGBs). In addition, he argued strongly for a civic exhibition of the survey results so that the local citizenry could participate democratically in major planning decisions. One measure of the far-sighted brilliance of Patrick Geddes is that both ideas – "survey before plan" and citizen participation in the planning process – strike us today as simple common sense. But while inventories are routinely done before preparing city plans today, many fail to include the full range of concerns that Geddes wanted to see addressed. To him, a survey should examine not just the physical and infrastructural environment, but the historical and cultural background of a place as well.

As an early prophet of regionalism, Geddes had a direct influence on environmental planners like Ian McHarg (p. 133) and, through Mumford and others, on the course of much urban planning practice during the New Deal period in America. For an insight into the origins of his thought, consult his early theoretical article "The Twofold Aspect of the Industrial Age: Paleotechnic and Neotechnic," *Town Planning Review*, 31 (1912), and Carl Sussman (ed.), *Planning the Fourth Migration: The Neglected Vision of the Regional Planning Association of America* (Cambridge, Mass.: MIT Press, 1976), which reprints the 1 May 1925 edition of *Survey* magazine devoted to popularizing Geddes's ideas in the U.S. and which includes articles by Mumford, Clarence Stein, Stuart Chase, and Benton MacKaye.

This selection is from Patrick Geddes, *Cities in Evolution* (London: Williams & Norgate, 1915). Geddes's other writings include *City Development: A Study of Parks, Gardens and Culture Institutes* (Edinburgh: Geddes & Co., 1904), essays in *Survey* magazine and a series of reports on planning cities in India.

Biographies of Geddes include Helen Meller, *Patrick Geddes: Social Evolutionist and City Planner* (London: Routledge, 1990) and Marshall Stalley, *Patrick Geddes: Spokesman for Man and the Environment* (New Brunswick, N.J.: Rutgers University Press, 1972), which contains a reprint of most of *Cities in Evolution*.

PATRICK GEDDES, "City Survey for Town Planning Purposes, of Municipalities and Government"

from *Cities in Evolution* (1915)

[...]

We come now to the need of City Surveys and Local Exhibitions as preparatory to Town Planning Schemes. It may but bring our whole argument together, and in a way, we trust, practically convincing to municipal bodies, and appealing also to the Local Government Boards – which in each of the kingdoms have to supervise their schemes – if we here utilize with slight abbreviation, a memorandum prepared in the Sociological Society's Cities Committee, and addressed to the authorities concerned, local and central alike.

SUMMARY OF THE CITIES COMMITTEE'S WORK

We welcomed and highly appreciated the Town Planning Act, and we early decided that it was not necessary for this Committee to enter into its discussion in detail, or that of its proposed amendments. We have addressed ourselves essentially to the problem of Town Planning itself, as raised by the study of particular types of towns and districts involved; and to the nature and method of the City Survey which we are unanimously of opinion is necessary before the preparation of any Town Planning Scheme can be satisfactorily undertaken. Schemes, however, are in incubation, alike by municipal officials, by public utility associations, and by private individuals, expert or otherwise, which, whatever their particular merits, are not based upon any sufficient surveys of the past development and present conditions of their towns, nor upon adequate knowledge of good and bad town planning elsewhere. In such cases the natural order, that of town survey before town planning, is being reversed; and in this way individuals and public bodies are in danger of committing themselves to plans which would have been widely different with fuller knowledge; yet which, once produced, it will be too late to replace, and even difficult to modify.

We have, therefore, during the past few years

addressed ourselves towards the initiation of a number of representative and typical City Surveys, leading towards Civic Exhibitions; and these we hope to see under municipal auspices, in conjunction with public museums and libraries, and with the co-operation of leading citizens representative of different interests and points of view. In Leicester and Saffron Walden, Lambeth, Woolwich, and Chelsea, Dundee, Edinburgh, Dublin, and other cities progress has already been made: and with the necessary skilled and clerical assistance, and moderate outlays, we should be able to assist such surveys in many other towns and cities. Our experience already shows that in this inspiring task, of surveying, usually for the first time, the whole situation and life of a community in past and present, and of thus preparing for the planning scheme which is to forecast, indeed largely decide, its material future, we have the beginnings of a new movement – one already characterized by an arousal of civic feeling, and the corresponding awakening of more enlightened and more generous citizenship.

RECOMMENDATION BY THE COMMITTEE

The preparation of a local and civic survey previous to the preparation of a Town Planning Scheme, though not actually specified in the Act, is fully within its spirit; and we are therefore most anxious that at least a strong recommendation to this effect should form part of the regulations for Town Planning Schemes provided for the guidance of local authorities by the Local Government Board. Without this, municipalities and others interested are in danger of taking the very opposite course, that of planning before survey. Our suggestion towards guarding against this is hence of the most definite kind, viz.:

Before proceeding to the preparation of a Town Planning Scheme, it is desirable to institute a Preliminary Local Survey – to include the collection and public exhibition of maps, plans, models, drawings, documents, statistics, etc., illustrative of Situation, Historic Development, Communications, Industry and Commerce, *Population, Town Conditions and Requirements, etc.*

We desire to bring this practical suggestion before local authorities, and also to ventilate it as far as may be in public opinion and through the press, and in communication to the many bodies whose interest in Town Planning Schemes from various points of view has been recognized in the Third Schedule of the Act, as lately amended by the Government in response to representations from our own and other societies.

DANGERS OF TOWN PLANNING BEFORE TOWN SURVEY

What will be the procedure of any community of which the local authorities have not as yet adequately recognized the need of the full previous consideration implied by our proposed inquiry, with its Survey and Exhibition? It is that the Town Council, or its Streets and Buildings Committee, may simply remit to its City Architect, if it has one, more usually to its Borough Surveyor or Engineer, to draw up the Town Planning Scheme.

This will be done after a fashion. But too few of these officials or of their committees have as yet had time or opportunity to follow the Town Planning movement even in its publications, much less to know it at first hand, from the successes and blunders of other cities. Nor do they always possess the many-sided preparation – geographic, economic, artistic, etc. – which is required for this most complex of architectural problems, one implying, moreover, innumerable social ones.

If the calling in of expert advice be moved for, the Finance Committee of the Town Council, the ratepayers also, will tend to discourage the employment of an external architect. Moreover, with exceptions, still comparatively rare, even the skilled architect, however distinguished as a designer of buildings, is usually as unfamiliar with town planning as can be the town officials; often, if possible, yet more so. For they have at least laid down the existing streets; he has merely had to accept them.

No doubt, if the plan thus individually prepared be so positively bad, in whole or in part, that its defects can be seen by those not specially acquainted with the particular town or with the quarter in question, the LGB [Local Government Board] can disapprove or modify. But even accepting what can be thus done at the distance of London, or even by the brief visit from an LGB advisory officer, the real danger remains. Not that of streets, etc., absurdly wrong perhaps; but that of the *low pass standard* – that of the mass of municipal art hitherto; despite exceptions, usually due to skilled individual initiative.

Town Planning Schemes produced under this too simple and too rapid procedure may thus escape rejection by the LGB rather than fulfil the spirit and aims of its Act; and they will thus commit their towns for a generation, or irreparably, to designs which the coming generation may deplore. Some individual designs will no doubt be excellent; but there are not as yet many skilled town planners among us. Even in Germany, still more in America (despite all recent praise, much of which is justified), this new art is still in its infancy.

As a specific example of failures to recognize and utilize all but the most obvious features and opportunities of even the most commanding sites, the most favourable situations, Edinburgh may be chosen. For, despite its exceptional advantages, its admired examples of ancient and modern town planning, its relatively awakened architects, its comparatively high municipal and public interest in town amenity, Edinburgh notoriously presents many mistakes, disasters, and even vandalisms, of which some are recent ones. If such things happen in cities which largely depend upon their attractive aspect, and whose town council and inhabitants are relatively interested and appreciative, what of towns less favourably situated, less generally aroused to architectural interest, to local vigilance and civic pride? Even with real respect to the London County Council and the record of its individual members, past or present, it must be said that this is hardly a matter in which London can expect the provincial cities to look to her for much light and leading as a whole, while her few great and monumental improvements are naturally beyond their reach.

In short, *passable* Town Planning Schemes may be obtained without this preliminary Survey and Exhibition which we desire to see in each town and city; but the best *possible* cannot be expected. From the confused growth of the recent industrial past, we tend to be as yet easily contented with any improvement: this, however, will not long satisfy us, and still less our successors. This Act seeks to open a new and better era, and to render possible cities which may again be beautiful: it proceeds from Housing to Town (Extension) Planning, and it thus raises inevitably before each municipality the question of town planning at its best – in fact of city development and city design.

METHOD AND USES OF PRELIMINARY SURVEY

The needed preliminary inquiry is readily outlined. It is that of a City Survey. The whole topography of the town and its extensions must be taken into account, and this more fully than in the past, by the utilization not only of maps and plans of the usual kind, but of contour maps, and, if possible, even relief models. Of soil and geology, climate, rainfall, winds, etc., maps are also easily obtained, or compiled from existing sources.

For the development of the town in the past, historical material can usually be collected without undue difficulty. For the modern period, since the railway and industrial period have come in, it is easy to start with its map on the invaluable "Reform Bill Atlas of 1832," and compare with this its plans in successive periods up to the present.

By this study of the actual progress of town developments (which have often followed lines different from those laid down or anticipated at former periods) our present forecasts of future developments may usefully be aided and criticized.

Means of communication in past and present, and in possible future, of course need specially careful mapping.

In this way also appears the need of relating the given town not only to its immediate environs, but to the larger surrounding region. This idea, though as old as geographical science, and though expressed in such a term as "County Town," and implicit in "Port," "Cathedral City," etc., etc., is in our present time only too apt to be forgotten, for town and country interests are commonly treated separately with injury to both. The collaboration of rustic and urban points of view, of county and rural authorities, should thus as far as possible be secured, and will be found of the greatest value. The recent agricultural development in Ireland begins to bring forward the need of a more intelligent and practical co-operation of town and country than has yet been attempted; and towards this end surveys are beginning, and are being already found of value.

Social surveys of the fulness and detail of Mr Booth's well-known map of London may not be necessary; but such broader surveys as those of Councillor Marr in his *Survey of Manchester*, or of Miss Walker for Dundee, and the like, represent the very minimum wherever adequate civic betterment is not to be ignored.

The preparation of this survey of the town's Past and Present may usually be successfully undertaken in association with the town's library and museum, with such help as their curators can readily obtain from the town-house, from fellow-citizens acquainted with special departments, and, when desired, from the Sociological Society's Cities Committee. Experience in various cities shows that such a Civic Exhibition can readily be put in preparation in this way, and without serious expense.

The urgent problem is, however, to secure a similar thoroughness of preparation of the Town Planning Scheme which is so largely to determine the future.

To the Exhibition of the City's Past and Present there therefore needs to be added a corresponding wall-space (a) to display good examples of town planning elsewhere; (b) to receive designs and suggestions towards the City's Future. These may be received from all quarters; some, it may be, invited by the municipality, but others independently offered, and from local or other sources, both professional and lay.

In this threefold Exhibition, then – of their Borough or City, Past, Present, and Possible –

the municipality and the public would practically have the main outlines of the inquiry needful before the preparation of the Town Planning Scheme clearly before them; and the education of the public, and of their representatives and officials alike, may thus – and so far as yet suggested, thus only – be arranged for. Examples of town plans from other cities, especially those of kindred site or conditions, will here be of peculiarly great value, indeed are almost indispensable.

After this exhibition – with its individual contributions, its public and journalistic discussion, its general and expert criticism – the municipal authorities, their officials, and the public are naturally in a much more advanced position as regards knowledge and outlook from that which they occupy at present, or can occupy if the short and easy off-hand method above criticized be adopted, obeying only the minimum requirements of the Act. The preparation of a Town Planning Scheme as good as our present (still limited) lights allow, can then be proceeded with. This should utilize the best suggestions on every hand, selecting freely from designs submitted, and paying for so much as may be accepted on ordinary architectural rates.

As the scheme has to be approved by the LGB, their inspector will have the benefit of the mass of material collected in this exhibition, with corresponding economy of his time and gain to his efficiency. His inspection would essentially be on the spot; any critic who may be appointed would naturally require to do this. His suggestions and emendations could thus be more easily and fully made, and more cheerfully adopted.

The selection of the best designs would be of immense stimulus to individual knowledge and invention in this field, and to a worthy civic rivalry also.

OUTLINE SCHEME FOR A CITY SURVEY AND EXHIBITION

The incipient surveys of towns and cities, above referred to, are already clearly bringing out their local individuality in many respects, in situation and history, in activities and in spirit. No single scheme of survey can therefore be drawn up so as to be equally applicable in detail to all towns alike. Yet unity of method is necessary for clearness, indispensable for comparison; and after the careful study of schemes prepared for particular towns and cities, a general outline has been drafted, applicable to all towns, and easily elaborated and adapted in detail to the individuality of each town or city. It is therefore appended, as suitable for general purposes, and primarily for that Preliminary Survey previous to the preparation of a Town Planning Scheme, which is the urgent recommendation of this Committee.

The survey necessary for the adequate preparation of a Town Planning Scheme involves the collection of detailed information upon the following heads. Such information should be as far as possible in graphic form, i.e. expressed in maps and plans illustrated by drawings, photographs, engravings, etc., with statistical summaries, and with the necessary descriptive text; and is thus suitable for exhibition in town-house, museum, or library; or, when possible, in the city's art galleries.

The following general outline of the main headings of such an inquiry admits of adaptation and extension to the individuality and special conditions of each town and city.

Situation, Topography, and Natural Advantages:

(a) Geology, Climate, Water Supply, etc.
(b) Soils, with Vegetation, Animal Life, etc.
(c) River or Sea Fisheries.
(d) Access to Nature (Sea Coast, etc.).

Means of Communication, Land and Water:

(a) Natural and Historic.
(b) Present State.
(c) Anticipated Developments.

Industries, Manufactures, and Commerce:

(a) Native Industries.
(b) Manufactures.
(c) Commerce, etc.
(d) Anticipated Developments.

Population:

(a) Movement.
(b) Occupations.
(c) Health.
(d) Density.
(e) Distribution of Well-being (Family Conditions, etc.).
(f) Education and Culture Agencies.
(g) Anticipated Requirements.

Town Conditions:

(a) Historical: Phase by Phase, from Origins onwards. Material Survivals and Associations, etc.
(b) Recent: Particularly since 1832 Survey, thus indicating Areas, Lines of Growth and Expansion, and Local Changes under Modern Conditions, e.g. of Streets, Open Spaces, Amenity, etc.
(c) Local Government Areas (Municipal, Parochial, etc.).
(d) Present: Existing Town Plans, in general and detail.
Streets and Boulevards. Open Spaces, Parks, etc.
Internal Communications, etc.
Water, Drainage, Lighting, Electricity, etc.
Housing and Sanitation (of localities in detail).
Existing activities towards Civic Betterment, both Municipal and Private.

Town Planning: Suggestions and Designs:

(A) Example from other Towns and Cities, British and Foreign.
(B) Contributions and Suggestions towards Town Planning Scheme, as regards:
(a) Areas.
(b) Possibilities of Town Expansion (Suburbs, etc.).
(c) Possibilities of City Improvement and Development.
(d) Suggested Treatments of these in detail (alternatives when possible).

A fuller outline for city activities in detail would exceed our present limits; moreover, it will be found to arise more naturally in each city as its survey begins, and in course of the varied collaboration which this calls forth. The preparation of such more detailed surveys is in progress in some of the towns above mentioned, and is well advanced, for instance, in Edinburgh and Dublin: and though these surveys are as yet voluntary and unofficial, there are indications that they may before long be found worthy of municipal adoption. The recent example of the corporation of Newcastle upon Tyne, towards establishing a Civic Museum and Survey, may here again be cited as encouraging, and even predicted as likely before long to become typical.

The question is sometimes asked, How can we, in our town or city, more speedily set agoing this survey and exhibition without the delay of depending entirely on private and personal efforts? Here the services of the Cities and Town Planning Exhibition may be utilized, as notably in the case of Dublin. In this way the city's survey is initiated in consultation with the local experts of all kinds; and the broad outline thus prepared is capable of later local development in detail, with economy of time and convenience of comparison with other cities. The Exhibition, with its civic surveys from other places, is also suggestive and encouraging to local workers: while the variety of examples of town planning and design from all sources are of course helpful to all interested in the preparation of the best possible local schemes.

LE CORBUSIER (CHARLES-EDOUARD JEANNERET)

"A Contemporary City"

from *The City of To-morrow and Its Planning* (1929)

Editors' introduction   Le Corbusier (1887–1969) was one of the genius founding fathers of the Modernist movement and of what has come to be known as the International Style in architecture. Painter, architect, city planner, philosopher, author of revolutionary cultural manifestos – Le Corbusier exemplified the energy and efficiency of the Machine Age. His was the bold, nearly mystical rationality of a generation that was eager to accept the scientific spirit of the twentieth century on its own terms and to throw off all preexisting ties – political, cultural, conceptual – with what it considered an exhausted, outmoded past.

Born Charles-Edouard Jeanneret, Le Corbusier grew up in the Swiss town of La Chaux-de-Fonds, noted for its watchmaking industry. He took his famous pseudonym after he had moved to Paris to pursue a career in art and architecture. From the first, his designs for modern houses – he called them "machines for living" – were strikingly original, and many people were shocked by the spare cubist minimalism of his designs. The real shock, however, came in 1922 when Le Corbusier presented the public with his plan for "a contemporary city of three million people." Laid out in a rigidly symmetrical grid pattern, the city consisted of neatly spaced rows of identical, strictly geometrical skyscrapers. This was not the city of the future, Le Corbusier insisted, but the city of today. It was to be built on the Right Bank, after demolishing several hundred acres of the existing urban fabric of Paris!

The "Contemporary City" proposal certainly caught the attention of the public, but it did not win Le Corbusier many actual urban planning commissions. Throughout the 1920s, 1930s, and 1940s, he sought out potential patrons wherever he could find them – the industrial capitalists of the Voisin automobile company, the communist rulers of the Soviet Union, and the fascist Vichy government of occupied France – mostly without success. Le Corbusier's real impact came not from cities he designed and built himself but from cities that were built by others and from the widespread adoption of certain planning principles that he pioneered. Most notable among these was the notion of "the skyscraper in the park," an idea that is today ubiquitous. Whether in relatively complete examples like Brasilia (where the new city was built from scratch), or in partial examples such as the skyscraper parks and the high-rise housing blocks that have been built in cities worldwide, the Le Corbusier vision has truly transformed the global urban environment.

Le Corbusier's "Contemporary City" plan has often been contrasted to Frank Lloyd Wright's "Broadacre" (p. 377), and the comparison of a thoroughly centralized versus a thoroughly decentralized plan is indeed striking.

Le Corbusier's boldness invites comparison with the original optimism of the post-World War II reconstruction and redevelopment efforts and even with the work of such visionary megastructuralists as Paolo Soleri (p. 454). Jane Jacobs (p. 104) may be counted as one of the severest critics and grassroots opponents of Corbusian city planning principles, and Allan Jacobs and Donald Appleyard's "Urban Design Manifesto" (p. 165) deliberately takes the form of a Le Corbusier pronouncement but rejects his program, opting instead for lively streets, participatory planning, and the integration of old buildings into the new urban fabric. Beneath all the sparkling clarity of Le Corbusier's urban designs are questions which must forever remain conjectural: How would democratic politics be practiced in a Corbusian city? What would social relationships be like amid the gleaming towers?

Le Corbusier's writings include *The City of To-morrow and Its Planning* (London: John Rodher (translated by Frederick Etchells from *Urbanisme*: 8th edn.), 1929. Reprinted 1947 by Architectural Press), *Concerning Town Planning* (London: Architectural Press (translated by Clive Entwistle from *Propos d'urbanisme*), and *L'Urbanisme des trois établissements humaines* (Paris: Éditions de Minuit, 1959).

Excellent accounts of Le Corbusier's ideas may be found in Robert Fishman's *Urban Utopias in the Twentieth Century* (New York: Basic Books, 1977) and Peter Hall's *Cities of Tomorrow* (Oxford: Basil Blackwell, 1988).

LE CORBUSIER (CHARLES-EDOUARD JEANNERET), "A Contemporary City"

from *The City of To-morrow and Its Planning* (1929)

The existing congestion in the centre must be eliminated.

The use of technical analysis and architectural synthesis enabled me to draw up my scheme for a contemporary city of three million inhabitants. The result of my work was shown in November 1922 at the Salon d'Automne in Paris. It was greeted with a sort of stupor; the shock of surprise caused rage in some quarters and enthusiasm in others. The solution I put forward was a rough one and completely uncompromising. There were no notes to accompany the plans, and, alas! not everybody can read a plan. I should have had to be constantly on the spot in order to reply to the fundamental questions which spring from the very depths of human feelings. Such questions are of profound interest and cannot remain unanswered. When at a later date it became necessary that this book should be written, a book in which I could formulate the new principles of Town Planning, I resolutely decided *first of all* to find answers to these fundamental questions. I have used two kinds of argument: first, those essentially human ones which start from the mind or the heart or the physiology of our sensations as a basis; secondly, historical and statistical arguments. Thus I could keep in touch with what is fundamental and at the same time be master of the environment in which all this takes place.

In this way I hope I shall have been able to help my reader to take a number of steps by means of which he can reach a sure and certain position. So that when I unroll my plans I can have the happy assurance that his astonishment will no longer be stupefaction nor his fears mere panic.

[...]

A CONTEMPORARY CITY OF THREE MILLION INHABITANTS

Proceeding in the manner of the investigator in his laboratory, I have avoided all special cases, and all that may be accidental, and I have assumed an ideal site to begin with. My object was not to overcome the existing state of things, but *by constructing a theoretically water-tight formula to arrive at the fundamental principles of modern town planning.* Such fundamental principles, if they are genuine, can serve as the skeleton of any system of modern town planning; being as it were the *rules* according to which development will take place. We shall then be in a position to take a special case, no matter what: whether it be Paris, London, Berlin, New York or some small town. Then, as a result of what we have learnt, we can take control and decide in what direction the forthcoming battle is to be waged. For the desire to rebuild any great city in a modern way is to engage in a formidable battle. Can you imagine people engaging in a battle without knowing their objectives? Yet that is exactly what is happening. The authorities are compelled to do something, so they give the police white sleeves or set them on horseback, they invent sound signals and light signals, they propose to put bridges over streets or moving pavements under the streets; more garden cities are suggested, or it is decided to suppress the tramways, and so on. And these decisions are reached in a sort of frantic haste in order, as it were, to hold a wild beast at bay. That beast is the great city. It is infinitely more powerful than all these devices. And it is just beginning to wake. What will to-morrow bring forth to cope with it?

We must have some rule of conduct.

We must have fundamental principles for modern town planning.

Site

A level site is the ideal site [for the contemporary city (Figure 1)]. In all those places where traffic becomes over-intensified the level site gives a chance of a normal solution to the

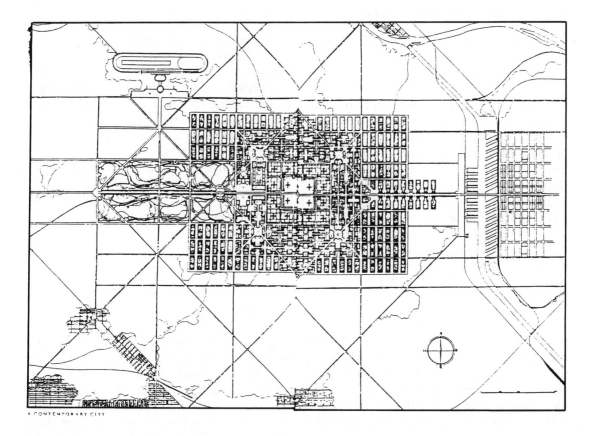

A CONTEMPORARY CITY

Figure 1

problem. Where there is less traffic, differences in level matter less.

The river flows far away from the city. The river is a kind of liquid railway, a goods station and a sorting house. In a decent house the servants' stairs do not go through the drawing room – even if the maid is charming (or if the little boats delight the loiterer leaning on a bridge).

Population

This consists of the citizens proper; of suburban dwellers; and of those of a mixed kind.

(a) Citizens are of the city: those who work and live in it.

(b) Suburban dwellers are those who work in the outer industrial zone and who do not come into the city: they live in garden cities.

(c) The mixed sort are those who work in the business parts of the city but bring up their families in garden cities.

To classify these divisions (and so make possible the transmutation of these recognized types) is to attack the most important problem in town planning, for such a classification would define the areas to be allotted to these three sections and the delimitation of their boundaries. This would enable us to formulate and resolve the following problems:

1 The *City*, as a business and residential centre.
2 The *Industrial City* in relation to the *Garden Cities* (i.e. the question of transport).
3 The *Garden Cities* and the *daily transport* of the workers.

Our first requirement will be an organ that is compact, rapid, lively and concentrated: this is the City with its well organized centre. Our second requirement will be another organ, supple, extensive and elastic; this is the *Garden City* on the periphery. Lying between these two organs, we must *require the legal establishment* of that absolute necessity, a protective zone which allows of extension, *a reserved zone* of woods and fields, a fresh-air reserve.

Density of population

The more dense the population of a city is the less are the distances that have to be covered. The moral, therefore, is that we must *increase the density of the centres of our cities, where business affairs are carried on.*

Lungs

Work in our modern world becomes more intensified day by day, and its demands affect our nervous system in a way that grows more and more dangerous. Modern toil demands quiet and fresh air, not stale air.

The towns of to-day can only increase in density at the expense of the open spaces which are the lungs of a city.

We must *increase the open spaces and diminish the distances to be covered.* Therefore the centre of the city must be constructed *vertically.*

The city's residential quarters must no longer be built along "corridor-streets", full of noise and dust and deprived of light.

It is a simple matter to build urban dwellings away from the streets, without small internal courtyards and with the windows looking on to large parks; and this whether our housing schemes are of the type with "set-backs" or built on the "cellular" principle.

The street

The street of to-day is still the old bare ground which has been paved over, and under which a few tube railways have been run.

The modern street in the true sense of the word is a new type of organism, a sort of stretched-out workshop, a home for many complicated and delicate organs, such as gas, water and electric mains. It is contrary to all economy, to all security, and to all sense to bury these important service mains. They ought to be accessible throughout their length. The various storeys of this stretched-out workshop will each have their own particular functions. If this type of street, which I have called a "workshop", is to be realized, it becomes as much a matter of construction as are the houses with which it is customary to flank it, and the bridges which carry it over valleys and across rivers.

The modern street should be a masterpiece of civil engineering and no longer a job for navvies.

The "corridor-street" should be tolerated no longer, for it poisons the houses that border it and leads to the construction of small internal courts or "wells".

Traffic

Traffic can be classified more easily than other things.

To-day traffic is not classified – it is like dynamite flung at hazard into the street, killing pedestrians. Even so, *traffic does not fulfil its function*. This sacrifice of the pedestrian leads nowhere.

If we classify traffic we get:

(a) Heavy goods traffic.
(b) Lighter goods traffic, i.e vans, etc., which make short journeys in all directions.
(c) Fast traffic, which covers a large section of the town.

Three kinds of roads are needed, and in superimposed storeys:

(a) Below-ground there would be the street for heavy traffic. This storey of the houses would consist merely of concrete piles, and between them large open spaces which would form a sort of clearing-house where heavy goods traffic could load and unload.

(b) At the ground floor level of the buildings there would be the complicated and delicate network of the ordinary streets taking traffic in every desired direction.

(c) Running north and south, and east and west, and forming the two great axes of the city, there would be great *arterial roads for fast one-way traffic* built on immense reinforced concrete bridges 120 to 180 yards in width and approached every half-mile or so by subsidiary roads from ground level. These arterial roads could therefore be joined at any given point, so that even at the highest speeds the town can be traversed and the suburbs reached without having to negotiate any cross-roads.

The number of existing streets should be diminished by two-thirds. The number of crossings depends directly on the number of streets; and *cross-roads are an enemy to traffic*. The number of existing streets was fixed at a remote epoch in history. The perpetuation of the boundaries of properties has, almost without exception, preserved even the faintest tracks and footpaths of the old village and made streets of them, and sometimes even an avenue ... The result is that we have cross-roads every fifty yards, even every twenty yards or ten yards. And this leads to the ridiculous traffic congestion we all know so well.

The distance between two bus stops or two tube stations gives us the necessary unit for the distance between streets, though this unit is conditional on the speed of vehicles and the walking capacity of pedestrians. So an average measure of about 400 yards would give the normal separation between streets, and make a standard for urban distances. My city is conceived on the gridiron system with streets every 400 yards, though occasionally these distances are subdivided to give streets every 200 yards.

This triple system of superimposed levels answers every need of motor traffic (lorries, private cars, taxis, buses) because it provides for rapid and *mobile* transit.

Traffic running on fixed rails is only justified if it is in the form of a convoy carrying an immense load; it then becomes a sort of extension of the underground system or of trains dealing with suburban traffic. *The tramway has no right to exist in the heart of the modern city.*

If the city thus consists of plots about 400 yards square, this will give us sections of about 40 acres in area, and the density of population will vary from 50,000 down to 6,000, according as the "lots" are developed for business or for residential purposes. The natural thing, therefore, would be to continue to apply our unit of distance as it exists in the Paris tubes to-day (namely, 400 yards) and to put a station in the middle of each plot.

Following the two great axes of the city, two "storeys" below the arterial roads for fast traffic, would run the tubes leading to the four furthest points of the garden city suburbs, and linking up with the metropolitan network ... At a still lower level, and again following these two main axes, would run the one-way loop systems for suburban traffic, and below these again the four great main lines serving the provinces and running north, south, east and west. These main lines would end at the Central Station, or better still might be connected up by a loop system.

The station

There is only one station. The only place for the station is in the centre of the city. It is the natural place for it, and there is no reason for putting it anywhere else. The railway station is the hub of the wheel.

The station would be an essentially subterranean building. Its roof, which would be two storeys above the natural ground level of the city, would form the aerodrome for aerotaxis. This aerodrome (linked up with the main aerodrome in the protected zone) must be in close contact with the tubes, the suburban lines, the main lines, the main arteries and the administrative services connected with all these ...

The plan of the city

The basic principles we must follow are these:

1 We must de-congest the centres of our cities.
2 We must augment their density.
3 We must increase the means for getting about.
4 We must increase parks and open spaces.

At the very centre we have the *station* with its landing stage for aero-taxis.

Running north and south, and east and west, we have the *main arteries* for fast traffic, form-

ing elevated roadways 120 feet wide.

At the base of the sky-scrapers and all round them we have a great open space 2,400 yards by 1,500 yards, giving an area of 3,600,000 square yards, and occupied by gardens, parks and avenues. In these parks, at the foot of and round the sky-scrapers, would be the restaurants and cafes, the luxury shops, housed in buildings with receding terraces: here too would be the theatres, halls and so on; and here the parking places or garage shelters.

The sky-scrapers are designed purely for business purposes.

On the left we have the great public buildings, the museums, the municipal and administrative offices. Still further on the left we have the "Park" (which is available for further logical development of the heart of the city).

On the right, and traversed by one of the arms of the main arterial roads, we have the warehouses, and the industrial quarters with their goods stations.

All around the city is the *protected zone* of woods and green fields.

Further beyond are the *garden cities*, forming a wide encircling band.

Then, right in the midst of all these, we have the *Central Station*, made up of the following elements:

(a) The landing-platform; forming an aerodrome of 200,000 square yards in area.
(b) The entresol or mezzanine; at this level are the raised tracks for fast motor traffic: the only crossing being gyratory.
(c) The ground floor where are the entrance halls and booking offices for the tubes, suburban lines, main line and air traffic.
(d) The "basement": here are the tubes which serve the city and the main arteries.
(e) The "sub-basement": here are the suburban lines running on a one-way loop.
(f) The "sub-sub-basement": here are the main lines (going north, south, east and west).

The city

Here we have twenty-four sky-scrapers capable each of housing 10,000 to 50,000 employees; this is the business and hotel section, etc., and accounts for 400,000 to 600,000 inhabitants.

The residential blocks, of the two main types already mentioned, account for a further 600,000 inhabitants.

The garden cities give us a further 2,000,000 inhabitants, or more.

In the great central open space are the cafes, restaurants, luxury shops, halls of various kinds, a magnificent forum descending by stages down to the immense parks surrounding it, the whole arrangement providing a spectacle of order and vitality.

Density of population

(a) The sky-scraper: 1,200 inhabitants to the acre.
(b) The residential blocks with set-backs: 120 inhabitants to the acre. These are the luxury dwellings.
(c) The residential blocks on the "cellular" system, with a similar number of inhabitants.

This great density gives us our necessary shortening of distances and ensures rapid inter-communication.

Note. The average density to the acre of Paris in the heart of the town is 146, and of London 63; and of the over-crowded quarters of Paris 213, and of London 169.

Open spaces

Of the area (a), 95 per cent of the ground is open (squares, restaurants, theatres).

Of the area (b), 85 per cent of the ground is open (gardens, sports grounds).

Of the area (c), 48 per cent of the ground is open (gardens, sports grounds).

Educational and civic centres, universities, museums of art and industry, public services, county hall

The "Jardin anglais". (The city can extend here, if necessary.)

Sports grounds: Motor racing track, Race-course, Stadium, Swimming baths, etc.

The protected zone (which will be the property of the city), with its aerodrome

A zone in which all building would be pro-hibited; reserved for the growth of the city as laid down by the municipality: it would consist of woods, fields, and sports grounds. The form-ing of a "protected zone" by continual purchase of small properties in the immediate vicinity of the city is one of the most essential and urgent tasks which a municipality can pursue. It would eventually represent a tenfold return on the capital invested.

Industrial quarters: types of buildings employed

For business: sky-scrapers sixty storeys high with no internal wells or courtyards ...

Residential buildings with "set-backs", of six double storeys; again with no internal wells: the flats looking on either side on to immense parks.

Residential buildings on the "cellular" prin-ciple, with "hanging gardens", looking on to immense parks; again no internal wells. These are "service-flats" of the most modern kind.

Garden cities: their aesthetic, economy, perfection and modern outlook

A simple phrase suffices to express the necessi-ties of tomorrow: WE MUST BUILD IN THE OPEN. The lay-out must be of a purely geometrical kind, with all its many and delicate implica-tions.

[...]

The city of to-day is a dying thing because it is not geometrical. To build in the open would be to replace our present haphazard arrange-ments, *which are all we have to-day*, by a *uniform* lay-out. Unless we do this *there is no salvation.*

The result of a true geometrical lay-out is *repetition.* The result of repetition is a *standard,* the perfect form (i.e. the creation of standard types). A geometrical lay-out means that mathematics play their part. There is no first-rate human production but has geometry at its base. It is of the very essence of Architecture. To introduce uniformity into the building of the city we must *industrialize building*. Building is the one economic activity which has so far resisted industrialization. It has thus escaped the march of progress, with the result that the cost of building is still abnormally high.

The architect, from a professional point of view, has become a twisted sort of creature. He has grown to love irregular sites, claiming that they inspire him with original ideas for getting round them. Of course he is wrong. For nowadays the only building that can be undertaken must be either for the rich or built at a loss (as, for instance, in the case of municipal housing schemes), or else by jerry-building and so robbing the inhabitant of all amenities. A motor-car which is achieved by mass production is a masterpiece of comfort, precision, balance and good taste. A house built to order (on an "interesting" site) is a masterpiece of incongruity – a monstrous thing.

If the builder's yard were reorganized on the lines of standardization and mass production we might have gangs of workmen as keen and intelligent as mechanics.

The mechanic dates back only twenty years, yet already he forms the highest caste of the working world.

The mason dates ... from time immemorial! He bangs away with feet and hammer. He smashes up everything round him, and the plant entrusted to him falls to pieces in a few months. The spirit of the mason must be disciplined by making him part of the severe and exact machinery of the industrialized builder's yard.

The cost of building would fall in the proportion of 10 to 2.

The wages of the labourers would fall into definite categories; to each according to his merits and service rendered.

The "interesting" or erratic site absorbs every creative faculty of the architect and wears him out. What results is equally erratic: lop-sided abortions; a specialist's solution which can only please other specialists.

We must build *in the open*: both within the city and around it.

Then having worked through every necessary technical stage and using absolute ECONOMY, we shall be in a position to experience the intense joys of a creative art which is based on geometry.

THE CITY AND ITS AESTHETIC

(The plan of a city which is here presented is a direct consequence of purely geometric considerations.)

A new unit *on a large scale* (400 yards) inspires everything. Though the gridiron arrangement of the streets every 400 yards (sometimes only 200) is uniform (with a consequent ease in finding one's way about), no two streets are in any way alike. This is where, in a magnificent contrapuntal symphony, the forces of geometry come into play.

Suppose we are entering the city by way of the Great Park. Our fast car takes the special elevated motor track between the majestic sky-scrapers: as we approach nearer there is seen the repetition against the sky of the twenty-four sky-scrapers; to our left and right on the outskirts of each particular area are the municipal and administrative buildings; and enclosing the space are the museums and university buildings.

Then suddenly we find ourselves at the feet of the first sky-scrapers. But here we have, not the meager shaft of sunlight which so faintly illumines the dismal streets of New York, but an immensity of space. The whole city is a Park. The terraces stretch out over lawns and into groves. Low buildings of a horizontal kind lead the eye on to the foliage of the trees. Where are now the trivial *Procuracies*? Here is the *city* with its crowds living in peace and pure air, where noise is smothered under the foliage of green trees. The chaos of New York is overcome. Here, bathed in light, stands the modern city [Figure 2].

Our car has left the elevated track and has dropped its speed of sixty miles an hour to run gently through the residential quarters. The "set-backs" permit of vast architectural perspectives. There are gardens, games and sports grounds. And sky everywhere, as far as the eye can see. The square silhouettes of the terraced roofs stand clear against the sky, bordered with the verdure of the hanging gardens. The uniformity of the units that compose the picture throw into relief the firm lines on which the far-flung masses are constructed. Their outlines softened by distance, the sky-scrapers raise immense geometrical facades all of glass, and in them is reflected the blue glory of the sky. An overwhelming sensation. Immense but radiant prisms.

And in every direction we have a varying spectacle: our "gridiron" is based on a unit of 400 yards, but it is strangely modified by architectural devices! (The "set-backs" are in counterpoint, on a unit of 600×400.)

The traveller in his airplane, arriving from Constantinople or Pekin it may be, suddenly sees appearing through the wavering lines of rivers and patches of forests that clear imprint which marks a city which has grown in accordance with the spirit of man: the mark of the human brain at work.

As twilight falls the glass sky-scrapers seem to flame.

This is no dangerous futurism, a sort of literary dynamite flung violently at the spectator. It is a spectacle organized by an Architecture which uses plastic resources for the modulation of forms seen in light.

A city made for speed is made for success.

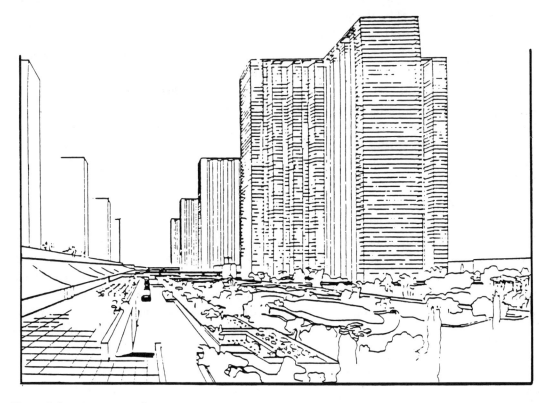

Figure 2 A contemporary city

FRANK LLOYD WRIGHT

"Broadacre City: A New Community Plan"

Architectural Record (1935)

Editors' introduction   For more than half a century, the question "Who is the greatest American architect?" could have only one answer: Frank Lloyd Wright (1867–1959). First with his revolutionary "prairie houses" that seemed to grow directly out of the Midwest landscape with their long, low cantilevered rooflines, and later with a series of commissions that included such masterpieces as the Imperial Hotel in Tokyo, the Guggenheim Museum in New York, and the breathtaking "Falling Water" in Western Pennsylvania, Wright became the spokesman for "organic architecture" and for a style of building that expressed "the nature of the materials."

To many, Wright's architecture and "the architecture of American democracy" were synonymous. As an unabashed egotist and something of a pioneer in the field of media celebrity, Wright encouraged the popular identification of himself with the American spirit. He cultivated an imperious image of plain-speaking, anticollectivist democracy and sought personally to embody the notions of radical individualism. As an artistic genius, Wright despised the popular philistinism of his day and attributed the observable decline of American popular culture to "the mobocracy" and to the unprincipled bankers and politicians who served its interests. By the 1920s and 1930s, Wright had become a social revolutionary but not, characteristically, of the socialist Left. Rather, Wright called for a radical transformation of American society in such a way as to restore earlier Emersonian and Jeffersonian virtues. And the physical embodiment of that utopian vision was Broadacre City.

Wright unveiled his model of Broadacre at Rockefeller Center, New York, in 1935. The article here reprinted represents his first and clearest statement of the revolutionary proposal whereby every citizen of the United States would be given a minimum of one acre of land per person, with the family homestead being the basis of the civilization as a whole and with government reduced to nothing more than a county architect who would be in charge of directing land allotments and the construction of basic community facilities. Many at the time thought the idea was totally outlandish, but Broadacre (and the small, efficient "Usonian" house) proved to be prophetic as sprawling suburban regions transformed the American landscape during the second half of the twentieth century.

Wright believed that two inventions – the telephone and the automobile – made the old cities "no longer modern," and he fervently looked forward to the day when dense, crowded conglomerations like New York and Chicago would wither and decay. In their place, Americans would reinhabit the rural landscape (and reacquire the rural virtues of individual freedom and self-reliance) with a "city" of independent homesteads in which people would be isolated enough from one another to insure family stability but connected enough, through modern telecommunications and transportation, to achieve a real sense of community. Borrowing an idea from the anarchist philosopher Kropotkin, Wright believed that the citizens of Broadacre would pursue a combination of manual and intellectual work every day, thus achieving a human wholeness that modern society and the modern city had destroyed. He also believed that a system of personal freedom and dignity through land ownership was the way to guarantee social harmony and avoid the class struggle.

Broadacre City invites immediate comparison with the very different models of Ebenezer Howard's Garden City (p. 346) and with Le Corbusier's cities based on towers in a park (p. 368). Intriguingly, the overall population density of Broadacre, on the one hand, and the Garden City and Corbusian visions, on the other, may not be all that different, depending on the actual acreage of the surrounding parkland or greenbelt. And both Wright's and Le Corbusier's plans are wedded to the automobile, one vision seeing a centralizing, the other a decentralizing, effect. But the most revealing comparison is the one Robert Fishman makes in his description of the now-emerging "technoburbs" (p. 485). One cannot help but wonder whether what seemed impossible in 1935 may actually be realized, with the help of computer-based telecommunications and the possibility of "telecommuting" to work over the Internet, as we approach the twenty-first century.

This selection is from *Architectural Record*, vol. 77 (April 1935).

There are many excellent biographies of Frank Lloyd Wright and even more critical analyses of his buildings and designs. The single most useful treatment of Broadacre can be found in Robert Fishman's *Urban Utopias of the Twentieth Century* (Cambridge, Mass.: MIT Press, 1982). But the very best sources on Wright are Wright himself, although his writing style is often quirky and hyperbolic. Of particular interest are *When Democracy Builds* (Chicago: University of Chicago Press, 1945), *Genius and the Mobocracy* (New York: Duell, Sloan & Pearce, 1949), and *The Living City* (New York: Horizon, 1958).

FRANK LLOYD WRIGHT, "Broadacre City: A New Community Plan"

Architectural Record (1935)

Given the simple exercise of several inherently just rights of man, the freedom to decentralize, to redistribute and to correlate the properties of the life of man on earth to his birthright – the ground itself – and Broadacre City becomes reality.

As I see Architecture, the best architect is he who will devise forms nearest organic as features of human growth by way of changes natural to that growth. Civilization is itself inevitably a form but not, if democracy is sanity, is it necessarily the fixation called "academic." All regimentation is a form of death which may sometimes serve life but more often imposes upon it. In Broadacres all is symmetrical but it is seldom obviously and never academically so.

Whatever forms issue are capable of normal growth without destruction of such pattern as they may have. Nor is there much obvious repetition in the new city. Where regiment and row serve the general harmony of arrangement both are present, but generally, both are absent except where planting and cultivation are naturally a process or walls afford a desired seclusion. Rhythm is the substitute for such repetitions everywhere. Wherever repetition (standardization) enters, it has been modified by inner rhythms either by art or by nature as it must, to be of any lasting human value.

The three major inventions already at work building Broadacres, whether the powers that over-built the old cities otherwise like it or not, are:

1   The motor car: general mobilization of the human being.

2   Radio, telephone and telegraph: electrical inter-communication becoming complete.
3   Standardized   machine-shop   production: machine invention plus scientific discovery.

The price of the major three to America has been the exploitation we see everywhere around us in waste and in ugly scaffolding that may now be thrown away. The price has not been so great if by way of popular government we are able to exercise the use of three inherent rights of any man:

1   His social right to a direct medium of exchange in place of gold as a commodity: some form of social credit.
2   His social right to his place on the ground as he has had it in the sun and air: land to be held only by use and improvements.
3   His social right to the ideas by which and for which he lives: public ownership of invention and scientific discoveries that concern the life of the people.

The only assumption made by Broadacres as ideal is that these three rights will be the citizen's so soon as the folly of endeavoring to cheat him of their democratic values becomes apparent to those who hold (feudal survivors or survivals), as it is becoming apparent to the thinking people who are held blindly abject or subject against their will.

The landlord is no happier than the tenant. The speculator can no longer win much at a game about played out. The present success-ideal, placing, as it does, premiums upon the wolf, the fox and the rat in human affairs and above all, upon the parasite, is growing more evident every day as a falsity just as injurious to the "successful" as to the victims of such success. Well – sociologically, Broadacres is release from all that fatal "success" which is, after all, only excess. So I have called it a new freedom for living in America. It has thrown the scaffolding aside. It sets up a new ideal of success.

In Broadacres, by elimination of cities and towns the present curse of petty and minor officialdom, government, has been reduced to one minor government for each county. The waste motion, the back and forth haul, that today makes so much idle business is gone.

Distribution becomes automatic and direct, taking place mostly in the region of origin. Methods of distribution of everything are simple and direct. From the maker to the consumer by the most direct route.

Coal (one-third the tonnage of the haul of our railways) is eliminated by burning it at the mines and transferring that power, making it easier to take over the great railroad rights of way; to take off the cumbersome rolling stock and put the right of way into general service as the great arterial on which truck traffic is concentrated on lower side lanes, many lanes of speed traffic above and monorail speed trains at the center, continuously running. Because traffic may take off or take on at any given point, these arterials are traffic not dated but fluescent. And the great arterial as well as all the highways become   great   architecture,   automatically affording within their structure all necessary storage facilities of raw materials, the elimination of all unsightly piles of raw material.

In the hands of the state, but by way of the county, is all redistribution of land – a minimum of one acre going to the childless family and more to the larger family as effected by the state. The agent of the state in all matters of land allotment or improvement, or in matters affecting the harmony of the whole, is the architect. All building is subject to his sense of the whole as organic architecture. Here architecture is landscape and landscape takes on the character of architecture by way of the simple process of cultivation.

All public utilities are concentrated in the hands of the state and county government as are matters of administration, patrol, fire, post, banking, license and record, making politics a vital matter to everyone in the new city instead of the old case where hopeless indifference makes "politics" a grafter's profession.

In the buildings for Broadacres no distinction exists between much and little, more and less. Quality is in all, for all, alike. The thought entering into the first or last estate is of the best. What differs is only individuality and extent. There is nothing poor or mean in Broadacres.

Nor does Broadacres issue any dictum or see any finality in the matter either of pattern or style.

Organic character is style. Such style has myriad forms inherently good. Growth is possible to Broadacres as a fundamental form, not as mere accident of change but as integral pattern unfolding from within.

Here now may be seen the elemental units of our social structure [Figure 1]: the correlated farm, the factory – its smoke and gases eliminated by burning coal at places of origin, the decentralized school, the various conditions of residence, the home offices, safe traffic, simplified government. All common interests take place in a simple coordination wherein all are employed: *little* farms, *little* homes for industry, *little* factories, *little* schools, a *little* university going to the people mostly by way of their interest in the ground, *little* laboratories on their own ground for professional men. And the farm itself, notwithstanding its animals, becomes the most attractive unit of the city. The husbandry of animals at last is in decent association with them and with all else as well. True farm relief.

To build Broadacres as conceived would automatically end unemployment and all its evils forever. There would never be labor enough nor could under-consumption ever

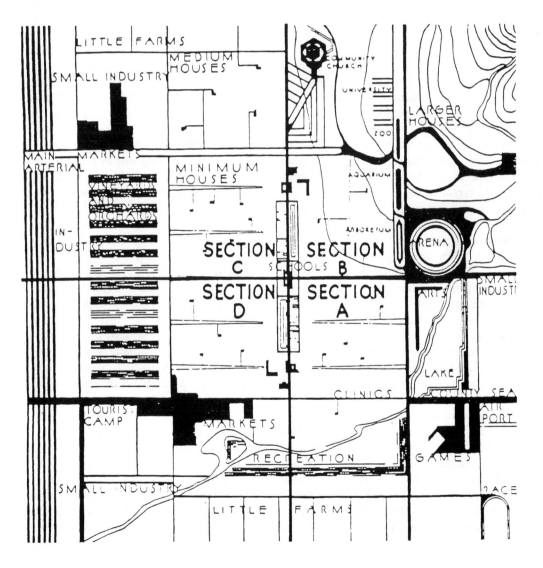

Figure 1

ensue. Whatever a man did would be done – obviously and directly – mostly by himself in his own interest under the most valuable inspiration and direction: under training, certainly, if necessary. Economic independence would be near, a subsistence certain; life varied and interesting.

Every kind of builder would be likely to have a jealous eye to the harmony of the whole within broad limits fixed by the county architect, an architect chosen by the county itself. Each county would thus naturally develop an individuality of its own. Architecture – in the broad sense – would thrive.

In an organic architecture the ground itself predetermines all features; the climate modifies them; available means limit them; function shapes them.

Form and function are one in Broadacres. But Broadacres is no finality! The model shows four square miles of a typical countryside developed on the acre as unit according to conditions in the temperate zone and accommodating some 1,400 families. It would swing north or swing south in type as conditions, climate and topography of the region changed.

In the model the emphasis has been placed upon diversity in unity, recognizing the necessity of cultivation as a need for formality in most of the planting. By a simple government subsidy certain specific acres or groups of acre units are, in every generation, planted to useful trees, meantime beautiful, giving privacy and various rural divisions. There are no rows of trees alongside the roads to shut out the view. Rows where they occur are perpendicular to the road or the trees are planted in groups. Useful trees like white pine, walnut, birch, beech, fir, would come to maturity as well as fruit and nut trees and they would come as a profitable crop meantime giving character, privacy and comfort to the whole city. The general park is a flowered meadow beside the stream and is bordered with ranks of trees, tiers gradually rising in height above the flowers at the ground level. A music-garden is sequestered from noise at one end. Much is made of general sports and festivals by way of the stadium, zoo, aquarium, arboretum and the arts.

The traffic problem has been given special attention, as the more mobilization is made a comfort and a facility the sooner will Broadacres arrive. Every Broadacre citizen has his own car. Multiple-lane highways make travel safe and enjoyable. There are no grade crossings nor left turns on grade. The road system and construction is such that no signals nor any lamp-posts need be seen. No ditches are alongside the roads. No curbs either. An inlaid purfling over which the car cannot come without damage to itself takes its place to protect the pedestrian.

In the affair of air transport Broadacres rejects the present airplane and substitutes the self-contained mechanical unit that is sure to come: an aerator capable of rising straight up and by reversible rotors able to travel in any given direction under radio control at a maximum speed of, say, 200 miles an hour, and able to descend safely into the hexacomb from which it arose or anywhere else. By a doorstep if desired.

The only fixed transport trains kept on the arterial are the long-distance monorail cars traveling at a speed (already established in Germany) of 220 miles per hour. All other traffic is by motor car on the twelve lane levels or the triple truck lanes on the lower levels which have on both sides the advantage of delivery direct to warehousing or from warehouses to consumer. Local trucks may get to warehouse-storage on lower levels under the main arterial itself. A local truck road parallels the swifter lanes.

Houses in the new city are varied: make much of fireproof synthetic materials, factory-fabricated units adapted to free assembly and varied arrangement, but do not neglect the older nature-materials wherever they are desired and available. House-holders' utilities are nearly all planned in prefabricated utility stacks or units, simplifying construction and reducing building costs to a certainty. There is the professional's house with its laboratory, the minimum house with its workshop, the medium house ditto, the larger house and the house of machine-age luxury. We might speak of them as a one-car house, a two-car house, a three-car house and a five-car house. Glass is extensively used as are roofless rooms. The roof is used often as a trellis or a garden. But where glass is extensively used it is usually for domestic purposes in the shadow of protecting overhangs.

Copper for roofs is indicated generally on the model as a permanent cover capable of being worked in many appropriate ways and giving a general harmonious color effect to the whole.

Electricity, oil and gas are the only popular fuels. Each land allotment has a pit near the public lighting fixture where access to the three and to water and sewer may be had without tearing up the pavements.

The school problem is solved by segregating a group of low buildings in the interior spaces of the city where the children can go without crossing traffic. The school building group includes galleries for loan collections from the museum, a concert and lecture hall, small gardens for the children in small groups and well-lighted cubicles for individual outdoor study: there is a small zoo, large pools and green playgrounds.

This group is at the very center of the model and contains at its center the higher school adapted to the segregation of the students into small groups.

This tract of four miles square, by way of such liberal general allotment determined by acreage and type of ground, including apartment buildings and hotel facilities, provides for about 1,400 families at, say, an average of five or more persons to the family.

To reiterate: the basis of the whole is general decentralization as an applied principle and architectural reintegration of all units into one fabric; free use of the ground held only by use and improvements; public utilities and government itself owned by the people of Broadacre City; privacy on one's own ground for all and a fair means of subsistence for all by way of their own work on their own ground or in their own laboratory or in common offices serving the life of the whole.

There are too many details involved in the model of Broadacres to permit complete explanation. Study of the model itself is necessary study. Most details are explained by way of collateral models of the various types of construction shown: highway construction, left turns, crossovers, underpasses and various houses and public buildings.

Anyone studying the model should bear in mind the thesis upon which the design has been built by the Taliesin Fellowship, built carefully not as a finality in any sense but as an interpretation of the changes inevitable to our growth as a people and a nation.

Individuality established on such terms must thrive. Unwholesome life would get no encouragement and the ghastly heritage left by overcrowding in overdone ultra-capitalistic centers would be likely to disappear in three or four generations. The old success ideals having no chance at all, new ones more natural to the best in man would be given a fresh opportunity to develop naturally.

PETER HALL

"The City of Theory"

from *Cities of Tomorrow: An Intellectual History of Urban Planning and Design in the Twentieth Century* (1988)

Editors' introduction   In this selection British geographer/planner Peter Hall reviews the evolution of city planning theory in the U.S. and Europe during the past four decades.

Until assuming the Bartlett Professorship of City Planning at University College, London in 1994, Peter Hall shuttled between the Department of City and Regional Planning of the University of California, Berkeley, and the University of Reading's Geography Department. He has traveled widely and written prolifically in urban geography and city planning.

Before World War II, city/town planning was defined as the craft of physical planning. Professors who had been educated as architects, landscape architects, and other design professionals dominated teaching and writing. They taught students to prepare self-contained, end-state physical plans like Raymond Unwin's plan for Letchworth: architectural drawings extended to city scale. Once a well-crafted, aesthetically pleasing, functional plan was complete on paper the early planning theorists believed that a city could be built just as a house is built from architectural drawings.

But, as Hall notes, few planners today or ever plan whole new towns from scratch. Rather they have to decide how to tie new housing, highways, parks, and sewer "systems" into existing cities. And city planning and building do not end the way house construction does.

During the 1960s, systems analysts who had been educated as economists, computer scientists, mathematical geographers, and engineers developed a competing paradigm of what city planning should be. They argued that city planning should be a science, not a craft. They felt planners could use quantitative and exact methodologies to plan urban transportation, utility, or other "systems" on an ongoing basis. The systems theorists thought plans should be mathematical models rather than end-state architectural drawings. Some systems planners suggested that physical plan documents written on paper were a waste of time.

But planning for what kind of city and for whom? Normative theorists, shaken by 1960s racial and class conflict in cities, felt city planning was too important to leave to technocratic systems analysts. They were more concerned with who the city was being built for and how equitable planning would be than quantitative technicalities. During the 1970s, Marxist theorists developed a particularly coherent body of urban theory in terms of class and race (but not, as Leonie Sandercock and Ann Forsyth point out (p. 408), in terms of gender). Marxist urban theory dominated much academic discourse through the 1970s.

Hall ends his tour of planning theory with some critical comments on the current divorce between planning theory and practice. He argues that too often academics debate each other's academic theories with little attention to actual practice or practitioners' needs. Finding academic planning theory irrelevant, city planning practitioners concern themselves only with the nuts and bolts of planning practice without the deeper understanding relevant theory could offer. Hall calls for an improved, reciprocal relationship between the two: theory that is informed by and relevant to actual planning practice and planning practice informed and improved by theory.

Other books by Peter Hall include *World Cities* (London: Weidenfeld & Nicolson, 3rd edn. 1984), *Urban and Regional Planning* (London: Routledge, 3rd edn. 1992), and *Great Planning Disasters* (London: Weidenfeld and Nicolson, 1982).

Other useful overviews of planning theory include John Friedmann, *Planning in the Public Domain: From Knowledge to Action* (Princeton, N.J.: Princeton University Press, 1987), Robert Burchell and George Sternlieb (eds.), *Planning Theory in the 1980s* (New Brunswick, N.J.: Rutgers University Press, 1978) and Andreas Faludi, *Planning Theory* (Elmsford, N.Y.: Pergamon Press, 1973).

PETER HALL, "The City of Theory"

from *Cities of Tomorrow: An Intellectual History of Urban Planning and Design in the Twentieth Century* (1988)

The chapter title ["The City of Theory"] might suggest total superfluity: for this book has been about nothing else than cities of theory, and attempts to bring them to actuality. And down to about 1955, that adequately describes the main current of twentieth-century planning history; such has been the central thesis. But from then on, it will not do. Hence the need for this chapter, and the title.

The reason is paradoxical: at that point, city planning at last became legitimate; but in doing so, it began to sow the seeds of its own destruction. All too quickly, it split into two separate camps: the one, in the schools of planning, increasingly and exclusively obsessed with the theory of the subject; the other, in the offices of local authorities and consultants, concerned only with the everyday business of planning in the real world. That division was not at first evident; indeed, during the late 1950s and most of the 1960s, it seemed that at last a complete and satisfactory link had been forged between the world of theory and world of practice. But all too soon, illusion was stripped aside: honeymoon was followed in quick succession during the 1970s by tiffs and temporary reconciliations, in the 1980s by divorce. And, in the process, planning lost much of its new-found legitimacy.

THE PREHISTORY OF ACADEMIC CITY PLANNING: 1930–1955

It was not that planning was innocent of academic influence before the 1950s. On the contrary: in virtually every urbanized nation, universities and polytechnics had created courses for the professional education of planners; professional bodies had come into existence to define and protect standards, and had forged links with the academic departments. Britain took an early lead when in 1909 ... the soap magnate William Hesketh Lever, founder of Port Sunlight, won a libel action against a newspaper and used the proceeds to endow his local University of Liverpool with a Department of Civic Design.

Stanley Adshead, the first professor, almost immediately created a new journal, the *Town Planning Review*, in which theory and good practice were to be firmly joined; its first editor was a young faculty recruit, Patrick Abercrombie, who was later to succeed Adshead in the chair first at Liverpool, then at Britain's second school of planning: University College London, founded in 1914. The Town Planning Institute (TPI) – the Royal accolade was conferred only in 1959 – was founded in 1914 on the joint initiative of the Royal Institute of British Architects, the Institution of Civil

Engineers and the Royal Institution of Chartered Surveyors; by the end of the 1930s it had recognized seven schools whose examinations provided an entry to membership (Cherry, 1974: 54, 56–60, 169, 218–22).

The United States was slower: though Harvard had established a planning course in 1909, neck and neck with Liverpool, it had no separate department until 1929. Nevertheless, by the 1930s America had schools also at MIT, Cornell, Columbia and Illinois, as well as courses taught in other departments at a great many universities across the country (Scott, 1969: 101, 266–7, 365–6; Wilson, 1974: 138–9). And the American City Planning Institute, founded in 1917 as a breakaway from the National Conference on City Planning, ten years later, became – mainly through the insistence of Thomas Adams – a full-fledged professional body on TPI lines, a status it retained when in 1938 it broadened to include regional planning and renamed itself the American Institute of Planners (Scott, 1969: 163; Birch, 1980: 26, 28, 31–2; Simpson, 1985: 126–7).

The important point about these, and other, initiatives was this: stemming as they did from professional needs, often through spin-offs from related professions like architecture and engineering, they were from the start heavily suffused with the professional styles of these design-based professions. The job of the planners was to make plans, to develop codes to enforce these plans, and then to enforce those codes; relevant planning knowledge was what was needed for that job; planning education existed to convey that knowledge together with the necessary design skills. So, by 1950, the utopian age of planning – the main theme of this book – was over; planning was now institutionalized into comprehensive land-use planning (Galloway and Mahayni, 1977: 65). All this was strongly reflected in the curricula of the planning schools down to the mid-1950s, and often for years after that; and these in turn were reflected in the books and articles that academic planners wrote. Land-use planning, Keeble told his British audience in 1959 and Kent reminded the American counterpart in 1964, was a distinct and tightly bounded subject, quite different from social or economic planning (Keeble,

1959: 1–2; Kent, 1964: 101). And these texts reflected the fact that city planners early adopted the thoughtways and the analytical methods that engineers developed for the design of public works, then applied them to the design of cities (Webber, 1968: 192–3).

The result, as Michael Batty has put it, was a subject that for ordinary citizens was "somewhat mystical" or arcane, as law or medicine were, but that was – in sharp contrast to education for these older professions – not based on any consistent body of theory; rather in it, "scatterings of social science bolstered the traditional architectural determinism" (Batty, 1979: 29). Planners acquired a synthetic ability not through abstract thinking, but by doing real jobs; in them, they used first creative intuition, then reflection. Though they might draw on bits and pieces of theory about the city – the Chicago School's sociological differentiation of the city, the land economists' theory of urban land rent differentials, the geographers' concepts of the natural region – these were employed simply as snippets of useful knowledge (Keeble, 1959: 2–2). In the important distinction later made by a number of writers (Hightower, 1969: 326; Faludi, 1985: 27), there was some theory *in* planning but there was no theory *of* planning. The whole process was very direct, based on a single-shot approach: survey (the Geddesian approach) was followed by analysis (an implicit learning approach), followed immediately by design.

True, as Abercrombie's classic text of 1933 argued, the making of the plan was only half the planner's job; the other half consisted of planning: that is, implementation (Abercrombie, 1933: 139); but it was nowhere assumed that some kind of continuous learning process was needed. True, too, the 1947 Act provided for plans – and the surveys on which they were based – to be quinquennially updated; the assumption was still that the result would be a fixed land-use plan. And, a decade after that, though Keeble's equally classic text referred to the planning process (Keeble, 1959: 2–1), by this he simply meant the need for a spatial hierarchy of related plans from the regional to the local, and the need at each scale for survey before plan. Nowhere is found a discussion of implementation or updating. Thus – apart from extremely generalized statements like Abercrombie's famous triad of "beauty, health and convenience" – the goals were left implicit; the planner would develop them intuitively from his own values, which were "expert" and apolitical. So in the classic British land-use planning system created by the 1947 Town and Country Planning Act, no repeated learning process was involved, since the planner would get it right first time (Batty, 1979: 29–32):

> The process was therefore not characterized by explicit feedback as the search "homed in" on the best plan, for the notion that the Planner had to learn about the nature of the problem was in direct conflict with his assumed infallibility as an expert, a professional ... The assumed certainty of the process was such that possible links back to the reality in the form of new surveys were rarely if ever considered ... This certainty, based on the infallibility of the expert, reinforced the apolitical, technical nature of the process. The political environment was regarded as totally passive, indeed subservient to the "advice" of the planners, and in practice, this was largely the case.

It was, as Batty calls it, the golden age of planning: the planner, free from political interference, serenely sure of his technical capacities, was left to get on with the job. And this was appropriate to the world outside, with which planning had to deal: a world of glacially slow change – stagnant population, depressed economy – in which major planning interventions would come only seldom and for a short time, as after a major war. Abercrombie, in the plan for the West Midlands he produced with Herbert Jackson in 1948, actually wrote that a major objective of the plan should be to slow down the rate of urban change, thus reducing the rate at which built structures became obsolescent: the ideal city would be a static, stable city:

> Let us assume ... that a maximum population has been decided for a town, arrived at after consideration of all the factors appearing to be relevant ... Allowance has been made for proper space for all conceivable purposes in the light of present facts and the town planner's experience and imagination. Accordingly, an envelope or green belt has been prescribed, outside which the

land uses will be those involving little in the way of resident population. The town planner is now in the happy position for the first time of knowing the limits of his problem. He is able to address himself to the design of the whole and the parts in the light of a basic overall figure for population. The process will be difficult enough in itself, but at least he starts with one figure to reassure him.
> (Abercrombie and Jackson, 1948, foreword)

American planning was never quite like that. Kent's text of 1964 on the urban general plan, though it deals with the same kind of land-use planning, reminds its students of "end-directions which are continually adjusted as time passes" (Kent, 1964: 98) And, because the planner's basic understanding of the interrelationship between socio-economic forces and the physical environment was largely intuitive and speculative, Kent warned his student readers,

> In most cases it is not possible to know with any certainty what physical design measures should be taken to bring about a given social or economic objective, or what social and economic consequences will result from a given physical-design proposal. Therefore, the city council and the city-planning commission, rather than professional city planners, should make the final value judgements upon which the plan is based.
> (Kent, 1964: 104)

But even Kent was certain that, despite all this, it was still possible for the planner to produce some kind of optimal land-use plan; the problem of objectives was just shunted off.

THE SYSTEMS REVOLUTION

It was a happy, almost dream-like, world. But increasingly, during the 1950s, it did not correspond to reality. Everything began to get out of hand. In every industrial country, there was an unexpected baby boom, to which the demographers reacted with surprise, the planners with alarm; only its timing varied from one country to another, and everywhere it created instant demands for maternity wards and child-care clinics, only slightly delayed needs for schools and playgrounds. In every one, almost simultaneously, the great postwar economic boom got under way, bringing pressures for new investment in factories and offices. And as boom generated affluence, these countries soon passed into the realm of high mass-consumption societies, with unprecedented demands for durable consumer goods: most notable among these, land-hungry homes and cars. The result everywhere – in America, in Britain, in the whole of western Europe – was that the pace of urban development and urban change began to accelerate to an almost superheated level. The old planning system, geared to a static world, was overwhelmed.

These demands in themselves would force the system to change; but, almost coincidentally, there were changes on the supply side too. In the mid-1950s there occurred an intellectual revolution in the whole cluster of urban and regional social studies, which provided planners with much of their borrowed intellectual baggage. A few geographers and industrial economists discovered the works of German theorists of location, such as John Heinrich von Thünen (1826) on agriculture, Alfred Weber (1909) on industry, Walter Christaller (1933) on central places, and August Lösch (1940) on the general theory of location; they began to summarize and analyse these works, and where necessary to translate them (Thünen, 1966; Weber, 1929; Christaller, 1966; Lösch, 1954). In the United States, academics coming from a variety of disciplines began to find regularities in many distributions, including spatial ones (Zipf, 1949; Stewart, 1947, 1956; Carrothers, 1956; Stewart and Warntz, 1958, 1959; Garrison, 1959–60). Geographers, beginning to espouse the tenets of logical positivism, suggested that their subject should cease to be concerned with descriptions of the detailed differentiation of the earth's surface, and should instead begin to develop general hypotheses about spatial distributions, which could then be rigorously tested against reality: the very approach which these German pioneers of location theory had adopted. These ideas, together with the relevant literature, were brilliantly synthesized by an American economist, Walter Isard, in a text that became immediately influential (Isard, 1960). Between 1953 and 1957, there occurred an instant revolution in human geography (John-

ston, 1979) and the creation, by Isard, of a new academic discipline uniting the new geography with the German tradition of locational economics. And, with official blessing – as in the important report of Britain's Schuster Committee of 1950, which recommended a greater social-science content in planning education – the new locational analysis began to enter the curricula of the planning schools (G.B. Committee, 1950).

The consequences for planning were momentous: with only a short timelag, "the discipline of physical planning changed more in the 10 years from 1960 to 1970, than in the previous 100, possibly even 1000 years" (Batty, 1979: 18). The subject changed from a kind of craft, based on personal knowledge of a rudimentary collection of concepts about the city, into an apparently scientific activity in which vast amounts of precise information were garnered and processed in such a way that the planner could devise very sensitive systems of guidance and control, monitored and if necessary modified. More precisely, cities and regions were viewed as complex systems – they were, indeed, only a particular spatially based subset of a whole general class of systems – while planning was seen as a continuous process of control and monitoring of these systems, derived from the then new science of cybernetics developed by Norbert Wiener (Wiener, 1948; Hall, 1982: 276).

There was thus, in the language later used in the celebrated work of Thomas Kuhn, a paradigm shift (Kuhn, 1962). It affected city planning as it affected many other related areas of planning and design. Particularly, its main early applications – already in the mid-1950s – concerned defence and aerospace; for these were the Cold War years, when the United States was engaging in a crash programme to build new and complex electronically controlled missile systems. Soon, from that field, spun off another application. Already in 1954, Robert Mitchell and Chester Rapkin – colleagues of Isard at the University of Pennsylvania – had published a book suggesting that urban traffic patterns were a direct and measurable function of the pattern of activities – and thus land uses – that generated them (Mitchell and Rapkin, 1954).

Coupled with earlier work on spatial inter-action patterns, and using for the first time the data-processing powers of the computer, this produced a new science of urban transportation planning, which for the first time claimed to be able scientifically to predict future urban-traffic patterns. First applied in the historic Detroit Metropolitan Area transportation study of 1955, further developed in the Chicago study of 1956, it soon became a standardized method-ology employed in literally hundreds of such studies, first across the United States, then across the world (Bruton, 1975: 17).

Heavily engineering-based in its approach, it adopted a fairly standardized sequence. First, explicit goals and objectives were set for the performance of the system. Then, inventories were taken of the existing state of the system: both the traffic flows, and the activities that gave rise to them. From this, models were derived which sought to establish these relation-ships in precise mathematical form. Then, fore-casts were made of the future state of the system, based on the relationships obtained from the models. From this, alternative solu-tions could be designed and evaluated in order to choose a preferred option. Finally, once implemented the network would be continually monitored and the system modified as necessary (Bruton, 1975: 27–42).

At first, these relationships were seen as operating in one direction: activities and land uses were given; from these, the traffic patterns were derived. So the resulting methodology and techniques were part of a new field, transporta-tion planning, which came to exist on one side of traditional city planning. Soon, however, American regional scientists suggested a crucial modification: the locational patterns of activ-ities – commercial, industrial, residential – were in turn influenced by the available transporta-tion opportunities; these relationships, too, could be precisely modelled and used for predic-tion; therefore the relationship was two-way, and there was a need to develop an interactive system of land-use–transportation planning for entire metropolitan or subregional areas. Now, for the first time, the engineering-based approach invaded the professional territory of the traditional land-use planner. Spatial inter-action models, especially the Garin–Lowry model – which, given basic data about employ-ment and transportation links, could generate a resulting pattern of activities and land uses – became part of the planner's stock in trade (Lowry, 1964, 1965; Batty, 1976). As put in one of the classic systems texts:

> In this general process of planning we partic-ularize in order to deal with more specific issues: that is, a specific real world system or subsystem must be represented by a specific conceptual system or subsystem within the general conceptual system. Such a particular representation of a system is called a model ... The use of models is a means whereby the high variety of the real world is reduced to a level of variety appropriate to the channel capacities of the human being.
> (Chadwick, 1971: 63–4, 70)

This involved more than a knowledge of computer applications – novel as that seemed to the average planner of the 1960s. It meant also a fundamentally different concept of planning. Instead of the old master-plan or blueprint approach, which assumed that the objectives were fixed from the start, the new concept was of planning as a process, "whereby programmes are adapted during their implementation as and when incoming information requires such chan-ges" (Faludi, 1973: 132). And this planning process was independent of the thing that was planned (Galloway and Mahayni, 1977: 68); as Melvin Webber put it, it was "a special way of deciding and acting", which involved a con-stantly recycled series of logical steps: goal-setting, forecasting of change in the outside world, assessment of chains of consequences of alternative courses of action, appraisal of costs and benefits as a basis for action strategies, and continuous monitoring (Webber, 1968: 278). This was the approach of the new British textbooks of systems planning, which started to emerge at the end of the 1960s, and which were particularly associated with a group of younger British graduates, many teaching or studying at the University of Manchester (McLoughlin, 1969; Chadwick, 1971). It was also the approach of a whole generation of subregional studies, made for fast-growing metropolitan areas in Britain during that heroic period of growth and change, 1965–75: Leicester–Leicestershire, Nottinghamshire–Derbyshire, Coventry–Warwickshire–Solihull, South Hampshire. All were heavily suffused with the new approach and the new techniques; in several the same key individuals – McLoughlin in Leicester, Batty in Derby – played a directing or a crucial consulting role.

But the revolution was less complete – at least, in its early stages – than its supporters liked to argue: many of these "systems" plans had a distinctly blueprint tint, in that they soon resulted in all-too-concrete proposals for fixed investments like freeway systems (Faludi, 1973: 146). Underlying this, furthermore, were some curious metaphysical assumptions, which the new systems planners shared with their blueprint elders: the planning system was seen as active, the city system as purely passive; the political system was regarded as benign and receptive to the planner's expert advice (Batty, 1979: 21). In practice, the systems planner was involved in two very different kinds of activity: as a social scientist, he or she was passively observing and analysing reality; as a designer, the same planner was acting on reality to change it – an activity inherently less certain, and also inherently subject to objectives that could only be set through a complex, often messy, set of dealings between professionals, politicians and the public.

The core of this problem was a logical paradox: despite the claims of the systems planners (Chadwick, 1971: 81), the urban planning system was different from (say) a weapons system. In this latter kind of system, to which the "systems approach" had originally and successfully been applied, the controls were inside the system; but here, the urban-regional system was inside its own system of control (Batty, 1979: 18–21). Related to this were other crucial differences: in urban planning, there was not just one problem and one overriding objective, but many, perhaps contradictory; it was difficult to move from general goals to specific operational ones (Altschuler, 1965: 20; Catanese and Steiss, 1970: 8); not all were fully perceived; the systems to be analysed did not self-evidently exist, but had to be synthesized; most aspects were not deterministic, but probabilistic; costs and benefits were difficult to quantify. So the claims of the systems school to scientific objectivity could not readily be fulfilled. Increasingly, members of the school came to admit that in such "open" systems, systematic analysis would need to play a subsidiary role to intuition and judgement; in other words, the traditional approach (Catanese and Steiss, 1970: 17, 21). By 1975 Britton Harris, perhaps the most celebrated of all the systems planners, could write that he no longer believed that the more difficult problems of planning could be solved by optimizing methods (Harris, 1975: 42).

THE SEARCH FOR A NEW PARADIGM

All this, in the late 1960s, came to focus in an attack from two very different directions, which together blew the ship of systems planning at least half out of the water. From the philosophical right came a series of theoretical and empirical studies from American political scientists, arguing that – at least in the United States – crucial urban decisions were made with a pluralist political structure in which no one individual or group had total knowledge or power, and in which, consequently, the decision-making process could best be described as "disjointed incrementalism" or "muddling through". Meyerson and Banfield's classic analysis of the Chicago Housing Authority concluded that it engaged in little real planning, and failed because it did not correctly identify the real power structure in the city; its elitist view of the public interest was totally opposed to the populist view of the ward politicians, which finally prevailed. Downs theorized about such a structure, suggesting that politicians buy votes by offering bundles of policies, rather as in a market. Lindblom contrasted the whole rational-comprehensive model of planning with what he found to be the actual process of policy development, which was characterized by a mixture of values and analysis, a confusion of ends and means, a failure to analyse alternatives, and an avoidance of theory. Altshuler's analysis of Minneapolis–St Paul suggested that the professional planner carried no clout against the political machine, which backed the highway-building engineers against them; they won by stressing expertise and concentrating on narrow goals, but theirs was a political game; the conclusion was that planners should recognize their own weakness, and devise strategies appropriate to that fact (Meyerson and Banfield, 1955; Downs, 1957; Lindblom, 1959; Altschuler, 1965b).

All these analyses arose from study of American urban politics, which is traditionally more populist, more pluralist, than most. Even there, Rabinowitz's study of New Jersey cities suggested that they varied greatly in style, from the highly fragmented to the very cohesive; while Etzioni, criticizing Lindblom, suggested that recent United States history showed examples of non-incremental decision-making, especially in defence (Rabinowitz, 1969, *passim*; Etzioni, 1968, *passim*). But, these reservations taken, the studies did at least suggest actuality was a very long way indeed from the cool, rational, Olympian style envisaged in the systems texts. Perhaps it might have been better if it had been closer; perhaps not. The worrisome point was that in practice, local democracy proved to be an infinitely messier business than the theory would have liked. Some concluded that if this was the way planning was, this was the way it should be encouraged to be: partial, experimental, incremental, working on problems as they arose (Bolan, 1967: 239–40).

That emerged even more clearly, because – as often seems to happen – in America the left-wing criticism was reaching closely similar conclusions. By the late 1960s, fuelled by the civil-rights movement and war on poverty, the protests against the Vietnam war and the campus free-speech movement, it was this wing that was making all the running. Underlying the general current of protest were three key themes, which proved fatal to the legitimacy of the systems planners. One was a widespread distrust of expert, top-down planning generally – whether for problems of peace and war, or for problems of the cities. Another, much more specific, was an increasing paranoia about the systems approach, which in its military applications was seen as employing pseudo-science and

incomprehensible jargon to create a smoke-screen, behind which ethically reprehensible policies could be pursued. And a third was triggered by the riots that tore through American cities starting with Birmingham, Alabama, in 1963 and ending with Detroit in 1967. They seemed to prove the point: systems planning had done nothing to ameliorate the condition of the cities; rather, by dismemberment of inner-city communities, it might actually have contributed to [the problems]. By 1967 one critic, Richard Bolan, could argue that systems planning was old-fashioned comprehensive planning, dressed up in fancier garb; both, alike, ignored political reality (Bolan, 1967: 239–40).

The immediate left-wing reaction was to call on planners themselves to turn the tables, and to practise bottom-up planning by becoming advocate-planners (Davidoff, 1965). Particularly, in this way they would make explicit the debate about the setting of goals and objectives, which both the blueprint and systems approaches had bypassed by means of their comfortable shared assumption that this was the professional planner's job. Advocacy planners would intervene in a variety of ways, in a variety of groups; diversity should be their keynote. They would help to inform the public of alternatives; force public planning agencies to compete for support; help critics to generate plans that were superior to official ones; compel consideration of underlying values. The resulting structure was highly American: democratic, locally grounded, pluralistic, but also legalistic in being based on conflict. But, interestingly, while demoting the planner in one respect, it enormously advanced his or her power in another: the planner was able to take many of the functions that the locally elected official exercised. And, in practice, it was not entirely clear how it would all work; particularly, how the process would resolve the very real conflicts of interest that could arise within communities, or how it could avoid the risk that the planners, once again, would become manipulators (Peattie, 1968: 85).

At any rate, there is more than a passing resemblance between the planner as a disjointed incrementalist, and the planner-advocate; and, indeed, between either of these and a third model set out in Bolan's paper of 1967, the planner as informal co-ordinator and catalyst, which in turn shades into a fourth: Melvin Webber's probabilistic planner, who uses new information systems to facilitate debate and improve decision-making. All are assumed to work within a pluralist world, with very many different competing groups and interests, where the planner has at most (and, further, should have) only limited power or influence; all are based, at least implicitly, on continued acceptance of logical positivism. As Webber put it, at the conclusion of his long two-part paper of 1968–69:

> The burden of my argument is that city planning failed to adopt the planning method, choosing instead to impose input bundles, including regulatory constraints, on the basis of ideologically defined images of goodness. I am urging, as an alternative, that planning tries out the planning idea and the planning method.
> (Webber, 1968–69: 294–5; cf. Rittel and Webber, 1973)

In turn, Webber's view of planning – which flatly denied the possibility of a stable predictable future or agreed goals – provided some of the philosophical underpinnings of the Social Learning or New Humanist approach of the 1970s, which stressed the importance of learning systems in helping cope with a turbulent environment (Schon, 1971; Friedmann, 1973). But finally, this approach divorced itself from logical positivism, returning to a reliance on personal knowledge which was strangely akin to old-style blueprint planning; and, as developed by John Friedmann of the University of California at Los Angeles, it finally resulted in a demand for all political activity to be decomposed into decision by minute political groups: a return to the anarchist roots of planning, with a vengeance.

So these different approaches diverged, sometimes in detailed emphasis, sometimes more fundamentally. What they shared was the belief that – at any rate in the American political system – the planner did not have much power and did not deserve to have much either; within a decade, from 1965 to 1975, these approaches together neatly stripped the planner of whatever

priestly clothing, and consequent mystique, s/he may have possessed. Needless to say, this view powerfully communicated itself to the professionals themselves. Even in countries with more centralized, top-down political systems, such as Great Britain, young graduating planners increasingly saw their roles as rather like barefoot doctors, helping the poor down on the streets of the inner city, working either for a politically acceptable local authority, or, failing that, for community organizations battling against a politically objectionable one.

Several historical factors, in addition to the demolition job on planning by the American theorists, contributed to this change: planners and politicians belatedly discovered the continued deprivation of the inner-city poor; then, it was seen that the areas where these people lived were suffering depopulation and deindustrialization; in consequence, planners progressively moved away from the merely physical, and into the social and the economic.

The change can be caricatured thus: in 1955, the typical newly graduated planner was at the drawing board, producing a diagram of desired land uses; in 1965 s/he was analysing computer output of traffic patterns; in 1975, the same person was talking late into the night with community groups, in the attempt to organize against hostile forces in the world outside.

It was a remarkable inversion of roles. For what was wholly or partly lost, in that decade, was the claim to any unique and useful expertise, such as that possessed by the doctor or the lawyer. True, the planner could still offer specialized knowledge on planning laws and procedures, or on how to achieve a particular design solution; though often, given the nature of the context and the changed character of planning education, s/he might not have enough of either of these skills to be particularly useful. And, some critics were beginning to argue, this was because planning had extended so thinly over so wide an area that it became almost meaningless; in the title of Aaron Wildavsky's celebrated paper, "If Planning Is Everything, Maybe It's Nothing" (Wildavsky, 1973: 130).

The fact was that planning, as an academic discipline, had theorized about its own role to such extent that it was denying its own claim to legitimacy. Planning, Faludi pointed out in his text of 1973, could be merely *functional*, in that the goals and objectives are taken as given; or normative, in that they are themselves the object of rational choice (Faludi, 1973: 175). The problem was whether planning was really capable of doing that latter job. As a result, by the mid-1970s planning had reached the stage of a "paradigm crisis" (Galloway and Mahayni, 1977: 66); it had been theoretically useful to distinguish the planning process as something separate from what is planned, yet this had meant a neglect of substantive theory, pushing it to the periphery of the whole subject. "Consequently, new theory is needed which attempts to bridge current planning strategies and the urban physical and social systems to which strategies are applied" (Galloway and Mahayni, 1977: 66).

THE MARXIST ASCENDANCY

That became ever clearer in the following decade, when the logical positivists retreated from the intellectual field of battle and the Marxists took possession. As the whole world knows, the 1970s saw a remarkable resurgence – indeed a veritable explosion – of Marxist studies. This could not fail to affect the closely related worlds of urban geography, sociology, economics, and planning. True, like the early neo-classical economists, Marx had been remarkably uninterested in questions of spatial location – even though Engels had made illuminating comments on the spatial distribution of classes in mid-Victorian Manchester. The disciples now reverently sought to extract from the holy texts, drop by drop, a distillation that could be used to brew the missing theoretical potion. At last, by the mid-1970s, it was ready; then came a flood of new work. It originated in various places and in various disciplines. In England and the United States the geographers David Harvey and Doreen Massey helped to explain urban growth and change in terms of the circulation of capital; in Paris, Manuel Castells and Henri Lefebvre developed sociologically based theories (Harvey, 1973, 1982, 1985a, 1985b; Castells, 1977, 1978; Lefebvre, 1968, 1972; Massey and Mee-

gan, 1982; Massey, 1984).

In the endless debates that followed among the Marxists themselves, a critical question concerned the role of the state (Carnoy, 1984). In France, Lokjine and others argued that it was mainly concerned, through such devices as macroeconomic planning and related infrastructure investment, directly to underpin and aid the direct productive investments of private capital. Castells, in contrast, argued that its main function had been to provide collective consumption – as in public housing, or schools, or transportation – to help guarantee the reproduction of the labour force and to dampen class conflict, essential for the maintenance of the system (Lokjine, 1977; Castells, 1977: 276–323; 1978: 15–36). Clearly, planning might play a very large role in both these state functions; hence, by the mid-1970s French Marxist urbanists were engaging in major studies of this role in the industrialization of such major industrial areas as Dieppe (Castells, 1978: 62–92).

At the same time, a specifically Marxian view of planning emerged in the English-speaking world. To describe it adequately would require a course in Marxist theory. But in inadequate summary, it states that the structure of the capitalist city, itself, including its land-use and activity patterns, is the result of capital in pursuit of profit. Because capitalism is doomed to recurrent crises, which deepen in the current stage of late capitalism, capital calls upon the state, as its agent, to assist it by remedying disorganization in commodity production, and by aiding the reproduction of the labour force. It thus tries to achieve certain necessary objectives: to facilitate continued capital accumulation, by ensuring rational allocation of resources; by assisting the reproduction of the labour force through the provision of social services, thus maintaining a delicate balance between labour and capital and preventing social disintegration; and by guaranteeing and legitimating capitalist social and property relations. As Dear and Scott put it: "In summary, planning is an historically-specific and socially necessary response to the self-disorganizing tendencies of *privatized* capitalist social and property relations as these appear in urban space" (Dear and Scott, 1981: 13). In particular, it seeks to guarantee collective provision of necessary infrastructure and certain basic urban services, and to reduce negative externalities whereby certain activities of capital cause losses to other parts of the system (ibid.: 11).

But, since capitalism also wishes to circumscribe state planning as far as possible, there is an inbuilt contradiction: planning, because of this inherent inadequacy, always solves one problem only by creating another (ibid.: 14–15). Thus, say the Marxists, nineteenth-century clearances in Paris created a working-class housing problem; American zoning limited the powers of industrialists to locate at the most profitable locations (Scott and Roweis, 1977: 1108). And planning can never do more than modify some parameters of the land development process; it cannot change its intrinsic logic, and so cannot remove the contradiction between private accumulation and collective action (ibid.: 1107). Further, the capitalist class is by no means homogeneous; different fractions of capital may have divergent, even contradictory interests, formed in consequence; thus, latter-day Marxist explanations come close to being pluralist, albeit with a strong structural element (Mollenkopf, 1983). But in the process, "the more that the State intervenes in the urban system, the greater is the likelihood that different social groups and fractions will contest the legitimacy of its decisions. *Urban life as a whole becomes progressively invaded by political controversies and dilemmas*" (Dear and Scott, 1981: 16).

Because traditional non-Marxian planning theory has ignored this essential basis of planning, so Marxian commentators argue, it is by definition vacuous: it seeks to define what planning ideally ought to be, devoid of all context; its function has been to depoliticize planning as an activity, and thus to legitimate it (Scott and Roweis, 1977: 1098). It seeks to achieve this by representing itself as the force which produces the various facets of real-world planning. But in fact, its various claims – to develop abstract concepts that rationally represent real-world processes, to legitimate its own activity, to explain material processes as the outcome of ideas, to present planning goals as derived from

generally shared values, and to abstract planning activity in terms of metaphors drawn from other fields like engineering – all these are both very large and quite unjustified (Cooke, 1983: 106–8). The reality, Marxists argue, is precisely the opposite: viewed objectively, planning theory is nothing other than a creation of the social forces that bring planning into existence (Scott and Roweis, 1977: 1099).

It makes up a disturbing body of coherent criticism: yes, of course, planning cannot simply be an independent self-legitimating activity, as scientific inquiry may claim to be; yes, of course, it is a phenomenon that – like all phenomena – represents the circumstances of its time. As Scott and Roweis put it:

> there is a definite mismatch between the world of current planning theory, on the one hand, and the real world of practical planning intervention on the other hand. The one is the quintessence of order and reason in relation to the other which is full of disorder and unreason. Conventional theorists then set about resolving this mismatch between theory and reality by introducing the notion that planning theory is in any case not so much an attempt to explain the world as it *is* but as it *ought* to be. Planning theory then sets itself the task of rationalizing irrationalities, and seeks to materialize itself in social and historical reality (like Hegel's World Spirit) by bringing to bear upon the world a set of abstract, independent, and transcendent norms.
>
> (ibid.: 1116)

It was powerful criticism. But it left in turn a glaringly open question, both for the unfortunate planner – whose legitimacy is now totally torn from him, like the epaulette from the shoulder of a disgraced officer – and, equally, for the Marxist critic: what, then, is planning theory about? Has it any normative or prescriptive content whatsoever? The answer, logically, would appear to be no. One of the critics, Philip Cooke, is uncompromising:

> The main criticism that tends to have been made, justifiably, of planning is that it has remained stubbornly normative ... in this book it will be argued that [planning theorists] should identify mechanisms which cause changes in the nature of planning to be brought about, rather than assuming such changes to be either the creative ideal-

izations of individual minds, or mere regularities in observable events.

(Cooke, 1983: 25, 27)

This is at least consistent: planning theory should avoid all prescription; it should stand right outside the planning process, and seek to analyse the subject – including traditional theory – for what it is, the reflection of historical forces. Scott and Roweis, a decade earlier, seem to be saying exactly the same thing: planning theory cannot be normative, it cannot assume "transcendent operational norms" (Scott and Roweis, 1977: 1099). But then they stand their logic on its own head, saying that "a viable theory of urban planning should not only tell us what planning is, but also what we can, and must, do as progressive planners" (ibid.).

This, of course, is sheer rhetoric. But it nicely displays the agony of the dilemma. Either theory is about unravelling the historical logic of capitalism, or it is about prescription for action. Since the planner-theorist – however sophisticated – could never hope to divert the course of capitalist evolution by more than a millimetre or a millisecond, the logic would seem to demand that s/he sticks firmly to the first and abjures the second. In other words the Marxian logic is strangely quietist; it suggests that the planner retreats from planning altogether into the academic ivory tower.

Some were acutely conscious of the dilemma. John Forester tried to resolve it by basing a whole theory of planning action on the work of Jürgen Habermas. Habermas, perhaps the leading German social theorist of the post-World War Two era, had argued that latter-day capitalism justified its own legitimacy by spinning around itself a complex set of distortions in communication, designed to obscure and prevent any rational understanding of its own workings (Bernstein, 1976, 1985; Held, 1980; McCarthy, 1981; Thompson and Held, 1982). Thus, he argued, individuals became powerless to understand how and why they act, and so were excluded from all power to influence their own lives,

as they are harangued, pacified, mislead [*sic*], and ultimately persuaded that inequality, poverty, and ill-health are either problems for which the victim is responsible or problems so "political" and "complex" that they can have nothing to say about them. Habermas argues that democratic politics or planning requires the consent that grows from processes of collective criticism, not from silence or a party line.

(Forester, 1980: 277)

But, Forester argues, Habermas's own proposals for communicative action provide a way for planners to improve their own practice:

By recognizing planning practice as normatively role-structured communication action which distorts, covers up, or reveals to the public the prospects and possibilities they face, a critical theory of planning aids us practically and ethically as well. This is the contribution of critical theory to planning: pragmatics with vision – to reveal true alternatives, to correct false expectations, to counter cynicism, to foster responsibility, engagement, and action. Critical planning practice, technically skilled and politically sensitive, is an organizing and democratizing practice.

(ibid.: 283)

Fine. The problem is that – stripped of its Germanic philosophical basis, which is necessarily a huge oversimplification of a very dense analysis – the practical prescription all comes out as good old-fashioned democratic common sense, no more and no less than Davidoff's advocacy planning of fifteen years before: cultivate community networks, listen carefully to the people, involve the less-organized groups, educate the citizens in how to join in, supply information and make sure people know how to get it, develop skills in working with groups in conflict situations, emphasize the need to participate, compensate for external pressures. True, if in all this planners can sense that they have penetrated the mask of capitalism, that may help them to help others to act to change their environment and their lives; and, given the clear philosophical impasse of the late 1970s, such a massive metaphysical underpinning may be necessary.

THE WORLD OUTSIDE THE TOWER: PRACTICE RETREATS FROM THEORY

Meanwhile, if the theorists were retreating in one direction, the practitioners were certainly reciprocating. Whether baffled or bored by the increasingly scholastic character of the academic debate, they lapsed into an increasingly untheoretical, unreflective, pragmatic, even visceral style of planning. That was not entirely new: planning had come under a cloud before, as during the 1950s, and had soon reappeared in a clear blue sky. What was new, strange, and seemingly unique about the 1980s was the divorce between the Marxist theoreticians of academe – essentially academic spectators, taking grandstand seats at what they saw as one of capitalism's last games – and the anti-theoretical, anti-strategic, anti-intellectual style of the players on the field below (Ambrose, 1986, *passim*; Reade, 1987, *passim*). The 1950s were never like that; then, the academics were the coaches, down there with the team.

This picture is of course exaggerated. Many academics did still try to teach real-life planning through simulation of real-world problems. The Royal Town Planning Institute enjoined them to become ever more practice-minded. The practitioners had not all shut their eyes and ears to what comes out of the academy; some even returned there for refresher courses. And if all this was true in Britain, it was even more so of America, where the divorce had never been so evident. Yet the picture does describe a clear and unmistakable trend; and it was likely to be more than a cyclical one.

The reason is simple: as professional education of any kind becomes more fully absorbed by the academy, as its teachers become more thoroughly socialized within it, as careers are seen to depend on academic peer judgements, then its norms and values – theoretical, intellectual, detached – will become ever more pervasive; and the gap between teaching and practice widen. One key illustration: of the huge output of books and papers from the planning schools in the 1980s, there were many – often those most highly regarded within the academic community – that were simply irrelevant, even

completely incomprehensible, to the average practitioner.

Perhaps, it might be argued, that was the practitioner's fault; perhaps too, we need fundamental science, with no apparent payoff, if we are later to enjoy its technological applications. The difficulty with that argument was to find convincing evidence that – not merely here, but in the social sciences generally – such payoff eventually comes. Hence the low esteem into which the social sciences had everywhere fallen, not least in Britain and the United States: hence too the diminished level of support for them, which – at any rate in Britain – had directly redounded on the planning schools. The relationship between planning and the academy had gone sour, and that is the major unresolved question that must now be addressed.

REFERENCES

Abercrombie, P. (1933) *Town and Country Planning.* London: Thornton Butterworth.

Abercrombie, P. and Jackson, H. (1948) *West Midlands Plan.* Interim and Confidential edition. 5 vols. London: Ministry of Town and Country Planning.

Altschuler, A.A. (1965a) "The Goals of Comprehensive Planning", *Journal of the American Institute of Planners* 31: 186–97.

——(1965b) *The City Planning Process.* Ithica, N.Y.: Cornell University Press.

Ambrose, P. (1986) *Whatever Happened to Planning?* London: Methuen.

Batty, M. (1976) *Urban Modelling: Algorithms, Calibrations, Predictions.* Cambridge: Cambridge University Press.

——(1979) "On Planning Processes" in B. Goodall and A. Kirby (eds) *Resources and Planning.* Oxford: Pergamon.

Bernstein, R. J. (1976) *The Restructuring of Social and Political Theory.* New York: Harcourt Brace Jovanovich.

——(1985) *Habermas and Modernity.* Cambridge, Mass.: MIT Press.

Birch, E. L. (1980a) "Advancing the Art and Science of Planning", *Journal of the American Planning Association* 46: 22–49.

Bolan, R. S. (1967) "Emerging Views of Planning", *Journal of the American Institute of Planners* 33: 233–45.

Bruton, M. (1975) *Introduction to Transportation Planning.* London: Hutchinson.

Carnoy, M. (1984) *The State and Political Theory.*

Princeton: Princeton University Press.

Carrothers, G. A. P. (1956) "An Historical Review of the Gravity and Potential Concepts of Human Interaction", *Journal of the American Institute of Planners* 22: 94–102.

Castells, M. (1977) *The Urban Question: A Marxist Approach*. London: Edward Arnold.

———(1978) *City, Class, and Power*. London: Macmillan.

Catanese, A. J. and Steiss, A. W. (1970) *Systemic Planning: Theory and Application*. Lexington: D. C. Heath.

Chadwick, G. (1971) *A Systems View of Planning: Towards a Theory of the Urban and Regional Planning Process*. Oxford: Pergamon.

Cherry, G. E. (1974) *The Evolution of British Town Planning*. London: Leonard Hill.

Christaller, W. (1966) *Central Places in Southern Germany* (trans. C. W. Baskin). Englewood Cliffs, N.J.: Prentice-Hall.

Cooke, P. N. (1983) *Theories of Planning and Spatial Development*. London: Hutchinson.

Davidoff, P. (1965) "Advocacy and Pluralism in Planning", *Journal of the American Institute of Planners* 31: 186–97.

Dear, M. S. and Scott, A. J. (1981) "Towards a Framework for Analysis" in M. S. Dear and A. J. Scott (eds) *Urbanization and Urban Planning in Capitalist Society*. London: Methuen, 3–16.

Downs, A. (1957) *An Economic Theory of Democracy*. New York: Harper Brothers.

Etzioni, A. (1968) *The Active Society*. London: Collier-Macmillan.

Faludi, A. (1973) *Planning Theory*. Oxford: Pergamon.

———(1985) "The Return of Rationality" in M. Breheny and A. Hooper (eds) *Rationality in Planning: Critical Essays on the Role of Rationality in Urban and Regional Planning*. London: Pion.

Forester, J. (1980) "Critical Theory and Planning Practice", *Journal of the American Planning Association* 46: 275–86.

Friedmann, J. (1973) *Retracking America: A Theory of Transactive Planning*. Garden City, N.Y.: Doubleday.

Galloway, T. D. and Mahayni, R. G. (1977) "Planning Theory in Retrospect: The Process of Paradigm Change", *Journal of the American Institute of Planners* 43: 62–71.

Garrison, W. (1959–60) "Spatial Structure of the Economy", *Annals of the Association of American Geographers* 49: 238–9, 471–82; 50: 357–73.

G.B. Committee on the Qualification of Planners (1950) *Report* (Cmd. 8059) (BPP 1950, 14). London: HMSO.

Hall, P. (1982) *Urban and Regional Planning*, 3rd edn. London: George Allen & Unwin.

Harris, B. (1975) "A Fundamental Paradigm for Planning" in *Symposium on Planning Theory*, vol. 1 (Planning Papers, 1). Philadelphia: Wharton, School.

Harvey, D. (1973) *Social Justice and the City*. London: Edward Arnold.

———(1982) *The Limits to Capital*. Oxford: Basil Blackwell.

———(1985a) *Consciousness and the Urban Experience: Studies in the History and Theory of Capitalist Urbanization*. Baltimore: Johns Hopkins University Press; Oxford: Basil Blackwell.

———(1985b) *The Urbanization of Capital: Studies in the History and Theory of Capitalist Urbanization*. Baltimore: Johns Hopkins University Press; Oxford: Basil Blackwell.

Held, D. (1980) *Introduction to Critical Theory: Horkheimer to Habermas*. Berkeley: University of California Press.

Hightower, H. C. (1969) "Planning Theory in Contemporary Professional Education", *Journal of the American Institute of Planners* 35: 326–9.

Isard, W. (1960) *Methods of Regional Analysis: An Introduction to Regional Science*. Cambridge, Mass.: MIT Press.

Johnston, R. J. (1979) *Geography and Geographers: Anglo-American Human Geography since 1945*. London: Edward Arnold.

Keeble, L. (1959) *Principles and Practice of Town and Country Planning*. London: Estates Gazette.

Kent, T. J. (1964) *The Urban General Plan*. San Francisco: Chandler.

Kuhn, T. S. (1962) *The Structure of Scientific Revolutions*. Chicago: University of Chicago Press.

Lefebvre, H. (1968) *Le Droit à la ville*. Paris: Éditions Anthropos.

———(1972) *Espace et politique: le droit à la ville II*. Paris: Éditions Anthropos.

Lindblom, C. E. (1959) "The Science of Muddling Through", *Public Administration Review* 19: 79–88.

Lokjine, J. (1977) *Le Marxisme, l'état, et la question urbaine*. Paris: PUF.

Losch, A. (1954) *The Economics of Location*, trans. W. H. Woglom and W. F. Stolper. New Haven, Conn.: Yale University Press.

Lowry, I. S. (1964) *A Model of Metropolis*. Santa Monica, Calif.: RAND Corporation. RM-4035-RC.

———(1965) "A Short Course in Model Design", *Journal of the American Institute of Planners* 31: 158–66.

McCarthy, T. A. (1978) *The Critical Theory of Jürgen Habermas*. Cambridge, Mass.: MIT Press.

McLoughlin, J. B. (1969) *Urban and Regional Planning: A Systems Approach*. London: RIBA Publication.

Massey, D. (1984) *Spatial Divisions of Labor: Social Structures and the Geography of Production*. London: Macmillan.

Massey, D. and Meegan, R. (1982) *The Anatomy of*

Job Loss: The How, Why and Where of Employment Decline. London: Methuen.

Meyerson, M. and Banfield, E. C. (1955) *Politics, Planning, and the Public Interest*. New York: Free Press.

Mitchell, R. B. and Rapkin, C. (1954) *Urban Traffic: A Function of Land Use*. New York: Columbia University Press.

Mollenkopf, J. (1983) *The Contested City*. Princeton: Princeton University Press.

Peattie, L. (1968) "Reflections on Advocacy Planning", *Journal of the American Institute of Planners* 34: 80–8.

Rabinowitz, F. (1969) *City Politics and Planning*. New York: Atherton Press.

Reade, E. (1987) *British Town and Country Planning*. Milton Keynes: Open University Press.

Rittel, H. W. J. and Webber, M. (1973) "Dilemmas in a General Theory of Planning", *Policy Sciences* 4: 155–69.

Schon, D. A. (1971) *Beyond the Stable State*. New York: Random House.

Scott, A. J. and Roweis, S. T. (1977) "Urban Planning in Theory and Practice: An Appraisal", *Environment and Planning* 9: 1097–119.

Scott, M. (1969) *American City Planning since 1890: A History Commemorating the Fiftieth Anniversary of the American Institute of Planners*. Berkeley: University of California Press.

Simpson, M. A. (1985) *Thomas Adams and the Modern Planning Movement: Britain, Canada and the United States, 1900–1940*. London: Mansell.

Stewart, J. Q. (1947) "Empirical Mathematical Rules Concerning the Distribution and Equilibrium of Population", *Geographical Review* 37: 461–85.

——(1956) "The Development of Social Physics", *American Journal of Physics* 18: 239–53.

Stewart, J. Q. and Warntz, W. (1958) "Macrogeography and Social Science", *Geographical Review* 48: 167–84.

Thompson, J. B. and Held, D. (1982) *Habermas: "Critical Debates"*. Cambridge, Mass.: MIT Press.

Thünen, J. H. von (1966) *Von Thünen's Isolated State*, trans. C. M. Wartenberg, ed. P. Hall. Oxford: Pergamon Press.

Webber, M. M. (1968–69) "Planning in an Environment of Change", *Town Planning Review* 39: 179–95, 277–95.

Weber, A. (1929) *Alfred Weber's Theory of the Location of Industries*, trans. C. J. Friedrich. Chicago: University of Chicago Press.

Wiener, N. (1948) *Cybernetics*. Cambridge, Mass.: MIT Press.

Wildavsky, A. (1973) "If Planning Is Everything, Maybe It's Nothing', *Policy Sciences* 4: 127–53.

Wilson, W. H. (1974) *Coming of Age in Urban America, 1915–1945*. New York: John Wiley.

Zipf, G. K. (1949) *Human Behavior and the Principle of Least Effort*. Cambridge, Mass.: Addison-Wesley.

FRANK S. SO and JUDITH GETZELS

"Introduction"

from *The Practice of Local Government Planning* (1988)

Editors' introduction   The Royal Town Planning Institute (RTPI) in the United Kingdom and its U.S. counterpart, the American Planning Association (APA), are national professional associations of practicing city planners. APA Deputy Executive Director Frank So and Judith Getzels – a planner with the city of Chicago – have edited a widely used anthology, *The Practice of Local Government Planning*, commonly called "the green book" by U.S. city planners. This selection draws on their experience and the green book's descriptions of planning practice to provide an overview of actual city planning practice in the U.S. today.

As this selection points out, the nature of the community in which a city planner works will affect what she or he actually does. The authors distinguish among older central cities, sunbelt cities, inner-ring suburbs, residential centers, high-growth suburban centers, and rural small towns. A planner working in a depressed U.S. Black ghetto as described by William Julius Wilson (p. 226) faces a declining economy, out-migration, deteriorating older housing, and resulting social ills. A planner for a suburban Levittown (p. 64), a technoburb (p. 485), or a technopole (p. 476) may be struggling to meet a whole different set of issues: rapid population growth, housing shortages, gender inequality, freeway congestion, environmental degradation, and competition for tax revenue from new development in the region. What makes the study of cities and city planning so fascinating is that each type of community faces a distinct set of challenging city planning issues.

Whatever the community, city planners are likely to follow a planning process with similar steps. So and Getzels describe a version of what is called *the rational planning model*: setting goals, study and analysis, plan or policy preparation, implementation, monitoring and feedback. Most city planning is informed by this model, though, as the authors correctly point out, planning in the real world is seldom as orderly as in textbooks. The process of planning results in plans: written documents expressing a vision for the city or region in words, tables, and maps. The authors provide an overview of different types of plans from comprehensive land use plans for an entire community through area plans, down to the level of site plans.

This selection is taken from Frank S. So and Judith Getzels (eds.), *The Practice of Local Government Planning* (Washington, D.C.: International City Management Association, 1988) which also contains chapters on planning for housing, transportation, environmental assessment, infrastructure, and other topics, written by city planning practitioners for practicing city planners.

City planning anthologies with chapters by specialists on different planning topics aimed more at academic audiences include Anthony J. Catanese and James C. Snyder, *Urban Planning* (New York: McGraw-Hill, 1988) and Jay Stein, *Classics in Urban Planning* (New York: McGraw-Hill, 1995).

Texts introducing the practice of U.S. city planning include S. Stuart Chapin, E. J. Kaiser, and David

Godschalk, *Urban Land Use Planning* (Champaign: University of Illinois Press, 1995), and Barry Cullingworth, *The Political Culture of Planning* (New York: Routledge, 1993).

Texts on regional and town planning in the U.K. include Peter Hall, *Urban and Regional Planning* (London: Routledge, 3rd edn. 1993) and J. B. Cullingworth and Vincent Nadin, *Town and Country Planning in Britain* (London: Routledge, 11th edn. 1994).

FRANK S. SO and JUDITH GETZELS, "Introduction"

from *The Practice of Local Government Planning* (1988)

PLANNING ENVIRONMENTS

The nature of local government planning can vary considerably in focus, substance, and style, depending on the type of community or area being planned. Planning for midtown Manhattan will be quite different from planning for the downtown of a rural Iowa community. This first section of the introduction provides an overview of a number of different environments in which planning is practiced: older central cities, Sun Belt cities, inner-ring, residential, and high-growth suburbs, small rural towns, and resort towns.

Older central cities

Older central cities such as Cleveland, Gary, and Newark, are what come to mind when the media refer to "the city." Most of these cities developed during the nineteenth century; their economies were based on smokestack industries; they were the early financial and retail centers; and they housed wave after wave of immigrants during the nineteenth and early twentieth centuries.

A number of related factors accelerated dislocations in economies of these cities. The federally supported development of the interstate highway system, for example, made it easy for middle-class families to move out of the cities into the suburbs and continue to commute to city jobs – at least for a while. Federal housing mortgage insurance programs lent support to this migration to the suburbs. Urban factory owners seeking to expand and modern-

ize their crowded old multi-story plants joined the exodus to the suburbs; land for efficient one-story factories was readily available at reasonable prices outside the city boundaries. Furthermore, quick and flexible truck access to these factories became possible as a result of their new locations on the new highways. Outmoded city plants were often simply abandoned; many of them still stand empty. The result for the cities was loss of middle-class populations as well as loss of industrial jobs.

During the 1950s, these older cities made efforts to improve and renew their declining central business districts – the source of a large portion of the tax revenue needed to run city government. Early efforts focused on the creation of pedestrian malls (perhaps to copy the suburban shopping centers), but it soon became clear that retailing was generally moving to the suburbs and that central business districts had to build their futures on banking, finance, government, and other service functions.

Other early efforts to rejuvenate the older cities focused on the construction of urban expressways, which public officials thought would bring in shoppers from the suburbs. In fact, the expressways simply made it easier to move to the suburbs.

During the 1970s and 1980s, changes in the nation's economy took their toll on older cities. In particular, many of the cities in the East and Midwest that had depended on smokestack industries such as steel and automobiles found their economies tumbling as these industries moved overseas. The decline in manufacturing employment created a decline in disposable income, which hurt retail business; decline in retail, in turn, created serious urban tax base problems. The economic decline and consequent shortage of jobs in some older central cities caused large numbers of young people to move away from these areas. This factor, combined with the more general migration of population to the suburbs, contributed to population decline in some older central cities.

Because of a complex interaction of social and economic factors, many older cities have serious housing problems. From the late 1940s through the early 1960s, the nation's public investment in urban housing was at its peak. In many instances, however, "urban renewal" consisted of totally clearing vast inner-city areas and building acres of high-rise public housing, an approach that turned out to be socially disastrous. Although parts of the urban housing market are vigorous – high-income apartment construction and the rejuvenation of declining residential areas by "urban pioneers" – the magnitude of housing needs continues to create significant challenges for older cities. For example, in the mid-1980s, sectoral unemployment, a decrease in the amount of inexpensive inner-city housing, and the deinstitutionalization of dependent populations worsened the problem of homelessness nationwide but put particular pressures on older central cities. Even the renewal of older neighborhoods, generally referred to as gentrification, is a cause of concern. Although planners and public officials alike are pleased to see declining areas renewed on a private basis, the purchase of housing by upper-income groups tends to displace lower-income residents.

The drop in federal housing support has placed an additional burden on cities, and planners have had to seek new ways to finance housing construction and rehabilitation. Many states have created housing authorities, and public–private partnerships are being forged to obtain new money from older urban financial institutions. In some high-growth downtown areas, cities charge fees to builders to create a pool of money that can be drawn on for housing loans.

Although older cities often appear to be a locus for national social and economic problems, they nevertheless remain the destination of immigrants seeking to build a new life. Immigrants tend to start from the bottom of the social and economic ladder and work their way up. To do this, they need inexpensive housing and suitable jobs – neither of which is easy to find in many older cities.

As bleak a picture as this is, older cities are and will be centers of commerce and services as well as good places to live. Planning in these cities may face formidable obstacles but is also an area of vigorous action and accomplishments.

Central business districts have come to emphasize services, rather than continue their past dependence on retailing. Retailing has come to be divided into those activities that are most economically delivered in suburban shopping centers and those that are most effectively delivered in a central area – such as department stores committed to a central anchor location. Central business districts have also been rejuvenated through the construction of new hotels, convention centers, and sports stadiums, all of which encourage tourism. Increasing tourism has been one of the primary goals of harbor, waterfront, and riverfront renewal programs. Older cities have also invested in centers for cultural activities and the arts. Federal and state funds have enabled many cities to retain or expand arts programs, including orchestras, dance, theatre, and fine arts.

Older cities have also come to recognize the importance of preserving historically significant downtown buildings and residential areas. The rich architectural legacy of older cities is increasingly seen as a valuable resource in the rejuvenation of urban areas. Along with historic preservation has come a greater interest in urban design. Cities are paying close attention to the creation of pedestrian plazas and other street-level amenities as well as to the design of new private buildings.

Economic development planning is crucial to the health of older central cities. Programs include business and job retention, job training, and the creation of financial mechanisms – such as tax abatement – to promote development. Cities even plan their capital facilities to improve the community as a business environment.

In spite of past difficulties, some older cities, such as Boston, San Francisco, and parts of Chicago and New York, are experiencing a turnaround reflected in significant new growth in downtown development. In fact, in such cities the development pressures are great enough to generate concern about traffic, parking, and the replacement of historically significant low-density buildings by high-rise, high-density buildings. In some cities, increased land values have driven up housing costs to the extent that the middle class has difficulty finding affordable housing.

Sun Belt cities

Sun Belt cities may be as old as cities in the North and East, but they are developing rapidly. Pleasant climates, coupled with a general shift of economic activity to the South and West, have created high rates of growth in cities such as Atlanta, Houston, Dallas, Phoenix, and Los Angeles. Suburbs near these cities are also high-growth areas. Some Sun Belt cities are business and financial centers for a regional economic hinterland. Central areas in such cities experience a variety of planning problems, such as boom-and-bust cycles in office development; insufficient public transit; and excessive automobile traffic (which is accompanied by air pollution). In some Sun Belt cities, such as Phoenix and Atlanta, efforts are being made to reverse sprawling development patterns by more intense, multinucleated development.

In rapidly growing cities, the climate for planning and development controls can undergo abrupt swings. On the theory that "growth is good," a city may go through a boom with little planning. It may then become clear that growth without quality has caused traffic congestion and air pollution and is generally destroying the "good life" that residents originally sought. The response may be more vigorous planning and regulatory mechanisms, which can set off yet another cycle in which major real estate interests experience losses and blame planning and land use controls – regardless of whether regulation is at fault.

Many growing Sun Belt cities in the South-west have developed in desertlike conditions and are now faced with a major natural resource problem: water. Urban and agricultural interests are often in conflict over the allocation of water. Some urban officials look to other regions for sufficient water supply, and future interregional political conflict on this issue is likely.

Inner-ring suburbs

In many ways the problems of older, inner-ring suburbs mirror those of central cities: because most of the land has been built out, these areas are not the focus of the kind of development interest that is being directed toward "outer-ring" suburbs. As the suburbs have matured, school enrollments have declined and local governments are faced with the special needs of an aging population. Competition with outlying regional shopping centers has damaged the commercial centers of many older suburbs: the traditional small central business districts are experiencing on a smaller scale the same decline in retail activities that the central cities have experienced. A variety of renewal and rehabilitation efforts have succeeded, however, in preserving the functions of the older suburban downtowns. Like that of older central cities, the housing stock of some older suburbs is aging. Given the decline in federal support for housing, these suburbs will have to look to the private market and to local government to help conserve the housing stock.

Residential suburbs

Residential suburbs include those that developed in the late 1940s and early 1950s as well as more recently. Suburban housing is predominantly single-family, with a small proportion of multifamily townhouse developments and low-rise apartment buildings. Residential suburbs generally include some commercial development, such as community and regional shopping centers, and business development along major arterial streets. Some suburbs may also sustain a limited amount of light industry along arterial streets or expressways.

The most common planning issues in such communities concern the orderly development of residential areas. Normally, zoning and land subdivision regulations can cope with new residential development. Increasingly, suburbs have begun to impose special fees or to require developers to participate in the financing of off-site improvements. Some suburban communities are still wary of the construction of multifamily dwellings, but this attitude is less common than it was in the past.

Public services and facilities are normally provided by the local governments, which provide police and fire protection (sometimes volunteer fire departments), libraries, and public schools. During the 1950s and 1960s, school construction often lagged behind need. However, as family size has decreased, or as families have postponed having children, shortages of schoolrooms are relatively rare, and some older suburbs are experiencing declines in school enrollment and are seeking new uses for school buildings.

As more business and industry move to suburban locations, suburban residents no longer look to the city's central business district as the primary place of employment. More and more suburban residents commute to jobs in other suburbs.

High-growth suburban centers

In the mid-1980s, a new type of suburb began to emerge that will pose significant challenges to planners. Some planners call them "centers," but there is as yet no common term for high-growth suburbs such as DuPage County, Illinois, and Route 1 near Princeton, New Jersey. The development of the "new" type of suburb began when the traditional suburb – consisting largely of single-family housing with a little multifamily housing and some business development – came to be seen by major businesses as a highly desirable location for office, research, or industrial facilities. The second phase of development occurred when enough businesses had relocated to the suburbs to transform them into job generators. High-rise office buildings and sprawling business parks now cluster along major suburban arterial streets and expressways. Regional offices for major insurance companies, research laboratories, and similar businesses and services are turning what were once residential suburbs into high-density, mixed-use developments. In some suburban centers, major business buildings and regional shopping centers are in close proximity. The total land and floor area devoted to commercial and business use may surpass the size of the central business district in many smaller cities.

These new suburban centers generate significant amounts of automobile traffic: few such communities have mass transit other than feeder bus service to commuter railroad lines. Thus, almost everyone drives to work, but most suburban expressways were built in an era when the journey to work was from suburb to central city. Now that work trips are from suburb to suburb, the cost of providing adequate roads presents a serious problem to local planners. First, suburban roads are generally considered local and therefore may not qualify for federal highway grants. Second, the density of development is so great and the land development pattern so set that no vacant land may be available for additional arterial streets. The result is suburban gridlock. Increasingly, local governments are requiring developers of shopping centers and office buildings to pay additional fees to finance roads beyond the boundaries of their own developments. Frustrated by the inability of local government to fund road improvements, some developers have chosen to finance road improvements on their own.

High rates of business growth in suburban centers have generated conflict between the development community and the local government on the one hand and citizen groups on the other. Developers and the local government see business and industrial growth, and the resulting tax revenues, as a desirable way to finance community services, especially in residential areas – which commonly do not pay their own way. Citizen groups, however, see high-density business development as destructive to the suburban way of life.

Suburban centers represent a new type of metropolitan development that is not like the old central city and not like the residential suburb of the last several decades. Because of the proliferation of neighboring suburban governments that share facilities – such as roads – and resources – such as water – intergovernmental planning mechanisms will be needed to deal with problems created by growth. The necessary cooperation may be difficult to achieve in areas where suburbs compete with each other to attract businesses.

Rural small towns

The rural small town is a distinct type of environment for planning. These often isolated communities serve as the centers for the county or township in an agricultural, resource-based, or other nonmetropolitan economy. They may have as few as 1,000 people; many are in the 2,500-to-5,000 population range. Many such communities have lost population to metropolitan areas: many have declined because of drops in the surrounding agricultural economy.

Small towns in poor or declining regions present special problems. Often, they do not have sufficient public funds to provide good public services. The cost of replacing a system of private wells and septic tanks with a modern water or sewerage system may be more than a small community can afford, and maintenance and replacement costs for public facilities can be quite high. Providing modern medical services is also a special problem for small communities.

In small rural towns, increased economic activity can be as much of a problem as poverty or decline. For example, a small community chosen as the site of a small industrial plant or in the vicinity of such a plant may have difficulty coping with the resulting growth. Local governments in rural areas often lack sufficient technical staff to analyze the private sector's development proposals. Moreover, they are not prepared to do the necessary public planning and must seek immediate help from private consultants or state technical assistance agencies. One of the most serious problems is providing public improvements such as sewer and

water facilities, which must be constructed *before* the local government begins to receive tax revenues from the new economic activities. Public debt must be carefully planned, and efforts must be made to negotiate with the private sector to install some facilities before they are needed. As new economic activity generates new housing needs, additional pressure is created for adequate public facilities. New populations require a host of public services, including schools, police protection, and fire protection.

A distinct category of rural small town is one whose economy is based on a resource such as oil or coal. Problems in such communities are often related to their economic dependence on a particular resource. If the resource becomes depleted, the local economy suffers. Miscalculation of the value of a resource can create problems, too. For example, in the mid-1970s a number of Great Plains towns expected to grow substantially because of oil shale deposits, but as world oil prices dropped during the 1980s, extracting oil from shale ceased to be economically feasible. Some small communities in Texas and Oklahoma have suffered because of the decline in oil prices and the decline of the U.S. oil industry.

Resort towns

The resort community is another planning environment that poses special challenges to planners. Resort communities in rural areas share many of the problems of other growing rural areas: growth in a rural environment often occurs without sufficient governmental oversight. Even when adequate technical planning services are available, rapid growth in a resort area can cause public services to lag behind the pace of development.

The fact that resort areas often take root in environmentally fragile areas poses special planning problems. A resort established in a beautiful natural area may find that growth takes its toll on the recreational value – open space, clean air, and a sense of wilderness.

A number of problems associated with resort areas are less related to growth than to the seasonal character of the communities. For example, the seasonal influx of tourists may create traffic jams for only part of the year, but the streets must be adequate to the stress of those months. Other systems, such as sewer and water facilities, are subject to the same temporary strains. In communities where there are a number of second homes, building code standards must be established on the basis of peak occupancy. In a number of communities, second homes are becoming year-round residences, but the local governments cannot provide adequate services for a year-round population.

PLANNING AND PLANS

Planning and plans are common to life, business, and government. To most of us, planning conveys the idea of preparing for the future or getting from here to there. This seems simple enough. However, within the context of local government, and to the various practitioners who work in it, *planning* and *plans* can have a variety of meanings depending on the situation. The discussion that follows describes what *planners* mean by "the planning process" and what various levels of "plans" are.

Planning as a process

At the most general level of planning and management, the planning process is divided into five major steps:

1 Basic goals. For local planning, determining basic goals may mean asking questions such as the following: Do we want to grow? Do we want to arrest decline? Do we want to be a center for high-tech industry? What balance do we want between investment in highways and in mass transit?

2 Study and analysis. Among other things, planners study land use, population trends, the economic base of the community, and physiographic features.

3 Plan or policy preparation. A plan or policy is prepared for the community as a whole or for a segment of it. It is a basic statement of how the community will develop, in what direction, and perhaps at what pace.

4 Implementation and effectuation. To carry out plans, planners use tools such as zoning ordinances, land subdivision regulations, capital improvements programs, and general guidelines for private development and public investment.

5 Monitoring and feedback. The last step determines, for example, how well the plans and policies are being carried out, whether the goals were realistic, and whether the study and analysis foresaw new occurrences. Feedback may become the basis for a redesign of the plans and even of the planning system.

These five steps describe the planning process in the abstract. In reality, most local planning consists of three steps: (1) examining inventories and trends in land use, population, employment, and traffic; (2) forecasting the "demand" (in some ways this is a "free market" approach); and (3) planning facilities and services of sufficient capacity to accommodate future demand. This traditional method of planning is an inexact process, depending as it does on forecasting. No matter how sophisticated the forecasting methods, trends are difficult to forecast – especially when a freewheeling entrepreneur makes a locational decision that will have major consequences for a city. Nevertheless, planners must become adept at analyzing a number of dependent interrelated systems.

Furthermore, public planners must be able to take responsibility for understanding what the community wants and for shaping the future of the community's land uses to reflect those desires. Although strong believers in the free market may not be comfortable with this notion, it is at the core of planning. Even some Sun Belt cities that initially welcomed a boomtown atmosphere are reassessing the role of public planning because of declining air quality, crowded streets and highways, and an inability to keep up with public service demand.

Multi-step planning

Planning agencies are now refining their procedures in order to help facilitate both forecasting and implementation of community goals. The first step consists of taking inventories and analyzing trends. In the second step, however, the forecasts are made on a different basis. Instead of assuming that the forecast is a given, the planning agency considers it to be a "what if" statement: the community can then evaluate the pluses and minuses of each forecast.

The third step is the identification of goals and objectives. Many communities have undertaken communitywide or business-led goal studies, which are useful ways of getting residents to think about the community. The identification of goals should be based on widespread participation; goals are not to be set by top officials. The role of the planning agency is to raise issues where there are choices. For example, what are the housing choices in the community? Are all income groups adequately served by the private market? Everyone wants a clean river in town, but how do we define "clean," and what are we willing to pay to clean up the river? How do we weigh standards for air pollution, noise, and water quality against economic development opportunities? Do we want to establish population density ceilings in particular areas?

The fourth step is to formulate, test, and compare alternative policies and plans. Unfortunately, only the most sophisticated transportation planning agencies have the methodological capacity to be precise in testing alternatives in terms of quantitative analysis, and even methods of transportation analysis have shortcomings ... Recently, interesting and useful efforts have been made to test plan or policy alternatives with a combination of quantitative and nonquantitative methods. However, these methods are most useful for answering very narrow policy questions. Given the complexity of interactions within urban areas with respect to land use, transportation, land economics, and so on, evaluating alternative general plans remains a difficult task.

The fifth step is to compare and evaluate alternative plans on the basis of such criteria as financial capacity, the extent to which community goals are met, public acceptability, the legal and social constraints on implementation, and the stress placed on limited resources or facilities.

The sixth step is to select the most acceptable plan and review the forecasts and assumptions. The purpose of this review is to consider two questions: How congruent are the plan and the data obtained in step one? How much compromise was necessary to create the preferred plan? For example, population forecasts may indicate the need for a variety of public facilities, but further analysis may show that public revenues will not permit the funding of those facilities. Thus, some desirable projects may be delayed, scaled down, or eliminated.

The seventh step is to prepare detailed plans for elements (e.g. housing, transportation) of the comprehensive plan and for community facilities and programs.

The eighth step is to implement plans and policies through both public and private means. Implementation usually involves regulation, some incentives, and some cooperation.

The final step is not a step at all but a continuous evaluation of the process as a whole. The purpose of the evaluation is to discover blind alleys, redo plans that seem impossible to implement, and change regulations that are creating problems.

Throughout the planning process, the planning agency conducts its own in-house work, hires consultants, consults with other local government departments, establishes task forces and advisory committees, confers with other governmental levels, and has numerous meetings with officials, technicians, and the public. The approach is complex and can be frustrating, yet it seems to be the only way we know to conduct the local democratic planning process. Thus, planning is not just a series of "rational" steps but is also constantly interwoven into a continuous process of agency management.

Plans

The preceding discussion emphasizes the process of planning, but planning must create products ... these products vary with the type and level of plan being prepared.

At the broadest and most general level is the comprehensive plan, at one time called the master plan and also known as the general plan. More recently, products of this kind have been called strategic plans. The comprehensive plan is a document (in multiple volumes for very large jurisdictions) that is the result of lengthy and intensive study and analysis. The geographic scope is the entire community and its regional environment. The time scale is long range or indefinite. Such a plan is comprehensive in that it tries to link long-range objectives to a number of interdependent elements, including population growth, economic development, land use, transportation, and community facilities.

The comprehensive plan discusses the principal issues and problems of growth or decline facing the community. It will also indicate the main trends that seem inevitable and that need the attention of public or public–private programs. Plans usually contain a mixture of suggestions, proposals for which the means of implementation have not yet been identified, and actual commitments of local governments. For at least a decade plans have tended not to be presented in map form because of the difficulty of identifying precise sites or dimensions; instead, most plans are a series of policy statements.

Depending on the size of the community, a comprehensive plan may also contain chapters on public utility and facility systems if general policies have been established for these systems. However, the degree of detail is nowhere near that in system plans ... System plans are more detailed than the comprehensive or general plans yet do not necessarily approach engineering specifications. A system plan summarizes the plans, policies, and programs for a specific network of communitywide facilities: the entire sewer system, the entire fire protection system, or the park and recreation system. System plans deal with specific facilities in specific places.

At the third level are area plans, which include details about certain geographic parts of the community. The most common type is a plan for the central business district. Other area plans are for industrial districts, civic and cultural centers, individual neighborhoods, the community or district encompassing several neighborhoods, and waterfronts. Details in area plans may go down to the block level. The area plan identifies the issues and problems facing a geographic area, develops plans for the future, and provides guidance to local decision makers reviewing private development proposals.

The style of planning can vary with the area. For example, a plan for a central business district may emphasize urban design components and the involvement of the private sector, whereas neighborhood-level planning involves citizen groups and neighborhood organizations.

The fourth type of plan is a detailed engineering plan for components of subsystems, such as trunk sewer lines, major water mains, and street extensions. These plans are based on system-wide plans and typically are prepared under the direction of the public works department.

At the fifth level are site plans for facilities such as libraries, fire stations, and neighborhood parks. Such facilities require land purchase, architectural and engineering drawings, scheduling in the capital improvements program, possible public hearings for site selection, meetings with neighborhood or community groups, and coordination with neighborhood development plans. System plans are considered separately from site plans, because linear systems provide the basic network for planned development. If the systems are not in, development may not occur. After they are constructed, the availability of utilities may accelerate development. In other words, these linear systems shape urban development.

The context of planning

Public planning is never as simple and direct as a textbook makes it sound. A planner must learn to be a jack-of-all-trades. Today's planner works in a complex intergovernmental web of plans, policies, and regulations. Planners must have the patience and the understanding to work in the changing world of politics. Planners must comply with a large body of land use law and must be ready to contribute to the making of that law. To make reasonable forecasts, planners need a working knowledge of practical economics. Planners must understand how a community's fiscal situation will limit or support the implementation of a plan. Planners must understand how to protect the natural environment and how to encourage development that most people will find aesthetically attractive.

LEONIE SANDERCOCK AND ANN FORSYTH

"A Gender Agenda: New Directions for Planning Theory"

Journal of the American Planning Association (1992)

Editors' introduction   In the twentieth century there have been a succession of "waves" of planning theory and many cross-currents, as described by Peter Hall (p. 383) . A new wave is theory about gender and planning. In the following selection Australian planners Leonie Sandercock and Ann Forsyth synthesize recent work on gender and city planning and sketch out "a gender agenda" for the future.

Leonie Sandercock is a visiting professor and lecturer in the Urban Planning Program at the University of California, Los Angeles. She was previously a professor and chair of the graduate Urban Studies Program at Macquarie University in Sydney, Australia. Her writings on city planning and the operation of the private real estate market in Australia have been influential both in Australian policy making and in the understanding of cities worldwide. Ann Forsyth, also originally from Australia, is an assistant professor of landscape architecture at the University of Massachusetts, Amherst.

Until recently, urbanists like Jane Jaccbs (p. 104) and Dolores Hayden (p. 143) who were concerned with gender issues were extremely rare. The global rise of feminism has changed that. A recent explosion of writing about gender and cities by women focuses on the uses of cities and the built environment by women, as distinct from men. This literature argues that male-planned cities reflect current (unequal) gender relations and often serve women poorly. Female homemakers may be isolated in single-family suburban homes, in an economically inferior status, unserved by public transit related to work sites or day care (if it exists at all), in buildings designed by male architects which reinforce patriarchal gender roles. Public spaces, it is argued, are generally designed by males and reflect predominantly male values and concerns.

More and more women are entering the planning profession, and women are increasingly joining the ranks of city planning school faculty. There is an increasing body of writings about how city planners can build new environments or retrofit old ones to better respond to working women, female-headed households, two-wage-earner nuclear families who share child rearing, lesbian lifestyles and other gender issues. If gender can no longer be ignored in planning practice, Sandercock and Forsyth argue that it should not be ignored in planning theory.

The first part of this selection describes currents in feminist thought which the authors argue should enrich planning theory. These include feminist theories of language and communication, critiques of epistemology and methodology which call for "connected knowing" (emphasizing both scientific reason and passion), feminist ethics, gender-sensitive definitions of the public and private domain, and other themes.

The second part of this selection lays out a "gender agenda" for planning education, research, and theory building. Sandercock and Forsyth would like to see initial efforts at rewriting the history of city planning broadened to provide a full account of women, not just as victims of male-dominated city planning, but as actors who have made a contribution. They argue that feminist theory can enrich planning theory. They feel that research and theory building can help change the culture of planning so that gender considerations become an accepted part of practice by all planners – male and female.

Note the connections between themes Peter Hall develops and the authors' account of emerging feminist planning theory. Women designers and architects in the planning-as-craft tradition are generating designs to meet women's needs; Marxist feminists are exploring the relationships between gender, class, and power; and systems-oriented women theorists are writing about how transit, day care, and other urban systems can better serve women's needs.

Leonie Sandercock's other books include *Cities for Sale* (London: Heinemann, 1976) and *Property, Politics, and Urban Planning: A History of Australian City Planning, 1890–1990* (New Brunswick, N.J.: Transaction Press, 1990).

Other books on women in cities and city planning include Catharine Stimpson, Elsa Dixler, Martha Nelson, and Kathryn Yatrakis (eds.), *Women and the American City* (Chicago: University of Chicago Press, 1981), Caroline Andrew and Beth Moore Milroy (eds.), *Life Spaces: Gender, Household, Employment* (Vancouver: University of British Columbia Press, 1988), Jo Little, Linda Peake, and Pat Richardson (eds.), *Women in Cities: Gender and the Urban Environment* (Basingstoke: Macmillan, 1988), Dolores Hayden, *Redesigning the American Dream* (New York: Norton, 1984), and Daphne Spain, *Gendered Space* (Chapel Hill, N.C.: University of North Carolina Press, 1992).

LEONIE SANDERCOCK and ANN FORSYTH, "A Gender Agenda: New Directions for Planning Theory"

Journal of the American Planning Association (1992)

"Women face problems of such significance in cities and society that gender can no longer be ignored in planning practice," says Leavitt (1986: 181). In "Toward a Woman-Centered University," Adrienne Rich speaks of the need to change the center of gravity within academia to encompass women's knowledge and experience (1979). Planners also must work to change the center of gravity within their field. Leavitt (1986), Wekerle (1980), Hayden (1981, 1984), Cooper Marcus and Sarkissian (1986), and Stimpson *et al.* (1981) write of the importance of gender as a focus in planning practice. The crucial connections between theory and practice are, however, still rare and tentative.

With the new wave of feminist thinking in the 1970s came a spate of research on women and the urban environment, but the integration of that rapidly growing body of work with theory and paradigms to explain women's urban experience was "still far in the future" (Wekerle, 1980). The 1980s witnessed some nourishing of attention to gender in policy questions in the "women and ..." literature (women and housing, women and transportation, women and economic development). But in the developed countries, of all of the subfields within planning, theory remains the most male dominated and the least influenced by any awareness of the importance of gender. (By contrast, for developing countries see Moser and Levi (1986) and Moser (1989).) The works of Hayden (1981,

1984) and Leavitt and Saegert (1989), as well as the literature on gender issues in international development, are path breaking and inspirational, but they are marginalized or ignored by most of the rest of planning theory. If gender can no longer be ignored in planning practice, how can the theoretical debates continue to be silent on the subject?

Of course, much depends on how we define planning theory. There is as little agreement within planning as to what constitutes planning theory, as there is within feminism as to what constitutes feminist theory. Not simply a semantic difficulty, it is a question of contested terrain. It is a political question. Just as feminists use competing theories to understand or explain the oppression and subordination of women, planners use competing theories to explain the role, practice, and effects of planning. Even more fundamentally, disagreement abounds as to the proper theoretical object of planning theory.

Planning theory can be delineated into three different emphases: planning practice, political economy, and metatheory (Sandercock and Forsyth, 1990). At one level are those authors who theorize about planning practice, both its processes and outcomes. In general, theories of planning practice involve analysis of the procedures, actions, and behavior of planners. They may also include an analysis of the context or concrete situation in which planners are working.

The political economy approach examines the nature and meaning of urban planning in capitalist society. This approach might encompass speculations about the relationships among capitalism, democracy, and reform. Generally this approach is disinterested in planning practice. Rather, this work begins with a general theory – most commonly some version of Marxism – and uses case studies from the planning arena to illustrate the prechosen theory.

The metatheory approach involves work that asks fundamental epistemological and methodological questions about planning. Its theoretical object is an abstract, general notion of planning as a rational human activity that involves the translation of knowledge into action. At this level, theorists are no longer necessarily talking specifically about urban or regional planning, but about planning as a generic activity and as a historical legacy of the Enlightenment.

Gender issues emerge in each of the three approaches and take the form of such themes as the economic status of women, the location and movement of women through the built environment, the connections between capitalist production and patriarchal relationships and between public and domestic life, how women know about the world and about what is good, and the forms of communication with which women are most comfortable or by which they are most threatened. An awareness of these issues is lacking in planning theory. The objective of this paper is not to present a singular feminist theory of planning practice. Rather it examines those aspects of feminist theory that seem to have the most to offer planning theory.

SPATIAL, ECONOMIC, AND SOCIAL RELATIONSHIPS

Contemporary Western feminism emerged from a particular urban form – the mid-twentieth-century capitalist city, "which expressed and reinforced differentiated gender roles" (Mackenzie, 1989: 110). As more women have become wage earners the physical constraints of this type of city have become apparent. Child care is rarely close to employment centers. When [it is] unavailable, women are severely constrained by the difficult decision between not having children and paying for child care in lost wages or lost time. Similarly, mass transit is scheduled for rational commutes to work rather than the erratic movements of women responsible for both domestic duties and paid work (Palm and Pred, 1976; Pickup, 1984). Theoretical accounts of these issues and the links among them emerge infrequently and only recently in the field of urban planning.

Feminist theory, however, has examined these issues. In a pioneering article, Ann Markusen (1980) argued that women's household work had been ignored by both Marxist and neoclassical economists, even though this work has a large impact on the use of cities. She examines these issues in relation to capitalism and patriarchy. Other feminist scholars are working on the relationship among capitalist urbanization, the built environment, and gender (Huxley, 1988; Mackenzie, 1989), or among household, community, and city (Leavitt and Saegert, 1989; Mackenzie, 1988). Some of this work has grown from attempts to develop a feminist Marxism.

Other feminists, dissatisfied with mainstream theories that define human relations primarily in terms of capitalist production in the official economy, have responded with subjectivist, communitarian, or hermeneutical approaches, and have emphasized the traditional, life-sustaining work of women. When the object of this work is to create new theories to better understand the context of planning, then it fits into the political economy approach to planning theory. When the primary object is to generate strategies and programs for change, then the work belongs with theories of feminist planning practice.

Dolores Hayden's article "What Would a Non-sexist City Be Like?" (1980) and her book *Redesigning the American Dream* (1984) provide the best-known and broadest theories and visions of feminist planning practice in developed nations. Theories that are broad in scope link different activities and scales of planning – home and transport, household sexual politics, work places, and the environment, for example – rather than just concentrating on one activity.

Hayden describes a diversity of women – single parents, poor women, battered wives, and so forth – and their different needs. This sense of women being at the same time a whole and also a collection of smaller populations grew during the 1980s, particularly as minority women began to speak out on women's issues (King, 1988). Women are divided by geographical, political, religious, class, and cultural boundaries. Yet the internationalized economy exacerbates the vulnerability of women, who continue to undertake the bulk of unpaid domestic work and are engaged in low-wage work and unorganized informal markets. Women are linked to each other more than ever by an international network of decisions. Immigrant workers, or nonmigrants working for mobile firms, exemplify this connection (Sassen-Koob, 1984).

Feminist theory is currently grappling with differences among women. The book title *All the Women Are White, All the Blacks Are Men, But Some of Us Are Brave* (Hull et al., 1982) reflects the vigorous exchange about whether feminist theory is ethnocentric, grounded only in the experience of white women, and whether adding in minority women is enough. Some feminists hold that theoretical categories need to be reformed in light of the distinct experiences of minority women (Barrett and McIntosh, 1985; Bhavnani and Coulson, 1986; Lugones and Spelman, 1983; Hooks, 1984). Planning theory must treat this diversity seriously. Theorists must also be able to determine when it is appropriate to distinguish between specific categories and when the experiences among women of different classes, races, and other backgrounds are actually congruent (Collins, 1990: 217–19).

Theorizing within this multiplicity of voices is a complex task, but not doing so can make "woman" as oppressive a category as "man" (Harding, 1986b). As yet, planning theory literature deals hardly at all with multiple oppressions by race, sexual preference, culture, and gender. Leavitt and Saegert's (1989) work on gender, race, and age among poor people is a notable exception. Outside planning there are more attempts.

LANGUAGE AND COMMUNICATION

Planning theorists are currently involved in debates over the types and uses of rational communication, the use of language as a means of empowerment, the construction of meaning (Marris, 1987), and microanalyses of communication as action and of listening as a crucial tool of social policy (Forester, 1989). Recent feminist scholarship has extended the scope of this important work.

Feminist theories of language often start by showing how language forms one's sense of reality, order, and place in the community. As such, language can be limiting as well as empowering (Spender, 1985; Collins, 1987).

Feminists have pointed to inequalities in the use of language; for example, to how men interrupt women more often than women interrupt men and to how men listen less intently to women than women listen to men (Spender, 1985: 41–50, 121–9). Important empirical studies are being conducted on how through language women come to know their world differently from each other and from men (Belenky *et al.*, 1986). Minority women have pointed to their distinct use and experience of language (Hooks, 1984; Williams, 1988; Collins, 1990). Empowering language and dominant forms of communications are frequently acquired through formal education. Where education is unequally distributed, inequalities in communication will be accentuated. The upbringing and life experience of many women have actively discouraged them from speaking out or speaking up for their own needs. And when women do speak, they are more ambivalent than men about speaking assertively and with authority and are less comfortable than men with the dominant rational, scientific modes of thought (Okin, 1989: 72).

Evidence of communication inequalities emerges in such areas as citizen participation. Professional jargon and argumentative speaking styles can alienate, confuse, or render women speechless. Although in practice residents and planners are likely to be somewhat "multi-lingual" (many planners are women, after all, and many men are sensitive to these issues), theory should address this need for appropriate styles of communication.

Theory needs to consider the assumption, implicit in pluralist political theory, that, if given the chance, all interest groups will articulate their demands in a roughly equivalent manner. Given the current socialization of women, particularly women who suffer multiple disadvantages because of class, race, education, health, and self-esteem, this simply may not be the case.

A feminist planner, experienced in neighborhood consultation and participatory planning, described her difficulties in encouraging people at public meetings to contribute equally, particularly when many women are socialized to believe they have nothing valuable to say. She responded to this problem in one large community meeting by asking people to sit in small groups and tell a story or anecdote about their neighborhood. People then had no trouble speaking out about their lives and their community. Previously silent or hesitant participants found that they too possessed knowledge. For example, women who were stuck in the suburbs all day talked about the problems of public transport for themselves and their family. The storytelling format gave a variety of people the courage to be more involved (Sarkissian, 1990).

Theories of professional communication and citizen representation and participation need to be developed to understand these complex inequalities in planning and to develop strategies to bring women out of silence. Balancing equality and special treatment is always a complicated task, but ignoring gender is a false equality.

METHODOLOGY AND EPISTEMOLOGY

The case for a feminist perspective on epistemology and methodology in planning is grounded in feminist critiques of content, theory, and method in the social sciences. The tendency in the social sciences has been to validate only scientific and technical knowledge and dismiss all other kinds of knowledge. Feminists are increasingly critical of the traditional dualism that pits reason against passion and rationality against politics, as if reason excludes passion, as if politics, by definition, were irrational. Instead, feminists argue for what Belenky *et al.* (1986) call "connected knowing," which emphasizes relationship, rather than separation between the self and the object of research, and for discussion of the politics of theory and method and of the origins and implications of theoretical hierarchies.

In her paper criticizing theory and method in geography, "On Being outside 'The Project,'" Christopherson (1989) notes recent work by feminists and other critical theorists in jurisprudence, history, philosophy, and aesthetics which discusses the relationship between theory construction and power. These feminists insist that theorists must identify their personal position relative to the theoretical object. By way of example, Collins (1990) elaborates four elements that shape her articulation of an Afrocentric feminist epistemology: concrete experience as a criterion of meaning; the use of dialogue in assessing knowledge claims; an ethic of caring that stresses a capacity for empathy and the appropriateness of emotions in dialogue; and an ethic of personal accountability. Feminists are certainly not alone in their critiques of positivist epistemology (Kuhn, 1962; Polanyi, 1958; Feyerabend, 1975), but their work originates in response to an alienation from the methods of research and definitions of knowledge that denigrate or ignore women's experiences and that refuse to consider the political content of knowledge creation.

John Friedmann's recent synthesis of planning theory, *Planning in the Public Domain: From Knowledge to Action*, is an example of planning theory's uncertainty about its knowledge base. Initially he defines his theoretical object – planning – as the linking of *scientific and technical knowledge* to action in the public domain. But in conclusion he turns away from purely technocratic planning and embraces subjective knowledge as the foundation of a radical planning approach – a stance more sympathetic to feminist critiques (Friedmann, 1987: 413–15).

A distinctively feminist epistemology would be controversial (Sandercock and Forsyth, 1992). Feminist insights, however, would expand the planner's perspective beyond scientific and technical knowledge to other ways of knowing. First, planners would accept that knowledge is gained through talking, especially through oral traditions and gossip, which Belenky *et al.* define as conversations among intimates, talk about feelings, about the personal, the particular, the petty, but not necessarily the trivial. "Gossip, like poetry and fiction, penetrates to the truth of things," say Belenky *et al.* It is a "special mode of knowing," which moves back and forth between large and small, between particular and general (Belenky *et al.* 1986: 116). Second, knowledge is gained through listening, which Forester (1989) insightfully describes as "the social policy of everyday life," and indispensable to those work-

ing in planning. Third, knowing is also tacit or intuitive (Polanyi, 1958). As microbiologist Barbara McLintock has argued, "Reason is not by itself adequate to describe and understand the vast complexity, indeed mystery, of living forms" (Keller, 1983: 199). Fourth, creating symbolic forms through painting, music, or poetry is a more important way of knowing and communicating than planners have yet been prepared to contemplate. (For example, graffiti, murals, and folk and rap songs are ways in which minorities express themselves.) And acting and reflecting on the meaning of action yields information about the world in a way that is unavailable through technical books and reports. This is the heart of the philosophy of learning by doing, practiced by Jane Addams in her community work in turn-of-the-century Chicago at Hull House (Addams, 1910), taken up by philosopher John Dewey who was a frequent visitor to Hull House (Dewey, 1980), and developed later in planning in the work of Donald Schon in his discussion of reflective practice (Schon, 1983).

All of these ways of knowing are inseparable from the subject who is doing the talking, listening, or acting. Knowledge thus is partially autobiographical, and, therefore, is gender based. Moreover, knowledge is a social construction. Different kinds of knowledge, including scientific and technical forms, must be shared through communication to construct meaning. The construction of meaning involves communication, politics, and passion. Knowledge is, therefore, an ongoing and unfinished business.

Expanding the ways of knowing leads to a rethinking of other methodological issues, such as how to go about research in planning. Again, the feminist social scientists can assist planners with these issues. Sociologists Judith Cook and Mary Fonow (1986) have outlined five basic principles of a feminist methodology:

1   to continuously and reflexively attend to the significance of gender and gender asymmetry as a basic feature of all social life, including the conduct of research;
2   to accept the centrality of consciousness raising as a specific methodological tool and as a general orientation, or way of seeing;

3   to challenge the norm of objectivity that assumes that the subject and object of research can be separated and that personal experiences are unscientific;
4   to be concerned with the ethical implications of feminist research, and recognition of the exploitation of women as objects of knowledge; and
5   to focus on the empowerment of women and transformation of patriarchal social institutions through research.

While a distinctive feminist method of research or a distinctive feminist epistemology would be unbalanced, it must be recognized with Westkott (1979) that knowledge is inherently dialectical and that feminist inquiry has emancipatory as well as critical power.

ETHICS IN PLANNING

Recently feminist attention has focused on ethics in response to the influential and controversial work of Carol Gilligan (1982), who with a group of colleagues published a series of studies critical of the work of Lawrence Kohlberg, a psychologist who advanced the theory that humans develop in a morally autonomous fashion, skilled in reasoning about rights and justice. Gilligan noticed that women rarely did as well as men in Kohlberg's studies, and proposed that this was not because of inferior moral development but rather because of their different development. She suggested that women tend to develop a morality of responsibility and care, based on relationships with loved ones in stark contrast to Kohlberg's prototypical liberal individuals with their focus on abstract reasoning about rights and justice (Gilligan, 1982; Gilligan et al., 1988; also Chodorow, 1978).

Although Gilligan originally suggested that these two moral orientations were mutually exclusive, her later work indicates that many people use both when finding the best solution to a problem (Johnston, 1988). Other studies have revealed that moralities of responsibility and care can be ascribed not only to women but to other disadvantaged and oppressed groups (Tronto, 1987; Collins, 1990). Other feminist philosophers have posed the possibility of an ethic based on "maternal thinking" (Ruddick, 1983) and have supported findings of altruistic tendencies in the general population (Mansbridge, 1988). Gilligan's work has come under attack for valorizing the consequences of women's oppression, pointing out that caring can lead to prejudice as well as altruism. Her insights remain an important empirical finding, while leaving unanswered the question of the origin of gender differences in the approach to ethical debates.

For planners, this expanded feminist ethic is a companion, although sometimes an uneasy one, to ideas of community. The new communitarian theorists offer sophisticated critiques of liberalism and offer alternatives with obvious links to feminist theories of care. They tend, however, to be complacent about traditional structures, such as the family or nation, which are hierarchically organized and oppressive to women (Sandel, 1982; MacIntyre, 1981). Feminists have proposed instead alternative models based on such communities as trade unions and political and self-help groups (Friedman, 1989).

Planning theory's sensitive analyses of community have often included critiques of romanticism (Jacobs, 1961; Bell and Newby, 1976; Heskin, 1991; Marris, 1987). Leavitt and Saegert's (1989) study of the residents of landlord-abandoned buildings in Harlem, a population predominantly black and female, is a pioneering empirical feminist work. They discovered that many of the residents had formed "community households," which shared economic and administrative burdens and drew on reciprocal social relations and attachment to place and the historical community of Harlem. Saegert and Leavitt describe the sensitivity required of planners to respect this sense of connection and care, rather than rely solely on economic criteria and formal democratic processes. Black feminist theorist Collins also discusses the centrality of an ethic of caring in African-American women's culture, but notes that institutional supports validating this ethic are virtually nonexistent (Collins, 1990: 215–17).

THE PUBLIC DOMAIN

The place of women in the public domain is a complex issue in planning. Beginning in the Victorian era and culminating in the progressive era, "the city of separate spheres" emerged in which a woman's proper place was perceived to be in the home (Wright, 1980; Brown, 1990). For domestics, however, who were usually immigrants and black women, that home was someone else's (Collins, 1990: 55). Twentieth-century metropolitan spatial form, with its "masculine cities and feminine suburbs" (Saegert, 1980), has reinforced the notion of separate spheres.

While sociologist Richard Sennett has discussed "the fall of public man" (1977), feminists in the past few decades have campaigned for the rise of public woman. The feminist political struggle in recent decades has had three components: (1) claiming women's right to be actors in the public domain and to work and participate fully in the life of the city; (2) carving out and protecting public space for women; and (3) redefining the nature and extent of the public domain. Some feminists argue that dramatic changes in metropolitan spatial structures and improvements in social and transportation policy are required to improve the opportunities for women who are also primary care-givers to participate in the political and economic life of the city. Second, feminist planners are still struggling to incorporate the issue of women's safety into land-use planning. Third, in challenging the definition of the public domain in liberal theory, feminists have shown that liberal theory has ignored the political nature of personal life, the interconnections between gender relations in the family and the paid workplace, and the fact that socialization for citizenship occurs in the domestic realm (Pateman, 1983; Okin, 1989; Hirschmann, 1989).

The feminist struggle has led to a variety of activist responses. One feminist stance is to say that the personal realm is political and that issues like domestic violence, which are traditionally seen as private issues, are actually public. A second strategy is to make a private issue, like sexuality or abortion, public until oppressive policies, programs, and plans are eliminated. A third strategy, often conducted by these same feminists, is to make private some actions and behaviors that have traditionally been seen as part of the public domain of planning. These include lobbying for the removal from public scrutiny of the family structure of households in residential areas or the sexual relationships of public housing tenants (information required for housing allocation and rental payments). The thrust of all these strategies is to redefine the meaning of public and private. While abolishing all divisions between the private realm and the larger world would be undesirable, feminists indicate that in the arena of urban planning the line between public and private or domestic life has been drawn to men's advantage. Thus the public domain is a physical construct that by definition represents a whole set of contested political and economic issues within planning.

Feminist analysis of the state can productively interact with planning theory. Feminist theory often characterizes the state as a kind of public patriarchy. Unquestionably its employees are divided by gender, with women concentrated in secretarial and clerical work and, at the senior level, primarily in human services. State policies about marriage, the family, legitimate violence, industrial subsidies, and schools tend to reproduce and form gender roles and relationships (Connell, 1990). Planners assist in this process when they create zoning policies that restrict cohabitation to only related individuals, forcing out or apart gay couples and communal households (Ritzdorf, 1989), or policies that attract industries with gender-segmented workforces to enterprise zones, thereby reinforcing different job options for men and women.

The involvement of planners in current moves to privatize public services also has a direct though complex effect on women. Women are more likely than men to receive public assistance, as single parents, as the dominant elderly population group, as residents in public housing, or as the majority users of public transport. This assistance has given women more choices, relieving them from some of the responsibilities formerly considered private or domestic, such as caring for children or older relatives, and giving them enough material resources to achieve some measure of independence.

The form privatization takes – corporate or community-based nonprofit group ownership, continued or cut resources – affects this trend toward greater independence. A limited-equity housing cooperative (like the ones studied by Leavitt and Saegert) is a far different form of privatization than ownership by an absentee corporate or unrestricted individual landlord. Feminists and planners need to consider this issue in all its complexity, which will mean dealing realistically and at many levels with issues of power and control in women's lives.

A GENDER RESEARCH AGENDA

A gender research agenda for planning theory concentrates on areas where feminist theory has had little to say: case studies of planning practice, practical and strategic gender interests, gender in the internal culture of planners, a gender-conscious reform of planning education, and the balance between multiple differences and equality.

STUDIES OF PLANNING PRACTICE

Feminist theory, unlike more academic theories, is related to and grows out of feminist practice. Studies of both feminist planning practice and the relationship of feminist activism to planning are needed. The case studies of traditional planning, however, seldom consider gender issues. Feminist planning needs what Krumholz and Forester (1990) have done for equity-based planning: an account of attempts to politicize gender issues in planning, followed by a theorizing of the successes and failures. Some international examples serve to inspire us: the Women's Committee of the Greater London Council (Brown, 1990); women's planning initiatives in Canada (Modlich, 1986); and the Dutch women movement's campaign against clustered deconcentration and their incorporation of social safety into city planning in Amsterdam and Eindhoven (Brown, 1990:

206–60). Surely there must be some home-grown equivalents.

Arguably the history of city planning should be rewritten, incorporating gender as a category of analysis. Feminist historiography has challenged the notion that the history of women is *always* the same as the history of men or that significant turning points in history have the same impact on both sexes (Lerner, 1979; Kelly, 1984; Scott, 1986). A gender-conscious approach to the writing of history produces a new set of questions about the history of city planning ideas and practice (Sandercock, 1990: 21–33) and develops a different sense of historical change. In the history of planning women have often suffered and been discriminated against because men or patriarchal capitalism have controlled their lives, but this is by no means the full story. Women have not simply been victims, they too have been actors, and recent work has begun to uncover their contributions (Hayden, 1981; Birch, 1983; Davis, 1983; Wirka, 1989).

PRACTICAL AND STRATEGIC GENDER INTERESTS

Feminist planners in developing countries have drawn a distinction between practical and strategic gender interests (Molyneux, 1985; Moser, 1989). Practical interests are derived directly from women's experiences in their gender relations and their interest in survival, given that context. The practical approach does not challenge current gender relations. Strategic gender interests are derived from a more theoretical or feminist analysis of women's subordination to men, and aim to alter those relationships. This theoretical construction seems worth exploring for its usefulness in planning in developed countries. It promises to provide a framework for linking the descriptive "women and ..." literature with explanations of why gender oppression occurs and with programs for fundamental change.

GENDER AND THE CULTURE OF PLANNERS

With more women entering the planning profession gender inequality is not merely an issue of the numerical dominance of men. Rather it is male dominance in the theories, standards, and ideologies used to guide planners' work – that is, in the internal culture of planners. By the late 1980s most planning schools were admitting roughly equal proportions of male and female students, but there nevertheless remain considerable structural inequalities between men and women in the planning profession. There are very few women running or even in the senior ranks of planning agencies. Women are concentrated in human services and social planning, professional areas with small and vulnerable budgets and relatively little prestige and power compared with development control, metropolitan strategy, or transportation planning. In essence, despite their growing numbers, women are still on the periphery rather than at the center of planning practice. Perhaps this will change over time, as women move up through the ranks in the next decade. Or are there structural impediments embedded in the culture of planners that need to be addressed (as there are for women in other professions)? Are women treated differently (from and by men) in the planning workplace? Do they experience difficulties in being heard, in being taken seriously, in being drawn into the confidences or information sharing that constitute the informal web of daily life in a planning office? Are women planners punished by their male peers if they speak out on women's issues? Do women planners simply not speak out on such issues from fear or from a perception that they would be marginalized in some way for doing so? In other words, is there a dominant male definition of the key issues and roles in the planning workplace that could be at once progressive in class terms and yet gender blind?

Two anecdotes suffice. A group of women planners in an Australian capital city, when asked whether they thought that the notion that planning policies are *not* gender neutral had percolated through the male ranks of the profession and become built-in to their daily prac-

tice and discussion, simply laughed at the apparent naivete of the question, at the hopelessness of the situation, and perhaps, too, at their own tendency to avoid the issue because of the discomfort it inevitably causes.

A feminist planner became the manager of community services for a large suburban municipality in Australia. The managers of all the other planning departments within that council were male. She knew that they all met together at the local pub at the end of the week. She suspected that important informal information exchange and power plays took place at these gatherings. She was not invited. Women traditionally have not been part of pub culture in Australian life. This planner was not a drinker and did not like the pub atmosphere. Yet she felt excluded and debated raising the matter with the boys. The issue likely has no solution; if she raised it and was invited to join the men, their conversation would no doubt be constrained by her presence. This problem is an example of how the internal culture of planners reflects the biases of the wider masculine culture, and poses dilemmas for professional women about whether to adjust their behavior accordingly, or whether to try to introduce more female ways of socializing into the workplace.

Research based on in-depth interviews could be done about the experience of women in the planning workplace to assess whether and to what extent the gender inequalities and biases of the wider society are being reinforced or challenged. (This is an omission in Forester's otherwise very perceptive 1989 work on the internal culture of planners.)

REFORM OF PLANNING EDUCATION

During a 1990 Australian government review of metropolitan strategy, a group of women planners were asked about gender issues in the local planning scene. The response was that consciousness of these issues was very low. The respondents added that recent women graduates of the local planning program were actively antifeminist. These new graduates, it seems, are afraid of being stereotyped and dismissed by male colleagues as "noisy feminists." Further questioning revealed that the planning school has no women on its faculty and that gender issues are not in the syllabus.

A recent introductory undergraduate planning course at the University of California at Berkeley had eighty-five students, male and female almost equally represented. Three of thirty lectures dealt specifically with the question of gender in planning history, theory, and practice, while the importance of gender was integrated into the rest of the subject matter. In student evaluations at the end of the course, 10 percent of the students, when asked "What was the worst thing about this class?", replied, "The emphasis on gender." One student complained that the course should have been titled "Feminist City Planning." This group ranked the instructor and the course at the lowest possible grade. On the other hand, some 30 percent noted the exploration of gender issues as one of the best things about the class, and ranked both course and instructor at the highest possible grade. This dramatic polarization reveals both the need for and the resistance to a gender-conscious approach to the teaching of planning. Some feminist planners indicate that attempts to introduce a more gender-sensitive curriculum in planning programs continue to be met with resistance and incomprehension by male-dominated faculties.

BALANCING DIFFERENCES AND EQUALITY

Feminism starts from an experience of difference – the differences between men and women, differences that in some way cause women to be disadvantaged. Recently, however, the focus in some feminist work has shifted to considerations of differences among women, which raises new and important questions. How do different groups of women use and experience cities? Do public spaces hold the same intimidation for middle-class and poor women, for African-Americans, mothers, Chicanas, Jewish women, or lesbians? How are experiences of lone parenting different for women from different communities? Taking account of the systematic differences among women, as well as the systematic differences among women and the men in their various communities, is an important task for gender-conscious planning.

THE ONGOING DEBATE

In "The 'Thereness' of Women: A Selective Review of Urban Sociology," Lyn Lofland asserts that in empirical and theoretical urban sociology, women are perceived as being part of the scene but not part of the action.

> [Women] are part of the locale or neighborhood or area described like other important aspects of the setting such as income, ecology or demography – but largely irrelevant to the analytic *action*. They reflect a group's social organization and culture, but they never seem to be in the process of creating it.
>
> (Lofland, 1975: 145)

In mainstream planning theory women have scarcely even been seen as subjects of theory. The problem, however, is far more subtle and complex than a simple tradition of exclusion. The paradigms on which planning and theorizing about it have been based are informed by characteristics traditionally associated with the masculine in our society. There is a need to rethink the foundations of the discipline, its epistemology, and its various methodologies. Feminist critiques and feminist literature need to be incorporated into the debates within planning theory.

REFERENCES AND FURTHER READING

Addams, Jane (1910) *Twenty Years at Hull House: With Autobiographical Notes.* New York: Macmillan.

Andrew, Caroline and Milroy, Beth Moore (eds.) (1988) *Life Spaces: Gender, Household, Employment.* Vancouver: University of British Columbia Press.

Barrett, Michele and McIntosh, Mary (1985) "Ethnocentrism and Socialist Feminist Theory," *Feminist Review* 20: 23–48.

Belenky, Mary, Clinchy, Blythe, Goldberger, Nancy and Tarule, Jill (1986) *Women's Ways of Knowing: The Development of Self, Voice, and Mind.* New York: Basic Books.

Bell, Colin, and Newby, Howard (1976) "Community, Communion, Class and Community Action: The Social Sources of the New Urban Politics" in D. T. Herbert and R. J. Johnson (eds.) *Spatial Perspectives on Problems and Policies*, vol. 2 of *Social Areas in Cities*. London: John Wiley.

Bell, Derrick (1985) *And We Are Not Saved: The Elusive Request for Racial Justice*. New York: Basic Books.

Bhavnani, Kum-Kum and Coulson, Margaret (1986) "Transforming Socialist Feminism: The Challenge of Racism," *Feminist Review* 23: 81–92.

Birch, Eugenie (1983) "From Civic Worker to City Planner: Women and Planning, 1890–1980" in Donald Krueckeberg (ed.) *The American Planner: Biographies and Reflections*. New York: Methuen.

Brown, Karen Rebecca (1990) "Rethinking the Man-Made Metropolis: The Relationship between Constructs of Gender and Planned Urban Form," B.A. honors thesis, Women's Studies, Brown University.

Caine, Barbara, Grosz, E. A. and de Lepervanche, Marie (1988) *Crossing Boundaries: Feminisms and the Critique of Knowledges*. Sydney: Allen & Unwin.

Castells, Manuel (1977) *The Urban Question*. London: Edward Arnold.

Chodorow, Nancy (1978) *The Reproduction of Mothering*. Berkeley: University of California Press.

Christopherson, Susan (1989) "On Being outside 'The Project'," *Antipode* 21(2): 83–9.

Clavel, Pierre (1986) *The Progressive City: Planning and Participation, 1969–1984*. New Brunswick, N.J.: Rutgers University Press.

Collins, Patricia (1990) *Black Feminist Thought: Knowledge, Consciousness and the Politics of Empowerment*. Boston: Unwin Hyman.

Connell, R. W. (1987) *Gender and Power: Society, the Person and Sexual Politics*. Stanford: Stanford University Press.

——(1990) "The State, Gender and Sexual Politics: Theory and Appraisal," *Theory and Society* 19: 507–44.

Cook, Judith and Fonow, Mary (1986) "Knowledge and Women's Interests: Issues of Epistemology and Methodology in Feminist Sociological Research," *Sociological Inquiry* 56(1): 2–29.

Cooper Marcus, Clare and Sarkissian, Wendy (1986) *Housing as if People Mattered: Site Design Guidelines for Medium-Density Family Housing*. Berkeley: University of California Press.

Davis, Allan (1983) "Playgrounds, Housing and City Planning" in Donald Krueckeberg (ed.) *Introduction to Planning History in the United States*. New Brunswick, N.J.: Center for Urban Policy Research, Rutgers University.

Delgado, Richard (1989) "Story Telling for Oppositionists and Others: A Plea for Narrative," *Michigan Law Review* 87: 2410–41.

Dewey, John [1929] (1980) *The Quest for Certainty: A Study of the Relation of Knowledge to Action*. New York: Perigree Books.

Fainstein, S. and Fainstein, N. (1982) *Urban Policy under Capitalism*. Beverly Hills, Calif.: Sage.

Faludi, Andreas (1986) *Critical Rationalism and Planning Methodology*. London: Pion.

Feyerabend, Paul (1975) *Against Method: Outline of an Anarchistic Theory of Knowledge*. London: New Left Books.

Fogelsong, Richard (1986) *Planning the Capitalist City: The Colonial Era to the 1920s*. Princeton, N.J.: Princeton University Press.

Forester, John (1989) *Planning in the Face of Power*. Berkeley: University of California Press.

Friedman, Marilyn (1989) "Feminism and Modern Friendship: Dislocating the Community," *Ethics* 99(1): 275–90.

Friedmann, John (1987) *Planning in the Public Domain: From Knowledge to Action*. Princeton: Princeton University Press.

Gilligan, Carol (1982) *In a Different Voice: Psychological Theory and Women's Development*. Cambridge, Mass.: Harvard University Press.

Gilligan, Carol, Ward, Janie and Taylor, Jill (eds.) (1988) *Mapping the Moral Domain: A Contribution of Women's Thinking to Psychological Theory and Education*. Cambridge, Mass.: Center for the Study of Gender, Education and Human Development, Harvard University.

Harding, Sandra (1986a) *The Science Question in Feminism*. Ithaca, N.Y.: Cornell University Press.

——(1986b) "The Instability of the Analytical Categories of Feminist Theory," *Signs* 11(4): 645–64.

Harding, Sandra and Hintikka, Merrill (eds.) (1983) *Discovering Reality: Feminist Perspectives on Epistemology, Metaphysics, Methodology, and Philosophy of Science*. Dortrecht: D. Reidel.

Harvey, David (1978a) "The Urban Process under Capitalism: A Framework for Analysis," *International Journal for Urban and Regional Research* 2(1): 101–31.

——(1978b) "Labour, Capital and Class Struggle around the Built Environment in Advanced Capitalist Societies" in Kevin Cox (ed.) *Urbanization and Conflict in Market Societies*. London: Methuen.

Hayden, Dolores (1980) "What Would a Non-sexist City Be Like? Speculations on Housing, Urban Design, and Human Work," *Signs* 5(3) (Supplement): S170–87.

——(1981) *The Grand Domestic Revolution: A History of Feminist Designs for American Homes, Neighborhoods and Cities*. Cambridge, Mass.: MIT Press.

——(1984) *Redesigning the American Dream: The Future of Housing, Work, and Family Life*. New York: W. W. Norton.

Heskin, Allan (1991) *The Struggle for Community.* Boulder, Colo.: Westview Press.

Hirschmann, Nancy (1989) "Freedom, Recognition, and Obligation: A Feminist Approach to Political Theory," *American Political Science Review* 83(4): 1227–44.

Hooks, Bell (1984) *Feminist Theory: From Margin to Center.* Boston: South End Press.

Hull, Gloria, Scott, Patricia Bell and Smith, Barbara (eds.) (1982) *All the Women Are White, All the Blacks Are Men, But Some of Us Are Brave: Black Women's Studies.* New York: Feminist Press.

Huxley, Margo (1988) "Feminist Urban Theory: Gender, Class and the Built Environment," *Transition* (Winter): 39–43.

Jacobs, Jane (1961) *The Death and Life of Great American Cities.* New York: Random House.

Jaggar, Alison and Bardo, Susan (eds.) (1989) *Gender/Body/Knowledge: Feminist Reconstructions of Being and Knowing.* New Brunswick, N.J.: Rutgers University Press.

Jaggar, Alison and Rothenberg, Paula (eds.) (1984) *Feminist Frameworks: Alternative Theoretical Accounts of the Relations Between Women and Men,* 2nd edn. New York: McGraw-Hill.

Keller, Evelyn Fox (1983) *A Feeling for the Organism: The Life and Work of Barbara McClintock.* San Francisco: W. H. Freeman.

Keller, Suzanne (ed.) (1981) *Building for Women.* Lexington, M.A.: Lexington Books.

Kelly, Joan Gadol (1984) *Woman, History and Theory: The Essays of Joan Kelly.* Chicago: University of Chicago Press.

King, Deborah (1988) "Multiple Jeopardy, Multiple Consciousness: The Context of a Black Feminist Ideology," *Signs* 14(1): 42–72.

Kohlberg, Lawrence (1981) *The Philosophy of Moral Development.* San Francisco: Harper & Row.

Krieger, Martin (1989) *Marginalization and Discontinuity: Tools for the Crafts of Knowledge and Decision.* New York: Russell Sage Foundation.

Krumholz, Norman and Forester, John (1990) *Making Equity Planning Work: Leadership in the Public Sector.* Philadelphia: Temple University Press.

Kuhn, Thomas (1962) *The Structure of Scientific Revolutions.* Chicago: University of Chicago Press.

Leavitt, Jacqueline (1986) "Feminist Advocacy Planning in the 1980s" in Barry Checkoway (ed.) *Strategic Perspectives in Planning Practice.* Lexington, Mass.: Lexington Books.

Leavitt, Jacqueline and Saegert, Susan (1989) *From Abandonment to Hope: Community-Households in Harlem.* New York: Columbia University Press.

Lerner, Gerda (1979) *The Majority Finds Its Past: Placing Women in History.* New York: Oxford University Press.

Lindblom, Charles (1990) *Inquiry and Change: The Troubled Attempt to Understand and Shape Society.* New Haven, Conn.: Yale University Press.

Lofland, Lyn (1975) "The 'Thereness' of Women: A Selective Review of Urban Sociology" in Marcia Millman and Rosabeth Moss Kanter (eds.) *Another Voice: Feminist Perspectives on Social Life and Social Science.* New York: Anchor Books.

Lugones, Maria and Spelman, Elizabeth (1983) "Have We Got Theory For You: Feminist Theory, Cultural Imperialism and the Demand for 'The Woman's Voice'," *Women's Studies International Forum* 6(6): 573–81.

MacIntyre, Alasdair (1981) *After Virtue: A Study in Moral Theory.* London: Duckworth.

Mackenzie, Suzanne (1988) "Building Women, Building Cities: Toward Gender Sensitive Theory in Environmental Disciplines" in Carolyn Andrew and Beth Moore Milroy (eds.) *Life Spaces: Gender, Household, Employment.* Vancouver: University of British Columbia Press.

——(1989) "Women in the City" in Richard Peet and Nigel Thrift (eds.) *New Models in Geography.* London: Routledge.

Majone, Giandomenico and Quade, Edward (1980) *Pitfalls of Analysis.* New York: John Wiley.

Mansbridge, Jane (ed.) (1988) *Beyond Self-Interest.* Chicago: University of Chicago Press.

Markusen, Ann (1980) "City Spatial Structure, Women's Household Work, and National Urban Policy," *Signs* 5(3) (Supplement): S23–44.

Marris, Peter [1982] (1987) *Meaning and Action: Community Planning and Conceptions of Change,* 2nd edn. London: Routledge & Kegan Paul.

Matrix (1984) *Making Space: Women in the Man-Made Environment.* London: Pluto Press.

Matsuda, Mari (1989) "Public Response to Racist Speech: Considering the Victim's Story," *Michigan Law Review* 87: 2320–81.

Millman, Marcia and Moss Kanter, Rosabeth (eds.) (1975) *Another Voice: Feminist Perspectives on Social Life and Social Science.* New York: Anchor Books.

Modlich, Regula (1986) "Women Plan Toronto," *Women and Environments* 8(1).

Molyneux, Maxine (1985) "Mobilization without Emancipation? Women's Interests, State, and Revolution in Nicaragua," *Feminist Studies* 11(2): 227–54.

Moser, Carolyn (1989) "Gender Planning in the Third World: Meeting Practical and Strategic Gender Needs," *World Development* 17(1): 1799–825.

Moser, Carolyn, and Levi, C. (1986) *A Theory and Methodology of Gender Planning: Meeting Practical and Strategic Gender Needs.* Gender and Planning Working Paper 11. London: Development Planning Unit, University College London.

Nicholson, Linda (ed.) (1990) *Feminism/Postmodernism.* New York: Routledge.

Okin, Susan Moller (1989) *Justice, Gender and the Family*. New York: Basic Books.

Palm, Risa and Pred, Alan (1976) *A Time-Geographic Perspective on the Problems of Inequality for Women*. Working Paper 236. Berkeley: Institute of Urban and Regional Development, University of California.

Paris, Chris (ed.) (1983) *Critical Readings in Planning Theory*. Oxford: Pergamon.

Pateman, Carole (1983) "Feminist Critiques of the Public/Private Dichotomy" in S. I. Benn and G. F. Gauss (eds.) *Public and Private in Social Life*. London: Croom Helm.

Pateman, Carole and Gross, Elizabeth (1986) *Feminist Challenges: Social and Political Theory*. Boston: Northeastern University Press.

Phillips, Anne (1987) *Divided Loyalties: Dilemmas of Sex and Class*. London: Virago.

Pickup, Laurie (1984) "Women's Gender-Role and Its Influence on Travel Behavior," *Built Environment* 10(1): 61–8.

Polanyi, Michael (1958) *Personal Knowledge: Towards a Post-critical Philosophy*. New York: Harper & Row.

Rich, Adrienne (1979) "Toward a Woman-Centered University" in *On Lies, Secrets and Silence*. New York: W. W. Norton.

Ritzdorf, Marsha (1989) "Regulating Separate Spheres: Municipal Land-Use Planning and the Changing Lives of Women," paper presented at the Conference of the Society for American City and Regional Planning History, 29 November.

Ruddick, Sara (1983) "Maternal Thinking" in Joyce Treblicot (ed.) *Mothering: Essays in Feminist Theory*. Savage, Md.: Rowman & Littlefield.

Saegert, Susan (1980) "Masculine Cities and Feminine Suburbs: Polarized Ideas, Contradictory Realities," *Signs* 5(3) (Supplement): S93–108.

Sandel, Michael (1982) *Liberalism and the Limits of Justice*. Cambridge: Cambridge University Press.

Sandercock, Leonie (1990) *Property, Politics and Urban Planning: A Political History of Australian City Planning 1890–1990*. New Brunswick, N.J.: Transaction Press.

Sandercock, Leonie and Forsyth, Ann (1990) *Gender: A New Agenda for Planning Theory*. Working Paper 521. Berkeley: Institute of Urban and Regional Development, University of California.

——(1992) "Feminist Theory and Planning Theory: The Epistemological Links," *Planning Theory Newsletter* (Winter). Turin: Dipartimento Interateneo Territorio.

Sarkissian, Wendy (1990) Personal communication.

Sassen-Koob, Saskia (1984) "From Household to Workplace: Theories and Survey Research on Migrant Women in the Labor Market," *International Migration Review* 18(4): 1114–67.

Schon, Donald (1983) *The Reflective Practitioner: How Professionals Think in Action*. New York: Basic Books.

Scott, Joan (1986) "Gender: A Useful Category in Historical Analysis," *American Historical Review* (December): 1053–75.

Sennett, Richard (1977) *The Fall of Public Man*. New York: Knopf.

Soja, Edward (1989) *Postmodern Geographies: The Reassertion of Space in Critical Social Theory*. New York: Verso.

Spender, Dale (1985) *Man Made Language*, 2nd edn. London: Routledge & Kegan Paul.

Stimpson, Catharine, Dixler, Elsa, Nelson, Martha and Yatrakis, Kathryn (eds.) (1981) *Women and the American City*. Chicago: University of Chicago Press. (Originally published in 1980 as a supplement to *Signs* 5(3).)

Tabb, W. K. and Sawers, L. (1978) *Marxism and the Metropolis*. Oxford: Oxford University Press.

Tronto, Joan (1987) "Beyond Gender Difference to a Theory of Care," *Signs* 12(4): 644–63.

Watson, Sophie (1986) "Women and Housing or Feminist Housing Analysis?" *Housing Studies* 1(1): 1–10.

——(1988) *Accommodating Inequality: Gender and Housing*. Sydney: Allen & Unwin.

Wekerle, Gerda (1980) "Women in the Urban Environment," *Signs* 5(3) (Supplement): S188–214.

Wekerle, Gerda, Peterson, Rebecca and Morley, David (eds.) (1980) *New Space for Women*. Boulder, Colo.: Westview Press.

Westkott, Nancy (1979) "Feminist Criticism of the Social Sciences," *Harvard Educational Review* 49(4): 422–30.

Williams, Patricia (1988) "On Being the Object of Property," *Signs* 14(1): 5–24.

——(1989) "The Obliging Shell: An Informal Essay on Formal Equal Opportunity," *Michigan Law Review* 87: 2128–59.

Wirka, Susan (1989) "Mary Kingsbury Simkhovitch and Neighborhood Planning in New York City, 1897–1909," Master's thesis, University of California, Los Angeles.

Wright, Gwendolyn (1980) *Moralism and the Model Home: Domestic Architecture and Cultural Conflict in Chicago, 1873–1913*. Chicago: University of Chicago Press.

PAUL DAVIDOFF

"Advocacy and Pluralism in Planning"

Journal of the American Institute of Planners (1965)

Editors' introduction   In both North America and Europe city planning professors have professional associations – the Association of Collegiate Schools of Planning (ACSP) for North America and the Association of European Schools of Planning (AESOP) for Europe. Members of each association meet once a year to present academic papers, discuss issues of interest to the profession, and renew old friendships. Every five years the two associations meet jointly, alternately in Europe and North America.

At the annual ACSP meeting the Paul Davidoff Award is presented to a city planning professor whose work exemplifies the practice and ideals of professor/activist Paul Davidoff, the author of this selection. It is an honor to receive the Davidoff award, because Davidoff exemplified professional commitment to vigorous advocacy on behalf of the less fortunate members of society.

During the 1960s, Davidoff, a lawyer and city planner, taught city planning students at Hunter College and simultaneously fought successfully to get racially integrated low-income housing built in exclusive white suburbs. This experience as an advocate for low-income minority residents shaped his view, presented in this selection, of what city planning could be like.

Most city or town planning is performed by a single local government agency that develops plans which, it feels, will best serve the welfare of the whole community as the agency perceives it, not of individual interest groups such as organizations of homeless people, merchants, environmentalists, or bicycle enthusiasts. While city planning commissions may explore many alternatives and consider conflicting interest group demands before finalizing plans, generally they end up with a single unitary plan.

Davidoff's vision for how planning might be structured was quite different. He argues that different groups in society have different needs which would result in fundamentally different plans if they were recognized. Business elites and other articulate, wealthy, and powerful groups have the skill and resources to shape city plans to serve their interests. But what about the poor and powerless? Davidoff argued that there should be planners acting as *advocates* articulating the interests of these and other groups much as a lawyer represents a client. For example, a planner might develop and advocate for a plan which would meet the needs of poor West Indian residents of London's Brixton neighborhood. Another planner might have a different plan representing the point of view of shopkeepers in the same area. And yet another might work with Brixton environmentalists to develop and advocate for a plan based on environmental concerns. A local planning commission could weigh the merits of the competing plans much as a court hears and weighs views from lawyers. Davidoff believed that the plan which would emerge from such a process would be better than a plan prepared by planning department staff without the interplay of competing advocate planners. And, Davidoff reasoned, the needs of the poor and powerless would be better met in city plans if – a big if – they were adequately represented.

Davidoff's view of planning profoundly influenced activist planners of the 1960s and 1970s, many of whom defined themselves as advocacy planners, developed plans to meet underrepresented groups, and advocated for their interests. "Equity planners" today continue this tradition.

Compare Davidoff's humanistic, grassroots, pluralistic approach to city planning with Le Corbusier's brilliant but elitist vision of an elite cadre of CIAM architects to impose on the fabric of cities the forms they felt modern machine culture demanded (p. 368). Compare Davidoff's views with Forester's comments on how planners working within the system can use their influence to empower stakeholders in the planning process (p. 434). Reflect on how city planning decisions are really made in the context of Mollenkopf's review of the academic literature on urban power (p. 258), and Stoker's review of urban regime theory (p. 269).

A critique of conventional city planning practice at the time of Davidoff's article is Alan Altschuler, *The City Planning Process: A Political Analysis* (Ithaca, N.Y.: Cornell University Press, 1965). An application of advocacy planning to women is Jacqueline Leavitt, "Feminist Advocacy Planning in the 1980s," in Barry Checkoway (ed.), *Strategic Perspectives in Planning Practice* (Lexington, Mass.: Lexington Books, 1986). Norman Krumholz and John Forester describe Krumholz's experience as the planning director of Cleveland, Ohio, who worked hard to make city planning responsive in *Making Equity Planning Work* (Philadelphia: Temple, 1990). For a radical critique of advocacy planning see Francis Fox Piven, "Whom Does the Advocate Planner Serve?" in Richard A. Cloward and Frances Fox Piven, *The Politics of Turmoil* (New York: Vintage, 1965). Piven sees advocacy planners as unwitting dupes of the system. She argues that angry and potentially violent groups will obtain more political leverage bargaining directly for themselves without professional intermediaries. She feels they need power, not plans.

Readings relating to advocacy and pluralism in the European planning context include R. Lees and M. May, *Community Action for Change* (London: Routledge & Kegan Paul, 1984), Noel Boaden, *Public Participation in Local Services* (Harlow: Longman, 1982), Geraint Parry, George Moyser, and Neil Day (eds.), *Political Participation and Democracy in Britain* (Cambridge: Cambridge University Press, 1992), and Chantal Mouffe (ed.), *Dimensions of Radical Democracy: Pluralism, Citizenship, Community* (London: Verso, 1992).

PAUL DAVIDOFF, "Advocacy and Pluralism in Planning"

Journal of the American Institute of Planners (1965)

The present can become an epoch in which the dreams of the past for an enlightened and just democracy are turned into a reality. The massing of voices protesting racial discrimination have roused this nation to the need to rectify racial and other social injustices. The adoption by Congress of a host of welfare measures and the Supreme Court's specification of the mean-ing of equal protection by law both reveal the response to protest and open the way for the vast changes still required.

The just demand for political and social equality on the part of the Negro and the impoverished requires the public to establish the bases for a society affording equal opportunity to all citizens. The compelling need for intelligent planning, for specification of new social goals and the means for achieving them, is manifest. The society of the future will be an urban one, and city planners will help to give it shape and content.

The prospect for future planning is that of a practice which openly invites political and social values to be examined and debated. Acceptance of this position means rejection of prescriptions for planning which would have the planner act solely as a technician. It has been argued that technical studies to enlarge the information available to decision makers must take precedence over statements of goals and ideals:

> We have suggested that, at least in part, the city planner is better advised to start from research into the functional aspects of cities than from his own estimation of the values which he is attempting to maximize. This suggestion springs from a conviction that at this juncture the implications of many planning decisions are poorly understood, and that no certain means are at hand by which values can be measured, ranked, and translated into the design of a metropolitan system.

While acknowledging the need for humility and openness in the adoption of social goals, this statement amounts to an attempt to eliminate, or sharply reduce, the unique contribution planning can make: understanding the functional aspects of the city and recommending appropriate future action to improve the urban condition.

Another argument that attempts to reduce the importance of attitudes and values in planning and other policy sciences is that the major public questions are themselves matters of choice between technical methods of solution. Dahl and Lindblom put forth this position at the beginning of their important textbook *Politics, Economics, and Welfare*:

> In economic organization and reform, the "great issues" are no longer the great issues, if they ever were. It has become increasingly difficult for thoughtful men to find meaningful alternatives posed in the traditional choices between socialism and capitalism, planning and the free market, regulation and laissez faire, for they find their actual choices neither so simple nor so grand. Not so simple, because economic organization poses knotty problems that can only be solved by painstaking attention to technical details – how else, for example, can inflation be controlled? Nor so grand, because, at least in the Western world, most people neither can nor wish to experiment with the whole pattern of socio-economic organization to attain goals more easily won. If, for example, taxation will serve the purpose, why "abolish the wages system" to ameliorate income inequality?

These words were written in the early 1950s and express the spirit of that decade more than that of the 1960s. They suggest that the major battles have been fought. But the "great issues" in economic organization, those revolving around the central issue of the nature of distributive justice, have yet to be settled. The world is still in turmoil over the way in which the resources of nations are to be distributed. The justice of the present social allocation of wealth, knowledge, skill, and other social goods is clearly in debate. Solutions to questions about the share of wealth and other social commodities that should go to different classes cannot be technically derived; they must arise from social attitudes.

Appropriate planning action cannot be prescribed from a position of value neutrality, for prescriptions are based on desired objectives. One conclusion drawn from this assertion is that "values are inescapable elements of any rational decision-making process" and that values held by the planner should be made clear. The implications of that conclusion for planning have been described elsewhere and will not be considered in this article. Here I will say that the planner should do more than explicate the values underlying his prescriptions for courses of action; he should affirm them; he should be an advocate for what he deems proper.

Determinations of what serves the public interest, in a society containing many diverse interest groups, are almost always of a highly contentious nature. In performing its role of prescribing courses of action leading to future desired states, the planning profession must engage itself thoroughly and openly in the contention surrounding political determination. Moreover, planners should be able to engage in the political process as advocates of the interests both of government and of such other groups, organizations, or individuals who are concerned with proposing policies for the future development of the community.

The recommendation that city planners represent and plead the plans of many interest groups is founded upon the need to establish an effective urban democracy, one in which citizens may be able to play an active role in the process of deciding public policy. Appropriate policy in democracy is determined through a process of political debate. The right course of action is always a matter of choice, never of fact. In a bureaucratic age great care must be taken that choices remain in the area of public view and participation.

Urban politics, in an era of increasing government activity in planning and welfare, must balance the demands for ever-increasing central bureaucratic control against the demands for increased concern for the unique requirements of local, specialized interests. The welfare of all and the welfare of minorities are both deserving of support; planning must be so structured and so practiced as to account for this unavoidable bifurcation of the public interest.

The idealized political process in a democracy serves the search for truth in much the same manner as due process in law. Fair notice and hearings, production of supporting evidence, cross-examination, reasoned decision are all means employed to arrive at relative truth: a just decision. Due process and two- (or more) party political contention both rely heavily upon strong advocacy by a professional. The advocate represents an individual, group, or organization. He affirms their position in language understandable to his client and to the decision makers he seeks to convince.

If the planning process is to encourage democratic urban government then it must operate so as to include rather than exclude citizens from participating in the process. "Inclusion" means not only permitting the citizen to be heard. It also means that he be able to become well informed about the underlying reasons for planning proposals, and be able to respond to them in the technical language of professional planners.

A practice that has discouraged full partici-

pation by citizens in plan making in the past has been based on what might be called the "*unitary plan.*" This is the idea that only one agency in a community should prepare a comprehensive plan; that agency is the city planning commission or department. Why is it that no other organization within a community prepares a plan? Why is only one agency concerned with establishing both general and specific goals for community development, and with proposing the strategies and costs required to effect the goals? Why are there not plural plans?

If the social, economic, and political ramifications of a plan are politically contentious, then why is it that those in opposition to the agency plan do not prepare one of their own? It is interesting to observe that "rational" theories of planning have called for consideration of alternative courses of action by planning agencies. As a matter of rationality it has been argued that all of the alternative choices open as means to the ends ought be examined. But those, including myself, who have recommended agency consideration of alternatives have placed upon the agency planner the burden of inventing "a few representative alternatives." The agency planner has been given the duty of constructing a model of the political spectrum, and charged with sorting out what he conceives to be worthy alternatives. This duty has placed too great a burden on the agency planner, and has failed to provide for the formulation of alternatives by the interest groups who will eventually be affected by the completed plans.

Whereas in a large part of our national and local political practice contention is viewed as healthy, in city planning where a large proportion of the professionals are public employees, contentious criticism has not always been viewed as legitimate. Further, where only government prepares plans, and no minority plans are developed, pressure is often applied to bring all professionals to work for the ends espoused by a public agency. For example, last year a Federal official complained to a meeting of planning professors that the academic planners were not giving enough support to Federal programs. He assumed that every planner should be on the side of the Federal renewal program. Of course government administrators will seek to gain the support of professionals outside of government, but such support should not be expected as a matter of loyalty. In a democratic system opposition to a public agency should be just as normal and appropriate as support. The agency, despite the fact that it is concerned with planning, may be serving undesired ends.

In presenting a plea for plural planning I do not mean to minimize the importance of the obligation of the public planning agency. It must decide upon appropriate future courses of action for the community. But being isolated as the only plan maker in the community, public agencies as well as the public itself may have suffered from incomplete and shallow analysis of potential directions. Lively political dispute aided by plural plans could do much to improve the level of rationality in the process of preparing the public plan.

The advocacy of alternative plans by interest groups outside of government would stimulate city planning in a number of ways. First, it would serve as a means of better informing the public of the alternative choices open, *alternatives strongly supported by their proponents*. In current practice those few agencies which have portrayed alternatives have not been equally enthusiastic about each. A standard reaction to rationalists' prescription for consideration of alternative courses of action has been "it can't be done; how can you expect planners to present alternatives which they don't approve?" The appropriate answer to that question has been that planners, like lawyers, may have a professional obligation to defend positions they oppose. However, in a system of plural planning, the public agency would be relieved of at least some of the burden of presenting alternatives. In plural planning the alternatives would be presented by interest groups differing with the public agency's plan. Such alternatives would represent the deepseated convictions of their proponents and not just the mental exercises of rational planners seeking to portray the range of choice.

A second way in which advocacy and plural planning would improve planning practice would be in forcing the public agency to compete with other planning groups to win political support. In the absence of opposition or alternative plans presented by interest groups the public agencies have had little incentive to improve the quality of their work or the rate of production of plans. The political consumer has been offered a yes–no ballot in regard to the comprehensive plan; either the public agency's plan was to be adopted or no plan would be adopted.

A third improvement in planning practice which might follow from plural planning would be to force those who have been critical of "establishment" plans to produce superior plans, rather than only to carry out the very essential obligation of criticizing plans deemed improper.

THE PLANNER AS ADVOCATE

Where plural planning is practiced, advocacy becomes the means of professional support for competing claims about how the community should develop. Pluralism in support of political contention describes the process; advocacy describes the role performed by the professional in the process. Where unitary planning prevails, advocacy is not of paramount importance, for there is little or no competition for the plan prepared by the public agency. The concept of advocacy as taken from legal practice implies the opposition of at least two contending viewpoints in an adversary proceeding.

The legal advocate must plead for his own and his client's sense of legal propriety or justice. The planner as advocate would plead for his own and his client's view of the good society. The advocate planner would be more than a provider of information, an analyst of current trends, a simulator of future conditions, and a detailer of means. In addition to carrying out these necessary parts of planning, he would be a *proponent* of specific substantive solutions.

The advocate planner would be responsible to his client and would seek to express his client's views. This does not mean that the planner could not seek to persuade his client. In some situations persuasion might not be necessary, for the planner would have sought out an employer with whom he shared common views about desired social conditions and the means toward them. In fact one of the benefits of advocate planning is the possibility it creates for a planner to find employment with agencies holding values close to his own. Today the agency planner may be dismayed by the positions affirmed by his agency, but there may be no alternative employer.

The advocate planner would be above all a planner. He would be responsible to his client for preparing plans and for all of the other elements comprising the planning process. Whether working for the public agency or for some private organization, the planner would have to prepare plans that take account of the arguments made in other plans. Thus the advocate's plan might have some of the characteristics of a legal brief. It would be a document presenting the facts and reasons for supporting one set of proposals, and facts and reasons indicating the inferiority of counter-proposals. The adversary nature of plural planning might, then, have the beneficial effect of upsetting the tradition of writing plan proposals in terminology which makes them appear self-evident.

A troublesome issue in contemporary planning is that of finding techniques for evaluating alternative plans. Technical devices such as cost–benefit analysis by themselves are of little assistance without the use of means for appraising the values underlying plans. Advocate planning, by making more apparent the values underlying plans, and by making definitions of social costs and benefits more explicit, should greatly assist the process of plan evaluation. Further, it would become clear (as it is not at present) that there are no neutral grounds for evaluating a plan; there are as many evaluative systems as there are value systems.

The adversary nature of plural planning might also have a good effect on the uses of information and research in planning. One of the tasks of the advocate planner in discussing the plans prepared in opposition to his would be to point out the nature of the bias underlying information presented in other plans. In this way, as critic of opposition plans, he would be performing a task similar to the legal technique of cross-examination. While painful to the planner whose bias is exposed (and no planner can

be entirely free of bias) the net effect of confrontation between advocates of alternative plans would be more careful and precise research.

Not all the work of an advocate planner would be of an adversary nature. Much of it would be educational. The advocate would have the job of informing other groups, including public agencies, of the conditions, problems, and outlook of the group he represented. Another major educational job would be that of informing his clients of their rights under planning and renewal laws, about the general operations of city government, and of particular programs likely to affect them.

The advocate planner would devote much attention to assisting the client organization to clarify its ideas and to give expression to them. In order to make his client more powerful politically the advocate might also become engaged in expanding the size and scope of his client organization. But the advocate's most important function would be to carry out the planning process for the organization and to argue persuasively in favor of its planning proposals.

Advocacy in planning has already begun to emerge as planning and renewal affect the lives of more and more people. The critics of urban renewal have forced response from the renewal agencies, and the ongoing debate has stimulated needed self-evaluation by public agencies. Much work along the lines of advocate planning has already taken place, but little of it by professional planners. More often the work has been conducted by trained community organizers or by student groups. In at least one instance, however, a planner's professional aid led to the development of an alternative renewal approach, one which will result in the dislocation of far fewer families than originally contemplated.

Pluralism and advocacy are means for stimulating consideration of future conditions by all groups in society. But there is one social group which at present is particularly in need of the assistance of planners. This group includes organizations representing low-income families. At a time when concern for the condition of the poor finds institutionalization in community action programs, it would be appropriate for planners concerned with such groups to find means to plan with them. The plans prepared for these groups would seek to combat poverty and would propose programs affording new and better opportunities to the members of the organization and to families similarly situated. The difficulty in providing adequate planning assistance to organizations representing low-income families may in part be overcome by funds allocated to local antipoverty councils. But these councils are not the only representatives of the poor; other organizations exist and seek help. How can this type of assistance be financed? This question will be examined below, when attention is turned to the means for institutionalizing plural planning.

THE STRUCTURE OF PLANNING

Planning by special interest groups

The local planning process typically includes one or more "citizens'" organizations concerned with the nature of planning in the community. The Workable Program requirement for "citizen participation" has enforced this tradition and brought it to most large communities. The difficulty with current citizen participation programs is that citizens are more often *reacting* to agency programs than proposing their concepts of appropriate goals and future action.

The fact that citizens' organizations have not played a positive role in formulating plans is to some extent a result of both the enlarged role in society played by government bureaucracies and the historic weakness of municipal party politics. There is something very shameful to our society in the necessity to have organized "citizen participation." Such participation should be the norm in an enlightened democracy. The formalization of citizen participation as a required practice in localities is similar in many respects to totalitarian shows of loyalty to the state by citizen parades.

Will a private group interested in preparing a recommendation for community development be required to carry out its own survey and analysis of the community? The answer would depend upon the quality of the work prepared by the public agency, work which should be public information. In some instances the public agency may not have surveyed or analyzed aspects the private group thinks important; or the public agency's work may reveal strong biases unacceptable to the private group. In any event, the production of a useful plan proposal will require much information concerning the present and predicted conditions in the community. There will be some costs associated with gathering that information, even if it is taken from the public agency. The major cost involved in the preparation of a plan by a private agency would probably be the employment of one or more professional planners.

What organizations might be expected to engage in the plural planning process? The first type that comes to mind are the political parties; but this is clearly an aspirational thought. There is very little evidence that local political organizations have the interest, ability, or concern to establish well-developed programs for their communities. Not all the fault, though, should be placed upon the professional politicians, for the registered members of political parties have not demanded very much, if anything, from them as agents.

Despite the unreality of the wish, the desirability for active participation in the process of planning by the political parties is strong. In an ideal situation local parties would establish political platforms which would contain master plans for community growth and both the majority and minority parties in the legislative branch of government would use such plans as one basis for appraising individual legislative proposals. Further, the local administration would use its planning agency to carry out the plans it proposed to the electorate. This dream will not turn to reality for a long time. In the interim other interest groups must be sought to fill the gap caused by the present inability of political organizations.

The second set of organizations which might be interested in preparing plans for community development are those that represent special interest groups having established views in regard to proper public policy. Such organizations as chambers of commerce, real estate boards, labor organizations, pro- and anti-civil rights groups, and anti-poverty councils come to mind. Groups of this nature have often played parts in the development of community plans, but only in a very few instances have they proposed their own plans.

It must be recognized that there is strong reason operating against commitment to a plan by these organizations. In fact it is the same reason that in part limits the interests of politicians and which limits the potential for planning in our society. The expressed commitment to a particular plan may make it difficult for groups to find means for accommodating their various interests. In other terms, it may be simpler for professionals, politicians, or lobbyists to make deals if they have not laid their cards on the table.

There is a third set of organizations that might be looked to as proponents of plans and to whom the foregoing comments might not apply. These are the ad hoc protest associations which may form in opposition to some proposed policy. An example of such a group is a neighborhood association formed to combat a renewal plan, a zoning change, or the proposed location of a public facility. Such organizations may seek to develop alternative plans, plans which would, if effected, better serve their interests.

From the point of view of effective and rational planning it might be desirable to commence plural planning at the level of city-wide organizations, but a more realistic view is that it will start at the neighborhood level. Certain advantages of this outcome should be noted. Mention was made earlier of tension in government between centralizing and decentralizing forces. The contention aroused by conflict between the central planning agency and the neighborhood organization may indeed be healthy, leading to clearer definition of welfare policies and their relation to the rights of individuals or minority groups.

Who will pay for plural planning? Some organizations have the resources to sponsor the development of a plan. Many groups lack the means. The plight of the relatively indigent association seeking to propose a plan might be analogous to that of the indigent client in search of legal aid. If the idea of plural planning makes sense, then support may be found from foundations or from government. In the beginning it is more likely that some foundation might be willing to experiment with plural planning as a means of making city planning more effective and more democratic. Or the Federal Government might see plural planning, if carried out by local anti-poverty councils, as a strong means of generating local interest in community affairs.

Federal sponsorship of plural planning might be seen as a more effective tool for stimulating involvement of the citizen in the future of his community than are the present types of citizen participation programs. Federal support could only be expected if plural planning were seen, not as a means of combating renewal plans, but as an incentive to local renewal agencies to prepare better plans.

The public planning agency

A major drawback to effective democratic planning practice is the continuation of that nonresponsible vestigial institution, the planning commission. If it is agreed that the establishment of both general policies and implementation policies are questions affecting the public interest and that public interest questions should be decided in accord with established democratic practices for decision making, then it is indeed difficult to find convincing reasons for continuing to permit independent commissions to make planning decisions. At an earlier stage in planning the strong arguments of John T. Howard and others in support of commissions may have been persuasive. But it is now more than a decade since Howard made his defense against Robert Walker's position favoring planning as a staff function under the mayor. With the increasing effect planning decisions have upon the lives of citizens the Walker proposal assumes great urgency.

Aside from important questions regarding the propriety of independent agencies which are far removed from public control determining public policy, the failure to place planning decision choices in the hands of elected officials has weakened the ability of professional planners to have their proposals effected. Separating planning from local politics has made it difficult for independent commissions to garner influential political support. The commissions are not responsible directly to the electorate and in turn the electorate is, at best, often indifferent to the planning commission.

During the last decade, in many cities power to alter community development has slipped out of the hands of city planning commissions, assuming they ever held it, and has been transferred to development coordinators. This has weakened the professional planner. Perhaps planners unknowingly contributed to this by their refusal to take concerted action in opposition to the perpetuation of commissions.

Planning commissions are products of the conservative reform movement of the early part of this century. The movement was essentially anti-populist and pro-aristocracy. Politics was viewed as dirty business. The commissions are relics of a not-too-distant past when it was believed that if men of good will discussed a problem thoroughly, certainly the right solution would be forthcoming. We know today, and perhaps it was always known, that there are no right solutions. Proper policy is that which the decision-making unit declares to be proper.

Planning commissions are responsible to no constituency. The members of the commissions, except for their chairman, are seldom known to the public. In general the individual members fail to expose their personal views about policy and prefer to immerse them in group decision. If the members wrote concurring and dissenting opinions, then at least the commissions might stimulate thought about planning issues. It is difficult to comprehend why this aristocratic and undemocratic form of decision making should be continued. The public planning function should be carried out in the executive or legislative office and perhaps in both. There has been some question about which of these branches of government would provide the best home, but there is much reason to believe that both branches would be made more cognizant of planning issues if they were each informed by their own planning staffs. To carry this division further, it would probably be advisable to establish minority and majority planning staffs in the legislative branch.

At the root of my last suggestion is the belief that there is or should be a Republican and Democratic way of viewing city development; that there should be conservative and liberal plans, plans to support the private market, and plans to support greater government control. There are many possible roads for a community to travel and many plans should show them. Explication is required of many alternative futures presented by those sympathetic to the construction of each such future. As indicated earlier, such alternatives are not presented to the public now. Those few reports which do include alternative futures do not speak in terms of interest to the average citizen. They are filled with professional jargon and present sham alternatives. These plans have expressed technical land use alternatives rather than social, economic, or political value alternatives. Both the traditional unitary plans and the new ones that present technical alternatives have limited the public's exposure to the future states that might be achieved. Instead of arousing healthy political contention as diverse comprehensive plans might, these plans have deflated interest.

The independent planning commission and unitary plan practice certainly should not co-exist. Separately they dull the possibility for enlightened political debate; in combination they have made it yet more difficult. But when still another hoary concept of city planning is added to them, such debate becomes practically impossible. This third of a trinity of worn-out notions is that city planning should focus only upon the physical aspects of city development.

AN INCLUSIVE DEFINITION OF THE SCOPE OF PLANNING

The view that equates physical planning with city planning is myopic. It may have had some historic justification, but it is clearly out of place at a time when it is necessary to integrate knowledge and techniques in order to wrestle effectively with the myriad of problems afflicting urban populations.

The city planning profession's historic concern with the physical environment has warped its ability to see physical structures and land as servants to those who use them. Physical relations and conditions have no meaning or quality apart from the way they serve their users. But this is forgotten every time a physical condition is described as good or bad without relation to a specified group of users. High density, low density, green belts, mixed uses, cluster developments, centralized or decentralized business centers are per se neither good nor bad. They describe physical relations or conditions, but take on value only when seen in terms of their social, economic, psychological, physiological, or aesthetic effects upon different users.

The profession's experience with renewal over the past decade has shown the high costs of exclusive concern with physical conditions. It has been found that the allocation of funds for removal of physical blight may not necessarily improve the overall physical condition of a community and may engender such harsh social repercussions as to severely damage both social and economic institutions. Another example of the deficiencies of the physical bias is the assumption of city planners that they could deal with the capital budget as if the physical attributes of a facility could be understood apart from the philosophy and practice of the service conducted within the physical structure. This assumption is open to question. The size, shape, and location of a facility greatly interact with the purpose of the activity the facility houses. Clear examples of this can be seen in public education and in the provision of low cost housing. The racial and other socioeconomic consequences of "physical decisions" such as location of schools and housing projects have been immense, but city planners, while acknowledging the existence of such consequences, have not sought or trained themselves to understand socioeconomic problems, their causes or solutions.

The city planning profession's limited scope has tended to bias strongly many of its recommendations toward perpetuation of existing social and economic practices. Here I am not opposing the outcomes, but the way in which they are developed. Relative ignorance of social and economic methods of analysis has caused planners to propose solutions in the absence of sufficient knowledge of the costs and benefits of proposals upon different sections of the population.

Large expenditures have been made on planning studies of regional transportation needs, for example, but these studies have been conducted in a manner suggesting that different social and economic classes of the population did not have different needs and different abilities to meet them. In the field of housing, to take another example, planners have been hesitant to question the consequences of locating public housing in slum areas. In the field of industrial development, planners have seldom examined the types of jobs the community needs; it has been assumed that one job was about as useful as another. But this may not be the case where a significant sector of the population finds it difficult to get employment.

"Who gets what, when, where, why, and how" are the basic political questions which need to be raised about every allocation of public resources. The questions cannot be answered adequately if land use criteria are the sole or major standards for judgment.

The need to see an element of city development, land use, in broad perspective applies equally well to every other element, such as health, welfare, and recreation. The governing of a city requires an adequate plan for its future. Such a plan loses guiding force and rational basis to the degree that it deals with less than the whole that is of concern to the public.

The implications of the foregoing comments for the practice of city planning are these. First, state planning enabling legislation should be amended to permit planning departments to study and to prepare plans related to any area of public concern. Second, planning education must be redirected so as to provide channels of specialization in different parts of public planning and a core focused upon the planning process. Third, the professional planning association should enlarge its scope so as to not exclude city planners not specializing in physical planning.

A year ago at the AIP convention it was suggested that the AIP Constitution be amended to permit city planning to enlarge its scope to all matters of public concern. Members of the Institute in agreement with this proposal should seek to develop support for it at both the chapter and national level. The Constitution at present states that the Institute's "particular sphere of activity shall be the planning of the unified development of urban communities and their environs and of states, regions and the nation *as expressed through determination of the comprehensive arrangement of land and land occupancy and regulation thereof.*" It is time that the AIP delete the words in my italics from its Constitution. The planner limited to such concerns is not a city planner, he is a land planner or a physical planner. A city is its people, their practices, and their political, social, cultural and economic institutions as well as other things. The city planner must comprehend and deal with all these factors.

The new city planner will be concerned with physical planning, economic planning, and social planning. The scope of his work will be no wider than that presently demanded of a mayor or a city councilman. Thus, we cannot argue against an enlarged planning function on grounds that it is too large to handle. The mayor needs assistance; in particular he needs the assistance of a planner, one trained to examine needs and aspirations in terms of both short- and long-term perspectives. In observing the early stages of development of Community Action Programs, it is apparent that our cities are in desperate need of the type of assistance trained planners could offer. Our cities require for their social and economic programs the type of long-range thought and information that have been brought forward in the realm of physical planning. Potential resources must be examined and priorities set.

What I have just proposed does not imply the termination of physical planning, but it does mean that physical planning be seen as part of city planning. Uninhibited by limitations on his work, the city planner will be able to add his expertise to the task of coordinating the operating and capital budgets and to the job of relating effects of each city program upon the others and upon the social, political, and economic resources of the community.

An expanded scope reaching all matters of public concern will make planning not only a more effective administrative tool of local government but it will also bring planning practice closer to the issues of real concern to the citizens. A system of plural city planning probably has a much greater chance for operational success where the focus is on live social and economic questions instead of rather esoteric issues relating to physical norms.

THE EDUCATION OF PLANNERS

Widening the scope of planning to include all areas of concern to government would suggest that city planners must possess a broader knowledge of the structure and forces affecting urban development. In general this would be true. But at present many city planners are specialists in only one or more of the functions of city government. Broadening the scope of planning would require some additional planners who specialize in one or more of the services entailed by the new focus.

A prime purpose of city planning is the coordination of many separate functions. This coordination calls for men holding general knowledge of the many elements comprising the urban community. Educating a man for performing the coordinative role is a difficult job, one not well satisfied by the present tradition of two years of graduate study. Training of urban planners with the skills called for in this article may require both longer graduate study and development of a liberal arts undergraduate program affording an opportunity for holistic understanding of both urban conditions and techniques for analyzing and solving urban problems.

The practice of plural planning requires educating planners who would be able to engage as professional advocates in the contentious work of forming social policy. The person able to do this would be one deeply committed to both the process of planning and to particular substantive ideas. Recognizing that ideological commitments will separate planners, there is tremendous need to train professionals who are competent to express their social objectives.

The great advances in analytic skills, demonstrated in the recent May issue of this journal [*Journal of the American Institute of Planners*] dedicated to techniques of simulating urban growth processes, portend a time when planners and the public will be better able to predict the consequences of proposed courses of action. But these advances will be of little social advantage if the proposals themselves do not have substance. The contemporary thoughts of planners about the nature of man in society are often mundane, unexciting or gimmicky. When asked to point out to students the planners who have a developed sense of history and philosophy concerning man's situation in the urban world one is hard put to come up with a name. Sometimes Goodman or Mumford might be mentioned. But planners seldom go deeper than acknowledging the goodness of green space and the soundness of proximity of linked activities. We cope with the problems of the alienated man with a recommendation for reducing the time of the journey to work.

CONCLUSION

The urban community is a system comprised of interrelated elements, but little is known about how the elements do, will, or should interrelate. The type of knowledge required by the new comprehensive city planner demands that the planning profession be comprised of groups of men well versed in contemporary philosophy, social work, law, the social sciences, and civic design. Not every planner must be knowledgeable in all these areas, but each planner must have a deep understanding of one or more of these areas and he must be able to give persuasive expression to his understanding. As a profession charged with making urban life more beautiful, exciting, and creative, and more just, we have had little to say. Our task is to train a future generation of planners to go well beyond us in its ability to prescribe the future urban life.

JOHN FORESTER

"Planning in the Face of Conflict"

Journal of the American Planning Association (1987)

Editors' introduction   While good city planning needs to be inspired by a vision of the end results, and should be informed by theory, in democracies planning is never achieved without conflict. Planners, citizens, local elected officials, developers, and others invariably have different views on what a city should be and how to get it built. Passions run high at important city planning commission meetings.

Consider the history of Letchworth, England, the world's first Garden City. Ebenezer Howard's inspiring vision (p. 346) catalyzed a movement to create Garden Cities along the lines he suggested. Raymond Unwin prepared a practical and attractive plan for Letchworth in 1903. Almost a century later Letchworth exists as a gracious city outside of London, the size Howard envisioned, surrounded by a greenbelt, with publicly owned land leased to the owners of gracious houses (many built by Unwin). Much of the increased land value created by the successful development has been invested back to the community just as Howard envisioned. But getting from Howard's vision to the completed city of Letchworth was tough work. The First Garden City Society fought neighboring landowners and hostile local officials who wanted nothing to do with what they considered outside socialist cranks. (Some locals suggested that they move the whole enterprise a few miles up the road to the local insane asylum!) When the project struggled financially, board members who wanted to keep all land in public ownership fought with members who wanted to sell some land for cash to keep the city growing. Later, when the city was financially successful, citizens fought directors to retain the "unearned increment" in increased land value that Howard had predicted for community use rather than stockholder profits. At every stage of the process a series of city planners had to navigate these troubled waters to a successful conclusion.

John Forester, a professor of city and regional planning at Cornell University, got down in the trenches with practicing city planners and others involved in city development to study what the practice of city planning is really like in the face of conflict. The following selection summarizes what he learned about the process and his ideas on how planners can be effective in the face of conflict.

Forester found that city planners need to help both developers and neighborhood residents through the complexities of the planning process. They have to be attentive to timing. Successful planners handle conflicts both through formal channels and informally. They have to respond to complex and contradictory duties – tugged this way by local politicians, that way by legal mandates, and yet another way by citizen demands. Through all of this, successful city planners must be true to professional norms and hold fast to their own visions of high-quality city development.

There are many lessons in Forester's work. People who want to be effective in translating city plans into action need to expect opposition and should not be surprised or worn down by what often seems an endless and frustrating process. They need to be aware of their own power and its limitations. They have to understand the interests of other actors in the city development process and form alliances. Finally, Forester argues, city planners can self-consciously follow any of a number of strategies to keep projects on track and achieve success – as rule enforcers, negotiators and mediators, resource people, or shuttle diplomats.

Consider the kind of conflicts you would expect if you were implementing plans to change any of the city types described in the selection by Frank So and Judith Getzels (p. 398). Compare Forester's insights with John Mollenkopf's observations on how to study urban power (p. 258).

John Forester builds on the ideas in this article in his book, *Planning in the Face of Power* (Berkeley and Los Angeles: University of California Press, 1989). Forester teamed up with former Cleveland city planning director Norman Krumholz to write an account of Krumholz's experience implementing socially responsible planning in *Making Equity Planning Work* (Philadelphia: Temple University Press, 1992).

Other books on the practice of city planning include Allan Altschuler, *The City Planning Process* (Ithaca, N.Y.: Cornell University Press, 1965) and Allan Jacobs, *Making City Planning Work* (Chicago: American Society of Planning Officials, 1976).

Books on conflict resolution in urban and environmental planning including Lawrence Susskind and J. Cruickshank, *Dealing with Differences* (New York: Basic Books, 1987), G. Bingham, *Resolving Environmental Disputes: A Decade of Experience* (Washington, D.C.: Conservation Foundation, 1986), and A. Talbott, *Settling Things: Six Case Studies in Environmental Mediation* (Washington, D.C.: Conservation Foundation, 1983).

JOHN FORESTER, "Planning in the Face of Conflict"

Journal of the American Planning Association (1987)

In the face of local land-use conflicts, how can planners mediate between conflicting parties and at the same time negotiate as interested parties themselves? To address that question, this article explores planners' strategies to deal with conflicts that arise in local processes of zoning appeals, subdivision approvals, special permit applications, and design reviews.

Local planners often have complex and contradictory duties. They may seek to serve political officials, legal mandates, professional visions, and the specific requests of citizens' groups, all at the same time. They typically work in situations of uncertainty, of great imbalances of power, and of multiple, ambiguous, and conflicting political goals. Many local planners, therefore, may seek ways both to negotiate effectively, as they try to satisfy partic-

ular interests, and to mediate practically, as they try to resolve conflicts through a semblance of a participatory planning process.

But these tasks – negotiating and mediating – appear to conflict in two fundamental ways. First, the negotiator's interest in the subject threatens the independence and the presumed neutrality of a mediating role. Second, although a negotiating role may allow planners to protect less powerful interests, a mediating role threatens to undercut this possibility and thus to leave existing inequalities of power intact. How can local planners deal with these problems? I discuss their strategies in detail below.

This article first presents local planners' own accounts of the challenges they face as simultaneous negotiators and mediators in local land-use permitting processes. Planning directors and staff in New England cities and towns, urban and suburban, shared their viewpoints with me during extensive open-ended interviews. The evidence reported here, therefore, is qualitative, and the argument that follows seeks not generalizability but strong plausibility across a range of planning settings.

The article next explores a repertoire of mediated negotiation strategies that planners use as they deal with local land-use permitting conflicts. It assesses the emotional complexity of mediating roles and asks: What skills are called for? Why do planners often seem reticent to adopt face-to-face mediating roles?

Finally, the article turns to the implications of these discussions. How might local planning organizations encourage both effective negotiation and equitable, efficient mediation? How might mediated-negotiation strategies empower the relatively powerless instead of simply perpetuating existing inequalities of power?

ELEMENTS OF LOCAL LAND-USE CONFLICTS

Consider first the settings in which planners face local permitting conflicts. Private developers typically propose projects. Formal municipal boards – typically planning boards and boards of zoning appeals – have decision-making authority to grant variances, special permits, or design approvals. Affected residents often have a say – but sometimes little influence – in formal public hearings before these boards. Planning staff report to these boards with analyses of specific proposals. When the reports are positive, they often recommend conditions to attach to a permit or suggest design changes to improve the final project. When the reports are negative, there are arguments to be made, reasons to be given.

Some municipalities have elected permit-granting boards; some have appointed boards. Some municipal ordinances mandate design review; others do not. Some local by-laws call for more than one planning board hearing on "substantial" projects, but others do not. Nevertheless, for several reasons, planners' roles in these different settings may be more similar than dissimilar.

Common planning responsibilities

First, planners must help both developers and neighborhood residents to navigate a potentially complex review process; clarity and predictability are valued goods. Second, the planners need to be concerned with timing. *When* a developer or neighborhood resident is told about an issue may be even more important than the issue itself. Third, planners typically need to deal with conflicts between project developers and affected neighborhood residents that usually concern several issues at once: scale, the income of tenants, new traffic, existing congestion, the character of a street, and so on. Such conflicts simultaneously involve questions of design, social policy, safety, transportation, and neighborhood character as well. Fourth, how much planners can do in the face of such conflicts depends not only upon their formal responsibilities, but also upon their informal initiatives. A zoning by-law, for example, can specify a time by which a planning board is to hold a public hearing, but it usually will not tell a planner how much information to give a developer or a neighbor, when to hold informal meetings with either or both, how to do it, just whom to invite, or how to negotiate with either party. So within the formal guidelines of zoning appeals, special permit applications, site plan and design reviews, planning staff can exercise substantial discretion and exert important influence as a result.

Planners' influence

The complexity of permitting processes is a source of influence for planning staff. Complexity creates uncertainties for everyone involved. Some planners eagerly use the resulting leverage, as an associate planning director explains, beginning with a truism but then elaborating:

> Time is money for developers. Once the money is in, the clock is ticking. Here we have some influence. We may not be able to stop a project that we have problems with, but we can look at things in more or less detail, and slow them down. Getting back to [the developers] can take two days

or two months, but we try to make it clear, "We're people you can get along with." So many developers will say, "Let's get along with these people and listen to their concerns ..."

He continues,

But we have influence in other ways too. There are various ways to interpret the ordinance, for example. Or I can influence the building commissioner. He used to work in this office and we have a good relationship ... his staff may call us about a project they're looking over and ask, "Hey, do you want this project or not?"

Planners think strategically about timing not only to discourage certain projects but to encourage or capture others. The associate director explains,

On another project, we waited before pushing for changes. We wanted to let the developer get fully committed to it; then we'd push. If we'd pushed earlier, he might have walked away ...

A director in another municipality echoes the point:

Take an initial meeting with the developer, the mayor, and me. Depending on the benefits involved – fiscal or physical – the mayor might kick me under the table; "Not now," he's telling me. He doesn't want to discourage the project ... and so I'll be able to work on the problems later ...

For the astute, it seems, the complexity of the planning process creates more opportunities than headaches. For the novice, no doubt, the balance shifts the other way.

But isn't everything, in the last analysis, all written down in publicly available documents for everyone to see? Hardly. Could all the procedures ever be made entirely clear? Consider the experience of an architect planner who grappled with these problems in several planning positions. The following conversation took place toward the end of my interview with this planner. The planner pulled a diagram from a folder and said, "Here's the new flow-chart I just drew up that shows how our design review process works. If you have any questions, let's talk. I think it's still pretty cryptic."

"If you think it's cryptic," interjected the zoning appeals planner, who was standing nearby and had overheard this, "just think what developers and neighborhood people will think!"

Both planners shook their heads and laughed, since the problem was all too plain: the arrows on the design review flow chart seemed to run everywhere. The chart was no doubt correct, but it did look complicated.

I recalled my first interview with the zoning appeals planner. Probing with a deliberately leading question, I had asked, "But what influence can you have in the process if everything's written down as public information, if it's all clear there on the page?"

The zoning appeals planner had grinned: "But that's just it! The process is not clear! And that's where I come in ..." The architect-planner developed the point further:

Where I worked before, the planning director wanted to adopt a new "policy and procedures" document that would have every last item defined. We were going to get it all clear. The whole staff spent a lot of time writing that, trying to get all the elements and subsections and so on clearly defined ... But it was chaos. Once we had the document, everyone fought about what each item meant ...

So clarity, apparently, has its limits!

Different actors, different strategies

Planning staff point almost poignantly to the different issues that arise as they work with developers and neighborhood residents. The candor of one planning director is worth quoting at length:

It's easy to sit down with developers or their lawyers. They're a known quantity. They want to meet. There's a common language – say, of zoning – and they know it, along with the technical issues. And they speak with one voice (although that's not to say that we don't play off the architect and the developer at times – we'll push the developer, for example, and the architect is happy because he agrees with us) ...

But then there's the community. With the neighbors, there's no consistency. One week one group comes in, and the next week it's another.

It's hard if there's no consistent view. One group's worried about traffic; the other group's not worried about traffic but about shadows. There isn't one point of view there. They also don't know the process (though there are cases where there are too many experts).

So at the staff level (as opposed to planning board meetings) we usually don't deal with both developers and neighbors simultaneously.

Although these comments may distress advocates of neighborhood power, they say much about the practical situation in which the director finds himself.

All people may be created equal, but when they walk into the planning department, they are simply not all the same. This director suggests that getting all the involved parties together around the table in the planners' conference room is not an obviously good idea, for several reasons. (It is, however, an idea we shall consider more closely below.)

First, the director suggests, planners generally know what to expect from developers; the developers' interests are often clearer than the neighbors', and project proponents may actually want to meet with the staff. Neighborhood residents may be less likely to treat planners as potential allies; after all, the planners are not the decision makers, and the decision makers can often easily ignore the planners' recommendations. Because developers may cultivate good relations with planning staff (this is in part their business, after all), while neighborhood groups do not, local planning staff may find meetings with developers relatively cordial and familiar, but meetings with neighborhood activists more guarded and uncertain.

Second, the planning director suggests that planners and developers often share a common professional language. They can pinpoint technical and regulatory issues and know that both sides understand what is being said. But on any given project, he implies, he may need to teach the special terms of the local zoning code to affected neighbors before they can really get to the issues at hand.

The planning director makes a third point. Developers speak with one voice; neighbors do not. When planners listen to developers talk, they know whom they're listening to, and they know what they're likely to hear repeated, elaborated, defended, or qualified next week. When planners listen to neighborhood residents, though, this director suggests, they can't be so sure how strongly to trust what they hear. "Who really speaks for the neighborhood?" the director wonders.

Planners must make practical judgments about who represents affected residents and about how to interpret their concerns. This director implies, therefore, that until planners find a way to identify "the neighborhood's voice," the problems of conducting joint mediated negotiations between developers and neighbors are likely to seem insurmountable. We return to this issue of representation below.

Inequalities of information, expertise, and financing

What about imbalances of power? Developers, typically, initiate site developments. Planners respond. Neighbors, if they are involved at all, then try to respond to both. Developers have financing and capital to invest; neighbors have voluntary associations and not capital, but lungs. Developers hire expertise; neighborhood groups borrow it. Developers typically have economic resources; neighbors often have time, but not always the staying power to turn that time into real negotiating power.

Where power relations are unbalanced, must mediated negotiation simply lead to coopting the weaker party? No, because, as we shall see below, mediated negotiation is not a gimmick or a recipe; it is a practical and political strategy to be applied in ways that address the specific relations of power at hand.

When either developers or neighborhood groups are so strong that they need not negotiate, mediated negotiation is irrelevant, and other political strategies are more appropriate. But when both developers and neighbors want to negotiate, planners can act both as mediators, assisting the negotiations, and as interested negotiators themselves. But how is this possible? What strategies can planners use?

PLANNERS' STRATEGIES: SIX WAYS TO MEDIATE LOCAL LAND-USE CONFLICTS

Consider the following six mediated-negotiation strategies that planning staff can utilize in the face of local land-use conflicts. They are *mediated* strategies because planners employ them to assure that the interests of the major parties legitimately come into play. They are *negotiation* strategies because (except for the first) they focus attention on the informal negotiations that may produce viable agreements even before formal decision-making boards meet.

Strategy one: The facts! The rules! (The planner as regulator)

The first strategy is a traditional response, pristine in its simplicity, but obviously more complex in practice. A young planner who handles zoning appeals and design review says:

> I see my role often as a fact finder so that the planning board can evaluate this project and form a recommendation; whether it's design review, special permits, or variances, you still need lots of facts . . .

Here of course is the clearest echo of the planner as technician and bureaucrat; the planner processes information and someone else takes responsibility for making decisions. But the echo quickly fades. A moment later, this planner continues,

> Our role is to listen to the neighbors, to be able to say to the board, "Okay, this project meets the technical requirements but there will be impacts . . ." The relief will usually then be granted, but with conditions . . . We'll ask for as much in the way of conditions as we think necessary for the legitimate protection of the neighborhood. The question is, is there a legitimate basis for complaint? And it's not just a matter of complaint, but of the merits.

This planner's role is much more complex than that of fact finder; it is virtually judicial in character. He implies, essentially, "I'm not just a bureaucrat, I'm a professional. I need to think

not only about the technical requirements, but about what's legitimate protection for the neighbors. Now I have to think about the merits!" Thinking about the merits, though, does not yet mean thinking about politics, the feelings of other agencies, the chaos at community meetings – it means making professional judgments and then recommending to the planning board the conditions that should be attached to the permits.

Consider now a slightly more complex strategy.

Strategy two: Premediate and negotiate – representing concerns

When developers meet with planners to discuss project proposals, neighborhood representatives rarely join them. Yet planners might nevertheless speak *for* neighborhood concerns as well as *about* them. A planning director in a municipality where neighborhood groups are well-organized, vocal, and influential notes,

> We temper our recommendations to developers. While we might accept A, the neighbors want D, and so we'll tell the developers to think about something in the middle – if they can make it work.

Here, the planner anticipates the concerns of affected residents and changes the informal staff recommendation accordingly to search for an acceptable compromise with the developers. He explains,

> What we do is premediate rather than mediate after the fact. We project people's concerns and then raise them; so we do more before [explicit conflict arises] . . . The only other way we step in and mediate, later, is when we support changes to be made in a project, changes that consider the neighbors' views; but that's later, after the public hearing . . .

Unlike the planner-regulator quoted above, this planning director relies on far more than his professional judgment when he meets with a developer. He will negotiate to reach project outcomes that satisfy local statutes, professional standards, and the interests of affected residents as well. His calculation is not only judicial, but explicitly political. He anticipates the concerns of interested community members. So he seeks to represent neighborhood interests – without neighborhood representatives.

Such premediation – articulating others' concerns well before they can erupt into overt conflict – involves a host of political, strategic, and ethical issues. What relationships does the planner have with neighborhood groups? In what senses can the planner "know what the community wants"? To which "key actors" might the planner "steer" the developer? How much information and how much advice should the planner give, or withhold?

Such questions arise whether or not project developers ever meet with neighbors. In many cases, where "neighborhoods" are sprawling residential areas, and where "the interests of the neighbors" seem most difficult to represent through actual neighborhood representatives, the planners' premediation may be the only mediation that takes place.

Strategy three: Let them meet – the planner as a resource

The planner's influence might be used in still other ways. The director continues:

> Regardless of how our first meeting with a developer goes, we recommend to them that they meet with neighbors and the neighbors' representatives [on the permit-granting board]. We usually can give the developer a good inkling about what to expect both professionally and politically. The same elected representative might say that a project is "okay" professionally, but not "okay" for them in their elected capacity. We try to encourage back and forth meetings . . .

The director, then, regularly takes the pulse of neighborhood groups and elected representatives. Working in city hall has its advantages: "We'll discuss a project with the representatives; we see them so much here, just in the halls, and they ask us to let them know what's happening in their parts of the city." So the director listens to the developers, listens to the neighbors, and "encourages back and forth meetings."

A planning director who seldom met jointly with neighbors and developers had an acute sense of other strategies he used:

> We . . . urge the applicants, the developers, to deal directly with the neighborhood for several reasons: First, if the neighbors are confronted at a hearing with glossy plans, they'll think it's all a *fait accompli*; so they'll just adopt the "guns blazing, full charge ahead" strategy, since they think it'll just be a "yea" or "nay" decision. Second, we tell them to talk to the neighbors since if they can come up with something that the neighbors will "okay," it'll be easier at the board of appeals. Third, we try to get them to meet one on one, or maybe as a group, but in as deinstitutionalized a way as possible, informally. We try to get the developers to sell their case that way; it'll get a much better hearing than at the big formal public hearings.

But why should planners be reluctant to convene joint negotiating sessions between developers and neighbors, yet still be willing to encourage both parties to meet on their own? Why don't these planners embrace opportunities to mediate local land-use conflicts face to face? One planner could hardly imagine such a mediating role:

> Work as a neutral between developers and neighbors? I don't know how I'd approach it. I'd just answer questions, suggest what could be done, and so on. That's what our role should be – although we should reach compromises between developers and neighbors. But we have to work within the rules – that's my reference point – to say what the rules of the game are; that's the job.

This planner's image of a "neutral" between disputing parties is less that of a mediator facilitating agreement than it is of a referee in a boxing match. The referee assures that the rules are followed, but the antagonists might still kill each other. No wonder planners might find this image of mediation unattractive!

A senior planner envisions further complications:

> If I could be assured I could be wholly independent, then I could mediate – but I still have to pay my bills . . . The planning department always has

some vested interests, as much as we try to stay objective, independent ... I work for a mayor, for the elected representatives, for 14 committees ... So there's always the question of compromise on my part: if the mayor says, "Tell me how to make this project work," for example. It took me a long time before I was able to say, "I'm going to have to say no." We have a very strong mayor ...

Strategy four: Perform shuttle diplomacy – probe and advise both sides

A planning director proposes another way to facilitate developer–neighbor negotiations:

> I feel more comfortable in shuttle diplomacy, if you will; trying to get the neighbors' concerns on the table, to get the developers to deal with them ... I'd rather bounce ideas off each side individually than be caught in the middle if they're both there. If both sides are there, I'm less likely to give my own ideas than if I'm alone with each of them.

Shuttle diplomacy, this director suggests, allows planners to address the concerns of each party in a professionally effective way. He explains:

> If I'm with the developer, I feel I can make a much more extreme proposal – "knock off three stories" – but I wouldn't dare say that if neighbors were there. The neighbors would be likely to pick up and run with it, and it could damage the negotiations rather than help them ... I'm willing to back off on an issue if the developer has a good argument, but the neighborhood might not, and then they might use my point as a club to hit the developer with: "Well, the planning director suggested that; it must be a good idea" ... and then I can't unsay it ...

This planning director is as concerned about how his suggestions, proposals, queries, and arguments will be understood and used as he is about what ought to be altered in the project at hand. He recognizes clearly that when he talks he acts politically and inevitably fuels one argument or another. He not only conveys information in talking, but he acts practically, influentially. He focuses attention on specific problems, shapes future agendas, legitimates a point of view, and suggests lines of further argument.

The director continued,

I might not want to concede to a developer that there won't be a traffic problem, because I want to push him to relieve a problem or a perceived problem ... but I could say to the neighbors aside, "Look, this will be no big deal; it'll be five trips, not fifty." I can say that in a private meeting, but in a public meeting if I say it to a neighborhood representative I'm insulting him, even if the developer snickers silently ... So I lose my ability to be frank with both sides if we're all together. Not that this should be completely shuttle diplomacy, but it has its place.

These comments suggest that planning staff can certainly mediate conflicts in local permitting processes, if not in ways that mediators are thought typically to act. The planners may not be independent third parties who assist developers and neighbors in face-to-face meetings to reach development agreements – but they might still mediate such conflicts as "shuttle diplomats."

Strategy five: Active and interested mediation – thriving as a non-neutral

We can consider a case that involves not a zoning appeal but a rezoning proposal. One planner, who had earlier worked as a community organizer, had convened a working group of five community representatives and five local business representatives to draft a rezoning proposal for a large stretch of the major arterial street in their municipality. She considers her work on that project a kind of mediation and reflects about how she as a planner acts as a mediator, dealing with substantive and affective issues alike:

> Am I in a position of having to think about everyone's interest and yet being trusted by no one? Sure, all the time. But I've been in this job for seven years, and I have a reputation that's good, fortunately ... Trust is an issue of your integrity and planning process. I talk to people a lot; communication is a big part of it ... My approach is to let people let off steam – let them say negative things about other people to me, and then in a different conversation at another time, I'll be sure to say something positive about that person – to try to let them feel that they can say whatever they want to me, and to try to confront them with the fact that the other person isn't just out to ruin the

process. But I'd do that in another conversation; I let them let off steam if they're angry.

This planner is well aware that distrust on all sides is an abiding issue, so she tries to build trust as she works. She works to assure others that she will listen to them and more; that she will acknowledge and respect their thoughts and feelings, whatever they have to say. She pays attention first to the person, then to the words. Then, as she establishes trust with her committee members and with others, she can also make sure, carefully, that real evidence is not ignored.

She realizes that anger makes its own demands, so she responds with an interested patience. She seeks throughout to mediate the conflicting interests of the groups with whom she's working:

> I also make a point to tell each side the other's concerns – categorically, not with names, but all the other sides' concerns ... Why's that important? I like to let people anticipate the arguments and prepare a defense, either to stand or fall on its own merits. For people to be surprised is unfortunate. It's better to let people know what's coming so they can build a case. They can hear an objection, if you can retain credibility, and absorb it; but in another setting they might not be able to hear it ... If they hear an objection first as a surprise, you're likely to get blamed for it. If concerns are raised in an emotional setting, people concentrate more on the emotion than on the substance. This is a concern of mine. In emotional settings, lots gets thrown out, and lots is peripheral, but possibly also central later ...

This planner is keenly aware that emotion and substance are interwoven, and that planners who focus only upon substance and try to ignore or wish away emotion do so at their own practical peril. Yet she is saying even more.

She knows that in some settings disputing groups can hear objections, understand the points at stake, and address them, while in other settings those points may be lost. She tries to present each side's concerns to the other so that they can be understood and addressed. Anticipating issues is central; learning of important objections late in the process will be mostly emotionally and financially, and planning staff are likely to share the blame. "Why didn't you tell us sooner ...?" the refrain is likely to sound.

Consider next, then, this planner-mediator's thoughts about the sort of mediation role she is performing. She continues,

> But what I do is different from the independent mediator model. In a job like mine, you have an on-going relationship with parties in the city. You have more information than a mediator does about the history of various individuals, about participating organizations, about the political history of city agencies, and so on. You also have a vested interest in what happens. You want the process to be credible. You want the product to be successful; in my case I want the city council to adopt the committee's proposal. And you're invested ... both professionally and emotionally. And then you have an opinion about particular proposals; you're a professional, you should have one, you should be able to look at a proposal and have an opinion.

Thus, she suggests, mediation has its place in local land-use conflicts, but the "rules of the game" will not be those that labor mediators follow. Indeed, planners who now mediate local land-use conflicts are not waiting for someone else to write the rules of the game, they are writing them themselves.

Strategy six: Split the job – you mediate, I'll negotiate

Consider finally a planning strategy that promotes face-to-face mediation with planning staff at the table – but as negotiators or advisors, not as mediators. A planning director explains:

> There's another way we deal with these conflicts; we might involve a local planning board member. For example, if there's a sophisticated neighborhood group that's well organized, we've brought in an architect from the board who's as good with words as he is with his pencil.... The chair of the board might ask the board member to be a liaison to the neighborhood, say, and sometimes he'll talk just to the neighbors, sometimes with both ...

Here the "process manager" comes from the planning board with highly developed "communications skills." How does the planner feel in these situations?

> It's more comfortable from my point of view, and the citizens', to have a board member in the convening role. I'm still a hired hand. It seems

more appropriate in a negotiating situation to have a citizen in that role and not an employee ... Since they've come from the neighborhoods, a board member is in a better position to bring neighbors and developers together – if they behave properly. Some board members are good communicators; some are more dynamic than others in pressing for specific solutions.

This planner identifies so strongly with the professional and political mandate of his position that he cannot imagine a role as neutral convener or mediator of neighborhood–developer negotiations. But that does not prevent mediation; it means rather that the planner retains a substantively interested posture while another party, here a planning board member, convenes informal, but organized, project negotiations between developers and neighbors. This planner's example makes the point:

> Take the example of the Mayfair Hospital site. The hospital was going to close, and the neighbors and the planning board were concerned about what might happen with the site. So Jan from the planning board got involved with the hospital and the neighborhood to look at the possibilities. Both the neighbors and the hospital set up re-use committees, and Jan and I went to the meetings. There was widespread agreement that the best use of the site would be residential – the neighbors definitely preferred that to an institutional use – but then there was a lot of haggling over scale, density, and so on. Ultimately, a special zoning district was proposed that included the site; the neighbors supported it, and it went to [the elected representatives] where they voted to rezone the several acres involved ...

When local planners feel they cannot mediate disputes themselves, then one strategy may be to search for informal, most likely volunteer, mediators. These ad hoc mediators might be "borrowed" from respected local institutions,

and their facilitation of meetings between disputing parties might allow planning staff to participate as professionally interested parties concerned with the site in question.

Table 1 summarizes the six approaches presented. Together, these approaches form a repertoire of strategies that land-use planners can use to encourage mediated negotiations in the face of conflicts in local zoning, special permit, and design review processes. To refine these strategies, local planning staff can build upon several basic theories and techniques of conflict resolution. Consider now the distinctive competences and sensitivities required by these strategies.

THE EMOTIONAL COMPLEXITY OF MEDIATED-NEGOTIATION STRATEGIES

More than a lack of independence keeps planners from easily adopting roles as mediators. The emotional complexity of the mediating role makes quite different demands upon planners than those that they have traditionally been prepared to meet. The community-organizer-turned-planner makes the point brilliantly:

> In the middle, you get all the flak. You're the release valve. You're seen as having some power, and you do have some ... Look, if you have a financial interest in a project, or an emotional one, you want the person in the middle to care about your point of view, and if you don't think they do, you'll be angry!
>
> ["So when planners try to be professional by appearing detached, objective, does it get people angry at them?" I asked.]
>
> Sure!

This comment cuts to the heart of planners'

Table 1 A repertoire of mediated-negotiation strategies used by local land-use planners in permitting processes

1 The Facts! The Rules! (The Planner as Regulator)
2 Pre-Mediate and Negotiate: Representing Concerns
3 Let Them Meet: The Planner as a Resource ...
4 Perform Shuttle Diplomacy: Probe and Advise Both Sides
5 Active and Interested Mediation – Thriving as a Non-neutral
6 Split the Job: You Mediate, I'll Negotiate

professional identities. Must "professional," "objective," and "detached" be synonymous? If so, this planner suggests, then planners' own striving for an independent professionalism will fuel the anger, resentment, and suspicion of the same people those planners presume to serve!

Thus we can understand the caution with which a planner speaks of his way of handling emotional participants in public hearings:

How do I deal with people's anger? I try to keep cool, but occasionally I get irritated. But that's how we're expected to behave, to be rational. It's all right for citizens to be irrational, but not the staff!

How does one keep cool, be rational, and still respond to the claims of an emotional public at formal hearings? This planner elaborates:

It's one thing to begin the discussion of a project [to present our analysis] and anticipate problems. But it's another thing to *rebut* a neighborhood resident in public in a gentle way … Part of the problem is that if you antagonize people it'll haunt you in the future … We're here for the long haul, and we have to try to maintain our credibility…

The planner's problem here is precisely *not* the facts of the case: the facts themselves may be clear enough. But how should the planner present the analysis that he feels must be made and how should he decide which arguments to make and which to hold back at a given time?

The biggest problem I have in the board meetings is when to respond and when to keep quiet. In a hearing, for example, I can't possibly respond to all the accusations and issues that come up. So I have to pick a direction, to deal with a generally felt concern. It's just not effective to enter into a debate on each point in turn; it's better to clarify things, to explain what's misunderstood…

This planner does much more than simply recapitulate facts. He tries to avoid an adversarial posture, even when he feels the situation is quite conflictual. He listens as much to the individuals and their concern as he does to each point. He knows that points and demands and positions may change as issues are clarified, but that if he cannot respond to people's concerns, he's in some trouble. Because he and his staff are there "for the long haul," he wants to be able to work with neighbors, community leaders, and elected representatives alike not just now but in the future as well. How he relates to the parties involved in local disputes, he suggests, is as important as what he has to say.

Another planner points to the skills involved:

Whom would I try to hire to deal with such conflicts? I'd look for someone who's a careful listener, someone who's good at explaining a position coherently, succinctly, quietly, in a calm tone … someone who could hear a point, understand it whether he or she agreed with it or not, and then verbalize a clear, concise response. Most people though – myself included – try to jump the gun and answer before it's appropriate. So I want someone who's able to stay cool and stay on the issues…

A community development director first mentions "a good listener" and then elaborates:

[To deal with these conflicting situations I'd want to hire staff] who won't say, "I know best," who won't get people's backs up just by their style. I'd want someone with some openness, with a sense of how things work who won't accept everything, but who won't offend people. They have to have critical judgment – to leave doors open, to give people a sense of involvement and a sense of the feasible – [someone who] can't be convinced of something that's not likely to work, just for the sake of getting agreement…

This planning director also points to the balance necessary between what planners say and how they say it. The "how" counts; he doesn't want staff who will "get people's backs up," "offend people," and not communicate an openness to others' concerns. Nor does he want someone who will sacrifice project viability for the temporary comfort of agreement. He asks for substantive judgment and the skills to manage a process.

Referring to the demands of working and negotiating with developers as they navigate the approval process, the director stresses the role of diplomacy:

We [planners] have access to information, to resources, to skills … so developers usually want to work with us. They have certain problems getting through the process … so we'll go to them and ask, "What do you want?" and we'll start a process of meetings … It's diplomacy; that's the real work. You have to have the technical skill … but that's the first 25 percent. The next 75 percent is diplomacy, working through the process.

Percentages aside, the point remains. To the

extent that planning practitioners and educators focus predominantly upon facts, rules, likely consequences, and mitigation measures, they may fail to attend to the pressing emotional and communicative dimensions of local land-use conflicts. Because the planning profession has not traditionally embraced the diplomat's skills, it should surprise no one that practicing planners envision mediating roles with more reticence than relish.

In the next section, we turn to administrative and political questions. What, initially, can be done in planning organizations to improve planners' abilities to mediate local land-use negotiations successfully? What about imbalances of power?

ADMINISTRATIVE IMPLICATIONS FOR PLANNING ORGANIZATIONS

What does this analysis imply for policymakers and planners who wish to build options for mediation into local review processes? Mediation may offer several opportunities, under conditions of interdependent power: a shift from adversarial to collaborative problem-solving; voluntary development controls and agreements; improved city–developer–neighborhood relationships enabling early and effective reviews of future projects; more effective neighborhood voice; and joint gains ("both gain" outcomes) for the municipality, neighbors, and developers alike. Such opportunities present themselves *only* when no single party is so dominant that it need not negotiate at all, that it is likely simply to get what it wants in any case.

Planners already use the strategies reviewed in diverse settings. Which strategy a planner uses, and at which times, depends largely on practical judgment: What skills does the planner have? How willing are developers or neighbors, or other agency staff, to meet jointly? Does enough time exist to allow early, joint meetings? Are the practical and political alternatives of any one party so attractive that they see no point in mediated negotiations?

No strategy is likely to be desirable in all circumstances, so no one approach will provide

the model to formalize into new zoning or permitting procedures. But to say that we should not formalize these strategies does not mean that we cannot regularly use them. How, then, can planners apply the mediated-negotiation strategies in local zoning, permitting, and design review processes?

First, planning staff must distinguish clearly the two complementary but distinct mandates they typically must serve: to press professionally, and thus to negotiate, for particular substantive goals (design quality or affordable housing, for example), and to enable a participatory process that gives voice to affected parties; thus, like mediators, to facilitate negotiations between disputants.

Second, planning staff need to adopt, administratively if not formally, a goal of supplementing (not substituting for) formal permitting processes with mediated negotiations: attempting to craft workable and voluntary tentative agreements before formal hearing dates.

Third, planning staff should examine each of the strategies reviewed here. They need to determine how each could work, given the size of their agency, their zoning and related by-laws, the political and institutional history of elected officials, neighborhood groups, and other agencies. Planning staff must ask which skills and competencies they need to develop to employ each of these strategies appropriately.

Fourth, planning staff must be able to show others – developers, neighborhood groups, public works department staff, elected and appointed officials – how and when mediated negotiations can lead to "both gain" outcomes and so improve the local land-use planning and development process. Planners also have to be clear about what mediated negotiation will *not* do: it will not solve problems of radically unbalanced power, for example. It can, however, refine an adversarial process into a partially collaborative one. It will not solve problems of basic rights, but it can often expand the range of affected parties' interests that developers will take into account. Mediated negotiations will neither necessarily co-opt project opponents (as skeptical neighborhood residents might suspect) nor stall proposals and projects (as skeptical developers and builders might suspect). Yet when each side can effectively threaten the other, when each side's interests depend upon the other's actions, then mediated negotiations may enable voluntary agreements, incorporate measures of control on both sides, allow "both gain" trades to be achieved, and do so more efficiently for all sides than pursuing alternative strategies (e.g. going to court or, sometimes, community organizing).

Fifth, planners need administratively to create an organized process to match incoming projects with one or more of the mediated-negotiation strategies and to review their progress as they go along. With staff training in negotiation and mediation principles and techniques, planning departments would be better able to carry out these strategies effectively once they have organized administratively to promote them.

DEALING WITH POWER IMBALANCES: CAN THE SIX STRATEGIES MAKE A DIFFERENCE?

The six strategies we have considered are hardly "neutral." Planners who adopt them inevitably either perpetuate or challenge existing inequalities of information, expertise, political access, and opportunity. Consider each approach, briefly, in turn.

To provide only the facts, or information about procedures, to whomever asks for them seems to treat everyone equally. Yet where severe inequalities exist, to treat the strong and the weak alike only ensures that the strong remain strong, the weak remain weak. The planner who pretends to act as a neutral regulator may sound egalitarian but nevertheless act, ironically, to perpetuate and ignore existing inequalities.

The premediation strategy can involve substantial discretion on the part of the planning staff. If the staff fail to put the interests of weaker parties "on the negotiating table," then here, too, inequalities will be perpetuated, not mitigated. If the staff do defend neighborhood interests in the development negotiations, they may challenge existing inequalities. But which "neighborhood interests" should the planning

staff identify? How should neighborhoods – especially weakly organized ones – be represented? These questions are both practical and theoretical and they have no purely technical, "recipe"-like answers.

At first glance, the strategy of letting developers and neighbors meet without an active staff presence seems only to reproduce the initial strengths of the parties. Yet depending on how the planning staff intervene, one party or another may be strengthened or weakened. At times planners have helped developers anticipate and ultimately evade the concerns of citizens who opposed projects. Yet planners may also provide expertise, access, information, and so on to strengthen weaker citizens' positions.

The same discretion exists for planning staff who act as shuttle diplomats. Here a planner may counsel weaker parties to help them both before and during actual negotiations by identifying concerns that might effectively be raised, experts or other influentials who might be called upon, prenegotiation strategies and tactics to be employed, and so on. The shuttle diplomat need not appear neutral to all parties but he or she does need to appear useful to, or needed by, those parties. Planners who act as "interested mediators" face many of the same problems and opportunities that shuttle diplomats confront. In addition, though, the activist mediator may risk being perceived by planning board members, officials, or elected representatives as making deals that preempt their own formal authority. Thus the invisibility of the shuttle diplomat has its advantages; the planners can give counsel discreetly, suggesting packages and "deals" but avoiding the glare – and the heat – of the limelight.

Finally, the strategy of separating mediation and negotiation functions also involves substantial staff discretion. Here, too, the ways that mediators and negotiators consider the interests and enable the voice of weaker parties will affect existing power imbalances.

Because negotiations always involve questions of relative power, they depend heavily upon the parties' *prenegotiation* work of marshalling resources, developing options, and organizing support. Thus politically astute planners need both organizing and mediated-negotiation skills if conflicts are to be addressed without pretending that structural power imbalances just do not exist. Finally, note that a planner who explicitly calls everyone's attention to class-based power imbalances, for example, may not obviously do better in any practical sense of the word than an activist mediator who knows the same thing and acts on it in just the same ways without explicitly framing the planning negotiations in those terms.

CONCLUSION

The repertoire of mediated-negotiation strategies inevitably requires that planners exercise practical judgment, both politically and ethically. These judgments involve who is and who is not invited to meetings; where, when, and which meetings are held; what issues should and should not appear on agendas; whose concerns are and are not acknowledged; how interventionist the planner's role is; and so on.

In local planning processes, then, planners often have the administrative discretion not only to mediate among conflicting parties, but to negotiate as interested parties themselves. Planning staff can routinely engage in the complementary tasks of supporting organizing efforts, negotiating, and mediating. In these ways, local planners can use a range of mediated-negotiation strategies to address practically existing power imbalances of access, information, class, and expertise that perpetually threaten the quality of local planning outcomes.

Mediated negotiations in local permitting processes will, of course, not resolve the structural problems of our society. Yet when local conflicts involve multiple issues, when differences in interests can be exploited by trading to achieve joint gains, and when diverse interests rather than fundamental rights are at stake, mediated-negotiation strategies for planners make good sense, politically, ethically, and practically.

PART 6

*T*he Future of the City

PART SIX

INTRODUCTION

The desire to peer into the future is a human trait as old as the biblical prophets and the oracle at Delphi. And the desire to project *urban* futures is at least as old as the vision of a "New Jerusalem" in the Book of Isaiah and Plato's description of the ideal city-state in *The Republic.* But the pace of futurist predictions seems to quicken at times when great cultural and historic shifts are taking place. Such was the case during the Industrial Revolution of the nineteenth century when fantasists such as Jules Verne captured the popular imagination. And such is the case today as the realization becomes every day more clear that the advanced economies of the world are entering a new information-based, postindustrial stage of development that promises to reveal new forms of urban civilization and human community.

In order to predict the shape of the emerging postmodern city, however, one must have a clear sense of the probable direction of the world urbanization process described by Kingsley Davis in "The Urbanization of the Human Population," (p. 2) the essay with which this volume begins. Will the percentage of the world's total population living in cities, now at about 50 percent, continue to increase in the decades and centuries to come? Will it, in the words of Frederick Law Olmsted, continue the "townward drift"? To what eventual level? 80 percent? 90? 100 percent? Or has urbanization reached its peak, ready to stabilize at more or less the present level? Or, perhaps, the line on the chart representing world urbanization will prove to be a bell curve, with the percentage of the human population living in cities going into a long, gradual decline until only a small fraction of the total population remains urbanized. This last possibility has spawned an intriguing, if highly conjectural, body of literature. Some, pondering the possible effects of modern transportation and telecommunications technologies, see a gradual withering away of earlier justifications for urban density. Others, particularly environmentalists, talk about urbanization reaching its natural limits and beginning to reverse in an age of ecological and economic constraints.

Today, the variety of possible futures from which to choose is extraordinarily diverse. In a way, each option seems like a mirror of some of our deepest hopes and/or deepest fears. Marshall McLuhan, the 1960s guru of communications theory, suggested that the whole world would one day become a "global village," with every member of humanity interacting with every other in a real-time simulacrum of the neolithic community. Some of the more radical members of the environmentalist movement have moved "back to nature" by establishing neolithic-style rural communes along the fringes of urbanized civilization, while other equally radical social activists have established "urban kibbutzim" in the very hearts of the inner cities. Techno-optimists see earth's future in space colonization projects. Techno-pessimists, allied with social pessimists like Mike Davis (p. 159), envision postapocalypse cities like the ones depicted in popular science-fiction films such as *Robocop, Terminator,* and *Blade Runner.*

Among the more interesting and useful urban futures of recent years are those of Constantin

Doxiadis and Paolo Soleri. Both men were trained as architects, and both may be counted as deeply humanistic philosophers. Both men predict a steady increase in the human population. And yet the futures they foresee – and propose – are radically different.

Doxiadis applies "ekistics," his "science of human settlements," to the existing, observable trends of worldwide population growth, as well as urban development patterns, and proclaims the emergence of Ecumenopolis, a worldwide city of twenty billion spread out along the seaboards of the major continents and internally organized into semi-independent communal "cells," each with a population of approximately 40,000 – just a little larger than the population size Ebenezer Howard recommended for Garden Cities.

Soleri looks at the same emerging realities and takes humanity in a radically different direction. He proposes constructing giant megastructures, each containing populations of millions, and leaving the rest of the planet to wilderness. The Soleri sketch of an arcology which opens Part 6 includes a tiny Empire State Building at the same scale to make sure the viewer understands just how huge the megastructures Soleri envisions really are. In Soleri's view, nature would develop on its own terms while a new stage of human community, inside the "arcologies," would thrive in human-constructed "neonature."

One may object to both Ecumenopolis and Arcology as being fantasies that are fundamentally utopian (in the sense of not having any useful application to present realities). But many utopias – those of Ebenezer Howard (p. 346), Le Corbusier (p. 368), and Frank Lloyd Wright (p. 377), for example – became, after modification, influential elements of actual planning practice. And even the most utopian aspects of Ecumenopolis and Arcology – Doxiadis's habitation cells and Soleri's neonature – suggest inescapable realities about cities everywhere. The conceptions may be mystical and exaggerated, but the realities they represent – the human will to small-scale community and the role of the built environment in the on-going cultural evolution of the human race – are essential ingredients of any future urban civilization.

Still, it is useful, when considering the future of the city, to come down to earth, to shorten the futurist perspective to the near term, and to project immediate futures based on present and observable trends. And among the most important such trends today are the parallel emergence of (1) a postindustrial, information-based economy and (2) a new, far-flung suburban ring of development that journalist Joel Garreau has dubbed "Edge City." These two developments, more than any others, are likely to determine the course of early twenty-first-century urban development, first in the advanced economies and later worldwide.

In the nineteenth century, middle-class suburbs developed outside major urban centers, spaced along commuter rail lines. In the twentieth century, the influence of the automobile turned once-attractive small-scale suburbs into an endless, congested sprawl. These first two stages in the development of suburbia depended on the existence of a vital central city, both as a center for production and employment and for cultural amenities. Today, all that seems to be changing. The new "Edge City" suburban ring is different from the earlier suburban developments in size, complexity, and even function. This is where most of the new houses, most of the new jobs, and even most of the new cultural centers are located. Increasingly, the major commute pattern is not from suburb to central city, but from suburb to suburb. Indeed, as Robert Fishman argues in *Bourgeois Utopias: The Rise and Fall of Suburbia* (1987), the new Edge City suburbs are not suburbs at all, but a fundamentally new kind of decentralized city that he calls "technoburbs" (p. 485).

California-based architect-planner Peter Calthorpe agrees. His "Pedestrian Pocket" developments are being built not as a further extension of traditional suburbia but in and for what he has variously called "the next American metropolis" and "the post-suburban metropolis." In one sense, Calthorpe's Pedestrian Pockets look backward to the Garden Cities of Ebenezer Howard – especially in their use of light-rail mass-transit options – but, in another sense, they look forward to an entirely new relationship between city and region, between individual and community. In short, Calthorpe's work responds to a future already in the process of becoming, characterized by "a dramatic shift in the nature and location of our workplace and a fundamental change in the character of our increasingly diverse households."

If Fishman has written the history (and suburban prehistory) of the newly emerging city of the future, and if Calthorpe has begun the design of its new, pedestrian-scale nodes, Manuel Castells and Peter Hall have surveyed its production centers in "Technopoles: Mines and Foundries of the Informational Economy" (p. 476). These "technopoles" are not the same as Fishman's "techoburbs," which are complete cities unto themselves. Some technopoles are entire cities, but others are specifically the workplaces of the new metropolis, the planned office-park and technology research developments – some highly successful, others dismal failures – that have been built and promoted to serve as the wealth-generating source-points (equivalent to what Lewis Mumford called the "factory camps" of the nineteenth century) of the postindustrial economy.

Castells and Hall argue that technopoles represent "a new industrial space," located in centers throughout Europe, Asia, and America and tied to a global "informational" economy fundamentally different from anything that has ever come before. In appearance, the technopoles are attractive and campus-like. The workers in the new technopoles are highly educated and well paid. But a number of paradoxes remain as troubling inconsistences in this technological new world order. First, as Saskia Sassen has pointed out in *Cities in a World Economy* (p. 70), a few already existing cities and regions – Tokyo, Los Angeles, Paris, London – resist decentralization and become increasingly important even as the new economic order globalizes. Second, a two-tier economy and a widening gulf between the educated elites and the ghettoized, marginalized urban populations seems to intensify rather than diminish in the cities of the information economy and the global marketplace. And third, the new urban order, abetted by the new economic realities, seems cut off from its past, from history and cultural tradition as sources of communal meaning and individual identity. A sense of estrangement may well be expected at great historic moments of human transformation, but it is not comforting. The newly emerging world will not be that of George Orwell's *Nineteen Eighty-Four*, but perhaps some version of Aldous Huxley's *Brave New World*.

Among those who share this sense of disquiet is Manuel Castells. In *The Informational City* (1989), Castells observes that the implicit tendency of the work-styles of the postindustrial economy is to detach themselves from traditional cultures, values, and communities. Information flows through networks and across vast distances, and "the historical emergence of the space of flows," he writes, supersedes "the meaning of the space of places." But men and women, as Doxiadis well understood, want to live in small-scale communities, not in computer networks or in on-line virtual realities. For Castells, then, the real challenge of the new informational city is to reconcile the "new techno-economic paradigm" and "place-based social meaning." "At the cultural level," he writes, "local societies, territorially defined, must preserve their identities, and build upon their historical roots, regardless of their economic and functional dependence upon the space of flows."

The program of cultural and communal resistance that Castells advocates is designed for the residents of the postsuburban technoburbs toiling in the technopoles, but another problem haunts the city of the future that is all too often forgotten. Dazzled by the extraordinary promise and challenge of our suburban, middle-class technological futures, we are too often blinded to the impacted, marginalized inner cities that techno-suburban futures seem to leave behind. In the ghettos and the barrios of the decaying central cities, whole populations continue to strive, but often with a declining sense of hope. In 1945, St. Clair Drake and Horace Cayton called these segregated, impoverished inner-city neighborhoods "social dynamite." In the U.S., U.K., and elsewhere, that dynamite has repeatedly exploded . . . and remains as a source of future explosions that calls into question the integrity, and perhaps even the viability, of any future city that may emerge. If the deepening gulf between urban rich and urban poor defines the contemporary social impasse, two broad paths seem possible as ways out. One, advocated by some nationalist groups, is communal autonomy and separate development. The other is integration, breaking down the class- and race-based walls of segregation that have grown up over the centuries between dominant and oppressed groups. Anthony Downs's "Alternative Futures for the American Ghetto" (p. 500) poses the prospects and difficulties of a wide range of urban ghetto enrichment and dispersal strategies.

No one, least of all Downs, thinks that solving the problem of inner-city poverty and race- and class-based segregation will be an easy task, nor that one solution is the only one worth considering. Clearly, there are many contentious issues of politics and urban governance, and even deeper concerns at the level of social structure and cultural development that will affect the future of cities. But as the technoburbs and the technopoles and the Pedestrian Pockets beckon, and as local economies and national sovereignties give way to global interdependence, the social dynamite is still there at the core of many cities, threatening to destroy urban civilization and to undermine the human community. Defusing that dynamite remains the unfinished business of the city of the future.

PAOLO SOLERI

"Arcology: The City in the Image of Man" and "The Characteristics of Arcology"

from *Arcology: The City in the Image of Man* (1969)

Editors' introduction   One need only glance at a Paolo Soleri architectural drawing (such as the one that opens Part 6) to know that one is in the presence of either an inspired visionary or a mad prophet. His "arcologies" – a combination of architecture and ecology – are megastructures so immense that they dwarf the outline of the Empire State Building that Soleri often includes as a scale reference. His techno-cities suggest populations of millions living a beehive existence in massive multicell units resembling the cooling towers of nuclear power plants. Is the Solerian vision a science-fiction fantasy, an Orwellian nightmare, or a new evolutionary stage in the progress of the human spirit?

Soleri was born in Turin, Italy, in 1919 and studied architecture at the Turin Architectural Institute. He worked with Frank Lloyd Wright at Taliesen West in Scottsdale, Arizona – ironic, given the fact that his arcologies are the diametrical antithesis of Broadacre City (p. 377) – and later founded his own Cosanti Foundation nearby where he began building – and doggedly continues to build – Arcosanti, the world's first arcology in the desert north of Phoenix, Arizona.

During the 1960s and 1970s, Soleri became the focus of an almost cult-like following, and students from around the world flocked to the Arcosanti site in Arizona's Paradise Valley to sit at the feet of the master and help build the dream. In addition, many adherents of the most radical tendencies of environmentalism adopted Soleri as their architectural guru because the arcology concept appeared to quarantine (destructive) humanity from (life-giving) nature. Soleri, however, proved to be full of surprises. As a deeply humanistic artist and as a personality of charm, gentleness, and wry humor, he was no cult leader and eschewed the status of guru. And as an environmentalist, his interest in nature was overwhelmingly of the human variety. In one analogy, Soleri compared his arcologies to ocean liners – campuslike temporary societies of unrelated people – and the implication that the natural world surrounding the arcology was as empty and uninviting as a vast ocean was unavoidable. Further, Soleri was quite explicit that the new arrangement of human life inside the arcology manifested a revolutionary new kind of environment, a "neonature," that was his true interest.

It has been said that Paolo Soleri takes the technological tendencies of Le Corbusier's "machine age" cities (p. 368) to an even higher plane. Others see his arcologies as models for cities in outer space or for earthbound cities in an age following nuclear war or global environmental disaster. Soleri himself sees no need to rely on catastrophe to usher in the new age. For him, the evolution of arcological neonature is merely an inevitable, and welcome, next step in the history of human progress. To pursue his philosophical projections further, consult *The Bridge between Matter and Spirit: Is Matter Becoming Spirit?* (Garden City, NY: Anchor, 1973), *The Omega Seed* (Garden City, NY: Anchor, 1981), and *Technology and Cosmogenesis* (New York: Paragon House, 1985).

PAOLO SOLERI, "Arcology: The City in the Image of Man" and "The Characteristics of Arcology"

from *Arcology: The City in the Image of Man* (1969)

ARCOLOGY: THE CITY IN THE IMAGE OF MAN

The concept is that of a structure called an arcology, or ecological architecture ... Such a structure would take the place of the natural landscape inasmuch as it would constitute the new topography to be dealt with. This man-made topography would differ from natural topography in the following ways:

1 It would not be a one-surface configuration but a multi-level one.
2 It would be conceived in such a way as to be the carrier of all the elements that make the physical life of the city possible – places and inlets for people, freight, water, power, climate, mail, telephone; place and outlets for people, freight, waste, mail, products, and so forth.
3 It would be a large-dimensioned sheltering device, fractioning three-dimensional space in large and small subspaces, making its own weather and its own cityscape.
4 It would be the major vessel for massive flow of people and things within and toward the outside of the city.
5 It would be the organizing pattern and anchorage for private and public institutions of the city.
6 It would be the focal structure for the complex and ever-changing life of the city.
7 It would be the unmistakable expression of man the maker and man the creator. It would be diverse and singular in all of its realizations. Arcology would be surrounded by uncluttered and open landscape.

The concept of a one-structure system is not incidental to the organization of the city but central to it. It is the wholeness of a biological organism that is sought in the making of the city, as many and stringent are the analogies between the functioning of an organism and the vitality of a metropolitan structure. Fundamental to both is the element of flow. Life is there where the flow of matter and energy is abundant and uninterrupted. With a great flow gradient the city acquires a cybernetic character.

The interacting of its components erases the space and time gaps that outphase the action–reaction cycles and ultimately break down the vitality of the system.

These are mechanical but fundamental premises for a functioning metropolitan life. In reality the idea is that of a very comprehensive "plumbing system" for the social animal, which the city is. The plumbing system consists of the previously mentioned man-made topography. Social, ethical, political, and aesthetic implications are left out, as they are valid and final only if and when physical conditions are realistically organized.

To dispel the aura of cerebralism or utopianism from the concept presented, there is another way to see the central problem of the city: The degree of fullness in each individual life depends on the reaching power unequivocally available to each person. In turn this reaching power is in direct proportion to the richness and variety of information coming to and going from the person. Information means not only sounds, sight, and so forth, but all the sensorial data, all the physical intermediaries that make any sensitivity possible; all kinds of inorganic, organic, organized, or man-made matter or material or instruments, from foodstuff to wireless, from toilets to television, from mothers' reprimands to theater. This wholeness of information must include packaged and remote information such as television, radio, telephone, and the communications media, as well as environmental information. Environmental information calls in the technology of transportation, distribution, and transfer, and calls for the no less fundamental quality of the environment itself.

This combination of remote and synthetic information and environmental information is indispensable to the nature of metropolitan life. In physical terms it means that the distances, the time, and the obstacles separating the person from all civilized institutions have to be scaled down to the supply of energy available to the person himself.

If we inject into the picture the sheer bulk of products and devices wanted by and forced upon each man, we can see the dimension and the absolute priority of the logistical problem. The burden of matter, part of the environmental information weighing on every man, is impressive and also irrational. This matter has to be transformed, manipulated, moved, serviced, stored, exchanged, rejected, and substituted – the warehouses of arcology will have to be enormous. One thing nomadism has not been able to teach us is frugality. What is the mechanism by which the rich and complex life of society can flow back into the structure of the city?

In a society where production is a successful and physically gigantic fact, the coordination and congruence of information, communication, transportation, distribution, and transference are the mechanics by which that society operates. It is not accidental that these are also dynamic aspects of another phenomenon, the most dynamic of all: life.

In every dynamic event of physical nature the elements of time and space, and this acceleration, speed, and deceleration, are crucial. The speed of light, a space and time shrinker, well serves the communication of information of the packaged kind – television, radio, telephone – the synthetic information. Thus a good supply of synthetic information can reach even the scattered suburbanite (for him environmental information is and remains monotone, bone stripped).

The picture is totally altered when we come to transportation and distribution. Unless the feeding in and feeding out of these two is highly centered and axialized, the laws of matter and energy will see that sluggishness and possibly stillness prevail. *Swiftness and efficiency are inversely proportional to dispersion. Scattered life is by definition deprived or parasitic.* This can be verified by approaching the problem from the opposite end: the environment is vital and living information; it is the bulk of information available to man.

Blighted environment is blighted information. The cause of blighted environment is the breakdown of environmental information occurring when there is no follow-through from synthetic information to transportation, distribution, and reach. When this occurs, the energies of the individual are exhausted in the struggle to keep the avenues of environmental information open, to keep the flow of things going. Man's mechanically low-grade energies are absorbed, not euphemistically, by cement, asphalt, steel, pollution, and all sorts of mechanical, static, and dynamic barriers in an ever-enlarging frame of space and time. The flow becomes sluggish, if it does not come to a standstill. This blighted environment is a direct consequence of sluggish or dying flow.

Impaired flow is ultimately the disproportion between the validity of the individual reach and the amount of energy that is expended to make the reach possible.

One may thus say that because of the biophysical make-up of our world, rich flow – that is, rich potentially – is the direct consequence of minimal separation between components. *Minimal separation between components cannot be achieved by using only two or three coordinates of space. Minimal separation between components is structured three-dimensionally, or it is not feasible.* The solid and not the surface is the environment where adequate flow is possible, thus where environmental information is rich and where life can flourish.

The surface of the earth, for all practical purposes, is by definition a two-dimensional configuration. *The natural landscape is thus not the apt frame for the complex life of society.* Man must make the metropolitan landscape in his own image: a physically compact, dense, three-dimensional, energetic bundle, not a tenuous film of organic matter. The man-made landscape has to be a multilevel landscape, a solid of three congruous dimensions. The only realistic direction toward a physically free community of man is toward the construction of truly three-dimensional cities. *Physical freedom, that is to say, true reaching power, is wrapped around vertical vectors . . .*

There is a further and reinforcing reason for verticality. As individuals we act horizontally and need horizontal dimensions up to six to ten times the vertical dimensions. Thus, the compactness and richness of social collective life can be found only vertically. *Around vertical vectors, megalopoly and suburbia can contract, moving from flat gigantism toward human and solid scale . . .*

If this concept is valid, as it seems to be in view of the nature of the physical and energetic world, then a dense urban structure is mandatory, regardless of the what, how, where, or when. A few generations of men reared and grown in an environment badly stripped of cultural and aesthetic scope may be sufficient for the brutalization of society. Signs that such brutalization is already at work are abundant and impressive. If man is quality against quantity, then the priority is clear. It is much too late for our present generation, bound to the spell of arrogance and license. It may even be quite late for the just born, but there is hope for the children of our children. The when is now, for lack of any reachable yesterday.

THE CHARACTERISTICS OF ARCOLOGY

A passenger liner is the closest ancestor of arcology. The common characteristics are compactness and definite boundary; the functional fullness of an organism designed for the care of many, if not most, of man's needs; a definite and unmistakable three-dimensionality.

Three main characteristics on the other hand are not common: the liner is structurally and functionally designed for motion within fluid; the liner is a shell for a temporary society of unrelated people; the liner is a sealed package connected to the outside only by way of synthetic information. Relieved of these three tyrannies, the liner, the concept of it, can open up and, retaining its organizational suppleness, become truly a "machine for living," that is to say, a physical configuration that makes man physically free.

We have then architecture as the materialization of the human environment and ecology as the physical, biological, and psychological balance of conditions that account for the specific site and its participation in the whole.

Arcology becomes the cleavage of the human in the body of matter and life, probing for the *ever-changing condition of the present in a manner congruous to the aesthetocompassionate nature of man.*

Arcology is then that architecture so complex in scope, so sound in structure, so infrastructurally subtle and pliable, so comprehensive, and of such miniaturizing force as to alter substantially the local ecology in the human direction.

Arcology is then, *morphologically*, that of the man-made (I will call it neonature), which parallels in one an ecology and an organism – an ecology in scale, pervasiveness, and balance, an organism in complexity and dynamism; *skeletally*, a structure of such dimension, scale, and organization as to be favorable to the interplay of the forces by which man and society grow; *functionally*, a compact, dense, and efficient organization caring for the intake, processing, storing, consuming, expelling, recycling of the elements needed by the complex life of man and society; *humanly*, an apt shelter for the multiple expressions and longing of man as an individual and man as a society; *formally*, a foundation for the aesthetogenesis of nature (into neonature).

If, for the sake of clarity, one separates the not-too-separable instrumentality from the scope (ends), one may say that the instrumental purpose of arcology is the definition of a well-rounded service system which, cutting into the waste of time and space, presents man with a few extra years of "positive" time, time to use to his personal, social advantage if he so pleases. That this may be invaluable lies in the assumption that life is precious enough and unique enough to demand rightly the best environmental conditions for its flowering and that coercion and frustration are inimical to life. Life is coerced by the environment man has produced and lives in. It is basically coerced by the very fact of the physical conditions he himself has compounded.

The time-waste brought about by spacewaste (functional and structural) by force of physical laws, including fatigue, results in cultural pauperism; thus, a waste of life at the level where such waste is unwarranted and unreasonable.

The achievement of the instrumental purpose of arcology coincides by force of physical laws with nature's conservation. The coincidence, which is also a reinforcing element in the qualitative scope of the life developing within the arcology itself, is a direct consequence of the identity of efficiency (in its full meaning, frugality) with axiality of life. Then instrumentality in its over-all power is vital to efficiency and thus, indirectly, is itself vital. *But the fruition of growth is in things that are not commensurable to that which would seem to be their cause.* While an apple is the fruition of a tree seeking continuity in the next apple tree, and in a sense all that is the new tree was already in the parent tree, the fruition of man is the creation of the "never been before and never to be again."

At the same time the observation that life has never been so rich is invalid in the two directions of ratio and history. The ratio fulfillment–wealth seems to dwindle constantly. This indicates an ultimate exhaustion of human values submerged by and in a mechanism of ever-powerfulness lost to man's purpose. Historically, the stage of affluence seems more a leveling of, rather than a stronger stimulus to, growth, as if affluence were at the same time cause and effect of a weakening in the thrust of evolution. Totalitarianism recognizes, or instinctively senses, this and capitalizes on it by putting ideals before affluence and in so doing, though possibly for the wrong reason, injects new purposefulness into individual motivations.

The mechanisms channeling life positively may consist of the replacement of comfort and security by joy. In joy, motivations are carried, uplifted, while in comfort and security they seem to be drugged, sinking into naught. Possibly then wealth would instrumentalize a joyful state instead of a security at any price, the negative side of conservatism. Joy comes from plenitude. Plenitude, though basically an inner condition, can be invited by an inspiring and stimulating environment and the feeling of working toward achievements that overreach one's own limitation and embrace not just oneness but otherness as well: therefrom, the fruitions of creativity.

The pertinence of arcology to the condition of man, the condition of joy or indifference, is direct and immediate. *Joy is then the burst of liveliness that comes with the fitness and coherence of a process that is developing under one's eyes; it is the opposite of senselessness and squandering.*

CONSTANTIN DOXIADIS

"Ecumenopolis, World City of Tomorrow"

Impact of Science on Society (1969)

Editors' introduction   Konstantinos (or Constantin) Doxiadis (1913–1975) was a brilliant and charismatic Greek architect and planner. If one were to assess his contributions to architecture and planning alone, his reputation would be assured. But what places Doxiadis in an imaginative class all his own is the development of a theory he called "ekistics" and a vision of the urban future he called "Ecumenopolis."

Doxiadis first used the word ekistics in 1942 while lecturing at the Athens Technical University. Derived from the Greek words for "home" and "settling down," ekistics was intended to be an entirely new discipline of human knowledge, what Doxiadis called "the science of human settlements." Reducing ekistic science to its basics, Doxiadis argued, "Human settlements consist of five basic elements, Nature, Man, Society, Shells, and Networks, which together form a system. Their goal is to make Man happy and safe." And what emerged from ekistic science – what the systematic study of ekistics revealed – was Ecumenopolis, "the World City of Tomorrow."

Doxiadis argued that the "main trends of present technological and economic progress cannot, and should not, be reversed." In fact, he wrote, all other considerations that traditionally have concerned urban theorists and planners – issues such as poverty, overcrowding, and racial and social conflict – are nothing more than "diseases which should not distract our attention." Furthermore, most of the plans put forward by others – including the abolition of automobiles, the colonization of outer space, back-to-nature movements, megastructures, and the establishment of communal utopias – he branded simply "escapist solutions." The "most dangerous escapist solutions," he wrote, "are those which advocate a return to small towns." And "still more dangerous is the theory recommending . . . the establishment of new satellite towns outside the large cities." Clearly Ebenezer Howard (p. 346), who advocated a system of garden cities each of about 32,000 people, did not see his vision as "escapist"; nor do Peter Calthorpe (p. 469) and other "new urbanists" of today see their theories as dangerous – though they find many features of historic small towns appealing and their designs are often for small communities.

Eschewing escapism in all its many forms, and embracing what he felt was the only realistic alternative, Doxiadis argued that "the most probable, logical and practical solution . . . is the progressive expansion of the present type of city as a result of the massive influx of an ever-increasing population" and saw Ecumenopolis as an emerging "universal system of life" and single "global settlement." Covering the coastal areas and most favored interior regions of all the habitable continents, Ecumenopolis would achieve a population of approximately 15 to 25 billion by the year 2200. What Doxiadis saw, quite simply, was a further and continual expansion, worldwide, of what Jean Gottman had identified as the Boston-to-Washington "Megalopolis" along the eastern seaboard of the United States (*Economic Geography*, 1957). Gottman had hopefully dubbed the immense conurbation "the Main Street of the nation." Lewis Mumford had called it "urban pathology" and "sprawling gigantism."

Although the vision of Ecumenopolis may appear to be a simple matter of projecting current population trends, and passively accepting existing technologies and human preferences, Doxiadis is more subtle than that. Although a major thrust of his argument is a devastating critique of decentralist and small-town-based planning visions, Doxiadis recognizes, on the basis of urban history, what he calls "the absolute need for man to live in small cities." Faced with a seeming paradox (the inevitability of Ecumenopolis vs. man's need for small-scale community), Doxiadis proposes that the World City will be unitary and continuous but will be made up of settlement "cells," units of habitation with populations of from 30 to 50,000 people. Whether or not this vision of a cellular structure will convince and/or satisfy the advocates of small-scale cities, Doxiadis has this in his favor: to date, the spreading world city – along the coasts of North and South America, Africa, China, and elsewhere – seems unchecked. Say what you will, Ecumenopolis may well be the wave of the future.

Doxiadis's important books on architecture and planning include *Architecture in Transition* (New York: Oxford University Press, 1963) and *Urban Renewal and the Future of the American City* (New York: National Association of Housing and Redevelopment Officials, 1966). The version of Ecumenopolis here reprinted, taken from a 1969 UNESCO publication, is perhaps the simplest and most direct explication of Doxiadis's theory. For a fuller exposition of the theory – in elaborate, if sometimes baffling, detail – consult *Ekistics: An Introduction to the Science of Human Settlements* (London: Oxford University Press, 1968) and *Ecumenopolis: The Inevitable City of the Future* (New York: Norton, 1979). For a critique of the tendencies inherent in Ecumenopolis, see Lewis Mumford's "The Myth of Megalopolis" in *The City in History: Its Origins, Its Transformations, and Its Prospects* (New York: Harcourt Brace, 1961).

CONSTANTIN DOXIADIS, "Ecumenopolis, World City of Tomorrow"

Impact of Science on Society (1969)

WHY THE CRISES IN OUR CITIES

About thirty-five years ago, when one talked of cities, the only questions raised were, as a rule, questions of the aesthetics of buildings: whether a particular house or monument was beautiful or ugly. Later, when the world began to suffer severely from the poor state of communications, all one heard on every hand was about the crisis in urban communications, and more particularly about too many motor-cars. Later still, social problems arose in certain countries, and people began to view the urban crisis from that particular aspect. In some countries, the problems were specifically racial, as in the United States, where the situation is more delicate than elsewhere. And so the urban crisis then took on the appearance of a social crisis.

Sometimes, also, the urban crisis was poorly understood, because each person tended to regard it from his own particular point of view. Certain people, in fact, referred to it as a crisis in small scale organic unity, that of the family; others saw it as resulting from the disappearance of small neighbourhoods and towns, and yet others as something inherent in large cities and big centres of population. Each one, in fact, saw only a single factor of the general crisis in space.

Actually, the crisis is nothing other than that

of the entire system. This is an essential principle we must understand: it is the crisis of a system we commonly refer to as the city, but which it would be more accurate to call the human settlement.

The crisis is a general one. We shall understand this if we consider the city from a rational point of view. To do so, we must try to view it under three aspects.

THE FIVE ELEMENTS

First we must try to understand of what it is composed. Five elements enter into its composition (Figure 1). The first of these is nature, the soil which gave it birth. By not taking this simple fact into account, our efforts have been doomed to failure. We have, in fact, polluted the atmosphere and the waters, destroyed beautiful country-sides, exhausted the natural resources, killed off the animals, insects and plants – in a word, annihilated the city's natural setting.

The second element is man, who is frequently left out of the calculations. All we need to do is look at a city from the air to realize that the most important place is allotted to motor-cars, and man occupies only the second place; that the city is covered with colossal buildings. We

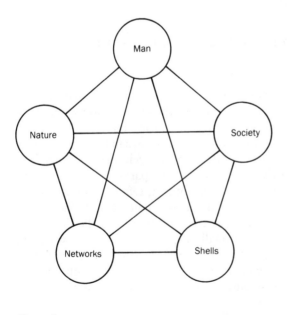

have so completely failed to recognize man's existence as to prevent our children from using the streets. In this way man is left exposed to various forms of psychosis and neurosis which are far more serious than the accidents which stain our streets with blood, for they are the diseases of a man who is no longer free to wander about and grows up, for the first time in history, with the feeling of being more at ease in the heart of nature than in the city.

Thirdly, society, painstakingly created by man, and producing, in turn, human settlements. We are incapable of creating a society. All we can create are enormous masses of people incapable of performing their normal functions. Men are more and more separated in space from each other; the necessary contacts between them are lacking. The women, left alone in the suburbs without a second car at their disposal, become "nervy", and the men who have to drive for several hours back and forth also become tense and nervous. It is curious to observe that when men are scattered over vast tracts of territory they lose contact with the small surface points of unity – the family, the neighbours. In this way we create a city with nothing human about it.

The fourth element is buildings in general, what the architectural trade refers to as "shells". Technically, there has certainly been progress. But does this progress serve man's true interests? This cannot be proved. On the other hand, we cannot help thinking that these great blocks isolate men and turn them into cave-dwellers. And the idea of wandering through car-choked streets admiring the beauty of some of the buildings as you go along is, strictly speaking, inconceivable.

The fifth and last element is the networks: highways, railways, water-supply systems, electricity and telecommunications. All these become more and more technically perfect every day. If they are underground systems, as in the case of water supply, electricity and telephone, they cannot possibly inconvenience men from the technical or aesthetic point of view. If, on the other hand, they are on the surface, such as certain electrical and telephone systems, they can be disadvantageous, at any rate aesthetically. But it is in the road system that failure has

Figure 1

been most marked. Motorways have the effect of breaking up a city's continuity and preventing it from functioning normally.

We therefore reach the conclusion that the failure of the system is due to the destruction of its elements and of the relationships between them. Because man cannot find joy in his home, because his habitation cannot offer him a better life, the entire city system suffers. Because the city expands rapidly, thanks to the motor-car and other centrifugal forces, it destroys the surrounding country-side and the entire system goes slowly from bad to worse.

[...]

INTENSIFICATION OF THE CRISIS

If we have succeeded in understanding the exact nature of the crisis and the reasons for it, we shall also be able to realize easily enough that it can only get worse and worse as time goes on, if things are allowed to remain as they are. It is because we have been unable to grasp this state of affairs that we find ourselves incapable of dealing with it rationally and have no assurance that we will be able to avert the worst.

Since the cause of the crisis in the system is essentially the latter's size, obviously as the size grows, the problems arising out of it will grow in the same proportion. Assuming that the world population at the end of the century will be double the present population of 3,500 millions (and more likely it will be something more), that means it will have reached 7,000 million. In the generation immediately following, that is to say, by the year 2030, the population will probably have quadrupled, but even if this were not so, it is bound to be very much higher than 7,000 million. If this rate of increase continues, we shall have reached a figure of over 20,000 million by the end of the twenty-first century. Such a population increase will call for a corresponding increase in the units which compose the main elements of the city.

But population is only one aspect of the question. A city is not composed only of human elements; there are others besides, such as buildings and mains of various kinds, which compli-cate the problem. To be able to deal with questions of buildings and mains, we have to know something about the economy. We know, of course, that the economic potential of the population is expanding. We may therefore expect per capita income to rise steeply, to at least double the present one in the course of the generation. This means that the gross revenue of a medium-sized town will have quadrupled.

As a first approximation, as the population increases, the need for surface space increases proportionately. However, since incomes go up, people demand more space for their dwellings and service networks. They also have more cars at their disposal and they insist on more room for them, too. And with rising prosperity, the mileage covered by each car constantly increases, so that new motorways have to be built. We can, therefore, say that it is not just the city itself which needs more room, but also every individual in it. This explains how it is that in a good many urban centers, over the past forty years, the surface area has multiplied twice or even three times. We are led to face this additional problem: that the demand for urban space is bound to increase at a faster rate than the population and, in certain cases, will greatly outstrip the growth of the economy.

We now see that, where we have a population with an increased economic potential and therefore insisting on more living space, our whole system of human settlements is bound to become much more complex than the actual growth in population would seem to justify. Likewise, the whole body of problems increases at a faster rate than does either the world population or the urban population.

ESCAPIST SOLUTIONS

Most people are not yet aware of the major problems. But there are some who understand them because they think and they make calculations, even though these may not always be very accurate. Such people endeavour to find solutions. At present these are, in fact, but escapist solutions. I propose to enumerate the main ones in the order of their appearance.

In the first category we can place solutions

based on various myths. These are, for example, the myth of optimism, which foresees the solution of all problems in emigration to other planets or in the abolishing of motor-cars; the myth founded upon imaginary concepts, such as the assertion that people are living today in high-density urban agglomerations, whereas the medium-sized town of today is in fact less densely populated than it was a generation ago; the myth that our problems would be solved by increasing the height of buildings, although, on the contrary, these enormous constructions create new problems without at all solving the human ones.

There is a whole series of other more realistic utopias, those which are based on some dream of reconstruction which is entirely divorced from logic. According to these, cities are no longer necessary.

There is still another form of utopia based on the application of the same abortive solutions to various problems which were tried at the end of the nineteenth century; these led to a host of utopian groups which founded utopian communities. This is a typical escapist solution.

Then there are escapist-motivated solutions which take the form of ideal cities and technological utopias. These advocate the creation of parking lots on the flat roofs of dwellings, or the construction of buildings shaped like huge metal tanks capable of moving from place to place.

The most dangerous escapist solutions are those which advocate a return to small towns. Actually, many of us have been born and raised in such towns and we still see them in our mind's eye and dream of going back to them. This form of utopia takes on different aspects, such as the ideal little towns like those imagined by Skinner with his *Walden Two*, or like those described in Aldous Huxley's last book, *Island*, in which there is a small island where people live in little towns.

Still more dangerous is the theory recommending as the ideal solution the establishment of new satellite towns outside the large cities. Yet do we not now possess the evidence of experience, showing that the satellite towns established sixty years ago have for the past thirty years been urban sectors and that the same fate has befallen those established thirty years ago?

THE PATH OF THE FUTURE

We have now reached the point where we must decide on the future road to follow. The question is: are we now capable of examining systematically the various practicable alternatives for the future which are open to us? I believe we are.

First among the roads we can follow is that of research into basic causes, and the first among these to be studied must be the world population increase. Even if a decision on birth control could be adopted immediately, two generations would go by before we could convince the inhabitants of remote villages in India or South America to apply it. This means that in all probability we will reach the figure of 7,000 million and then 12,000 million before the population increase can be arrested.

Given this increase in world population, it is permissible to ask whether the urban population must necessarily rise too. Could we not arrange to keep this population in the countryside? That is something quite out of the question. Man's belief in the freedom of the individual (which all peoples are coming to hold as firmly as their belief in human progress) makes it impossible for us to intervene directly in a man's decisions. We cannot say: "Live in the villages, even if you are not needed for rural work to produce food, which can today be produced by a reduced number of people."

The general increase in farm productivity will sustain the swelling of urban populations and the decrease of the rural population. The result will be that, in a world population of 7,000 million in the year 2000, 5,000 million will be city dwellers. Consequently, the urban population will not simply have doubled, as is sometimes naively thought, but will have quadrupled. And when the world population reaches 12,000 million, the lowest levelling-off point, 10,000 million people will be city-dwellers, six or seven times the present number.

Let us now consider the third road open to us. Given the fact of the increase in the urban population, might it not be possible to restrict the growth of our cities by directing the surplus population to new towns? We should give this solution serious thought. We could, indeed, build new towns to absorb that population if the necessary funds were available; for such towns call for a bigger capital investment per head for fewer services, especially during the first few years, the first decades, the first generations, until they reach the size of our present-day cities.

But why do we want the new towns to reach the size of today's cities? The answer is that only towns of a certain size can give men a greater number of options. Some people will say that even a town of modest size can have a theatre and a hospital, and, indeed, towns of 50,000, 80,000 or 250,000 inhabitants (this last being the fashionable figure just now) will be attractive to a certain proportion of the population.

The answer to this argument is simple. There was a time when a man was presumably content in a village of 700 inhabitants, which could support a primary school. What people forgot was that such a village could well have insisted on having a secondary school, a vocational school, and a university for its children.

Some will still argue that small towns like this can even meet the cost of maintaining a theatre. But where is the man who will be content with just one theatre, on the model of the small cities of ancient Greece, where the theatre was only obliged to open its doors during important festivals? Might he not well prefer a city with five, ten or twenty theatres, where he could choose between various productions? And why would he be content with a hospital with 200 beds if his disease calls for the attention of a number of specialists, which only university centres are able to provide? In fact, we cannot logically conceive of a city of fixed size which can satisfy our needs. The larger a city the more the needs it serves, which is why people are increasingly attracted to cities.

Should we enlarge our present cities or should we build new ones? The answer is that, theoretically, we could build new ones, provided we make them at least as large as the present ones. In view, however, of the fact that the exodus is from small cities to large ones and

that, whatever the size of the new cities we wish to build, their actual construction is bound to take a considerable number of years – one, two or possibly three generations – the population flow will obviously be away from them. Consequently they will prove a failure, for we cannot possibly force these generations to accept dictated solutions to problems which involve their being told where they are to live.

So the answer to this difficult question is as follows: evolutionary and constructive forces will inevitably lead to the growth of cities of the present type in response to the need to satisfy all the requirements of the inhabitants. This does not mean that a certain number of cities of a new type will not be built, but the building of them will be difficult, and will affect only a small proportion of the population.

Thus we are led to the following conclusion: the most probable, logical and practical solution among the three we have been discussing is the progressive expansion of the present type of city as a result of the massive influx of an ever-increasing population.

TOWARDS ECUMENOPOLIS

Our present cities are developing into increasingly complex systems. Starting with the city which develops in concentric circles, we finally reach the one which is strung out along the main artery linking it up with the nearest town, port or coast. We thus pass naturally from the city we are familiar with to a system of cities linked together, forming an urban complex with great numbers of inhabitants.

This brings us at last to the following conclusions: under the growing pressures of these various forces – economic, biological, demographic, etc. – we are gradually creating a bigger and bigger system of settlements, a system which, left to develop blindly, can only worsen daily and eventually bring us to catastrophe. This system will very quickly assume world proportions. From the megalopolis we shall pass to cities extending over continents, and thence to Ecumenopolis, or world-city. Its advent is inevitable. Any strict analysis reveals that there is nothing logical, rational or practical we can do to avoid it.

Ecumenopolis will be shaped by the forces engendered in cities of the present type as they attract huge populations in the future; by great systems for transportation, the inevitable magnet for industry and other activities; and by forces of an aesthetic nature, such as the attraction exerted by the seaboard on increasing numbers of people.

People will want to enjoy aesthetic pleasures at home; they will want to be able to build their houses overlooking an attractive valley, or along the coast with beaches opening before them, even though the crowded city centre is some distance away. At the same time, we must bear in mind the attraction of the vast plains, where water abounds, where the climate is mild.

All the above allows us gradually to form an idea of what the universal city will look like. As a result of research conducted by the Athens Centre of Ekistics we can already imagine to some degree how it will appear within a century or a century and a half.

Ecumenopolis, this world-city that will englobe the whole of humanity, will be a frightening conurbation, but, as we made clear earlier, we have no evidence that enables us to conclude that a better sort of city can be created. Once we are convinced that this city is inevitable, we can only form one conclusion: if it is built on today's lines, according to present-day trends, it will be a city doomed to destruction, that which Lewis Mumford referred to some time ago as a necropolis – city of the dead.

There is still, of course, another road that could be followed: to avoid it altogether. But, as has been already pointed out, this is not a logical or practical solution. I would like to emphasize here that we have no reason to claim today that we know any more about the reasons why it would be a good thing to avoid establish-

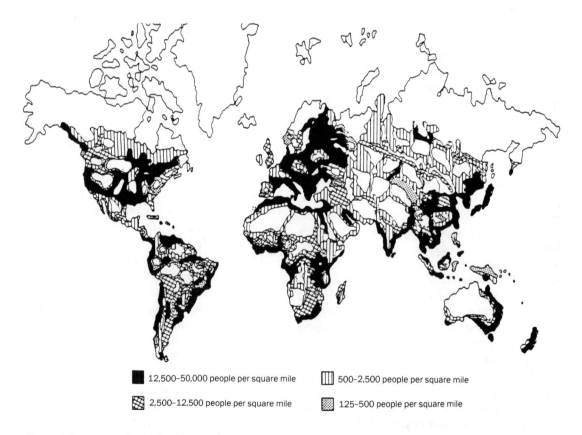

■ 12,500–50,000 people per square mile   ▥ 500–2,500 people per square mile

▨ 2,500–12,500 people per square mile   ▦ 125–500 people per square mile

Figure 2 Ecumenopolis, 100–150 years from now

ing a universal city than did the citizens of ancient Athens, about 3,000 years ago, when Theseus decided to concentrate the rural population in one town, the tiny city of Athens, with only a few thousand inhabitants. How could they tell then whether or not they should avoid establishing this initial town in the plain of Athens? Doubtless similar arguments were used then in favor of the scheme and against it as are used today in the case of the universal city.

It is high time we accepted our responsibilities and started working toward something which must be done right. To do this, we must understand that the real challenge does not lie in whether or not to create the world-city; it lies in creating it correctly, taking into account the human factor, so that man who, at present, sees his values disintegrating around him, may be able to find them again.

THE OUTLINES OF ECUMENOPOLIS

In the preceding sections of this study, I have tried above all to clarify the problem so it can be fully understood, for understanding is an essential condition for success. If we fail today to deal with this problem, it will be because we have not understood it.

In Athens we are presently applying ourselves to the collection of data on human settlements. This systematized knowledge forms an organized discipline which is becoming a science, called "ekistics" – the science of human settlements.

We must realize that ekistics cannot be restricted merely to understanding the problem; it must also lead to solutions for tomorrow. How is it that man in the past possessed the necessary strength, imagination and courage to build permanent settlements when he was still a hunter? How is it that he then went on to build villages, towns, industrial cities and metropolises? Why shouldn't we today have the necessary courage to conceive and build the world-city? To do it, we need, in addition to science, technology and art. Thus, we shall have to make ekistics a science, a technology and an art, all in one. If we set to work in this way, we

shall come to realize that we really can create Ecumenopolis. It is of no special importance to us to know exactly what the size of the city will be. For it will not make much difference to us that, going in certain directions, we would pass through hundreds of miles of urban centers. What will really matter is to know that, after a journey of ten or twenty minutes or of one to five hours, as the case may be, we can be certain of finding the country-side. When we see the problem in this light, we shall understand that size and shape are of no special concern; what matters is a proper balance between elements. We shall then affirm this conclusion; that nature must be converted into a gigantic network with tentacles penetrating deeply into all parts of the universal city so as to reach every residential area – a system of woodlands transformed into parks, intersected by avenues and gardens, within easy reach of our homes.

The size of a city should not worry us if we know that we can control the atmosphere and keep it unpolluted. There are small towns where the atmosphere is contaminated by a great number of cars and large towns where the atmosphere is clean. What is important is to ensure that pollution from industrial plants and vehicular traffic is under control. Then we will be able to breathe better air in a large city than we could in a small town without proper pollution control.

Proceeding in this way enables us to understand, little by little, how the elements of nature will penetrate the city. A similar approach can establish the nature of the various networks. Transportation problems have nothing whatever to do with the size of a city. They are the result of lack of organization and because we have not yet learned that men and machines cannot exist on the same footing.

Urban transportation will function properly when it is placed beneath the surface, like arteries in the human body. As soon as we grasp this fact, we can take the first steps in the right direction – indeed, we have already done so. At one time, water was carried in surface conduits; the same was true – and still is in many places – of sewage drains; overhead electric and telephone wires are still a common sight.

The day will come when all such installations

will be below the surface. Goods will be transported through underground tubes. Some of these already exist. In Canada, important networks of the kind are under construction for the transport of industrial products.

In the near future, no one will object to using underground roadways, just as no one made objections when the subways began transporting people at speeds of 15–20 miles an hour in London, Paris and New York, considerably faster than they had been used to in their horse-drawn cabs. Before very long, we shall be travelling underneath our cities at speeds of 60–200 miles an hour, spending perhaps between 5 and 10 minutes below ground, instead of driving for hours on roads, constantly irritated by the stop and go of traffic lights.

These new transportation networks will be much more satisfactory and will make it possible to have cities spread over very much wider areas while being much better organized.

When this programme has been carried out, we will then attain the solution which is of prime importance to us: freeing the surface of the earth for man to enjoy and to use for the development of his artistic gifts. In a word, the earth's surface will be used in harmony with man's way of life. We harken back thus to the time, thousands of years ago, when man was both a researcher and a guinea-pig in the vast laboratory of life and did the experiments which enabled him to build throughout the world those beautiful cities which we still admire: ancient Athens, Florence, the old Paris and old London, as well as Williamsburg in the United States. An intrinsic worth attached to these cities because they had been built on a human scale, to man's own measurements.

A careful study of the cities of the past shows that they never exceeded more than about 1 mile in length or about 1.5 square miles in area, and included no more than 50,000 inhabitants, when they were at their most successful. Cities which were much bigger were, in fact, the capitals of large empires and were never able to retain their organization for very long. They often deteriorated into anarchy, as in the case of Rome and Byzantium. If they hoped to sustain an organized and integral life of their own, they had to be carefully planned from the start, like Peking and Changan (modern Sian), two ancient Chinese capitals.

Generally, then, any cities which exceeded the usual, the reasonable maxima were doomed to fail, were short-lived, and offer us no solution. Those that do offer a solution were the small cities of 30,000 to 50,000 inhabitants, covering an area of about 1.5 square miles. If we examine their structure rationally, we shall realize that we must return to something similar if we want to organize our life properly.

We thus reach what seems to be a paradox: on the one hand, the inevitable huge Ecumenopolis; on the other, the absolute need for man to live in small cities. But this only appears paradoxical. For following such reasonings to their logical conclusion, we arrive at a gigantic city of superhuman dimensions, made up of small units.

Thus, our thought processes have led us to the construction of huge cities composed of small towns, of vast urban complexes served by underground transportation systems, leaving the surface of the ground free, at man's disposal, and supplied with every human amenity. The conclusion we reach then is that Ecumenopolis, the world-city, will be made up of cells of 30,000 to 50,000 people.

In practice, we are already beginning to build such cities. Islamabad, the new capital of Pakistan, intended for 2.5 million inhabitants, has been laid out in this way. Before such cities are even finished, life there is already in full swing and anyone can go and study them in operation. It is very important to keep on studying them until they have been brought to perfection. Then, by applying similar principles, it will be possible to transform some of the older cities.

Indeed, these principles have been applied to certain limited areas or even to certain cities which are planning the organization of the entire system on this sound basis. One example is Philadelphia (United States), which is now engaged in a gradual urban renewal project which will house 10,000 families on ground once covered with slums. There is also the immense urban region of Detroit, now in course of development and planned to accommodate by the year 2000 more than 10 million inhabitants enjoying maximum amenities.

So, after examining the nature of the crisis of the cities and the various escapist solutions, we have gradually synthesized a solution. This solution enables us to envisage the development of human settlements in a practical manner and to build in such a way as to offer men a much happier form of existence by combining the advantages of the small towns of old – which were certainly considerable from the point of view of a humane way of life – with those of the large cities which alone are capable of enlarging our freedoms and chances of development.

PETER CALTHORPE

"The Pedestrian Pocket"

from Doug Kelbaugh (ed.), *The Pedestrian Pocket Book* (1989)

Editors' introduction   Peter Calthorpe (born 1949) is an urban futurist very much rooted in both the realities of the present and the traditions of the past. As a practicing architect who also teaches at the University of California, Berkeley, Calthorpe is a successful designer/builder engaged in the ever-expanding housing market of the suburban areas of northern California. And as a leading proponent of ecology and environmentalism as applied to urban design, he is a prophet of a new kind of twenty-first-century community, the "Pedestrian Pocket," that is descended directly from Ebenezer Howard's Garden Cities (p. 346).

Working as a researcher for the California Energy Commission and the United States Department of Energy, Calthorpe wrote extensively and lectured around the world on the necessity of ecologically sensitive design and energy-efficient building based on the application of passive solar techniques. For a time, he was a partner of Sim Van der Ryn, the California state architect in the administration of progressive governor Jerry Brown. Together, they published *Sustainable Communities*, an influential volume that helped spread the ideas of solar energy, recycling, appropriate technology, and environmentalist approaches to urban planning and design. And in a chapter of that book entitled "A Short History of Twentieth-Century New Towns," Calthorpe addressed the development of the modern urban planning tradition from the original visions of Howard, through the contributions of Le Corbusier and Frank Lloyd Wright, to the prophetic postmodernism of Leon Krier and others. What was needed, the article seemed to say, was a viable alternative to the modernist urban planning trap of problematic inner cities surrounded by the cultural wasteland of sprawl suburbia.

In *The Pedestrian Pocket Book*, Calthorpe examines the "profound mismatch between the old suburban patterns ... and the post-industrial culture in which we now find ourselves," and the similarities between his solution and the one proposed by Howard in 1898 are striking. Both the Garden Cities and the Pedestrian Pockets are surrounded by greenbelts of permanent agricultural land. Both are relatively dense developments, allowing residents to walk to the urban center in a short period of time. Both combine residential, commercial, and workplace elements; and where the Garden City was served by a railroad connection, the Pedestrian Pocket avoids the typical suburban monoculture of the automobile by a system of light-rail transit connectors.

Although the source of the Pedestrian Pocket is the Garden City, the real application of the Calthorpe plan will be – indeed, already is – in the blossoming new ring of suburban development currently springing up around the old metropolitan cores, the area that journalist Joel Garreau has dubbed "Edge City" and which Robert Fishman calls "technoburbs" (p. 485). In his most recent book, *The Next American Metropolis*, Calthorpe has further refined and matured the pedestrian pocket idea to fit the emerging realities of Edge City technoburbia with what he calls TODs or "transit-oriented developments." Calthorpe is the most practical of urban visionaries because his visions represent "a response to a transformation that has already expressed itself: the transformation from the industrial forms of segregation and centralization to the decentralized and integrated forms of the post-industrial era." This, he writes, is the result of "a culture adjusting itself" to new realities.

Andres Duany and Elizabeth Plater-Zyberk, Jaime Correa, Steven Peterson and Barbara Littenberg, Mark Schimmenti, Daniel Solomon and a number of other architects and planners are designing human-scale communities with design aspects similar to the ones Calthorpe espouses. Because their architecture draws on traditional small-town elements these architects are sometimes referred to as neotraditionalists; their work as "the new urbanism."

This selection is from Doug Kelbaugh (ed.), *The Pedestrian Pocket Book* (Princeton, N.J.: Princeton Architectural Press, 1989). Other books by Peter Calthorpe include *Sustainable Communities* (San Francisco: Sierra Club Books, 1986) co-edited with Sim Van der Ryn, and *The Next American Metropolis* (Princeton, N.J.: Princeton Architectural Press, 1993).

Peter Katz, *The New Urbanism: Towards an Architecture of Community* (New York: McGraw-Hill, 1994) provides an overview of designs by Peter Calthorpe and other of the "new urbanists." See also James Howard Kunstler's *The Geography of Nowhere* (New York: Simon & Schuster, 1993) for a lively description of Calthorpe and other new urbanists' work.

PETER CALTHORPE, "The Pedestrian Pocket"
from **Doug Kelbaugh (ed.), *The Pedestrian Pocket Book* (1989)**

There is a profound mismatch between the old suburban patterns of settlement we have evolved since World War II and the post-industrial culture in which we now find ourselves. This mismatch is generating traffic congestion, a dearth of affordable and appropriate housing, environmental stress, a loss of open space, and lifestyles that burden working families and isolate the elderly and singles living alone. This mismatch has two primary sources: a dramatic shift in the nature and location of our work place and a fundamental deviation in the character of our increasingly diverse households.

Traffic congestion in the suburbs signals a strong change in the structure of our culture. The computer and service industries have led to the decentralization of the work place, causing new traffic patterns and "suburban gridlock." Where downtown employment once dominated, suburb-to-suburb traffic now produces greater commuting distances and time. Throughout the country, over 40 percent of all commuting trips are now between suburbs.

These new patterns have seriously eroded the quality of life in formerly quiet suburban towns. In the San Francisco Bay area, for example, 212 of the region's 812 miles of suburban freeway are regularly backed up during rush hours. That figure is projected to double within the next twelve years. As a result, recent polls have traffic continually heading the list as the primary regional problem, with the difficulty of finding good affordable housing running a close second.

Home ownership has become a troublesome – if not unattainable – goal, even with our double-income families. Affordable housing grows ever more elusive, and families have had to move to less expensive but more peripheral sites, consuming irreplaceable agricultural land and overloading roads. In 1970 about half of all families could meet the expense of a median-priced single-family home; today less than a quarter can.

Moreover, the basic criteria for housing have changed dramatically as single occupants, single parents, the elderly, and small double-income families redefine the traditional home. Our old suburbs were designed around a stereotypical household which is no longer prevalent. Over 73 percent of the new households in the 1980s lack at least one component of the traditional husband, wife and children model. Elderly people over 65 make up 23 percent of the total number of new homeowners, and single parents represent an astonishing 20 percent. Certainly the traditional three-bedroom, single-family residence is relevant to a decreasing segment of the population. The suburban dream becomes even more complicated when one considers the problem of affordability.

In addition to these dominant questions of traffic and housing, longer-range consequences of pollution, air quality, open-space preservation, the conversion of prime agricultural land, and growing infrastructure costs add to the crisis of post-industrial sprawl. These issues are manifested in a growing sense of frustration – placelessness – with the fractured quality of our suburban megacenters. The unique qualities of place are continually consumed by chain-store architecture, scaleless office parks and monotonous subdivisions.

THE SERVICE ECONOMY: DRIVING DECENTRALIZATION

As new jobs have shifted from blue collar to white and grey, the computer has allowed the decentralization of the new service industries into mammoth low-rise office parks on inexpensive and often remote sites. The shift is dramatic: from 1973 to 1985 five million blue-collar jobs were lost nationwide while the service and information fields gained from 82 to 110 million jobs. This translated directly into new office complexes, with 1.1 billion square feet of office space constructed. Nationwide, these complexes have moved outside the central cities, with the percentage of total office space in the suburbs shifting from 25 percent in 1970 to 57 percent in 1984.

Central to this shift is a phenomenon called the "back office," the new sweatshop of the post-industrial economy. The typical back office is large, often with a single floor area of one to two acres. About 80 percent of its employees are clerical, 12 percent supervisory and only 8 percent managerial. In a survey of criteria for back-office locations, forty-seven major Manhattan corporations ranked cost of space first, followed by the quality of the labor pool and site safety. These criteria lead directly to the suburbs where land is inexpensive, parking is easy, and (most importantly) the work force is supplemented by housewives – college-educated, poorly paid, nonunionized, and dependable.

This low-density office explosion has rejuvenated suburban growth just as urban "gentrification" has run its course. The young urban professional has recently made a family commitment and feels the draw of the suburbs. Most of the growth areas in the United States – office parks, shopping malls and single-family dwelling sub-divisions – have a suburban character. Although such growth continually seems to reach the limits of automobile congestion and building moratoriums, there are no readily available alternatives that will enrich the dialogue between growth and no-growth factions, between public benefit and private gain, between the environmentalist and the businessperson.

THE PEDESTRIAN POCKET: A POST-INDUSTRIAL SUBURB

Single-function land-use zoning at a scale and density that eliminates the pedestrian has been the norm for so long that Americans have forgotten that walking can be part of their daily lives. Certainly, the present suburban environment is not walkable, much to the detriment of children, their chauffeur parents, the elderly, and the general health of the population. Urban redevelopment is a strong and compelling alternative to the suburban world but does not seem to fit the character or aspirations of major parts of our population and of many businesses. Mixed-use New Towns are no alternative, as the political consensus needed to back the massive infrastructure investments is lacking. By default, growth is directed mainly by the location of new freeway systems, the economic strength of the region and standard single-use zoning practices. Environmental and local opposition to growth only seems to spread the problem, either transferring the congestion to the next county or creating lower and more auto-dependent densities.

Much smaller than a New Town, the Pedestrian Pocket is defined as a balanced, mixed-use area within a quarter-mile or a five-minute walking radius of a transit station. The functions within this 50- to 100-acre zone include housing, offices, retail, day care, recreation, and parks. Up to two thousand units of housing and one million square feet of office space can be located within three blocks of the transit station using typical residential densities and four-story office configurations.

The Pedestrian Pocket accommodates the car as well as transit and walking. Parking is provided for all housing and commercial space. The housing types are standard low-rise, high-density forms such as three-story walk-up apartments and two-story townhouses. Only the interrelationships and adjacent land use have changed. People have a choice: walk to work or to stores within the Pedestrian Pocket; take the light rail to work or to shop at another station; car pool on a dedicated right-of-way; drive on crowded freeways. In a small Pedestrian Pocket, homes are within walking distance of a neighborhood shopping center, several three-acre parks, day care, various services, and two thousand jobs. Within four stops of the light rail in either direction (ten minutes), employment is available for 16,000, or the amount of back-office growth equivalent to that of one of the nation's highest-growth suburbs over the last five years.

This mix of uses supports a variety of transportation means: walking, bus, light rail, car pool, and standard automobile. The goal is to create an environment that offers choices. Providing comfortable mid-day pedestrian access to retail, services, recreation, and civic functions is essential in order to encourage people to car pool. Similarly, the location of the station, whether bus or rail, near home or work and the realistic opportunity to handle errands without a car are tied to an individual's decision to use mass transit. A Pocket configuration that allows easy access by car to all commercial and residential development maintains the freedom of choice. The result is the best of both worlds.

The Pedestrian Pocket is located on a dedicated right-of-way which evolves with the development. Rather than bearing the large cost of a complete rail system as an initial expense, this right-of-way facilitates mass transit by providing exclusively for car pools, van pools, bikes, and buses. As the cluster matures, transit investments are made for light rail in the developed right-of-way. But the growth of this land-use pattern is not dependent on this investment; the system is designed to support many modes of traffic and to phase light rail into place when the population is great enough to support it.

The Pedestrian Pocket system would eventually act in concert with new light rail lines, reinforcing ridership and connecting existing employment centers, towns and neighborhoods with new development. Light rail lines are currently under construction in many suburban environments, such as, in California alone, Sacramento, San Jose, San Diego, Long Beach, and Orange County. They emphasize the economies of using existing right-of-ways and a simpler, more cost-effective technology than heavy rail. In creating a line of Pedestrian Pockets, the public sector's role is merely to organize the transit system and set new zoning guidelines, leaving development to the private sector. Much of the cost of the transit line can be covered by assessing the property owners benefiting from the increased densities.

The light rails in current use provide primarily a park-and-ride system to connect low-density sprawl with downtown commercial areas. In contrast, the Pedestrian Pocket system is decentralized, linking many nodes of high-density housing with many commercial destinations. Peak-hour traffic is multidirectional, reducing congestion and making the system more efficient. Bus systems, along with car-pool systems, can tie into the light rail. Several of the Pockets on a line have large parking facilities for park-and-ride access, allowing the existing suburban development to enjoy the services and opportunities of the Pockets. However, the location of the office, stores and services adjacent to the station and each other avoids the need for secondary mass transit or additional large parking areas.

The importance of the Pedestrian Pocket is that it provides balanced growth in jobs, housing, and services, while creating a healthy mass-transit alternative for the existing community. The key lies in the form and mix of the Pocket. The pedestrian path system must be carefully designed and form a primary order for the place. If this is configured to allow the pedestrian comfortable and safe access, up to 50 percent of a household's typical automobile trips can be replaced by walking, car pool and light rail journeys. Not only does this produce a better living environment within the Pocket, but the reduction of traffic in the region is significant and in many cases essential.

HOUSING: DIVERSITY IN NEEDS AND MEANS

Housing in the Pedestrian Pocket is planned to provide each of the primary household types with affordable homes that meet their needs. Families with children, single parents or couples need an environment in which kids can move safely, in which day care is integrated into the neighborhood, and in which commuting time is reduced. The townhouses and duplexes proposed for the Pedestrian Pocket allow these families to have all this as well as an attached garage, land ownership and a small private yard. These building types are more affordable to build and maintain than their detached counterparts yet still offer individual ownership and a private identity. The common open space, recreation, day care, and convenient shopping render these houses even more desirable. Group play areas are located off the townhouses' private yards and are connected to the central park and the commercial section by paths. One-third of the housing in a Pocket is of this type.

For singles and "empty-nesters," traditional two- and three-story apartment buildings or condominiums keep costs down while allowing access to the civic facilities, retail services and recreational amenities of the extended community. This segment of the population is traditionally more mobile and thus has an option of either rental or ownership housing. Elderly housing is located close to the parks, light rail and service retail; this eliminates some of the distance and alienation typical of housing facilities for the elderly. The housing is formed into courtyard clusters of two-story buildings which provide a private retreat area and the capacity for common facilities for dining and social activities. Residence in a pedestrian community allows the elderly to become a part of our everyday culture again and to enjoy the parks, stores, and restaurants close at hand.

Several parks double as paths to the station area, a route which is pleasant and free of automobile crossings. The housing overlooking the parks provides security surveillance and twenty-four-hour activity. Each Pocket offers a different arrangement of day-care buildings and general recreational facilities in its parks. Although the housing forms small clusters, the central park and facilities tend to unify the neighborhood, giving it an identity and commonality missing in most of our suburban tracts. An organization (much like a condominium homeowner's organization), which includes landlords, townhouse owners, tenants, office managers, and worker representatives, maintains the centers.

The goal of this tight mix of housing and open space is not just to provide more appropriate homes for the different users or to offer the convenience of walking but hopefully to reintegrate the currently separated age and social groups of our diverse culture. The shared common spaces and local stores may create a rebirth of our lost sense of community and place.

COMMERCE AND COMMUNITY

Jobs are the fuel of new growth, of which the service and high-technology fields are the spearhead. For example, the San Francisco Bay region has currently about 63 percent of all its jobs in these areas. That percentage is expected to increase in the next twenty years, adding about 200,000 new jobs in high technology and 370,000 new jobs in service. Retail activity and housing growth always follow in proportion to these primary income generators. The Pedestrian Pocket provides a framework that allows jobs and housing to grow in tandem.

The commercial buildings in the Pocket offer retail opportunities at their ground floor and offices above. The retail stores enjoy the local walk-in trade from offices and housing, as well as exposure to light rail and drive-in customers. All the stores face a "Main Street" on which the light rail line, the station and convenience parking for cars are mixed. This multiple exposure and access, along with the abundance of office workers, creates a strong market for the theaters, library, post office, food stores, and other convenience stores located in the one hundred thousand square feet of retail.

The offices above the retail stores provide space for small entrepreneurial businesses, start-up firms and local community services. Behind these offices, parking structures capable of accommodating one-half the workers in all the commercial space are located. Presumably, the other half of the employees walk, car pool, or arrive by light rail.

There is a 500,000 to 1,000,000 square foot potential in two to four office buildings per Pedestrian Pocket. These four-story buildings, with 60,000 square feet per floor, fit the size and cost criteria of most back-office employers. The buildings form a courtyard open to the station on one side and the park on the other. Office employees share day-care facilities and open space with the neighborhood.

The commercial mix attempts to balance housing with a desirable job market, stores, entertainment, and services. But the commercial facilities and the offices are not entirely financially dependent on the local housing; access by automobile from the existing neighborhoods and by light rail from other Pockets augments the market. Similarly the transportation system makes a pool of employees available from a twenty-mile range.

REGIONAL PLANNING AND THE PEDESTRIAN POCKET

Pedestrian Pockets are not meant to stand alone as developments; they are intended to form a network offering long-range growth within a region. They will vary considerably given the complexities of place and their internal makeup. Some may be larger than the sixty-acre model we've been using as an example: the quarter-mile walking radius actually encloses 120 acres. Pockets may offer different focuses, with one providing a regional shopping center, one, a cultural center, or a third, housing and recreation. Some may be used as redevelopment tools to provide economic incentives in a depressed area; others may rejuvenate an aging shopping area; the remaining Pockets may be located in new areas zoned for low-density sprawl and in this way save much of the land from more drastic development.

Pockets and their rail lines also connect to the existing assets of an area. The system links the major towns, office parks, shopping areas, and government facilities and allows those from earlier communities to gain access to the Pocket system. Many new light rail systems, built only to connect existing low-density development, are experiencing some resistance from people not wanting to leave their cars. The importance of rezoning for a comfortable walking distance from house to station is to ease people out of their cars, to give them an alternative which is convenient and pleasing. There is evidence that in time such planning will succeed: in a study of San Francisco's rail transit system, BART, it was discovered that fully 40 percent of those who lived and worked within a five-minute walk of the station used the train to get to work.

To test this regional planning concept I chose an area north of San Francisco, combining Marin and Sonoma counties. Many consider the area prime turf for new post-industrial sprawl. Sonoma is projected to have a 61 percent growth in employment in the next twenty years, the highest in the Bay region. Combined, these two counties are to grow by about 88,000 jobs and 63,000 households in the next fifteen years. Of the new jobs, around 60,000 will be in the service, high-technology and knowledge fields, the equivalent of twenty million square feet of office and light industrial space. With standard planning techniques, this growth will consume massive quantities of open space and necessitate a major expansion of the freeway system. The result will still involve frustrating traffic jams.

Instead, twenty Pedestrian Pockets along a new light rail line accommodate this office growth with matching retail facilities, businesses and approximately 30,000 new houses. Several additional pockets dedicated primarily to homes allow two-thirds of the area's housing demand to be met while linking the counties' main cities with a viable mass-transit system. A recently acquired, Northwestern Pacific railroad abandoned right-of-way, which would connect a San Francisco ferry terminal to the northernmost county seat, forms the spine for such a new pattern of growth.

SOCIAL AND ENVIRONMENTAL FORM

It is easy to talk quantitatively about the physical and environmental consequences of our new sprawl but very difficult to postulate their social implications. Many argue that there is no longer a causal relationship between the structure of our physical environment and that of our human well-being or social health. We are adaptable, they claim, and our communities form around interest groups and work rather than around any sense of place or group of individuals. Our center is abstract, not grounded in place, and our social forms are disconnected from home and neighborhood. Planners complicate the issue by polarizing urban and suburban forms. Some advocate a rigorous return to traditional city forms and almost pre-industrial culture, while others praise the evolution of the suburban megalopolis as the inevitable and desirable expression of our new technologies and hyper-individualized culture. However rationalized, these new forms have a restless and hollow feel, reinforcing our mobile state and the instability of our families. Moving at a speed that allows only generic symbols to be recognized, we cannot wonder that the man-made environment seems trite and overstated.

In proposing the Pedestrian Pocket the practical comes first; the Pedestrian Pocket preserves land, energy and resources, reduces traffic, renders homes more affordable, allows children and the elderly more access to services, and decreases commuting time for working people. The social consequences are less quantitative but perhaps equally compelling. They have to do with the quality of our shared world.

Mobility and privacy have increasingly displaced the traditional commons, which once provided the connected quality of our towns and cities. Our shared public space has been given over to the car and its accommodation, while our private world has become bloated and isolated. As our private world grows in breadth, our public world becomes more remote and impersonal. As a result, our public space lacks identity and is largely anonymous, while our private space strains toward a narcissistic autonomy. Our communities are zoned black or white, private or public, my space or nobody's. The automobile destroys the urban street, the shopping center destroys the neighborhood store, and the depersonalization of public space grows with the scale of government. Inversely, private space is taxed by the necessity of providing for many activities that were once shared and is further burdened by the need to create identity in a sea of monotony. Although the connection between such social issues and development is elusive and complex, it must be addressed by any serious theory of growth.

In one way, Pedestrian Pockets are utopian – they involve the directed choice of an ideal rather than of laissez-faire planning, and they make certain assumptions about social well-being. But by not assuming a transformation of our society or its people, they avoid the full label, and its subsequent pitfalls, of most utopian schemes. They represent instead a response to a transformation that has already expressed itself: the transformation from the industrial forms of segregation and centralization to the decentralized and integrated forms of the post-industrial era. And perhaps, Pedestrian Pockets express the positive environmental and social results of a culture adjusting itself to this new reality.

MANUEL CASTELLS and PETER HALL

"Technopoles: Mines and Foundries of the Informational Economy"

from *Technopoles of the World* (1994)

Editors' introduction   Approaching the twenty-first century, the world is experiencing a revolution in high technology as profound as the Industrial Revolution of the nineteenth century. Technology and science parks and even entire cities built around high technology are emerging around the world. Unlike nineteenth-century cities, which produced manufactured goods such as textiles, steel, or lumber, these new centers produce information and innovative ideas.

An astute observer of Manchester, England, at the beginning of the Industrial Revolution could discern the outlines of a new physical form, social structure, and economy unlike any prior city of that time. Today careful studies of California's Silicon Valley, Japan's "technopolis sites," France's science city of Sophia-Antipolis and other "mines and foundries of the information age" can inform our understanding of what many technology-driven cities of the future may be like. Spanish sociologist-planner Manuel Castells and British geographer-planner Peter Hall are engaged in just such studies. They have literally traveled the world studying technology centers. Castells and Hall suggest the French word "technopole" to describe cities or areas within cities devoted to research and innovation in high technology.

What technopoles are like is of more than academic interest as countries around the world scramble to promote successful high-tech cities which can function effectively as milieux of innovation. Where they have succeeded, technopoles have provided jobs, wealth, and future prospects. But the globe is also littered with failed efforts to promote such cities based more on boosterism and hope than careful analysis and realism.

Technopoles are startlingly different from the cutting edge cities of the industrial era. Clean and populated mainly by an affluent elite, they have little in common with Manchester and other gritty nineteenth-century industrial cities with their pollution and wretched slum areas hidden from the grand boulevards and fashionable sections frequented by the rich, as depicted by Engels (p. 47).

Note the parallels between this selection and Saskia Sassen's description of cities in the global economy (pp. 70, 300). Like Sassen, the authors of this selection found no evidence that the largest global cities such as London, New York, and Tokyo are withering; indeed, they are milieus of innovation in their own rights. Compare Castells and Hall's description of technopoles which were consciously designed as centers for advanced technology with Robert Fishman's description of the more diffuse technoburbs growing spontaneously in many metropolitan areas (p. 485).

This selection is taken from Castells and Hall, *Technopoles of the World* (London: Routledge, 1994). Other writings on high technology and urbanization by these authors include Manuel Castells (ed.), *High Technology, Space, and Society* (Beverly Hills and London: Sage, 1985) and Ann Markusen, Peter Hall, and Amy Glasmeier, *High-Tech America: The What, How, Where and Why of* the Sunrise Industries (Boston: George Allen & Unwin, 1986).

MANUEL CASTELLS and PETER HALL, "Technopoles: Mines and Foundries of the Informational Economy"

from *Technopoles of the World* (1994)

There is an image of the nineteenth-century industrial economy, familiar from a hundred history textbooks: the coal mine and its neighboring iron foundry, belching forth black smoke into the sky, and illuminating the night heavens with its lurid red glare. There is a corresponding image for the new economy that has taken its place in the last years of the twentieth century, but it is only just imprinting itself on our consciousness. It consists of a series of low, discreet buildings, usually displaying a certain air of quiet good taste, and set amidst impeccable landscaping in that standard real-estate cliche, a campus-like atmosphere.

Scenes like these are now legion on the periphery of virtually every dynamic urban area in the world. They appear so physically similar – outside Cambridge, England, or Cambridge, Massachusetts; Mountain View, California, or Munich, Germany – that the hapless traveler, dropped by parachute, would hardly guess the identity of the country, let alone the city. The developments they represent go under a bewildering variety of names, which invariably permute a few key elements like Techno, Science, Twenty-first Century, Park, Plaza, Polis, and -topia. In France, where there are certainly as many of them as anywhere else, they go under a generic name, *technopole*. It is so evocative that in this book we have decided to appropriate it for the English language.

Generally, technopoles are planned developments. Some are pure private sector real-estate investments, and these happen to be among the most numerous but least interesting. A significant number, however, have resulted from various kinds of cooperation or partnership between the public and private sectors. They are promoted by central or regional or local governments, often in association with universities, together with the private companies that occupy the resulting spaces. And these technopoles, the more interesting ones, are invariably more than just plots to rent. They also contain significant institutions of a quasi-public or nonprofit type, such as universities or research institutes, which are specifically implanted there in order to help in the generation of new information. For this is the function of the technopole: it is to generate the basic materials of the informational economy.

Quite a number of the people in the buildings of these new technopoles do not usually make anything, though somewhere else, often not many miles away, in rather similar buildings – sometimes of slightly less elegance – other people are making the things they invent here. The things may be computers or VCRs or CD players, word processing or spreadsheet software, artificial systems, high-technology ceramics, genetically engineered drugs, or a thousand other new products. What the things have in common is that they embody information that has essentially been created here. These high-technology products – hardware and software, bulky products and almost immaterial ones – are the products and symbols of a new economy, the informational economy. The information they embody has been created in technopoles, and invariably the embodiment of the information into the products also occurs in technopoles, which thus constitute the mines and foundries of the informational age.

The informational economy has been less noticed than the industrial economy it is replacing, and technopoles have had less attention from academic analysts than factories and mills. Though there are books about science parks in individual countries, and isolated articles about bigger experiments like the Japanese technopolis program, there is no account that tries to bring together, in one descriptive-analytic account, the most important ventures in constructing technopoles worldwide.

This book has been written to try to fill that gap. In order to write it, we have literally traveled the world – from Silicon Valley to Siberia, from the Côte d'Azur of France to the middle of Korea, from South Australia to Andalucia. We have intensively studied more than a dozen technopoles worldwide: some long-developed and mature, some hardly even begun; some wildly successful, some apparent failures. In this book we try to tell how each began, how it has taken shape, what it is trying to achieve, and how well it has succeeded. And then we try to sum up our experience.

To start, however, we need to understand the true significance of the technopole phenomenon. These developments have not suddenly sprouted by some kind of accident, or just because of a passing fashion. On the contrary: they are deliberate attempts, by farseeing public and private actors, to help control and guide some exceedingly fundamental transformations that have recently begun to affect society, economy, and territory, and are beginning to redefine the conditions and processes of local and regional development.

THREE CONTEMPORARY ECONOMIC REVOLUTIONS

Technopoles in fact explicitly commemorate the reality that cities and regions are being profoundly modified in their structure, and conditioned in their growth dynamics, by the interplay of three major, interrelated, historical processes:

1 A technological revolution, mainly based in information technologies (including genetic engineering), at least as momentous historically as the two industrial revolutions based on the discovery of new sources of energy.

2 The formation of a global economy: that is, the structuring of all economic processes on a planetary scale, even if national boundaries and national governments remain essential elements and key actors in the strategies played out in international competition. By a global economy we understand one that works in real time as a unit in a worldwide space, be it for capital, management, labor, technology, information or markets. Even firms that are anchored in and aimed at domestic markets depend on the dynamics and logic of the world economy through the intermediation of their customers, suppliers, and competitors. The acceleration of the process of European integration and the creation of the new European Economic Area emphasize these tendencies towards globalization and interdependence in the world economy.

3 The emergence of a new form of economic production and management, that – in common with a number of economists and sociologists – we term informational. It is characterized by the fact that productivity and competitiveness are increasingly based on the generation of new knowledge and on the access to, and processing of, appropriate information. As the pioneer work of Robert Solow and the subsequent stream of econometric research by the "aggregate production function" school of thought have shown, the last half-century has been characterized by a new equation in the generation of productivity, and thus of economic growth. Instead of the quantitative addition of capital, labor, and raw material, typical of the function of productivity growth in both agrarian and industrial economies, the new economy, emerging in advanced industrial countries since the 1950s, has increasingly depended for its productivity growth on what econometric equations label the "statistical residual," which most experts translate in terms of the inputs from science, technology, and the management of information in the production process. It is this recombination of factors, rather than the addition of factors, that appears to be critical for the generation of wealth in our economy.

Furthermore, the informational economy seems to be characterized by new organizational forms. Horizontal networks substitute for vertical bureaucracies as the most productive form of organization and management. Flexible specialization replaces standardized mass production as the new industrial form best able to adapt to the variable geometry of changing world demand and versatile cultural values. This is not equivalent, as it is sometimes argued, to saying that small and medium businesses are the most productive forms of the new economy. Major multinational corporations continue to be the strategic nerve centers of the economy, and some of its most innovative actors. What is changing is the organizational form, both for large corporations and small businesses. Networks are the critical form for the flexible process of production. They include networks between large firms, between small and large firms, between small firms themselves, and within large firms that are decentralizing their internal structure, breaking it up in quasi-independent units, as so dramatically illustrated by the recent restructuring of IBM to offset its losses.

INFORMATION AND INNOVATION

These three processes are interlinked. The informational economy is a global economy because the productive capacity generated by the new productive forces needs constant expansion in a world market dominated by a new hierarchy of economic power, which is decisively dependent on information and technology, and is less and less conditioned – nonrenewable energy sources temporarily excepted – by the cost of labor and raw materials. The technological revolution provides the necessary infrastructure for the process of formation of the global, informational economy, and it is fostered by the functional demands generated by this economy. New information technologies are critical for the processes and forms of the new economy, on at least three levels.

First, they provide the material basis for the integration of economic processes worldwide, while keeping the necessary organizational flexibility for such processes. For instance, microelectronics-based manufacturing allows advanced standardization of parts of a given industrial product, produced in various locations, for assembly near the final market, while providing the necessary flexibility for producing in short runs or in large quantities, depending upon changing demand. The increasing integration of telecommunications and computing forms the technological infrastructure of the new global economy, as railways provided the material basis for the formation of national markets in nineteenth-century industrialization.

Second, industrial producers of new technologies have been the fastest growing sectors in the world economy in the last 25 years, and in spite of business cycles they have certainly not yet reached their mature stage, driven as they are by constant innovation. Thus, such sectors play the role of growth engines for the development of countries and regions, with their greatest potential at the upper levels of the technological ladder, in industries characterized by a strict spatial division of labor between the innovation function, advanced fabrication, assembly, testing, and customized production. The more countries and regions are able to generate the development of these new, technologically-advanced industries, the greater their economic potential in the global competition.

Third, this information-driven technological transformation of the global economy requires a rapid modernization process of all sectors of the economy so that they are able to compete in an open economy. Thus, whether we consider the fate of nations, regions, or cities, technological diffusion becomes even more critical than the development of high-technology production.

In theory, such technological modernization could proceed quite independently from the design and production of advanced technological devices. However, empirical evidence shows that the technological potential of countries and regions is directly related to their ability to produce, indeed manufacture, the most advanced technological products, which constitute technological inputs that condition the improvement of products and processes in downstream industries. This is for three reasons:

1 Technological innovation, and the application of such innovations, depends on the process of learning by doing, rather than off-the-shelf operation manuals. Thus, the greater the capacity of a country and region to design and produce advanced technological inputs, the greater its ability to adapt these technologies to productive processes elsewhere, creating a synergistic interaction between design, production, and utilization.

2 All technical division of labor becomes, over time, a social division of labor. This means that in a world governed by competition through comparative advantage, countries or regions specializing in the production of inputs that are required by other industrial structures have a definite advantage. The technological component of products thus becomes a decisive dividing line in the trade between countries. Following Ricardo's classical rule, Portugal specialized in wine and England in manufactured textiles; but, before long, the best port wine was the favorite drink of English gentlemen enriched by the product of their textile mills. In a similar manner, if Amstrad becomes a packaging and marketing device for Korean computer parts and ICL becomes a front store for Fujitsu, it may not be long before City of London stockbrokers will find that the trading language of their shopfloor has changed from English to Japanese, or perhaps Korean. The point is that the balance of competitive advantage in both these cases, and indeed in all cases in the long run, is with the technologically-advanced partner. Nations ignore this rule at their peril: importing other people's technologies in order to develop value-added services may employ a few people, but the resulting employment growth is likely to be both modest and highly volatile, as a comparison of the recent course of the Japanese and German economies with the British and American ones will amply demonstrate.

In sum, the technological basis of countries and regions becomes critical for growth because, ultimately, the deficit in the balance of trade between high-value, high-technology producers, and low-technology, low-value producers creates an untenable disequilibrium.

Research by Dosi and Soete on comparative trade patterns has demonstrated the fundamental role of high-technology manufacturing and the technological level of industrial sectors in international competitiveness. Thus, if countries or regions do not generate sufficient surplus to import and adapt new technologies, they will be unable to afford the imports necessary for the modernization of their traditional industries.

3 Third, the culture of the technologically-advanced, information-based society cannot be productively consumed if there is no significant level of innovation in the social fabric. To be sure, the middle classes in developing countries can buy VCRs and personal computers. But only in a country, in a region, in a locality, where innovative informational processes are taking place can the generation of new ideas and new forms of organization and management occur in a creative manner. In other words, what is characteristic of the new informational economy is its flexibility, its productive adaptation to the conditions and demands of each society, of each culture, of each organization. To replicate the industrial organization of standardized mass production in the informational age, merely by buying the use of the technology without truly using its potential, is like using word-processing capacity to standardize the work of typing pools, instead of automating the process and upgrading secretarial work to the programming of more complex tasks.

Technological innovation, the production of technologically-advanced devices, and technological diffusion cannot be entirely disjointed processes. Obviously not many regions in the world can excel in all three dimensions, and some inter-regional and international division of labor will always take place. However, no country or region can prosper without some level of linkage to sources of innovation and production. If this sounds an impossible task, it is because of an exceedingly simplistic notion about high-technology innovation and production. High technology is shorthand for a whole array of new products and processes that goes far beyond microelectronics, even if micro-electronics was the original core of the techno-logical revolution. Informatics (hard and soft), telecommunications, genetic engineering, advanced materials, renewable energy, specialty chemicals, information processing, bioelectron-ics, and so many other fields and subfields of technological innovation, advanced manufac-turing, and technological services, offer so many opportunities that the scope of the new industrial geography, with its different levels of specialization and its diversity of markets, is broader by far than that generally accepted.

CITIES AND REGIONS: THE NEW ECONOMIC ACTORS

What we are witnessing, then, is the emergence of a new industrial space, defined both by the location of the new industrial sectors and by the use of new technologies by all sectors. At the same time, such new industrial space is globally interdependent, both in inputs and markets, triggering a restructuring process of gigantic dimensions that is felt by cities and regions around the world.

Indeed, the most fascinating paradox is the fact that in a world economy whose productive infrastructure is made up of information flows, cities and regions are increasingly becoming critical agents of economic development: as Goodman puts it, the last entrepreneurs. Pre-cisely because the economy is global, national governments suffer from failing powers to act upon the functional processes that shape their economies and societies. But regions and cities are more flexible in adapting to the changing conditions of markets, technology, and culture. True, they have less power than national gov-ernments, but they have a greater response capacity to generate targeted development pro-jects, negotiate with multinational firms, foster the growth of small and medium endogenous firms, and create conditions that will attract the new sources of wealth, power, and prestige. In this process of generating new growth, they compete with each other; but, more often than not, such competition becomes a source of innovation, of efficiency, of a collective effort to create a better place to live and a more effective place to do business.

In their search for the new sources of eco-nomic growth and social wellbeing, cities and regions are stimulated both negatively and pos-itively by comparative international experience. Those areas that remain rooted in declining activities – be they manufacturing, agriculture, or services of the old, noncompetitive kind – become industrial ruins, inhabited by disconso-late, unemployed workers, and ridden by social discontents and environmental hazards. New countries and regions emerge as successful locales of the new wave of innovation and investment, sometimes emerging from deep agricultural torpor, sometimes in idyllic corners of the world that acquire sudden dynamism. Thus, Silicon Valley and Orange County in California; Arizona, Texas, Colorado, in the western United States; Bavaria in Germany; the French Midi, from Sophia-Antipolis via Mont-pellier to Toulouse; Silicon Glen in Scotland; the electronics agglomeration in Ireland; the new developments in southern Europe, from Bari to Málaga and Seville; and, above all, the newly industrializing countries of Asia (South Korea, Taiwan, Hong Kong, Singapore, Malaysia) that in two decades have leapt straight from being traditional agricultural societies – albeit with high levels of literacy and education – to being highly competitive economies based on strong electronics sectors.

Such role models, both positive and negative, have a dramatic influence on the collective consciousness of countries, regions, and local-ities, as well as on the development projects of their respective governments. Many regions in the industrialized and industrializing world have dreamed of becoming the next Silicon Valleys, and some of them went headlong into the business. A hasty, hurried study by an opportunistic consultant was at hand to provide the magic formula: a small dose of venture capital, a university (invariably termed a "Tech-nology Institute"), fiscal and institutional incen-tives to attract high-technology firms, and a degree of support for small business. All this, wrapped within the covers of a glossy brochure, and illustrated by a sylvan landscape with a futuristic name, would create the right conditions to out-perform the neighbors, to become the locus of the new major global industrial center. The world is now littered with the ruins of all too many such dreams that have failed, or have yielded meager results at far too high a cost. Indeed it would almost seem, as some scholars have argued, that the whole world has become gripped by "high-technology fantasies," which signify virtually nothing.

And yet, the late twentieth century has seen an undeniable major redistribution of technological innovation and industrial entrepreneurialism; the world's economic geography has very fundamentally changed. The fact that local and regional governments have stampeded to join the new model of development does demonstrate their perception that we are indeed in the midst of a transition to a new productive form, and that managing the process requires institutional initiatives working through and upon the market. True, image-making and high-technology ideology are pervasive elements of this new brand of regional policy. But this is because, for good or for ill, image-making has become a central basis for successful competition in our latter-day economy and culture. By trying positively to harness the new technologies to their own ends, localities and regions are asserting their control over events; they are vigorously denying that they are condemned to live within the old logic of spatial divisions of labor that locks them into particular functions determined by events long ago. As in any process of competition and entrepreneurial initiative, there will be creative destruction – as well as (with due apologies to Schumpeter) destructive creation, when a region bases its future on military-related high-technology production. Yet this drive to innovate and invest is successfully building new industrial spaces, and is thus producing a new and quite extraordinary wave of worldwide reindustrialization that denies the myths of postindustrialism.

TECHNOPOLES AND MILIEUX OF INNOVATION

This effort to innovate and develop *de novo* very often takes the form of creating and nurturing what we have called "technopoles." We need now a more precise definition; under this name we include various deliberate attempts to plan and promote, within one concentrated area, technologically innovative, industrial-related production: technology parks, science cities, technopolises and the like. Our study will try to assess how these different developments perform (or fail to perform) their role as engines of the new round of economic development and as organizing nodes of the new industrial space. Comprehension of the technopole phenomenon has been so blurred by political, ideological, and business biases that any serious study must start from a careful empirical analysis of how these centers are created and developed, and of the factors that account for their differential success, according to a set of criteria that must be established at the start.

However, our study of the technopole phenomenon soon led us to the conclusion that we should not be constrained by the boundaries artificially set by the promoters of the technopole idea. In other words, we must go back to seek the historic sources of inspiration of the technopole strategy. We should look into the formation and operation of those innovative industrial complexes that first changed the dynamics of world competition: Silicon Valley, Boston's Route 128, the Los Angeles military-industrial complex, the Tokyo industrial district, the post-1945 industrialization of Bavaria.

Furthermore, in our inquiry we came to the conclusion that most of the older major metropolises, such as Paris or London, indeed remain among the major innovation and high-technology centers of the world, and certainly of their respective countries. Thus, the focus of our study gradually shifted from exclusive concentration on the deliberately-planned technopoles, to extend both to their implicit role models and their true parents: that is, to the semi-spontaneous technopoles and to the giant metropolitan technopoles that cast such a huge shadow over the new start-ups and their aspiring imitators. And that in turn led us to consider, in all its complexity, the meaning of that pregnant but elusive concept, milieux of innovation.

By milieux of innovation we understand the social, institutional, organizational, economic, and territorial structures that create the conditions for the continuous generation of synergy and its investment in a process of production that results from this very synergistic capacity, both for the units of production that are part of the milieu and for the milieu as a whole.

Developing such milieux of innovation has now become a critical issue for economic development, and a matter of political and social prestige. And thus image-making, industrial projects, state policies, and the new economic geography mix in a confusing game of simultaneous doing and labeling. Any attempt to analyze the interaction between technological development, industrialization, and regional development on the basis of international experience must start with a clear distinction between the various kinds of realities to which terms like technopoles or technology parks, or any of the other labels, refer. This is not just a semantic question, since each type of technopole must be analyzed and evaluated according to the implicit or explicit goals it is trying to achieve.

A TYPOLOGY OF TECHNOPOLES: OUTLINE OF THE BOOK

While the eventual purpose of this book [*Technopoles of the World*] is to analyze and thus understand the process of formation of innovative industrial milieux, leading to truly dynamic regional or local economic growth, we start with a more modest aim: to tell the story as it actually is, in terms of the case studies of real places, before we proceed into the analysis. So the typology of technopoles we propose here is an empirical one: these are the various kinds of technologically-innovative milieux that we actually find in today's world. Some may have more ambitious goals, some more modest ones, but they are all presented here as they are: as specific forms of territorial concentration of technological innovation with a potential to generate scientific synergy and economic productivity. Our taxonomy, accordingly, arises

from the facts of the international experience in all its varied forms.

The first type of technopole consists of industrial complexes of high-technology firms that are built on the basis of innovative milieux. These complexes, linking R&D and manufacturing, are the true command centers of the new industrial space. Some are created entirely out of the most recent wave of global industrialization, characterized by the new high-technology firms; the most prominent worldwide is Silicon Valley, which we have accordingly selected so that we may study and report on the actual history of an industrial myth. Other new complexes, however, develop out of old industrial regions which go through a process of transformation and reindustrialization; the most important example is Boston's Route 128, which accordingly becomes the second of our case studies.

These new techno-industrial complexes arise without deliberate planning, though even there governments and universities did play a crucial role in their development. But other experiences are indeed the result of conscious institutional efforts to replicate the success of such examples of spontaneous growth. Thus, most of our analytic efforts will focus on the experiences of planned techno-industrial development.

The next type of technopole we distinguish, accordingly, can broadly be called science cities. These are strictly scientific research complexes, with no direct territorial linkage to manufacturing. They are intended to reach a higher level of scientific excellence through the synergy they are supposed to generate in their secluded scientific milieux. We have chosen to study four major cases of deliberate attempts to create scientific excellence by concentrating human and material resources in such a secluded science center, in four very different contexts: the Siberian city of Akademgorodok, the major Japanese experiment at Tsukuba; the Korean creation at Taedok; and the new concept of the multinuclear science city currently under development in the Kansai region of Japan.

A third type of technopole aims to induce new industrial growth, in terms of jobs and production, by attracting high-technology manufacturing firms to a privileged space. Innovation functions are not excluded from such projects, but they are mainly defined in terms of economic development. We label them "technology parks," because that is the most usual way in which they describe themselves. However, the name should not obscure the reality, which is a deliberately-established high-technology business area, resulting from government- or university-related initiatives. In this quite loose category, we have analyzed three experiences, ranging from the most tightly-planned government-originated park, through a mixed scheme, to the loosest university initiative: the cases of Hsinchu in Taiwan, Sophia-Antipolis in France, and Cambridge in England.

Fourth, we have analyzed the design of entire technopolis programs as instruments of regional development and industrial decentralization. Here the choice was obvious, since there is only one major such program worldwide: the Technopolis program in Japan.

Having looked at these planned cases, and having reflected on them, we came to a conclusion that surprised us. Despite all this activity, it remains true that over the years and decades most of the world's actual high-technology production and innovation still comes from areas that are not usually heralded as innovative milieux, and indeed may have few of their physical features: the great metropolitan areas of the industrialized world. So we determined that we should study them as quintessential innovative milieux. We found a fundamental distinction between the old metropolises that kept their leading technological role (Tokyo, Paris, London), the metropolises that lost their role as advanced manufacturing centers (New York and Berlin), and the newly-arriving technological-industrial metropolises that in fact took their place (Los Angeles and Munich).

Finally, we decided that it might be interesting to make a progress report on two current attempts to create innovative milieux, in which [we] are [ourselves] involved: Adelaide's Multi-function Polis and Seville's Cartuja '93, two antipodean experiences that should yield valuable lessons for any other place, or other group of people, interested to join the great adventure of planning the territories of the next technological age.

These works in progress conclude our case studies. In two final chapters [of *Technopoles of the World*], we try to draw the threads together. Chapter 9 seeks to distill the lessons that these very disparate experiences appear to teach us. And Chapter 10 builds on it to make some tentative suggestions for a policy of technopole-building. In these chapters, necessarily, we are somewhat speculative and judgmental. We are dealing with some of the largest and certainly some of the potentially most important projects anywhere in the world today. These are our judgments on them, and not everyone may necessarily agree with them. We hope that at least they will trigger a debate, and perhaps further studies. If they do, then our purpose will have been satisfied.

ROBERT FISHMAN

"Beyond Suburbia:
The Rise of the Technoburb"

from *Bourgeois Utopias: The Rise and Fall of Suburbia* (1987)

Editors' introduction   Robert Fishman is a professor of history at Rutgers University who established his academic reputation with his first book, the magisterial *Urban Utopias in the Twentieth Century* (1977), a study of the work of Ebenezer Howard, Le Corbusier, and Frank Lloyd Wright. For his second book, he decided to address a totally prosaic, nonvisionary subject – the history of suburbia – only to discover that "the suburban ideal" was, in the final analysis, yet another form of utopia, the utopia of the middle class.

Much of the literature of suburbia – especially that of the automobile-based tract developments of the post-World War II era – has been overwhelmingly negative. Titles like *The Crack in the Picture Window* (John Keats), *The Split Level Trap* (Richard Gordon), and *The Crabgrass Frontier* (Kenneth Jackson) give some sense of the tone of much suburban analysis, although a notable, much more sympathetic exception is Herbert Gans's *The Levittowners* (p. 64). And while many – including Lewis Mumford, Jane Jacobs, and Dolores Hayden – disdain contemporary suburbia as a cultural wasteland, still others have decried it as an environmental and ecological disaster, despoiling the rural countryside with endless sprawl. What none of these analyses recognizes, however, is the power of what Fishman calls suburbia's "extraordinary hold over the middle-class mind."

The suburban ideal, more than suburbia itself, is the real focus of *Bourgeois Utopias: The Rise and Fall of Suburbia* (New York: Basic Books, 1987), and the logic of his analysis leads Fishman to many surprising insights and conclusions. In the medieval period and up through the eighteenth century, suburbs were clusters of houses on the outskirts of towns inhabited by the poor. When suburbs were first established for the upper and middle classes, the ideal was to create a perfect synthesis of urban sophistication and rural virtue. Here was a conception as utopian as that of any visionary social reformer but with an important difference: "Where other modern utopias have been collectivist," writes Fishman, "suburbia has built its vision of community on the primacy of private property and the individual family."

What the suburbia that Herbert Gans described in *The Levittowners* has evolved into today is "techno-burbia," a dominant new urban reality that can no longer be considered suburbia in the traditional sense. In Fishman's view, the new techno-burbs surrounding the old urban cores do not represent "the suburbanization of the United States," as Kenneth Jackson would have it, but "the end of suburbia in its traditional sense and the creation of a new kind of decentralized city." That suburbia has become the city itself is, perhaps, the final irony of modern urbanism . . . and the first principle of what Peter Calthorpe calls the next American metropolis (*The Next American Metropolis*, New York: Princeton Architectural Press, 1993). For other views of the emerging postmodern suburbia, consult journalist Joel Garreau's *Edge City* (New York: Anchor, 1992) and Manuel Castells, *The Informational City* (Oxford: Basil Blackwell, 1989).

ROBERT FISHMAN, "Beyond Suburbia: The Rise of the Technoburb"

from *Bourgeois Utopias: The Rise and Fall of Suburbia* (1987)

If the nineteenth century could be called the Age of Great Cities, post-1945 America would appear to be the Age of Great Suburbs. As central cities stagnated or declined in both population and industry, growth was channeled almost exclusively to the peripheries. Between 1950 and 1970 American central cities grew by 10 million people, their suburbs by 85 million. Suburbs, moreover, accounted for at least three-quarters of all new manufacturing and retail jobs generated during that period. By 1970 the percentage of Americans living in suburbs was almost exactly double what it had been in 1940, and more Americans lived in suburban areas (37.6 percent) than in central cities (31.4 percent) or in rural areas (31 percent). In the 1970s central cities experienced a net out-migration of 13 million people, combined with an unprecedented deindustrialization, increasing poverty levels, and housing decay.

[...]

From its origins in eighteenth-century London, suburbia has served as a specialized portion of the expanding metropolis. Whether it was inside or outside the political borders of the central city, it was always functionally dependent on the urban core. Conversely, the growth of suburbia always meant a strengthening of the specialized services at the core.

In my view, the most important feature of postwar American development has been the almost simultaneous decentralization of housing, industry, specialized services, and office jobs; the consequent breakaway of the urban periphery from a central city it no longer needs; and the creation of a decentralized environment that nevertheless possesses all the economic and technological dynamism we associate with the city. This phenomenon, as remarkable as it is unique, is not suburbanization but a new city.

Unfortunately, we lack a convenient name for this new city, which has taken shape on the outskirts of all our major urban centers. Some have used the terms "exurbia" or "outer city." I suggest (with apologies) two neologisms: the "technoburb" and the "techno-city." By "technoburb" I mean a peripheral zone, perhaps as large as a county, that has emerged as a viable socioeconomic unit. Spread out along its highway growth corridors are shopping malls, industrial parks, campuslike office complexes, hospitals, schools, and a full range of housing types. Its residents look to their immediate surroundings rather than to the city for their jobs and other needs; and its industries find not only the employees they need but also the specialized services.

The new city is a technoburb not only because high tech industries have found their most congenial homes in such archetypal technoburbs as Silicon Valley in northern California and Route 128 in Massachusetts. In most technoburbs such industries make up only a small minority of jobs, but the very existence of the decentralized city is made possible only through the advanced communications technology which has so completely superseded the face-to-face contact of the traditional city. The technoburb has generated urban diversity without traditional urban concentration.

By "techno-city" I mean the whole metropolitan region that has been transformed by the coming of the technoburb. The techno-city usually still bears the name of its principal city, for example, "the New York metropolitan area"; its sports teams bear that city's name (even if they no longer play within the boundaries of the central city); and its television stations appear to broadcast from the central city. But the economic and social life of the region increasingly bypasses its supposed core. The techno-city is truly multicentered, along the pattern that Los Angeles first created. The technoburbs, which might stretch over seventy miles from the core in all directions, are often in more direct communication with one another – or with other techno-cities across the country – than they are with the core. The techno-city's real structure is aptly expressed by the circular superhighways or beltways that serve so well to define the perimeters of the new city. The beltways put every part of the urban periphery in contact with every other part without passing through the central city at all.

[...]

The old central cities have become increasingly marginal, while the technoburb has emerged as the focus of American life. The traditional suburbanite – commuting at ever-increasing cost to a center where the available resources barely duplicate those available much closer to home – becomes increasingly rare. In this transformed urban ecology the history of suburbia comes to an end.

PROPHETS OF THE TECHNO-CITY

Like all new urban forms, the techno-city and its technoburbs emerged not only unpredicted but unobserved. We are still seeing this new city through the intellectual categories of the old metropolis. Only two prophets, I believe, perceived the underlying forces that would lead to the techno-city at the time of their first emergence. Their thoughts are therefore particularly valuable in understanding the new city.

At the turn of the twentieth century, when the power and attraction of the great city was at its peak, H. G. Wells daringly asserted that the technological forces that had created the industrial metropolis were now moving to destroy it. In his 1900 essay "The Probable Diffusion of Great Cities," Wells argued that the seemingly inexorable concentration of people and resources in the largest cities would soon be reversed.

In the course of the twentieth century, he prophesied, the metropolis would see its own resources drain away to decentralized "urban regions" so vast that the very concept of "the city" would become, in his phrase, "as obsolete as 'mailcoach.'"

Wells based his prediction on a penetrating analysis of the emerging networks of transportation and communication. Throughout the nineteenth century, rail transportation had been a relatively simple system favoring direct access to large centers. With the spread of branchlines and electric tramways, however, a complex rail network had been created that could serve as the basis for a decentralized region. (As Wells wrote, Henry E. Huntington was proving the truth of his propositions for the Los Angeles region.)

Wells pictured the "urban region" of the year 2000 as a series of villages with small homes and factories set in the open fields, yet connected by high speed rail transportation to any other point in the region. (It was a vision not very different from those who saw Los Angeles developing into just such a network of villages.) The old cities would not completely disappear, but they would lose both their financial and their industrial functions, surviving simply because of an inherent human love of crowds. The "post-urban" city, Wells predicted, will be "essentially a bazaar, a great gallery of shops and places of concourse and rendezvous, a pedestrian place, its pathways reinforced by lifts and moving platforms, and shielded from the weather, and altogether a very spacious, brilliant, and entertaining agglomeration." In short, the great metropolis will dwindle to what we would today call a massive shopping mall, while the productive life of the society would take place in the decentralized urban region.

Wells's prediction was taken up in the late 1920s and early 1930s by Frank Lloyd Wright, who moved from similar assumptions to an even more radical view. Wright had actually seen the beginnings of the automobile and truck era; he was, perhaps not coincidentally, living mostly in Los Angeles in the late 1910s and early 1920s. Wright, like Wells, argued that "the great city was no longer modern" and that it was destined to be replaced by a decentralized society.

He called this new society Broadacre City. It has often been confused with a kind of universal suburbanization, but for Wright "Broadacres" was the exact opposite of the suburbia he despised. He saw correctly that suburbia represented the essential extension of the city into the countryside, whereas Broadacres represented the disappearance of all previously existing cities.

As Wright envisioned it, Broadacres was based on universal automobile ownership combined with a network of superhighways, which removed the need for population to cluster in a particular spot. Indeed, any such clustering was necessarily inefficient, a point of congestion rather than of communication. The city would thus spread out over the countryside at densities low enough to permit each family to have its own homestead and even to engage in part-time agriculture. Yet these homesteads would not be isolated; their access to the superhighway grid would put them within easy reach of as many jobs and specialized services as any nineteenth century urbanite. Traveling at more than sixty miles an hour, each citizen would create his own city within the hundreds of square miles he could reach in an hour's drive.

Like Wells, Wright saw industrial production inevitably leaving the cities for the space and convenience of rural sites. But Wright went one step further in his attempt to envision the way that a radically decentralized environment could generate that diversity and excitement which only cities had possessed.

He saw that even in the most scattered environment, the crossing of major highways would possess a certain special status. These intersections would be the natural sites of what he called the roadside market, a remarkable anticipation of the shopping center: "great spacious roadside pleasure places these markets, rising high and handsome like some flexible form of pavilion – designed as places of cooperative exchange, not only of commodities but of cultural facilities." To the roadside markets he added a range of highly civilized yet small scale institutions: schools, a modern cathedral, a center for festivities, and the like. In such an environment, even the entertainment functions of the city would disappear. Soon, Wright devoutly wished, the centralized city itself would disappear.

Taken together, Wells's and Wright's prophecies constitute a remarkable insight into the decentralizing tendencies of modern technology and society. Both were presented in utopian form, an image of the future presented as somehow "inevitable" yet without any sustained attention to how it would actually be achieved. Nevertheless, something like the transformation that Wells and Wright foresaw has taken place in the United States, a transformation all the more remarkable in that it occurred without a clear recognition that it was happening. While diverse groups were engaged in what they believed was "the suburbanization" of America, they were in fact creating a new city.

[...]

TECHNOBURB/TECHNO-CITY: THE STRUCTURE OF THE NEW METROPOLIS

To claim that there is a pattern or structure in the new American city is to contradict what appears to be overwhelming evidence. One might sum up the structure of the technoburb by saying that it goes against every rule of planning. It is based on two extravagances that have always aroused the ire of planners: the waste of land inherent in a single family house with its own yard, and the waste of energy inherent in the use of the personal automobile. The new city is absolutely dependent on its road system, yet that system is almost always in a state of chaos and congestion. The landscape of the technoburb is a hopeless jumble of housing, industry, commerce, and even agricultural uses. Finally, the technoburb has no proper boundaries; however defined, it is divided into a crazy quilt of separate and overlapping political jurisdictions, which make any kind of coordinated planning virtually impossible.

Yet the technoburb has become the real locus of growth and innovation in our society. And there is a real structure in what appears to be wasteful sprawl, which provides enough logic and efficiency for the technoburb to fulfill at least some of its promises.

If there is a single basic principle in the structure of the technoburb, it is the renewed linkage of work and residence. The suburb had separated the two into distinct environments; its logic was that of the massive commute, in which workers from the periphery traveled each morning to a single core and then dispersed each evening. The technoburb, however, contains both work and residence within a single decentralized environment.

By the standards of a preindustrial city where people often lived and worked under the same roof, or even of the turn of the century industrial zones where factories were an integral part of working class neighborhoods, the linkage between work and residence in the technoburb is hardly close. A recent study of New Jersey shows that most workers along the state's growth corridors now live in the same county in which they work. But this relative dispersion must be contrasted to the former pattern of commuting into urban cores like Newark or New York. In most cases traveling time to work diminishes, even when the distances traveled are still substantial; as the 1980 census indicates, the average journey to work appears to be diminishing both in distance and, more importantly, in time.

For commuting within the technoburb is multidirectional, following the great grid of highways and secondary roads that, as Frank Lloyd Wright understood, defines the community. This multiplicity of destinations makes public transportation highly inefficient, but it does remove that terrible bottleneck which necessarily occurred when work was concentrated at a single core within the region. Each house in a technoburb is within a reasonable driving time of a truly "urban" array of jobs and services, just as each workplace along the highways can draw upon an "urban" pool of workers.

Those who believed that the energy crisis of the 1970s would cripple the technoburb failed to realize that the new city had evolved its own pattern of transportation in which a multitude of relatively short automobile journeys in a multitude of different directions substitutes for that great tidal wash in and out of a single urban core which had previously defined commuting. With housing, jobs, and services all on the periphery, this sprawl develops its own form of relative efficiency. The truly inefficient form would be any attempted revival of the former pattern of long distance mass transit commuting into a core area. To account for the new linkage of work and residence in the technoburb, we must first confront this paradox: the new city required a massive and coordinated relocation of housing, industry, and other "core" functions to the periphery; yet there were no coordinators directing the process. Indeed, the technoburb emerged in spite of, not because of, the conscious purposes motivating the main actors. The postwar housing boom was an attempt to escape from urban conditions· the new highways sought to channel traffic into the cities; planners attempted to limit peripheral growth; the government programs that did the most to destroy the hegemony of the old industrial metropolis were precisely those designed to save it.

This paradox can be seen clearly in the area of transportation policy. Wright had grasped the basic point in his Broadacre City plan: a fully developed highway grid eliminates the primacy of a central business district. It creates a whole series of highway crossings, which can serve as business centers while promoting the multidirectional travel that prevents any single center from attaining unique importance. Yet, from the time of Robert Moses to the present, highway planners have imagined that the new roads, like the older rail transportation, would enhance the importance of the old centers by funneling cars and trucks into the downtown area and the surrounding industrial belt. At most, the highways were to serve traditional suburbanization; in other words, the movement from the periphery to the core during morning rush hours and the reverse movement in the afternoon. The beltways, those crucial "Main Streets" of the technoburb, were designed simply to allow interstate traffic to avoid going through the central cities.

The history of the technoburb, therefore, is the history of those deeper structural features of modern society first described by Wells and Wright taking precedence over conscious intentions. For purposes of clarity I shall now divide this discussion of the making of the techno-city into two interrelated topics: housing and job location.

Housing

The great American postwar housing boom was perhaps the purest example of the suburban dream in action, yet its ultimate consequence was to render suburbia obsolete. Between 1950 and 1970, on the average, 1.2 million housing units were built each year, the vast majority as suburban single family dwellings; the nation's housing stock increased by 21 million units or over 50 percent. In the 1970s the boom continued even more strongly: twenty million more new units were added, almost as many as in the previous two decades. It was precisely this vast production of new residences that shifted the center of gravity in the United States from the urban core to the periphery and thus ensured that these vital and expanding areas could no longer remain simply bedroom communities.

This great building boom, which seems so characteristic of post-1945 conditions, in fact had its origins early in the twentieth century in the first attempts to universalize suburbia throughout the United States. It can be seen essentially as a continuation of the 1920s building boom, which had been cut off for two decades by the Depression and the war. As George Sternlieb reminds us, the American automobile industry in 1929 was producing as many cars per capita as it did in the 1980s, and real estate developers had already plotted out subdivisions in out-lying areas that were only built up in the 1960s and 1970s.

[…]

Even the late 1970s combination of stagnant real income with high interest rates, gasoline prices, and land values did not diminish the desirability of the new single family house. In 1981 a median American family earned only 70 percent of what was needed to make the payments on the median priced house; by 1986, the median family could once again afford the median house. Single family houses still constitute 67 percent of all occupied units, down only 2 percent since 1970 despite the increase in costs; moreover, a survey of potential home buyers in 1986 showed that 85 percent intended to purchase a detached, single family suburban house, while only 15 percent were looking at condominium apartments or townhouses. The "single," as builders call it, is still alive and well on the urban periphery.

This continuing appeal of the single should not, however, obscure the crucial changes that have transformed the meaning and context of the house. The new suburban house of the 1950s, like its predecessors for more than a century, existed precisely to isolate women and the family from urban economic life; it defined an exclusive zone of residence between city and country. Now a new house might adjoin a landscaped office park with more square feet of new office space than in a downtown building, or might be just down the highway from an enclosed shopping mall with a sales volume that exceeds those of the downtown department stores, or might overlook a high tech research laboratory making products that are exported around the world. No longer a refuge, the single family detached house on the periphery is preferred as a convenient base from which both spouses can rapidly reach their jobs.

Without the simultaneous movement of jobs along with housing, the great "suburban" boom would surely have exhausted itself in ever longer journeys to workplaces in a crowded core on overburdened highways and mass transit facilities. And the new peripheral communities would have been in reality the "isolation wards" for women that critics have called them, instead of becoming the setting for the reintegration of middle-class women into the work force as they have. The unchanging image of the suburban house and the suburban bedroom community has obscured the crucial importance of this transformation in work location, the subject of the next section.

Job location

As those who have tried to plan the process have painfully learned, job location has its own autonomous rules. The movement of factories away from the urban core after 1945 took place independently of the housing boom and probably would have occurred without it. Nevertheless, the simultaneous movement of housing and jobs in the 1950s and 1960s created an unforeseen "critical mass" of entrepreneurship and expertise on the perimeters, which allowed the technoburb to challenge successfully the two century long economic dominance of the central city.

[. . .]

At the same time, the growing importance of trucking meant that factories were no longer as dependent on the confluence of rail lines which existed only in the old factory zones. Workers had their automobiles, so factories could scatter along the periphery without concern about the absence of mass transit. (The scattering of aircraft plants and other factories in Los Angeles in the 1930s prefigured this trend.) The process gained momentum as a result of thousands of uncoordinated decisions in which managers allowed their inner city plants to run down and directed new investment toward the outskirts . . .

These changes in job location during the 1950s and 1960s were, however, only a prelude to the real triumph of the technoburb: the luring of both managerial office employment and advanced technological laboratories and production facilities from the core to the peripheries. This process may be divided into three parts. First came the establishment of "high tech" growth corridors in such diverse locations as Silicon Valley, California; Silicon Prairie, between Dallas and Forth Worth; the Atlanta Beltway; Route 1 between Princeton and New Brunswick, New Jersey; Westchester County, New York; Route 202 near Valley Forge, Pennsylvania; and Route 128 outside Boston. The second step was the movement of office bureaucracies, especially the so-called back office, from center city high-rises to technoburb office parks; and the final phase was the movement of production-service employment – banks, accountants, lawyers, advertising agencies, skilled technicians, and the like – to locations within the technoburb, thus creating that vital base of support personnel for larger firms.

Indeed, this dramatic surge toward the technoburb has been so sweeping that we must now ask whether Wright's ultimate prophecy will be fulfilled: the disappearance of the old urban centers. Is the present-day boom in downtown office construction and inner city gentrification simply a last hurrah for the old city before deeper trends in decentralization lead to its ultimate decay?

In my view, the final diffusion that Wells and Wright predicted is unlikely, if only because both underestimated the forces of economic and political centralization that continue to exist in the late twentieth century. If physical decentralization had indeed meant economic decentralization, then the urban cores would by now be ghost towns. But large and powerful organizations still seek out a central location that validates their importance, and the historic core of great cities still meets that need better than the office complexes on the outskirts. Moreover, the corporate and government headquarters in the core still attract a wide variety of specialized support services – law firms, advertising, publishing, media, restaurants, entertainment centers, museums, and more – that continue to make the center cities viable.

The old factory zones around the core have also survived, but only in the painfully anomalous sense of housing those too poor to earn admission to the new city of prosperity at the periphery. The big city, therefore, will not disappear in the foreseeable future, and residents of the technoburbs will continue to confront uneasily both the economic power and elite culture of the urban core and its poverty. Nevertheless, the technoburb has become the true center of American society.

THE MEANING OF THE NEW CITY

Beyond the structure of the techno-city and its technoburbs, there is the larger question: what is the impact of this decentralized environment on our culture? Can anyone say of the technoburb, as Olmsted said of the suburb a century ago, that it represents "the most attractive, the most refined, and the most soundly wholesome forms of domestic life, and the best application of the arts of civilization to which mankind has yet attained"? Most planners in fact say the exact opposite. Their indictment can be divided into two parts. First, decentralization has been a social and economic disaster for the old city and for the poor, who have been increasingly relegated to its crowded, decayed zones. It has resegregated American society into an affluent outer city and an indigent inner city, while erecting ever higher barriers that prevent the poor from sharing in the jobs and housing of the technoburbs.

Second, decentralization has been seen as a cultural disaster. While the rich and diverse architectural heritage of the cities decays, the technoburb has been built up as a standardized and simplified sprawl, consuming time and space, destroying the natural landscape. The wealth that postindustrial America has generated has been used to create an ugly and wasteful pseudocity, too spread out to be efficient, too superficial to create a true culture.

The truth of both indictments is impossible to deny, yet it must be rescued from the polemical overstatements that seem to afflict anyone who deals with these topics. The first charge is the more fundamental, for it points to a genuine structural discontinuity in post-1945 decentralization. By detaching itself physically, socially, and economically from the city, the technoburb is profoundly antiurban as suburbia never had been. Suburbanization strengthened the central core as the cultural and economic heart of an expanding region; by excluding industry, suburbia left intact and even augmented the urban factory districts.

Technoburb development, however, completely undermines the factory district and potentially threatens even the commercial core. The competition from new sites on the outskirts renders obsolete the whole complex of housing and factory sites that had been built up in the years 1890 to 1930 and provides alternatives to the core for even the most specialized shopping and administrative services.

This competition, moreover, has occurred in the context of a massive migration of southern blacks to northern cities. Blacks, Hispanics, and other recent migrants could afford housing only in the old factory districts, which were being abandoned by both employers and the white working class. The result was a twentieth century version of Disraeli's "two nations." Now, however, the outer reaches of affluence include both the middle class and the better-off working class – a majority of the population; while the largely black and Hispanic minority are forced into decaying neighborhoods, which lack not only decent housing but jobs.

This bleak picture has been modified somewhat by the continued ability of the traditional urban cores to retain certain key areas of white collar and professional employment; and by the choice of some highly paid core workers to live in high-rise or recently renovated housing around the core. Compared both to the decaying factory zones and to peripheral expansion, the "gentrification" phenomenon has been highly visible yet statistically insignificant. It has done as much to displace low income city dwellers as to benefit them. The late twentieth century American environment thus shows all the signs of the two nations syndrome: one caught in an environment of poverty, cut off from the majority culture, speaking its own languages and dialects; the other an increasingly homogenized culture of affluence, more and more remote from an urban environment it finds dangerous.

[...]

The case against the technoburb can easily be summarized. Compared even to the traditional suburb, it at first appears impossible to comprehend. It has no clear boundaries; it includes discordant rural, urban, and suburban elements; and it can best be measured in counties rather than in city blocks. Consequently the new city lacks any recognizable center to give meaning to the whole. Major civic institutions seem scattered at random over an undifferentiated landscape.

Even planned developments – however harmonious they might appear from the inside –

can be no more than fragments in a fragmented environment. A single house, a single street, even a cluster of streets and houses can be and frequently are well designed. But true public space is lacking or totally commercialized. Only the remaining pockets of undeveloped farmland maintain real openness, and these pockets are inevitably developed, precipitating further flight and further sprawl.

The case for the techno-city can only be made hesitantly and conditionally. Nevertheless, we can hope that its deficiencies are in large part the early awkwardness of a new urban type. All new city forms appear in their early stages to be chaotic. "There were a hundred thousand shapes and substances of incompleteness, wildly mingled out of their places, upside down, burrowing in the earth, aspiring in the earth, moldering in the water, and unintelligible as any dream." This was Charles Dickens describing London in 1848, in his novel *Dombey and Son* (Chapter 6). As I have indicated, sprawl has a functional logic that may not be apparent to those accustomed to more traditional cities. If that logic is understood imaginatively, as Wells and especially Wright attempted to do, then perhaps a matching aesthetic can be devised.

We must remember that even the most "organic" cityscapes of the past evolved slowly after much chaos and trial and error. The classic late nineteenth century railroad suburb – the standard against which critics judge today's sprawl – evolved out of the disorder of nineteenth century metropolitan growth. First, planners of genius like John Nash and Frederick Law Olmsted comprehended the process and devised aesthetic formulas to guide it. These formulas were then communicated – slowly and incompletely – to speculative builders, who nevertheless managed to capture the basic idea. Finally, individual property owners constantly upgraded their holdings to eliminate discordant elements and bring their community closer to the ideal.

We might hope that a similar process is now at work in the postsuburban outer city. As a starting point for a technoburb aesthetic, there are Wright's Broadacre City plans and drawings, which still repay study for anyone seeking a vision of a modern yet organic American landscape. More useful still is the American New Town tradition, starting from Radburn, New Jersey, with its careful designs intended to reconcile decentralization with older ideas of community. Already, New Town designs have been adopted by speculative builders, not only in a highly publicized project like James Rouse's Columbia, Maryland, but in hundreds of smaller planned communities, which are beginning to leave their mark on the landscape.

At the level of civic architecture there is Wright's Marin County Civic Center to serve as a model for public monuments in a decentralized environment. The multilevel, enclosed shopping mall has attained a spaciousness not unworthy of the great urban shopping districts of the past, while newly built college campuses and campuslike office complexes and research centers contribute significantly to the environment. Some commercial highway strips have been rescued from cacophony and have managed to achieve a liveliness that is not tawdry. (This evolution parallels the evolution of the nineteenth century urban core, originally a remarkably ugly cluster of small buildings and large signs, which was transformed into a reasonably dignified center for commerce by the turn of the century.)

Most importantly, there is a growing sense that open land must be preserved as an integral part of the landscape, through regional land use plans, purchases for parklands, and tax abatements for working farms. These governmental measures, combined with thousands of small scale efforts by individuals, could create a fitting environment for the new city. These efforts, moreover, could provide the starting point for a more profound diversification of the outer city. An increased understanding and respect for the landscape of each region could lead to a growing rejection of a mass culture that erases all such distinctions.

The techno-city, therefore, is still under construction, both physically and culturally. Its economic and social successes are undeniable, as are its costs. Most importantly, the new pattern of decentralization has fundamentally altered the urban form on which suburbia had depended for its function and meaning. Whatever the fate of the new city, suburbia in its traditional sense now belongs to the past.

MANUEL CASTELLS

"The Reconstruction of Social Meaning in the Space of Flows"

from *The Informational City* (1989)

Editors' introduction   The information revolution sweeping the world today has profound implications for the future of cities. The power of computers is increasing and the cost of computing is dropping at astonishing rates. Fax machines, modems, fiber-optic cable, communication satellites, a global electronic (e-mail) system, videoconferencing, the Internet, information highways, virtual reality, and multimedia are proceeding apace.

Manuel Castells was born in Spain, educated as a sociologist in France, and is currently a professor of city and regional planning at the University of California, Berkeley. As a young man Castells fled Franco's authoritarian and intellectually stifling Spain for the freedom and intellectual excitement of Paris. He became a neo-Marxist, crafting sophisticated theories on the role of the capitalist state and grassroots urban protest movements. Later, Castells turned his attention to the implications of high technology and the information revolution for cities.

Castells has taught and worked for progressive change all over the world. Currently he divides his time between teaching at Berkeley and work with the Spanish government in Madrid.

Castells sees information technologies as the fundamental instrument of the new organizational logic transforming the world today. Accordingly he uses the adjective "informational" as a type of city as "industrial" or "colonial" city might have been used in the nineteenth century. Castells is interested in how information technology will restructure relationships between rich and poor regions, labor and capital, centralization and decentralization of services, governments and nongovernmental entities, the individual and society.

Castells argues that what he calls the "space of flows" will increasingly govern the actions of power-holding organizations rather than territorially based institutions operating in the "space of places." Industry and services will be organized worldwide around the operation of their information-generating units. Castells envisages powerful, secretive, multinational institutions not tied to any particular place as the dominant institutions of the future.

Will local and even national governments wither in importance with the information dominance of powerful multinational institutions? Will the information revolution lead to greater social inequality between rich and poor nations? Are "dual cities" where rich and powerful professional managers manipulate impoverished masses, both blocks and continents away, inevitable? Will mass urban social movements emerge to reassert popular power against such an Orwellian future? And can they succeed against so powerful and subtle a global system? Thirty years ago, radicals could identify and work to overthrow a territorially based dictator like Francisco Franco. But who and where is the enemy in the emerging space of flows?

In "The Reconstruction of Social Meaning in the Space of Flows," Castells argues that despite dangerous aspects of the emerging world order, the future of the informational city is not predetermined. Territorially defined local societies can preserve their identities. Grassroots organizations may reassert their identities and enhance their power – perhaps by using new information technology such as citizens' data banks, interactive communication systems, and community-based multimedia centers. Local governments can develop a central role in organizing the social control of places, rather than becoming passive pawns in a global economy they neither understand or control.

Many of the visionary writers in this anthology predicted that the information (and transportation) technology of their times would undermine old, and make possible new, city patterns. Ebenezer Howard argued that Garden Cities were possible because they could communicate by telegraph and send goods by railroad (p. 346). Frank Lloyd Wright foresaw instant communication and rapid transportation in Broadacre City: by pneumatic tube and helicopter (p. 377)!

This selection is from *The Informational City* (Oxford: Basil Blackwell, 1989) – Castells's most complete statement of his ideas on the informational city. Related material is in *High Tech, Space, and Society* (Beverly Hills: Sage, 1985) edited by Castells, and *Technopoles of the World* (London: Routledge, 1994) jointly authored with Peter Hall (p. 476). Castells's earlier writing includes *The Urban Question* (London: Edward Arnold, 1977) and *The City and the Grassroots* (Berkeley: University of California, 1983).

MANUEL CASTELLS, "The Reconstruction of Social Meaning in the Space of Flows"

from *The Informational City* (1989)

At the end of this analytical journey, we can see a major social trend standing out from all our observations: the historical emergence of the space of flows, superseding the meaning of the space of places. By this we understand the deployment of the functional logic of power-holding organizations in asymmetrical networks of exchanges which do not depend on the characteristics of any specific locale for the fulfillment of their fundamental goals. The new industrial space and the new service economy organize their operations around the dynamics of their information-generating units, while connecting their different functions to disparate spaces assigned to each task to be performed; the overall process is then reintegrated through communication systems. The new professional-managerial class colonizes exclusive spatial segments that connect with one another across the city, the country, and the world; they isolate themselves from the fragments of local societies, which in consequence become destructured in

the process of selective reorganization of work and residence. The new state, asserting its sources of power in the control and strategic guidance of knowledge, fosters the development of an advanced technological infrastructure that scatters its elements across undifferentiated locations and interconnected secretive spaces. The new international economy creates a variable geometry of production and consumption, labor and capital, management and information – a geometry that denies the specific productive meaning of any place outside its position in a network whose shape changes relentlessly in response to the messages of unseen signals and unknown codes.

New information technologies are not in themselves the source of the organizational logic that is transforming the social meaning of space: they are, however, the fundamental instrument that allows this logic to embody itself in historical actuality. Information technologies could be used, and can be used, in the pursuit of different social and functional goals, because what they offer, fundamentally, is flexibility. However, their use currently is determined by the process of the socio-economic restructuring of capitalism, and they constitute the indispensable material basis for the fulfillment of this process.

The supersession of places by a network of information flows is a fundamental goal of the restructuring process that has been analyzed. This is because the ultimate logic of restructuring is based on the avoidance of historically established mechanisms of social, economic, and political control by the power-holding organizations. Since most of these mechanisms of control depend upon territorially based institutions of society, escaping from the social logic embedded in any particular locale becomes the means of achieving freedom in a space of flows connected only to other power-holders, who share the social logic, the values, and the criteria for performance institutionalized in the programs of the information systems that constitute the architecture of the space of flows. The emergence of the space of flows actually expresses the disarticulation of place-based societies and cultures from the organizations of power and production that continue to dominate society without submitting to its control. In the end, even democracies become powerless confronted with the ability of capital to circulate globally, of information to be transferred secretly, of markets to be penetrated or neglected, of planetary strategies of political-military power to be decided without the knowledge of nations, and of cultural messages to be marketed, packaged, recorded, and beamed in and out of people's minds.

What emerges from this restructuring process manifested in the space of flows is not the Orwellian prophecy of a totalitarian universe controlled by Big Brother on the basis of information technologies. It is a much more subtle, and to some extent potentially more destructive, form of social disintegration and reintegration. There is no tangible oppression, no identifiable enemy, no center of power that can be held responsible for specific social issues. Even the issues themselves become unclear, or paradoxically so explicit that they cannot be treated

because they constantly refer to a higher level of social causality which cannot be grasped. The fundamental fact is that social meaning evaporates from places, and therefore from society, and becomes diluted and diffused in the reconstructed logic of a space of flows whose profile, origin, and ultimate purpose are unknown, even for many of the entities integrated in the network of exchanges. The flows of power generate the power of flows, whose material reality imposes itself as a natural phenomenon that cannot be controlled or predicted, only accepted and managed. This is the real significance of the current restructuring process, implemented on the basis of new information technologies, and materially expressed in the separation between functional flows and historically determined places as two disjointed spheres of the human experience. People live in places, power rules through flows.

Nevertheless, societies are not made up of passive subjects resigned to structural domination. The meaninglessness of places, the powerlessness of political institutions are resented and resisted, individually and collectively, by a variety of social actors. People have affirmed their cultural identity, often in territorial terms, mobilizing to achieve their demands, organizing their communities, and staking out their places to preserve meaning, to restore whatever limited control they can over work and residence, to reinvent love and laughter in the midst of the abstraction of the new historical landscape. But, as I have shown elsewhere in my cross-cultural investigation of urban social movements, these are more often reactive symptoms of structural contradictions than conscious actions in pursuit of social change. Faced with the variable geometry of the space of flows, grassroots mobilizations tend to be defensive, protective, territorially bounded, or so culturally specific that their codes of self-recognizing identity become non-communicable, with societies tending to fragment themselves into tribes, easily prone to a fundamentalist affirmation of their identity. While power constitutes an articulated functional space of flows, societies deconstruct their historical culture into localized identities that recover the meaning of places only at the price of breaking down communication among different cultures and different places. Between ahistorical flows and irreducible identities of local communities, cities and regions disappear as socially meaningful places. The historical outcome of this process could be the ushering in of an era characterized by the uneasy coexistence of extraordinary human achievements and the disintegration of large segments of society, along with the widespread prevalence of senseless violence – for the impossibility of communication transforms other communities into "aliens," and thus into potential enemies. The globalization of power flows and the tribalization of local communities are part of the same fundamental process of historical restructuring: the growing dissociation between techno-economic development and the corresponding mechanisms of social control of such development.

These trends are not ineluctable. They can be reversed, and should be reversed, by a series of political, economic, and technological strategies that could contribute to the reconstruction of social meaning in the new historical reality characterized by the formation of the space of flows as the space of power and functional organizations. While the focus of this book [*The Informational City*] has been primarily analytical, outside normative debate about policies, I believe it is important, in concluding, to explore possible ways out of the destructive dynamics identified by this research.

The new techno-economic paradigm imposes the space of flows as the irreversible spatial logic of economic and functional organizations. The issue then becomes how to articulate the meaning of places to this new functional space. The reconstruction of place-based social meaning requires the simultaneous articulation of alternative social and spatial projects at three levels: cultural, economic, and political.

At the cultural level, local societies, territorially defined, must preserve their identities, and build upon their historical roots, regardless of their economic and functional dependence upon the space of flows. The symbolic marking of places, the preservation of symbols of recognition, the expression of collective memory in actual practices of communication, are fundamental means by which places may continue to

exist as such, without having to justify their existence by the fulfillment of their functional performance. However, to avert the danger of over-affirmation of a local identity without reference to any broader social framework of reference at least two additional strategies are required: on the one hand, they must build communication codes with other identities, codes that require the definition of communities as sub-cultures able to recognize and to communicate with higher-order cultures; and on the other they must link the affirmation and symbolic practice of cultural identity to economic policy and political practice. They may thereby overcome the dangers of tribalism and fundamentalism.

Localities – cities and regions – must also be able to find their specific role in the new informational economy. This is possibly the most difficult dimension to integrate into a new strategy of place-based social control, since a precise and major characteristic of the new economy is its functional articulation in the space of flows. However, localities can become indispensable elements in the new economic geography because of the specific nature of the informational economy. In such an economy, the main source of productivity is the capacity to generate and process new information, itself dependent upon the symbolic manipulating ability of labor. This informational potential of labor is a function of its general living conditions, not only in terms of education, but in terms of the overall social milieu that constantly produces and stimulates its intellectual development. In a fundamental sense, social reproduction becomes a direct productive force. Production in the informational economy becomes organized in the space of flows, but social reproduction continues to be locally specific. While the overall logic of the production and management system still operates at the level of flows, the connection between production and reproduction – a key element of the new productive forces – requires an adequate linkage to the place-based system of formation and development of labor. This linkage must be explicitly recognized by each locality, so that locally-based labor will be able to provide the skills required in the production system at the precise point of its connection in the network of productive exchanges. Labor – and, indeed, individual citizens – must develop an awareness of the precise role of their place-based activities in the functional space of flows. On the basis of such an awareness they will be better placed to bargain for the control of the overall production system as it relates to their interests. Yet this economic bargaining power on the part of the informational labor force is highly vulnerable if it is not backed up by the social strength provided by cultural identity, and if it is not articulated and implemented by renewed political power from local governments.

Local governments must develop a central role in organizing the social control of places over the functional logic of the space of flows. It is only through the reinforcement of this role that localities will be able to put pressure on economic and political organizations to restore the meaning of the local society in the new functional logic. This statement runs counter to the widespread opinion that the role for local governments will diminish in an internationalized economy and within the functional space of flows. I believe that it is precisely because we live in such a world that local governments can and must play a more decisive role as representatives of civil societies. National governments are frequently as powerless as local to handle unidentifiable flows. Furthermore, since the origin and destination of the flows cannot be controlled, the key issue has become flexibility and adaptability to the potential and requirements of the network of flows in each specific situation as it relates to a given locality. Because local governments defend specific interests, linked to a local society, they can identify such interests and respond flexibly to the requirements of the flows of power, so identifying the best bargaining position in each case. In other words, in a situation of generalized lack of control, the more specific the bargaining agenda, and the more flexible the capacity of response, both positive and negative, to the network of flows, the greater will be the chances of restoring some level of social control. It may be instructive to recall that the formation of the world economy in the fourteenth to sixteenth centuries led to the emergence of city-states as

flexible political institutions able to engage in worldwide strategies of negotiation and conflictive articulation with transnational economic powers. The current process of total internationalization of the economy may also lead to the renaissance of the local state, as an alternative to the functionally powerless and institutionally bureaucratized nation states.

Nevertheless, for local governments to assume such a fundamental role they must extend their organizational capacity and reinforce their power in at least two directions. First, by fostering citizen participation they should mobilize local civil societies to support a collective strategy toward the reconstruction of the meaning of the locality in a conflictive dynamics with the placeless powers. Community organization and widespread, active citizen participation are indispensable elements for the revitalization of local governments as dynamic agents of economic development and social control. Secondly, and in so doing, they must connect with other organized, self-identified communities engaged in collective endeavor, taking care to avoid tribalism and acting on the material basis of work and power. Local governments will be unable to control the logic of the space of flows if they remain confined to their locality, while flows-based organizations select their locations at their convenience, playing localized social and political actors one against the other. Local governments attempting to restore social control of the development process need to establish their own networks of information, decision making, and strategic alliances, in order to match the mobility of power-holding organizations. In other words, they must reconstruct an alternative space of flows on the basis of the space of places. In this way they can avoid the deconstruction of their locales by the placeless logic of flows-based organizations.

Interestingly enough both these strategies – active citizen participation and a nation-wide or worldwide network of local governments – could be implemented most effectively on the basis of new information technologies. Citizens' data banks, interactive communication systems, community-based multimedia centers are powerful tools to enhance citizen participation on the basis of grassroots organizations and local governments' political will. On-line information systems linking local governments across the world could provide a fundamental tool in countering the strategies of flows-based organizations, which would then lose the advantage deriving from their control of asymmetrical information flows. Information technologies could provide the flexible instrument to reverse the logic of domination of the space of flows built by the process of socio-economic restructuring. However, the technological medium alone will not be able to transform this process in the absence of social mobilization, political decisions, and institutional strategies that would enable local governments to challenge collectively the power of flows and to reinstate the counterpower of places.

These reflections are not intended to provide a specific policy agenda for political action and social change, given the generality of the analysis presented in this book. They aim simply at opening a debate, in both scholarly and political circles, that could begin to address the fundamental challenge posed by the emergence of the space of flows to the meaning of our cities and to the welfare of our societies. The policy orientations I have suggested may appear uto-pian. But sometimes a utopian vision is needed to shake the institutions from shortsightedness and stasis and to enable people to think the unthinkable, thus enhancing their awareness and their control of the inevitable social transformation. What we must prevent at all costs is the development of the one-sided logic of the space of flows while we keep up a pretence that the social balance of our cities has been maintained. Unless alternative, realistic policies, fostered by new social movements, can be found to reconstruct the social meaning of localities within the space of flows, our societies will fracture into non-communicative segments whose reciprocal alienation will lead to destructive violence and to a process of historical decline.

However, if innovative social projects, represented and implemented by renewed local governments, are able to master the formidable forces unleashed by the revolution in information technologies, then a new socio-spatial structure could emerge made up of a network of local communes controlling and shaping a network of productive flows. Maybe then our historic time and our social space would converge towards the reintegration of knowledge and meaning into a new Informational City.

ANTHONY DOWNS

"Alternative Futures for the American Ghetto"

Daedalus (1968)

Editors' introduction   Since the nineteenth-century settlement house movement, programs have been developed by government and private philanthropy to deal with the problems of poor, minority slum areas. Sometimes government programs try to enrich the quality of life in the poorest urban areas through job training, public health programs, housing rehabilitation, educational enrichment, crime prevention and substance abuse programs. Other programs seek to disperse ghetto area residents through the push of urban renewal or the pull of portable housing vouchers.

Writing at the time of U.S. Black ghetto riots in the mid-1960s, Anthony Downs lays out alternative ghetto enrichment and dispersal strategies. While Downs is writing about Black ghettos in the U.S., much of what he has to say is relevant to urban slums worldwide.

Anthony Downs is a senior fellow at the Brookings Institution – a Washington, D.C., think tank. He has written extensively over the past three decades on poverty, race, housing, urban sprawl, traffic congestion, metropolitan planning, and other urban problems. Downs often takes the logic of strategies which have been suggested or tried on a modest scale to their logical limit: what would it really take to completely disperse the population of every poor Black ghetto in America? How much would it really cost to completely eliminate traffic congestion? How much housing at what cost would it really require to provide for every American household a decent, safe, and sanitary affordable housing unit?

Often, as in this selection, Downs concludes that strategies to achieve broad social goals would require government action and more funding (usually much more than can realistically be expected). This emphasis on government programs and spending differentiates Downs from conservatives like Charles Murray (p. 233), who oppose government spending to solve urban problems. But Downs is no bleeding-heart liberal. He advocates triage strategies for urban neighborhoods – leaving the worst neighborhoods to die while directing scarce resources to poor but salvageable neighborhoods. This puts him at odds with many liberals. So does the argument advanced in this selection that dispersal of Black ghettos will be accepted by the white majority in America only if Blacks are dispersed into white areas in such a way that the white majority remains numerically and culturally dominant.

Consider how African-American writers W. E. B. Dubois (p. 57) and William Julius Wilson (p. 226) have described Black ghetto conditions over the past century. How would they react to each of Downs's alternative futures? What would Black nationalists think of dispersal strategies and the "law of cultural dominance?" What would Charles Murray predict would be the effect of massive government programs to enrich the quality of ghetto life? Would the enrichment and dispersal strategies work today in light of Wilson's description of how Black urban ghettos have changed since Downs's article was written?

This selection is from *Daedalus*, vol. 97, no. 4 (Fall 1964) and is reprinted in Anthony Downs,

Urban Problems and Prospects (Chicago: Markham, 1970). Other books by Anthony Downs include *Stuck in Traffic* (Washington, D.C.: Brookings Institution, and Cambridge, Mass.: The Lincoln Institute of Land Policy, 1992), *New Visions for Metropolitan America* (Washington, D.C.: Brookings Institution, and Cambridge, Mass.: The Lincoln Institute of Land Policy, 1992), *Opening Up the Suburbs: An Urban Strategy for America* (New Haven, Conn.: Yale University Press, 1973), *Inside Bureaucracy* (Boston: Little, Brown, 1967), and *An Economic Theory of Democracy* (New York: Harper, 1957).

Other writings about American black ghettos and government policy towards them include St. Clair Drake and Horace Cayton, *Black Metropolis* (Chicago: University of Chicago Press, 1945), Kenneth B. Clark, *Dark Ghetto: Dilemmas of Social Power* (New York: Harper & Row, 1965), Lee Rainwater, *Behind Ghetto Walls: Black Families in a Federal Slum* (Chicago: Aldine, 1970), Daniel P. Moynihan, *The Negro Family: The Case for National Action* (Washington, D.C.: Office of Policy Planning and Research, U.S. Department of Labor, 1965), Elliot Liebow, *Tally's Corner: A Study of Negro Streetcorner Men* (Boston: Little, Brown, 1967).

Important government analyses of the causes of and cures for urban rioting in the U.S. and the U.K. include U.S. National Advisory Committee on Civil Disorders, *Report* (New York: Dutton, 1968), popularly referred to as the Kerner Commission Report, and G.B. Home Office, *The Brixton Disorders 10–12 April, 1981: Report of an Inquiry by the Rt. Hon. The Lord Scarman, O.B.E. (Cmnd. 8427)* (BPP 1981–2) (London: HMSO, 1981), popularly referred to as the Scarman Report.

ANTHONY DOWNS, "Alternative Futures for the American Ghetto"

Daedalus (1968)

[...]

Because of the immense complexity of our society, an infinite number of alternative future strategies regarding ghettos could conceivably be designed. But for purposes of practical consideration, this number must be narrowed drastically to a few major choices facing us. Selecting these few is inescapably arbitrary – there is no "scientific" way to do it. I believe, however, that the narrowing of alternative ghetto futures can best be accomplished by focusing upon the major choices relating to the following three questions:

To what extent should future nonwhite population growth be concentrated within the central cities, as it has been in the past twenty years?

To what extent should our white and non-white populations be residentially segregated from each other in the future?

To what extent should society redistribute income to relatively depressed urban areas or population groups in society in a process of "enrichment"?

Each of these questions can be answered with any one of a whole spectrum of responses from one extreme to the other. But for purposes of analysis, I believe we can usefully narrow these answers down to just two points on the spectrum for each question. This allows us to reduce the alternatives to the following:

Degree-of-concentration alternatives

1 Continue to concentrate nonwhite population growth in central cities or perhaps in a few older central cities. (*Concentration*)
2 Disperse nonwhite population growth widely throughout all parts of metropolitan areas. (*Dispersal*)

Degree-of-segregation alternatives

1 Continue to cluster whites and nonwhites in

residentially segregated neighborhoods, regardless of where they are within the metropolitan area. (*Segregation*)

2 Scatter the nonwhite population, or at least a fraction of it, "randomly" among white areas to achieve at least partial residential integration. (*Integration*)

Degree-of-enrichment alternatives

1 Continue to provide relatively low-level welfare, educational, housing, job training, and other support to the most deprived groups in the population – both those who are incapable of working, such as the vast majority of public-aid recipients, and those who might possibly work, but are unemployed because of discrimination, lack of desire, or any other reason. (*Non-enrichment*)

2 Greatly raise the level of support to welfare, educational, housing, job-training, and other programs for the most deprived groups, largely through federally aided programs. (*Enrichment*)

Even narrowing the alternatives in this fashion leaves a logical possibility of eight different combinations. A number of these can, however, be ruled out as internally inconsistent in practice. For example, I believe it is extremely unlikely that any strategy of dispersing the nonwhite population throughout metropolitan areas could be accomplished without provision of substantially greater incentives to both nonwhites (to get them to move) and whites (to increase their willingness to accept large numbers of nonwhite in-migrants without strong resistance). Thus no combination of both dispersal and non-enrichment need be considered.

Similarly, in the very long run, concentration of future nonwhite population growth within central cities is probably inconsistent with integration. Many of those cities will become so preponderantly nonwhite that integration within their borders will be impossible. Admittedly, it may take two or more decades for this to occur in some central cities, and it might never occur in others. Nevertheless, some types of integration (such as in the public schools) will become impossible long before that if a concentration policy is followed. For these reasons, I will consider only one special combination containing both concentration and integration. This consists of continued concentration, but a build-up of a gradually expanding inner-city

core of fully integrated housing and public facilities created through massive urban renewal. For reasons explained below, this strategy would require a significant enrichment program too.

This whole process of elimination leaves five basic alternative strategies relevant to future development of ghettos. For convenience, each has been assigned a short name to be used throughout the remainder of this article, summarized as follows:

1 *Present policies*: concentration, segregation, and non enrichment.

2 *Enrichment only*: concentration, segregation, enrichment.

3 *Integrated core*: concentration, integration (in the center only), enrichment.

4 *Segregated dispersal*: dispersal, segregation, enrichment.

5 *Integrated dispersal*: dispersal, integration, enrichment.

Before these strategies are examined in detail, two things about them should be emphasized.

First, they apply to individual metropolitan areas. Therefore it would be at least theoretically possible to adopt different strategies toward the ghetto in different metropolitan areas. There are, in fact, some convincing reasons why this would be an excellent idea.

Second, these strategies are formed from relatively extreme points on the relevant ranges of possibilities. Hence they could actually be adopted in various mixtures, rather than in forms set forth above. This further strengthens the case for using a variety of approaches across the country. For purposes of analysis, however, it is fruitful to examine each of these strategies initially as though it were to be the sole instrument for coping with ghetto problems in all metropolitan areas.

THE PRESENT-POLICIES STRATEGY

In order to carry out this strategy, we need do nothing more than we do now. Even existing federal programs aimed at aiding cities ... will continue or accelerate concentration, segregation, and non-enrichment, unless those programs are colossally expanded.

I do not wish to imply that present federal and local efforts in the anti-poverty program, the public housing program, the urban renewal program, health programs, educational programs, and many others are not of significant benefit to residents of ghettos. They are. Nevertheless, as both recent investigations and recent violence have emphasized, existing programs have succeeded neither in stemming the various adverse trends operating in ghetto areas nor in substantially eliminating the deplorable conditions there. Therefore, the strategy of continuing our present policies and our present level of effort is essentially not going to alter current conditions in ghettos.

This may make it seem silly to label continuation of present policies as a specific anti-ghetto strategy. Yet failure to adopt effective policies is still a strategy. It may not be a successful one, but it nevertheless is an expression of society's current commitment and attitude toward the ghetto.

Thus, if we maintain our current programs and policies, segregated areas of residence in our central cities will continue to expand rapidly and to suffer from all the difficult problems inherent in both racial and economic ghettos.

THE ENRICHMENT-ONLY STRATEGY

The second fundamental ghetto future strategy I call "enrichment only." This approach is aimed at dramatically improving the quality of life within the confines of present ghetto areas and those nearby areas into which ghettos will expand in the future if concentration continues. I presume that any such policy would apply to the poverty meaning of ghetto more than the racial one – that is, any enrichment strategy would aim at upgrading the lowest-income and most disadvantaged citizens of our central cities, regardless of race. Nevertheless, a sizeable proportion of such persons are nonwhites. Moreover, programs aimed at reducing racial discrimination in employment and in the quality of public services would form an important part of any strategy aimed at upgrading the most deprived groups. So the enrichment-only strategy would still concentrate upon the same areas as if it were to follow a racial policy.

The basic idea underlying the enrichment-only strategy (and part of every other strategy involving enrichment) is to develop federally financed programs that would greatly improve the education, housing, incomes, employment and job-training, and social services received by ghetto residents. This would involve vastly expanding the scale of present programs, changing the nature of many of them because they are now ineffective or would be if operated at a much larger scale, and creating incentives for a much greater participation of private capital in ghetto activities. Such incentives could include tax credits for investments made in designated ghetto areas, wage subsidies (connected with training but lasting longer than such training so as to induce employers to hire unskilled ghetto residents), rent or ownership supplements for poor families, enabling them to rent or buy housing created by private capital, and others.

It is important to realize that the enrichment-only strategy would end neither racial segregation nor the concentration of nonwhites in central cities (and some older adjoining suburbs). It would help many Negroes attain middle-class status and thus make it easier for them to leave the ghetto if they wanted to. Undoubtedly many would. But, by making life in central-city attractive without creating any strong pressures for integration or dispersal of the nonwhite population, such a policy would increase the in-migration of nonwhites into central cities. This would speed up the expansion of racially segregated areas in central cities, thereby accelerating the process of "massive transition" of whole neighborhoods from white to nonwhite occupancy.

THE INTEGRATED-CORE STRATEGY

This strategy is similar to the enrichment-only strategy because both would attempt to upgrade the quality of life in central-city ghettos through massive federally assisted programs. The integrated-core strategy would also seek, however, to eliminate racial segregation in an ever expanding core of the city by creating a socially, economically, and racially integrated community there. This integrated core would be built up through large-scale urban renewal programs, with the land re-uses including scattered-site public housing, middle-income housing suitable for families with children, and high-quality public services – especially schools.

All of these re-uses would be based upon "managed integration" – that is, deliberate achievement of a racial balance containing a majority of whites but a significant minority of Negroes. Thus, the integrated-core strategy could be carried out only if deliberate racial discrimination aimed at avoiding de facto segregation becomes recognized by the Supreme Court as a legitimate tactic for public agencies. In fact, such recognition will probably be a necessity for any strategy involving a significant degree of integration in public schools, public housing, or even private residential areas. This conclusion was ... recognized by the Chicago Board of Education, its staff, and its consultants, who all recommended the use of quotas in schools located in racially changing neighborhoods to promote stable integration.

The integrated-core strategy essentially represents a compromise between an ideal condition and two harsh realities. The ideal condition is development of a fully integrated society in which whites and Negroes live together harmoniously and the race of each individual is not recognized by anyone as a significant factor in any public or private decisions.

The first harsh reality is that the present desire of most whites to dominate their own environment means that integration can only be achieved through deliberate management and the willingness of some Negroes to share schools and residences as a minority. The second harsh reality is the assumption that it will be impossible to disperse the massive Negro ghettos of major central cities fast enough to prevent many of those cities from eventually becoming predominantly, or even almost exclusively, Negro in population. The development of predominantly Negro central cities, with high proportions of low-income residents, ringed by predominantly white suburbs with much wealthier residents, might lead to a shattering

polarization that would split society along both racial and spatial lines.

This strategy seeks to avoid any such polarization by building an integrated core of whites and nonwhites in central cities, including many leaders of both races in politics, business, and civic affairs. Negro leadership will properly assume the dominant position in central-city politics in many major cities after Negroes have become a majority of the municipal electorates there. By that time, integration of leadership within those cities will, it is to be hoped, have become a sufficient reality so that leaders of both races can work together in utilizing the central city's great economic assets, rather than fighting one another for control over them.

Thus, the integrated-core strategy postulates that a significant movement toward racial integration is essential to keep American society from "exploding" as a result of a combined racial–spatial confrontation of central cities vs. suburbs in many large metropolitan areas. It also postulates that development of integration in the suburbs through massive dispersal cannot occur fast enough to avoid such a confrontation. Therefore, integration must be developed on an "inside-out" basis, starting in the core of the central city, rather than in the suburbs.

THE CONCEPT OF DISPERSAL

The two dispersal strategies concerning the future of ghettos are both based upon a single key assumption: that the problems of ghettos cannot be solved so long as millions of Negroes, particularly those with low incomes and other significant disadvantages, are required or persuaded to live together in segregated ghetto areas within our central cities. These strategies contend that large numbers of Negroes should be given strong incentives to move voluntarily from central cities into suburban areas, including those in which no Negroes presently reside.

To illustrate what "large numbers" really means, let us postulate one version of dispersal which I call the "constant-size ghetto strategy." This strictly hypothetical strategy aims at stopping the growth of existing central-city ghettos by dispersing enough Negroes from central cities to the suburbs (or to peripheral central-city areas) to offset potential future increases in that growth. Taking the period from 1970 through 1975, estimates made by the National Advisory Commission on Civil Disorders show that the nonwhite population of all U.S. central cities taken as a whole would, in the absence of any dispersal strategy, expand from about 13.6 million to about 15.5 million. Thus, if dispersal of nonwhites were to take place at a scale large enough to keep central-city racial ghettos at their 1970 level during the five subsequent years, there would have to be an out-movement of 1.9 million Negroes into the suburbs. This amounts to 380,000 per year.

From 1950 to 1960, the suburban Negro population of all U.S. metropolitan areas grew a total of only 60,000 per year. In that decade, the white population of suburban portions of our metropolitan areas (the so-called "urban fringe") increased about 1,720,000 persons per year. Thus, 96.6 percent of all suburban population growth consisted of whites. From 1960 to 1966, the Negro population growth in all suburban areas declined sharply to a rate of 33,300 per year. In fact, there was actually in-migration of Negroes from suburbs to central cities. But the white population in all suburbs went up by an average of 1,750,000 per year. Thus the proportion of suburban growth made up of whites climbed to 98.1 percent – an even higher fraction than in the decade from 1950 to 1960.

Undoubtedly, some of this white population increase was caused by an exodus of whites from central cities in response to Negro growth therein. If future Negro population growth in central cities were stopped by a large-scale dispersion policy, then white population growth in the suburbs would be definitely smaller than it was from 1950 through 1966. The size of the resulting decline would depend upon the fraction of white exodus from central cities that occurs in response to Negro growth, as opposed to such other factors as rising incomes, the aging central-city housing stock, and shifts in life-cycle position. If whites leave central cities in a one-to-one ratio with the expansion of Negro population therein, then a cessation of Negro ghetto growth would result in a large drop in white suburban growth. In that case, future suburban population increases would consist of about 23 percent Negroes (based on very rough calculations). This contrasts with proportions of less than 5 percent from 1950 through 1960 and less than 3 percent from 1960 through 1966.

Clearly, such dispersal would represent a radical change in existing trends. Not only would it stop the expansion of Negro ghettos in central cities, but it would also inject a significant Negro population into many presently all-white suburban areas. It is true that policies of dispersal would not necessarily have to be at this large a scale. Dispersal aimed not at stopping ghetto growth, but merely at slowing it down somewhat, could be carried out at a much lower scale. Yet even such policies would represent a marked departure from past U.S. practice.

Such a sharp break with the past would be necessary for any significant dispersal of Negroes. Merely providing the *opportunity* for Negroes to move out of ghettos would, at least in the short run, not result in many moving. Even adoption of a vigorously enforced nation-wide open-occupancy law applying to *all* residences would not greatly speed up the present snail's-pace rate of dispersion. Experience in those states that have open-occupancy ordinances decisively proves this conclusion.

Hence, positive incentives for dispersion would have to be created in order to speed up the rate at which Negroes voluntarily move from central cities and settle in suburban areas. (Certainly no policy involving *involuntary* movement of either whites or Negroes should ever be considered.) Such incentives could include rent supplements, ownership supplements, special school-support bonus payments linked to the education of children moving out from ghettos, and other devices which essentially attach a subsidy to a person. Then, when the person moves, he and the community into which he goes get credit for that subsidy. This creates incentives both for him to move and for the community to accept him gladly. Both of the strategies involving dispersal would thus represent radical changes in existing practices.

SEGREGATED VS. INTEGRATED DISPERSAL

One of the fundamental purposes of any dispersal strategy is providing Negro Americans with real freedom of choice concerning housing and school accommodations. The experience of other ethnic groups indicates that Negroes would exercise that choice in suburban areas in a combination of two ways. Some individual Negro households would become scattered "randomly" in largely white residential areas. But other Negro households – probably a larger number – would voluntarily cluster together. This would create primarily Negro neighborhoods, or even primarily Negro suburban communities. Such a combination of both *scattering* and *clustering* would occur even if Negro households had absolutely no fear of hostility or antagonism from white neighbors. It is unrealistic to suppose, however, that *all* prejudice against Negro neighbors can be eliminated from presently all-white suburbs in the immediate future. As a result, even if a dispersal strategy is carried out, there will still be some external pressure against Negro newcomers. This will encourage an even higher proportion of incoming Negro households to cluster together than would do so in the absence of all fears and antagonism. Moreover, public policies to accomplish dispersion might include deliberate creation of some moderate-sized clusters of Negro families, as in scattered-site public housing developments.

Once all-Negro clusters appear in previously all-white suburbs, there is a high probability that they will turn into "ghetto-lets" or "mini-ghettos." The same forces that produced ghettos in central cities are likely to repeat themselves in suburbs, though in a much less pathological form. Those pressures are a rapidly expanding Negro population, the "Law of Cultural Dominance" among whites, and at least some restriction of Negro choice in areas far removed from existing all-Negro neighborhoods. Therefore, once a Negro cluster becomes large enough so that Negro children dominate a local elementary school, the typical phenomenon of white withdrawal from the local residential real estate market is likely to occur. This has already taken place regarding Jews and gentiles in many suburban areas. Thus, any dispersal strategy that does not explicitly aim at preventing segregation, too, will probably create new segregated neighborhoods in the suburbs.

This new form of *de facto* segregation will, however, have far less damaging effects upon Negroes than existing segregation concentrated in central cities. In the first place, if Negro clusters are deliberately created in almost all parts of the metropolitan area at once, whites will be unable to flee to "completely safe" suburbs without accepting impractically long commuting journeys. This will reduce the white propensity to abandon an area after Negroes begin entering it. Moreover, the presence of some Negroes in all parts of suburbia will also make it far easier for individual Negro families to move into all-white neighborhoods on a scattered basis. Thus any dispersal policy that really disperses Negroes in the suburbs will immediately create an enormous improvement in the real freedom of residential choice enjoyed by individual Negro families. This will be true even if most of these families actually choose to remain in Negro clusters.

Second, any dispersal strategy would presumably be accompanied by strongly enforced open-occupancy laws applying to all housing. At present, these laws do not lead to scattering, but they would in the climate of a dispersal strategy. Then Negro willingness to move into all-white areas would rise sharply and white antagonism toward such move-ins would drop.

Third, *de facto* residential segregation need not lead to segregated suburban schools. In relatively small communities, such as most suburbs, it is easy to bus students to achieve stable racial balance. Thus, the formation of clustered Negro housing would not have to cause the quality-of-education problems that now exist in central-city ghettos. True, if a given suburb became predominantly Negro, its schools might become quite segregated. In that case, school systems in adjoining suburbs might have to merge or at least work out student exchange procedures with the segregated community in order to counteract segregation. This may be difficult to accomplish (though in the climate of a dispersal strategy it would be at least think-able). Hence it is possible some segregated school systems might appear in suburban areas. But Negro families would still have far more opportunities than they do now to move to areas with integrated schools.

A dispersal strategy that did not succeed in initially placing Negro households in almost all parts of the metropolitan area would be more likely to generate "ghetto-lets." Hence, if dispersal tactics call for initially concentrating on dispersion only to a few suburbs, it is quite possible that segregated dispersal would result. This implies that integrated dispersal could be attained in only two ways. Either the initial dispersal strategy must place Negroes in almost all suburban communities, or specific integration-furthering mechanisms – such as school and residential quotas – must be adopted.

[...]

COPYRIGHT INFORMATION

PROLOGUE

1 THE EVOLUTION OF CITIES

2 PERSPECTIVES ON URBAN FORM AND DESIGN

3 URBAN SOCIETY AND CULTURE

4 URBAN POLITICS, GOVERNANCE, AND ECONOMICS

5 URBAN PLANNING: VISIONS, THEORY, AND PRACTICE

6 THE FUTURE OF THE CITY

INDEX